Chalfant 1992

The Historical Jesus

The Historical Jesus

The Life of a Mediterranean Jewish Peasant

John Dominic Crossan

HarperSanFrancisco

A Division of HarperCollins*Publishers*

FIRST EDITION

Library of Congress Cataloging-in-Publication Data

Crossan, John Dominic,
    The historical Jesus: the life of a Mediterranean Jewish peasant/
John Dominic Crossan. —1st ed.
        p.   cm.
    Includes bibliographical references and index.
    ISBN 0-06-061607-5
    1. Jesus Christ—Biography.   2. Jesus Christ—Biography—History
and criticism.   3. Jesus Christ.   I. Title.
BT301.2.C76   1991
232.9'01—dc20
    [B]   90-56451
                                                                          CIP

91   92   93   94   95   RRD(H)   10   9   8   7   6   5   4   3   2   1

This edition is printed on acid-free paper that meets the
American National Standards Institute Z39.48 Standard.

for
Sarah,
Frank, and Michelle

Contents

✧ Overture ✧
The Gospel of Jesus

In the beginning was the performance; not the word alone, not the deed alone, but both, each indelibly marked with the other forever. He comes as yet unknown into a hamlet of Lower Galilee. He is watched by the cold, hard eyes of peasants living long enough at subsistence level to know exactly where the line is drawn between poverty and destitution. He looks like a beggar, yet his eyes lack the proper cringe, his voice the proper whine, his walk the proper shuffle. He speaks about the rule of God, and they listen as much from curiosity as anything else. They know all about rule and power, about kingdom and empire, but they know it in terms of tax and debt, malnutrition and sickness, agrarian oppression and demonic possession. What, they really want to know, can this kingdom of God do for a lame child, a blind parent, a demented soul screaming its tortured isolation among the graves that mark the edges of the village? Jesus walks with them to the tombs, and, in the silence after the exorcism, the villagers listen once more, but now with curiosity giving way to cupidity, fear, and embarrassment. He is invited, as honor demands, to the home of the village leader. He goes, instead, to stay in the home of the dispossessed woman. Not quite proper, to be sure, but it would be unwise to censure an exorcist, to criticize a magician. The village could yet broker this power to its surroundings, could give this kingdom of God a localization, a place to which others would come for healing, a center with honor and patronage enough for all, even, maybe, for that dispossessed woman herself. But the next day he leaves them, and now they wonder aloud about a divine kingdom with no respect for proper protocols, a kingdom, as he had said, not just for the poor, like themselves, but for the destitute. Others say that the worst and most powerful demons are not found in small villages but in certain cities. Maybe, they say, that was where the exorcised demon went, to Sepphoris or Tiberias, or even Jerusalem, or maybe to Rome itself, where its arrival would hardly be noticed amidst so many others already in residence. But some say nothing at all and ponder the possibility of catching up with Jesus before he gets too far.

Even Jesus himself had not always seen things that way. Earlier he had received John's baptism and accepted his message of God as the imminent apocalyptic judge. But the Jordan was not just water, and to be baptized in it was to recapitulate the ancient and archetypal passage from imperial bondage to national freedom. Herod Antipas moved swiftly to execute John, there was no apocalyptic consummation, and Jesus, finding his own voice, began to speak of God not as imminent apocalypse but as present healing. To those first followers from the peasant villages of Lower Galilee who asked how to repay his exorcisms and cures, he gave a simple answer, simple, that is, to understand but hard as death itself to undertake. You are healed healers, he said, so take the Kingdom to others, for I am not its patron and you are not its brokers. It is, was, and always will be available to any who want it. Dress as I do, like a beggar, but do not beg. Bring a miracle and request a table. Those you heal must accept you into their homes.

That ecstatic vision and social program sought to rebuild a society upward from its grass roots but on principles of religious and economic egalitarianism, with free healing brought directly to the peasant homes and free sharing of whatever they had in return. The deliberate conjunction of magic and meal, miracle and table, free compassion and open commensality, was a challenge launched not just at Judaism's strictest purity regulations, or even at the Mediterranean's patriarchal combination of honor and shame, patronage and clientage, but at civilization's eternal inclination to draw lines, invoke boundaries, establish hierarchies, and maintain discriminations. It did not invite a political revolution but envisaged a social one at the imagination's most dangerous depths. No importance was given to distinctions of Gentile and Jew, female and male, slave and free, poor and rich. Those distinctions were hardly even attacked in theory; they were simply ignored in practice.

What would happen to Jesus was probably as predictable as what had happened already to John. Some form of religiopolitical execution could surely have been expected. What he was saying and doing was as unacceptable in the first as in the twentieth century, there, here, or anywhere. Still, the exact sequence of what happened at the end lacks multiple independent accounts, and the death is surer in its connection to the life than it is in its connection to the preceding few days. It seems clear that Jesus, confronted, possibly for the first and only time, with the Temple's rich magnificence, symbolically destroyed its perfectly legitimate brokerage function in the name of the unbrokered kingdom of God. Such an act, if performed in the volatile atmosphere of Passover, a feast that celebrated Jewish liberation from inaugural imperial oppression, would have been quite enough to entail crucifixion by religiopolitical agreement. And it is now impossible for us to imagine the offhand brutality, anonymity, and indifference with which a peasant nobody like Jesus would have been disposed of.

What could not have been predicted ~~and might not have~~ been expected was that the end was not the end. Those who had originally experienced divine power through his vision and his example still continued to do so after his death—in fact, even more so, because now it was no longer confined by time or place. A prudently neutral Jewish historian reported, at the end of the first century, "When Pilate, upon hearing him accused by men of the highest standing amongst us, had condemned him to be crucified, those who had in the first place come to love him did not give up their affection for him. And the tribe of the Christians, so called after him, has still to this day not disappeared." And an arrogant Roman historian reported that, at the start of the second century, "Christus, the founder of the name [of Christian], had undergone the death penalty in the reign of Tiberius, by sentence of the procurator Pontius Pilatus, and the pernicious superstition was checked for the moment, only to break out once more, not merely in Judaea, the home of the disease, but in the capital itself, where all things horrible or shameful in the world collect and find a vogue." Jesus' own followers, who had initially fled from the danger and horror of the crucifixion, talked eventually not just of continued affection or spreading superstition but of resurrection. They tried to express what they meant by telling, for example, about the journey to Emmaus undertaken by two Jesus followers, one named and clearly male, one unnamed and probably female. The couple were leaving Jerusalem in disappointed and dejected sorrow. Jesus joined them on the road and, unknown and unrecognized, explained how the Hebrew Scriptures should have prepared them for his fate. Later that evening they invited him to join them for their evening meal, and finally they recognized him when once again he served the meal to them as of old beside the lake. And then, only then, they started back to Jerusalem in high spirits. The symbolism is obvious, as is the metaphoric condensation of the first years of Christian thought and practice into one parabolic afternoon. Emmaus never happened. Emmaus always happens.

If we ask, however, which of all the words placed on his lips actually go back to the historical Jesus, it is possible to offer at least a reconstructed inventory. But, as you read them, recall that, in the light of the preceding paragraphs, these words are not a list to be read. They are not even a sermon to be preached. They are a score to be played and a program to be enacted.

Carry no purse, no bag, no sandals, nor two tunics. Whatever house you enter, eat what is set before you; heal the sick in it and say to them, "The kingdom of God has come upon you."

Ask, and it will be given to you; seek, and you will find; knock, and it will be opened for you.

The kingdom of God will not come with signs that can be checked beforehand; nor will they say, "Here it is!"or "There!" because the kingdom of God is already among you.

You have ears, use them!

Whoever receives you, receives not you but me; whoever receives me, receives not me but the one who sent me.

Whoever divorces his wife and marries another commits adultery, and whoever marries a woman divorced from her husband commits adultery.

What goes into your mouth will not defile you, but what comes out of your mouth, that will defile you.

Those who enter the kingdom of God are like infants still being suckled.

You are the light of the world!

No prophet is acceptable in his village; no physician heals those who know him.

Human beings will be forgiven all their sins.

A woman in the crowd raised her voice and said to him, "Blessed is the womb that bore you, and the breasts that you sucked!" But he said, "Blessed rather are those who hear the word of God and keep it!"

Forgive, and you will be forgiven.

The first will be last and the last first.

Whatever is hidden will be made manifest, whatever is covered up will be uncovered.

A sower went out to sow. And as he sowed, some seed fell along the path, and the birds came and devoured it. Other seed fell on rocky ground, where it had not much soil, and since it had no root it withered away. Other seed fell among thorns and the thorns grew up and choked it, and it yielded no grain. And other seeds fell into good soil and brought forth grain, growing up and increasing and yielding thirtyfold and sixtyfold and a hundredfold.

The kingdom of God is like a mustard seed, the smallest of all seeds. But when it falls on tilled ground, it produces a great plant and becomes a shelter for birds of the sky.

No one after lighting a lamp puts it in a cellar or under a bushel, but on a stand, that those who enter may see the light.

Be wise as serpents and innocent as doves.

To one who has will more be given; from one who has not, it will be taken away.

Blessed are the destitute.

If you follow me, you carry a cross.

A man planted a vineyard, and let it out to tenants, and went into another country. When the time came, he sent a servant to the tenants, that they should give him some of the fruit of the vineyard; but the tenants beat him, and sent him away empty-handed. And he sent another servant; him also they beat and treated shamefully, and sent him away empty-handed. And he sent yet a third; this one they wounded and cast out. Then the owner of the vineyard said, "What shall I do? I will send my beloved son; it may be they will respect him." But when the tenants saw him, they said to themselves, "This is the heir; let us kill him, that the inheritance may be ours."

Blessed are the reviled.

I will destroy this Temple and no one will be able to rebuild it.

The harvest is great but the laborers are few. Pray the Lord of the harvest to send out laborers.

Why have you come out into the desert? To see a reed shaken by the wind? To see a man clothed in soft clothing? Those who are gorgeously appareled and live in luxury are in kings' courts. What then did you come out to see? A prophet? Yes, I tell you, and more than a prophet.

When you see a cloud rising in the west, you say at once, "A shower is coming"; and so it happens. And when you see the south wind blowing, you say, "There will be scorching heat" and it happens. You know how to interpret the appearance of earth and sky; but why do you not know how to interpret the present time?

They showed Jesus a gold coin and said to him, "Caesar's men demand taxes from us." He said to them, "Give Caesar what belongs to Caesar, give God what belongs to God."

Blessed are those who weep.

To save your life is to lose it; to lose your life is to save it.

Who is not against you is for you.

It is like a fisherman who cast his net into the sea and drew it up from the sea full of small fish. Among them he found a fine large fish. He threw all the small fish back into the sea and chose the large fish without difficulty.

I have cast fire upon the world, and see, I am guarding it until it blazes.

Do you think that I have come to give peace on earth? No, I tell you, but rather division; for henceforth in one house there will be five divided, three against two and two against three; they will be divided, father against son and son against father, mother against daughter and daughter against her mother, mother-in-law against her daughter-in-law and daughter-in-law against her mother-in-law.

It is as if a man should scatter seed upon the ground, and should sleep and rise night and day, and the seed should sprout and grow, he knows not how. The earth produces of itself, first the blade, then the ear, then the full grain in the ear. But when the grain is ripe, at once he puts in the sickle, because the harvest has come.

You see the mote in your brother's eye, but do not see the beam in your own eye. When you cast the beam out of your own eye, then you will see clearly to cast the mote from your brother's eye.

A city built on a high mountain and fortified cannot fall, nor can it be hidden.

What I tell you in the dark, utter in the light; and what you hear whispered, proclaim upon the housetops.

If a blind man leads a blind man, both will fall into a pit.

It is not possible for anyone to enter the house of a strong man and take it by force unless he binds his hands; then he will be able to ransack his house.

Do not be anxious about your life, what you shall eat, nor about your body, what you shall put on. Consider the ravens: they neither sow nor reap, they have neither storehouse nor barn, and yet God feeds them. Consider the lilies, how they grow; they neither toil nor spin; yet I tell you, even Solomon in all his glory was not arrayed like one of these. Instead, seek his kingdom, and these things shall be yours as well.

Woe to the Pharisees, for they are like a dog sleeping in the manger of oxen, for neither does he eat nor does he let the oxen eat.

Among those born of women, from Adam until John the Baptist, there is no one so superior to John that his eyes should not be lowered before him. Yet whichever one of you comes to be a child will be acquainted with the kingdom and will become superior to John.

No servant can serve two masters; for either he will hate the one and love the other, or he will be devoted to the one and despise the other.

No one drinks old wine and immediately desires to drink new wine.

No one puts a new patch on an old garment, and no one puts new wine into old wineskins.

Whoever does not hate his father and mother cannot become a disciple to me. And whoever does not hate his brothers and sisters cannot become a disciple to me.

The kingdom may be compared to a man who sowed good seed in his field; but while men were sleeping, his enemy came and sowed weeds among the wheat, and went away. So when the plants came up and bore grain, then the weeds appeared also. And the servants of the householder came and said to him, "Sir, did you not sow good seed in your field? How then has it weeds?" He said to them, "An enemy has done this." The servants said to him, "Then do you want us to go and gather them?" But he said, "No; lest in gathering the weeds you root up the wheat along with them. Let both grow together until the harvest; and at harvest time I will tell the reapers, 'Gather the weeds first and bind them in bundles to be burned, but gather the wheat into my barn.'"

There was a rich man who had much money. He said, "I shall put my money to use so that I may sow, reap, plant, and fill my storehouse with produce, with the result that I shall lack nothing." Such were his intentions, but that same night he died.

There was a man who (wanted) to invite guests and when he had prepared the dinner, he sent his servant to invite the guests. He went to the first and said to him, "My master invites you." He said, "I have claims against some merchants. They are coming to me this evening. I must go and give them my orders. I ask to be excused from the dinner." He went to another and said to him, "My master invites you." He said to him, "My friend is going to be married, and I am to prepare the banquet. I shall not be able to come. I ask to be excused from the dinner." He went to another and said to him, "My master invites you." He said to him, "I have just bought a farm, and I am on my way to collect the rent. I shall not be able to come. I ask to be excused." The servant returned and said to his master, "Those whom you invited to the dinner have asked to be excused." The master said to his servant, "Go outside to the streets and bring back those whom you happen to meet, so that they may dine."

Blessed are the hungry.

A man said to him, "Tell my brothers to divide my father's possessions with me." He said to him, "O man, who has made me a divider?"

The Kingdom is like a merchant who had a consignment of merchandise and who discovered a pearl. The merchant was shrewd. He sold the merchandise and bought the pearl alone for himself.

Foxes have holes, and birds of the air have nests; but the human being has nowhere to lay its head.

Why do you wash the outside of the cup? Do you not realize that the one who made the inside made the outside too?

If you have money, do not lend it at interest, but give it to one from whom you will not get it back.

The Kingdom is like a certain woman. She took a little leaven, concealed it in some dough, and made it into large loaves.

The disciples said to him, "Your brothers and your mother are standing outside." He said to them, "Those here who do the will of God are my brothers and my mother."

They said to Jesus, "Come let us pray today and let us fast." Jesus said, "What is the sin that I have committed, or wherein have I been defeated? But when the bridegroom leaves the bridal chamber, then let them fast and pray."

The Kingdom is like a shepherd who had a hundred sheep. One of them, the largest, went astray. He left the ninety-nine and looked for that one until he found it. When he had gone to such trouble, he said to the sheep, "I care for you more than the ninety-nine."

The kingdom of heaven is like treasure hidden in a field, which a man found and covered up; then in his joy he goes and sells all that he has and buys that field.

The scribes and elders and priests were angry because he reclined at table with sinners.

Love your enemies and pray for those who abuse you.

He was casting out a demon that was dumb; when the demon had gone out, the dumb man spoke, and the people marveled. But some of them said, "He casts out demons by Beelzebul, the prince of demons." But he said to them, "Every kingdom divided against itself is laid waste, and a divided household falls. And if Satan also is divided against himself, how will his kingdom stand? For you say that I cast out demons by Beelzebul."

If I cast out demons by Beelzebul, by whom do your sons cast them out? Therefore they shall be your judges. But if it is by the finger of God that I cast out demons, then the kingdom of God has come upon you.

Beware of the scribes, who like to go about in long robes, and to have salutations in the marketplaces and the best seats in the synagogues and the places of honor at feasts.

Salt is good; but if salt has lost its saltness, how will you season it?

If any one strikes you on the right cheek, turn to him the other also; and if any one would sue you and take your coat, let him have your cloak as well; and if any one forces you to go one mile, go with him two miles.

One of the disciples said to him, "Lord, let me go and bury my father." But Jesus said to him, "Follow me, and leave the dead to bury their own dead."

Another said, "I will follow you, Lord; but let me first say farewell to those at my home." Jesus said to him, "No one who puts his hand to the plow and looks back is fit for the kingdom of God."

You are as lambs in the midst of wolves.

What father among you, if his son asks him for bread, will give him a stone? Or if he asks for a fish, will give him a serpent? If you then, who are evil, know how to give good gifts to your children, how much more will your Father who is in heaven give good things to those who ask him!

Are not five sparrows sold for two pennies? And not one of them is forgotten before God. Why, even the hairs of your head are all numbered. Fear not; you are of more value than many sparrows.

Where your treasure is, there will your heart be also.

From the days of John the Baptist until now the kingdom of God has suffered violence, and men of violence take it by force. For all the prophets and the law prophesied until John.

Peter came up and said to him, "Lord, how often shall my brother sin against me, and I forgive him? As many as seven times?" Jesus said to him, "I do not say to you seven times, but seventy times seven."

A man going on a journey called his servants and entrusted to them his property; to one he gave five talents, to another two, to another one, to each according to his ability. Then he went away. He who had received the five talents went at once and traded with them; and he made five talents more. So also, he who had the two talents made two talents more. But he who had received the one talent went and dug in the ground and hid his master's money. Now after a long time the master of those servants came and settled accounts with them. And he who had received the five talents came forward, bringing five talents more, saying, "Master, you delivered to me five talents; here I have made five talents more." His master said to him, "Well done, good and faithful servant; you have been faithful over a little, I will set you over much; enter into the joy of your master." And he also who had the two talents came forward, saying, "Master, you delivered to me two talents; here I have made two talents more." His master said to him, "Well done, good and faithful servant; you have been faithful over a little, I will set you over much; enter into the joy of your master." He also who had received the one talent came forward, saying,

"Master, I knew you to be a hard man, reaping where you did not sow, and gathering where you did not winnow; so I was afraid, and I went and hid your talent in the ground. Here you have what is yours." But his master answered him, "You wicked and slothful servant! You knew that I reap where I have not sowed, and gather where I have not winnowed? Then you ought to have invested my money with the bankers, and at my coming I should have received what was my own with interest. So take the talent from him, and give it to him who has the ten talents."

He said to them, "The kings of the Gentiles exercise lordship over them; and those in authority over them are called benefactors. But not so with you; rather let the greatest among you become as the youngest, and the leader as one who serves. For which is the greater, one who sits at table, or one who serves? Is it not the one who sits at table? But I am among you as one who serves."

It is easier for a camel to go through the eye of a needle than for a rich man to enter the kingdom of God.

Love your neighbor like your soul; guard your neighbor like the pupil of your eye.

Become passersby.

It is impossible to mount two horses or to stretch two bows.

Blessed is the one who has suffered.

Split a piece of wood, and I am there. Lift up the stone, and you will find me there.

The Kingdom is like a certain woman who was carrying a jar full of meal. While she was walking on the road, still some distance from home, the handle of the jar broke, and the meal emptied out behind her on the road. She did not realize it; she had noticed no accident. When she reached her house, she set the jar down and found it empty.

The kingdom is like a certain man who wanted to kill a powerful man. In his own house he drew his sword and stuck it into the wall in order to find out whether his hand could carry through. Then he slew the powerful man.

If you are offering your gift at the altar, and there remember that your neighbor has something against you, leave your gift there before the altar and go; first be reconciled to your neighbor, and then come and offer your gift.

Do not swear at all, either by heaven, for it is the throne of God, or by the earth, for it is his footstool, or by Jerusalem, for it is the city of the great King. And do not swear by your head, for you cannot make one hair white or black. Let what you say be simply yes or no; anything more than this comes from evil.

Exalt yourself and you will be humbled; humble yourself and you will be exalted.

The Kingdom may be compared to a king who wished to settle accounts with his servants. When he began the reckoning, one was brought to him who owed him ten thousand talents; and as he could not pay, his lord ordered him to be sold, with his wife and children and all that he had, and payment to be made. So the servant fell on his knees, imploring him, "Lord, have patience with me, and I will pay you everything." And out of pity for him the lord of that servant released him and forgave him the debt. But that same servant, as he went out, came upon one of his fellow servants who owed him a hundred denarii; and seizing him by the throat he said, "Pay what you owe." So his fellow servant fell down and besought him, "Have patience with me, and I will pay you." He refused and went and put him in prison till he should pay the debt. When his fellow servants saw what had taken place, they were greatly distressed, and they went and reported to their lord all that had taken place. Then his lord summoned him and said to him, "You wicked servant! I forgave you all that debt because you besought me; and should not you have had mercy on your fellow servant, as I had mercy on you?" And in anger his lord delivered him to the jailers, till he should pay all his debt.

The Kingdom is like a householder who went out early in the morning to hire laborers for his vineyard. After agreeing with the laborers for a denarius a day, he sent them into his vineyard. And going out about the third hour he saw others standing idle in the marketplace; and to them he said, "You go into the vineyard too, and whatever is right I will give you." So they went. Going out again about the sixth hour and the ninth hour, he did the same. And about the eleventh hour he went out and found others standing; and he said to them, "Why do you stand here idle all day?" They said to him, "Because no one has hired us." He said to them, "You go into the vineyard too." And when evening came, the owner of the vineyard said to his steward, "Call the laborers and pay them their wages, beginning with the last, up to the first." And when those hired about the eleventh hour came, each of them received a denarius. Now when the first came, they thought they would receive more; but each of them also received a denarius. And on receiving it they grumbled at the householder, saying, "These last worked only one hour, and you have made them equal to us who have borne the burden of the day and the scorching heat." But he replied to one of them, "Friend, I am doing you no wrong; did you not agree with me for a denarius? Take what belongs to you, and go; I choose to give to this last as I give to you."

There are eunuchs who have been so from birth, and there are eunuchs who have been made eunuchs by men, and there are eunuchs who have made themselves eunuchs for the sake of the kingdom of heaven.

A man had two sons; and he went to the first and said, "Son, go and work in the vineyard today." And he answered, "I will not"; but afterward he repented and went. And he went to the second and said the same; and he answered, "I go, sir," but did not go. Which of the two did the will of his father?"

A man was going down from Jerusalem to Jericho, and he fell among robbers, who stripped him and beat him, and departed, leaving him half dead. Now by chance a priest was going down that road; and when he saw him he passed by on the other side. So likewise a Levite, when he came to the place and saw him, passed by on the other side. But a Samaritan, as he journeyed, came to where he was; and when he saw him, he had compassion, and went to him and bound up his wounds, pouring on oil and wine; then he set him on his own beast and brought him to an inn, and took care of him. And the next day he took out two denarii and gave them to the innkeeper, saying, "Take care of him; and whatever more you spend, I will repay you when I come back."

Which of you who has a friend will go to him at midnight and say to him, "Friend, lend me three loaves; for a friend of mine has arrived on a journey, and I have nothing to set before him"; and he will answer from within, "Do not bother me; the door is now shut, and my children are with me in bed; I cannot get up and give you anything"? Though he will not get up and give him anything because he is his friend, yet because of his importunity he will rise and give him whatever he needs.

A man had a fig tree planted in his vineyard; and he came seeking fruit on it and found none. And he said to the vinedresser, "Lo, these three years I have come seeking fruit on this fig tree, and I find none. Cut it down; why should it use up the ground?" And he answered him, "Let it alone, sir, this year also, till I dig about it and put on manure. And if it bears fruit next year, well and good; but if not, you can cut it down."

For which of you, desiring to build a tower, does not first sit down and count the cost, whether he has enough to complete it? Otherwise, when he has laid a foundation, and is not able to finish, all who see it begin to mock him, saying, "This man began to build, and was not able to finish." Or what king, going to encounter another king in war, will not sit down first and take counsel whether he is able with ten thousand to meet him who comes against him with twenty thousand? And if not, while the other is yet a great way off, he sends an embassy and asks terms of peace.

What woman, having ten silver coins, if she loses one coin, does not light a lamp and sweep the house and seek diligently until she finds it? And when she has found it, she calls together her friends and neighbors, saying, "Rejoice with me, for I have found the coin which I had lost."

There was a man who had two sons; and the younger of them said to his father, "Father, give me the share of property that falls to me." And he divided his living between them. Not many days later, the younger son gathered all he had and took his journey into a far country, and there he squandered his property in loose living. And when he had spent everything, a great famine arose in that country, and he began to be in want. So he went and joined himself to one of the citizens of that country, who sent him into his fields to feed swine. And he would gladly have fed on the pods that the swine ate; and no one gave him anything. But when he came to himself he said, "How many of my father's hired servants have bread enough and to spare, but I perish here with hunger! I will arise and go to my father, and I will say to him, 'Father, I have sinned against heaven and before you; I am no longer worthy to be called your son; treat me as one of your hired servants.'" And he arose and came to his father. But while he was yet at a distance, his father saw him and had compassion, and ran and embraced him and kissed him. And the son said to him, "Father, I have sinned against heaven and before you; I am no longer worthy to be called your son." But the father said to his servants, "Bring quickly the best robe, and put it on him; and put a ring on his hand, and shoes on his feet; and bring the fatted calf and kill it, and let us eat and make merry; for this my son was dead, and is alive again; he was lost, and is found." And they began to make merry. Now his elder son was in the field; and as he came and drew near to the house, he heard music and dancing. And he called one of the servants and asked what this meant. And he said to him, "Your brother has come, and your father has killed the fatted calf, because he has received him safe and sound." But he was angry and refused to go in. His father came out and entreated him, but he answered his father, "Lo, these many years I have served you, and I never disobeyed your command; yet you never gave me a kid, that I might make merry with my friends. But when this son of yours came, who has devoured your living with harlots, you killed for him the fatted calf!" And he said to him, "Son, you are always with me, and all that is mine is yours. It was fitting to make merry and be glad, for this your brother was dead, and is alive; he was lost, and is found."

There was a rich man who had a steward, and charges were brought to him that this man was wasting his goods. And he called him and said to him, "What is this that I hear about you? Turn in the account of your stewardship, for you can no longer be steward." And the steward said to himself, "What shall I do, since my master is taking the stewardship away from me? I am not strong enough to dig, and I am ashamed to beg. I have decided what to do, so that people may receive me into their houses when I am put out of the stewardship." So, summoning his master's debtors one by one, he said to the first, "How much do you owe my master?" He said, "A hundred measures of oil." And he said to him, "Take your bill, and sit down quickly and write fifty." Then he said to another, "And how much do you owe?" He said, "A hundred measures of wheat." He said to him, "Take your bill, and write eighty."

There was a rich man, who was clothed in purple and fine linen and who feasted sumptuously every day. And at his gate lay a poor man named Lazarus, full of sores, who desired to be fed with what fell from the rich man's table; moreover the dogs came and licked his sores. The poor man died and was carried by the angels to Abraham's bosom. The rich man also died and was buried; and in Hades, being in torment, he lifted up his eyes, and saw Abraham far off and Lazarus in his bosom. And he called out, "Father Abraham, have mercy upon me, and send Lazarus to dip the end of his finger in water and cool my tongue; for I am in anguish in this flame." But Abraham said, "Son, remember that you in your lifetime received your good things, and Lazarus in like manner evil things; but now he is comforted here, and you are in anguish. And besides all this, between us and you a great chasm has been fixed, in order that those who would pass from here to you may not be able, and none may cross from there to us."

In a certain city there was a judge who neither feared God nor regarded man; and there was a widow in that city who kept coming to him and saying, "Vindicate me against my adversary." For a while he refused; but afterward he said to himself, "Though I neither fear God nor regard man, yet because this widow bothers me, I will vindicate her, or she will wear me out by her continual coming."

Two men went up into the Temple to pray, one a Pharisee and the other a tax collector. The Pharisee stood and prayed thus with himself, "God, I thank thee that I am not like other men, extortioners, unjust, adulterers, or even like this tax collector. I fast twice a week, I give tithes of all that I get." But the tax collector, standing far off, would not even lift up his eyes to heaven, but beat his breast, saying, "God, be merciful to me a sinner!" This man went down to his house justified rather than the other.

Once again, those words are not a list to be read. They are not even a sermon to be preached. They are a score to be played and a program to be enacted. This book is an account of their inaugural orchestration and initial performance. In the end, as in the beginning, now as then, there is only the performance.

✧ Prologue ✧
The Historical Jesus

> Trying to find the actual Jesus is like trying, in atomic physics,
> to locate a submicroscopic particle and determine its charge.
> The particle cannot be seen directly, but on a photographic
> plate we see the lines left by the trajectories of larger particles
> it put in motion. By tracing these trajectories back to their
> common origin, and by calculating the force necessary to
> make the particles move as they did, we can locate and
> describe the invisible cause. Admittedly, history is more
> complex than physics; the lines connecting the original figure
> to the developed legends cannot be traced with mathematical
> accuracy; the intervention of unknown factors has to be
> allowed for. Consequently, results can never claim more than
> probability; but "probability," as Bishop Butler said, "is the very
> guide of life."
>
> Morton Smith (1978:6)

Historical Jesus research is becoming something of a scholarly bad joke. There were always historians who said it could not be done because of historical problems. There were always theologians who said it should not be done because of theological objections. And there were always scholars who said the former when they meant the latter. Those, however, were negative indignities. What is happening now is rather a positive one. It is the number of competent and even eminent scholars producing pictures of Jesus at wide variance with one another.

One example will suffice to illustrate the present problem. Daniel J. Harrington's presidential address to the Catholic Biblical Association at Georgetown University on August 6, 1986, has been published both in its original text (1987a) and in an "adapted and expanded" version (1987b). In that latter article he gives "a short description of seven different images of Jesus that have been proposed by scholars in recent years, the differences relating to the different Jewish backgrounds against which they have chosen to locate their image of the historical Jesus" (36). There is Jesus as a political revolutionary by S. G. F. Brandon (1967), as a magician by Morton Smith (1978), as a Galilean charismatic by Geza Vermes (1981, 1984), as a Galilean rabbi by Bruce Chilton (1984), as a Hillelite or proto-Pharisee by

Harvey Falk (1985), as an Essene by Harvey Falk (1985), and as an eschatological prophet by E. P. Sanders (1985).

Not every work in that list has the same persuasive potential, but the
plurality is enough to underline the problem. Even under the discipline of
attempting to envision Jesus against his own most proper Jewish background, it seems we can have as many pictures as there are exegetes. Several of those works, and others that could easily be added, for example,
Borg (1984) or Horsley (1987), contain elements and insights that must
surely be retained in any future synthesis. But that stunning diversity is an
academic embarrassment. It is impossible to avoid the suspicion that historical Jesus research is a very safe place to do theology and call it history,
to do autobiography and call it biography.

The problem of multiple and discordant conclusions forces us back to
questions of theory and method. Methodology in Jesus research at the end
of this century is about where methodology in archaeological research was
at the end of the last. When an archaeologist digs into an ancient mound
more or less at random, takes what looks most precious or unique, and hur-
ries home to some imperial museum, we have not scholarly archaeology
but cultural looting. Without scientific stratigraphy, that is, the detailed
location of every item in its own proper chronological layer, almost any conclusion can be derived from almost any object. But although contemporary
archaeology knows very well the absolute importance of stratigraphy, contemporary Jesus research is still involved in textual looting, in attacks on the
mound of the Jesus tradition that do not begin from any overall stratigraphy, do not explain why this or that item was chosen for emphasis over
some other one, and give the distinct impression that the researcher knew
the result before beginning the search.

I knew, therefore, before starting this book that it could not be another
set of conclusions jostling for place among the numerous scholarly images
of the historical Jesus currently available. Such could, no matter how good
it was, but add to the impression of acute scholarly subjectivity in historical
Jesus research. This book had to raise most seriously the problem of methodology and then follow most stringently whatever theoretical method was
chosen.

My methodology for Jesus research has a triple triadic process: the
campaign, the strategy, and the tactics, as it were. The first triad involves
the reciprocal interplay of a macrocosmic level using cross-cultural and
cross-temporal social *anthropology*, a mesocosmic level using Hellenistic
or Greco-Roman *history*, and a microcosmic level using the *literature* of
specific sayings and doings, stories and anecdotes, confessions and interpretations concerning Jesus. All three levels, anthropological, historical,

and literary, must cooperate fully and equally for an effective synthesis. Let me insist on and underline that point. I presume an equal and interactive cooperation in which weakness in any element imperils the integrity and validity of the others. Such triadic equality is extremely hard to come by at the moment. My method, then, demands an equal sophistication on all three levels at the same time. Consider an example. Possibly the key chapter of this book is the thirteenth, "Magic and Meal." The discussion of Jesus' healing, in that chapter, involves an integration of anthropological studies, from Ioan Lewis on ecstatic religion (1971) to Allan Young on the anthropologies of illness and sickness (1982) and Peter Worsley on non-Western medical systems (1982), and historical studies, from John Hull on Hellenistic magic and the synoptic tradition (1974) to David Aune on magic in early Christianity (1980). Jesus' eating, in that chapter, involves a similar integration of anthropological studies such as Peter Farb and George Armelagos's study of the anthropology of eating (1980) and historical studies such as Dennis Smith's study of social obligation in the context of communal meals (1980). But both anthropological and historical levels demand an equal sophistication on the literary or textual level, an acute sensitivity to the chronology of stratification, the multiplicity of attestation, and the interweaving of retention, mutation, and creation within the Jesus tradition itself.

Throughout this book I use several other anthropological models and typologies, for example, Gerhard Lenski's *Power and Privilege: A Theory of Social Stratification* (1966), Ted Robert Gurr's *Why Men Rebel* (1970), and Bryan Wilson's *Magic and the Millennium: A Sociological Study of Religious Movements of Protest Among Tribal and Third-World Peoples* (1973), but no amount of anthropological modeling can obscure the fact that any study of the historical Jesus stands or falls on how one handles the literary level of the text itself. Hence the necessity for a second and third triad focusing directly on that textual level. But allow me first to back up a little.

The ordinary reader may well wonder why there is any problem at all with the literary or textual level of the Jesus tradition. Have we not, for this first-century Mediterranean Jewish peasant, four biographies by Matthew, Mark, Luke, and John, individuals all directly or indirectly connected with him and all composing within, say, seventy-five years after his death? Is that not as good or even better than we have for the contemporary Roman emperor, Tiberius, for whom we have biographies by Velleius Paterculus, Tacitus, Suetonius, and Dio Cassius, only the first of whom was directly connected with him, the others composing from seventy-five to two hundred years after his death? What, then, is the literary problem for the Jesus textual tradition?

It is, at heart, precisely that fourfold record, even if there were no external documents whatsoever, that constitutes the literary problem. If you read those four texts vertically, as it were, from start to finish and one after another, you get a generally persuasive impression of unity, harmony, and agreement. But if you read them horizontally, focusing on this or that unit and comparing it across two, three, or four versions, it is disagreement rather than agreement that strikes one most forcibly. By even the middle of the second century, pagan opponents, like Celsus, and Christian apologists, like Justin, Tatian, and Marcion were well aware of those discrepancies, even if only between, say, Matthew and Luke. The solution was to reduce that plurality to unity in one of the two obvious ways: either eliminate all Gospels save one, the solution of Marcion, or laminate all of them into a single narrative, the solution of (and one that probably even predates) Justin and his student Tatian. Those twin solutions are, in a way, still implicitly operative today. Problem: there are twin versions of the Lord's Prayer. Solution: cite Matthew and ignore Luke. Problem: there are two versions of Jesus' birth story. Solution: put the shepherds and the Magi together at the manger.

Over the last two hundred years, however, comparative work on the Gospels has slowly but surely established certain results and conclusions. First, Gospels are found not only inside but also outside the New Testament itself. Second, the four intracanonical ones represent neither a total collection nor a random sampling of all those available but were deliberately selected by a process in which others were rejected for reasons not only of content but even of form. Third, retention, development, and creation of Jesus materials are found alike within both intracanonical and extracanonical sources. Fourth, differences and discrepancies between accounts and versions are not due primarily to vagaries of memory or divergences in emphasis but to quite deliberate theological interpretations of Jesus. Finally, and in summary, the continuing presence of the risen Jesus and the abiding experience of the Spirit gave the transmitters of the Jesus tradition a creative freedom we would never have dared postulate were it not forced upon us by the evidence. Even, for example, when Matthew or Luke are using Mark as a source for what Jesus said or did or what others said or did to Jesus, they are unnervingly free about omission and addition, about change, correction, or creation in their own individual accounts — but always, of course, subject to their own particular interpretation of Jesus. The Gospels are neither histories nor biographies, even within the ancient tolerances for those genres. They are what they were eventually called, Gospels or good newses, and thereby comes a double warning. "Good" is always such within some individual's or community's opinion or interpretation. And "news" is not a word we usually pluralize again as "newses."

The Jesus tradition, therefore, contains three major layers, one of retention, recording at least the essential core of words and deeds, events and happenings; another of development, applying such data to new situations, novel problems, and unforeseen circumstances; and a final one of creation, not only composing new sayings and new stories, but, above all, composing larger complexes that changed their contents by that very process. "In the first century and early second century, "as Helmut Koester summarized the situation, "the number of gospels in circulation must have been much larger, at least a good dozen of which we at least have some pieces, and everybody could and did rewrite, edit, revise, and combine, however he saw fit" (1983:77). That, in starkest outline, is the textual problem of the Jesus tradition. So how does one search back through those sedimented layers to find what Jesus actually said and did, and, especially, how does one do so with some scholarly integrity and some methodological validity? I have, by the way, no presumption whatsoever that those others layers are illicit, invalid, useless, or detrimental. I do not like to call that first layer "authentic," as if the other two were inauthentic. I talk of original, developmental, and compositional layers, or of retention, development, and creation, but I reject absolutely any pejorative language for those latter processes. Jesus left behind him thinkers not memorizers, disciples not reciters, people not parrots.

My methodology's second triad focuses specifically on that textual problem derived from the very nature of the Jesus tradition itself. The first step is inventory. That initial step involves a complete declaration of all the major sources and texts, both intracanonical and extracanonical, to be used. They must be placed in their historical situation and literary relationship not because that eliminates controversy but so that a reader knows where one stands on every issue. Every step of that inventory is more or less controverted, but that fact demands rather than excuses a clear stand on each problem.

The second step is stratification, the positioning of each source or text in a chronological sequence so that the reader knows what is being dated from, say, 30 to 60, 60 to 80, 80 to 120, and 120 to 150 C.E. Thus, for example, the inventory for this book is established within those four strata (appendix 1).

The third step is attestation. This loops back to the inventory but presents that now stratified data base in terms of multiplicity of independent attestation for each complex of the Jesus tradition within those sources or texts. The fundamental word there is *independent.* If a unit appears in Matthew, Mark, Luke, and John, we have four versions but how many independent ones? It might be two, Mark and John, or sometimes

only one, Mark alone. And every one of those judgments must be worked
out for every single complex in the stratified inventory (see appendix 1).

Finally, there is the third triad, which focuses on the methodological
manipulation of that inventory already established according to chronological hierarchy of stratification and numbered hierarchy of attestation. The
first of its three elements involves a focus on the *sequence of strata*. The
investigation must begin with the first stratum and work from there to the
second, third, and fourth. But this step emphasizes the tremendous importance of that first stratum. It is, in terms of methodological discipline, data
chronologically closest to the time of the historical Jesus. Chronologically
most close does not, of course, mean historically most accurate. In abstract
theory, a unit from the fourth stratum could be more original than one
from the first stratum. But in terms of method, that is, of scholarly discipline and investigative integrity, study must begin with the first stratum.
This book, for instance, will work almost exclusively with that stratum. I
have, however, no presumption that one should work only with it. It is simply the exigencies of space that preclude expanding into the other strata in
this book. I do presume that one should work in sequence through those
strata and that proper method demands an emphasis on the primary stratum that no other stratum can claim. From it one establishes a working
hypothesis about the historical Jesus that can then be tested against subsequent strata. In my Overture, for example, and in appendix 1 as well, I have
given a full indication of what I consider historical Jesus material from all
four strata, but I must emphasize that judgments on the second, third, and
fourth levels were made on, after, and in the light of conclusions concerning that crucial first stratum.

The second element of my final triad is *hierarchy of attestation*. My
methodology begins with the first stratum and, within it, with those complexes having the highest count of independent attestation. A first-stratum
complex having, say, sevenfold independent attestation must be given very,
very serious consideration. I admit, once again, that for reasons of space, in
this book, I have had to group complexes around themes such as "John and
Jesus," but hierarchy of attestation within the first stratum has always been
the guiding principle. And, although in abstract theory there could be just
as much development and creation in that first stratum as in any of the
other three, my method postulates that, at least for the first stratum, everything is original until it is argued otherwise.

The final element is a *bracketing of singularity*. This entails the complete avoidance of any unit found only in single attestation even within the
first stratum. It is intended as a safeguard and an insurance. Something
found in at least two independent sources from the primary stratum can-

not have been created by either of them. Something found there but only in single attestation could have been created by that source itself. Plural attestation in the first stratum pushes the trajectory back as far as it can go with at least formal objectivity. Let me insist here, again, on the distinction between theory and method. I agree that, in theory, a unit found only in a single source from the third stratum might be just as original as one found in fivefold independent attestation from the first stratum. When I started my own work on the historical Jesus over twenty years ago, I placed tremendous emphasis on 447 *The Good Samaritan* [3/1] in Luke 10:29–37 (1973). I still accept everything I said about that unit, and nothing in this book denies the picture of Jesus derived from it. But that was not, in retrospect, a very good method. If I can start there, somebody else can start anywhere else, for instance, with 405 Cities of Israel [3/1] in Matthew 10:23. My inventory's statistics also indicate caution with singularity. There are 522 complexes in that inventory. Of those, 180 have more than one independent attestation: 33 have multiple (4 or more), 42 have triple, 105 have double attestation. There are 342 with only a single attestation. In summary, then, two-thirds of the complexes in the Jesus tradition as inventoried in appendix 1 have only a single attestation.

An example may assist that abstract description. In my inventory's primary stratum is the following item:

20 *Kingdom and Children* [1/4]
   (1) *Gos. Thom.* 22:1–2
   (2) Mark 10:13–16 = Matt. 19:13–15 = Luke 18:15–17
   (3) Matt. 18:3
   (4) John 3:1–10

I term that a *complex*. It has four *sources;* that is, it has fourfold independent attestation, as indicated by the numbers in rounded brackets. It contains six *units*. In this book, however, the focus is not so much on *units*, on citing this or that text or event and asking if Jesus said it or did it, but on *complexes* and on asking whether the core of the complex goes back to Jesus, even allowing for development and creation within it. Did Jesus, in other words, make, in whatever words, some correlation between Kingdom and Children? Whenever I cite a complex, therefore, I record it like this: 20 *Kingdom and Children* [1/4]. The initial number, 20 in this case, tells you where to find that complex, according to chronology of stratum and plurality of attestation, within the inventory of appendix 1. The terminal numbers, [1/4] in this case, remind us constantly what stratum [1/] and attestation [/4] is involved. My *methodological* rule of thumb is that the lower the number left of that stroke and the higher the number to its right, the more seriously the complex must be taken. I realize, by the way, that appendix 1 contains data dense enough to be almost unreadable. But, without sending the size and price of this book beyond reason, I have tried to give you there the full inventory on which it is based. I have also designated each complex as, in my judgment, originally from Jesus (+) or not (−). I have also used the designation ± for certain cases whose metaphorical or metonymical content rendered such positivistic simplicities magnificently irrelevant.

It is clear, I hope, that my methodology does not claim a spurious objectivity, because almost every step demands a scholarly judgment and an informed decision. I am concerned, not with an unattainable objectivity, but with an attainable honesty. My challenge to my colleagues is to accept those formal moves or, if they reject them, to replace them with better ones. They are, of course, only *formal* moves, which then demand a *material* investment. Different scholars might invest those formal moves with widely divergent sources and texts, but historical Jesus research would at least have some common methodology instead of a rush to conclusion that could then be only accepted or denied.

About quotations, especially because this book would have been much shorter without them: I have cited in full those *primary* documents on which my conclusions are based. I do not presume that most readers, even scholarly ones, always look up references, and I have chosen, therefore, to cite in full. With Josephus, for example, it is necessary to cite the two usually divergent accounts he has of almost every incident for the first three quarters of the first century of the common era. Reference or paraphrase cannot replace citation, particularly in that case. Angle brackets (< >), by the way, indicate that the enclosed content was, in an editor's opinion, omitted from the manuscript in question. In quoting *secondary* literature I spend no time citing other scholars to show how wrong they are. Those who are cited represent my intellectual debts and suggest where the reader may go for wider argumentation.

A final word of thanks. I am very grateful to the Department of Religious Studies, the College of Liberal Arts and Sciences, and the administration of De Paul University, which granted my request for a sabbatical leave to work on this book in the Winter Quarter of 1988–89.

PART I

Brokered Empire

Roman, remember by your strength to rule
Earth's peoples — for your arts are to be these:
To pacify, to impose the rule of law,
To spare the conquered, battle down the proud.

> *Virgil,* Aeneid 6.851–853 *(Fitzgerald 190)*

The city of Rome has never been an important center of
trade.... Perhaps no major city in Western history has had so
little commercial and economic importance as has ancient,
medieval, and modern Rome.

> *William I. Davisson and James E. Harper (175)*

From the time Rome became an imperial city until today she
has been a parasite-city, living on gifts, rents, taxes, tribute.
That does not make Rome any less a city, only a different kind
of city from Genoa.

> *Sir Moses I. Finley (125)*

Rome attempted, not merely to cope with the large quantities
of people it had brought together, but to give to its otherwise
degraded mass culture an appropriate urban guise, reflecting
imperial magnificence. To investigate this contribution one
must fortify oneself for an ordeal: to enjoy it, one must keep
one's eyes open, but learn to close one's nose to the stench,
one's ears to the screams of anguish and terror, one's gullet to
the retching of one's own stomach. Above all, one must keep
one's heart on ice and check any impulse to tenderness and pity,
with a truly Roman stolidity. All the magnitudes will be stretched
in Rome: not least the magnitude of debasement and evil.

> *Lewis Mumford (214)*

✧ 1 ✧

Then and Now

> The voices that speak to us from antiquity are overwhelmingly
> those of the cultured few, the elites. The modern voices that
> carry on their tale are overwhelmingly those of white, middle-
> class, European and North American males. These men can,
> and do, laud imperialistic, authoritarian slave societies. The
> scholarship of antiquity is often removed from the real world,
> hygienically free of value judgements. Of the value judgements,
> that is, of the voiceless masses, the 95% who knew how "the
> other half" lived in antiquity.
>
> The peasants form no part of the literate world on which
> most reconstructions of ancient history focus. Indeed, the
> peasants — the pagani — did not even form part of the lowly
> Christian (town dweller's) world. They are almost lost to
> historical view, because of their illiteracy and localism.
>
> *Thomas F. Carney (xiv, 231 note 123)*

The first century of the common era is obscured from our contemporary view by three giant filters. The past is recorded almost exclusively in the voices of elites and males, in the viewpoints of the wealthy and the powerful, in the visions of the literate and the educated. That already constricted report is available sometimes through the deliberate decision of later dominations but also through the vagaries of chance and luck, fate and accident. Either way, further constrictions. And our present looks back to the past, to that already doubly filtered past, dependent, of course, on where one's present is located, but, let us say in individualistic, democratic, urban, middle-class America, often with ethnocentric presumptions it is not even aware of projecting.

Some demographic statistics from the past may serve, therefore, not as proofs about anything but as warnings about everything. Bruce Malina speaks of classes and masses. "The preindustrial city contained no more than ten percent of the entire population under its direct and immediate control. And of this ten percent that constituted the preindustrial urban population, perhaps less than two percent belonged to the elite or high

3

class" (1981:72). Thomas Carney writes of death and taxes. On death: "We are used to a society in which very few infants are lost at birth or prior to weaning. Death, happily, tends to be remote from our experience, if we are below 30. People do not start dying in any numbers until their late fifties or, generally, their sixties or later. In preindustrial society, however, probably a third of the live births were dead before they reached the age of six. By sixteen something like 60% of these live births would have died, 75% by twenty-six, and 90% by forty-six. Very few—3% maybe—reached their sixties" (88). On taxes: "In general, resources extracted from the tax base were mostly redistributed to the men of the apparatus—who mostly invested their official gains in large estates. Taxation was generally regressive.... At best they protected the tax base; they rarely developed it—more often, indeed, they eroded it.... They took a larger share, in fact, than did the elites in more primitive societies before them, or in industrial societies after them" (341).

How, then, is it even possible for us to imagine the face of a Mediterranean Jewish peasant through those triple filters and across the gulf of those millennia? Three major sources help at least somewhat to counter those three filters just mentioned. First, on the macrocosmic level, there are anthropological or sociological studies and models, especially those using trans-temporal and cross-cultural disciplines. Next, on the mesocosmic and more local level, there are archaeological digs and discoveries. Finally, on the microcosmic level, there are papyrus documents and archives, documentary texts predominantly from Egypt in which ordinary peasants have preserved an individual voice and a personal presence normally denied them by their illiteracy and their poverty.

A Friendly Sea in a Hostile Landscape

Three terse judgments, sharp as Mediterranean shadows. "The Mediterranean," in the words of Jane Schneider, "is something of a paradox: a friendly sea surrounded by a hostile landscape" (3). "All Mediterranean societies," in the words of Julian Pitt-Rivers, "face the sea and their enemies—and customers—on the far side of it" (1977:ix). "A double constraint," in the words of Fernand Braudel, "has always been at the heart of Mediterranean history: poverty and the uncertainty of the morrow" (1.245). But even to speak of the social and cultural anthropology of the Mediterranean basin demands three steps, each controversial in its possibility and fraught with difficulties in its execution.

The first step proposes a valid pan-Mediterranean construct open to anthropological investigation. John Davis limits this Mediterranean unity exclusively to historical contacts. Early in his book *The People of the Mediterranean* he describes that unity as, "those institutions, customs and practices which result from the conversation and commerce of thousands of years, the creation of very different peoples who have come into contact round the mediterranean shores" (13). That same judgment is reiterated at the book's conclusion: "over the millennia it has proved impossible for mediterranean people to ignore each other. They have conquered, colonised, converted; they have traded, administered, intermarried—the contacts are perpetual and inescapable" (255).

Jeremy Boissevain, in reviewing Davis's book, argues for a more profound unity, that of ecology. "The Mediterranean is more than just a field of interaction, commerce, and conquest. In spite of his materialist analysis of honour, Davis, in my view, has missed the most obvious materialist parameters that together give the region its distinctive signature: sea, climate, terrain, and mode of production. . . . These materialist parameters, placed in a comparative historical framework, provide a basis on which various differences and similarities characteristic of mediterranean societies may be usefully compared. . . . Mediterranean men have done a great deal besides 'converse' and 'exchange'. . . . Men and women around the middle sea have also worked hard to solve similar problems of production under comparable physical conditions" (Boissevain et al. 83).

David Gilmore, in an invited reply to Davis's book and Boissevain's review, pushes this ecological basis for circum-Mediterranean unity even further by specifying Boissevain's use of Fernand Braudel, who began his huge and magnificent study *The Mediterranean and the Mediterranean World in the Age of Philip II* by devoting three hundred pages to ecology. He claims that Boissevain, "is missing the most important implication of Braudel's work, which is not simply that the Mediterranean is ecologically homogeneous, but rather that this unity derives from the consistent juxtaposition of opposites within nations, the close proximity of rugged topography with fertile riverine basins. It is this intranational contrast between remote, inaccessible mountain peaks and rich agricultural valleys that lies at the heart of mediterranean ecosystems. Throughout the region, one finds independent, egalitarian communities of peasants, tribesmen, or pastoralists in the marginal hills and in the adjacent plains something vastly different—the latifundium, the great estate, the commercial farm, heir to the Roman villa . . . often worked by day laborers under harsh conditions" (Boissevain et al. 88).

Writing for the same symposium of invited responses, Thomas Crump adds some other qualifications to the proposed ecological unity of the Mediterranean. "Boissevain is right to refer to the geophysical factors discussed by Braudel [but] he fails to note three critical sociocultural factors which give the area a quite distinctive character. The first, and perhaps the most important, is that almost every region of the Mediterranean has at some time in the past—generally more than 300 years ago—been very much more important than it is now. . . . The second factor is that the general hierarchical structure of Mediterranean societies has always been based on cities. . . . The third factor is that for more than 2,000 years every mediterranean society of any importance has had the use of a written language" (Boissevain et al. 86).

It seems, then, that we are dealing with a valid unity-in-diversity called Mediterranean society. But it is built up in interactive layers from geography and ecology, through technology and economics, and on to culture and politics.

The second step is particularly difficult for researchers trained to do specifically located fieldwork. Scholars begin with detailed ethnographies, say, of Andalusian villagers or Greek shepherds or Berber and Bedouin tribes. Next comes the call for comparison, from Davis, and for explanation of what such comparison means, from Boissevain. Analytically comparative social and cultural anthropology within the Mediterranean construct is precisely what the next step demands.

Consider, for example, a specific and indeed fascinating ethnographic case study conducted by Julian Pitt-Rivers between 1949 and 1952 and published as *The People of the Sierra* in 1954. It is one of the earlier results of the postwar surge in Mediterranean anthropology centered around E. E. Evans-Pritchard at Oxford University. The focal point of his investigation was Grazalema, or Alcalá, as he called it to protect the innocent, an Andalusian pueblo in the Sierra de Cádiz. It is hardly possible to work comparatively with contemporary Grazalema and, say, ancient Nazareth, just because both are Mediterranean hill-villages with a population of about two thousand inhabitants. Before any such trans-temporal comparisons can be attempted, the data from Andalusia or anywhere else has to be analytically compared with other contemporary data to establish modern Mediterranean constants. Only the results of such analysis will have any chance of valid retrojection to the Mediterranean of two thousand years ago. I would note in passing, however, that reading even such isolated and contemporary accounts of traditional societies is an excellent therapeutic against presuming that an ancient Galilean village is like, say, a modern American one, only much smaller, older, and without electrical utilities or electronic toys.

In a recent article on the current state of Mediterranean anthropology, David Gilmore, presuming the ecological constants, summarizes the other ones that have been suggested within the Mediterranean construct. There are sociocultural constants: "a strong urban orientation; a corresponding disdain for the peasant way of life and for manual labor; sharp social, geographic, and economic stratification; political instability and a history of weak states; 'atomistic' community life; rigid sexual segregation; a tendency towards reliance on the smallest possible kinship units (nuclear families and shallow lineages); strong emphasis on shifting ego-centered, noncorporate coalitions; an honor-and-shame syndrome which defines both sexuality and personal reputation . . . most villagers share an intense parochialism . . . and intervillage rivalries are common . . . There is a general gregariousness and interdependence of daily life characteristic of small, densely populated neighborhoods . . . [There is] institutionalized hostile nicknaming. . . . The evil eye belief is widespread" (1982:178–79). Later he calls that belief, "probably one of the few true Mediterranean universals. It is also one of the oldest continuous religious constructs in the Mediterranean area" (1982:198). There are also religious, marital, and political constants: "religion plays an important institutionalized role in both north and south, as do priests, saints, and holy men . . . Dotal marriage [dowry] is practiced in only 4 percent of the world's cultures, and is limited geographically to eastern Eurasia and the mediterranean basin . . . At the micropolitical level . . . emphasis on informal personal power rather than formal institutions is reflected in the reliance on patronage" (1982:179).

The third step, then, is to control critically the retrojection of those constants from the modern to the ancient Mediterranean, and, that, to compound the problem, involves moving not only from now to then but from fieldwork among people to library work among texts. It must be said immediately that such forays have usually been conducted from ancient history into modern anthropology rather than in the opposite direction.

John Davis, who seems to have honed his writing style by watching fishmongers fillet fish, castigates his anthropological peers for ignoring history but then savages Pitt-Rivers's essay on honor for "hugger-mugger . . . impression of potpourri . . . conceptual confusion which allows historical events, literature of the sort studied by literary critics, and folklore to *tend to illustrate* whatever real thing the general structure may be" (253) and for "elegant use of historical and literary sources which, in a more methodology-minded age, demands careful and critical analysis of the kinds of reasoning underlying the introduction of wayward material" (257). But at least Pitt-Rivers was trying to move from now to then and from field to text.

He tried even more formally and deliberately in a later book on the anthropology of Mediterranean sexuality that began once again with the Sierra de Cádiz in the early 1950s but ended with Shechem and the text of

Genesis 34. His basic intuition on that text is that "the limits of endogamy and exogamy are debated throughout the length of Genesis" so that its stories ask repeatedly but implicitly, "how closely related must you be in order to be one people and how other must you be in order to be a spouse? Other sex? Other family? Other lineage? Other tribe? Other nation?" (1977:154). One answer is given in the earlier nomadic situation of political dependence. In Genesis 12, 20, and 26 the patriarchs are willing to give their wives (as "sisters") to settled power brokers in exchange for pasture, a "form of sexual hospitality...amply testified from ethnographies of many nomadic people, who use their women as a means of establishing relations with the sedentary population" (1977:159). A very different answer is given in their later sedentary situation of political independence. There are two significant transitions in the new answer of Genesis 34. Not only are wives no longer given in sexual hospitality to outsiders, but neither are daughters to be given to them in marriage. And the guardians of this new answer are the new generation, the woman's brothers rather than her father. So Simeon and Levi destroy Shechem and his city rather than allow him to marry Dinah even after all the male citizens accepted circumcision. In Genesis 34:30 Jacob protests against their action, but the brothers get the last word, in 34:31, "Should he treat our sister as a harlot?" Notice, however, that in 34:28 the sons of Jacob take with them not only all the property of the murdered Shechemites but their wives as well. The politics of sex is exactly the same in Genesis 12, 20, 26, and in 34: superiors take the inferiors' women but do not give them their own. The difference is that in the former case the patriarchs are inferior, in the latter they are superior.

Pitt-Rivers had mentioned earlier that "there is however one area of the world which, though it is noted for being traditionally organised in corporate and even kin groups, refuses to exchange women: the Mediterranean" (1977:120). He is willing, therefore, to generalize from Genesis 34 and suggest that "it records in the cryptic fashion of such legends a truth about the origin of Mediterranean civilisation" (1977:171) so that, "the fate of Shechem represents...not only the sexual revolution that initiated the Mediterranean concept of honour, but the starting point of the history of Mediterranean civilisation itself" (1977:186).

Be that as it may, the three steps are now complete. It is possible and instructive to take a proposed Mediterranean constant, in this case the politics of sexual honor, and study it both across present space and past time and from fieldwork to biblical text. Mediterranean anthropology in particular, not to speak of other anthropology in general, can serve as a necessary discipline in situating archaeological artifacts or controlling how we imag-

ine the long-ago lives of ordinary people who once filled their world but
never filled its literature.

Through the Eyes of Others

Larcia Horaea, freedwoman of another Roman freedwoman and wife
of that freedwoman's son, proclaimed on her first-century B.C.E. epitaph,
"My last day made its judgment; death snatched away my soul but did not
take my life's honour" (Lefkowitz & Fant 135). Two millennia later Jeremy
Beckett proclaimed, "The refinement of the notion of honour is perhaps
Mediterranean anthropology's most impressive achievement to date" (Boissevain et al. 85). In 1965, for example, after three Mediterranean confer-
ences between 1959 and 1963, John G. Peristiany edited a collection of
essays entitled *Honour and Shame* and sub-titled *The Values of Mediterranean Society*. Its individual essays contained primarily ethnographic fieldwork but also one literary study and included, in terms of economy, settled
villagers, transhumant herders, and desert nomads; in terms of geography,
both the northern shore, from Andalusia to Greece and Cyprus, and the
southern shore from Egypt to Algeria; and in terms of religion, both Christian and Muslim groups.

What does honor and shame mean for those Mediterranean groups
and societies for whom they are basic, fundamental, and pivotal values?
Julian Pitt-Rivers, speaking from fieldwork in Andalusia in the early fifties,
says, "Honour is the value of a person in his own eyes, but also in the eyes
of his society. It is his estimation of his own worth, his *claim* to pride, but
it is also the acknowledgement of that claim, his excellence recognized by
society, *his right* to pride" (Peristiany 21 = Pitt-Rivers 1977:1). That is clear
but seems also a little prosaic, general, or even universal.

In another essay, however, the profundity of those values becomes
much clearer. Pierre Bourdieu, speaking from fieldwork among the Berber
tribesmen of Algerian Kabylia in the late fifties, says more acutely, "The
point of honour is the basis of the moral code of an individual who sees
himself always through the eyes of others, who has need of others for his
existence, because the image he has of himself is indistinguishable from
that presented to him by other people. . . . Respectability, the reverse of
shame, is the characteristic of a person who needs other people in order to
grasp his own identity and whose conscience is a kind of interiorization of
others, since these fulfil for him the role of witness and judge. . . . He who
has lost his honour no longer exists. He ceases to exist for other people, and
at the same time he ceases to exist for himself" (Peristiany 211, 212). And

although, of course, honor and shame differs programmatically between women and men, those preceding quotations could apply alike to female as well as male members of such societies.

In his introduction to that collection, Peristiany attempted to move beyond discrete ethnographic description to formulate a general cross-cultural hypothesis concerning groups and societies for whom honor and shame are basic, fundamental, and pivotal values. Its importance warrants a lengthy citation. "It is not possible to read about honour and shame in these six Mediterranean societies without making frequent mental excursions and involuntary comparisons with the *gesta* of chivalry, with school gangs, with street corner societies, etc. What do these groups have in common? This, it seems to me, is the crux of the problem. The papers collected here may allow the formulation of a *tentative,* an exploratory, answer. Honour and shame are the constant preoccupation of individuals in small scale, exclusive societies where face to face personal, as opposed to anonymous, relations are of paramount importance and where the social personality of the actor is as significant as his office. Within the minimal solidary groups of these societies, be they small or large families or clans, spheres of action are well defined, non-overlapping and non-competitive. The opposite is true outside these groups. What is significant in this wider context is the insecurity and instability of the honour-shame ranking. . . . In this insecure, individualist, world where nothing is accepted on credit, the individual is constantly forced to prove and assert himself. Whether as the protagonist of his group or as a self-seeking individualist, he is constantly 'on show,' he is forever courting the public opinion of his 'equals' so that they may pronounce him worthy" (11). What is most striking about his hypothesis is that it concerns not only Mediterranean nomads, shepherds, or peasants, but also gangs of warrior elites from ancient jousting lists to modern street corners.

At that stage, however, the problem comes full circle. If honor and shame can be so universalized, how is it at all a useful Mediterranean characteristic? A much later collection of articles is very helpful on that precise point. "Mediterranean honor," according to David Gilmore's introduction, "is a 'libidinized' social reputation; and it is this eroticized aspect of honor—albeit unconscious or implicit—that seems to make the Mediterranean variant distinctive." Again: "Mediterranean . . . unity is at least partly derived from the primordial values of honor and shame, and these values are deeply tied up with sexuality and power, with masculine and gender relations." Again: "If a gender-based honor-and-shame moral system defines a Mediterranean World, then this category emerges not simply as an example of butterfly collecting, but as a mutually intelligible framework of moral choices by which people communicate and gain an identity both with and within the group" (1987:3, 16, 17). That same specification is underlined in the collection's concluding essay by Stanley Brandes. "It is this pervasive sexuality that is particularly characteristic of Mediterranean value systems, of Mediterranean codes of honor and shame. In this, the codes may be distinguished from parallel moral systems elsewhere," in Japan, for example (Gilmore, 1987:125).

In his 1977 survey of Mediterranean anthropology, John Davis claims, "There are three main forms of stratification which have been observed in the mediterranean: bureaucracy, class and honour. Each of them is related to the distribution of wealth, more or less directly. They are, for the purpose of analysis, ideal types, distinct elementary forms which, in substantive politics, are intertwined, mixed in varying degrees, variously important. Each is associated with an appropriate mode of political representation — again, ideal types, elementary forms, which in the hugger-mugger of actual political activity have variable importance. These are: insistence on citizen's rights; class struggle; patronage" (76).

Those three stratification systems are exemplified very clearly in Peristiany's own essay in that collection he also edited. His fieldwork concentrated on the Greek Cypriot mountain village of Alona in the middle 1950s. Stratification by bureaucracy and power is clear when the villager has to approach a government civil servant and when "in the impersonal interaction between citizen and civil servant the only claim upon the latter's *philotimo* is that of his own sectional interests, and these call for the assertion of his administrative dignity, for arrogance and the marking of social distance" (186). Stratification by wealth and class is clear "when the returned expatriate who had achieved success in a city environment wished to trade on this success as a means of achieving immediate recognition in the village . . . [and] considered . . . further that his financial success raised him above the confines of the village hierarchy" (178). But neither of those other stratifications is confused by the villagers with their own hierarchy of honor and shame. Peristiany concludes by comparing honor and honesty: "The punctiliousness of honour must be referred to the code of an exclusive and agonistic microsociety; that of honesty to an inclusive, egalitarian macrosociety. Duty, in the first instance, is to those with whom one shares honour. In the second, the un-Greek macrosociety, one's duty is to all fellow citizens or, even further, to all humans. . . . Honour is active. Here insecurity and the daily reevaluation of one's standing breed constant self-assertion and even heroism. The ideals of honesty and equality breed passive conformity and are more congenial to a conception of duty wide in its application, but more accommodating in its expectations" (189–90).

The comparison of honor and shame with other stratification systems intensifies the problem. It is relatively easy to understand the bases and advantages of stratification systems based on class or status, wealth or power, possessions or authority. But why is there a stratification system based on honor and shame? Why are there those relatively objective systems based on control of goods or services but also this subjective or, better, intersubjective system based on honor and shame?

Davis himself asks the question quite bluntly. "The final point is to raise the question—why does honour exist?" And he also points to a fascinating attempt to answer it. "It must be frankly admitted that only the excellent Jane Schneider has asked and attempted to answer that question in print" (100).

This is how, according to Jane Schneider, the move from ecology to society operates within Mediterranean pastoralism: "Unlike [pastoralism in] Central Asia . . . pastoralism in the Mediterranean was challenged by the continuous expansion of agriculture for centuries preceding the industrial revolution. Because transport by sea was easy, Iron Age technologies for the production of agricultural surpluses diffused into dry and mountainous zones which might otherwise have remained pastoral, broken only by scattered communities of marginal, autochthonous cultivators. Particularly on the less arid European side, landlords devoted vast regions to the production of wheat for export, simply because of the facility with which it could be transported by sea. . . . In much of the Mediterranean, pastoralism and agriculture coexisted, competing for the same resources in a way which fragmented the social organization of each type of community and blurred the boundary between them. In the absence of the state, pastoral communities, and agricultural communities in their midst, developed their own means of social control—the codes of honor and shame—which were adapted to the intense conflict that external pressures had created within them, and between them" (3). We are dealing, in other words, with a harsh ideology for an equally harsh ecology, with limited and unstable social unities arising from limited and unstable natural resources. Pastoral societies, whether nomadic and moving over an extended territory or transhumant and moving back and forth between one set area and another, are controlled by what might be termed Schneider's Law: "the more vulnerable and pressured a pastoral society, the smaller and more independent of each other are its basic economic units" (6). When one considers the difficulties of Mediterranean pastoralism, "facing extremes of temperature and tempest, periodic drying out of pastures and water sources, treacherous migratory routes and predatory animals," it is easy to see that "pastoralists, to survive, must be selfish . . . appropriately they make selfishness a virtue" (5).

When I first read the descriptions of Mediterranean honor and shame societies in Peristiany's collection, I wondered why any group would invent a stratification code that seemed to guarantee instability and insecurity, tension and combativeness. Schneider's analysis reminds us that "the more difficult it is to find large extensions of suitable grazing land, to have regular access to adequate supplies of water and a predictable route of migration, the more extrafamilial organization becomes not only difficult to achieve but an outright handicap in the management of herds" (6). Hence, what I have termed Schneider's Law, namely, the greater the external pressure on pastoralism, the less the internal organization of pastoralism, is exemplified by her across the following huge ecological sweep. "One can imagine a gradient which goes from predominantly pastoral Central Asia through the Mediterranean to predominantly agricultural Western Europe—from the horse-raising, camel-riding nomads of Asia to the camel-raising, horse-riding nomads of the Middle East, to the transhumant sheep and goat herders of North Africa and Eastern Europe, and finally to the low-status shepherds and goatherds and the high-status 'ranchers' of Spain and Italy, who are little more than specialists within agricultural communities. This gradient of pastoral-agrarian interaction is roughly paralleled by a graded complexity of social organization among pastoralists" (7).

There is, however, an obvious and immediate problem. One could at least imagine a single large nuclear family quite self-sufficient in its ability to maintain and expand its flocks and herds and to obtain and control access to needed pasture and water. But it would necessarily and inevitably have to go outside itself for wives and husbands. Scarcest of all those scarce resources, therefore, are marriage partners, because these by definition cannot come from within the nuclear family.

Although Schneider is speaking of honor and shame primarily among Mediterranean pastoralists and marginal agriculturists, her language makes it possible at least to imagine wider application: "As a political phenomenon, honor can attach to any human group from the nuclear family to the nation state. The problem of honor becomes salient when the group is threatened with competition from equivalent groups. It is especially salient when small particularistic groups, such as families, clans, or gangs, are the principal units of power, sovereign or nearly so over the territories they control. Concern for honor also grows when contested resources are subject to redivision along changing lines, when there is no stable relationship between units of power and precisely delimited patrimonies, i.e., when the determination of boundary lines is subject to continual human intervention. Finally, concern with honor arises when the definition of the group is problematical; when the social boundaries are difficult to maintain, and

internal loyalties are questionable. Shame, the reciprocal of honor, is especially important when one of the contested resources is women, and
women's comportment defines the honor of social groups. Like all ideologies, honor and shame complement institutional arrangements for the distribution of power and the creation of order in society" (2).

A family or a group may run its affairs quite well on the principle of
homo homini lupus, that is, of acting toward one another as wolves would
never do, but what happens when mates are needed? If, for example, there
were only two nuclear families in the entire world, they could compete with
each other to their hearts' content for everything else desirable, but they
would have to cooperate with each other for mates.

I suppose, however, one could imagine a noncooperative system even
there. Speaking of Mediterranean pastoralists, Schneider says that "women
are contested resources, much like sheep," and again, "women . . . are contested resources much like pastures and water, so much so that kidnap-
pings, abductions, elopements, and the capture of concubines appear to
have been frequent occurrences, at least in the past" (20, 18). But that is
hardly a satisfactory system or a satisfactory explanation, since women,
even if seen as another contested resource, are also a very special and even
unique resource among such resources. The future of the family depends
on the individuality of the new wife in a way it hardly does on the individuality of sheep, or pasture, or well. There must be, then, some way not only
of acquiring this special resource but also of guaranteeing its quality.
Hence the almost mythological importance of virginity in Mediterranean
codes of honor and shame. This serves, as Schneider notes, to obviate
intrafamilial tensions between brother and brother or even brother and
father because it unifies them in concern about the purity of their women.
But there is much more to it than that. Virginity is the living symbol and
incarnate emblem of the group's closed-off combativeness. It is easy to
understand the importance of Mary, as Virgin-Mother, in such circumstances. She is exactly what one wishes for but can never obtain: maternity
without the loss of virginity, progeny without the necessity of sex, and,
therefore, competition for resources without the need to cooperate for the
most important one. In the words of Julian Pitt-Rivers, "When it is said that
'we fight with those with whom we intermarry' or vice versa . . . [it means]
that we, as individuals, give our daughters to members of the groups with
whom we, as a collectivity, have relations of conflict. The two types of relationship, collective hostility and affinity through marriage, are the opposed
aspects of an ambivalence and it is the second which qualifies the first and
sets limits to it, bringing it under the control of the longer-term interests
represented by the descendants who result from intermarriage" (1977:123).

Honor and shame, then, could be defined as the ideology of small, discrete, and unstable groups competing permanently for basic resources that are attained insecurely and maintained precariously but where conflict must be reluctantly transposed into cooperation for the most precious resource of all, marriageable women.

Can Anything Good Come from Nazareth?

Compare Nazareth as seen first through literary and then through archaeological lenses. Leaving aside Christian sources, Jack Finegan sums up what we have about it from earliest other texts. "In the Old Testament Jos. 19:10–15 gives a list of the towns of the tribe of Zebulon . . . but does not mention Nazareth. Josephus, who was responsible for military operations in this area in the Jewish War . . . gives the names of forty-five towns in Galilee, but does not say anything about Nazareth. The Talmud also, although it refers to sixty-three Galilean towns, does not mention Nazareth" (27). From Jewish literary texts, then, across almost one thousand five hundred years, nothing.

The very first mention of Nazareth in any non-Christian text comes from a fragmented inscription on a piece of dark gray marble excavated at Caesarea in August of 1962 and dating from the third or fourth century of the common era. In 70 C.E., during the First Roman-Jewish War, the Temple of Jerusalem was totally destroyed by the future emperor Titus, and, at the end of the Third Roman-Jewish War in 135 C.E., the defeated Jews were expelled from the territory of Jerusalem, renamed Aelia Capitolina by the emperor Hadrian. The surviving priests, divided from ancient times into twenty-four courses that took weekly turns in Temple service, were eventually reorganized and resettled in various Galilean towns and villages. A list of those assignments was affixed to the wall of Caesarea's synagogue built around the year 300 C.E. The restored line reads: "The eighteenth priestly course [called] Hapizzez, [resettled at] Nazareth." Both communal relocation and synagogal inscription served, no doubt, both to recall the Second Temple's past and to await a Third Temple's future (Vardaman; Avi-Yonah). But archaeology knows more about Nazareth than this rather late first non-Christian mention of its name.

Between 1955 and 1960 the Franciscan scholar Bellarmino Bagatti excavated at Nazareth beneath both the demolished older Church of the Annunciation and other Franciscan property extending north-eastward toward their Church of Saint Joseph. He summarized his discoveries by saying, "Chronologically we have: tombs of the Middle Bronze Period [c. 2000–1500 B.C.E.]; silos with ceramics of the Middle Iron Period [c. 900–539

B.C.E.]; and then, uninterruptedly, ceramics and constructions of the
Hellenistic Period [c. 332–63 B.C.E.] down to modern times" (Bagatti
1.29–32). The remnants from those earlier occupations are, however, quite
limited, while those of that final one are much more extensive. Thus,
despite some hints of an ancient lineage, "It is in the second century B.C.E.
that extensive remains are to be found, which suggests that this is the
period of the refounding of the village. . . . This implies that the village was
less than two hundred years old in the first century C.E." (Meyers &
Strange 57, 184 note 36). It was also and only in the late second century that
the Jewish dynasty of the Hasmoneans succeeded in conquering the Greek
city of Samaria, which blocked their northward thrust for control of the
Plain of Esdraelon and annexation of Galilee. The refounding of Nazareth
may well reflect that territorial expansion.

The tombs, both those discovered by Bagatti and others known from
earlier explorations, would have been placed outside the village and serve,
in fact, to delimit its circumference for us. Looking at their locations on the
plans drawn up by Bagatti (1.28) or Finegan (27), one realizes just how small
the village actually was and also that Bagatti's excavations were located
pretty much at its heart. The vast majority of the tombs are chambers with
several burial shafts cut horizontally into the walls so that a body could be
inserted head first. Because of those shafts or niches, they are called *loculi*
graves in Latin or *kokim* graves in Hebrew. One tomb from the Nazareth
necropolis, for example, had six balanced shafts on either side of the burial
chamber and a thirteenth one in the back wall. Artifacts found when that
tomb was excavated in 1923 span the first half millennium of the common
era and indicate "that the village, even though it ran into difficulties in the
war of 70, was never abandoned" and that "the tomb was in use for many
centuries" (Bagatti 1.237). The use of such multishafted burial chambers is
quite significant because, as Jack Finegan observed, "from about 200 B.C.
[they] became virtually the standard type of Jewish tomb," so that "it may
fairly be said that this type of tomb virtually became the canonical form of
the Jewish family grave" (28, 185). Another conclusion from archaeology,
therefore, is that Nazareth was a very Jewish village in the Roman era.

Bagatti also discovered many grottoes inside the ancient village, as well
as cisterns for water, presses for olives, vats for oil, millstones and silos for
grain. The conclusion is "that the principal activity of these villagers was
agriculture. Nothing in the finds suggests wealth" (Meyers & Strange 56).

Three qualifications must be added to that picture of Nazareth as a
Jewish agricultural hamlet in the early Roman period. The first one is from
regional topography, and it underlines both the differentiation between
Upper and Lower Galilee and the location of Nazareth in the southern-

most part of that latter region. The four ranges of Lower Galilean hills reach heights of over one thousand feet and run so as to create west-east valleys between them. But the Meiron range in Upper Galilee reaches a height of almost four thousand feet and far more effectively isolates that area than do the much smaller hill ranges of Lower Galilee (Freyne 1980a:xvi, 9–16). Eric Meyers concludes from this regionalism that "it is intriguing to ask whether the negative reflections of the later sages on 1st century Galilee and some of the clichés in the New Testament are due more to the degree of accommodation to Hellenism in the south [Lower Galilee] than to a presumed rural agricultural Judaism. The latter would have been more characteristic of those living in the mountains of the north [Upper Galilee]" (1975–76:97; see also 1979:698–699). Furthermore, the Nazareth range is the southernmost of those four sets of Lower Galilean hills. The villages of the northern three ranges stay close to the base of their hills, while the Nazareth range has far more sites closer to its top. This derives from its softer and more porous rock, which allows for springs much farther up the slope (Freyne, 1980a:11). The village of Nazareth, then, at an elevation of over a thousand feet and with its single ancient spring, is exactly what the terrain dictated. But that, of course, isolated the village off the beaten track.

A second qualification comes from political geography. "A *major city*," says Ian Hopkins, following what is called Central Place Theory, "contains within its region a number of *smaller cities* and each of these serves a region with *towns*, each of which is surrounded by a region of *villages*. The key factors which determine this pattern of settlement location are commerce, especially local marketing functions, and administrative functions, through which the cities serve the towns and the towns the villages" (19, my italics). For Lower Galilee, that relative hierarchy, determined more by political autonomy than mere population density, was represented by Bethshan/ Scythopolis as its *major city*, Sepphoris and Tiberias as its *smaller cities*, Capernaum and Magdala/Tarichaeae as its *towns*. Nazareth, clearly a *village*, is closest, not to one of those towns, but, at three or four miles distance, to Sepphoris, a smaller city.

Aulus Gabinius, proconsul of Syria between 57 and 55 B.C.E., organized Palestine into five administrative districts after the Roman conquest and made Sepphoris the capital of the Galilean district, presumably thereby validating its already leading position (JW 1.170; JA 14.91). In 4 B.C.E., during the revolts after Herod the Great's death, Sepphoris was apparently the rebel center in Lower Galilee. Its royal arsenals were taken by Judas, son of Ezekias, and, in retaliation, Quinctilius Varus, proconsul of Syria, had the city destroyed and its inhabitants sold into slavery (JW 2.56,

68; JA 17.271, 289). Herod Antipas, having received Galilee and Perea as his tetrarchy in 3 B.C.E., "fortified Sepphoris to be the ornament of all Galilee, and called it Autocratoris" (JA 18.27), presumably more or less immediately and presumably as his capital city. But, then, probably between 17 and 20 C.E., Antipas built an entirely new city on the western shore of Lake Gennesaret, called it Tiberias in honor of the emperor, gave it an entirely Greek constitution and a primarily Jewish population, and made it his new capital, with Sepphoris reduced to a subordinate position. Those roles were reversed, however, by Felix, Roman procurator between 52 and 60 C.E. (JA 18.36–38; Life 37–38). When the First Roman-Jewish War broke out in 66 C.E., Sepphoris, predominantly Jewish and strategically important, remained staunchly loyal to Rome, because of its earlier destruction for rebellion in 4 B.C.E. and/or its recent restoration to capital status around 54 C.E. Its inhabitants were described by Josephus as "the only people of that province [Galilee] who displayed pacific sentiments" (JW 3.30). Tiberias, on the other hand, and despite dissident elements, was predominantly pro-rebellion, and was spared destruction only by the speed with which it surrendered to Vespasian's forces (Life 349–352). But Sepphoris remained, in the words of Seán Freyne, "a Jewish aristocratic city in the heart of fertile Galilee, given its position of prominence by the Romans originally and aware that this was dependent on their continued good pleasure. This explains the striking uniformity and consistency of its attitudes throughout the revolt, but it also helps to explain the Galileans' detestation of it, despite their sharing similar religious loyalties" (1980a:128).

When Josephus, in the defensive history of his Galilean leadership, speaks of Sepphoris as "situated in the heart of Galilee, surrounded by numerous villages" (Life 346), Nazareth is among those unnamed villages, which must be seen not as isolated entities but as satellites of a provincial capital "of considerable importance in late antiquity" (Meyers, Netzer & Meyers 4). The main west-east road through Galilee ran from Ptolemaïs on the Mediterranean coast through Sepphoris to Tiberias on the Sea of Galilee. Ptolemaïs itself was on the Via Maris, the coastal Way of the Sea, that most ancient Palestinian highway of international commerce and conquest that opened Sepphoris and its environs to cosmopolitan influence. Sepphoris was also the terminus of the north-south mountain road from Jerusalem. Two roads, therefore, and possibly carrying quite different types of influence, converged in Sepphoris so that the village or hamlet of Nazareth, while certainly off the beaten track, was not very far off a fairly well beaten track. To understand Nazareth, therefore, demands consideration not only of its rural aspects but also of its relationship to an urban provincial capital that contained, in the summary statement of Andrew Overman, "courts, a fortress, a theater seating 3-4000, a palace, a colonnaded street on top of the acropolis, two city walls, two markets (upper and lower), archives, the royal bank, and the arsenal . . . [and a] population . . . around 30,000" (164).

A last, and possibly most important qualification, comes from comparative demography. Even with much more archaeology still to be done, certain results already demand a very different view of Lower Galilee in the first century of the common era. There was, according to Andrew Overman, "an unusually large number of urban and larger village centers in lower Galilee, an area roughly 15 miles by 25 miles . . . this makes lower Galilee one of the most densely populated regions of the entire Roman Empire." Therefore, he continues, "one is never more than a day's walk from anywhere in lower Galilee, if that. . . . One could not live in any village in lower Galilee and escape the effects and ramifications of urbanization. . . . Life in lower Galilee in the first century was as urbanized and urbane as anywhere else in the empire" (165, 168). And the other side of that geographical proximity and demographic density was cultural continuity. "Did," Douglas Edwards asks, "a significant cultural antagonism exist in lower Galilee between rural areas that were largely conservative, Aramaic speaking enclaves and Hellenistic, urbane, Greek oriented urban areas?" His answer, based on the work of Martin Goodman, is emphatically negative. "The hostility . . . that Tiberias and Sepphoris attracted was as a result of political disputes, not a 'cultural split.' Indeed, there existed 'a cultural continuum from city to country'" (181–182).

The name of Nazareth, then, may be absent from non-Christian literature, but its peasants lived in the shadow of a major administrative city, in the middle of a densely populated urban network, and in continuity with its hellenized cultural traditions. In the words of Eric Meyers, "the isolation that often is associated with the Galilean personality is . . . quite inappropriate when we speak of Jesus of Nazareth, who is growing up along one of the busiest trade routes of ancient Palestine at the very administrative center of the Roman provincial government" (1979:698). And in those of Thomas Longstaff, "it is no longer possible to think of Jesus as a simple peasant from Nazareth (dare one say 'a good old country boy'?) nor to describe the disciples as 'hillbillies from Galilee.' Their lives, and those of the many who followed them, were certainly affected by the all-pervasive presence of the Roman city" (14).

Do Not Forget Me

If ancient literary sources presume primarily the vision of an elite, even if only of a quite relative and even contended elite, there are also documentary sources to be considered. Egypt, because its bureaucrats were very busy and its sands were very dry, has preserved papyrus documents by the tens of thousands. Here, at least, we get direct and immediate evidence for life at the other end of the spectrum of power and influence. These are not the literary reflections of the aristocracy but rather the archival reflections of the peasantry. "The three principal sources of papyrus documents," according to John White, "have been town and village rubbish heaps, some as high as thirty feet, ancient collapsed buildings and, finally, tombs and cemeteries." Furthermore, it was "estimated in 1981 that some 25,000 papyri of Roman date alone had already been published and that twice that number from the same period still remained to be edited and published" (4–5). Here are two examples of such peasant documentation, discovered around the turn of the century on the west bank of the Nile about one hundred twenty miles south of Cairo in the excavated rubbish dumps of ancient Oxyrhynchus, the modern El Bahnasa.

The first example is simple but at once tender and terrible. The worker Hilarion writes to his wife Alis on June 18 in the year 1 B.C.E.

> Hilarion to his sister Alis many greetings, likewise to my lady Berous and to Apollonarion. Know that we are even yet in Alexandria. Do not worry if they all come back (except me) and I remain in Alexandria. I urge and entreat you, be concerned about the child and if I should receive my wages soon, I will send them up to you. If by chance you bear a son, if it is a boy, let it be, if it is a girl, cast it out [to die]. You have said to Aphrodisias, "Do not forget me." How can I forget you? Therefore I urge you not to worry. (Year) 29 of Caesar [Augustus], Payni 23. (White 111–12; see also Hunt & Edgar 1.294–95; Davis 1933:1–7)

Hilarion was married in the Egyptian custom to his sister Alis. Their mother was named Berous, and they already had one son called Apollonarion. Hilarion and some companions had left their home at Oxyrhynchus and traveled north to work in Alexandria. The pregnant Alis, having heard nothing nor received anything from him, transmitted her concern through Aphrodisias, who was also traveling to the capital. The letter is Hilarion's response to her concern. That is an isolated case, a flash of light in the darkness that surrounds Alis and Hilarion forever. The second example is much fuller and more detailed. These are papyri that furnish a veritable history of a peasant artisan.

Scattered across the first two published volumes of the Oxyrhynchus Papyri are texts referring either directly or indirectly to a weaver named Tryphon, an Egyptian contemporary and more or less social equal of Jesus. These archival papyri, spanning five generations, are documentary rather than literary, are preserved as the random gift of Egypt's climate, and furnish at least an outline biography for a member of the lower classes. One ordinarily expects to hear of such persons only if they drew upon themselves the welcome or unwelcome attention of the upper classes. But here we have a perfect case of objective and documentary data concerning an ancient life located at the lower end of the social, economic, and political hierarchy.

Augustus imposed on Egypt a head-tax to be levied on all males between the age of fourteen and sixty, save, of course, for the privileged classes. Census lists for taxation required, therefore, both names and ages. And on a copy of one such official listing, from the years 11 to 12 C.E., we first meet with Tryphon at three years of age. His paternal great-grandfather, the elder Didymus, is mentioned only by name and is presumably dead. The elder Didymus's son, Tryphon's paternal grandfather, also named Tryphon, was then sixty-four. The elder Tryphon appears as the head of an extended family all paying taxes from the same household. He and his wife Timotos had three children, the younger Didymus aged thirty-seven, Dionysius aged thirty-two, and the elder Thoönis aged twenty-one. Dionysius and his wife Thamounion were the parents of the younger Tryphon, born around 8 C.E. Then, in a listing for the next year, Tryphon has a new brother, the younger Thoönis, aged one year (P. Oxy. 288, 314; Grenfell & Hunt 2.280–284, 306).

The next documents are from the early twenties C.E. About 21 C.E., Tryphon, almost certainly the elder, had a horoscope prepared for an individual who had been born at 10:00 P.M. on September 28 of some year between 15 and 37 C.E. (P. Oxy. 235; Grenfell & Hunt 2.137–139). A tear in the papyrus renders the precise year of Tiberius' reign uncertain, but, at a pure guess, the individual might have been Tryphon's third grandson, Onnophris, born to Dionysius and Thamounion after Tryphon and Thoönis the youngers, around 21 C.E.? Be that as it may, and whatever the meaning of the horoscopes for Tryphon the elder, taxes had now become a reality for Tryphon the younger. We have his tax receipts for the years between 22 and 25 C.E. and it includes those of his father for 24 to 25 C.E. They were paying four different types of taxes. The first and most important was the handicraft tax, in their case, on weaving. This was levied on all, either female or male, who worked for wage or profit and even, apparently, before the age of fourteen. Tryphon, for example, started paying at least some weaving taxes even before he was eligible, at fourteen, for the poll tax. Soon, however, he was paying as much or even more than his father. Consider, for example, the tenth year of Tiberius, or 23 to 24 C.E. in our reckoning. Tryphon, who was then about fifteen or sixteen, paid, in several installments, a weaving tax of 39.75 drachmae (P. Oxy. 288, 311; Grenfell & Hunt 2.280–284, 304). There were also three other taxes for that same year.

> The tenth year of Tiberius Caesar Augustus, Mecheir 13, paid through
> Diogenes, banker, by Tryphon son of Dionysius for poll-tax in the Hippo-
> drome quarter, including charge for transport, 8 drachmae, and on the
> 24th of Pharmouthi by the same poll-tax 4 drachmae. On Pauni 21, dies
> Augustus, for pig-tax 2 drachmae 1½ obols. On Epeiph 16, for embank-
> ment-tax 6 drachmae. (P. Oxy. 288; Grenfell & Hunt 2.280–284; Hunt &
> Edgar 2.482–485)

The full *poll-tax* rate for the Oxyrhynchite nome was sixteen drachmae, but
the metropolites were allowed to pay only twelve drachmae. The *dike-tax*
was "the only tax whose rate was uniform throughout the province,"
according to Naphtali Lewis, and "went to pay for supplies and materials . . . it was paid in addition to, not as a substitute for, the labour on the
dikes required . . . of the peasantry." On the *pig-tax*, "we can only speculate:
one suggestion is that it provided the Greek and Roman temples with sacrificial animals, thus acting as an incentive to the Egyptian farmers to raise
an animal that was anathema to their religion" (170–171). It did not mean,
in other words, that Tryphon's family kept pigs.

Cumulatively, therefore, with six obols to the drachma, Tryphon's four
taxes for 23 to 24 C.E. came to sixty drachmae. On Naphtali Lewis's price
index of goods and services in first-century Egypt, that is the equivalent, for
example, of the wages for about twenty days of legionary service or forty
days of household industrial labor (208).

Sometime around the start of the thirties C.E. Tryphon married Demetrous, but the marriage, as can be seen from a torn papyrus complaint of
between 30 and 35 C.E., did not go well.

> To Alexandrus, strategus, from Tryphon, son of Dionysius, of the city of
> Oxyrhynchus. I married Demetrous, daughter of Heraclides, and I for
> my part provided for my wife in a manner that exceeded my resources.
> But she became dissatisfied with our union, and finally left the house
> carrying off property belonging to me a list of which is added below. I
> beg, therefore, that she be brought before you in order that she may
> receive her deserts, and return to me my property. This petition is with-
> out prejudice to the other claims which I have or may have against her.
> The stolen articles are: a . . . worth 40 drachmae . . . (P. Oxy. 282; Grenfell
> & Hunt 2.272–273, plate 7)

The verb "carrying off" is in the plural and, as the editors note, it "indicates
that Demetrous had an accomplice . . . very likely her mother." We shall
meet them both again later on.

What happened next casts some retrospective light on that divorce. It
seems quite likely that it was Tryphon's interest in another woman named

Saraeus that caused Demetrous's displeased departure. In any case, on May 22 of 36 C.E., he entered into a very careful agreement with Saraeus.

> Tryphon, son of Dionysius, a Persian of the Epigone, to Saraeus, daughter of Apion, under the wardship of Onnophris, son of Antipater, greeting. I acknowledge the receipt from you at the Serapeum at Oxyrhynchus through the bank of Sarapion, son of Kleandrus, of . . . a total sum of 72 drachmae of silver . . . in consideration of which I have consented (to our marriage). And I will repay to you the 72 drachmae of silver [by October 27 of 36 C.E.] . . . If I do not repay in accordance with the above terms I will forfeit to you the said sum with the addition of half its amount, for which you are to have the right of execution upon me and all my property, as in accordance with a legal decision . . .
> (P. Oxy. 267; Grenfell & Hunt 2.243–247)

They intended, expressly, to enter an "unrecorded marriage," that is, to live together for a trial period without a regular contract, and they sealed the arrangement with a deposit-loan from Saraeus to Tryphon. A non-dowry, as it were, for a non-marriage. Because Tryphon agreed, in effect, to a five-month loan with a 50 percent penalty for nonrepayment, I conclude that he wanted the trial cohabitation even more than did Saraeus or her family. The experimental union must have worked out quite well, because Saraeus did not take back her deposit-loan on the specified date. Indeed, at the bottom of the original 36 C.E. contract it is noted that the "dowry" was paid back to Saraeus only on June 9 of 43 C.E. My guess, in the light of subsequent papyri, is that they decided to end their trial period after seven years and that the loan's return represented part of that regularization process.

There are two other interesting details evident in that cohabitation contract. First, somebody named Leon had to sign "on behalf of Tryphon because he did not know how to write for himself." Saraeus and her guardian Onnophris were also illiterate. Second, Tryphon is called "a Persian of the Epigone." This epithet denotes "as a rule, indigent people, granted loans on rather harsh and, to some extent, degrading terms . . . [since] this clause deprived [them] of the traditional right of every Egyptian to seek shelter in a temple. . . . It seems that the obligation of being styled 'Persian of the Epigone' was imposed on the debtor only . . . all [Persians of the Epigone] mentioned in the contracts are little men" (Tcherikover et al. 1.51).

For that same 36 C.E. we have the following document, described but not transcribed by its editors: "Contract between Thamounion, acting with her son Tryphon, and Abarus a weaver, apprenticing to him her son Onnophris .. for two years" (P. Oxy. 322; Grenfell & Hunt 2.306). I would guess that Dionysius, Tryphon's father, was already dead by 36 C.E., so that

Tryphon himself, as eldest son, furnished the obligatory male presence for the contract of his mother Thamounion and his brother, the younger Onnophris, named after her father, the elder Onnophris. The boy, by the way, was not yet fourteen (P. Oxy. 275; Grenfell & Hunt 262–264 note for line 17).

For the next year, 37 C.E., there are two untranscribed texts. The first is described as a "Petition to Sotas, strategus, from Tryphon, complaining of an assault by Demetrous and her mother upon his wife Saraeus" (P. Oxy. 315; Grenfell & Hunt 2.306). In the light of preceding texts, no comment is required on that complaint. The second text is described as an "Acknowledgement by [Thamounis], daughter of Onnophris, Persian of the Epigone, of the loan of 16 drachmae from her son Tryphon." By 37 C.E., despite Demetrous and possibly because of Saraeus, things were a little better for Tryphon. There is also a third untranscribed papyrus from some date after 37 C.E.: "Beginnings of 27 lines of an agreement between Tryphon and Saraeus concerning the nurture of their infant daughter . . . Cancelled" (P. Oxy. 321; Grenfell & Hunt 2.306). Their marriage was still unofficial in 37 C.E., and the birth of their first child demanded some nurturing agreement. But that second agreement, like their initial cohabitation agreement, must have been superseded in 42 C.E. by a regularized marriage contract.

In 44 C.E. we hear again about Tryphon's brother, the younger Thoönis, the middle sibling between himself and the younger Onnophris. The letter is sent to the official scribes of the bureaucratic region.

> From Thamounion, daughter of Onnophris, of the city of Oxyrhynchus, with her guardian Sarapion, son of Sarapion. My son Thoönis, son of Dionysius, who has no trade, registered in the quarter of Temouenouthis, some time ago removed abroad. Wherefore I ask that his name be entered in the list of persons removed . . . and I swear . . . that the aforesaid statement is correct, and that Thoönis possesses no means. . . . If I swear truly may it be well with me, but if falsely the reverse. (P. Oxy. 251; Grenfell & Hunt 2.203–204)

Taxes demanded accurate and up-to-date census lists, and a legitimate move from one's recorded place necessitated deregistration. Even though Thoönis was about thirty-four years of age, it is the resident Thamounion who swears out the removal form. Notice, by the way, that the family had been registered in the Hippodrome section of Oxyrhynchus on their taxation receipts for 22 to 25 C.E. but had now moved to the Temouenouthis section of the city. Those terms "denote an area larger than that of a street with the houses fronting it ... but somewhat less than that implied by 'quarter.' Oxyrhynchus had at least fourteen" such sections (Grenfell and Hunt 2.189–190).

Tryphon's next documentation is another set of tax receipts. These are for the years between 45 and 50 C.E., and, like the earlier ones for 22 to 25 C.E., they indicate the same fourfold taxation of weaving, poll, pig, and embankment, now paid, of course, in the Temouenouthis section of the city.

The last two years, however, were somewhat more eventful than his tax receipts would indicate. Sometime around the middle forties C.E. a second child, the boy Apion, was born to Tryphon and Saraeus. Then, in 49 C.E., Saraeus, represented by Theon, was sued by a man named Pesouris, represented by Aristocles. The text is from the minutes of the court proceedings before the strategus Tiberius Claudius Pasion, civil and judicial administrator of the Oxyrhynchite nome.

> In court, Pesouris *versus* Saraeus.
> Aristocles, advocate for Pesouris, said: "Pesouris, my client ... picked up from the gutter a boy foundling, named Heraclas. He put it in the defendant's charge. This nurse was there for the son of Pesouris. She received her wages for the first year when they became due, she also received them for the second year. In proof of my assertions there are the documents in which she acknowledges receipt. The foundling was being starved, and Pesouris took it away. Thereupon Saraeus, waiting her opportunity, made an incursion into my client's house and carried the foundling off. She now justifies its removal on the ground that it was free-born. I have here, firstly, the contract with the nurse; I have also, secondly, the receipt of the wages. I demand their recognition."
> Saraeus: "I weaned my own child, and the foundling belonging to these people was placed in my charge. I received from them my full wages of 8 staters. Then the foundling died, and I was left with the money. They now wish to take away my own child."
> Theon: "We have the papers relating to the foundling."
> The strategus: "Since from its features the child appears to be that of Saraeus, if she and her husband will make a written declaration that the foundling entrusted to her by Pesouris died, I give judgement in accordance with the decision [i.e., laws] of our lord the prefect, that she have her own child on paying back the money she has received." (P. Oxy. 37; Grenfell & Hunt 1.79–81)

The facts are clear enough: Pesouris, having appropriated Apion as or instead of his slave-son Heraclas, found himself swiftly dispossessed of the infant by Saraeus's resourceful action. When, however, Pesouris still proved recalcitrant, Tryphon had a street scribe write for him to the prefect of Egypt in 49 or 50 C.E.

> To Gnaeus Vergilius Capito, from Tryphon, son of Dionysius, of the city of Oxyrhynchus. Syrus [Pesouris], son of Syrus, entrusted to the keeping of my wife Saraeus, daughter of Apion . . . a boy foundling named Her-aclas, whom he had picked up from the gutter, to be nursed. The found-ling died, and Syrus tried to carry off into slavery my infant son Apion. I accordingly applied to Pasion, the strategus of the nome, by whom my son was restored to me in accordance with what you, my benefactor, had commanded, and the minutes entered by Pasion. Syrus, however, refuses to comply with the judgment, and hinders me in my trade. I therefore come to you, my preserver, in order to obtain my rights. Farewell. (P. Oxy. 38; Grenfell & Hunt 1.81–82)

There is no difficulty in a poor person sending a petition to the prefect; the difficulty is in getting an efficacious reply. Two untranscribed papyri from 50 to 51 C.E. indicate that Alexandria failed to respond and that Tryphon had to take up the affair, once again, with the local strategus. The first is described as a "Fragment of a petition addressed to Tiberius Claudius Pasion, strategus, by Tryphon." The second is the "Latter part of a petition, addressed probably to the strategus, by Tryphon, complaining of an assault upon him and his wife Saraeus by a woman and other persons unnamed" (P. Oxy. 316, 324; Grenfell and Hunt 2.306). I presume that Pesouris is giv-ing in to Tryphon with the same reluctance earlier displayed by Demetrous.

A year later in 52 C.E. Tryphon was in more direct contact with Alexan-drian authority. His documents contained two copies of the following official statement.

> Release from service was granted by Gn. Vergilius Capito, prefect of Upper and Lower Egypt, to Tryphon, son of Dionysius, weaver, suffering from cataract and shortness of sight, of the metropolis of Oxyrhynchus. Examination was made in Alexandria. (P. Oxy. 38 = 317; Grenfell & Hunt 1.83 = 2.306)

At the age of forty-four, the weaver's trade had taken its toll on Tryphon's eyes, but it had also released him from any future military service.

In 54 C.E. Tryphon bought a "weaver's loom . . . measuring three weav-ers' cubits less two palms, and containing two rollers and two beams" from Ammonius, son of Ammonius, for twenty silver drachmae (P. Oxy. 264; Grenfell & Hunt 2.3234–235). It may have been intended for his son Apion, because, in 56 C.E., Apion paid the standard thirty-six drachmae for the weavers' tax in the Temouenouthis section of the city (P. Oxy. 310; Grenfell & Hunt 2.304). I cannot imagine that he was already fourteen by that year.

If he was, that legal confusion in 49 C.E. was between a seven-year-old Apion and a two-year-old Heraclas! We must presume, I think, that Apion started weaving and paying appropriate taxes a few years before he reached the age of poll-tax, as his father Tryphon had done before him.

By the middle of the fifties, then, Tryphon's cottage industry may have doubled if he, despite his failing eyesight, and now his son Apion as well were both weaving. Hence, presumably, another major purchase from the year 55 C.E.

> Tryphon, son of Dionysius, about . . . years old, of middle height, fair, with a long face and a slight squint, and having a scar on his right wrist, has bought from his mother Thamounis' cousin, Pnepheros, son of Papontos, also an inhabitant of Oxyrhynchus, about 65 years old, of middle height, fair, having a long face and a scar above his . . . eyebrow and another on his right knee, (the document being drawn up in the street) one half of a three-storied house inherited from his mother, together with all the entrances and exits and appurtenances, situated by the Serapeum at Oxyrhynchus in the southern part of the street called Temegenouthis to the west of the lane leading to "Shepherds' Street," its boundaries being, on the south and east, public roads, on the north, the house of the aforesaid Thamounis, mother of Tryphon the buyer, on the west, the house of Tausiris, sister of Pnepheros the seller, separated by a blind alley, for the sum of 32 talents of copper; and Pnepheros undertakes to guarantee the half share which is sold perpetually in every respect with every guarantee. (P. Oxy. 99; Grenfell & Hunt 1.161–163)

First of all, there is the purchase price, in which, for the first time, we run into copper rather than silver coinage. One talent was worth 6000 drachmae, so 32 copper talents was 192,000 copper drachmae. The exchange rate, in the first century, was about 450 copper drachmae to one silver drachma. The purchase price, in other words, was about 426 silver drachmae. And there was, by the way, a tax of 10 percent on the transaction. Next, there is the close relationship of the family houses, one next to another on the corner. Finally, there is that mention of "Shepherds' Street." Recall the loom that Tryphon had bought from Ammonius, son of Ammonius, in 54 C.E. In that same year, the younger Ammonius wrote to his father requesting "in a note the record of the sheep, how many more you have by the lambing beyond those included in the first return" (P. Oxy. 297; Grenfell & Hunt 2.297–298). That seems to indicate that they were involved in weaving wool from sheep rather than linen from flax. And the mention of Tryphon's relations congregated near "Shepherds' Street" might also indicate the same trade. "Egypt was famous," according to Naphtali Lewis, "for two of its manufactures, linen and papyrus. . . . The weaving . . . remained basically a 'cottage industry,' practiced throughout the land. . . . The weavers of the much-prized linens were the aristocrats of the craft, which was handed down from one generation to the next, with weavers often co-operating to train one another's children" (134–135). It may well be that Tryphon's family were not among those "aristocrats" but were weavers in wool rather than in linen.

Between 55 and 59 C.E. Tryphon's documentation is primarily about loans, one going out and three coming in. In 57 C.E. Tryphon made a loan to one Dioscorus, son of Zenodorus, "Persians of the Epigone," on terms as harsh as his own from Saraeus twenty years before. It was for 52 drachmae for about three months, and the terms for nonrepayment were "the addition of one half, with proper interest for the overtime." Tryphon had, nevertheless, to include a copy of the loan in a letter to his friend Ammonas asking him to get the overdue repayment as soon as possible (P. Oxy. 269; Grenfell & Hunt 2.250–252). The other three loans, however, are all coming in to Tryphon. First, in 55 C.E., he borrowed and repaid 104 drachmae from one Thoönis, son of Thoönis, probably a relative but not to be confused with either Tryphon's uncle or son of that same name. We have, incidentally, that worthy's tax receipts for several years between 65 and 83 C.E., and he was not himself a weaver (P. Oxy. 289; Grenfell & Hunt 2.284–288). Next, in 59 C.E., Antiphanes, son of Heraclas, lent Tryphon 160 drachmae, which he later repaid (P. Oxy. 318, 306; Grenfell & Hunt 2.306, 304). Finally, in an untranscribed text, "Tryphon, Saraeus, and Onnophris, Tryphon's brother" borrowed and repaid 314 drachmae to one "Tryphaena, acting with her son-in-law Dionysius" (P. Oxy. 320; Grenfell & Hunt 2.305–306).

The final document is from 66 C.E. It is a contract of apprenticeship very similar to that made for Tryphon's brother Onnophris, just mentioned, and the weaver Abarus way back in 36 C.E. Prices, however, have crept up a little, and the contract is now for one rather than two years.

> Tryphon agrees that he has apprenticed to Ptolemaeus his son Thoönis, whose mother is Saraeus, daughter of Apion, and who is not yet of age, for a term of one year from this day, to serve and to perform all the orders given him by Ptolemaeus in respect of his weaver's art in all its branches of which Ptolemaeus has knowledge. The boy is to be fed and clothed during the whole period by his father Tryphon, who is also to be responsible for all the taxes upon him, on condition of a monthly payment to himself by Ptolemaeus of 5 drachmae on account of victuals, and at the termination of the whole period of a payment of 12 drachmae on account of clothing. (P. Oxy. 275; Grenfell & Hunt 2.262–264)

The apprenticeship theory was that the boy got free training; the master got free assistance but had to keep the apprentice in food and clothing. Because Thoönis, like his uncle Onnophris before him, was living at home during his apprenticeship, their family got a refund for food and clothing from the master. The boy had to make up any missed days, and there was also a fine of one hundred drachmae to master and to treasury for taking the boy away before the year was up. Notice, once again, that the boy is under age but is still liable to some taxes, presumably the handicraft tax, which must have been payable at whatever age one started production. Maybe, by 66 C.E., Tryphon's eyesight was so bad that he could no longer work even enough to teach his younger son the family trade.

I said, at the start of this section, that Tryphon was an Egyptian contemporary and more or less social equal of Jesus. A word, then, about weavers and carpenters, even before we get, at the start of chapter 3, to Gerhard Lenski's placement of artisans below peasants in the social hierarchy of agrarian societies. Ramsay MacMullen, discussing Roman social relations in the first three common era centuries, noted that "pedigree would be a matter of common knowledge, announced in one's very name . . . 'Weaver' or 'Carpenter' declared plebeian origins" (1974:107–108). Later, in an appended "Lexicon of Snobbery" he cites a collection of terms used by "Greek and Roman authors to indicate the range of prejudice felt by the literate upper classes for the lower" (1974:139–140; see also 17–18, 198 note 82). Those terms include "weaver," both of wool (*eriourgos*) and linen (*linourgos*), and "carpenter" (*tektōn*), the same term used for Jesus in Mark 6:3 and for Joseph in Matthew 13:55. It scarcely matters, by the way, which of those readings is more correct: "a man usually took up whatever work his family handed down to him" (1974:98). There is, actually, not just snobbery but some truth at work in all those accusations tossed at peasants by their literate describers and aristocratic oppressors throughout the centuries. Peasants, we read, are dull, dumb, and dishonest; they are slow, stupid, lazy, and indifferent. James Scott, however, has argued, from fieldwork among Malaysian peasants around 1980, that those ascendancy detractions accurately describe but inaccurately recognize what are actually the "weapons of the weak . . . the tenacity of self-preservation—in ridicule, in truculence, in irony, in petty acts of noncompliance . . . in resistant mutuality, in the disbelief in elite homilies, in the steady grinding efforts to hold one's own against overwhelming odds—a spirit and practice that prevents the worst and promises something better" (1985:350). Or, from another world: Lost English huntsman to Irish peasant in late nineteenth century Donegal: "Did the gentry pass this way, my good man?" "They did that, your honor." "How long ago?" "About three hundred years ago, your honor." A small victory, surely, but as fact or fiction, that story has been around Ireland for a century.

In any case, the Tryphon papyri, and tens of thousands like them, let us glimpse directly and immediately the long-ago lives of very, very ordinary people, female and male, urban and rural, peasant and laborer, at least in Egypt. They recall, forcibly and precisely, the exact details of ancient lives. And they challenge us to extrapolate from Egypt to Palestine along the constancies of peasant existence. Do not forget me.

✧ 2 ✧

War and Peace

WHEREAS Providence . . . has . . . adorned our lives with the
highest good: *Augustus* . . . and has in her beneficence granted
us and those who will come after us [a Savior] who has made
war to cease and who shall put everything [in peaceful] order . . .
with the result that the birthday of our God signalled the
beginning of Good News for the world because of him . . .
herefore . . . the Greeks in Asia *Decreed* that the New Year begin
for all the cities on September 23 . . . and the first month shall ..
be observed as the Month of Caesar, beginning with 23
September, the birthday of Caesar.

    Decree of calendrical change on marble steles in the Asian
temples of Rome and Augustus (Danker 217)

Two epic poems define contradictory visions of the assassinated Julius Caesar, his adopted son and testamented heir Octavian, Augustus to be, and
the Julio-Claudian dynasty that they founded. Virgil's epic, written
between 29 and 19 B.C.E., created a mythology of the new Principate:

The Trojan Caesar comes, to circumscribe
Empire with Ocean, fame with heaven's stars.
Julius his name, from Iulus handed down:
All tranquil shall you take him heavenward
In time, laden with plunder of the East,
And he with you shall be invoked in prayer . . .
And grim with iron frames, the gates of War
Will then be shut.
    (Virgil, *Aeneid* 1.286–94; Fitzgerald 13)

Lucan's counterepic, written in the early sixties C.E. as that dynasty
stumbled to its end under Nero, proposed an ideology of the lost Republic:

Caesar could no longer endure a superior,
nor Pompey an equal.
Which had the fairer pretext for warfare,
we may not know:

each has high authority to support him;
for, if the victor had the gods on his side,
the vanquished had Cato.
                    (Lucan, *The Civil War* 1.125–28;
                                        Duff 12–13)

*great
line !*

It took courage to suggest that the cause of Julius Caesar, Augustus,
and the Principate had *only* the victory-giving gods on its side while Pompey, Brutus, and Cassius had Cato, sainted in life and martyred in death, on
theirs. And it was dangerously sarcastic for Lucan to do so having just apos-
trophized Nero among the gods in the dedication of his poem. But Lucan
turned history into poetry, which cost him his career at Nero's command,
and he then turned poetry into conspiracy, which cost him his life, in a
warm bath of his own blood, again at Nero's command. That, however, was
almost a hundred years after Octavian defeated Anthony at Actium. How
did the *Pax Romana*, the peace established by Augustus, look closer up?

A Shrine to Augustan Peace

Between 13 and 9 B.C.E. Augustus erected the *Ara Pacis Augustae* in the
same Campus Martius that already contained his imperial mausoleum. This
Altar of Augustan Peace was surrounded by a walled enclosure decorated with
sculptured scenes. The overall plan counterpoised Augustus and the imperial
family on the south wall with the Senate and People of Rome on the north
wall, and the historic mythology of Rome, from Aeneas to Romulus and
Remus, on the west wall with the cosmic mythology of Rome, symbolized
by Terra Mater and Roma, on the east wall (*CAH* 10, plan 2 after p. 581).
    There is only one slight hint of war in the entire ensemble, and it takes
a close inspection to see it. Among the figures of the imperial family in the
southeast corner there is a single male wearing army uniform rather than
the togas worn by all the rest. It is most probably Drusus, brother of
Tiberius, who was campaigning in Germany when the slabs were being prepared and who, having pushed Roman power to the Elbe, died there in the
very year the *Ara* itself was dedicated (*CAH Volume of Plates* 4.116–17). But
that merest hint of war is more than balanced by the emphasis on children
not only among the imperial family but also among the Roman populace
on the opposing wall. And above all, it is completely obliterated by the Terra
Mater as the dominant symbol of Augustan peace (Rostovtzeff 1.44; *CAH
Volume of Plates* 4.120–21).
    The central figure of that frieze is a seated and draped woman
representing Terra Mater, or Mother Earth. She is seated on a rock in the

countryside, with two children on her lap, surrounded by symbols of fertility. Behind her, to left and right, are ears of corn and heads of poppies; below her, to left and right, are a resting cow and a drinking sheep; beside her, to left and right, are allegorical female figures seated respectively on swan and sea-dragon and representing either rivers and seas or air and water. This is Augustan peace as the whole earth, not just Rome or even Italy, returned to fertility and security, taken back from the male warrior and restored to the female mother.

It was, of course beautiful pictorial propaganda. But a very similar vision speaks out from another contemporary monument, at once personal rather than official and intensely poignant rather than blatantly triumphant. It is a Roman husband's epitaph for a dead and dearly loved wife.

The epitaph, described by Nicholas Horsfall "as considerably the longest Latin inscription erected by a private individual" (85) and by Gregory Horsley as "the single most impressive statement of the depth of the marriage-bond . . . in the later Graeco-Roman world" (3.35), began as a husband's funeral oration for his dead wife, buried sometime within the two final decades of the first century before the common era. It belongs therefore to the genre of *laudatio funebris,* that typically Roman format of which about fifty examples are extant and in which the deceased is praised either by a family member or a political associate (Kierdorf 137–49). The speech was addressed to her during the funeral ceremonies and then inscribed on two tightly adjacent marble slabs, presumably as part of her tomb. No names are mentioned in the extant sections, and, although it was once thought that the couple might be Q. Lucretius Vespillo, consul in 19 B.C.E., and his wife, Turia, that seems rather unlikely, so that the protagonists of what has been termed the *Laudatio Turiae* must be left for the present unknown. That, at least, is the consensus of recent scholarship, from Marcel Durry in 1950, through Erik Wistrand in 1975, and up to Nicholas Horsfall in 1983.

The First Triumvirate of Pompey, Crassus, and Caesar lost Crassus to defeat and death by the Parthians at Carrhae in 53 B.C.E and then degenerated in 49 B.C.E. into civil war between Pompey, who had been married to Caesar's daughter Julia until her death in 54 B.C.E. , and Caesar himself. The fragmented opening of the eulogy plunges the reader immediately into those death throes of the Roman Republic. Its format of biographical address records how the Wife,

> became an orphan suddenly before the day of our wedding, when both
> your parents were murdered together in the solitude of the countryside.
> It was mainly due to your efforts that the death of your parents was not

left unavenged. For I had left for Macedonia, and your sister's husband
Cluvius had gone to the province of Africa. (I.3–6; Wistrand 18–19)

Wife-to-be and Husband-to-be had sided with the Pompeians against
Caesar. They chose the wrong side. One year later Pompey was defeated by
Caesar at Pharsalus on the Thessalian plains of central Greece and then
assassinated by a renegade Roman near an Egyptian beach.

The Husband details all his Wife-to-be did for him during his flight and
exile, taking "all the gold and jewellery from your own body," and finally
appealing in the name of Caesar's explicitly proclaimed clemency to those
who represented the absent Caesar in Italy. Her pleas were successful, he
was repatriated (probably in 49 or 48 B.C.E.), and they were married soon
afterward.

But prominent among those who assassinated Caesar on March 15 of
44 were former Pompeians, like Brutus and Cassius, whom he had pardoned and even promoted. Caesar's clemency cost him his life, and the
Second Triumvirate of Anthony, Lepidus, and Octavian, dead Caesar's
adopted son and appointed heir, would not make the same mistake. By 43
B.C.E., as soon as they had consolidated their power, and even before they
set out for battle against Brutus and Cassius in Greece, they drew up
proscription lists against their enemies. But they did so in a way that
guaranteed not only political revenge and confiscated wealth but also
human horror and civil terror.

In such a situation the names of Pompeians who fought against Caesar
and were then amnestied and repatriated by him became obvious candidates for execution. The Husband, presumably as such an amnestied Pompeian, was on the proscription lists. The language of the epitaph becomes
suddenly very guarded, speaking only of "our intimate and secret plans and
private conversations" and mentioning vaguely how "I was saved by your
good advice . . . [as you] prepared a safe hiding-place for me . . . I was hidden and my life was saved" (II.4–10; Wistrand 24–25). Those unspecified
plans may well have involved flight to areas still controlled by the enemies
of the Triumvirate and a renewed military role in the resistance. It would
have been a dangerous and futile option. By the fall of 42 B.C.E. both Cassius and Brutus were dead by their own hands after defeat in the battles of
Philippi, and with them died any lingering hopes for the Republic's return.
By 35 B.C.E. Sextus Pompeius was also defeated and dead. The Wife had
advised hiding rather than flight, and this time she had saved his life at considerable danger to herself and her sister's family. One presumes that they
had agreed to hide him on their properties as the somewhat safer place.
But, of course, to hide a proscribed person brought proscription on oneself.

The Wife's strategy was to hide her husband until his proscription could be revoked by showing that he was not guilty in any way of the death of Caesar or of disloyalty to the new Triumvirate. They managed, somehow, to get an edict attesting to the Husband's good standing from Octavian, still absent with Anthony for or after Philippi. But, Lepidus, representative of the Triumvirate in Italy, refused to acknowledge the edict, infuriated no doubt by its presumptive intrusion into his own area of command. Only the Wife's courage and constancy finally forced him to accept it. The Wife had saved her husband's life twice, once under each Triumvirate.

As the text continues, the Wife offered to save him once again. They were unable to have children, and she offered to divorce him but without any separation of property, to let him marry another woman and have children with her and to treat those children as if they were her own.

> I must admit that I flared up so that I almost lost control of myself; so horrified was I by what you tried to do that I found it difficult to retrieve my composure. To think that separation should be considered between us before fate had so ordained, to think that you had been able to conceive in your mind the idea that you might cease to be my wife while I was still alive, although you had been utterly faithful to me when I was exiled and practically dead! (II.40–43; Wistrand 28–29)

As the Husband brings the inscription to conclusion, pain and even desperation repeatedly break the surface of the expected formulas of grief and farewell.

> Would . . . that I had died leaving you still alive and that I had you as a daughter to myself in place of my childlessness. . . . You bequeathed me sorrow through my longing for you and left me a miserable man without children to comfort me. . . . But along with you I have lost the tranquillity of my existence. When I recall how you used to foresee and ward off the dangers that threatened me, I break down under my calamity. . . . Natural sorrow wrests away my power of self-control and I am overwhelmed by sorrow. I am tormented by two emotions: grief and fear—and I do not stand firm against either . . . (II.51–54, 60–64; Wistrand 28–31)

Far from allowing her to become his ex-wife and "sister," he had adopted her in his will as his daughter so that her rights of inheritance and powers of precedence would be greatly enhanced. But all to no avail. She died before him.

That magnificent text, in which the political and the private, the social and the personal intertwine so poignantly and which stands as warning against any too glib descriptions of the Roman patriarchal family, reminds us of how real Augustan propaganda was for many Romans. "When peace," it says, "had been restored throughout the world and the lawful political order reestablished, we began to enjoy quiet and happy times" (II.25–26; Wistrand 26–27). That is how even a Republican and Pompeian aristocrat could describe the advent of Augustus.

Beggared of Paternal Estate

A somewhat darker picture emerges from the Augustan poets, from Virgil, Horace, and Propertius, all three of whom had lost their properties during the civil wars. There can be no doubt, therefore, of their horror of civil strife. It had touched them personally and they remember it vividly.

Publius Virgilius Maro, born near Mantua on the ides of October in 70 B.C.E., had his lands commandeered for the victorious veterans of Philippi in 42 B.C.E. and was almost killed for resisting dispossession.

> Lycidas, Oh! we have struggled through, but only
> To suffer this grief undreamed, that a soldier-stranger
> Should grab our dear little farm and bellow to us:
> "These fields are mine; uproot yourselves, you fossils."
> Beaten and down, for Luck must dip full circle,
> We are sending him now these kids (may they breed him mischief!).
> (Virgil, *Eclogues* 9.2–6; Lind 71)

Quintus Horatius Flaccus, born five years after Virgil but at the other end of Italy, joined the republicans Brutus and Cassius as an officer against Octavian and Anthony at Philippi. After their defeat he escaped to Italy but found his father dead and his lands confiscated. He described that situation in a verse-letter of around the year 20 B.C.E. to Julius Florus, a friend in the retinue of Tiberius. Note, in passing, that Anthony, the actual victor of the second and decisive battle at Philippi goes prudently unmentioned.

> The tide of civil strife flung me, a novice in war, amid weapons that were
> to be no match for the strong arms of Caesar Augustus. Soon as Philippi
> gave me discharge therefrom, brought low with wings clipped and beg-
> gared of paternal home and estate, barefaced poverty drove me to writ-
> ing verses. (Horace, *Epistles* 2.2:47–52; Fairclough 428–29)

Sextus Propertius, the youngest of the three, was born around 50 B.C.E. in Umbria, probably at Assisi. He too lost his patrimony in the confiscations after Philippi.

When you were young—too young—you lost your father
and every day you fared a little worse:
the great house and the fields, the stabled oxen,
seized and allotted soldiers of the state.
(Propertius, *Elegies* 4.1; Carrier 161)

Three poets, then, from one end of the Italian peninsula to the other and none from Rome itself, but all three impoverished by the Triumvirate after Philippi. And three poets all taken under the protective patronage of C. Cilnius Maecenas, the pen of Augustus as Marcus Agrippa was his sword and just as expert in the new order's literature, diplomacy, and mythological image making as the latter was in its war, administration, and military strength. Three poets, in other words, almost destroyed by Octavian but then saved by Augustus.

An aside on Ovid, that other great Augustan poet, who was born later and lived much longer than any of them: He experienced neither destruction nor salvation from Augustus. And possibly because of that he preferred the elegant dalliance of *The Art of Love* to joining in poetic support of the Augustan program of military and moral rearmament. It was from the viewpoint of poetry probably just as well. In that book, wedged irrelevantly and irreverently between advice on finding possible lovers at gladiatorial shows or at parties, stands a section of about forty lines on Gaius Caesar's fatal expedition against Parthia. For example,

Father Mars, father Caesar, bestow your grace on his going:
One of you is a god; some day the other will be.
If I'm a prophet at all, you will win, and my anthems will praise you;
Loud shall be my song, uttering paeans of praise.
(Ovid, *The Art of Love* 1.203–6; Humphries 111)

That hymn of "ghastly political sycophancy" is so much in place bad politics, in tone bad poetry, and in time bad prophecy, that one is almost forced to ponder parody (Humphries 7). Augustus could scarcely have been amused by a poetic projection of Gaius' future triumph as, in context, a good place to pick up women. And when future triumph became past disaster, Augustus, mourning his shattered dynastic hopes after Gaius' death, was surely, in retrospect, less and less amused. Late in the year 8 C.E. he banished Ovid to isolated Tomis on the western coast of the Black Sea. The explicit reason was the licentiousness of that ten-year-old book, the real reason some imperial crime about which Ovid knew too much, but the result was a decade of exile and death at the back of the Roman beyond.

Against the Britons and the Asians

To return to those other three both Augustan-aged and Augustan-minded poets, once again cynicism comes easily, all too easily. The triad's restored or restituted lands could be taken as an Augustan bribe for poetic propaganda. Here, for example, from Ezra Pound's *Homage to Sextus Propertius* of 1917 is one such view.

> Upon the Actian marshes Virgil is Phoebus' chief of police
> > He can tabulate Caesar's great ships.
> He thrills to Ilian arms,
> > He shakes the Trojan weapons of Aeneas.
> And casts stores on Lavinian beaches.
> Make way, ye Roman authors,
> > > > > clear the streets O ye Greeks
> For a much larger Iliad is in the course of construction
> > > > > > (and to Imperial order)
> Clear the streets O ye Greeks.
> > > > > > > (Pound, 1934:34)

The jibe is cheap, however, since their poetry is too immortal to be insincere. And, besides, as Pound himself would learn later on, poetry and autocracy are not necessarily antithetical.

The problem is not poetic insincerity, the possibility of court poets being bought, paid, and kept for purposes of political propaganda. Virgil, Horace, and Propertius were all sincerely committed to the new order. They had personally experienced Augustan salvation. They were themselves metonymic condensations of what Italy had experienced. But there is another and much darker problem lurking behind their most enthusiastic lines. Watch its progress across three stages.

The first stage dates from the year 40 B.C.E. Caesar was four years dead, already deified at Rome and avenged at Philippi. Octavian and Anthony had agreed on peace between them and sealed the pact of Brundisium by the marriage of Anthony to the former's sister Octavia. Virgil wrote his *Fourth Eclogue*, dedicated to C. Asinius Pollio, one of that year's consuls and, even before Maecenas, Virgil's patron. The poem dreams of a new-born or soon-to-be-born infant, who will grow up in a time of ecstatic peace, himself that time's rhapsodic symbol.

> But when maturing years make you a man,
> Even the merchant will give up the sea,

The pine will not become a trading ship,
For every land will furnish everything.
The soil will not endure the hoe, nor vines
The pruning hook; the vigorous plowman will
Release his oxen from their yokes; no dyes
Will teach bright-colored falsehood to pure wool:
The ram, in the meadow by himself, will blush
Sweet crimson murex-color, then will change
His fleece to saffron, while, spontaneously,
Vermilion clothes the young lambs as they graze.
                    (Virgil, *Eclogues* 4.37–45; Wender 51.52)

One can well debate what if any child of flesh and blood is there intended or even how seriously Virgil takes it all. But, at this first stage, peace is peace for all the world in a golden age of fertility without toil and prosperity without strife. And that, of course, is still the vision that, over twenty-five years later, the *Ara Pacis* sculptures froze in stone for all who passed to see.

But a different and darker stage had already appeared a decade after Virgil's rhapsody. Actium was over, a terribly mediocre consummation in which Anthony's land forces sallied forth primarily to surrender and Anthony's sea forces copied that successful maneuver. Once again mythology took over. It was not now a peaceful mythology of the fertile earth. It was rather a vision in which civil war between Octavian and Anthony, twinned Roman warlords, was transmuted into Octavian leading the hosts of the civilized West against Anthony, or better Cleopatra, and the hordes of the barbarian East. The poetry is better, but the cost is higher. Here, then, is Actium in apotheosis.

Propertius, hearing Virgil out of the corner of his ear, earlier proposed with tongue in cheek to write an *Iliad* about his mistress Cynthia and "our wars of love, waged breast to breast, and naked" (*Elegies* 2.1; Carrier 57). Later, however, he wrote of Actium but still with remnant truth about the other side.

I think of Anthony, and the strangled groaning
of his lost legions there at Actium drowned
when he turned back his fleet for love of Egypt
hunting a shelter never to be found.
Such victories are Caesar's fame and glory;
the hand that conquered sheathed the sword in peace.
    . . .

Actium, where Caesar's fleet was harbored
and storm-worn ship and sailor may find relief.
Here were the whole world's navies; they lay at anchor,
some of them fated for joy, some doomed to grief.
Egyptian and Roman: shameful that Roman weapons
should be hurled from those ships of Anthony and the queen.
Caesar's are here, their sails filled with Jove's blessing,
as they fight for all that a fatherland can mean.

                (Propertius, *Elegies* 2.16, 4.6; Carrier 83, 175)

The battle is Rome against Egypt but here, at least, it is still recognized that Romans fought for Anthony, although Anthony himself is scarcely seen as Roman any longer. The mythological battle lines are much clearer in Virgil.

Augustus Caesar leading into battle
Italians, with both senators and people,
Household gods and great gods. . . .
Then came Antonius with barbaric wealth
And a diversity of arms, victorious
From races of the Dawnlands and Red Sea,
Leading the power of the East, of Egypt,
Even of distant Bactra of the steppes.
And in his wake the Egyptian consort came
So shamefully. . . . The queen
Amidst the battle called her flotilla on
With a sistrum's beat, a frenzy out of Egypt,
Never turning her head to see
Twin snakes of death behind, while monster forms
Of gods of every race, and the dog-god
Anubis barking, held their weapons up
Against our Neptune, Venus, and Minerva.

                (Virgil, *Aeneid* 8:678–700; Fitzgerald 254)

That is much, much better: better myth, better propaganda. Our gods against the mongrel gods of every race. Our people, the Italians, against a polyglot of arms. Our Augustus against a frenzy out of Egypt.

The third stage was already evident in the *Odes,* which Horace published in 23 B.C.E. even before the posthumous publication of Virgil's *Aeneid* in 19 B.C.E. Whether Augustus was securing his frontiers or enlarging his empire, the mythology is now of peaceful Roman center and war-filled barbarian periphery, not just West against East but center against both West and East. Two examples will suffice.

In the years between 27 and 25 B.C.E. Augustus, it was said, was considering an expedition against Britain, and Aelius Gallus, prefect of Egypt, was undertaking one against Arabia.

Guard Caesar bound for Britain at the world's end,
Guard our young swarm of warriors on the wing now
To spread the fear of Rome
Into Arabia and the Red Sea coasts.
Alas, the shameful past — our scars, our crimes, our
Fratricides! This hardened generation
Has winced at nothing, left
No horror unexplored. What profanations
Has fear of heaven kept our young men's hands from?
What altars have they spared? O on fresh anvils
Reforge our blunted swords
To point at Caspian and Arab hearts!
                    (Horace, *Odes* 1.35; Michie 90–91)

Augustan peace is real and still has much to do with fertility of field and prosperity of city. And it would be untrue to confine its benefits to Rome or even to Italy alone. But peace at home now goes hand in hand with war abroad. Maybe peace is retained at home precisely by wars maintained abroad. Another example, and one where the racism and jingoism is underlined by the translation, possibly without linguistic but certainly with moral right. Horace is speaking of Apollo.

He shall ward off bitter famines,
Plagues and grim wars from the Romans,
Sending all such visitations
To the Britons and the Asians,
Moved by these our supplications.
                    (Horace, *Odes* 1.21; Michie 58–59)

To see how all of that looked over a hundred years later and from the viewpoint of the British, read the magnificent speech created by Tacitus in a biography of his father-in-law, Gnaeus Julius Agricola, governor of Britannia between 77 and 84 C.E. The British general Calgacus describes the Roman Empire just before his decisive encounter with its military might.

Harriers of the world, now that earth fails their all devastating hands
they probe even the sea: if their enemy has wealth, they have greed; if
he is poor, they are ambitious; East and West have glutted them; alone
of mankind they behold with the same passion of concupiscence waste
alike and want. To plunder, butcher, steal, these things they misname

empire [*imperium*]; they make a desolation and call it peace. Children and kin are by the law of nature each man's dearest possession: they are swept away from us by conscription to be slaves in other lands; our wives and sisters, even when they escape a soldier's lust, are debauched by self-styled friends and guests: our goods and chattels go for tribute; our lands and harvests in requisitions of grain; life and limb themselves are used up in levelling marsh and forest to the accompaniment of gibes and blows. Slaves born to slavery are sold once for all and are fed by their masters free of cost; but Britain pays a daily price for her own enslavement, and feeds the slaves. (Tacitus, *Agricola* 30–31; Stuart 18–19; Wengst 52–53)

One forgives Tacitus, who is, as Ramsay MacMullen put it, "in certain respects an utter fool" (1974:58), much for that speech alone.

None of this is intended to deny a valid meaning to Roman and Augustan peace. But it was a Roman and Italian peace from a Roman and Italian civil war. And just as the war had ravaged certain provinces outside Italy, so did the peace benefit them as well. But we have moved a long way from peace as the whole earth ecstatic with fertility, to peace as the victory of West over East, to peace as the still center of a permanently war-torn periphery. Rome and Italy had learned what other great empires also learn. An imperial heartland can export its violence elsewhere and call it law and order, can even call it peace.

✧ 3 ✧

Slave and Patron

Class, then, essentially a relationship, *is* above all the collective
social expression of the *fact of exploitation* (and of course of
resistance to it): the division of society into economic classes is
in its very nature the way in which exploitation is effected, with
the propertied classes living off the non-propertied. I admit that
in my use of it the word "exploitation" often tends to take on a
pejorative colouring; but essentially it is a "value-free"
expression, signifying merely that a propertied class is freed
from the labour of production through its ability to maintain
itself out of a surplus extracted from the primary producers,
whether by compulsion or by persuasion or (as in most cases) by
a mixture of the two.

G. E. M. de Ste. Croix (1975:26)

Either slave and master or client and patron would have been the more
expected combinations for this chapter's title. But the conjunction of slave
and patron is quite deliberate, and Thomas Carney sets the moral situation
that justifies it. "The ugly fact," he says, "was that, given the low level of technology in antiquity, someone had to go without—without proper family life,
material sufficiency, basic human dignity and life space—in order to generate a surplus. Absolute power over another human being, the incontroverti-
ble right to treat another as a human instrument or an object of one's passions
dehumanizes both parties. That is what slavery, any form of slavery, means.
As an institution it perfectly complements patronage. Together, these two
practices go far to account for the authoritarianism in antiquity's societies,
with their spectrums of hierarchical statuses" (214–215). The title's combination also underlines the fact that in ancient Rome the relationship of
patron and client had as its oldest realization and possibly permanent shadow
the link between a master-patron and his freed slave.

Social Strata in Agrarian Societies

Gerhard Lenski has proposed a theory of social stratification as a cross-
cultural model for "the distributive process in human societies—the pro-

43

cess by which scarce values are distributed" (x), that is, who gets the material or economic surplus. If, for instance, ten people produce ten units of produce apiece, need only eight apiece for survival, and therefore have two apiece for surplus, one can easily imagine twin extremes: Society A in which all alike have two units of surplus or Society B in which nine have no surplus and one person has twenty units of it.

One of his book's very great virtues is its deliberate balancing of the two major approaches within the social sciences: the conservative or functional tradition and the radical or conflictual tradition. "Conflict theorists, as their name suggests, see social inequality as arising out of the struggle for valued goods and services in short supply. Where the functionalists emphasize the common interests shared by the members of a society, conflict theorists emphasize the interests which divide. Where functionalists stress the common advantages which accrue from social relationships, conflict theorists emphasize the element of domination and exploitation. Where functionalists emphasize consensus as the basis of social unity, conflict theorists emphasize coercion. Where functionalists see human societies as social systems, conflict theorists see them as stages on which struggles for power and privilege take place" (16–17). Lenski works toward a synthesis of both approaches, and it is especially that synthetic approach that renders his work so valuable.

Lenski's model divides human societies, primarily by technology and only secondarily by ecology, into hunting and gathering, simple horticultural, advanced horticultural, agrarian, and industrial societies. All of those societies not only were known from time past but were available somewhere in our contemporary world when social anthropologists first began scientific study of their specific characteristics, complexities, and differences. Within that typology, for example, the Roman Empire was an agrarian society, a generic type characterized by "the invention of the plow . . . the discovery of how to harness animal power, and the discovery of the basic principles of metallurgy. The latter made possible the forging of iron plowshares (a great advance over their wooden predecessors) . . . [also] the invention of the wheel and the sail, which greatly facilitated the movement of men and goods" (190). It was distinguished, on the one hand, from simple horticultural societies using the digging stick or advanced horticultural societies using the hoe, terracing, irrigation, fertilization, and metal tools. It was distinguished, on the other, from industrial societies, where "the raw materials used are far more diversified, the sources of energy quite different, and the tools far more complex and efficient" (298).

One can obviously debate Lenski's master-model in whole or in part, but I accept it as a basic discipline to eliminate the danger of imposing presuppositions from advanced industrial experience on the world of an ancient agrarian empire. "One fact," concludes Lenski, "impresses itself on almost any observer of agrarian societies, especially on one who views them in a broadly comparative perspective. This is the fact of *marked social inequality*. Without exception, one finds pronounced differences in power, privilege, and honor associated with mature agrarian economies. These differences surpass those found in even the most stratified horticultural societies of Africa and the New World, and far exceed those found in simple horticultural or hunting and gathering societies" (210).

Agrarian societies have, according to Lenski's view, nine classes but with an abysmal gulf separating the five upper from the four lower ones. The *Ruler* was really a separate class because "all agrarian rulers enjoyed significant proprietary rights in virtually all of the land in their domains" (215-216). Next, was the *Governing Class*, which averaged out around one percent of the population, but "on the basis of available data, it appears that *the governing classes of agrarian societies probably received at least a quarter of the national income of most agrarian states, and that the governing class and ruler together usually received not less than half*" (228). The *Retainer Class* averaged out around 5 percent of the population and ranged from scribes and bureaucrats to soldiers and generals, but all united in "service to the political elite," (243) for whom they were absolutely indispensable as groups and totally expendable as individuals. The *Merchant Class* confronted the governing class on the level of market rather than authority. They probably evolved upward from the lower classes, but "in virtually every mature agrarian society merchants managed to acquire a considerable portion of the wealth, and in a few instances a measure of political power as well" (250). The *Priestly Class*, "last but not least among the privileged elements in agrarian societies," owned, for example, 15 percent of the land of Egypt in the twelfth century B.C.E. and 15 percent of the land of France in the eighteenth century C.E. (256-257). At some times, in some places, and with some religions more than others, "*the priestly class tended to function as the preserver of the ancient Redistributive Ethic of primitive societies, where the accumulation of goods in private hands had served as a form of communal insurance rather than as private property*" (266).

On the other side of the great divide was, above all, the *Peasant Class*, the vast majority of the population. Put abstractly: "the burden of supporting the state and the privileged classes fell on the shoulders of the common people, and especially on the peasant farmers who constituted the substantial majority of the population" (266). Put concretely: "in the sixteenth century, Toyotomi Hideyoshi, the then effective ruler of Japan, abolished all taxes except the land tax, which he then set at two-thirds of the total crop. This is probably the best indication we have of the *total* take of the political elite" in the average agrarian state (267). Put bluntly and brutally: "the great majority of the political elite sought to use the energies of the peasantry to the full, while depriving them of all but the basic necessities of life" (270).

The *Artisan Class* averaged around 5 percent of the population. "In most agrarian societies, the artisan class was originally recruited from the ranks of the dispossessed peasantry and their noninheriting sons and was continually replenished from these sources," but it must be emphasized that "despite the substantial overlap between the wealth and income of the peasant and arti-san classes, the median income of artisans apparently was not so great as that of peasants" (278). Hence, of course, their place in the hierarchy of power and privilege. The *Unclean and Degraded Classes,* like the untouchables in Hindu society, were those whose origins or occupations separated them downward from the great mass of peasants and artisans. Porters, miners, prostitutes, for example, or the Chinese rickshaw puller who, despite the romanticism of early Western movies about the Orient, had a life expectancy of about five years (281). Finally, there was the *Expendable Class,* averaging between 5 and 10 percent of the population in normal times. "These included a variety of types, ranging from petty criminals and outlaws to beggars and underemployed itinerant workers, and numbered all those forced to live solely by their wits or by charity" (281). The expendables were not just deviants, but, as their terrible title suggests, they existed because "despite high rates of infant mortality, the occasional practice of infanticide, the more frequent practice of celibacy, and adult mortality caused by war, famine, and disease, agrarian societies usually produced *more people than the dominant classes found it profitable to employ*" (281–282).

At the end of his discussion of those nine classes, Lenski gives a diagram by way of graphic summary (284). Two details are immediately striking about his diagram. It does not look like the classic pyramid of power. It looks much more like a ship's decanter: very, very wide toward the base and tapering upward, with a needlelike shaft that would, in true scale, go right off the page. Furthermore, not all those classes receive flat horizontal bands across the diagram. Several of them sweep upward so that, in terms of power and privilege, lower members of a higher class may be well below higher members of a lower class. Finally, there was "considerable mobility" between those classes, but what must be remembered is that "in the long run, in all these societies, downward mobility was much more frequent than upward" (289–290).

Paradoxes in Roman Slavery

When we try to imagine the situation of slaves in the Augustan age, we have, however, to accept a wide spectrum of ambiguity and ambivalence.

Agricultural and especially plantation slaves had certainly a far worse life than domestic or household slaves. Marcus Porcius Cato, great-grandfather of the later Stoic saint and Republican martyr with the same famous name, wrote an agricultural manual around 160 B.C.E. and gave this general advice.

> Sell worn-out oxen, blemished cattle, blemished sheep, wool, hides, an old wagon, old tools, an old slave, a sickly slave, and whatever else is superfluous. The master should have the selling habit, not the buying habit. (Cato, *On Agriculture* 2.7; Hooper & Ash 8–9)

And Marcus Terentius Varro, pardoned by Caesar for having fought against him under Pompey, proscribed by the Triumvirate for having been pardoned by Caesar, survived the civil wars to write an agricultural treatise in 37 B.C.E. when already about eighty years old. In it he gave this succinct analysis.

> I turn to the means by which land is tilled. . . . Some divide these into . . . three: the class of instruments which is articulate, the inarticulate, and the mute; the articulate comprising the slaves, the inarticulate comprising the cattle, and the mute comprising the vehicles. (Varro, *On Agriculture* 1.17; Hooper & Ash 224–25)

Those guides give a glimpse of agricultural slavery from the master's point of view. How did it look from that of the slaves?

In between Cato and Varro, for example, there were two major three-year revolts on the Sicilian slave plantations in 135 and 104 B.C.E. Diodorus Siculus, as his nickname shows a native of Sicily, writing a history of Rome in the late first century before the common era, described the precipitating conditions of the first rebellion. Both text and tone may be derived from Posidonius, another Greek historian of Rome but from earlier in that same century.

> The Sicilians . . . began to purchase a vast number of slaves, to whose bodies, as they were brought in droves from the slave markets, they at once applied marks and brands. . . . But they treated them with a heavy hand in their service, and granted them the most meagre care, the bare minimum for food and clothing. . . . The slaves, distressed by their hardships, and frequently outraged and beaten beyond all reason, could not endure their treatment. (Diodorus of Sicily, *Library of History* 34/35:2.1, 2, 4; Oldfather et al. 12.56–59)

That is one extreme, the inhuman brutality of agricultural slavery on the *latifundia* or agrofactories, the large plantations worked by slave labor.

At the other extreme is the situation of someone like Tiro, Cicero's slave and then freedman, secretary and then biographer, who preserved for posterity those hundreds of letters that, as D. R. Shackleton Bailey noted, "were never meant to become public property" and to which "nothing comparable has survived out of the classical world: not the 'literary' letters of Plato, Seneca, and Pliny. . . . In Cicero's letters we see a Roman Consular, on any reasonable estimate one of the most remarkable men of his eventful time, without his toga" (xii).

In April of the year 53 B.C.E., while Cicero was on his estate at Cumae north of Puteoli on the Campanian coast, Tiro was seriously ill, presumably at Cicero's Tusculum estate just southeast of Rome. Cicero wrote four letters to Tiro within the week of April 10 to 17, and they indicate a quite extraordinary relationship between master and slave, even if that slave was just about to be manumitted and receive both freedom and new name, Marcus Tullius Tiro, from his patron and benefactor.

Cicero, having heard of Tiro's illness, immediately sent a personal messenger, Menander or Andricus, to report about his condition. But, unable to await the messenger's return, he followed with a letter.

> I shall consider that you have done me every possible favour, if I see you in good health. I await with the greatest anxiety the arrival of Menander [or: Andricus], whom I sent to you. As you love me, take care of your health, and mind you join us when you have made a complete recovery. Goodbye. April 10th. (Cicero, *Letters to His Friends* 16.13; Williams 3.348–49)

That same morning, even with the first letter sent, Menander or Andricus returned with news of Tiro, and a second and fuller letter followed fast on the heels of the first one.

> Andricus did not join me until the day after I expected him; so I had a night full of fear and misery. Your letter added nothing at all to my information as to your condition, but all the same it relieved me. I have nothing to amuse me, no literary work at hand; I cannot bring myself to touch it, until I see you. Please give orders that your doctor shall be promised whatever fee he asks. I am writing to that effect to Ummius [Cicero's Tusculum steward?]. I am told that you are distressed in mind, and that your doctor says that you are suffering in health as a result of it. As you love me, arouse from slumber your literary talents, and that culture which makes you so precious to me. You must now be well in mind, so as to be so in body. I beg of you to ensure this as much for my sake as for your own. Retain Acastus' services, so that you may be waited upon with greater comfort. Keep yourself safe for me; the day of my promise is at hand—indeed I shall definitely fix it now—it will be the day you arrive. Again and again, goodbye. Noon, April 10. (Cicero, *Letters to His Friends* 16.14; Williams 3.348–51)

That is, from master to slave, a quite extraordinary letter. Indeed, you would never guess it was such a letter were it not for that sensitive and terminal inducement to recovery: as soon as you return here you will receive your freedom.

Better news arrived with one Aegypta two days later, and Cicero wrote a third letter to Tiro on April 12.

> Aegypta joined me here on April 12th. Although he reported that you were entirely rid of your fever and were going on nicely, yet his telling me that you had been unable to write caused me some anxiety; and all the more so, because Hermia, who ought to have arrived on the same day, has not done so. You could not believe how anxious I am about your health: if you relieve me from that anxiety, I will relieve you of all your duties. I should write a longer letter if I thought you were now able to enjoy the reading of it. Concentrate your wits, of which I have the highest opinion, upon keeping yourself safe for my benefit, as well as your own. Use every care (I say it again and again) in looking after your health. Good-bye.
>
> P.S. Since the above was written Hermia has turned up. I have got your letter, though your poor handwriting is very shaky; and no wonder, after so serious an illness. I sent you Aegypta to stay with you, because he is not without culture, and is, I believe, fond of you; and with him a cook, for you to make use of. Good-bye. (Cicero, *Letters to His Friends* 16.15; Williams 3.350–53)

Once again that is neither the tone nor the content expected in a letter from master to slave.

The final letter in this series was written on April 17, with Cicero expecting to meet by the end of the month with the fully recovered Tiro at Formiae farther north along the coast.

> Yes indeed, I am anxious that you should join me, but I am afraid of your travelling. You have been very seriously ill, and you are exhausted from fasting, and taking purgatives, and the violence of the attack itself. Serious illnesses are apt to be followed by serious complications, if any mistake is made. Then, again, to the two days you will have been on the road to Cumae there will be added the five succeeding days needed for your return. I want to be at Formiae on the 28th inst. See to it, my dear Tiro, that I find you there in robust health.... My promise will be fulfilled on the appointed day (I have given you the etymology of the word *fides*). Mind you make a complete recovery. We are "in attendance" here. Good-bye! April 17. (Cicero, *Letters to His Friends* 16.10; Williams 3.336–39)

The promise of imminent manumission is repeated and Cicero declares himself "in attendance," a legal term meaning that he is ready to grant Tiro his freedom whenever he is ready.

An Anti-economic Ideology

Thomas Carney's splendid book *The Shape of the Past* studies "the leading sectors or master institutions of antiquity—bureaucracy, city life, economics and the military" (xvi), but with one very special feature in his discussion of economics. He knows quite well and explains quite emphatically the quantum differences between antiquity and modernity with regard to all four institutions. On the bureaucracy, then and now: In theory, at least, modern governmental bureaucracy is supposed to be a "rational, planned organization to maximize efficiency and productivity," but "there was in antiquity no concept of bureaucracy as a rationally ordered, politically neutral instrumentality, meant to serve the public . . . bureaucrats in this tradition were officials regulating a subject population in the interests of an overlord" (72–73). On the city, then and now: "The gulf between an ancient city and a modern one is immense. A whole series of intermediary forms is involved, each built upon its predecessor" (86). On the army, then and now: "In Antiquity a high degree of ingenuity was expended upon warfare, with a low to moderate amount of attention given to economic matters. The situation in the Middle Ages was just the opposite," and "Military matters dominated the attention of the ancients as much as economic matters preoccupy men in industrial societies" (275 note 15, 236). But despite such immense differences for bureaucracy, city, and military between then and now, it is only in turning to the economy that the chapter uses quotation marks and becomes: "'Economics' in Antiquity" (137). Why, granted those admitted sea changes in their meaning, speak of the so-called economy but not of the so-called bureaucracy, city, or army? Why quotation marks only for "economics" and nothing else across the centuries from preindustrial to postindustrial society?

Carney himself does not directly explain those quotations marks, but their reason was already quite clear from his preceding chapters. The Augustan age of the Roman Empire was a period of immense commercial activity, but it was done within and despite a fundamentally anti-economic ideology. Here, for example, are a series of quotations across forty pages before Carney even gets to his chapter on the ancient economy. "Authoritarian thought-ways were pervasive in this hierarchically ordered and power-ridden society, especially among the military elite. So was an anti-economic ethos: large estates, conferring a gentleman's existence, were the one form of wealth accepted as socially desirable.... The life style of The Great called for landlordism as its base. This life style produced a set of values — such as conspicuous consumption — which ... involved devaluing entrepreneurial and innovative activity in general.... Historically, the great step forward that launched humanity towards industrialism seems to have been associated with the development among the elite of attitudes supportive of entrepreneurial endeavours.... Wealth was just as avariciously sought as in any capitalist society, but on a 'seize or squeeze' principle, not by generating it through increased production. Capital was formed in antiquity by taking it from someone else, either as booty in war or as taxes squeezed out of a toiling peasant population.... The case for entrepreneurialism was ... never articulated in antiquity.... Preindustrial society did not in fact produce a body of economic thought" (61, 93, 95, 97, 99). Think of all the theory, thought, and teaching that went into ancient rhetoric; think then of all the anti-thinking that went into ancient economics.

Two examples of such ancient anti-economics will suffice, especially as they are absolutely classic statements of that ethos. Marcus Porcius Cato, whose agricultural treatise of 160 B.C.E. was mentioned earlier, began his manual with this overture.

> It is true that to obtain money by trade is sometimes more profitable, were it not so hazardous; and likewise money-lending, if it were as honourable. Our ancestors held this view and embodied it in their laws, which required that the thief be mulcted double and the usurer four-fold; how much less desirable a citizen they considered the usurer than the thief, one may judge from this. And when they would praise a worthy man their praise took this form: "good husbandman," "good farmer"; one so praised was thought to have received the greatest commendation. The trader I consider to be an energetic man, and one bent on making money; but, as I said above, it is a dangerous career and one subject to disaster. On the other hand, it is from the farming class that the bravest men and the sturdiest soldiers come, their calling is most highly respected, their livelihood is most assured and is looked on with the least hostility, and those who are engaged in that pursuit are least inclined to be disaffected. (Cato, *On Agriculture* 1.1–4; Hooper & Ash 2–3)

That is a remarkably clear hierarchy, and it is also a moral one: farmer, trader, thief, moneylender. "This dominant value system has been described as 'Catonism,' a mind-set characteristic of a traditionalist, landed upper class. Components are as follows ... advocacy of the sterner virtues ... moral regeneration ... militaristic aims and values ... anti-intellectual and anti-cosmopolitan ... despises foreigners ... hostile to trade and commerce ... inhibits the development of labour, and provides an environment

wherein industrial capitalism has little chance. . . . Catonist views seem
always to have commanded respect in antiquity wherever they were voiced.
No voices were raised against them in praise of a business ethic. Traders and
artisans were not, as a general rule, held in high esteem. Inarticulate and
powerless, they developed no ethos of their own. Rather, they accepted, perforce, the low valuation socially defined as theirs by the superbly articulate
dominant culture of the elite . . . the Business Outlook had no articulate
champions among the philosophies of antiquity" (Carney 101, 219).

The same moral value system is found over a hundred years later in one
of Cicero's last writings. His *De Officiis*, a treatise on moral duties written
in the last gloomy years of his life when and because he had nothing better
to do, was formatted as a letter to his son Marcus, then studying philosophy
at Athens with all the total dedication of a very well financed undergradu-
ate far from home. Here is Cicero's moral judgment on the various occupations given not just as his own opinion but as that which "we have been
taught." Note particularly the reasons for this presumably traditional
assessment.

> Now in regard to trades and other means of livelihood, which ones are to
> be considered becoming to a gentleman and which ones are vulgar, we
> have been taught, in general, as follows. First, those means of livelihood
> are rejected as undesirable which incur people's ill-will, as those of tax-
> gatherers and usurers. Unbecoming to a gentleman, too, and vulgar are
> the means of livelihood of all hired workmen whom we pay for mere
> manual labour, not for artistic skill; for in their case the very wages they
> receive is a pledge of their slavery. Vulgar we must consider those also
> who buy from wholesale merchants to retail immediately; for they would
> get no profits without a great deal of downright lying; and verily, there is
> no action that is meaner than misrepresentation. And all mechanics are
> engaged in vulgar trades; for no workshop can have anything liberal
> about it. Least respectable of all are those trades which cater to sensual
> pleasures:
>
>> Fishmongers, butchers, cooks, and poulterers,
>> And fishermen,
>
> as Terence says. Add to these, if you please, the perfumers, dancers, and
> the whole *corps de ballet* [better: vaudeville performers].
> But the professions in which either a higher degree of intelligence
> is required or from which no small benefit to society is derived—
> medicine and architecture, for example, and teaching—these are proper
> for those whose social position they become. Trade, if it is on a small
> scale, is to be considered vulgar; but if wholesale and on a large scale,
> importing large quantities from all parts of the world and distributing to

many without misrepresentation, it is not to be greatly disparaged. Nay, it even seems to deserve the highest respect, if those who are engaged in it, satiated, or rather, I should say, satisfied with the fortunes they have made, make their way from the port to a country estate, as they have often made it from the sea into port. But of all the occupations by which gain is secured, none is better than agriculture, none more profitable, none more delightful, none more becoming to a freeman. (Cicero, *De Officiis* 1.150–51; Miller 152–155)

The vulgar occupations are given in descending order: tax-gatherers and usurers, manual laborers, retailers, mechanics, food sellers and preparers, entertainers. The liberal occupations are given in ascending order: doctors, architects, and teachers; then merchants but only if they are large-scale and minimally engaged in barter or, especially, if it is more or less a one-shot or temporary venture plowed immediately or eventually back into land. Above all, once more at the summit stands agriculture, the agriculture, that is, not of the tenant farmer and the day laborer but of the landed gentry and the ancestral estate.

If the Roman elites programmatically disdained business, but not, of course, its results, and theoretically denigrated commerce, but not, of course, its effects, whence came the dynamism for the age of Augustan commercial expansion? Enter the immortal Trimalchio.

The Frog-Prince's Passion for Trade

In Tiro's case we heard the story primarily from the side of Cicero. There is one very special example, however, in which we hear, albeit refracted through glorious fiction, the voice of a freedman himself, and it serves to focus much wider questions concerning ancient economics and Mediterranean clientage.

Petronius, born in either the early or late twenties of the common era and named either Titus or Gaius, was governor of Bithynia and temporary replacement consul in 60 and 61 C.E. His even more temporary ascendancy as Nero's *Arbiter Elegantiae*, or master of elegant frivolity, began to decline when his enemy Gaius Ofonius Tigellinus became one of the two commanders of the Imperial Guard in 62 C.E. Accused, like Lucan, of participation in Piso's conspiracy against Nero, he was forced to commit suicide in 66 C.E. He died at Cumae, a Campanian seaside town like the unnamed one he described so brilliantly in his novel the *Satyricon*, written probably in 61 C.E. when he was at the height of imperial favor (Corbett 11–29).

The satirical novel follows the adventures of two students, the narrator, Encolpius, and his friend Ascyltos, along with a younger companion,

Giton, and an older companion, Eumolpus. It has been rightly described as "a great work . . . a unique work, the only mature realistic novel that we possess from the ancient world, and almost certainly the only such work that was then produced . . . we have to wait till the Spanish picaresque novels of the sixteenth century before we again meet anything like it" (Lindsay 7). The heart of the novel's extant chapters is a banquet at the home of one Trimalchio in *Satyricon* 27–78 (Heseltine 38–157; Lindsay 69–128). That feast, of course, reflects the social situation in the time of Nero, but during it we learn about Trimalchio's early life, and that biography is both part and type of Augustan society. Mikhail Rostovtzeff says of Trimalchio that "the active part of his life fell certainly in the life of Augustus," that he "was one type of his age," and that, in fact, he was one of "the leading type of men who figured in the economic life of the time of Augustus" (57). Petronius paints him, of course, with a pompous vulgarity far larger than life, but for the satire to work the type must be authentic. Paul Veyne declares this programmatically in an excellent article. "Fictional though it is, this life must be taken seriously. We would even propose taking Trimalchio as an actual person and relocating his biography among the data of his times. The *Satyricon* will then appear as fundamentally realistic and even typical; it is an excellent historical document" (213).

A first and mythological summary of Trimalchio's biography is painted on the entrance wall to his house, but he gives a second and more detailed story to his guests toward the end of the dinner.

> When I came out of Asia, I was about as tall as this candlestick. In fact I used to measure myself against it, every day, and rub oil from the lamp round my lips to make my beard sprout. Still, I was my master's pet for fourteen years. There's nothing wrong in doing whatever your master orders. And I gave his wife what she wanted too. You know what I mean. I'll leave it at that. No one can say I'm the sort that boasts. Anyway, as the gods willed, I became the real master in the house and the other fellow hadn't any thoughts he could call his own. You can guess the rest. I was named joint-heir with Caesar and I came into an estate good enough for a senator. But a man's not satisfied with nothing. I got a passion for trade. I won't keep you long—I built five ships, put a cargo of wine in—wine was worth its weight in gold at the time—and set off for Rome. You might think I'd fixed the whole thing. Every ship was wrecked; a fact, I'm not romancing. Neptune swallowed up thirty million in one day. But do you think I was downhearted? Heavens, no, I no more kept the taste of the loss in my system than if it had never happened. I built another fleet, bigger, better, with a larger layout. No one could say I didn't have pluck. You know, a big ship has got a big sort of strength

about it. I put in another cargo of wine, bacon, beans, perfumes, slaves. And here's where Fortunata showed the stuff she's made of. She sold all her jewellery, all her clothes, and put a hundred gold pieces in my hand. That was the leaven that made my fortune rise. When the gods give a push, things happen quick. I turned in a cool ten million from the one trip. Straight-off I bought up all the estates that had been my master's. I built a mansion and bought slaves and cattle. Whatever I touched, grew like honeycomb. When I came to have more than all the revenues of the land of my birth, I dropped speculation. Retired from direct trade and went in for financing freedmen. (Petronius, *Satyricon* 75–76; Lindsay 125–26)

From slave to bookkeeper and bailiff, from catamite to accountant, and then from heir and entrepreneur to landowner and lender. One recalls Carney's laconic comment, "The history of antiquity resounds with the sanguinary achievements of Aryan warrior elites. But it was the despised Levantines, Arameans, Syrians and Greeklings who constituted the economic heroes of antiquity" (197).

It is not too surprising, therefore, that such a dual relationship led to Trimalchio's testamentary manumission, becoming at the moment of his master's death his freedman, his heir and, also, of course, a Roman citizen. But he was not just a freedman or even a rich freedman. He was what Paul Veyne has called an "independent freedman" (224). His patron's will mentions no familial legacies but only the polite and prudent one for the emperor. Presumably the mistress is already dead, so there is no patron's family with continuing rights over Trimalchio. He is free, rich, and on his own. It is possibly not a surprising status for freedmen of families decimated by decades of civil war.

With his patron's death Trimalchio could have settled down to a life of leisure on his newly acquired estates. Instead, directly opposing the ideology whereby, as Carney reminds us, "land, not capital, was of critical importance in antiquity . . . it was land, not capital, that produced resources in antiquity" (181, 182), he sold his entire inheritance for liquid financing. I hesitated above to use the word *unique* because maybe, even here, Trimalchio is still a type. But, at least, it must be emphasized that in selling all his inherited land to establish liquid capital, he is flying in the face of tradition. Be it as individual or type, and be it only for a moment, the spirit of capitalism appears here far ahead of its time.

The next step was just as bold. Instead of going in with others in a shared-risk association, he built his own ships, bought his own cargo, and, gambling everything on the dearth and thus inflated price for Campanian vintage, sent five wine-laden ships up the coast to Rome. Gambled everything and lost everything. He says he lost thirty million sesterces in that single disastrous storm, but that is also the exact same amount he later leaves on his epitaph. For Petronius, thirty million seems to be a round number for a very large amount or all one has. Thus, for example, he says of one Titus that "thirty millions fell into his lap when his father came to a sticky end" and of Eumolpus that "in Africa he had thirty millions sunk in farm-estates and bonds" (Lindsay 91, 178). Hence, and simply, Trimalchio had turned all his inherited lands into liquid capital, had risked it all on one lonely throw of the dice, and lost. Only his wife Fortunata, "this nightclub tart [taken] . . . off the sale-platform and made . . . an honest woman," saved him for a second chance.

Notice, by the way, that, despite that initial disaster, he stuck with shipping. He even wanted them on his tomb: "See that you put ships sailing along with all their sails set on my monument" (*Satyricon* 71; Lindsay 121). He was absolutely correct. Ignore the vaunted Roman roads or, better still, see them as modern economic historians view them. "The excellent Roman roads were built for military purposes. They might be put to commercial purposes, but their routes were not chosen with commercial purposes in mind, nor did their builders consider the convenience of the merchant. They regularly took the straightest route and the quickest line of march with little consideration of making grades that carts could climb. The roads were not laid out to connect the hinterland to local rivers, but to connect the center of the Empire to the periphery of defense. Moreover land transport was very awkward. The horse was hardly used, for the horseshoe was unknown or little used and the Roman harness choked the team. With such a harness, it has been estimated, no team of horses could pull a load heavier than 500 kilograms. A single ass in modern harness can pull as much. The wagon lacked the whiffle tree and traces and so steered badly. It lacked the brake so that steep climbs and descents were dangerous. Tandem harnessing was unknown. Consequently pack animals were more important than carts" (Davisson & Harper 238). If one responds that those roads were built for military rather than commercial purposes, Sir Moses Finley, another ancient economic historian, would reply, "Roman armies could march long distances along the roads; they could neither be fed or clothed nor armed from long distances by those routes." The reason is clear. "The ox was the chief traction animal of antiquity, the mule and the donkey his near rivals, the horse hardly at all. All three are slow and hungry. The transport figures in Diocletian's edict of maximum prices [at the end of the third century] imply that a 1200-pound wagon-load of wheat would double in price in 300 miles, that a shipment of grain by sea from one end of the Mediterranean to the other end would cost less (ignoring the risks) than carting it seventy-five miles" (128, 126).

Trimalchio, therefore, had to counter not only an anti-economic ideology but serious deficiencies in the technology of traction and transportation. Trimalchio, "ignoring the risks," chose ships.

And then he did something as pedestrian as his opening gambit was unpredictable. Having sold his entire landed inheritance for liquid and high-risk capital, having then lost it and regained it, he retired from trade and put it all back in land. In fact the motif of land, ever more land, runs like a refrain through the entire dinner conversation.

> Straight-way I bought up all the estates that had been my master's. . . .
>
> Trimalchio owns estates as far as a kite can fly. . . .
>
> Anything here that makes your mouths water is the produce of a country estate of mine that I haven't seen yet. They tell me it's on the boundary of Terracina and Tarentum [in the heel of Italy]. My aim at the moment is to collect adjacent properties all across Sicily. Then if I feel like going to Africa, I can do it by travelling the whole way through my own territory. . . .
>
> If I could only extend my estates as far as Apulia [eastward], I'd have gone far enough for this life.
>
> (*Satyricon* 37, 48, 76; Lindsay 1960:80, 94–95, 127)

In the end, then, and so presumably even in the beginning, it was not land for capital, it was land for capital for more, much more, land. Note that he first bought back precisely those lands he had sold; he redeemed his own landed inheritance. Not trade and commerce but lands and loans are now his life. He was, in the deft phrase of Paul Veyne, only an interim capitalist (232).

That biography emphasizes one striking difference between then and now, between ranks and classes, between classes and revolutions.

The juridical and legal distinctions of Roman society into ranks or castes involved the senatorial and equestrian orders at the top. But then comes a major anomaly between order and power. When the equestrian Augustus became emperor, he and his dynasty vaulted far above the senatorial elite, and, with order and power no longer synonymous, the days of the senatorial aristocracy were numbered. Too-powerful senators became a doomed species. At the bottom of society were the free, the freed, and the slaves. But, here too there was a major social anomaly involving wealth, corresponding to that involving power at the top level. A freed slave, as we saw with Trimalchio, could become both instant millionaire and instant Roman citizen. In terms of wealth, but not of rank or power, he could vault above even some senatorial dignitaries. And that anomaly could not last for long. Too-rich freedmen were also a doomed species. But none of those anomalies served to create a middle class. The time was not ripe, so that, as Sir Moses Finley has insisted, there was no "powerful capitalist class between the land-owning aristocracy and the poor" (49). Ramsay Mac-Mullen puts it even more forcibly. "What could have induced the Romans to be so blind? Surely they saw that, in their gathering of wealth by conquest, they gathered a giant market. Surely *someone* realized that the great swelling of cities in later Republican Italy offered perfectly extraordinary economic opportunities, especially in luxury goods, services, trades, and crafts. But no; with unteachable conservatism, rich Romans turned to the land, and even those of relatively modest means could not lower themselves to the running of an arms factory or fuller's mill. That left a vacuum, promptly filled by Greek freedmen.... The manners and values manifested by the likes of Trimalchio, prominent as provincial decurions, had the profoundest effect on the civilization of the empire" (1974:126).

Sir Ronald Syme wrote a great work on Augustus that he called *The Roman Revolution*. But there was no revolution in the Marxist sense. To quote again from Davisson and Harper, "In Marxian thought a revolution — the French revolution is the classic example — is the act by which a newly arrived class takes violent control of the state and its apparatus of power. Marx went on to argue that a new class was the result of new 'relations of production.' That is, the sources of its wealth differentiated the new class from the previous possessors of political power. The French Revolution was a 'bourgeois' revolution and brought to power persons whose wealth came from trade and manufacturing rather than land" (187). No such revolution took place in Rome. Trimalchio, the multimillionaire freedman, lived like the landed members of the senatorial and equestrian orders. In ostentation he was their parody, but in wealth he was their peer. He could never enter their ranks nor ever wanted to do so. He was, in fact, the mini-emperor of a mini-empire. But it was questionable how long such a social anomaly as he represented would be tolerated. He was not middle class, because there was no middle class in antiquity. For such a class to exist would have required not only financial worth but political power and ethical status as well. In terms, not of present and personal biography, but of future and corporate destiny, Trimalchio and his type were, in the terse formulations of Paul Veyne, but lost souls on dead-end streets, stillborn capitalists, aborted bourgeoisie (227, 230–231). Still ... Forget the banality of his final poetry or the vulgarity of his final table; bracket the fact that he fled back to the land as soon as he made his commercial fortune; remember only that past moment when he sold all his land for capital. That was the moment when Petronius and his Trimalchio flirted even if only for an instant with the future.

A Map of Patronal Society

If antiquity, unlike modernity, had no middle class, what did its social structure look like? The comparison is spelled out very clearly by Thomas Carney. He describes antiquity as "a society based on patronage, not class stratification; so little pyramids of power abounded . . . Thus society resembled a mass of little pyramids of influence, each headed by a major family—or one giant pyramid headed by an autocrat—not the three-decker sandwich of upper, middle, and lower classes familiar to us from industrial society . . . The client of a power wielder thus becomes a powerful man and himself in turn attracts clients. Even those marginal hangers-on to power attract others, more disadvantageously placed, as their clients. So arise the distinctive pyramids of power—patron, then first order clients, then second and third order clients and so on—associated with a patronage society. It is quite different from the three-layer sandwich of a class society" (63, 90, 171). Indeed, one might even say, going back to an earlier statement, that, if the Romans thought of land as we do of capital, they thought of patronage as we do of investment.

The processes of patronage and clientage appear rather positive in the light of a Tiro or a Trimalchio. Patron and client seem better alternatives than master and slave and may even right somewhat that preceding injustice. But patronage is more than manumission, and patronal society is a much more pervasive and possibly also a much more corruptive process than might at first appear. G. E. M. de Ste. Croix, for example, has calculated, "A surprising number of the surviving letters of such influential men as Cicero, Pliny the Younger and M. Cornelius Fronto—over eighty of Cicero's, nearly twenty of Fronto's, and fifteen of Pliny's to the emperor Trajan alone—are entirely devoted to recommendations of their friends and clients for office, promotion or other privileges. Whole towns might benefit by favours obtained through one of their citizens from the emperor or some great man; and it became customary for municipalities to adopt distinguished men, sometimes by the dozen, as their *patroni*" (1954:40).

Here, then, is a minimal cartography of the patronal process, with deliberate emphasis on its basic distinctions across about two hundred years of indefatigable Roman letter writing.

In terms of the patron, first of all, the contact may be either direct or indirect, depending on whether an intermediate broker is absent or present to the process. For example, the preceding cases of Tiro and Trimalchio were directly negotiated between owner-patron and slave-client. Remember, of course, that the term *broker* should never be taken in our sense of an impersonal, neutral, or bureaucratic intermediary. It is always to be understood within what Carl Landé has called "the dyadic basis of clientelism," where "the only element essential to the definition is that the relationship must connect two individuals with each other by a direct personal tie" (Schmidt et al. xiii–xiv). A broker, in this sense, is one who sustains a double dyadic alliance, one as client to a patron and another as patron to a client.

Marcus Cornelius Fronto, acclaimed as the greatest orator of the first half of the second century, was both tutor and friend to Marcus Annius Verus and Lucius Verus, adopted sons and designated heirs to the emperor Antoninus Pius, who ruled between 138 and 161 C.E. Sometime around the year 150 C.E. Fronto needed something from the emperor, but instead of writing directly to him, he routed it through Marcus.

> *To my Lord.*
> Saenius Pompeianus, whom I have defended in many cases, since he
> took up the contract for farming the taxes of Africa, is from many causes
> a stand-by in my affairs. I commend him to you that, when his accounts
> are scrutinised by our Lord your Father, you may be induced both by my
> recommendation and your constant practice to extend to him that
> characteristic kindness, which you habitually show to all. Farewell, my
> sweetest Lord. (Fronto, *Ad M. Caes.* v.34; Haines 1.232–235)

Is it only the jaundiced modern eye that notes those many previous cases against Pompeianus, the criteria for the present accounting as Fronto's recommendation and Marcus' kindness rather than Pompeianus' accuracy and integrity, and concludes that filial brokerage was possibly advisable in this case?

Similarly, after Marcus became the emperor Marcus Aurelius in 161 C.E. and Lucius Verus was his co-emperor, Fronto wrote "To my Lord Verus Augustus" in 166 C.E. and declared,

> All the favours I have had to ask from my Lord your brother I have pre-
> ferred to ask and obtain through you.
>   (Fronto, *Ad Verum Imp.* ii.8; Haines 2.240–241)

Once again, brokerage was preferred, but now it is by brother rather than by son.

Next, in terms of status, the relationship may be horizontal or vertical depending on whether it is between social equals or unequals. Because most definitions and discussions of patronal society rightly underline the latter relationship, it is worth drawing some attention to the former one, especially in the early Principate.

An example of a horizontal relationship is the case of Cicero and Manius Acilius Glabrio, and, by the way, notice again how important brokerage is in this situation. They are social equals, so that the patron-client relationship is not one of permanent hierarchical inequality but rather of delicate, reciprocal, and alternating indebtedness. It is more precisely and politely termed *amicitia,* or friendship, but the term must be understood in their sense and not necessarily in ours. It began, probably in the fifties B.C.E., with Cicero defending Acilius in two capital cases.

> Acilius . . . is under the greatest obligation to me; for I have twice successfully defended him on a charge involving his civic status [*iudicio capitis*]; and it is not his nature to be ungrateful, and he shows me marked deference. (Cicero, *Letters to His Friends* 7.30; Williams 2.88–89)

Cicero would not at the time have submitted a bill to Acilius for his legal and oratorical representation. To have done so would have concluded and closed their mutual indebtedness and thereby violated the ethics of *amicitia,* or friendship, as such alternating patronage and clientage was called. The give-and-take of reciprocal and alternating indebtedness between social equals in which neither party could ever really be "paid up" because any precise or exact computation of the "balance sheet" was quite impossible supplied the moral cement for the edifice of patronal society. The networking web of patrons, brokers, and clients spreads continuously, with each nodal person capable of moving up or down among those possibilities for new individuals.

In 45 B.C.E., that is, between Caesar's victory over Pompey in 48 B.C.E. and his assassination in 44 B.C.E., the Pompeian Cicero had limped back to Rome under clemency, but the Caesarian Acilius was proconsul of Achaia. Then the letters started to arrive from Cicero. The "bill" would be paid in installments, as it were, and it would be "paid" as favors done to friends of Cicero rather than directly to Cicero himself. The patronal web enlarges to double dyads as Cicero becomes a broker between the now powerful Acilius and his own clients. There are no less than ten letters commending Sicilian friends of Cicero to Acilius in the year 45 B.C.E. alone. One example will suffice, one in which Cicero acknowledges that he does seem to have a lot of very special friends in Sicily.

> *Cicero to Manius Acilius Glabrio, Proconsul.*
> In the community of Halesa [in the mid-northern coast of Sicily]—and a highly refined and distinguished community it is—I am closely united by bonds of both hospitality and intimacy with the two Clodii, M. Archagathus and C. Philo. But I am afraid that, because I am most

particularly recommending so many people to you, I may be suspected
of making all my recommendations equally strong as a sort of bid for
popularity—though indeed, as far as you are concerned, both I and all
my friends are abundantly satisfied with what you do. But I would really
have you believe that this family, and these members of it, are very
closely bound to me by long-standing friendship, and mutual services,
and goodwill. For that reason I beg of you with more than ordinary ear-
nestness to do all you can for them in every possible way, so far as your
honour and position permit. If you do so, I shall be extremely grateful.
(Cicero, *Letters to His Friends* 13.32; Williams: 3.100–101)

As Richard Saller asked rhetorically in his superb study of personal
patronage under the Principate, "How many favors was Acilius required to
perform before he absolved his debt to Cicero?" (16).

An example of a vertical relationship, and again a brokered one, is the
case of Trajan, Pliny, and Harpocras. It may well strike the modern reader
as magnificently trivial or even supremely absurd. Here the broker is Pliny
the Younger, writing, in 98–99 C.E., to the emperor Trajan on behalf of his
masseur Harpocras. There are four extant letters, but I cite only the salient
parts.

To the Emperor Trajan.
Having been attacked last year by a severe and dangerous illness, I
employed a physician whose care and diligence, Sir, I cannot sufficiently
reward, but by your gracious assistance. I intreat you therefore to make
him a citizen of Rome; for he is the freedman of an alien. His name is
Harpocras; his patroness (who has been dead a considerable time) was
Thermuthis, the daughter of Theon.

To the Emperor Trajan.
I return you thanks, Sir, for your ready compliance with my desire, in . . .
making Harpocras my physician a citizen of Rome. But when, agreeably
to your directions, I gave in an account of his age and estate, I was
informed by those who are better skilled in these affairs than I pretend
to be, that as he is an Egyptian, I ought first to have obtained for him
the freedom of Alexandria, before he was made free of Rome. I confess,
indeed, as I was ignorant of any difference in this case between Egyptians and other aliens, I contented myself with only acquainting you that
he had been manumitted by a foreign lady, long since deceased. However, it is an ignorance I cannot regret, since it affords me an opportu-
nity of receiving from you a double obligation in favour of the same
person. That I may legally therefore enjoy the benefit of your goodness,
I beg you would be pleased to grant him the freedom of the city of Alexandria, as well as that of Rome. And that your gracious intentions may

not meet with any farther obstacles, I have taken care, as you directed, to send an account to your freedmen of his age and fortune.

The Emperor Trajan to Pliny.
It is my resolution, in pursuance of the maxim observed by the princes my predecessors, to be extremely cautious in granting the freedom of the city of Alexandria: however, since you have obtained of me the freedom of Rome for your physician Harpocras, I cannot refuse you this other request. You must let me know to what district he belongs, that I may give your letter to my good friend Pompeius Planta, governor of Egypt.

To the Emperor Trajan.
I cannot express, Sir, the pleasure your letter gave me, by which I am informed that you have made my physician Harpocras a citizen of Alexandria; notwithstanding your resolution to follow the maxim of your predecessors in this point, by being extremely cautious in granting that privilege. Agreeably to your directions, I acquaint you that Harpocras belongs to the nome of Memphis. I entreat you then, most gracious Emperor, to send me as you promised a letter to your good friend, Pompeius Planta, governor of Egypt. (Pliny, *Letters* 10.5, 6, 7, 10; Melmoth 2.282–285, 290–291)

The Latin word used by Pliny really means a masseur rather than a physician. For example, at the start of Trimalchio's story he is in the bathhouse, and "under his eyes three masseurs were drinking Falerian wine" (*Satyricon* 28; Lindsay 70). As Sherwin-White comments, "this specialist . . . was concerned with convalescence rather than cures. He directed a course of exercise and massage intended for wealthy convalescents. . . . The elder Pliny . . . regarded the genus as money-making quacks" (566). Patronage on the edge of absurdity?.

Finally, as for the client, the recipient can be a person, as in all the preceding cases, or a group. A city, just as well as an individual, could be client to a powerful patron. Back to where we started, with Fronto; in this letter, dated possibly between 157 and 161 C.E., he advises his native city of Cirta in North African Numidia on potential patrons. I cite only the key section.

Fronto to the Triumvirs and Senators of Cirta.
Wherefore my advice to you is to choose for your patrons, and send resolutions to that effect to, those who at present stand highest at the bar—Aufidius Victorinus, whom you will have on your burgess-roll if the Gods favour my designs, for I have betrothed my daughter to him, nor could I have better consulted the interests either of myself in the matter of

posterity or of my daughter in the matter of her whole life, than when I chose such a son-in-law, a man of such character and great eloquence; Servilius Silanus also, an excellent and most eloquent man, you will have as your patron by burgess right, since he comes from the neighbouring and friendly state of Hippo Regius; Postumius Festus you cannot do wrong in electing as your patron in consideration of his character and eloquence, himself also a native of our province and of no distant state. (Fronto, *Ad Amicos* ii.11; Haines 1.292–295)

The patronal webs, then, involved not only individuals as patrons and clients, either vertically between social unequals or horizontally between equals, and either directly without brokerage or indirectly with it, but also individuals as patrons with groups as clients, either associations, societies, cities, municipalities, or even larger entities. Also, and especially, in several of the preceding cases, we catch a glimpse of patronal linkage between provinces and capital, between local and Roman aristocracies.

To understand the prevalence of patronage, certain features of Roman life must be remembered. From the viewpoint of the emperor: "With regard to the recruitment of administrators," according to Richard Saller, "Rome during the Principate had markedly little formal machinery by comparison with other great, enduring pre-industrial empires (e.g., the Chinese and Ottoman). Rather than developing palace schools or competitive examinations (as in Turkey and China, respectively), emperors relied on a network of private connections to bring leading candidates to their attention. While the emperor had a limited bureaucracy through which he could reach his subjects, there were few formal, impersonal mechanisms through which the subjects could initiate contacts with the central government. Hence, many of these contacts, which in a more developed bureaucracy would take the form of written applications, could be made only through patron-client networks in the Roman empire" (205–206). From the viewpoint of the nobility: "The need to maintain 'friendships' turned in part on the fact," according to Arthur Hands, "that even in a money economy there were still a considerable number of services essential to comfort and security which could not be bought for money. . . . In the aristocratic state it was almost exclusively among men of like status that men of quality needed such friendships; their 'friends' supplied services analogous to those provided by bankers, lawyers, hotel owners, insurers and others today" (32–33). From the viewpoint of the people, again from Saller: "The kind of patronage . . . between the municipal and Roman aristocracies . . . represents only the thin, upper crust of patronage relationships. By all criteria which a recent collection of studies has listed as conducive to patronage between landowners and the laboring classes, conditions were ripe throughout the empire for patronage to permeate the society from top to bottom. We can catch only the briefest glimpses of patronage relationships with the lower classes. . . . That is unfortunate, because it was these relationships which provided the crucial economic and social infrastructure for the élite patronage" (194).

In the Roman Mediterranean, therefore, the web of patronage and clientage, with accounts that could never be exactly balanced because they could never be precisely computed, was the dynamic morality that held society together. What was wrong, for example, about offering money for such favors was that cash, being calculable, foreclosed the delicate unbalance of indebtedness and closed off the relationship for the future. Cash could, of course, be involved, as in a slave buying freedom, but it was still the master's grace that allowed the slave to do so. No wonder, therefore, that de Ste. Croix called "patronage and clientship .. as it were the mainspring of Roman public life" (1954:40).

The Bedrock of Political Life

Imagine, then, two more or less ideal types of society: a *patronal* society whose moral ideology expects offices and benefits by right of assistance from an influential power broker and a *universal* society whose ethical theory expects them by right of request to an appropriate civil servant. In the former case, for example, in the Roman world, influence was a moral duty: the emperors needed it, the moralists praised it, and countless inscriptions publicly proclaimed it. In the latter case, influence may occur but should not, and, when it does, it is handled quietly and secretly.

Carl Landé, however, having distinguished between "group politics and dyadic politics," with the former based on general laws and the latter on personal relations, concluded that "the model of a group-based political system . . . corresponds rather closely to the actual political systems of present-day Western Europe and North America. But there is no modern state that can be adequately described solely in terms of our dyadic model" (Schmidt et al. 506, 509). That presumes an evolutionary movement from the patronal and personal to the universal and general, from dyads to groups, and from society under influence to society under law. It also presumes that universalism under impersonal law is the only efficient and effective way to run advanced industrial and technological societies. But then, of course, there may also be industrio-patronal societies such as Japan . . .

Like honor and shame at the start of chapter 1, patronage and clientage are not exclusively Mediterranean phenomena, but they are profoundly characteristic of its unity and continuity. In the words of John Davis, "From the wholesale market in Athens to the desert of western Cyrenaica, to the plains of south-eastern Portugal, men take up postures of subordination in order to gain access to resources—to market expertise, to water, to dried milk from welfare agencies. Submission to a patron is commoner and more widespread in the mediterranean than bureaucracy, or fascism, or communism, or any of the varieties of democracy: it can exist without any of them, and co-exists with all of them. It is an independent *sui generis* mode of political representation . . . it is the bedrock of political life in most of those mediterranean communities which anthropologists have studied" (146–147). Notice one feature of that description, especially in comparison with Mediterranean patronage in the Roman era. I deliberately included under Roman patronage relations between equals as well as unequals, although the former cases could be legitimately isolated under a rubric such as friendship (*amicitia*), or, in our terms, nepotism or cronyism. It is, however, relations between social or categorical unequals that Davis underlines, and this raises certain moral questions.

Current anthropological studies of patronage and clientage underline the disparity in power between the protagonists. Here are descriptions from some major recent works. Ernest Gellner says that "patronage is unsymmetrical, involving inequality of power; it tends to form an extended system; to be long-term, or at least not restricted to a single isolated transaction; to possess a distinctive ethos; and, whilst not always illegal or immoral, to stand outside the officially proclaimed formal morality of the society in question," and John Waterbury agrees that "the most fundamental characteristic of patron-client relations is that they are asymmetrical, one party being demonstrably more powerful or prestigious than the other" (Gellner & Waterbury 4, 329). Shlomo Eisenstadt and Louis Roniger go even farther and claim that "paradoxical situations . . . are the major features of the patron-client nexus—the most important among which are, first, a rather peculiar combination of inequality and asymmetry in power with seeming mutual solidarity expressed in terms of personal identity and interpersonal sentiments and obligations; second, a combination of potential coercion and exploitation with voluntary relations and mutual obligations; third, a combination of emphasis on such mutual obligations and solidarity or reciprocity between patrons and clients with the somewhat illegal or semilegal aspect of the relations" (Eisenstadt & Lemarchand 277 = Eisenstadt & Roniger 1980:50–51 = 1984:49). Such paradoxes press the moral question even more obviously.

The ethical problem was emphasized by James Scott's use of the word *exploitation* in the two programmatic anthologies published in 1977. In one he had an article entitled "Patronage or Exploitation?" (Gellner & Water-

bury 21), and in the other he asked, "When are vertical structures of defer-
ence legitimate, and when are they viewed as exploitative?" (Schmidt et al.
496). The moral issue was emphasized even more by Anthony Hall's article,
also in that latter collection. He proposed "a broad distinction between
those [patron-client relations] based on overt acceptance of traditional values by the subordinate (patrimonial) and those based increasingly on more
obvious forms of repression by the powerful because their legitimacy is
slowly decreasing (repressive)." That would seem to make the former cases
ethically acceptable and the latter not. But as Hall goes on to exemplify the
former patrimonial relations in northeast Brazil, he mentions that they
were "based to a large extent on general acceptance by the rural mass of the
prevailing socio-economic system and value structure which allowed them
to be exploited; as long as the system of patronage provided them with a living they returned their loyalty to the master" (Schmidt et al. 511). We end
up, in other words, with two main types of patronage, one exploitative and
the other repressive, or, if one prefers, one smoothly and one crudely
repressive.

In his extremely useful 1982 survey of Mediterranean anthropology,
David Gilmore notes that "Mediterranean societies are all undercapitalized
agrarian civilizations. They are characterized by sharp social stratification
and by both a relative and absolute scarcity of natural resources. There is
little social mobility. Power is highly concentrated in a few hands, and the
bureaucratic functions of the state are poorly developed. These conditions
are of course ideal for the development of patron-client ties and a dependency ideology . . . patronage relations provide a consistent ideological support for social inequality and dependency throughout the Mediterranean
area." Thus, if some scholars imagine a "simple model of vertical integration thought patronage" so that "patronage is seen basically as a mode of
integration between social classes," others, to the contrary, see it "more
starkly as an elite instrument for class domination. It is interpreted as an
imposed relation of dependence which 'masks' underlying exploitation or
dominance" (192–93). And the same judgment, by the way, may well apply
to nation-patrons and nation-clients. René Lemarchand claims that "the
questions raised by power asymmetries within and among nations lie at the
heart of the 'development or underdevelopment' syndrome. To frame these
questions in clientelistic terms is not meant to minimize the contribution
of dependency theory to our understanding of modern economic imperialism, but merely to suggest an alternative perspective from which to look at
the relationship of Third World elites to the international system" (Eisenstadt & Lemarchand 29).

Whether, then, in the ancient or modern world, and whether between

individuals or nations, the patron and client relationship is one of exploitation at best and repression at worst. Like the relationship of master and
slave, it is presumably (we hope) a dying phenomenon—even if the death
watch, as in the former case, takes centuries.

In Heaven as It Is on Earth

Patronage and clientage have been discussed so far primarily as modes
of social relationship and political organization. But they can organize
heaven just as well as earth. They can be religious and theological just as
well as social and political, and usually both if either. Thus, for example, in
a conceptual essay, Anthony Hall defines the term *patron* as "a person of
power, status, authority and influence . . . an employer, a ceremonial spon-
sor or even a protecting saint, but is only relevant in relation to a less powerful person or 'client' whom he can help or protect" (Schmidt et al. 510). And
in a bibliographical article in that same anthology, James Scott has a section, "Religious Clientelism," in which he maintains that "the relationship
between a 'saint,' prophet, or religious teacher and his followers may often
be viewed as a patron-client relationship despite the fact that grace and
divine inspiration supplement the material resources of the patron. In
some societies, networks of religious patronage may constitute a 'shadow'
social structure in potential conflict with secular forms of authority. In others, religious clientelism may become the predominant mode of authority"
(Schmidt et al. 491). Finally, in a fascinating comparison between politics
and religion on contemporary Malta, Jeremy Boissevain shows how "the
relation between social and religious change is evident in the congruence
between mortal and immortal patrons and brokers. Both types seem to
have thrived in periods when power was concentrated in the hands of a few,
when economic and political uncertainty prevailed, when widespread poverty induced dependency. . . . In Malta, as elsewhere in Europe, the saints
are marching out" (Gellner & Waterbury 94).

That conjunction of mortal and immortal patronage, of political and
religious clientage, reaches from the contemporary to the ancient Mediterranean. In a brilliant article, G. E. M. de Ste. Croix has shown how "the
three main stages in the evolution of *suffragium*," the word from which we
get our *suffrage*, furnish us "in miniature" with "the political history of
Rome" (1954:33, 48), and, after a slight time lag, with the ecclesiastical history of early Catholic Christianity.

During the Republic, the word meant the vote of free people,
although, of course, votes might often be bought or co-opted. But by the
end of the common era's second century, *suffragium* came to mean

"influence, interest, patronage, by a powerful man" (1954:38). Such patronage was ideally based on the moral obligation of reciprocity, but, where and as that ethos disintegrated, patronal influence could be bought and paid for in cash. Finally, then, "not later than the end of the fifth century," the word *suffragium* came "to mean not only the influence which the great man exercises but also the actual sum of money or other bribe given him in return for exercising it" (1954:47). That, however, is only the political side of the story. There is also a religious counterpart. The historical evolution of *suffragium* in terms of earthly power within Roman imperialism is mirrored in terms of heavenly power within Catholic Christianity.

The first usage, *suffragium*-as-vote, appears by the middle of the third century in connection with the election of bishops. "In the early Christian church, the one way in which the mass of the laity might on occasion hope to exercise a decisive influence was in the election of a bishop of their choice. But in the ecclesiastical as in the secular sphere, decision from below (in so far as it existed) tended to be replaced by decision from above; and in the long run the ordinary laity lost the voice they seem to have possessed in the early days. St. Cyprian, bishop of Carthage for some ten years prior to his martyrdom in 258, several times uses the expression *suffragium plebis* or *populi* or *omnium* in relation to the election of bishops; but it is certain, despite some rather ambiguous expressions, that he is not thinking of any popular vote: it is the comprovincial bishops whose *iudicium* is to decide the choice, in the presence of the laity (*plebe praesente*), whose *suffragium* can only be expressed in the form of acclamations. . . . Cyprian seems to be the earliest surviving writer to advocate this method of electing bishops, which he represents as the only proper one" (1954:35–36). Such popular acclamatory concurrence was considered essential, at least theoretically, into the fourth and fifth centuries, and popular acclamation alone sufficed to elect very special bishops like Saint Martin of Tours or Saint Ambrose of Milan even in the second half of the fourth century. But by the middle of the sixth century, the participation of the laity in episcopal elections was a thing of the past.

The second stage, *suffragium*-as-influence, also finds its counterpart in religious usage. "By the later fourth century the term *patrocinium* has begun to be applied to the activity of the apostles and martyrs on behalf of the faithful: in the writings of St. Ambrose, and later Prudentius, St. Augustine, St. Paulinus of Nola and others, the martyrs are the most powerful of *patroni*. . . . The expression *suffragium* then finds its way into everyday religious terminology, in the sense of 'intercession.' Just as the terrestrial patron is asked to use his influence with the emperor, so the celestial patron, the saint, is asked to use his influence with the Almighty. . . . As in the terrestrial sphere, so in the celestial, the lack of a patron might be fatal, for even the Almighty could hardly be trusted to give the right verdict unless an approach could be made to him through an influential intermediary" (1954:46). Ordinary pagan Romans, having grown up in an earthly world of patronage and clientage, would not find the heavenly world of Christianity too alien a place for late fourth century conversion.

Finally, there is the third usage, *suffragium*-as-bribe. "From the fifth century onwards we begin to hear frequently of simony, the sale or purchase of ecclesiastical preferment or spiritual gifts, an offence with which the Church seems not to have been seriously troubled under the pagan empire, but which now becomes rife. It need not surprise us to find the word *suffragium* applied to the corrupt practices by which bishoprics were so often procured. . . . Here again we find the unpleasant customs of the secular world imposing themselves also in the ecclesiastical sphere" (1954:47).

A footnote to that general process whereby earthly became the model for heavenly patronage brings the wheel full circle. Jeremy Boissevain, speaking of ideological differences between contemporary Protestants and Catholics, says about the latter, "The importance of intermediaries, especially in the political field, is summed up neatly in the proverb often quoted by Sicilians and Maltese: 'You can't get to heaven without the help of saints,' for political patrons in both cultures are referred to as saints" (1974:80). Saints were first called patrons, and now patrons are called saints.

All of this comes strikingly together in a text of the Stoic philosopher Epictetus, who lived between about 55 and 135 C.E. and will be seen in much greater detail in the next chapter. Note in this excerpt how easily one moves from earthly to heavenly patronage.

> A man has heard that the road which he is taking is infested with rob-
> bers; he does not venture to set forth alone, but he waits for a company,
> either that of an ambassador, or of a quaestor, or of a proconsul, and
> when he has attached himself to them he travels along the road in
> safety. So in this world the wise man acts. Says he to himself: "There are
> many robber-bands, tyrants, storms, difficulties, losses of what is most
> dear. Where shall a man flee for refuge? How shall he travel secure
> against robbery? To whom shall he attach himself? To So-and-so, the rich
> man, or the proconsul? And what is the good of that? He himself is
> stripped, groans, sorrows. Yes, and what if my fellow-traveller himself
> turn upon me and rob me? What shall I do? I will become a friend of
> Caesar; no one will wrong me if I am a companion of his. But, in the
> first place, the number of things I must suffer and endure in order to
> become his friend! and the number of times, and the number of persons

by whom I must first be robbed! And then, even if I do become his
friend, he too is mortal. And if some circumstance lead him to become
my enemy, where indeed had I better retire? To a wilderness? What,
does not fever go there? What, then, is to become of me? Is it impossible
to find a fellow-traveller who is safe, faithful, strong, free from the suspicion of treachery?" Thus he reflects and comes to the thought that, if he
attach himself to God, he will pass through the world in safety. (Epictetus,
Discourses 4.1:91–98; Oldfather 2.274–277)

That is less a parallelism of earthly and heavenly patronage than it is a
single chain of hierarchical patronage that moves progressively upward
from earth to heaven without a break in the linkage. And, one must admit
with Barbara Levick that such a passage "provokes reflections on the swift
progress of monotheism in the society of the Empire." Maybe the reason is
that "Christianity gave access, on a basis of merit and effort and through an
incorruptible intermediary, to a reliable authority" (151). But if, hopefully
without ethnocentric moral imperialism, one finds earthly patronage and
clientage a less than ideal way of organizing human relationships, their
heavenly counterparts may also be less than ideal. Whether in heaven as it
is on earth, or on earth as it is in heaven, systemic relational models such as
those of slave and master or of client and patron may be part of a world for
whose passing one might not mourn.

✧ 4 ✧

Poverty and Freedom

The Cynics sought happiness through freedom. The Cynic
conception of freedom included freedom from desires, from
fear, anger, grief and other emotions, from religious or moral
control, from the authority of the city or state or public officials,
from regard for public opinion and freedom also from the care
of property, from confinement to any locality and from the care
and support of wives and children. . . . The Cynics scoffed at the
customs and conventionalities of others, but were rigid in
observance of their own. The Cynic would not appear
anywhere without his wallet, staff and cloak, which must
invariably be worn, dirty and ragged and worn so as to leave the
right shoulder bare. He never wore shoes and his hair and beard
were long and unkempt.

Farrand Sayre (7, 18)

The concept of freedom in Cynicism represents a striving after
freedom from something: freedom from all care about food,
clothing, house, home, marriage, children, etc.; freedom from
all ties which morality, law, state, and community life in general
may put upon the individual; furthermore freedom from
passions, ambitions, intellectual, cultural and religious
demands, etc., and finally freedom from life itself with the right
to leave it voluntarily if the demand for freedom entails it. . . .
But the problem becomes considerably more difficult if we
search for more positive things.

Ragnar Höistad (15–16)

Both Vittorio Lanternari and Bryan Wilson have written fascinating studies
on religious movements of protest among tribal and Third-World peoples,
but that latter work is especially useful because it proposes a sevenfold
typology based on the diverse ways in which people *respond to the world*
when salvation from evil is no longer found adequately within the standard
religious resources of their tradition. Granted, of course, the multivalent
meaning of evil and therefore of any transcendent salvation from it, and

using *God* as "the convenient symbol for supernatural power, however that power is conceived and designated in particular cultures," he established seven reactions grouped in three sets according to where the emphasis falls along the movement of *response/to/the world* (22–26).

The first group is *Conversionists* who, as subjectivists, place primary emphasis on *response* to the world. They believe that "God will change us." Since the world is corrupt because people are corrupt, salvation comes only through "a profoundly felt, supernaturally wrought transformation of the self." Next are two groups who, as relationists, place primary emphasis on response *to* the world. *Manipulationists* believe that "God calls us to change perception." People must learn the right means, facilities, techniques so as "to alter their relation to the world, to see the world differently." *Thaumaturgists* believe that "God will grant particular dispensations and work specific miracles." Salvation is conceived much more narrowly than in the preceding case, is particularistic, personal, local, and magical and is very difficult to generalize, organize, and ideologize. Finally, there are four groups who, as objectivists, place primary emphasis on response to *the world*. *Revolutionists* believe that "God will overturn" the world. In this case, "only the destruction of the world, of the natural, but more specifically of the social, order, will suffice." This presumes divine and imminent action, with or without human participation. *Introversionists* believe that "God calls us to abandon" the world. It is so irredeemably evil that one must withdraw completely, either alone or with and into "a separated community preoccupied with its own holiness and its means of insulation from the wider society." *Reformists* believe that "God calls us to amend" the world. This response is very close to secular improvement programs except that it presumes "supernaturally-given insights about the ways in which social organization should be amended." *Utopians* believe that "God calls us to reconstruct" the world. This presumes "some divinely given principles" of reconstruction, is much more radical than the reformist alternative, but, unlike the revolutionist option, insists much more on the role human beings must take in the process.

I presume that Wilson's typology has both trans-temporal as well as trans-cultural validity, and I focus on one of his types, the *introversionist* response, in the first century of the common era. If one thinks of Mediterranean civilization located at the crossroads of, on the one hand, honor and shame, and, on the other, patronage and clientage, each with both horizontal and vertical, human and divine dimensions, one can also begin to imagine "the fullest possible withdrawal from it." But where could one stand to get such leverage? How could one, for example, withdraw from Greco-Roman civilization?

Diogenes or Daedalus?

"By the middle of the first century of our era, elements of the Cynic and Stoic tenets were fairly well merged," according to Cora Lutz, "in the teachings of the popular philosophers" (28 note 127). Cynicism was founded by Diogenes of Sinope, who lived from about 400 to about 320 B.C.E. and was born on the mid-southern coast of the Black Sea. The term itself comes from *kyon*, the Greek word for dog, and it was used of Diogenes by Aristotle, as if quoting a well-known nickname. It was originally a derogatory term for the provocative shamelessness with which Diogenes deliberately flouted basic human codes of propriety and decency, custom and convention, doing, as the third-century historian of philosophy Diogenes Laertius delicately puts it, "everything in public, the works of Demeter and Aphrodite alike" (6.69; Hicks 2.70–71). Stoicism was founded by Zeno of Citium, who lived from about 333 to about 264 B.C.E. and was born on the southeastern coast of Cyprus. That title comes, more demurely, from the Athenian agora's Stoa Poikile, where Zeno taught for many years. Both philosophies sought the happiness of inner freedom and personal self-sufficiency, but where Stoicism found it in detachment from the world, Cynicism found it in abandonment of the world. Insofar as they interacted together, and especially on the popular level, Cynicism was practical and radical Stoicism; Stoicism was theoretical and moderate Cynicism. Take, for example, the case of Seneca.

Lucius Annaeus Seneca—Seneca the Younger—Stoic philosopher, author, and multimillionaire, lived between about 4 B.C.E. and 65 C.E. As tutor to Nero, his responsibility for imperial virtue and vice remained somewhat ambiguous, but he was, in the end, ordered to commit suicide for alleged participation in the anti-Neronic conspiracy headed by Gaius Calpurnius Piso. Despite his extreme wealth, he was greatly influenced by the Cynic philosopher Demetrius, who lived in his household during the years between 51 and 65 C.E. when Seneca was composing his *Epistulae Morales*, moral treatises fictionalized as letters to his friend Gaius Lucilius. One can see, for instance, the difference between the theoretical dispassion of the Stoic Seneca (I have but do not care) and the practical dispossession of the Cynic Demetrius (I do not have but do not care) in this story:

> When Gaius Caesar [Caligula] wanted to give Demetrius two hundred
> thousand, he laughingly refused it, not even deeming it a sum the
> refusal of which was worth boasting about. . . . "If he meant to tempt
> me," said he, " he ought to have tested me by offering me his whole king-
> dom." (Seneca, *De Beneficii* 7.11; Basore et al. 3.482–483)

In terms of possessions, Stoics sought to have as if they had not, Cynics to have not as if they had. Be that as it may, and however Seneca balanced extreme wealth and a Cynic chaplain, the influence of Demetrius lies behind this text:

> How, I ask, can you consistently admire both Diogenes and Daedalus? Which of these two seems to you a wise man—the one who devised the saw, or the one who, on seeing a boy drink water from the hollow of his hand, forthwith took his cup from his wallet and broke it, upbraiding himself with these words: "Fool that I am, to have been carrying superfluous baggage all this time!" and then curled himself up in his tub and lay down to sleep. . . . If mankind were willing to listen to this sage, they would know that the cook is as superfluous as the soldier. . . . Follow nature, and you will need no skilled craftsmen. (Seneca, *Epistulae Morales* 90.14–16; Basore et al. 5.402–405)

"Surveying the state of Cynicism at the end of the Augustan age," according to Donald Dudley, "we should not be inclined to predict for it a revival and at least another five hundred years of life. But history was repeating itself, at least, in so far as it ever does; that is to say that the conditions which had proved favourable for the growth of Cynicism after the death of Alexander were being reproduced in the early years of the first century A.D. The Imperial system, though an enormous gain in efficiency of administration, had taken the interest out of politics; there was a great increase in cosmopolitanism; finally luxury was more rampant than ever, and philosophy, even Stoicism, had compromised with it. There was a demand for a simpler, practical creed, which Cynicism was to meet. The 'lion's array' of Diogenes would again find worthy wearers; Cynicism was to be, not reborn, but revived" (124).

The struggle, in other words, is of nature against culture, Cynicism against civilization, Diogenes against Daedalus; and, of course, one recognizes the irony of the aristocratic Seneca writing for the former of those dichotomies. But at least, and however illusionary it may be, the appeal to nature posits a vantage point from which a radical critique of culture becomes possible. And though none of this may be directly revolutionary in the sense of instigating imperial assassinations, it still has an acutely political edge. A few paragraphs earlier in that same epistle (at 90.10), Seneca said, "A thatched roof once covered free men; under marble and gold dwells slavery." The ambiguity is obvious: was it, morally, marble and gold that themselves enslaved, or was it, politically, tyrannical rule symbolized by them that did it?

Cynicism is not, in other words, just a moral attack on Greco-Roman civilization; it is a paradoxical attack on civilization itself. To cite a much later example, the emperor Julian, who lived from 331 to 363 C.E., could say this about Cynicism itself, whatever his difficulties with certain of its contemporary practitioners:

> Cynicism is a branch of philosophy, and by no means the most insignificant or least honourable, but rivalling the noblest . . . It seems to be in some ways a universal philosophy, and the most natural, and to demand no special study whatsoever. (Julian, *Oration 6: To the Uneducated Cynics*; Wright 2.8–9, 22–23)

That we are dealing with "a universal philosophy" is clear from the epilogue to Donald Dudley's history of Cynicism, which sweeps from Oriental mysticism, through Greco-Roman Cynicism, on to Christian monasticism, and secular Anarchism (209–213). It is also clear in that the social protest that Bryan Wilson termed *introversionism* and described as the "fullest possible withdrawal" from the world found its ancient Greco-Roman incarnation in Cynicism. But, despite any quite legitimate historical links from India to Diogenes or from Greco-Roman Cynicism to Christian monasticism, it is necessary to insist that, with all of them, we are but dealing with divergent manifestations of one of the great and fundamental options of the human spirit. I would also insist that though Wilson's *revolutionism* and *introversionism* could stand at opposite poles as the most active and social against the most passive and personal forms of response, they could, on the one hand, also become indistinguishable in the center of their continuum; and, on the other, radical negation, even at its most passive, is never apolitical.

Free Under Father Zeus

Musonius Rufus, Etruscan by birth but Stoic by choice, lived from about 30 to about 100 C.E. and has been described as the "apostle of moral liberty" and "the Roman Socrates" (Lutz 3–4). He argued, despite an acceptance of standard gender roles, "that women too should study philosophy" since both women and men had the same reason, senses, body, and "inclination" to virtue, goodness, and justice (Lutz 38–41). And, having answered "should daughters receive the same education as sons?" in the affirmative, he faced an objection ever ancient and ever new.

> "Come now," I suppose someone will say, "do you expect that men should learn spinning the same as women, and that women should take part in gymnastic exercises the same as men?" No, that I should not demand. But I do say that, since in the human race man's constitution is

stronger and woman's weaker, tasks should be assigned which are suited
to the nature of each; that is the heavier tasks should be given to the
stronger and the lighter to the weaker. Thus spinning and indoor work
would be more fitting for women than for men, while gymnastics and
outdoor work would be more suitable for men. Occasionally, however,
some men might more fittingly handle certain of the lighter tasks and
what is generally considered women's work, and again, women might do
heavier tasks which seem more appropriate for men whenever conditions of strength, need, or circumstance warranted. For all human tasks,
I am inclined to believe, are a common obligation and are common for
men and women, and none is necessarily appointed for either one exclusively, but some are more suited to the nature of one, some to the other,
and for this reason some are called men's work and some women's. But
whatever things have reference to virtue, these one would properly say
are equally appropriate to the nature of both, inasmuch as we agree that
virtues are in no respect more fitting for the one than the other.
(Musonius Rufus, Fragment IV; Lutz 46–47)

Hand in hand with such social egalitarianism went an equal political
egalitarianism, and it is well to remember that Musonius Rufus was twice
banished from Rome, once by Nero and again by Vespasian. His argument
"that kings also should study philosophy" is not just the old ideal of the
philosopher-king but has a certain daring reciprocity to it. If the true king
should be a philosopher, is not the philosopher the true king?

For my part, I believe that the good king is straightway and of necessity
a philosopher, and the philosopher a kingly person. . . . Even if he does
not have many subjects obedient to him, he is not for that reason less
kingly, for it is enough to rule one's wife and children or, for that matter,
only oneself (Musonius Rufus, Fragment IV; Lutz 64–67)

Everyone can be a king, and only those who can rule themselves are
truly royal. Over against the actualities of political and imperial dominion
stands a royalty of freedom in the kingdom of the free. "Did anyone," he
asks rhetorically, "ever exhibit greater freedom of speech . . . and . . . were
any of his contemporaries freer than Diogenes?" (Lutz 74–75).

The archetypal encounter is, therefore, that between Diogenes and
Alexander, which "could only have occurred on the occasion of Alexander's
visit to the Isthmus [of Corinth] in 336 B.C. to meet representatives from
the Greek states and make preparations for his invasion of Asia" (Sayre 59).
This oft-told tale was already known to Cicero, writing in 45 B.C.E.

But Diogenes, certainly, was more outspoken, in his quality of Cynic,
when Alexander asked him to name anything he wanted: "Just now," he

said, "stand a bit away from the sun!" Alexander apparently had inter-
fered with his basking in the heat. (Cicero, *Tusculan Disputations* 5.92;
King 518–519)

Think, by the way, of how that anecdote sounded not just to the
progeny of Diogenes but to the emulators of Alexander. The question was
not just one of beggary against royalty but of where true beggary and true
royalty reside. Those quite subversive implications were spelled out
emphatically by one of Musonius Rufus' own pupils, Epictetus, whose
work I quoted at the end of the last chapter.

Born in Hierapolis in Phrygia, Epictetus "was the one Greek philosopher who, despite the monistic and necessitarian postulates of his philosophy, conceived of his God in as vivid a fashion as the writers of the New
Testament, and almost as intimately as the founder of Christianity himself." Born the slave son of a slave mother, "an all-engulfing passion for independence and liberty so preoccupied him in his youth, that throughout his
life he was obsessed with the fear of restraint, and tended to regard mere
liberty, even in its negative aspect alone, as almost the highest conceivable
good" (Oldfather 1.vii–viii). He lived from about 55 to about 135 C.E., was
allowed by his master Epaphroditus, Nero's freedman secretary, to hear
Musonius Rufus' lectures, and, eventually freed, was banished along with
the other philosophers by Domitian in 89 C.E. He established a school in
Nicopolis, Augustus' memorial to Actium on the western coast of Greece,
and, since, like Socrates, he left nothing behind him in writing, we know his
teachings only from what W. A. Oldfather has described as "a stenographic
record of the *ipsissima verba* of the master" by his pupil Flavius Arrian
(1.xiii).

Epictetus was, of course, a Stoic, but his sympathy for Cynicism is
clear from a glance at the indexes to the Loeb edition, where Diogenes far
outnumbers Zeno. For my present purpose, however, I restrict discussion
to his chapter "On the Calling of a Cynic" in 3.22 but remembering, even
there, that we are reading the commentary of a Stoic. He asks, in a justly
famous passage,

> And how is it possible that a man who has nothing, who is naked, house-
> less, without a hearth, squalid, without a slave, without a city, can pass a
> life that flows easily? See, God has sent you a man to show you that it is
> possible. Look at me, who am without a city, without a house, without
> possessions, without a slave; I sleep on the ground; I have no wife, no
> children, no praetorium, but only the earth and heavens, and one poor
> cloak. And what do I want? Am I not without sorrow? Am I not without
> fear? Am I not free? When did any of you see me failing in the object of

my desire? or ever falling into that which I would avoid? did I ever blame God or man? did I ever accuse any man? did any of you ever see me with sorrowful countenance? And how do I meet with those whom you are afraid of and admire? Do not I treat them like slaves? Who, when he sees me, does not think that he sees his king and master? (Epictetus, *Discourses* 3.22:45–49; Oldfather 2.146–147)

Notice, in the flow of that passage, the sequence from "nothing" to "free" to "king," the logic of poverty leading to freedom leading to royalty. This is the heart of the Cynic challenge and the place where the Stoic Epictetus speaks not only about but within Cynicism. I gloss each of those three points with commentary from elsewhere in that same chapter.

Poverty, first of all. Epictetus is very concerned that the externals of Cynicism may be mistaken for its internals. But, even while warning against that danger, he never suggests abandoning those externals. He simply insists that internal poverty must beget external and that external must not replace internal.

So do you [would-be Cynics] also think about the matter carefully; it is not what you think it is. "I wear a rough cloak even as it is, and I shall have one then; I have a hard bed even now, and so I shall then; I shall take to myself a wallet and a staff, and I shall begin to walk around and beg from those I meet, and revile them. . . . " If you fancy the affair to be something like this, give it a wide berth; don't come near it, it is nothing for you. . . .

Lo, these are words [the long quotation from 3.22:45–49 given above] that befit a Cynic, this is his character, and his plan of life. But no, you say, what makes a Cynic is a contemptible wallet, a staff, and big jaws; to devour everything you give him, or to stow it away, or to revile tactlessly the people he meets, or to show off his fine shoulder. (Epictetus, *Discourses* 3.22:9–10, 50; Oldfather 2.132–135, 148–149)

It is obvious that Epictetus is speaking to an audience of the poorer classes, whose normal poverty is not that different, in externals, from Cynic poverty. But, he insists, while accepting those externals voluntarily, it is the internals that count.

Next is freedom. This comes not only from a physical poverty that renders one impervious both to desire and loss, but especially from a spiritual poverty that renders one oblivious both to attack and assault.

For this too is a very pleasant strand woven into the Cynic's pattern of life; he must needs be flogged like an ass, and while he is being flogged he must love the men who flog him, as though he were the father or brother of them all. But that is not your way. If someone flogs you, go stand in the midst and shout, "O Caesar, what do I have to suffer under your peaceful rule? let us go before the Proconsul." But what to a Cynic is Caesar, or a Proconsul, or anyone other than He who has sent him into the world, and whom he serves, that is, Zeus? . . .

Now the spirit of patient endurance the Cynic must have to such a degree that common people will think him insensate and a stone; nobody reviles him, nobody beats him, nobody insults him; but his body he has himself given for anyone to use as he sees fit. (Epictetus, *Discourses* 3.22:54–56, 100; Oldfather 2.148–151, 166–167)

It is fascinating to watch the Christian nervousness of some earlier translators in handling that passage. Elizabeth Carter compares it with Matthew 5:39–44 but notes "that Christ specifies higher injuries and provocations than Epictetus doth; and requires of *all* his followers, what Epictetus describes only as the duty of one or two *extraordinary* persons, as such" (Rouse 260 note 11). Not true.

Finally, there is the theme of true royalty, and, on this, notice that the same Greek word is used for the "*sceptre* of Zeus" and the "*staff* of Diogenes" in 3.22:34, 57 (my italics).

Where will you find me a Cynic's friend? . . . He must share with him his sceptre and kingdom. . . .

See to what straits we are reducing our Cynic [if he marries], how we are taking away his kingdom from him . . .

and yet shall the Cynic's kingship [or: kingdom] not be thought a reasonable compensation [for celibacy]. (Epictetus, *Discourses* 3.22:63, 75, 79; Oldfather 2.152–153, 156–159)

Poverty, freedom, and royalty, then, because the Cynic "has been sent by Zeus to men, partly as a messenger . . . and partly . . . as a scout" (3.22:23–24), so that he walks the earth as "one who shares in the government of Zeus" (3.22:95).

The Skin of My Feet for Shoes

Abraham Malherbe warns that "Cynic-Stoic" is "a hyphenation that has contributed to obscurity about what is Cynic and what is Stoic." To avoid such obscurity he emphasizes that "a valuable but neglected source for the history of Cynicism is the Cynic letters. Most of these letters come from the Augustan age and purport to have been written by such ancient worthies of the sect as Antisthenes, Diogenes and Crates and by such non-Cynics as Anacharsis, Heraclitus, Hippocrates and Socrates and his followers, all of whom are represented as advancing Cynic views. The value of these letters lies in the fact that they are Cynic writings which provide evidence of Cynicism at the time when it was experiencing a reawakening. . . . The picture of Cynicism that emerges from the letters is of a rich diversity that compels us to be more circumspect in using the Stoic writers as authorities on Cynicism" (2–3). Or, in the description of F. Gerald Downing, "The Cynic Epistles are imagined letters of early Cynic teachers, and of others conscripted to the Cynic cause (Heraclitus, Socrates). The letters seem to come from a wide spread of dates, some pre-Christian, some contemporary with the beginnings of Christianity, others as late as the second century C.E. By and large they represent a radical, severe, and less literary and so, perhaps, more 'populist' strand of Cynicism than in our other sources" (1988:192).

The titles for my present and preceding sections are taken from those fictionalized Cynic letters, the former from *Pseudo-Diogenes* 34 and the latter from *Pseudo-Anacharsis* 5 (Malherbe 144–145, 42–43). We know, for example, that *Pseudo-Anacharsis* 5 was available by at least 45 B.C.E. because Cicero quoted it in full in his *Tusculan Disputations* 5.90 (King 516–517).

> [To Hanno] For me, a Scythian cloak serves as my garment, the skin of
> my feet as my shoes, the whole earth as my resting place, milk, cheese
> and meat as my favorite meal, hunger as my main course. (*Pseudo-*
> *Anacharsis* 5; Malherbe 42–43)

This fictional letter claims for Cynicism "Anacharsis, a Scythian prince [who] visited Greece in the early sixth century B.C. in a quest for wisdom [and] as a type of the 'noble savage' . . . captured the imagination of the Greeks" (Malherbe 6). Already, therefore, in the pre-Christian period, it was clear that Cynicism involved not just a theoretical position on philosophy but a practical decision on dress, food, and shelter. It was this programmatic and external poverty that made Cynicism so overtly obvious and so popularly recognizable.

"To say," according to Leif Vaage, "that Greco-Roman Cynicism was principally a way of life is to say that the way of life of Greco-Roman Cynics principally characterized them. This way of life can be summarized shortly. The standard uniform of the Cynics was a cloak, a wallet, a staff. Typically, their life included barefooted itinerancy viz. indigence, sleeping on the ground or in the baths and other public buildings, a diet of water and vegetables. They were found usually in the market-place. They begged" (1987:374–375). One could probably add uncut hair and beard, as well. We are dealing, of course, with deliberately antisocial symbolism, and the point, say, of an anticultural dress was not that it be uniform for all Cynics but that it be anticonventional for all Cynics. What they sought, as Vaage emphasizes, was "self-sufficiency . . . to free themselves from the system of desires which they perceived to enthrall Greco-Roman culture" and to practice "forthrightness . . . and shamelessness" as an "implicit or explicit critique of typical values of Greco-Roman civilization" (1987:375–380).

Consider, for example, their code of anti-dress as mentioned repeatedly in the fictional letters of Diogenes, "the prophet of indifference," especially those in 1–29, which form "an early collection . . . dated from the first century B.C. or even earlier" (Malherbe 17).

> [To Hicetas] Do not be upset, Father, that I am called a dog and put on a double, coarse cloak, carry a wallet over my shoulders, and have a staff in my hand . . . living as I do, not in conformity with popular opinion but according to nature, free under Zeus. . . .
>
> [To Apolexis] I have laid aside most of the things that weigh down my wallet, since I learned that for a plate a hollowed out loaf of bread suffices, as the hands do for a cup. . . .
>
> [To Antipater] I hear that you say I am doing nothing unusual in wearing a double, ragged cloak and carrying a wallet. Now I admit that none of these is extraordinary, but each of them is good when undertaken out of conscious determination. . . .
>
> [To Anaxilaus] I have recently come to recognize myself to be Agamemnon, since for a scepter I have my staff and for a mantle the double, ragged cloak, and by way of exchange, my leather wallet is a shield. . . .
>
> [To Agesilaus] Life has a sufficient store in a wallet. . . .
>
> [To Crates] Remember that I started you [Crates] on your life-long poverty . . . consider the ragged cloak to be a lion's skin, the staff a club, and the wallet land and sea, from which you are fed. For thus would the spirit of Heracles, mightier than every turn of fortune, stir in you. (*Pseudo-Diogenes* 7, 13, 15, 19, 22, 26; Malherbe 98–119)

In Cynic tradition, therefore, cloak, wallet, and staff had become almost an official triad. And lack of sandals can be found not only with the wild Scythian Anacharsis but even with Musonius Rufus on the Stoic side of the Stoic-Cynic hyphenation.

> Wearing one chiton is preferable to needing two, and wearing none but only a cloak is preferable to wearing one. Also going barefoot is better than wearing sandals, if one can do it, for wearing sandals is next to being bound, but going barefoot gives the feet great freedom and grace when they are used to it. (Musonius Rufus, Fragment XIX; Lutz 122–123)

The argument is urbanely pragmatic and Stoically moderate, but the result is still bare feet. A similar phenomenon is mentioned in the letters fictionally attributed to Socrates, a collection of seven epistles that, as Malherbe suggests, probably "come from the first century or even earlier" (27).

> I have chosen a life of poverty. . . . I willingly refuse gifts not only from living friends, but also from friends who have died and left gifts to me. . . . I am satisfied to have the plainest food and the same garment summer and winter, and I do not wear shoes at all. (*Pseudo-Socrates* 6; Malherbe 232–233)

Whether we talk of cloak, wallet, and staff, or of bare feet and long hair, what is significant is not that all Cynics looked exactly alike but that all Cynics looked sufficiently different from what was normal by contemporary social standards to be recognized as programmatically divergent.

The deliberate and anticultural poverty of the Cynic could entail not only vagrancy but also itinerancy, and it was probably this particular feature that the staff itself emphasized. Diogenes himself had been called by divine oracle to elevate his exilic poverty into a philosophic position and so also was Dio of Prusa, nicknamed Chrysostom or "golden-tongued,"a native of Bithynia and student of Musonius Rufus. He lived between about 40 and at least 112 C.E. and, banished from both Rome and Bithynia by Domitian in 82 C.E., he turned his fourteen-year banishment into a calculated philosophical mission. "Wherever he roamed," in the words of Walter Liefeld, "he carried the message of the ideal kingship in contrast to the dominion of the emperor" (1967:52). We keep seeing glimpses of what he must have looked like in his *Discourses*.

> Someone who is unkempt and wears his garment closely wrapped about him and has no companions on his walks, a man who makes himself the first target for examination and reproof. . . . I am well aware that it is customary for most people to give the name of Cynic to men who dress as I do; and . . . consider them to be not even of sound mind to begin with, but a crazy wretched lot. . . . I wear my hair long . . . someone in a cloak but no tunic, with flowing hair and beard. (Dio Chrysostom, *Discourses* 33.14; 34.2; 35.2; 72.3; Cohoon & Crosby 3.284–285, 336–339, 390–391; 5.176–177)

He became, in other words, a typical or even archetypal wandering preacher in the classic Cynic style, but, from Walter Liefeld again, "the appeal and message of the Cynics was not calculated to win the approval of the better Roman classes. They offended the Roman *gravitas*, stirred the lower classes, and openly opposed rulers who failed to live up to the Cynic-Stoic ideal of kingship. This political activity brought not only persecution but suspicion on wandering preachers in general" (162). And that brings up the question of class.

In the Army of the Dog

Ronald Hock, in a dissertation on Paul's ideal of the working apostle, concludes that "discussions of the philosopher's means of support go back to the clash between Socrates and the sophists over the propriety of charging fees for teaching. . . . Thus, in the first century A.D. . . . the options included charging fees (preferred by Stoics and Aristotelians), begging (preferred by Cynics), and requiring yearly contributions (developed by Epicureans). These conventional practices, however, were to some extent opposed and debated. For example within the Cynic school some philosophers refused to beg their support and instead advocated still another alternative: working to support oneself" (1974:84). And, in considering those last two options of begging or working, two points must be kept in mind.

At least theoretically and ideologically even if not practically and experientially, begging by Cynics could be distinguished from begging by beggars as follows (in that pre-Christian collection of the fictionalized letters of Diogenes seen above):

> [To Metrocles] Be bold, not only with regard to your dress, name, and
> way of life . . . but also in begging people for sustenance, for it is not at
> all disgraceful. . . . It is all right to beg, if it is not for a free gift or for
> something worse in exchange, but for the salvation of everyone; that is,
> to ask people for things that accord with nature, and to ask with a view
> to doing the same things as Heracles, the son of Zeus, and to be able to
> give back something much better than what you receive yourself. . . .
> Socrates used to say that sages do not beg but demand back, for every-
> thing belongs to them, just as it does to the gods. And this he tried to
> infer from the premises that the gods are masters of all, that the prop-
> erty of friends is held in common, and that the sage is a friend of god.
> Therefore, you will be begging for what is your own.
>   [To Crates] Ask for bread even from the statues in the market place
> as you enter it. In a way, such a practice is good, for you will meet men
> more unfeeling than statues. (*Pseudo-Diogenes* 10, 11; Malherbe 102–105)

And if begging could be defended as appropriate, working also needed its own defense, for, as we have seen in the preceding chapter and as Ronald Hock emphasizes, "that Greeks, especially philosophers, despised manual labor cannot be doubted" (1974:22). That meant, of course, that manual labor just as much as begging could be, for a philosopher, a deliberate countercultural activity, a calculated repudiation of hierarchical social values. The classic example is Musonius Rufus, who, in Fragment XI, sets the ideal philosophical school not in the city but in the country and around a sage who does "manual labor just like a peasant" (Lutz 82–83). Cynic begging or Cynic working, then, each needed a defense in Greco-Roman society, but there was one very special problem with the former that did not arise with the latter: sincerity and integrity.

Lucian, who lived between about 120 and about 180 C.E., was born in Samosata on the upper reaches of the Euphrates. His witty and irreverent writings, especially his satiric dialogues, were intended, so says the Loeb introduction, "not to reform society nor to chastise it, but simply to amuse it" (Harmon et al. 1.viii). It is clear that Lucian could admire a Cynic, as he does in his account of the second-century C.E. philosopher Demonax.

> He did not ... alter the details of his life in order to gain the wonder and attract the gaze of men he met, but led the same life and ate the same food as everyone else, was not in the least subject to pride, and played his part in society and politics. (Lucian, *Demonax* 5; Harmon et al. 1.146–147)

He had, in other words, little of what made Cynics Cynics, which was, precisely and deliberately, those externals that one could not fail to see, could not refuse to notice. It is equally clear that, for Lucian, the polar opposite of a Demonax is a Peregrinus Proteus. He was a wandering preacher, first a Christian, having been both converted and excommunicated in Palestine, and then a Cynic with "his hair long ... dressed in a dirty mantle ... a wallet slung at his side, the staff ... in his hand" as described in *The Passing of Peregrinus* 15 (Harmon et al. 5.16–17). Finally, banished from Rome, he announced at the Olympic Games of 161 C.E. that he would immolate himself publicly at those of 165 C.E. Peregrinus claimed, Lucian admits, that his dramatic suicide was "for the sake of his fellow men, that he [might] teach them to despise death and endure what is fearsome" (5.26–27), yet he consistently and even vehemently impugns his motives, intentions, and purposes. He "never fixed his gaze on the verities, but always did and said everything with a view to glory and the praise of the multitude even to the extent of leaping into fire" (5.46–49). Lucian, of course, knew nothing whatsoever about Peregrinus' integrity of character or sincerity of motivation. As Luke Johnson put it in discussing the conventions of ancient polemic, whoever your opponents were, "they were all lovers of pleasure, lovers of money, and lovers of glory" (432). This is underlined by the fact that Lucian's contemporary, Aulus Gellius, who lived between about 123 and 169 C.E., records the following:

When I was in Athens, I met a philosopher named Peregrinus, who was later surnamed Proteus, a man of dignity and fortitude, living in a hut outside the city. And visiting him frequently, I heard him say many things that were in truth helpful and noble. (Aulus Gellius, *Attic Nights* 12.11; Rolfe 2.392–393)

As with the intensely disliked Peregrinus so with the equally disliked Cynics, one should be careful of taking Lucian's analysis of motivation as anything more than the standardized rhetorical vituperation of opponents.

Lucian did not like Cynics, and the more Cynic they were, the less he liked them. In *Philosophies for Sale* Zeus, with the aid of Hermes, holds an auction in which incarnated philosophies and prospective buyers get to talk to one another. This is from the Cynic-for-sale section:

First, after taking you in charge, stripping you of your luxury and shackling you to want, I will put a short cloak on you. Next I will compel you to undergo pains and hardships, sleeping on the ground, drinking nothing but water and filling yourself with any food that comes your way. As for money, in case you have any, if you follow my advice you will throw it into the sea forthwith. You will take no thought of marriage or children or native land: all that will be sheer nonsense to you, and you will leave the home of your fathers and make your home in a tomb or a deserted tower or even a jar [like Diogenes]. Your wallet will be full of lupines, and of papyrus rolls written on both sides. Leading this life you will say that you are happier than the Great King and if anyone flogs you or twists you on the rack, you will think there is nothing painful in it. . . . The traits that you should possess in particular are these: you should be impudent and bold, and should abuse all and each, both kings and commoners, for thus they will admire you and think you manly. Let your language be barbarous, your voice discordant and just like the barking of a dog: let your expression be set, and your gait consistent with your expression. In a word, let everything about you be bestial and savage. Put off modesty, decency and moderation, and wipe away blushes from your face completely. Frequent the most crowded place, and in those very places desire to be solitary and uncommunicative, greeting nor friend nor stranger; for to do so is abdication of the empire [of freedom]. Do boldly in full view of all what another would not do in secret; choose the most ridiculous ways of satisfying your lust; and at the last, if you like, eat a raw devilfish or squid, and die. This is the bliss we vouchsafe you. . . .

But at all events it is easy, man, and no trouble for all to follow; for you will not need education and doctrine and drivel, but this road is a short cut to fame. Even if you are an unlettered man, a tanner or a fishman or a carpenter or a money-changer — there will be nothing to hinder you from being wondered at, if only you have impudence and boldness and learn how to abuse people properly. (Lucian, *Philosophies for Sale* 9–11; Harmon et al. 2.466–471)

The buyer takes the auctioned Cynic home for two obols because he "might do at a pinch for a boatman or a gardener." I have given that quotation in full because it is, despite an edge of caricature, probably the fullest and fairest description of popular Cynicism that we have from antiquity. I focus here, however, on that final barb about Cynicism's availability even to illiterate manual workers.

Lucian, in another comic dialogue, links the alleged insincerity of Peregrinus to that of lower-class Cynics. A personified Philosophy comes to protest before Zeus and Apollo. Her accusation is against the Cynics.

There is an abominable class of men, for the most part slaves and hirelings . . . or learning such trades as . . . cobbling, building, busying themselves with fuller's tubs, or carding wool. . . . Their trades, however, were petty, laborious, and barely able to supply them with just enough. To some, moreover, servitude seemed grievous and (as indeed it is) intolerable . . . so, resorting to good old Desperation, inviting the support, too, of Hardihood, Stupidity, and Shamelessness, who are their principal partisans, and committing to memory novel terms of abuse .. they very plausibly transform themselves in looks and apparel to counterfeit my very self. . . . It does not require much ceremony to don a short cloak, sling on a wallet, carry a staff in one's hand, and . . . slang everyone. (Lucian, *The Runaways* 12–14; Harmon et al. 5.68–71)

If this continues, warns Philosophy, "all the men in the workshops . . . will leave their trades deserted" as manual labor is abandoned for beggary and debauchery hidden under Cynic apparel "in the army of the dog."

Once again, with lower-class Cynicism as with Peregrinus, I accept Lucian's description of fact but not his analysis of motive. Of course, then as now, there were lower-class actions and operations whose integrity or sincerity was less than ideal. But so, then as now, were the activities of the elites and the aristocracies. When, for example, Donald Dudley discusses Cynicism in the second century C.E. he follows Lucian in accepting "the influx into the movement of a large number of charlatans" (144). But such strictures against "Cynicism as the 'philosophy of the proletariat'" (147) do not beget a parallel questioning of the motivations of Dio Chrysostom, who, after fourteen years of exiled and impoverished itinerancy "abandoned the vagrant Cynic life to become the friend of Trajan, a person of great influence in the affairs of his native province of Bithynia, and a kind of unofficial but influential intermediary between the Roman government and the Greek states generally" (148).

My point is not that Dio was insincere, any more than Seneca before him. But then neither necessarily was Peregrinus. And lower-class Cynics were no more or less sincere than upper-class Cynics. But insofar as the lower classes adopted Cynicism, they would beget from the literate upper classes a double denigration, one because of their philosophy and another because of their class.

PART II

Embattled Brokerage

... the great God, whom no hands of men fashioned
in the likeness of speechless idols of polished stone.
For he does not have a house, a stone set up as a temple,
dumb and toothless, a bane which brings many woes to men,
but one which it is not possible to see from earth nor to measure
with mortal eyes, since it was not fashioned by mortal hand.
                    Sibylline Oracles 4:6–11, from about 100 C.E. *(OTP 1.384)*

What happens when the structure of society is such that a part
of the society feels itself so systematically excluded from
participation in the redemptive media that it cannot "make it"
within the present situation, that it cannot attain salvation? At
this point we may expect to find strategies to unblock access to
power. The nature of the strategies will depend on the type of
society and the forms of perceived deprivations. Political
revolution, crusades, witchcraft and millenarism are some of the
possibilities. If millenarian activities and movements appear,
they will develop according to a specifiable pattern.
                                        Sheldon R. Isenberg (28)

The close connection between the temple and sectarianism is
also shown by the fact that the important stages in the
development of Jewish sectarianism coincide with the
important stages in the history of the second temple. Sects
appeared in inchoate form in the Persian period when the
newly built temple was trying to establish its legitimacy. They
emerged fully developed in the second century B.C.E. after the
temple had been profaned by Epiphanes and purified by the
Maccabees. Sects disappeared after 70 C.E., because the
destruction of the temple removed one of the chief focal points
of sectarianism. . . . In ancient Judaism sectarian alienation,
whatever its origin, generally expressed itself in polemics

against the central institutions of society (notably the temple), its authority figures (notably the priests), and its religious practices (notably purity, Sabbath, and marriage law). The "cutting edge" of sectarianism was not theology but practice.

Shaye J. D. Cohen (1987:132, 168)

✧ 5 ✧

Aristocrat and Historian

Flavius Josephus, or Joseph ben Matthias . . . [is] certainly the
single most important source for the history of the Jewish
people during the first century C.E.
Harold W. Attridge (CRINT 2.2.185)

Josephus may be most unreliable historically when he himself
has played an active role in the events being described
David M. Rhoads (15)

Josephus . . . can invent, exaggerate, over-emphasize, distort,
suppress, simplify, or, occasionally, tell the truth. Often we
cannot determine where one practice ends and another begins.
Shaye J. D. Cohen (1979:181)

Here, from Publius Cornelius Tacitus, senator, consul, provincial governor,
orator, and historian, always prudent and always the aristocrat, writing in
the early years of the second century C.E., is a terse description of the first
sixty years of Jewish and Roman relations.

> The first Roman to subdue the Jews and set foot in their temple by right
> of conquest was Gnaeus Pompey [63 B.C.E.]: thereafter it was a matter of
> common knowledge that there were no representations of the gods
> within, but that the place was empty and the secret shrine contained
> nothing. The walls of Jerusalem were razed, but the temple remained
> standing. Later, in the time of our civil wars, when these eastern prov-
> inces had fallen into the hands of Mark Antony, the Parthian prince,
> Pacorus, seized Judaea, but was slain by Publius Ventidius, and the Par-
> thians were thrown back across the Euphrates: the Jews were subdued
> by Gaius Sosius [40–37 B.C.E.]. Antony gave the throne to Herod, and
> Augustus, after his victory, increased his territory. After Herod's
> death . . . the kingdom was divided into three parts and given to Herod's
> sons [4 B.C.E.].
> (Tacitus, *Histories* 5.9; Moore & Jackson 2.190–191)

Those three Herodian princes, none of whom Tacitus bothers even to name, were Herod Archelaus, ethnarch of Idumea, Judea, and Samaria, from 4 B.C.E. until 6 C.E., when Rome, after exiling him to Gaul, assumed direct prefectural control of his territories; Herod Antipas, tetrarch of Galilee and Perea, from 4 B.C.E. until 39 C.E., when Rome, after exiling him also to Gaul, gave his territories to a next-generation Herodian, Agrippa I; and Herod Philip, tetrarch of territories to the north and northeast of the Sea of Galilee, from 4 B.C.E. to 33 or 34 C.E., when, after a peaceful reign over his mostly non-Jewish subjects, he died without benefit of exile to Gaul. With the first generation of Herodian princes gone from the Palestinian scene, and apart from a brief period between 41 and 44 C.E. when Herod Agrippa I was king of all his grandfather's earlier holdings, Roman procurators backed by auxiliary forces ruled directly over all of Palestine, with, however, legal and military intervention always possible by the legate of Syria backed by legionary forces.

At least Hold Historical Truth in Honor

The Jewish historian Josephus was born into the priestly aristocracy of Jerusalem in 37 C.E., appeared at Rome before Nero to defend some fellow priests in 64 C.E., returned to become "general" of the Jewish revolt in Galilee, and eventually surrendered to Vespasian in 67 C.E. Having foretold that his captor would become emperor, he was released when that prophecy was accomplished in 69 C.E. He observed the siege and fall of Jerusalem as interpreter for Titus and returned to Rome under patronage of the new Flavian dynasty of Vespasian, emperor in 69–79, Titus in 79–81 and Domitian in 81–96 C.E. He died probably around the end of the first century. So, at least for the First Roman-Jewish War, he was a participant and eyewitness on both the Jewish and Roman sides. Yet, as the epigraphs to this chapter suggest, Josephan accuracy cannot always be taken for granted. How, then, does one learn to read Josephus between the extremes of either acritical paraphrase or corrosive agnosticism?

Josephus' first work was the *Jewish War*, with portions already presented to Vespasian between 75 and 79 C.E., the first six books published under Titus between 79 and 81 C.E., and the seventh added under Domitian, presumably in the early 80s C.E. Next came the much longer but not nearly as well-written *Jewish Antiquities* in twenty books, with a completed first edition published in 93–94 C.E. The *Life*, its short autobiographical appendix, may have been part of that first edition or else added in a revised version, probably before 96 C.E. Finally, *Against Apion*, or *On the Antiquity of the*

Jews, in two books was written after the *Antiquities* and possibly under the new emperor Nerva between 96 and 98 C.E.

The two major problems in using Josephus as a historian are already evident in that sequence of subjects. There is, first of all and in the words of Shaye Cohen, "the development of the historian from a Roman apologist to a religious nationalist" (1979:240). One would hardly have predicted from his first publication the direction taken by the second, let alone the fourth one.

The *Jewish War,* from whose prologue come the two main subtitles of this section, was written within imperial patronage, pension, and palace and was intended primarily to defend the actions of Rome and especially the burning of the Temple and the razing of Jerusalem in the war of 66–74 C.E. Nobody from the highest aristocracy on either side is guilty of anything. Titus, on the Roman side, shines with a martial heroism matched only by his compassionate restraint, and he gets three speeches to underline his position, in *Jewish War* 3.472–484; 6.34–53; 6.328–350. So, on the Jewish side, the Herodian Agrippa II and the high priests Ananus and Jesus tried to stop the war and save the city, each of them with a single speech, in *Jewish War* 2.345–407; 4.162–192; 4.239–269. Since speeches were, in ancient historiographical fashion, created by the historian, they are especially useful in seeing overtly what lies elsewhere as covert tendentiousness. There one sees most clearly at work Josephus the apologist for Roman imperialism and Jewish aristocracy. Or again, after a long digression on the Roman army in *Jewish War* 3.70–107, Josephus concludes,

> If I have dwelt at some length on this topic, my intention was not so much to extol the Romans as to console those whom they had vanquished and to deter others who may be tempted to revolt. (Josephus, *Jewish War* 3.108–109)

Contrast that with the collection of Roman decrees protecting Jewish rights and practices in *Jewish Antiquities* 16.160–173, which concludes,

> Now it was necessary for me to cite these decrees since this account of our history is chiefly meant to reach the Greeks in order to show them that in former times we were treated with all respect and were not prevented by our rulers from practicing any of our ancestral customs but, on the contrary, even had their co-operation in preserving our religion and our way of honouring God. (Josephus, *Jewish Antiquities* 16.174)

Finally, his last work, *Against Apion,* is a powerful polemic not just against the contemporary anti-Jewish slanders of the popular Greco-Egyptian Apion but against all earlier Hellenistic attacks as well. It is also a forceful apology for the Jewish experience and tradition, rising to a striking climax at its conclusion.

> I would therefore boldly maintain that we have introduced to the rest of the world a very large number of beautiful ideas. What higher justice than obedience to the laws? What more beneficial than to be in harmony with one another, to be a prey neither to disunion in adversity, nor to arrogance and faction in prosperity; in war to despise death, in peace to devote oneself to crafts or agriculture; and to be convinced that everything in the whole universe is under the eye and direction of God. (Josephus, *Against Apion* 2.293–294)

The point is not that Josephus changed from being pro-Roman to anti-Roman or from anti-Jewish to pro-Jewish. He was, in his own way, always both pro-Roman and pro-Jewish, and those attitudes never changed. *But he began as apologist for Romans to Jews, and he ended as apologist for Jews to Romans.* In reading through his works, therefore, one must constantly and carefully consider where the specific writing is located along that line of change and development. Granted that we are always dealing with subtle omissions, additions, and alterations, in delicate emphases, nuances, and balances, it is precisely those variations that must be assessed in terms of that Josephan progression.

The second major problem is actually a facet of the first, but it concerns primarily the first three writings. The *Jewish War* not only describes the period from 66 to 74 C.E., but it also prefaces that primary subject with a review of the preceding period from 175 B.C.E. to 66 C.E. Thus, when the later *Jewish Antiquities* describes the period from the creation of the world until the outbreak of the war in 66 C.E., there is a first overlap in the Josephan corpus between *Jewish War* 1.31–2.279 and *Jewish Antiquities* 12.237–20.258 for the years between 175 B.C.E. and 66 C.E.

There is also, however, a second overlap. Justus of Tiberias, another Jewish historian, whose wartime motivations were possibly as ambivalent and his intentions as ambiguous in the late sixties as those of Josephus himself, launched an attack on Josephus probably after the death of Agrippa II in the early nineties. He portrayed Josephus' Galilean activities in the years 66–67 C.E. as the work of a brutal and venal tyrant who forced others to revolt against their will and who was primarily responsible for Tiberias' insurrection against Rome. His purpose seems to have been the restoration of his native Tiberias to the local eminence it lost to Sepphoris in the fifties. Indeed, that may well have been exactly what he hoped to obtain during the war itself, namely, the destruction of Sepphoris and the exaltation of Tiberias. Be that as it may, Josephus immediately replied to his assault with the *Life*, a defense that, apart from a few general autobiographical details at its start and completion, is primarily concerned with the period when he was "general" of the rebellion in Galilee. Since he had already told about that event in his first publication, there is an overlap between *Jewish War* 2.430–3.114 and *Life* 20–411 for the years 66 and 67 C.E.

Detailed study of those two overlaps, one for the years between 175 B.C.E. and 66 C.E. and the other for the years 66 and 67 C.E., does not reassure one about the historical objectivity of Josephus. Indeed, it was precisely an analysis of those passages that led Shaye Cohen to the extremely negative judgment cited at the beginning of this chapter. But two conclusions from his brilliant dissertation on Josephus are somewhat more hopeful in indicating how it might be possible to read Josephus even or especially against himself.

When Josephus was creating those overlaps he did not always simply revise what he himself had written earlier. Instead, and much more often, he went back to the basic sources used earlier and rewrote them for his new purpose. Here, following the penetrating analyses of Shaye Cohen, are how those overlaps look in terms of Josephan methodology. First, the account of the Hasmonean dynasty from 142 to 37 B.C.E. in *Jewish Antiquities* 13.225–14.491 is primarily a direct revision of the earlier *Jewish War* 1.51–357. But, then, the account of Herod the Great from 37 to 4 B.C.E. in *Jewish Antiquities* 15–17 is not just a revision of the earlier *Jewish War* 1.358–2.117 but a rewritten version of its basic source. Next, and in general, the account of the years from Herod's death in 4 B.C.E. to the start of the war in 66 C.E. follows mostly that second method. *Jewish Antiquities* 18.1–20.251 is again not just a revision of *Jewish War* 2.118–276 but uses several sources, one of which was also used in that earlier version. It should be noted, however, that the short section on Gessius Florus, the last procurator before the war in 64 to 66 C.E., is taken directly into *Jewish Antiquities* 20.252–257 from the earlier *Jewish War* 2.277–279. Finally, *Life* 20–411 on Josephus' Galilean generalship in 66 and 67 C.E. is, once again, not just a revision of the earlier *Jewish War* 2.430–3.114 but a rewritten version of its original source. That source was not necessarily anyone else's work but probably a chronologically sequential outline or *hypomnema* such as any competent Hellenistic historian would prepare before getting down to the actual writing itself. It is also possible, of course, that such a personally prepared *hypomnema* may be the common source used for the years 4 B.C.E. to 66 C.E. in *Jewish War* 2.118–276 and *Jewish Antiquities* 18.1–20.251 (Cohen 1979:51–66). That sounds very complicated, but it has one very clear result. When one reads two versions of something in Josephus, say for those years of the first common era century with which I am primarily concerned, one should not simply choose either version at random and much less conflate the two into a sensible compromise. Instead, each must be read critically as one version of a basic source, be that Josephus' own prepared outline or the work of another, but now arranged apologetically and thematically according to the basic Josephan development from apologist of Rome to Judaism in the *Jewish War* but of Judaism to Rome in the *Jewish Antiquities*.

There is a second important conclusion from Shaye Cohen's insightful study of Josephus. Having quoted another historian's judgment that "Thucydides was such a remarkably objective historian that he himself has provided sufficient material for his own refutation," he concludes "that Josephus provides enough data to refute his own account" but that this "is a sign of sloppiness and incompetence rather than conscientiousness and objectivity" (1979:181). Granted, of course, Josephus was no Thucydides, even if the Jewish historian detailing, in the first century C.E., how his people had lost a disastrous war to the Romans was probably watching from the corners of both eyes the Athenian historian detailing, in the fifth century B.C.E., how his people had lost a disastrous war to the Spartans. The important thing for our purposes is that, whether from objectivity or subjectivity, conscientiousness or sloppiness, Josephus does furnish us with adequate data to read him critically and coherently against himself. In what follows, therefore, I absolutely avoid that happy paraphrastic synthesis that mars so much scholarly usage of Josephus, and, instead, I cite both texts wherever parallels are present, interpret any significant differences, and base conclusions only on such analyses.

I Cannot Conceal My Private Sentiments

It will not do, therefore, to dismiss Josephus as a Flavian flunky and, doubting everything he says, pick and choose what suits one's own concerns. Neither will it do to dismiss him as a Jewish traitor. Compare, for example, the following statements made before the walls of a doomed Jerusalem.

> The Romans . . . attributed every reverse to some treachery on my part, and were constantly and clamourously demanding of the Emperor that he should punish me as their betrayer [also]. (Josephus, *Life* 416)

> Never may I live to become so abject a captive as to abjure my race or to forget the traditions of my forefathers. (Josephus, *Jewish War* 6.107)

The accusation by the Roman soldiers has, in the Greek original, a telltale "also" that indicates that they considered Josephus ready to betray them as he had just betrayed his own people (Cohen, 1979:228 note 98). All in all, however, his own assessment seems, for once, much more fair and accurate.

What is needed, therefore, is a reading of Josephus that is coherently and consistently critical. It must acknowledge, as seen in the preceding section, both his methods and his motivations, and it must assess change and development within each area. It must also acknowledge his biases and prejudices. And, as he admits in the quotation from the prologue of the *Jewish War* that heads this section, "I cannot conceal my private sentiments." Those presuppositions basically fall into two categories, the religiopolitical, which has always been noted, and the socioeconomic, which requires much more emphasis than it has heretofore received.

God Now Rested over Italy

Josephus' religiopolitical prejudices or presuppositions could hardly be more obvious, and they derive directly from the biblical traditions of prophetic historiography. Now with the Romans, just as earlier with the Egyptians or the Assyrians, the Babylonians or the Persians, the Greeks or the Syrians, whatever happens to the Jews and the current world empire is interpreted in terms of God's punitive and salvific designs (*CRINT* 2.2.203–206).

First, concerning the Roman Empire in general and the Flavian dynasty in particular, Josephus' theological position is absolutely clear, consistent, and repeated like a major motif throughout the *Jewish War*. A few samples will suffice.

> The Romans . . . to whom Fortune has transferred her favours . . . [Now] divine assistance . . . is ranged on the side of the Romans, for, without God's aid, so vast an empire could never have been built up.
>
> Moved, may be, also by God, who was already shaping the destinies of empire [Nero sends Vespasian to Palestine].
>
> Vespasian was led to think that divine providence had assisted him to grasp the empire and that some just destiny had placed the sovereignty of the world within his hands.
>
> Titus . . . was still at Alexandria, assisting his father [Vespasian] to establish the empire which God had recently committed to their hands.
>
> Fortune, indeed, had from all quarters passed over to them [the Romans], and God who went the round of the nations, bringing to each in turn the rod of empire, now rested over Italy.
>
> You are warring not against the Romans only, but also against God . . . [For] the Deity has fled from the holy places and taken His stand on the side of those with whom you are now at war.
>
> (Josephus, *Jewish War* 2.360, 391; 3.6; 4.622; 5.2, 367, 378, 412)

Note, of course, that, whether named for Greco-Roman consumption Fate, Destiny, or Fortune, it is always the Jewish God that Josephus has in mind.

Next, concerning the Jews in general and the revolutionaries in particular, the conclusions from the preceding presuppositions are just as clear, consistent, and repetitive.

> God, I suppose ... had already turned away even from His sanctuary and ordained that that day [the defeat of Cestius in November 66 C.E.] should not see the end of the war.
>
> It was by an act of God, who was preserving John [of Gischala from capture in Galilee] to bring ruin upon Jerusalem.
>
> They imagined ... that Ananus [the former high priest] would be everywhere, inspecting the sentries at all hours. Such, indeed, had been his practice on other nights, but on this one it was omitted; not through any remissness on his part, but by the over-ruling decree of Destiny that he and all his guards should perish.
>
> But it was, I suppose, because God had, for its pollutions, condemned the city to destruction and desired to purge the sanctuary by fire, that he thus cut off those who clung to them with such tender affection. (Josephus, *Jewish War* 2.539; 4.104, 297, 323)

Not only has God given imperial rule to the Romans, but God had also decreed the destruction of Jerusalem precisely because of the crimes of the revolutionaries.

Finally, concerning Josephus' own role in all of this, both those previous strands come together. The Romans are the Babylonians, Titus is Nebuchadnezzar, Josephus is, of course, Jeremiah, and the Second Temple will fall on the same day that the First Temple was lost almost seven hundred years previously. Once again, the texts speak for themselves.

> Since [Josephus prays to God] it pleases thee who didst create the Jewish nation, to break thy work, since fortune has wholly passed to the Romans, and since thou hast made choice of my spirit to announce the things that are to come, I willingly surrender to the Romans and consent to live; but I take thee to witness that I go, not as a traitor, but as thy minister.
>
> When the king of Babylon besieged this city, our king Zedekiah having, contrary to the prophetic warnings of Jeremiah, given him battle, was himself taken prisoner and saw the town and the temple levelled to the ground. Yet, how much more moderate was that monarch than your leaders, and his subjects than you! For ... neither the king nor the people put him [Jeremiah] to death. But you ... assail with abuse and missiles me who exhort you to save yourselves.

> The temple . . . God, indeed long since, had sentenced to the flames; but now in the revolution of the years had arrived the fated day, the tenth of the month Lous, the day on which of old it had been burnt by the king of Babylon.
>
> One may well marvel at the exactness of the cycle of Destiny; for, as I said, she waited until the very month and the very day on which in bygone times the temple had been burnt by the Babylonians. (Josephus, *Jewish War* 3.351–354; 5.391–393; 6.250, 268)

Those religiopolitical presuppositions, about the Romans, the Jews, and Josephus himself, are quite clear and consistent, especially in the *Jewish War*, and they have been well emphasized in past scholarship. Josephus' socioeconomic presuppositions, however, need and have seldom obtained an equal emphasis.

Tyrants and Their Bands of Marauders

Josephus' socioeconomic prejudices are extremely important, however, because, as David Rhoads put it in summing up the climax of the revolutionary situation from 6 to 74 C.E., "the war was not only a national revolt against Rome, it was also a class war among the Jews" (178). The same point is made, although in somewhat more muted fashion, by Shaye Cohen. "The fact that the conflict was also a civil war between the upper and lower classes does not imply that only the lower classes had economic grievances" (1979:189 note 19). Or again: "The great revolt of 66–70 A.D. was in large part, especially in its early phases, a civil struggle among Jews — between the rich and the poor, between the upper classes and the lower, between the city dwellers and the country folk" (1988:222). It was actually that in all its phases, right to the bitter end. "The significant point here," according to Tessa Rajak, "is that Josephus, for all that he fought briefly with the Jewish rebels, had no more sense of identification with the Jewish oppressed and dispossessed than the upper classes elsewhere seem to have had with theirs" (85).

Richard Horsley, in a series of compelling articles and books during the last decade, has forcibly raised the question of the socioeconomic realities obscured by Josephus' rhetoric but still visible behind its facade. He says of Josephus that, in general, he "is biased against, and even hostile to, the common people . . . [his] works are self-serving, pro-Roman, defensive of the Jewish elite, certainly antirevolutionary, and, in effect, antipeasant" (Horsley & Hanson: xix–xx). And, in particular, he "is a hostile witness who despises the popular leaders and movements [in Galilee] which he was attempting to control as a representative of the government in Jerusalem" (Horsley 1988:183). In reading Josephus, therefore, it is necessary to acknowledge not only that his religiopolitical presuppositions render him generally inimical to the revolt but that his socioeconomic presuppositions render him particularly inimical to lower-class participation, let alone leadership, in its processes.

My interest here is not primarily in the social situation at the time of the First Roman-Jewish War in the late sixties of the first common era century but rather in the social situation of its earliest decades. But I am convinced by Horsley's invaluable work that the most proximate background for Jesus must be the full trajectory of peasant social unrest, which can be mapped across a hundred years before it comes to a first and awful consummation in the revolt against Rome. In the rest of this chapter, therefore, and following Horsley's lead, I attempt to disentangle the various socially distinct strands in first-century social unrest, to pay special attention to evidence of popular, lower-class, or peasant protests and reactions, and, above all, to read Josephus despite and against himself. Before proceeding, however, a glance from the Jewish aristocrat Josephus to the Roman aristocrat Tacitus is required.

Sub Tiberio Quies

Tacitus, describing those relations between imperial Rome and Palestinian Jewry that led up to their first war, selected only certain incidents for inclusion. There are four such cases, three in the *Histories* and one in the *Annals*.

> After Herod's death, a certain Simon assumed the name of king without waiting for Caesar's decision. He, however, was put to death by Quin[c]tilius Varus, governor of Syria; the Jews were repressed; and the kingdom was divided into three parts and given to Herod's sons [4 B.C.E.]. Under Tiberius all was quiet [14–37 C.E.]. Then, when Caligula ordered the Jews to set up his statue in their temple, they chose rather to resort to arms, but the emperor's death put an end to their uprising [40–41 C.E.]. The princes now being dead or reduced to insignificance, Claudius made Judea a province [once again] and entrusted it to Roman knights or to freedmen [44 C.E.]; one of the latter, Antonius Felix [52–60 C.E.], practised every kind of cruelty and lust, wielding the power of king with all the instincts of a slave.... Still the Jews' patience lasted until Gessius Florus [64–66 C.E.] became procurator: in his time war began. (Tacitus, *Histories* 5.9–10; Moore & Jackson 2.190–193)

> Felix was fostering crime by misconceived remedies, his worst efforts being emulated by Ventidius Cumanus ... when the growth of the mischief forced them to interpose the army of their troops, the troops were

beaten, and the province would have been ablaze with war but for the intervention of Quadratus, the governor of Syria. (Tacitus, *Annals* 12.54; Moore & Jackson 3.394–395)

The last five Roman governors of Palestine were Ventidius Cumanus in 48–52, Antonius Felix in 52–60, Porcius Festus in 60–62, Lucceius Albinus in 62–64, and Gessius Florus in 64–66 C.E. I ignore until later the problematic sequence of Felix and Cumanus in Tacitus' second text and emphasize here two major points from the twin texts.

In detailing the reasons for the Roman-Jewish War, Tacitus emphasized exclusively the malfeasance of the Roman procurators immediately preceding the outbreak of hostilities in the summer of 66 C.E. He indicts Felix and Florus specifically, and that indictment is later extended back to include Cumanus. Tacitus, in other words, is ready to blame the Romans rather than the Jews for the war. Admittedly, "Romans" here excludes his own *senatorial* order, since it is imperial policy that sent members of the *equestrian* order and, in the unique case of Felix, a *freedman,* to rule Palestine. Indeed, it takes repeated interventions by the Syrian legate, a governor of *senatorial* rank, to remedy problems in Palestine. Nevertheless, and even acknowledging that bias, procuratorial malgovernment beginning at least by 48 C.E. must be taken very seriously as a cause of the First Roman-Jewish War.

There is, next, that famous statement concerning the years between 14 and 37 C.E., "Under Tiberius all was quiet." How quiet was quiet? Notice what Tacitus is doing in those texts. He proceeds emperor by emperor, but he is concerned only with rebellions that necessitated *direct intervention by the Roman legate in Syria backed by the three or later four legions of the army of the Euphrates.* The Roman governors in Palestine, who had only auxiliary forces at their command, are not even mentioned apart from those specific situations. Tacitus is recording, in other words, only those smaller rebellions that led up to the war itself.

First, under Augustus in 4 B.C.E., in the revolts after Herod's death, Quinctilius Varus intervened from Syria with savage reprisals and a force of three legions plus auxiliary troops. Then, under Caligula in 41 C.E., in what Tacitus calls a rebellion against that emperor's threatened desecration of the Temple, Petronius intervened from Syria with two legions. Next, under Claudius in 52 C.E., Jewish rebellion against the venality of the procurator Cumanus necessitated intervention by Ummidius Quadratus from Syria. Finally, under Nero in 66 C.E., the malfeasance of the governor Florus resulted in open rebellion, the defeat of Cestius Gallus intervening from Syria with one legion, and the start of the war. When, therefore, between

Augustus and Caligula, Tacitus says, *"Sub Tiberio quies,"* all he means is that under Tiberius there were no revolts in Palestine *necessitating intervention from the Syrian legate backed by his legionary forces.* "Quiet" means that the Palestinian governors could handle any problems, including those they themselves had created, and such affairs were therefore of no interest to Roman history or to Tacitus. That is not exactly the same as saying that under Tiberius all was peaceful or that there was no social unrest in Palestine in the years between 14 and 37 C.E., and that will be important to remember throughout the rest of this book. Remember also the connotations of "all quiet on the western front."

✧ 6 ✧

Visionary and Teacher

The Near East and Mediterranean types of apocalypticism are
certainly the most literarily elaborated. . . . However, if we widen
our scope, we will find striking phenomenological parallels in
the cultures of the Americas, Africa and Oceania, which can
hardly be explained with reference to early historical
connections with the above area, or by way of diffusion. . . . The
revitalization of mythic material and its reinterpretation with
reference to the contemporaneous situation is a recurrent
feature in these movements.

Tord Olsson (Hellholm 28, 29)

In the proceedings of the International Colloquium on Apocalypticism held
at Uppsala in August of 1979, Tord Olsson suggested, "If we consider the
data from the fields of social anthropology and comparative religion, we can
observe that revelatory world-views are regularly actualized in situations of
conflict or crisis, real or imagined, or in the context of fear of such situations. One type of situation emerges when the social organization, including access to central power, has been affected by a decrease in intra-system
communication so that the cultural integration of a certain group is jeopar-
dized. This decrease is no doubt the operating factor in the change process
in which a group is forced into an organizational and cultural niche.
Another type of situation arises when the cultural integrity of a community
or group is exposed to external influence, *e.g.* in the form of war, colonialism, and political or religious propaganda" (Hellholm 30–31). There are
three important points in that cross-cultural proposal. Apocalypticism is,
first of all, one possible response to a profound attack on cultural integrity,
to a combined religiopolitical and socioeconomic threat. Next, it may be
either a real or an imagined danger; it is perception that counts. And,
finally, another distinction is equally important. It may be internal or external; it may be the reaction of a group that once had power or status but is
now marginalized and disenfranchised within a changing society, or it may
be the response of an entire society colonized within an imperial situation.

Apocalypticism is usually called millennialism (or millenarianism or millenarism) within the wider scope of comparative anthropology. "To the purist," admits Sylvia Thrupp, introducing the papers of a 1960 conference on revolutionary religious movements, "the millennium can properly refer only to the fixed period of 1000 years that is found in the Judaic-Christian tradition. In our perspective, however, the term may be applied figuratively to any conception of a perfect age to come, or a perfect land to be made accessible. The picture will vary according as time is fitted into the scheme of the cosmos. The perfect age may come by an act of regeneration, time being bent back, as it were, to recapture some state of harmony in which the world began. It may have some of this quality of early freshness and yet come as time is running out. It will then last for a period that is fixed, variable, or indeterminate, and it may even form part of a cycle of ages. Or it may be an age to last indefinitely, with no doom ahead" (Thrupp 12). Norman Cohn, speaking on medieval millennialism during that same conference, described as millennial "any religious movement inspired by the phantasy of a salvation which is to be (a) collective, in the sense that it is to be enjoyed by the faithful as a group; (b) terrestrial, in the sense that it is to be realised on this earth and not in some otherworldly heaven; (c) imminent, in the sense that it is to come both soon and suddenly; (d) total, in the sense that it is utterly to transform life on earth, so that the new dispensation will be no mere improvement on the present but perfection itself; (e) accomplished by agencies which are consciously regarded as supernatural" (Thrupp 31).

Anti-Hellenistic apocalypticism is to be understood, then, within that wider framework of anthropological millennialism, for, as Samuel Eddy put it, "Resort to prophecy is a universal response of beaten men" (335). In his analysis of the Near Eastern response to Greek imperialism Eddy concluded that "while the countries differed in their anti-Hellenism, nonetheless when opposition did occur, it took forms that were generally similar. Egypt, Persis, and Judah all prophesied the downfall of the Greek regime, and all three fought with weapons against it to make this dream come true. . . . There were three main motives for the religious resistance, and . . . these were interlocking. First, there was the effort to regain native rule as an end in itself. Second, there was the effort to regain native rule as a means of ending social upheaval and economic exploitation. Third, there was the effort to regain native rule to protect law and religion" (324, 330).

Eddy also proposed "four basic kinds of resistance: passive, militant, messianic, and proselytic" (335). Passive resistance appeared in all dissenting cultures and involved a return to archaic legends about one's own most ancient heroes. Militant resistance is known most clearly in Palestine and

Egypt but possibly in Persia as well. It was always accompanied by messianic resistance that invoked the intervention of a divine being who would expel the Greeks and restore the land not only to native normalcy but to idyllic fertility and rhapsodic peace. Proselytic resistance was found only in Persia and Palestine, and it sought to persuade or even force nonbelievers to conversion within the messianic victory. What is most interesting in all this is Eddy's suggestion that we are dealing with responses susceptible to cross-cultural modelling. "The four types of resistance were all of them normal human responses to domination by an alien culture which threatens to end or modify the old. . . . The reaction of the American Indian, for example, to American imperialism was the same. The Indians suffered loss of independence, economic hardship, and the breakdown of their order of society, and they experienced nativistic revivals passively advocating continued belief in Indian culture by Indians, undertook militant wars of religion like that led by the Prophet and Tecumseh, believed in messianic movements emphasizing high morality, like those in the Pacific Northwest, and even began proselytism among themselves, as in the case of Indian Shakerism or the Peyote cult" (340).

That fourfold typology of religiopolitical reaction to overbearing cultural seductiveness, overpowering military superiority, overwhelming economic exploitation, and overweening social discrimination is already comparatively if inchoately cross-cultural and trans-temporal. It must be made fully and programmatically so by widening it into that sevenfold typology seen earlier in Bryan Wilson's magnificent sociological study of religious movements of protest among tribal and Third-World peoples. For example, his concluding comments on *Revolutionist* or millennial responses to colonialism are very important for a sympathetic understanding of that reaction. The length of this quotation underlines its importance. "Millennialism always promises social transformation, and although always erroneous, it none the less creates a new conscious expectation of social change. Sometimes it prompts men to begin to make the millennium. The new age does not come, but the effort of work, organization, and the futuristic (or restorative) ethic has important consequences. A new framework of order is established . . . a new conception of the social organization of the collectivity occurs: a glimmering sense of a different future is acquired. The idea of social change is grasped. The deities who hitherto have sanctioned custom, now—suddenly—become the initiators of change (even if that change is restoration). When men acquire a notion of the ancestors or the spirits initiating change they have experienced a radical transformation of consciousness. This transformation is perhaps rooted more in millennialism—despite its inherent incapacity to fulfil the promised change it proclaims — than in any other single historical phenomenon" (494–495).

Three levels of background are presumed, therefore, behind this chapter's analysis of Jewish apocalypticism. The macrolevel is the cross-cultural study of millennialism as a very specific response to certain forms and certain circumstances of religiopolitical colonialism. The mesolevel is the wider historical environment created by the millennial rejection of cultural imperialism in the Hellenistic Near East. The microlevel is that full spectrum of inclusivism and exclusivism within which Judaism and paganism reacted mutually to each other in the Greco-Roman period. What must never be forgotten is that, on the one hand, Jews were not alone, then or thereafter, in their anticolonial apocalypticism and, on the other, not all Jews, maybe not even a majority of Jews, agreed or even sympathized with that millennial dream.

The Coming of the Fifth Kingdom

Scribes and teachers belong, as you recall from Gerhard Lenski's typology of agrarian social stratification in the last chapter, not to the *governing* but to the *retainer* class. Their strength, ranging from high scholarship to mere literacy, was in their bureaucratic, organizational, and pedagogical skills. Their weakness was their total dependence on the governing class. And, as experts in the high literate tradition, they were generally conservative and establishmentarian unless, of course, that tradition contained within itself an ancient strain of egalitarian social criticism. Note, for example, the bitter socioeconomic invectives against the governing class from the *Book of the Epistle of Enoch* in 1 *Enoch* 91–107 during the early second century B.C.E. (*OTP* 2.72–88).

What happened, however, after the sixties of the second century B.C.E. was far different from the towering visions of millennial consummation that had been produced in that dramatic decade. The age of the pious did not "approach a thousand years," as imagined in *Jubilees* 23:27. "The devil" did not "have an end," nor was "sorrow . . . led away with him," as promised in *Testament of Moses* 10:1. No "everlasting kingdom" was "given to the people of the saints of the most high," nor did "all dominions . . . serve and obey them," as pledged in Daniel 7:27. And, finally, all the sheep, all the beasts, and all the birds were not finally united so that the Lord "rejoiced with great joy because they had all become gentle and returned to his house," as climactically envisaged in the Animal Apocalypse at 1 *Enoch* 90:33 (*OTP* 2.102; 1.931; 1.71). What actually happened was that first there were the Maccabees, and then there were the Romans. And so, apocalyptic vision, millennial dream, and transcendental hope continued to be written anew or reread again.

Their King Shall Be the Lord Messiah

Eighteen pedagogical rather than liturgical psalms, known collectively as the *Psalms of Solomon,* survive from some literate Jewish group around the middle of the first century B.C.E. They are attributed fictionally but fittingly to Solomon, the son of David, and three of them, *Psalms of Solomon* 2, 8, and 17, have datable allusions, especially to Pompey, who, invited to mediate between the feuding Hasmonean princes Judas Aristobulus II and John Hyrcanus II, overpowered the former after a three-month siege of the Temple in the fall of 63 B.C.E. and reinstated the latter but with an imposed tribute and without a royal title. In general, therefore, these psalms can be dated during or soon after the period between 63 and 48 B.C.E. They have been attributed to the Pharisees or even the Essenes, but it is better to leave them to unspecified scribal circles with a strong didactic bent.

In any case, even with Pompey ingloriously dead, Rome still ruled over Palestine. Those behind the psalms show no intention of rising against Rome. They are not necessarily pacifists, but certainly realists. Reduced to impotence by Roman military might, they turn once again to the ancient millennial dream. Deliverance is to come from a leader who, though human and operating upon this earth, is touched with an aura of the divine: he is sinless, all virtuous, and by his word alone, without any recourse to warfare, he will restore a purified Israel to rule over the purified nations of a purified earth.

> See, Lord, and raise up for them their king,
> the son of David, to rule over your servant Israel
> in the time known to you, O God.
> And he will have gentile nations serving under his yoke. . . .
> There will be no unrighteousness among them in his days,
> for all shall be holy,
> and their king shall be the Lord Messiah.
> (For) he will not rely on horse and rider and bow,
> nor will he collect gold and silver for war.
> Nor will he build up hope in a multitude for a day of war. . . .
> He will strike the earth with the word of his mouth forever.
>   (*Psalms of Solomon* 17:21, 29, 32–33, 35; *OTP* 2.667–668)

Note, by the way, that of those "two messianic titles, 'Son of David' and 'Lord Messiah,' the former [is] the first instance and the latter the only instance of such usages in Jewish literature" (*OTP* 2.646). And this messianic leader does not use violence, neither the actual violence of normal warfare nor the transcendental violence of angelic destruction. The terrible irony is that, just as the millennial hopes of Daniel 7–12 had awaited the angels and received instead the Hasmoneans, so now the *Psalms of Solomon* awaited the Lord Messiah, the Son of David, and received instead the execrable Herod, the son of Antipater. Yet it is surely proper to mourn rather than mock those visions of a perfect world so deeply embedded in the human heart as to appear again and again, ever defeated and ever repeated. At their best they kept alive a hope for perfect justice within which smaller gains might be achieved as means and methods, strategies and tactics were slowly and painfully learned. At their worst they seduced people into believing that means and methods, strategies and tactics were no longer necessary.

Our Blood Will Be Avenged Before the Lord

The Testament of Moses was written, according to George Nickelsburg's proposal, in late 167 B.C.E., but chapters 6 and 7 were added much later. The original apocalypse proclaimed the millennial hope against Syrian colonialism and Jewish collaboration. This was now updated to include the evil days of both Hasmonean and Herodian dynasties and to speak against Roman colonialism and Jewish collaboration before the promised eschatological consummation. The revised version dates, most likely, from "the months or years following Herod's death" (Nickelsburg 1981:213), say, the first decade of the first common era century.

> The powerful kings [the Hasmoneans] will rise over them, and they will
> be called priests of the Most High God. They will perform great impiety
> in the Holy of Holies. And a wanton king [Herod], who will not be of
> priestly family will follow them . . . for thirty-four years [37–4 B.C.E.] he
> will impose judgments upon them as did the Egyptians. . . . And he will
> beget heirs who will reign after him for shorter periods of time. After his
> death there will come into their land a powerful king of the West who
> will subdue them; and he will take away captives, and a part of their
> temple he will burn with fire. He will crucify some of them around their
> city. (*Testament of Moses* 6:1–2, 6–9; *OTP* 2.930)

That final statement refers to the uprisings after the death of Herod that were quelled, as we shall see in more detail later on, by the Syrian legate, Quinctilius Varus, and the interim procurator of Judea, his finance minister Sabinus, who burned part of the Temple in overcoming the rebels. Once again, however, there is no hint of human or divine violence in the actualization of this millennial dream. It was not there in the original version from 167 B.C.E., and it is still not there in the additions from around the turn of the era.

The Son of Man to Whom Righteousness Belongs

In Genesis 5:24, "Enoch walked with God; and he was not [found any longer on earth], for God took him [to heaven]." That apotheosis made him, of course, an obvious source for otherworldly discoveries and revelations. The oldest of the three works fictionally attributed to his authorship is *1 Enoch* or the *Ethiopic Apocalypse of Enoch*, a composite five-book treatise that grew and developed from the third century B.C.E. to the end of the first century C.E.:

1. *The Book of the Watchers* (1–36): third century B.C.E.
2. *The Book of the Similitudes* (37–71): early first century C.E.
3. *The Book of Astronomical Writings* (72–82): third century B.C.E.
4. *The Book of Dream Visions* (83–90): 164–160 B.C.E.
5. *The Book of the Epistle of Enoch* (91–107): early second century B.C.E.

The final text to be considered here is the last of those five units, the *Book of the Similitudes/Parables of Enoch*, now extant as *1 Enoch* 37–71. The composition, including three revelatory discourses in *1 Enoch* 38–44, 45–57, 58–59, an original conclusion in 70, and another but later conclusion in 71, is dated, most likely, between "around the turn of the era" (Nickelsburg 1981:223) and "the early or mid first century C.E." (Collins 1984a:143).

The seer Enoch does not receive this "vision of wisdom" as a review of future history but as a journey through the present heavens. Reassurance comes not from the inevitabilities of historical change as empires rise and fall but from the constancies of celestial order as sun, moon, and stars move in their mandated rhythms. Encouragement comes not from time and history, as in other Jewish apocalypses, but from space and cosmos, as in the two earliest ones, *The Book of Astronomical Writings* in *1 Enoch* 72–82 and *The Book of the Watchers* in *1 Enoch* 1–36.

We are back, then, with earthly disharmony starting from and correlating with angelic discord. Heavenly and earthly warfare are but twin facets of a single cosmic struggle between good and evil, with the final judgment coming alike and simultaneously to them both. And the outcome of that last judgment has been preset by God from ages past, from the very moment the evil angels first rebelled, so that Enoch can actually see its future implementation during his heavenly journey. His revelation is not just that it will happen but that he has seen it happening.

In the *Psalms of Solomon* 17–18 the millennial consummation focused around a single figure called the Son of David or the Lord Messiah. No such focus appeared in the *Testament of Moses,* but it does again in the *Book of the Similitudes* with the Elect One. He is the agent of God's final judgment, and, according to George Nickelsburg, he "combines the titles, attributes, and functions of the one like a son of man from Daniel 7, the Servant of the Lord in Second Isaiah, and the Davidic Messiah. 'Son of man' is not a title. It is a Semitic way of saying 'man,' and it is almost always qualified: 'that son of man,' 'the son of man who has righteousness'" (1981:215). This humanlike figure is more than the personification or even the champion of God's people, it is their mythical equivalent, their celestial archetype, their eternal complement, their heavenly counterpart. It is also worth noting that, in the *Psalms of Solomon,* the Son of David, the Lord Messiah, rules over a magnificently irenic and inclusive world, but, in the *Book of the Similitudes,* that Son of Man, the Elect One, separates good from evil in a far more punitive and exclusive world. It is even possible, for instance, that the group for which the book spoke was sectarian in character even within Judaism itself.

World Power Passed to the Roman People

The millennial visions of the Persian *Bahman Yasht* (Eddy 343–349) and the Jewish ones of Daniel 2 and 7 (Collins 1984a:21–26) imagined a succession of four world powers, and both those apocalyptic reviews of history's past were fictionally portrayed as prophecies of history's future. For the Persian seer, the four kingdoms were the Assyrian, Medean, Persian, and Greek empires, and they were to be consummated by a fifth empire with imperial rule restored to Ahura Mazda, a savior king, and the Persian people. For the Jewish seer, the four were the Babylonian, Medean, Persian, and Greek empires, and they were to be consummated by a fifth empire with imperial rule replaced by Yahweh, the angelic hosts, and the Jewish people.

The fifth empire came, however, neither as Persian nor Jewish restoration but as Roman colonization. And Rome itself was quite capable of using that revised sequence for its own political propaganda. Caius Velleius Paterculus, writing in 30 C.E., records the following:

> Aemilius Sura says in his book on the chronology of Rome: "The Assyrians were the first of all races to hold world power, then the Medes, and after them the Persians, and then the Macedonians. Then through the defeat of Kings Philip and Antiochus, of Macedonian origin,

followed closely upon the overthrow of Carthage, the world power
passed to the Roman people." (Velleius Paterculus, *Compendium of
Roman History* 1.6; Shipley 14–15)

Sura must have written that in the early decades of the second century
B.C.E. as technological superiority in war was passing from the Macedonian
phalanx to the Roman legion.

By the end of the first century C.E., even a Jewish author could concede, with however little enthusiasm, that Rome was the fifth empire. *The
Fourth Sibylline Oracle,* a religiopolitical prophecy against the Macedo-
nians, possibly non-Jewish and possibly as early as the third century B.C.E.,
was revised by a Jewish author after Rome had destroyed the Temple in 70
C.E. Between the original oracle of four empires in 4.49–101 and the subsequent apocalyptic consummation in 4.173–192, there was later inserted a
description of Roman hegemony in 4.102–172.

> A leader of Rome will come to Syria who will burn
> the Temple of Jerusalem with fire, at the same time slaughter
> many men and destroy the great land of the Jews with its broad roads.
> (*Sibylline Oracle* 4:125–127; *OTP* 1.387)

Instead of the fifth empire as the cosmic theocracy of Yahweh and the
vindication of the faithful Jewish people, the fifth empire was simply the
Romans instead of the Greeks. Apocalyptic judgment and millennial consummation were once again postponed.

No Lord but God

There is a very pressing preliminary problem between this and the
preceding chapter. The importance of the apocalyptic vision within Judaism was underlined by the texts still extant, yet one reads scarcely anything
about the endurance of that millennial dream within Josephus. How is that
discrepancy to be explained?

Josephus, in fact, had a very particular and very personal reason for not
emphasizing Jewish apocalyptic beliefs or messianic hopes. His life had
been spared because of his correct prediction, in 67 C.E., of Vespasian's
future elevation to emperor. His prediction, described in the *Jewish War*
3.399–402, was also known to the Roman historians Suetonius and Cassius
Dio (Stern 1976–80:2.122, 371). But that prophecy was delivered as a fulfillment of Jewish apocalyptic messianism.

> What more than all else incited them to the war [even as the Temple
> burned] was an ambiguous oracle . . . found in their sacred scriptures, to

the effect that at that time one from their country would become ruler of the world. This they understood to mean someone of their own race, and many of their wise men went astray in their interpretation of it. The oracle, however, in reality signified the sovereignty of Vespasian who was proclaimed Emperor in Jewish soil. (Josephus, *Jewish War* 6.312–313)

That stunning application of Jewish messianism to Vespasian had saved Josephus' life in Galilee. It is hardly likely, then, that Josephus would explain too clearly or underline too sharply the existence of alternative apocalyptic or messianic fulfillments before or apart from Vespasian himself. We therefore will have to read Josephus somewhat against himself; we will have to find apocalypticism and messianism between the lines of his explicit descriptions. My specific proposal is that the revolts described by Josephus as that of the Fourth Philosophy, or of the Sicarii, are activist manifestations of apocalypticism or messianism. In other words, what was already described in this chapter and what will now be described belong to the same intellectual and social world. It is the world of *retainer* revolt, and it extends from scribalism to activism, from passive resistance to active terrorism, and from martyrdom to militancy. And its slogan was: No Lord but God.

An Intrusive Fourth School of Philosophy

Herod Archelaus lasted as ethnarch of Idumea, Judea, and Samaria only from the death of his father Herod the Great in 4 B.C.E. until 6 C.E., when the Romans deposed him and took over direct control of his territory through a governor of equestrian rank. Coponius, its first *praefectus*, was appointed in 6 C.E., while P. Sulpicius Quirinius, *legatus Augusti pro praetore*, was governor of Syria, but with senatorial rank. This administrative change demanded a census, registration of property, and assessment of taxation throughout the absorbed areas of Palestine.

> Under his [Coponius'] administration, a Galilean, named Judas, incited his countrymen to revolt, upbraiding them as cowards for consenting to pay tribute to the Romans and tolerating mortal masters, after having God for their Lord. This man was a sophist [that is, a teacher] who founded a sect [that is, a school of thought] of his own, having nothing in common with the others. Jewish philosophy, in fact, takes three forms. The followers of the first school are called Pharisees, of the second Sadducees, of the third Essenes. (Josephus, *Jewish War* 2.117–118)

That notation is straightforward enough, and its apologetic intention is quite clear. Judas the Galilean and his ideologically rebellious *sect* are mentioned in first place so that they can be separated completely from the subsequent *three forms of Jewish philosophy,* given as the Pharisees, Sadducees, and Essenes in 2.119 but then described as the Essenes in 2.120–161, the Pharisees in 2.162–163, 166a, and the Sadducees in 2.164–165, 166b. One is led to conclude that those latter forms, which are explained for Josephus' Hellenistic readers with deliberate parallelism between Pharisees and Stoics, Sadducees and Epicureans, Essenes and Pythagoreans, have nothing rebellious, dangerous, or subversive about them. That point is underlined by the length and prominence given to the Essenes, even though Josephus still claims, in 2.162, that the Pharisees "hold the position of the leading sect" over the other two groups. Judas and his followers are totally outside the official triad and a world apart from those deliberately emphasized Essenes, but, on the other hand, no great importance is given to them. They are, one might presume, a mere passing phenomenon of the year 6 C.E.

Josephus returns twice to the subject of Judaism's three philosophies or schools of thought in the later *Jewish Antiquities.* In the first instance, he mentions the Pharisees, Sadducees, and Essenes in 13.171 and then discusses them as the Pharisees in 13.172a, the Essenes in 13.172b, and the Sadducees in 13.173. That comment is made without any contextual connection, is placed against the general background of the 140s B.C.E., is fairly impartial in its length per group, and, of course, can say nothing about Judas the Galilean in 6 C.E. The second instance, however, is in precise parallel position to that in *Jewish War* 2.119–166, and now the differences are striking. Whereas in the *Jewish War* Judas received only two paragraphs out of fifty, he now receives ten out of twenty-two. Instead of being mentioned only before the official philosophic trilogy, he now frames it before and after. And instead of being merely a *sect,* he is now elevated to a *fourth philosophy.* We now hear of Judas in 18.4–10; then the three ancient philosophies are mentioned in 18.11 as the Essenes, Sadducees, and Pharisees but discussed as the Pharisees in 18.12–15, the Sadducees in 18.16–17, the Essenes in 18.18–22; and finally Judas appears again in 18.23–25. Yet those twin framing units about Judas are not only quite different from the earlier one in *Jewish War* 2.117–118, they are also rather different from each other. This is the opening frame.

> But a certain Judas, a Gaulanite from the city of Gamala [east of the Sea of Galilee], who had enlisted the aid of Saddok, a Pharisee, threw himself into the cause of rebellion. They said that the assessment carried with it a status amounting to downright slavery, no less, and appealed to the nation to make a bid for independence. *They urged that in case of success the Jews would have laid the foundation of prosperity, while if they*

failed to obtain any boon, they would win honour and renown for their
lofty aim; and that Heaven would be their zealous helper to no lesser end
than the furthering of their enterprise until it succeeded—all the more if
with high devotion in their hearts they stood firm and did not shrink from
the bloodshed that might be necessary. Since the populace, when they
heard their appeals, responded gladly, the plot to strike boldly made serious progress; and so these men sowed the seed of every kind of misery,
which so afflicted the nation that words are inadequate. When wars are
set afoot that are bound to rage beyond control, and when friends are
done away with who might have alleviated the suffering, when raids are
made by great hordes of brigands and men of the highest standing are
assassinated, it is supposed to be the common welfare that is upheld, but
the truth is that in such cases the motive is private gain. They sowed the
seed from which sprang strife between factions and the slaughter of fellow citizens. . . . Here is a lesson that an innovation and reform in ancestral traditions weighs heavily in the scale of leading to the destruction of
the congregation of the people. In this case certainly, Judas and Saddok
started among us an intrusive fourth school of philosophy . . . planting
the seeds of those troubles which subsequently overtook it [the body pol-
itic], all because of the novelty of this hitherto unknown philosophy.
(Josephus, *Jewish Antiquities* 18.4–9, italics added)

The length of that quotation underlines its importance, and I have
italicized the section where apocalyptic motivation is hidden behind a Josephan screen of Hellenistic urbanity. On the one hand, Judas now leads not
some isolated sect but a fourth philosophy or ideology, albeit a novel and
intrusive one. And it is not so absolutely separated from the three earlier
options that a Pharisee cannot be involved in its inception. On the other,
Josephus speaks as if this new vision was the single root cause of everything
that was to happen for the next sixty years. This creates the impression of
a single coherent, concerted, and coordinated ideological program leading
from the refusal of taxation in 6 C.E. to the war against Rome in 66 C.E. It
must be asserted flatly and immediately that this is a pure construct of Josephan imagination and one that is contradicted by his own subsequent
accounts. He is surely correct to say that Judas' proposal was novel since,
after all, the Jewish nation had been under various imperial overlords for
around six hundred years. But, no doubt, Judas could have gone back a
thousand years to 2 Samuel 24, when God sent a plague to punish the
census taken up by David, and responded that his philosophy was older
than any of the other three. The more significant point is not whether it
was or was not new but whether it was or was not the seedbed of all that was
to follow. And here the answer must be a firm negative. With regard to
Judas' fourth philosophy and all that was to follow, Josephus' causative

claim is simply compositional design; his originative allegation is pure narrative simplification.

Indeed, after that opening frame's accusation of responsibility for the nation's eventual disaster, one is hardly ready to read either the content or the tone of this closing frame. Once again I italicize what I consider to be Josephus' restatement of their millennial ideology.

> As for the fourth of the philosophies, Judas the Galilean set himself up as leader of it. This school agrees in all other respects with the opinions of the Pharisees, except that they have a passion for liberty that is almost unconquerable, since they are convinced that God alone is their leader and master. *They think little of submitting to death in unusual forms and permitting vengeance to fall on kinsmen and friends if only they may avoid calling any man master. Inasmuch as most people have seen the steadfastness of their resolution amid such circumstances, I may forgo any further account. For I have no fear that anything reported of them will be considered incredible. The danger is, rather, that report may minimize the indifference with which they accept the grinding misery of pain.* The folly that ensued began to afflict the nation after Gessius Florus, who was governor [64–66 C.E.], had by his overbearing and lawless activities provoked a desperate rebellion against the Romans. (Josephus, *Jewish Antiquities* 18.23–25, italics added)

Now the fourth philosophy gets a far more laudatory description, is like the Pharisees in all things but one, and is responsible for civil strife only much later and only in conjunction with procuratorial malfeasance. The ambivalence of Josephus' reactions to the fourth philosophy in those frames actually mirrors a similar ambivalence at the end of the *Jewish War*. There he had excoriated the lives of the Sicarii but then glorified their deaths.

The final mention of Judaism's major schools of thought is in Josephus' *Life*, which, even though appended to the *Antiquities*, talks only of three sects, philosophies, or ideological groups.

> At about the age of sixteen I determined to gain personal experience of the several sects into which our nation is divided. These, as I have frequently mentioned, are three in number—the first that of the Pharisees, the second that of the Sadducees, and the third that of the Essenes. I thought that, after a thorough investigation, I should be in a position to select the best. So I submitted myself to hard training and laborious exercises and passed through the three courses. Not content, however, with the experience thus gained, on hearing of one named Bannus, who dwelt in the wilderness, wearing only such clothing as trees provided, feeding on such things as grew of themselves, and using frequent

ablutions of cold water, by day and night, for purity's sake, I became his devoted disciple. With him I lived for three years and, having accomplished my purpose, returned to the city. Being now in my nineteenth year, I began to govern my life by the rules of the Pharisees, a sect having points of resemblance to that which the Greeks call the Stoic school. (Josephus, *Life* 10–12)

Leaving aside the Hellenistic typicality of that process, and the precocious atypicality of its speed, there are again only three philosophies in Judaism. Yet most of those three years were spent with a fourth option, not named as a fourth philosophy but attached to a specifically named individual. One could hardly have blamed an ancient reader for mentally correlating the four options of *Jewish Antiquities* 18.4–25 with those four options in its appended *Life* 10–12. And a modern reader like Tessa Rajak has wondered whether "this stay with Bannus may have brought him into contact not just with a religious community in search of purity, such as the Qumran sect, but with a group of political activists. . . . However, if there was any quasi-revolutionary thinking among Josephus' desert companions, this was an approach which Josephus would have encountered only to reject it totally" (38–39). Indeed, unless his claim that he was a Pharisee from the fifties C.E. is sheer opportunism from the nineties C.E., that choice may well have represented primarily a rejection of the desert option with all its dangerous religiopolitical overtones.

Back to Judas the Galilean, whose nickname, by the way, reminds us that his activity was not conducted in his native region but presumably as a teacher in Jerusalem. Josephus does not even tell us what happened to him, and we know only that he did not succeed from this vague record in Acts 5:37. "Judas the Galilean arose in the days of the census and drew away some of the people after him; he also perished and all who followed him were scattered." All in all, despite and against Josephus' elevation of the ideology's creative effects from *Jewish War* 2.117–118 into *Jewish Antiquities* 18.4–10,23–25, one must conclude, with David Rhoads, that "the revolt of Judas the Galilean in Judea in 6 C.E. was relatively small and ineffective" (59). It was of millennial inspiration since it seems most likely, as Richard Horsley has suggested, that Jewish apocalypticism lies behind the "veiled, Hellenistic language" of those sections I italicized above in *Jewish Antiquities* 18.5, 23, 24 (1979b:443). He has also suggested that the ideology was "a nonviolent, nonrevolutionary resistance" (1987:89). This is probably also correct, at least for the situation in 6 C.E. Judas may well have been advocating passive resistance rather than active rebellion, although, of course, such fine distinctions would have been lost completely on the

Romans. It was Josephus, then, who elevated it from idea to sect to philosophy, from nonviolent to violent action, and from passing incident to abiding situation.

The Sons of Judas the Galilean

Judas the Galilean may not have started either sect or philosophy, revolt or rebellion, but he did have an ideology, and he did start a family. Judea alone was under direct Roman rule from 6 to 41 C.E. but along with the rest of the country, came under Herod Agrippa I between 41 and 44 C.E. On his death the entire country came under direct Roman rule. The first prefects, now called procurators, were Cuspius Fadus in 44–46 and the apostate Jew Tiberius Julius Alexander, nephew of the philosopher Philo, in 46–48 C.E.

> Claudius . . . sent as procurators, first Cuspius Fadus, and then Tiberius Alexander, who [plural] by abstaining from all interference with the customs of the country kept the nation at peace. (Josephus, *Jewish War* 2.220)

> The successor of Fadus was Tiberius Alexander . . . who . . . did not stand by the practices of his people. . . . It was in the administration of Tiberius Alexander, that the great famine occurred in Judaea. . . . Besides this James and Simon, the sons of Judas the Galilean, were brought for trial and, at the order of Alexander, were crucified. This was the Judas who, as I explained above, had aroused the people to revolt against the Romans while Quirinius was taking the census of Judaea. (Josephus, *Jewish Antiquities* 20.100–102)

We know nothing else about James or Simon, and Josephus refrains from making any explicit claims of continuity with Judas beyond paternity. We do not know if they were teachers or in what precise activity they were involved or whether it happened in Galilee or Judea. We may presume, however, that they did something construed as rebellious by the Romans. And just as we heard of their father when the Romans first took direct rule over Judea, so we hear of his sons when the Romans first spread that direct rule to the entire country. One can only wonder, therefore, whether there was both genealogical and ideological continuity from Judas to his crucified sons. And was their action still nonviolent?

Hidden Daggers and Hidden Faces

Even when Josephus was claiming Judas' ideology as a fourth philosophy, he never gave it a name as he did the other three, the Pharisees, Sadducees, and Essenes. But sometime between 52 and 60 C.E., when Felix was procurator, we hear for the first time of a group whom Josephus calls the Sicarii. How, if at all, do they relate to the ideology of "no lord but God"?

> But while the country was thus cleared of these pests [that is, the social bandits to be discussed later] a new species of bandits was springing up in Jerusalem, the so-called *sicarii*, who committed murders in broad daylight in the heart of the city. The festivals were their special seasons, when they would mingle with the crowd, carrying short daggers [*sicae* in Latin] concealed under their clothing, with which they stabbed their enemies. Then, when they fell, the murderers joined in the cries of indignation and, through this plausible behaviour, were never discovered. The first to be assassinated by them was Jonathan the high-priest; after his death there were numerous daily murders. The panic created was more alarming than the calamity itself; every one, as on a battlefield, hourly expected death. Men kept watch at a distance on their enemies and would not trust even their friends when they approached. Yet, even while their suspicions were aroused and they were on their guard, they fell; so swift were the conspirators and so crafty in eluding detection. (Josephus, *Jewish War* 2.254–257)

That is a very clear description. A new type of bandit, brigand, outlaw, has appeared in the mid-fifties C.E. They are not rural bandits, about whom we shall see much more later on, but urban terrorists. Their method was not open robbery in the countryside but secret assassination in the city. Their tactics are instantly recognizable against our own contemporary experience. The festivals not only gave maximum anonymity, they also guaranteed maximum publicity. The festival was an ancient mass medium. No doubt a relatively small group, they produced, as Josephus himself recognized, terror out of all proportion to their actual murders. Their first victim was not Ananias, son of Nebedaeus, the current high priest between 47 and 59 C.E., but Jonathan, high priest between 36 and 37 C.E. and probably the most powerful extant member of the Ananus family. It was a precise, deliberate, and calculated choice. "'Terrorism is the weapon of the weak'— or so goes Brian Crozier's now famous generalization," as cited by Richard Horsley, comparing ancient and modern terrorism. "It is especially well suited to the struggles of colonized peoples against foreign domination, since the 'normal' means of 'legitimate' coercion have been closed to them. Terror is particularly tempting for small conspiratorial groups that lack a power base among the people. Often it is directed primarily against fellow nationals who are collaborating or at least cooperating with the foreigners" (1979b:439). So it was Jonathan, the Jewish high priest, and not Felix, the Roman procurator, who was the first assassinated in the terror campaign of the Sicarii. What was new, by the way, was not the assassin's hidden dagger but the assassin's hidden face. Josephus records in *Jewish Antiquities* 15.281 how "ten of the citizens conspired together, swearing to undergo any danger and placing daggers under their clothes" to assassinate Herod. But Herod, with a better secret police than Julius Caesar, moved swiftly to abort the conspiracy.

The parallel account about the Sicarii in *Jewish Antiquities* is, however, totally different: there is nothing about them as a new breed of outlaw, and, although Jonathan is murdered with concealed daggers, the murder is brought about by the procurator Felix, who turns rural bandits into urban assassins.

> Felix [decided] to bribe Jonathan's most trusted friend, a native of Jerusa-
> lem named Doras, with a promise to pay a great sum, to bring in
> brigands to attack Jonathan and kill him. Doras agreed and contrived to
> get him murdered by the brigands in the following way. Certain of the
> brigands went up to the city as if they intended to worship God. With
> daggers concealed under their clothes, they mingled with the people
> about Jonathan and assassinated him. As the murder remained
> unpunished, from that time forth the brigands with perfect impunity
> used to go to the city during the festivals and, with their weapons simi-
> larly concealed, mingle with the crowds. In this way they slew some
> because they were private enemies, and others because they were paid
> to do so by someone else. They committed these murders not only in
> other parts of the city but even in some cases in the temple; for there
> too they made bold to slaughter their victims, for they did not regard
> even this as a desecration. This is the reason why, in my opinion, even
> God Himself, for loathing of their impiety, turned away from our city
> and, because He deemed the temple to be no longer a clean dwelling
> place for Him, brought the Romans upon us and purification by fire
> upon the city. (Josephus, *Jewish Antiquities* 20.163–166)

That is probably best described as a radically tendentious revision of the earlier data and must be read with critical discrimination. It is part of the even greater responsibility attributed to the last procurators in *Jewish Antiquities* over the already great culpability assigned to them in the *Jewish War*. Felix, in effect, invented the Sicarii, and they, in effect, brought on the Temple's destruction. It was Felix who turned rural brigands into urban ter-rorists in order to have Jonathan killed. I think it better, therefore, to depend completely on *Jewish War* 2.254–257 and bracket completely the parallel in *Jewish Antiquities* 20.163–166. Despite that deliberate Josephan confusion, the Sicarii must be carefully distinguished from the bandits: in their location, city against country; in their methods, assassination against robbery; in their intention, anonymity against notoriety; and in their results, terror against anger; and, above all, in their social class, literate scribes and teachers of the retainer class against illiterate farmers and shepherds of the peasant class.

What about the Sicarii during the revolt against Rome? Insofar as precise moments are discernible, the First Roman-Jewish War more or less irrevocably broke out with a split within the priestly aristocracy, a breach within the operational unity of the governing class. Eleazar, son of the Ananias who had been high priest in 47–59 C.E., was Captain of the Temple, more or less equivalent to deputy high priest, in 66 C.E. He persuaded the lower priests to terminate the twice-daily sacrifices on behalf of the emperor and people of Rome. The reason, however, was much wider than mere anti-Roman sentiment. In *Jewish War* 2.409–417 it is stated as manifesto: "to accept no gift or sacrifice from a foreigner." What is at stake is the complete purification of the Temple through separation from any pagan influence or contact whatsoever. Civil war broke out immediately in Jerusalem: on one side, holding the western upper city, were those who opposed the war, led by the chief priests, and, on the other, holding the Temple and the lower city due south of it, were Eleazar and those who had joined him. *Jewish War* 2.424 records a week-long stalemate.

At this point I propose reading three texts that Josephus records as quite separate and successive events but that I think must all refer to the same incident.

(1) And now some of the most ardent promoters of hostilities banded together and made an assault on a fortress called Masada; and having gained possession of it by stratagem, they slew the Roman guards and put a garrison of their own in their place.

(2) The eighth day was the feast of wood-carrying, when it was customary for all to bring wood for the altar, in order that there might be an unfailing supply of fuel for the flames, which are always kept burning. The Jews in the Temple [Eleazar's forces] excluded their opponents from this ceremony, but along with some feebler folk numbers of the *sicarii* — so they called the brigands who carried a dagger in their bosom — forced their way in; these they enlisted in their service and pressed their attacks more boldly than before.

(3) At this period a certain Menahem, son of Judas surnamed the Galilean — that redoubtable doctor [skillful teacher] who in old days, under Quirinius, had upbraided the Jews for recognizing the Romans as masters when they already had God — took his intimate friends off with him to Masada, where he broke into king Herod's armoury and provided arms both for his fellow-townsmen and for other brigands; then, with these men for his bodyguard, he returned like a veritable king to Jerusa-

lem, became the leader of the revolution, and directed the siege of the palace. (Josephus, *Jewish War* 2.408, 425, 433–434)

If it is correct to read those first two texts in the light of the third one as all referring to the same event, that event becomes quite clear. Menahem, son or possibly grandson of Judas the Galilean, and, like him, a teacher, led his Sicarii followers in an attack on Masada, the well-fortified and well-provisioned Herodian fortress on the southwestern shore of the Dead Sea. Menahem, having armed both his own Sicarii and local peasants as well, returned to Jerusalem at their head and, if I read Josephus aright, with the panoply of a messianic claimant. He was initially, and perforce, more or less allied with Eleazar against the antiwar aristocracy. But it was clearly the arrival of these new and now well-armed forces that broke the stalemate and helped Eleazar to prevail.

Eleazar, however, had no intention of turning the revolution over to Menahem, whose followers had meanwhile caught and killed Ananias and his brother Ezechias.

The partisans of Eleazar now rose against him; they remarked to each other that, after revolting from the Romans for love of liberty, they ought not to sacrifice this liberty to a Jewish hangman and to put up with a master who, even were he to abstain from violence, was anyhow far below themselves; and that if they must have a leader, anyone would be better than Menahem. So they laid their plans to attack him in the Temple, whither he had gone up in state to pay his devotions, arrayed in royal robes and attended by his suite of armed fanatics [literally: zealots].... A few succeeded in escaping by stealth to Masada, among others Eleazar, son of Jairus and a relative of Menahem, and subsequently despot of Masada. Menahem himself, who had taken refuge in the place called Ophlas and there ignominiously concealed himself, was caught, dragged into the open, and after being subjected to all kinds of torture, put to death. His lieutenant, along with Absalom, his most eminent supporter in his tyranny, met with a similar fate. (Josephus, *Jewish War* 2.442–448)

The snobbery of that "far below ourselves" may be from Eleazar or Josephus or both. It is, in any case, the *governing* class talking about not the *peasant* but the *retainer* class. Aristocrats do not consider themselves "above" peasants but beyond them somewhere, in another world. An aristocratic priest might need, however, to assert superiority over an upstart teacher. One can also, by the way, assess the tendentiousness of Josephus' description of Menahem's fate not only by that passage's rhetorical overtones but also by the fact, recorded in his *Life* 21, that he himself "sought asylum in the inner court of the Temple" until "Menahem and the chief-tains of the band of brigands had been put to death." The aristocracy, how-ever dissident or rebellious, was back in charge of the war.

The surviving Sicarii retreated to their secure base on Masada and took no further part in a war they could not lead. They are mentioned a few times later, for example, in *Jewish War* 4.399–400, when they attacked nearby Engaddi, in 4.503–508 and 653, when Simon bar Giora tried unsuccessfully to have them rejoin the war, and in 7.409–419, when those who had escaped to Egypt and there attacked "certain Jews of rank" were handed over to the Romans by their Alexandrian fellow Jews. Finally, having given absolutely no military assistance even during Jerusalem's last desperate days, they and their families still atop Masada died by their own hands just before Flavius Silva's mopping-up operations could finally reach them in 73 or 74 C.E.

What, in retrospect and summary, of the continuity repeatedly under-lined by Josephus in those preceding texts between Judas the Galilean in the early years of the first century and the Sicarii between its mid-fifties and mid-seventies? In telling their final fate on Masada, Josephus summarizes the connection once again.

> [The] fortress was called Masada; and the Sicarii who had occupied it
> had at their head a man of influence named Eleazar. He was a descen-
> dant of the Judas who, as we have previously stated, induced multitudes
> of Jews to refuse to enroll themselves, when Quirinius was sent as cen-
> sor to Judaea. For in those days the Sicarii clubbed together against
> those who consented to submit to Rome and in every way treated them
> as enemies, plundering their property, rounding up their cattle, and set-
> ting fire to their habitations; protesting that such persons were no other
> than aliens, who so ignobly sacrificed the hard-won [or: highly prized] lib-
> erty of the Jews and admitted their preference for the Roman yoke. Yet,
> after all, this was but a pretext, put forward by them as a cloak for their
> cruelty and avarice, as was made plain by their actions. For the people
> did join with them in the revolt and take their part in the war with
> Rome, only, however, to suffer at their hands still worse atrocities; and
> when they were again convicted of falsehood in this pretext, they only
> oppressed the more those who in righteous self-defence reproached
> them with their villainy. (Josephus, *Jewish War* 7.252–258)

That marvelously ambiguous "in those days" makes it deliberately pos-sible to connect the actions of the Sicarii either with the first-mentioned Eleazar or the second-mentioned Judas. Thus, one could imagine the Sicarii operative for almost seventy years. I consider that sheer Josephan tendentiousness and reread all of that preceding data against his interpreta-tion along the following lines.

There is *genealogical* continuity from Judas of Galilee in 6 C.E., to Simon and Judas between 46 and 48 C.E., and on to Menahem and Eleazar, between 66 and 73 C.E. There is *functional* continuity as learned teachers between Judas and Menahem, and possibly with the others as well. There is *ideological* continuity concerning "no Lord but God" between Judas, Eleazar, and some of the Sicarii who escaped to Alexandria before Masada fell. The speech of Eleazar in *Jewish War* 7.323 mentions "neither to serve the Romans nor any other save God" and, in 7.418–419 the Sicarii, delivered over to the Romans by the Alexandrian Jews refuse, under every torture, "to call Caesar lord." There is not, however, despite and against Josephus himself, any *operational* continuity between Judas and the Sicarii. Judas of Galilee, most likely, advocated passive resistance. His sons, Judas and Simon may or may not have already turned to violence. The Sicarii certainly did, and their strategies were classical terrorist ones, but they started those actions only in the mid-fifties C.E. The ideology was always elitist and urban, the purview of learned teachers. It is only Josephus' deliberate attempt to lump all unapproved insurgents into one great bandit mass that could mislead David Rhoads into concluding that "the Sicarii were lower-class revolutionaries from the Judean countryside" (121).

We saw earlier the ambivalence between Josephus' twin comments on the fourth philosophy in *Jewish Antiquities* 18.4–10 as against 18.23–25. The same ambivalence had already surrounded the Sicarii when he came to conclude the last book of his *Jewish War*, since, by that time and for him, they were the end of a rebellious line that had started with the novel ideology of the fourth philosophy in 6 C.E. Josephus is now fiercely ambivalent about the Sicarii. Appalled by their lives, he is enthralled by their deaths, on Masada and in Alexandria. But, of course, that allowed him to climax his *Jewish War* not with the Flavian triumph at Rome as detailed in 7.116–162 but with the heroic deaths of the Jewish Sicarii at Masada and Alexandria as detailed in 7.275–419 (Rajak 220–221). In the end, as so often with terrorism, the Sicarii lost a cause and left a legend.

✧ 7 ✧

Peasant and Protester

> As participation in determining the shape of their own lives is
> denied to a colonized people, they may retreat further into their
> own cultural or religious traditions. Their religious traditions
> and rites take on increased importance as the only dimension of
> their life that remains under their own control. As a way of
> preserving some semblance of dignity, colonized people tend to
> focus all the more on their distinctive religious traditions, rules,
> and rituals as symbols of their former freedom and self-
> determination. This tends to make them all the more sensitive
> about violation of these symbols.
> *Richard A. Horsley (1987:128)*

The book from which that epigraph is taken speaks of "a spiral of violence"
in colonial and imperial situations. It distinguishes a first stage of *injustice,*
which is the structural violence of colonialism and the institutional violence
of imperialism themselves. Next comes the indigenous reaction of *protest and
resistance,* ranging all the way from passive withdrawal through strikes and
demonstrations to banditry and terrorism. The third stage is *repression,* ranging likewise from intimidation through harassment to imprisonment and dis-
appearance, torture, and death. Finally, there is *revolt,* when and if that
preceding stage escalates to unbearable levels (24–26).

That spiral of violence concerns, moreover, not just the small minority
who are the upper classes but the vast ordinary majority who are the lower
classes. From now on and throughout this second part of the book I focus
on that majority, with close dependence on the work of Richard Horsley,
who, over the last decade, has elaborated a very convincing typology of
popular movements in first-century Roman Palestine. I quote two statements of his as programmatic guides for what is to follow. "Two events," he
says, "that took place in Jewish Palestine during the mid–first century C.E.
have been highly significant for subsequent history: the career and death of
Jesus of Nazareth and the great Jewish revolt of 66–70. . . . In both of these
events the Jewish peasantry was the dynamic force, the original source of
historical change and its ramifications. . . . Yet until very recently, the mod-

ern Western assumption has been that the common people have had little to do with the making of history. Insofar as any have ever been aware of the existence of peasants, it is commonly believed that they were simply very conservative folk pursuing their traditional way of life and 'vegetating in the teeth of time'" (Horsley & Hanson: xi–xii). And, even more succinctly, "About the only time that ordinary people made the pages of literary historical sources was when they caused trouble for the elite" (Horsley 1988:83). And yet, no matter how important the Great Tradition of the aristocracy may be both for itself and even for the Little Tradition of the peasantry, it is that latter matrix that is the most direct, immediate, and primary background for a peasant farmer or artisan like Jesus of Nazareth. I turn then quite deliberately from the elite society emphasized in the last chapter to consider peasant society in the next chapters.

Vegetating in the Teeth of Time

The classic definition of peasant society is that of A. L. Kroeber in his monumental 1948 work on anthropology. "Peasants are definitely rural," he asserted, "yet live in relation to market towns; they form a class segment of a larger population which usually contains also urban centers, sometimes metropolitan capitals. They constitute part-societies with part-cultures. They lack the isolation, the political autonomy, and the self-sufficiency of tribal populations; but their local units retain much of their old identity, integration, and attachment to soil and cults" (284). Those "part-" words indicate that the peasantry, as a major societal type, is being defined in a way that is not just rural or occupational but structural and relational. A similar Janus-like definition appears in a classic 1956 text by Robert Redfield: "We are looking at rural people in old civilizations, those rural people who control and cultivate their land for subsistence and as a part of a traditional way of life and who look to and are influenced by gentry or townspeople whose way of life is like theirs but in a more civilized form" (31).

Both those preceding descriptions seem relatively benign, far removed, indeed, from the *peasant* class seen earlier in Lenski's typology for agrarian states and empires. Two definitions from the mid-sixties, however, spell out much more clearly what it means for peasants to be "part of" larger entities such as preindustrial cities or agrarian empires, or to be "influenced by gentry or townspeople." Notice, for example, the slight shift from the language of participation to that of exploitation in George Foster's 1967 description: "If the primary criterion for defining peasant society is structural—the relationship between the village and the city (or state)—it is clear that the major focuses of interest will be found in these ties. They have a number of aspects, including the social, economic, religious, jural, historical, and emotional. But in all, it seems to us that the critical common denominator is that peasants have very little control over the conditions that govern their lives. . . . Peasants are not only poor, as has often been pointed out, but they are relatively powerless" (Potter et al. 8).

It is, however, only in Eric Wolf's 1966 monograph, published the same year as Lenski's typology, that the full exploitative connotation of Kroeber's "part-" is emphatically underlined. "In primitive societies, surpluses are exchanged directly among groups or members of groups; peasants, however, are rural cultivators whose surpluses are transferred to a dominant group of rulers that uses the surpluses both to underwrite its own standard of living and to distribute the remainder to groups in society that do not farm but must be fed for their specific goods and services in turn . . . [It] is only when a cultivator is integrated into a society with a state — that is, when the cultivator becomes subject to the demands and sanctions of power-holders outside his social stratum — that we can appropriately speak of peasantry" (3–4, 11). For both Lenski and Wolf, then, a peasantry is defined in terms of an outside power, be it city, state, or empire, that appropriates its agricultural surplus to itself.

Any residual illusions that such arrangements are benign may be removed by considering an example given by Wolf. It is for "a 40-acre farm in Mecklenburg, northeastern Germany, during the fourteenth and fifteenth centuries" (5). Its total annual *yield* was 10,200 pounds of grain crops. Of that, 3,400 pounds was immediately stored as *seed* for the next sowing and 2,800 pounds as *feed* for the four horses. Of the remaining 4,000 pounds, 2,700 pounds went for *rent* to the landowner. In the end, therefore, only 1,300 pounds were left for the peasant family "yielding a per capita daily ration of 1600 calories" (9). Since the physiological minimum is somewhere between 2000 and 3000 calories per day, that family would have to augment its daily caloric intake through other methods.

George Dalton, an economic anthropologist, having just concluded that "anyone who attempts to make generalizations which are true for all peasants, past and present, in Europe, Asia, Latin America, the Caribbean, and the Middle East, is necessarily confined to Kroeber's definition" (404), immediately proceeds beyond it by claiming that "peasants of all times and places are structured inferiors. In traditional peasantries, their inferiority is structured legally and reinforced via dependent land tenure" (406). It is well, therefore, to consider what might be rational behavior in a system of structured inferiority when considering those standard accusations hurled at peasants: that they are untrusting and suspicious, aggressive and competitive, passive, stubborn, and stupid. Two examples will have to suffice.

In a justly famous article of 1965, George Foster wrote that "the model of cognitive orientation that seems to me best to account for peasant behavior is the 'Image of Limited Good.' By 'Image of Limited Good' I mean that broad areas of peasant behavior are patterned in such fashion as to suggest that peasants view their social, economic, and natural universes—their total environment—as one in which all of the desired things in life such as land, wealth, health, friendship and love, manliness and honor, respect and status, power and influence, security and safety, *exist in finite quantity* and *are always in short supply*, as far as the peasant is concerned. Not only do these and all other 'good things' exist in finite and limited quantities, but in addition *there is no way directly within peasant power to increase the available quantities*" (Potter et al. 304). A vision of limited good seems quite rational if your caloric intake is pushed to the minimum and your appropriated surplus is pushed to the maximum. Or, again, from Eric Hobsbawm, writing in 1973: "The normal strategy of the traditional peasantry is passivity. It is not an ineffective strategy, for it exploits the major assets of the peasantry, its numbers and the impossibility of making it do some things by force for any length of time, and it also utilises a favourable tactical situation, which rests on the fact that no change is what suits a traditional peasantry best. A communally organised traditional peasantry, reinforced by a functionally useful slowness, imperviousness and stupidity—apparent or real—is a formidable force" (1973a:13).

It is important at this point to recall, once again, the work of James Scott. It is important because from here on I am depending on ancient literate descriptions of peasant protest, rebellion, and revolt. Such events are recorded only when they have already achieved a level of intensity forcing awareness of their presence on elitist observers. Yet, what Scott has shown so persuasively about contemporary Malaysian peasants is equally true of ancient Mediterranean peasants. "Most subordinate classes throughout most of history have rarely been afforded the luxury of open, organized, political activity. Or, better stated, such activity was dangerous, if not suicidal. . . . For all their importance when they do occur, peasant rebellions—let alone revolutions—are few and far between. The vast majority are crushed unceremoniously. . . . For these reasons it seemed to me more important to understand what we might call *everyday* forms of peasant resistance—the prosaic but constant struggle between the peasantry and those who seek to extract labor, food, taxes, rents, and interest from them. Most forms of this struggle stop well short of outright collective defiance. Here I have in mind the ordinary weapons of relatively powerless groups: foot dragging, dissimulation, desertion, false compliance, pilfering, feigned ignorance, slander, arson, sabotage, and so on. These . . . forms of class struggle . . . require little or no coordination or planning; they make use of implicit understandings and informal networks; they often represent a form of individual self-help; they typically avoid any direct, symbolic confrontation with authority. . . . When such stratagems are abandoned in favor of more quixotic action, it is usually a sign of great desperation" (1985:xv–xvi; see also 1990). Furthermore, and more profoundly, as Scott had proposed in an earlier article, "the little tradition [of the peasantry] does not merely represent some parochial version of the great tradition [of the gentry]. Rather, the little tradition often constitutes a 'shadow society—a pattern of structural, stylistic, and normative opposition to the politico-religious tradition of ruling elites'" (1977:211). Those insightful analyses must be kept constantly in mind throughout the second part of this book, where, whenever Josephus speaks, and in whatever terms, of peasant protest, we can be certain we are seeing but the tip of the iceberg, even or especially when that tip has achieved lethally dangerous proportions. "The subordinate classes—especially the peasantry," warns a final summary from Scott, "are likely to be more radical at the level of ideology than at the level of behavior, where they are more effectively constrained by the daily exercise of power" (1985:331; see all of 304–350).

The Threat of an Agrarian Strike

There are seven main incidents to be reviewed, and I have summarized these for easy reference in appendix 2. The first example occurred in 4 B.C.E. after Herod's death but before his son Archelaus had gone to Rome to plead his testamentary case before Caesar and receive eventual control of Idumea, Judea, and Samaria.

> [Archelaus] went forth to the Temple. . . . Speaking from a golden throne
> on a raised platform, he greeted the multitude . . . it would be his earnest
> and constant endeavour to treat them better than they had been treated
> by his father. Delighted at these professions, the multitude at once
> proceeded to test his intentions by making large demands. One party
> clamoured for a reduction of the taxes, another for the abolition of the
> duties [on sales], a third for the liberation of prisoners. To all these
> requests, in his desire to ingratiate himself with the people, he readily
> assented. (Josephus, *Jewish War* 2.4 = *Jewish Antiquities* 17.204–205)

The parallel versions are so close in that case as not to need double citation. And, because of Archelaus' special situation, the protests and appeals were successful. Those popular protests, however, eventually turned into the Passover massacre of 4 B.C.E.

Two separate incidents concerning the Jews and one concerning the Samaritans are recorded from the governorship of Pontius Pilate between 26 and 36 C.E. Only the Jewish ones are considered here; the Samaritan case, which brought about Pilate's dismissal, will be discussed below under millennial prophecy.

The first episode is that of the *Iconic Standards*. It must have happened soon after Pilate's appointment in the winter of 26 to 27 C.E. I consider, by the way, that the incident of the *Aniconic Shields* in Philo's *Embassy to Gaius* 199–305 is but another version of this same event. The differences between Josephus' and Philo's accounts are the expected ones between twin versions of the same situation, especially in a rhetorical context where Philo is contrasting a villainous Pilate with an idyllic Tiberius. I follow Josephus' version.

> Pilate, being sent by Tiberius as procurator to Judaea, introduced into Jerusalem by night and under cover the effigies of Caesar which are called standards. This proceeding, when day broke, aroused immense excitement among the Jews . . . considering their laws to have been trampled under foot, as those laws permit no images to be erected in the city. (Josephus, *Jewish War* 2.169)

> Now Pilate, the procurator of Judaea, when he brought his army from Caesarea and removed it to winter quarters in Jerusalem, took a bold step in subversion of the Jewish practices, by introducing into the city the busts [embossed medallions] of the emperor that were attached to the military standards, for our law forbids the making of images. It was for this reason that the previous procurators, when they entered the city, used standards that had no such ornaments. Pilate was the first to bring the images into Jerusalem and set them up, doing it without the knowledge of the people, for he entered at night. (Josephus, *Jewish Antiquities* 18.56)

The ordinary people of Jerusalem went to Caesarea, gathering country reinforcements as they went, and implored Pilate to remove the offending emblems. He refused, and "they fell prostrate around his house and for five whole days and nights remained motionless in that position," as *Jewish War* 2.171 tells the story, in contrast to the more laconic "they did not cease entreating him" in *Jewish Antiquities* 18.57. To break this sit-down strike, Pilate hid his soldiers in the stadium, had the demonstrators come there for an audience, and then threatened them with immediate death unless they submitted. When all immediately and simultaneously offered to accept martyrdom, Pilate was himself forced to submit rather than massacre so many.

The second incident is that of the *Temple Funds*. It cannot be dated with any precision, but Josephus makes it, from a literary point of view, almost a parallel companion piece to the preceding episode. Indeed, the demonstrations at Caesarea and Jerusalem form a diptych in Josephus, and one may wonder if literary harmony may have overcome historical accuracy in the details.

> He provoked a fresh uproar by expending upon the construction of an aqueduct the sacred treasure known as Corbonas; the water was brought from a distance of 400 furlongs. . . . He, foreseeing the tumult, had interspersed among the crowd a troop of his soldiers, armed but disguised in civilian dress with orders not to use their swords, but to beat any rioters with cudgels. (Josephus, *Jewish War* 2.175–176)

> He spent money from the sacred treasury in the construction of an aqueduct to bring water into Jerusalem, intercepting the source of the stream at a distance of 200 furlongs . . . tens of thousands assembled . . . some too even hurled insults and abuse of the sort that a throng will commonly engage in. He thereupon ordered a large number of soldiers to be dressed in Jewish garments, under which they carried clubs. . . . They, however, inflicted much harder blows than Pilate had ordered, punishing alike both those who were rioting and those who were not. (Josephus, *Jewish Antiquities* 18.60–62)

In the *Antiquities* version the Jewish disguise of the soldiers no longer makes any sense. It did in the former version because the disguised soldiers had *infiltrated* the crowd from the very beginning. The logic of that tactic derives from Pilate's previous experience. In the *Iconic Standards* incident he had suddenly confronted a Jewish crowd with armed soldiers and, confronted with mass unresisting martyrdom, had been forced to back down. In the *Temple Funds* case he planned to stampede the crowd into either violent action or headlong flight. I presume, therefore, that both events happened in relatively close proximity to each other, soon after Pilate first became governor.

The popular demonstrations against Pilate in the twenties or thirties pale completely before the one against Gaius Caligula between 39 and 41 C.E. "This protest against Gaius's plan to install a statue of himself in the Jewish Temple was clearly," in the words of Richard Horsley, "the largest, most widespread popular outcry during the whole period from the imposition of direct Roman rule until the outbreak of the great revolt in 66" (1987:114). The story of *Caligula's Statue* is told not only in the parallel texts of Josephus' *Jewish War* 2.185–203 and *Jewish Antiquities* 18.261–309 but also by Philo in his *Embassy to Gaius* 203–348, and the details increase greatly as one moves across those three descriptions.

All three texts agree that Caligula, having decided to place in Jerusalem's Temple a statue of himself as Zeus incarnate, ordered Petronius, his new Syrian legate, to do so by taking two legions into Judea. Those two legions, about twelve thousand soldiers if at full complement, represented half the forces stationed at Antioch to guard the eastern approaches of the empire. Two legions was also the striking force brought south by Varus against revolts in Jerusalem and all over Palestine in 4 B.C.E. With Caligula obviously expecting resistance, Petronius moved southward immediately and put his troops into quarters for the winter of 39 to 40 C.E. at Ptolemaïs on the Phoenician seacoast due west of Galilee (Schürer-Vermes 1.397). But then follows an interesting divergence between Philo and Josephus.

> He also sent for the magnates of the Jews, priests and magistrates. . . . For he thought that if he could start by appeasing them he could use them to instruct all the rest of the population to abstain from opposition. . . . Smitten by his first words . . . they stood riveted to the ground, incapable of speech, and then while a flood of tears poured from their eyes as from fountains they plucked the hair from their beards and heads. . . . While they were thus lamenting, the inhabitants of the holy city and the rest of the country hearing what was afoot marshalled themselves as if at a single signal . . . and issued forth in a body leaving cities, villages and houses empty and in one rush sped to Phoenicia where Petronius chanced to be. . . . They were divided into six companies, old men, young men, boys, and again in their turn old women, grown women, maidens. (Philo, *Embassy to Gaius* 222–225)

In that version, even though Petronius starts with the authorities, it is the masses who act. The former lament, but the latter, without any mention of leadership from priesthood or aristocracy, march from Jerusalem to Ptolemaïs gathering numbers from the peasantry as they go. "The Jews descended," says Philo's rampant rhetoric, "like a cloud and occupied the whole of Phoenicia" (226). The men emphasized that they were unarmed, had brought their wives and children with them, were loyal both to Rome and Gaius, "but if we cannot persuade you, we give up ourselves for destruction that we may not live to see a calamity worse than death" (229–233). Petronius faced, as Pilate once had been, with the prospect of mass unresisting martyrdom, decided to stall on the statue's construction and to write to Caligula telling him, not the truth of the Jewish nonviolent challenge, but that

> The wheat crop was just ripe and so were the other cereals, and he
> feared that the Jews in despair for their ancestral rites and in scorn of
> life might lay waste the arable land or set fire to the cornfields on the
> hills and the plain. (Philo, *Embassy to Gaius* 249)

In Philo, Petronius speaks first to the Jewish authorities who came to
him at his bidding and then to the crowds who came to him unbidden. But
it is the latter rather than the former who persuade him to stall Caligula. In
Josephus, however, it is the crowds who instigate the proceedings, and only
after hearing them does he call in the Jewish authorities more or less to
mediate with their own people.

> The Jews assembled with their wives and children in the plain of
> Ptolemaïs and implored Petronius to have regard first for the laws of
> their fathers, and next for themselves. Yielding so far to this vast multi-
> tude and their entreaties, he left the statues and his troops at Ptolemaïs
> and advanced into Galilee, where he summoned the people, with all per-
> sons of distinction, to Tiberias. (Josephus, *Jewish War* 2.192–193)

> Many tens of thousands of Jews came to Petronius at Ptolemaïs with
> petitions not to use force to make them transgress and violate their
> ancestral code. . . . He gathered up his friends and attendants and has-
> tened to Tiberias. . . . As before, many tens of thousands faced Petronius
> on his arrival at Tiberias. (Josephus, *Jewish Antiquities* 18.263, 269)

Both of Josephus' accounts, the shorter one in *Jewish War* and the
much longer one in *Jewish Antiquities,* agree with Philo that the men were
accompanied by their entire families and that they offered themselves as
unresisting martyrs against Caligula's statue and Petronius' legions. It is not
possible, therefore, to consider the theme of massive unresisting martyrdom a Josephan creation to exculpate the ordinary people from any hint
of armed anti-Roman resistance. That is also important for the light it casts
back on those earlier challenges to Pilate. Basically, we are dealing with the
same phenomenon: massive unarmed and nonviolent refusal to cooperate
based on a declared willingness to die rather than give in.

There is also, however, the agricultural aspect of the demonstrations,
and this appears in all three texts, but with one very basic difference. In
Philo it was the time of harvesting, and there was an alleged fear of arson
against that year's crops. In Josephus it was the time of sowing, and there
was a real fear of, in our terms, a strike against next year's crops. I do not
think, by the way, that those are separate events but simply divergent versions of the same incident, and, of the two, Josephus has the better one.

[Petronius] saw that the country was in danger of remaining unsown —
for it was seed-time and the people had spent fifty days idly waiting
upon him. (Josephus, *Jewish War* 2.200)

Aristobulus, the brother of King Agrippa, together with Helcias the
elder and other most powerful members of this house, together with the
civic leaders, appeared before Petronius and appealed to him, since he
saw the deep feelings of the people, not to incite them to desperation
but to write to Gaius telling how incurable was their opposition to
receiving the statue and how they had left their fields to sit protesting,
and ... since the land was unsown, there would be a harvest of banditry,
because the requirement of tribute could not be met.... He now convened the Jews, who arrived in many tens of thousands, at Tiberias, [and
after addressing them] dismissed the assembly ... and requested those in
authority to attend to agricultural matters and to conciliate the people
with optimistic propaganda. (Josephus, *Jewish Antiquities* 18.273–274,
279, 284)

So, to his honor, Petronius gave in. Meanwhile, in Rome, Agrippa I, as
we saw above, had persuaded Caligula to abandon the statue project, but
the letter so ordering Petronius crossed with Petronius' own letter telling
Caligula that he could not or would not take it onward to Jerusalem. Caligula responded by ordering Petronius to commit suicide, and only Caligula's
assassination in early 41 C.E. saved Petronius' life.

That is a quite extraordinary incident, not only for the presence of profound human decency in Petronius or the absence of concerned leadership
in the Jewish elites, but especially for the carefully planned activism of the
peasantry. First, they came with their entire families so that it was clearly
not an armed insurrection. Next, they waited in peaceful demonstration
around Petronius for forty or fifty days and, presumably, intended to go on
doing so until he relented. Further, they declared themselves willing to die
as martyrs before accepting the statue's installation in their Temple.
Finally, of course, as the peasants knew quite well and as the land-owning
aristocracy pointed out to Petronius, there was no sowing being done by
anyone since, once again, whole families had come to demonstrate and to
protest.

Note, for future reference, the aristocratic awareness that unsown
seeds reaped only a harvest of banditry. But, for now, I emphasize the
degree of political consciousness, of strategic and tactical planning, and of
sheer crowd control necessary for what Richard Horsley has rightly called a
"peasant strike, at least in Galilee" (1986a:39). To symbolize the conscious
agricultural basis of the entire operation, as soon as Petronius had given in,

God straightway sent a heavy shower that was contrary to general anticipation, for that day, from morning on, had been clear and the sky had
given no indication of rain. Indeed, the entire year had been beset by so
great a drought that it caused the people to despair of rainfall even if at
any time they saw the sky overcast. (Josephus, *Jewish Antiquities* 18.285;
no *Jewish War* parallel)

No doubt the peasants could not have succeeded in the long run
except for Petronius' humanity, Agrippa I's intercession, and, above all,
Caligula's most timely assassination. Still they, without any leadership from
the *governing* class, had evolved and executed a magnificently orchestrated
plan of passive resistance. The question whether such an operation was led
exclusively from the *peasant* class or had behind it scribes and teachers
from the *retainer* class will be left as an open question.

After Caligula came Claudius between 41 and 54 C.E. During his reign,
with Cumanus as governor of Palestine in 48 to 52 C.E., two peaceful popular protests are recorded. A third one, which escalated into revolt and
brought the Syrian legate's military intervention for the third time in about
half a century, will be discussed in more detail later on.

The first incident involved the Roman troops stationed, as was their
custom, on the roofs of the Temple's porticoes for the feast of Passover and
is on the borderline between peaceful and violent protest.

One of the soldiers, raising his robe, stooped in an indecent attitude, so
as to turn his backside to the Jews, and made a noise in keeping with his
posture. (Josephus, *Jewish War* 2.224)

One of the soldiers uncovered his genitals and exhibited them to the
multitude. (Josephus, *Jewish Antiquities* 20.108)

The crowd was enraged at this blasphemous insult and hurled stones,
according to *Jewish War* 2.225, or insults, according to *Jewish Antiquities*
20.110, at Cumanus himself. He ordered reinforcements into the Antonia
fortress, which overlooked the Temple from the north, the people pan-
icked, and, although not even attacked, crushed themselves in their thousands while trying to escape.

The second incident is closely linked to the preceding one in both time
and theme. It took place during punitive reprisals against villages about a
dozen miles northwest of Jerusalem. Since this aspect of the case involved
brigands, it will be seen in more detail in a later chapter. What is of interest
here is the public protest that ensued after a very specific action.

A soldier, finding in one village a copy of the sacred law, tore the book in
pieces and flung it into the fire. At that the Jews were roused as though

it were their whole country which had been consumed in the flames; and, their religion acting like some instrument to draw them together, all on the first announcement of the news hurried in a body to Cumanus at Caesarea, and implored him not to leave unpunished the author of such an outrage on God and on their law. (Josephus, *Jewish War* 2.229–231)

One of the soldiers, who had found a copy of the laws of Moses that was kept in one of the villages, fetched it out where all could see and tore it in two while he uttered blasphemies and railed violently. The Jews, on learning of this, collected in large numbers, went down to Caesarea, where Cumanus happened to be, and besought him to avenge not them but God, whose laws had been subjected to outrage. For, they said, they could not endure to live, since their ancestral code was thus wantonly insulted. (Josephus, *Jewish Antiquities* 20.115–116)

That last sentence, present only in the *Antiquities* account, may simply express the depths of their despair or else refer to the tactic of mass unresisting martyrdom seen already. Both versions agree that Cumanus responded by having the soldier executed.

There is even a final incident recorded under Nero, emperor between 54 and 68 C.E., when it was already very late for peaceful protest. It probably happened at Passover of 65 C.E. under Florus, the last governor before the war.

So long as Cestius Gallus remained in Syria discharging his provincial duties, none dared even to send a deputation to him to complain of Florus; but when he visited Jerusalem on the occasion of the feast of unleavened bread, the people pressed round him, and a crowd of not less than three millions implored him to have compassion on the calamities of the nation, and loudly denounced Florus as the ruin of the country. (Josephus, *Jewish War* 2.280)

That last peaceful protest, whose historically incredible numbers bespeak its rhetorically desperate situation, begets but promises, too little and too late.

We have explicit evidence, then, from that preceding section, of seven public protests: one before Archelaus against Herod's legacy in 4 B.C.E., two before Pilate against himself soon after 26 C.E., one more before Petronius against Caligula in 40 to 41 C.E., another two before Cumanus against individual Roman soldiers between 48 and 52 C.E., and a final one before Gallus against Florus in 65 C.E. Only the first and the last ones were socioeconomic in content; all the others were religiopolitical. But, for the ordinary people, religious protest may well have been the only way that social, economic, or political oppression could be challenged. Indeed, what

Jean-Pierre Lémonon points out about the case of the *Iconic Standards* might well be broadened to include all those peaceful protests: Josephus' "insistence on attachment to ancestral traditions hides the anti-Roman character of the Jewish demonstration" (152). In any case, all those demonstrations were nonviolent, all had very specific objectives, and four out of the seven achieved those objectives without loss of life. With Archelaus and Petronius, they won; with Pilate and Cumanus, they won once and lost once, each time; with Gallus and Florus it was too late.

✧ 8 ✧

Magician and Prophet

> New thaumaturgical movements represent a deviant religious
> response—a sectarian religious response—largely because of the
> newness of their ritual procedures and organizational forms.
> They become a protest against traditional religious practice—
> itself highly thaumaturgical—because they pit new measures,
> and (often) new conceptions of social nexus, against the old. As
> a "protest" such new movements are muted comments on the
> inadequacy of previous procedures rather than an articulate
> condemnation. Their practice, however, is often enough to
> make evident at least a temporary rejection of older procedures,
> and of those who control them. . . . Thaumaturgical belief is not
> only the pristine religious orientation, it is also more persistent
> than millennialism. The many little failures of magic are less
> disturbing to believers than the one big periodic failure of the
> millennium, and are more easily explained away.
>
> *Bryan Wilson (192, 492–493)*

In Bryan Wilson's typology of religiopolitical protest among colonized peoples there appear not only thaumaturgical or magical but also millennial or revolutionary prophets, or, more simply, magicians and prophets. Thus, even though the former attempt to change, more immediately, the sorry state of the individual rather than that of the group, it would be unwise to consider them apolitical or neutral. No matter what their individual intentions or explicit proclamations, their activities represent, in many ways, an extremely radical challenge to any established religiopolitical system whether local or colonial. "One possible indication of popular resistance to the idea that the equation resources/needs has been inscribed once and for all in the heavens, and translated on earth in a rigid system of sacred times (calendar) and places (temples), is," according to Gildas Hamel, "the great importance given to 'holy' or 'pious' men. Their deeds, i.e., prayers and miracles, had the particularity of being 'out of season,' or at least outside of the prescribed way of relating to God. They even displayed the hubris towards God (or the Gods) by accepting the danger to their life, or sanity, of an immediate relationship with the divine powers, in return for rains, a cure, or other material benefits" (206)

A word about terminology: Wilson's title for such individuals is *thaumaturge*, and that benefits from the inoffensiveness that accompanies little-used linguistic roots. Geza Vermes, to whose work this chapter is deeply indebted, speaks of the charismatic or the holy man. Once again the terms are quite inoffensive, this time because they are so general and vague. The more ordinary term for what they describe is *magician*, and I prefer to use it despite some obvious problems. The title *magician* is not used here as a pejorative word but describes one who can make divine power present *directly through personal miracle* rather than *indirectly through communal ritual.* Despite an extremely labile continuum between the twin concepts, magic renders transcendental power present concretely, physically, sensibly, tangibly, whereas ritual renders it present abstractly, ceremonially, liturgically, symbolically. Deceit, fakery, and trickery are no doubt possible in either of those situations, but they are no more inevitable or ineluctable in the former than in the latter or in any other religious operations, promises, and procedures. *Magic,* like *myth,* is a word and a process that demands reclamation from the language of sneer and jeer. Magic is used here as a neutral description for an authentic religious phenomenon, and its potential abuse no more destroys its validity than do similar possibilities elsewhere. But if, in the end, the title magician offends, simply substitute thaumaturge, miracle worker, charismatic, holy one, or whatever pleases, but know that we speak of exactly the same activity in any case, namely, personal and individual rather than communal and institutional access to, monopoly of, or control over divine power.

Elijah and Elisha

There is one very special strand of the biblical prophetic tradition that uniquely combines oracular political prophecy and popular individual magic. This is the saga of Elijah and Elisha between 880 and 840 B.C.E. in 1 Kings 16 to 2 Kings 10, which narrates the bloody replacement of Omri's dynasty by that of Jehu and the equally bloody replacement of Baal's worship by that of Yahweh.

That integrated double cycle is, most significantly, a northern tradition, arising soon after the unified monarchy of David and Solomon had split into the separate monarchies of Judah in the south and Israel in the north. Furthermore, especially the Elijah but also the Elisha cycle have deliberate resonances with the Exodus traditions that could be construed as anywhere from anti- to para- to ultra-Mosaic versions.

First, Elijah, for example, is fed miraculously on "a cake baked on hot stones and a jar of water," so that "he arose, and ate and drank, and went in the strength of that food forty days and forty nights to Horeb the mount of God." A journey through the wilderness, miraculous food, and then a meeting with God at Mount Sinai or, as the northern traditions call it, Mount Horeb. And the resemblances or anti-resemblances continue. Compare the twin accounts, as each prophet meets God atop the sacred mountain.

> [For God and Moses] there were thunders and lightnings, and a thick cloud upon the mountain, and a very loud trumpet blast . . . and Mount Sinai was wrapped in smoke, because the Lord descended upon it in fire; and the smoke of it went up like a kiln, and the whole mountain quaked greatly. (Exodus 19:16–19)

> [For God and Elijah] the Lord passed by, and a great and strong wind rent the mountains, and broke in pieces the rocks before the Lord, but the Lord was not in the wind; and after the wind an earthquake, but the Lord was not in the earthquake; and after the earthquake a fire, but the Lord was not in the fire; and after the fire a still small voice. (1 Kings 19:11–12)

But Elijah's "still, small voice" of God, which is almost a deliberate caricature of Moses' great trumpet blast that "grew louder and louder," carried a terrible message in 1 Kings 19:15–18. Elijah is told to appoint Hazael as king of Syria, Jehu as king of Israel, and Elisha as his own successor, "and him who escapes from the sword of Hazael shall Jehu slay; and him who escapes from the sword of Jehu shall Elisha slay." This initial mandate binds the double cycle together as Elijah makes Elisha his disciple in 1 Kings 19:19–21 and then his successor in 2 Kings 2:1–14. And it is Elisha rather than Elijah who establishes the ascendancy of Hazael over Syria and Jehu over Israel in 2 Kings 8:13 and 9:1–3.

Next, that transition from Elijah to Elisha in 2 Kings 2:1–14 took place at the Jordan. Whereas Moses did not even enter the Promised Land but was buried in the midst of Moab, Elijah is taken up to heaven like Enoch. But, beforehand, "Elijah took his mantle, and rolled it up, and struck the water, and the water was parted to the one side and to the other, till the two of them could go over on dry ground." Then, afterward, when Elisha had inherited the mantle and a double share of power, "he took the mantle of Elijah . . . and struck the water . . . and . . . the water was parted to the one side and to the other; and Elisha went over." What God had done for all Israel through Moses at the Red Sea in Exodus 14–15 and through Joshua at the Jordan in Joshua 3 is now done through and for Elijah and Elisha alone.

Finally, Elisha himself, in 2 Kings 3:4–20, obtains miraculous water in the wilderness of Edom for the kings of Israel and Judah as they march against Mesha, king of Moab.

All that Exodus parallelism or anti-parallelism renders Elijah-Elisha the northern equivalent of the Mosaic liberation traditions, which may have been, by now, much too associated with the southern Temple at Jerusalem. But, apart from that, there are two very special features of the northern tradition itself.

There is, first of all, the problem of rain. In Palestine, according to Gildas Hamel's summary, "The rains fall only during the 'rainy season,' i.e., from October to April (mostly in December, January, and February), and never from May 15 to September—three quarters of the rain has normally fallen by the end of February" (209). Across the entire Mediterranean basin, but especially in Palestine, timing, quantity, and quality of rain must work together in delicate harmony. Hours of heavy rain in September, for example, after months of aridity, could wash away topsoil completely. Not too much and not too little; not too soon and not too late. Of course, there were also dangers from wars and pests, but the rains were paramount. Rain was life itself; to control the rain was to control life itself.

When Solomon had completed the Temple at Jerusalem, for example, he prayed at its inauguration,

> When heaven is shut up and there is no rain because they have sinned
> against thee, if they pray toward this place, and acknowledge thy name,
> and turn from their sin, when thou dost afflict them, then hear thou in
> heaven, and forgive the sin of thy servants, thy people Israel . . . and
> grant rain upon the land, which thou hast given to thy people as an
> inheritance. (1 Kings 8:35–36 = 2 Chronicles 7:26–27)

Since the Temple was the link between heaven and earth, it was the place where rain was obtained in answer to fidelity or at least to repentance. But, then, in 1 Kings 17:2, at the start of the Elijah-Elisha saga, Elijah announced, "As the Lord the God of Israel lives, before whom I stand, there shall be neither dew nor rain these years, except by my word." And, in 1 Kings 18:41–45, he proved his miraculous power over the rain. The question lies implicit: is, then, a northern Elijah as good as a southern Temple?

And, secondly, there are the miracles—not just public and communal miracles like control of the rainfall but private and individual miracles that are, it would seem, deliberately intercalated in 1 Kings 17–18 between the start and conclusion of the inaugural rain narrative. Thus, after Elijah announces his control of the rain in 17:1, he is miraculously fed in the desert by ravens in 17:2-7, multiplies the meal and oil of the pagan widow at Sidonian Zarephath in 17:8-16, and raises her son from the dead in 17:17-24. Only then, in 18:1-46, does the rain story conclude. Elijah has been given power by God over rain, food, and death, over, in other words, all of life. There is also a very important footnote to that last miracle. It was clear from the prayer placed on Solomon's lips at the Temple's inauguration that sin and drought were a continuum, the former begetting the latter and the latter certifying the former. So also was there, moving from the communal to the personal, a continuum between sin and sickness or death. The bereaved widow said to Elijah in 1 Kings 17:18, "What have you against me, O man of God? You have come to me to bring my sin to remembrance, and to cause the death of my son!" Whether, therefore, by magic or miracle, by prayer or ritual, by prophet or Temple, control over rain and health was equally control over sin and evil.

Miracles multiply, from the sublime to the ridiculous, as the saga continues with Elisha. There is again the combination of national or even international emphasis side by side with personal and individual emphasis as well. Apart from the miraculous streams in the wilderness of Edom seen already in 2 Kings 3:4-20, there is the cure of Naaman, leprous commander of the Syrian army, in 2 Kings 5:1-19a, the foretelling of the Syrian army's rout in 2 Kings 6-7, and of Hazael's ascendancy to the Syrian throne in 2 Kings 8:7-15. Then, at the other end of the spectrum occur certain miracles of a somewhat more limited nature. Elisha cures contaminated water at Jericho in 2 Kings 2:15-22, curses and has bears kill some taunting youths in 2:23-25, cures contaminated pottage in 4:38-41, multiplies barley loaves in 4:42-44, and makes an iron ax head float on the Jordan in 6:1-7. Finally, there is a set of miracles in 2 Kings 4 that read suspiciously like a variant or developed version of the Elijah set in 1 Kings 17. Elisha multiplies the remnant oil of a poor widow in 4:1-7, promises a son to a wealthy but barren woman whose husband was old in 4:8-17, and then raises the late-born son from the dead in 4:18-37.

The Elijah-Elisha saga establishes a northern tradition of prophecy quite different from the better-known southern one. They are not just prophets of deed as well as word. It is rather that their deeds operate not only on the national and international or communal and corporate plane, they also operate on the private, personal, and individual level. And they heal not only the very rich but also the very poor. Above all, they combine magic and prophecy, and, as prophetic magicians or magical prophets, they continue, develop, and enlarge a combination already present in the inaugural Mosaic model.

Magicians Rabbinized

Those stories about Elijah and Elisha as prophetic magicians find no continuing tradition within the Hebrew Bible itself. The reason is obvious: the Temple, with its priesthood, was the place where sins were forgiven, rains were guaranteed, and healings were possible. But, at least by the centuries immediately before and after the common era, there is evidence that miraculous making of rain and miraculous healing of body were still a live tradition. But just as, throughout this second part of the book, I am usually reading the Josephan corpus against itself, so, in this specific section, I am reading the rabbinical corpus against itself. Also, I am using the simplest form of transcription for Hebrew names and titles, even when citing from scholarly works that use more complicated formats.

Honi in the Circle

In 65 B.C.E., with the Hasmonean dynasty stumbling toward its own destruction by rival claimants, Hyrcanus II, one of the two sons of Alexander Jannaeus, had besieged the other son, Aristobulus II, in the Temple. Josephus tells this story about Honi or, as he calls him, Onias.

> Now there was a certain Onias, who, being a righteous man and dear to God, had once in a rainless period prayed to God to end the drought, and God had heard his prayer and sent rain; this man hid himself when he saw that the civil war continued to rage, but was taken to the camp of the Jews and was asked to place a curse on Aristobulus and his fellow-rebels, just as he had, by his prayers, put an end to the rainless period. But when in spite of his refusals and excuses he was forced to speak by the mob, he stood up in their midst and said: "O God, king of the universe, since these men standing beside me are Thy people, and those who are besieged are Thy priests, I beseech Thee not to hearken to them against these men nor to bring to pass what these men ask Thee to do to those others." And when he had prayed in this manner the villains among the Jews who stood round him stoned him to death.
> (Josephus, *Jewish Antiquities* 14.22–24)

Notice how Josephus emphasizes prayer rather than magic, and he, of course, is much in favor of not cursing priests imprisoned by besiegers in the Temple! Honi's refusal cost him his life, but it is with the earlier, rainmaking activity that I am primarily concerned here. It is that which recalls the tradition of Elijah.

That earlier miracle is told in greater detail in the *Mishnah*, the official codification of rabbinic law produced in Palestine around the year 200 C.E. by Judah the Patriarch. That title comes from a verb meaning "to repeat," that is, to study and pass on a tradition, a root that also names those "repeaters" who did so in the two preceding centuries as *tannaim*. It contains sixty-three tractates organized into six orders or divisions but is quoted by tractate only.

The story in *Mishnah, Taanith* 3:8, can now be studied with a methodology enormously refined from the study of Adolf Büchler in 1922 (196–264), through that of Geza Vermes in 1973 (1981:69–72), to the brilliant application of Jacob Neusner's methods by William Scott Green in 1979. I follow Green's analysis very closely below and begin with his insight that, since this is the only miracle recorded of preceding sages in the *Mishnah* and since "the power to perform miracles had little place in early rabbinic Judaism" (628), it requires careful stratigraphic study to see why it is there at all.

Here is the text, in my slightly simplified version of Green's alphabetical presentation and with some explanatory inserts added in square brackets.

A. They sound (the shofar) on account of any calamity which may befall the community, except for too much rain [lest it betray doubt that God, against his own promise in Genesis 9:8–17, might flood the earth once again].

B. Once they said to Honi the Circle-maker, "Pray so that rains will fall."

C. He said to them, "Go out and bring in the Passover ovens so that they will not melt."

D. And he prayed, but rains did not fall.

E. He made a circle and stood inside it.

F. And he said, "Master (of the Universe), your children have turned their faces to me because I am like a son of the house before you.

G. I swear by your Great Name that I am not moving from here until you have mercy on your children."

H. The rains began to drip.

I. He said, "I did not ask for this, but for rains of (sufficient amount to fill) cisterns, ditches, and caves."

J. They fell with vehemence.

K. He said, "I did not ask for this, but for rains of benevolence, blessing, and graciousness."

L. They fell as he ordered them,

M. until Israel went up from Jerusalem to the Temple Mount because of the rains.

N. They said to him, "Just as you prayed for them to fall, so pray for them to cease."

O. He said to them, "Go out and see if the Stone of Strayers has been washed away [and only with such a flood, would I dare pray for them to cease!]."

P. Simeon b. Shetah sent (a message) to him.

Q. He said to him, "You deserve to be excommunicated but what shall I do to you? For you act petulantly before the Omnipresent like a son who acts petulantly before his father, yet he does his will.

R. And concerning you Scripture says, 'Let your father and mother be glad, and let him who bore you rejoice'" (Proverbs 23:25).

(*Mishnah, Taanith* 3:8; Green 626–627)

It is necessary to separate at least three major and successive layers in that text, possibly more sublayers, but at least the three main ones.

First, there is the core of the text and its oldest stratum in the Honi tradition at C, E–L. That must have had some opening phrase, but, as we shall see, it is now lost forever behind that later B. In any case, and however the request was formulated, it received in C a magnificently certain and absolutely secure response: Get ready for lots of rain! And, by the way, that Passover dating is significant, for, as Gildas Hamel noted, "Nisan (April) was the month of the last rain . . . this spring rain was of decisive importance for the harvest because it caused the heads of wheat to form and develop" (213). Originally C proceeded directly into E–L, whose triadic construction obviates any possibility of coincidence and proves the precision of Honi's control over the rain. It also introduces a playful note into the process, for Honi is like a firstborn son or heir apparent with whom God interacts quite differently than with his other children. But it is the magical circle and the oath of immobility that constrains God to act lest, without rain, Honi perjure himself by departure and God be instrumental in his crime. We begin, in other words, with what William Scott Green termed an "ancient Jewish magical rite" (635).

Next, however, there is PQR, the first step in the rabbinization of a magician. The Honi tradition may have been too powerfully popular to ignore, so, despite the rabbinic dislike for miracles and magic, a first attempt at absorption was made by appending PQR to the earlier C, E–L. The subunit in PQ gives a grudging and ambiguous acceptance of Honi's exceptional action. But in having excommunication threatened by Simeon ben Shetah, a contemporary Pharisee whom later rabbinical tradition considered among its forebears, Honi himself becomes "a member of the Pharisaic, and by extension, the rabbinic group" (Green 638). And the second subunit, the text from Proverbs 23:25, brings Honi within the approval of Scripture itself. I find it hard to imagine that the rabbis would ever have passed on the Honi tradition without some cauterization such as PQR, and I find it unnecessary to postulate any separate existence for PQR apart from such prophylaxis. The unit in C, E–L and PQR redeems Honi's person by bringing him within Pharisaism and Scripture, but much more is still needed to redeem his action.

The third stratum is the entire A–R unit. The opening, in A, gives the subject under legal discussion. But this is not really taken up until MNO, which explains that, while one can pray for rain to start, one should not pray for it to cease. That these frames had originally nothing whatsoever to do with the story of Honi is clear from internal and external indications. Internally, Honi had just obtained a perfectly appropriate and adequate rainfall in E–L and not the destructive downpour presumed in MNO. Externally, that same piece of MNO tradition appears in the *Tosefta* or "supplement" to the *Mishnah,* which is organized in parallel orders and tractates but contains interpretations that are *baraita* or "external" to that authoritative collection. This parallel collection of rabbinic law was published after the *Mishnah* probably toward the end of the third century C.E. In the present case, it contains an independent version of the MNO unit.

> A. To a certain pious man (*hasid*) did they say, "Pray, so it will rain."
> B. He prayed and it rained.
> C. They said to him, "Just as you have prayed so it would rain, now pray so the rain will go away."
> D. He said to them, "Go and see if a man is standing on Keren Ofel [a high rock] and splashing his foot in the Qidron Brook. [Then] we shall pray that the rain will stop.
> E. Truly it is certain that the Omnipresent will never again bring a flood to the world,
> F. For it is said, *There will never again be a flood* (Genesis 9:11)."
> (*Tosefta, Taanith* 2:13; Neusner ad locum)

There, with prayer and not magic, and with prayer to start but not to stop, is the proper rabbinical ideal personified by the *hasidim,* ultra-pietistic observers of the law, "figures characterized in rabbinic literature by their ethical supererogation and extreme legal practices" (Green 631).

But Honi was no *hasid,* and the prayer of Honi was not pietistic but magical, or, better, it was not prayer at all but magic. The request for prayer in B of the *Mishnah* account is closely parallel to that in A of the *Tosefta* account, and although, recalling Josephus' version, it is always possible that they asked for prayer and obtained magic, it is probably better to consider that an earlier opening request is now replaced by that B. But, in the present *Mishnah* composition, the serenity of C is construed as arrogance, and the prayer, in the first half of D, is refused by God in the second half. Notice, however, that from B through D to MNO, Honi's action has now become prayer. If, in the second stratum, there was an ambiguous approval for his magic, that magic has now, by the third stratum, become completely transmuted into prayer.

Further details about Honi are supplied in the two *Talmuds*, works that contain units of *Mishnah* and consequent *Gemara*, that is, "completion" or commentary by the *amoraim* or "speakers" of the centuries after its completion. The *Yerushalmi*, also known as the *Jerusalem* or *Palestinian Talmud*, was compiled in Palestine in the early fifth century C.E. and comments on thirty-nine of the *Mishnah*'s sixty-three tractates. The *Babli*, also known as the *Babylonian Talmud*, was compiled in Babylon between the fifth and seventh centuries C.E., and, although it comments on only thirty-six and a half tractates of the *Mishnah*, it is between three and four times as long as the *Yerushalmi*.

First of all, that entire appropriation process comes to a fitting consummation in the *Babylonian Talmud*, where Honi is further rabbinized, at *Taanith* 23a, in several different ways. In recording the *Mishnah* story, the circle is now glossed as a fulfillment of Habakkuk 2:1, "I will take my stand to watch, and station myself on the tower"; he is twice addressed as "Rabbi"; he claims, in proper rabbinical style, that "I have received a tradition"; and he participates in the sacrificial ritual of the Temple in order to stop the excessive rainfall. Or, again, his actions fulfill Job 22:28–30, "You will decide on a matter, and it will be established for you, and light will shine on your ways. For God abases the proud, but he saves the lowly. He delivers the innocent man; you will be delivered through the cleanness of your hands." And, best of all, he is shown as meditating on Psalm 126:1, "When the Lord restored the fortunes of Zion, we were like those who dream," so that "when he came to the House of Study he would explain to the rabbis all their difficulties." It is also worth noting that, in glossing the *Mishnah*'s statement that Honi acted toward God like a petulant son, this expanded version adds,

> Thus he says to him, Father [Abba] take me to bathe in warm water [and he does], wash me in cold water [and he does], give me nuts, almonds, peaches, and pomegranates and he gives them unto him. (*Babylonian Talmud, Taanith* 23a; Epstein ad locum)

That is the first of only two times when God is addressed as "Abba" in rabbinical literature; the second we shall see in a moment.

Finally, we hear of two grandsons continuing the Honi tradition of miraculous rainmaking, and that brings the tradition well into the first century C.E. One story concerns Honi's son's son, Abba Hilkiah. When the scholars come to ask him "to pray for rain," he goes through a most complicated series of acts, all of which are later explained away as virtue rather than magic. And, before they even get to present their request,

He said to his wife, I know the scholars have come on account of rain,
let us go up to the roof and pray, perhaps the Holy One, Blessed be He,
will have mercy and rain will fall, without having credit given to us.
(*Babylonian Talmud, Taanith* 23ab; Epstein ad locum)

The other story concerns Honi's daughter's son, Hanan ha-Nehba, and
once again there is a strong negation of personal power or individual magic.

> A. Hanan ha-Nehba was the son of the daughter of Honi the Circle-
> Drawer. When the world was in need of rain, the Rabbis would send him
> school children and they would take hold of the hem of his garment and
> say to him, Father, Father [Abba, Abba], give us rain.
> B. Thereupon he would plead with the Holy One, Blessed be He,
> [thus], Master of the Universe, do it for the sake of these who are unable
> to distinguish between the Father [Abba] who gives rain and the father
> [abba] who does not. (*Babylonian Talmud, Taanith* 23b; Epstein ad
> locum)

The combination of B and A looks like another appropriation device.
In A there is no mention of prayer and Hanan is approached exactly the
way Honi was in the earliest strata of his tradition. But the presence of B
explicitly differentiates between the magical power of Hanan and the
divine power of God. That is also the second and final time that God is
addressed as "Abba" in rabbinical literature. Both cases are in the context of
miracle workers and their imperious, childlike control of the divine power.

Honi the magician, then, had been progressively metamorphosed into
Pharisee, *hasid,* and rabbi. And, if by the time of the *Mishnah,* the magician
had become a rabbi among rabbis, by the time of the *Babylonian Talmud,*
he had become a rabbi above rabbis, "a master of rabbinic law, the greatest
sage of his generation" (Green 646). Notice, of course, that neither Honi
nor his two grandsons are ever explicitly called "Rabbi" in those texts.

Two separate but equally important points derive from the perdurance
of that rabbinized magician, Honi the Circle-Maker. He was probably a
peasant, but his magic was too powerfully present and had moved, at least
by the story of his death, from the Little into the Great Tradition. It could
not be ignored or avoided but had to be included and co-opted. Next, and
above all, "the power to bring rain, formerly the prerogative of the priests
and the cult, now became the function of the rabbi and his Torah . . . The
inclusion in Mishnah of the account of a popular rain-maker and the transformation of him into a rabbi would have been one way of documenting the
claim that the new religion of the rabbis had superseded the old religion of
the priests" (Green 641). All of this forcibly emphasizes that, for priests, for

rabbis, or for any institutionalized remedy for moral and natural disaster, the individual prophetic or charismatic magician always poses an implicit problem about validity that could readily escalate into an ideological challenge about legitimacy.

Hanina, Man of Deed

In considering Hanina ben Dosa, a miracle worker who lived, like Jesus of Nazareth, prior to the destruction of the Second Temple in the first century C.E., there is again the necessity for rigorous stratigraphic methodology in studying the rabbinical texts. I am building here on the preliminary work of Geza Vermes (1981:72–80), who has gathered together the major texts in one convenient location (1972–73a), but especially on the more stringent analyses of Seán Freyne (1980b) and Baruch Bokser (1985). I am also extending the principles and conclusions of Bill Green's research on the Honi traditions to the Hanina ones as well. In charting their general trajectory I presuppose two major rabbinical motivations. First, *magic must become prayer*, and, second, *magician must become rabbi*. Only when and if those processes are accomplished will a major magician survive within the rabbinical corpus. Minor magicians, of course, can be safely ignored.

The parameters of the problem may be seen by looking at two units concerning Hanina in the *Mishnah*.

> When R. Hanina ben Dosa died, men of good deeds [or: men of might, workers of miracles] ceased. (*Mishnah, Sotah* 9:15; Danby 306)

> They tell of R. Hanina ben Dosa that he used to pray over the sick and say, "This one will live," or " This one will die." They said to him, "How knowest thou?" He replied, "If my prayer is fluent in my mouth, I know that he is accepted; and if it is not I know that he is rejected." (*Mishnah, Berakoth* 5:5; Danby 6)

Note that, from the very beginning and when first we meet him, he is already called a rabbi, but this is simply the most obvious feature of the rabbinization process. "Despite attempts to insinuate the contrary," notes Vermes, "it is likely that Hanina was not a rabbi, a professional religious teacher" (1972–73a:62). "It seems very improbable," agrees Freyne, "that Hanina ever functioned as a Rabbi in the restricted sense of propounder of halachic teaching—the normal meaning of the title after 70 C.E." (1980b:224). On the other hand, Freyne is more correct than Vermes in maintaining "that 'man of deed' should be differentiated from *hasid*, and that in regard to Hanina the tendency was to assimilate the two roles" (1980b:238). "Indeed," according to Dennis Berman, summarizing his own doctoral dissertation, "the sources carefully distinguish between hasidim and 'men of deed.'" The man of deed is the miracle worker or magician, but "the hasid is zealous in ritual observance and scrupulous in his conduct; he is intensely devout and perfectly righteous . . . [he] is also an ideal of the active life, but he is distinguished by his radicalism, spiritual fervor and zeal for the law" (17, 20). To term Hanina, or Honi, a *hasid* is simply part of the rabbinization process and should not be followed by contemporary analysis.

In that first Mishnaic quotation, then, Hanina is hyperbolically praised as the greatest among "men of deed." He was, according to Vermes, in disagreement with both Büchler and Safrai, "not a social worker or promoter of public welfare (for which, incidentally, no evidence appears in the sources), but, as has been long believed, the most celebrated miracle-worker in rabbinic Judaism" (1972-73a:39).

The second quotation, however, neatly subjects magic to prayer and Hanina to heaven. Hanina, in the words of Vermes, "humbly asserts that if the words of his prayer are not his own, but are placed in his mouth by God, they are efficacious. If, on the other hand, inspiration is lacking and no healing words emerge, there is no cure for none is intended by heaven" (1972-73a:30). I am, however, much less sure than Vermes about the originality of that attribution (1972-73a:49). According to *Tosefta, Berakoth* 3:3, "R. Aqiba says, 'If one's prayer is fluent, this is a good sign for him. But if not, it is a bad sign for him'" (Neusner ad locum). I consider it much more likely that a saying of Rabbi Akiba was used to rabbinize Hanina than that an authentic Hanina saying was transferred to Akiba.

That establishes the guiding line for my analysis: a man of deed must be translated into a man of prayer; healings must be subjected to heaven in ways acceptable to the rabbinical tradition. But since the Hanina traditions are far more numerous and diverse than the Honi ones, I place my main emphasis on two cases in which multiple versions of the same incident are recorded and where at least a segment of the trajectory can be most plausibly reconstructed. Notice, however, that I determine that sequence not by successive dates along a documentary trajectory but by successive stages along a rabbinization trajectory.

The Distant Child

The central theme in the first stream of tradition is the relationship between Hanina and a distant and endangered child. Here, following my heuristic principle of magic becoming prayer, is the earliest recoverable version, the earliest retrievable stage along the rabbinization trajectory.

A. Our Rabbis taught: It happened that the daughter of Nehonia the digger of wells [to provide water for the pilgrims who traveled to Jerusalem on the three festivals] once fell into a big pit. When people came and informed R. Hanina b. Dosa (about it), during the first hour he said to them "She is well," during the second he said to them, "She is still well," but in the third hour he said to them, "She has by now come out (of the pit)."

B. They then asked her, "Who brought you up?"—Her answer was: "A ram (providentially) came to my help with an old man leading it."

C. They then asked R. Hanina b. Dosa, "Are you a prophet?" He said to them, "I am neither a prophet, nor the son of a prophet. I only exclaimed: Shall the thing to which that pious man has devoted his labour become a stumbling-block to his seed?"

D. R. Aha, however, said: Nevertheless, his son died of thirst, (thus bearing out what the Scripture says), *And it shall be very tempestuous round about him,* [Psalm 50:3] which teaches that the Holy One, blessed be He, is particular with those round about Him even for matters as light as a single hair. (*Babylonian Talmud, Baba Kamma* 50a = *Yebamoth* 121b; Epstein ad locos)

Notice that in A there is no mention whatsoever of prayer. Further, it is not clear whether Hanina miraculously saved her or miraculously announced that she had been normally saved by others. In any case, BCD are somewhat biting attempts to contain the miracle. In B the girl is saved by Abraham and Isaac from Genesis 22 and not by Hanina, a fact under-lined in the parallel *Yebamoth* 121b version, whose only significant differ-ence is that it has Hanina himself ask the girl this question. In C she is saved by a general providential incongruity and not by Hanina. Nehonia, by the way, is presumably the individual, in *Mishnah, Shekalim* 5:1, described as "the trench-digger" (Danby 157). Further, Hanina, citing Amos 7:14, admits he is no prophet. Finally, in D, the Babylonian and Amoraic Rabbi Aha bar Jacob deflates the whole tradition. Lest the preservation of Honi's daughter from death by drowning, that is, too much water, impugn the sovereign freedom of God, he asserts that his son died of the opposite fate, death by thirst, too little water. As usual, of course, Hanina is already called a rabbi.

What is most striking about that complex is that three separate anti-Hanina codicils in BCD are appended to the story in A before it was accept-able. But they are all external additions, so we can still see the original story without any internal editorialization. And we can see what bothered the rabbis so much about it: there is no mention of prayer either requested or furnished.

The second stage in the development of the Distant Child tradition replaces Nehonia with Johanan ben Zakkai and thus brings Hanina into close conjunction with the founder and first leader of the rabbinical academy at Jamnia or Yavneh. It also moves us into the politics of Yavneh as the rabbis regrouped in that Judean coastal town after the Second Temple's destruction in 70 C.E.

> A. On another occasion it happened that R. Hanina b. Dosa went to study Torah with R. Johanan ben Zakkai. The son of R. Johanan ben Zakkai fell ill. He said to him: Hanina my son, pray for him that he may live. He put his head between his knees and prayed for him and he lived.
>
> B. Said R. Johanan ben Zakkai: If Ben Zakkai had stuck his head between his knees for the whole day, no notice would have been taken of him.
>
> C. Said his wife to him: Is Hanina greater than you are? He replied to her: No; but he is like a servant [who has permission to go at any time] before the king, and I am like a nobleman [who has permission to go only at fixed times] before the king. (*Babylonian Talmud, Berakoth* 34b; Epstein ad locum)

There is a perfectly even balance maintained in A. Hanina is student and "son" of Johanan but performs a miracle at his request. And, like a good rabbi, he studies Torah and responds through prayer. B, however, introduces an invidious comparison against Johanan, and C, in rebuttal, counters with a like one against Hanina. Note, in passing, that Hanina's posture recalls Elijah's on Mount Carmel in 1 Kings 18:42: "he bowed himself down upon the earth, and put his face between his knees." Was that, by the way, magic or prayer?

There is, of course, absolutely no biographical data contained in that incident either about Hanina's rabbinical study or Johanan's saved son, and it is extremely unwise to draw either chronological or geographical conclusions from it. The point of the Johanan miracle is to rephrase the pre–70 C.E. Nehonia story in a post–70 C.E. Yavnian environment wherein magician and rabbi must be harmonized. But, once again, the controversial nature of Hanina is emphasized by the BC codicils appended to the delicately balanced A.

The third stage of the traditions' development has two substages within it, and their comparison is also very instructive. Once again we are immersed in rabbinical politics, on the presumption that Rabban Gamaliel is not Gamaliel I from the pre–70 C.E. period but "Gamaliel II, the teacher who ousted Yohanan ben Zakkai from the presidency at Yavneh and dominated the Palestinian scene in the late first and early second century"

(Vermes 1972–73a:59). His supporters still needed to absorb Hanina, so they deliberately retold the Nehonia story but now with Gamaliel II replacing Yohanan ben Zakkai. Here is the first stage in that absorption.

> It happened that Rabban Gamaliel's son fell ill, and he sent two pupils to R. Hanina ben Dosa in his town. He said to them: Wait until I go to the upper room. He went to the upper room, then came down. He said to them: I am assured that Rabban Gamaliel's son has now recovered from his illness. They noted (the time). In that hour he asked for food. (*Palestinian Talmud, Berakoth* 9d; Vermes 1972–73a:31)

Notice, immediately, that there is no mention of prayer in that unit, although, of course, one could presume that prayer was what was happening in the upper room. That absence is, however, safely muted by its attachment to *Mishnah, Berakoth* 5:5, where, as we saw, Hanina's magic was safely rabbinized as God-controlled prayer.

Whatever inadequacies are still present in that first substage are more than compensated by the second substage of this third level in the development of the Distant Child tradition. Here is that version, which, incidentally, is placed just before the Johanan version in the *Babylonian Talmud*.

> A. Our Rabbis taught: Once the son of R. Gamaliel fell ill. He sent two scholars to R. Hanina b. Dosa to ask him to pray for him. When he saw them he went up to an upper chamber and prayed for him. When he came down he said to them: Go, the fever has left him;
>
> B. They said to him: Are you a prophet? He replied: I am neither a prophet nor the son of a prophet, but I have learnt this from experience. If my prayer is fluent in my mouth, I know that he [the sick man] is accepted; but if not, I know that he is rejected.
>
> C. They sat down and made a note of the exact moment. When they came to R. Gamaliel, he said to them: By the temple service! You have not been a moment too soon or too late, but so it happened; at that very moment the fever left him and he asked for water to drink. (*Babylonian Talmud, Berakoth* 34b; Epstein ad locum)

Compare, first of all, that AC unit with the preceding substage in *Palestinian Talmud, Berakoth* 9d. Here, prayer is both explicitly requested and explicitly accorded. Next, in B, the unit about prayer fluency from *Mishnah, Berakoth* 5:5, which had explicitly subjected Hanina's prayer to the discretion of God, is interpolated inside the story replacing the externally appended C unit ("Are you a prophet?") from the original Nehonia story in *Babylonian Talmud, Baba Kamma* 50a. The magician is now securely rabbinized and securely associated with the great Rabbi Gamaliel II.

The Lizard's Bite

I begin discussion of the Lizard's Bite with a unit in the *Mishnah* that does not concern Hanina in any way. It speaks of the concentration at prayer practiced by any fervent *hasid*.

> The pious men of old [*hasidim*] used to wait an hour before they said the Tefillah [the Eighteen Benedictions], that they might direct their heart to God. Even if the king salutes a man he may not return the greeting; and even if a snake was twisted around his heel he may not interrupt his prayer. (Mishnah, *Berakoth* 5:1; Danby 5)

But then, in a much later document, there occurs a piece of tradition about Hanina, and here, despite assimilations, we can still see the original story that began the development of the Lizard's Bite tradition.

> A. Our Rabbis taught: In a certain place there was once a lizard [*arvad*] which used to injure people. They came and told R. Hanina b. Dosa. He said to them: Show me its hole. They showed him its hole, and he put his heel over the hole, and the lizard came out and bit him, and it died.
> B. He put it on his shoulder
> C. and brought it to the Beth ha-Midrash and said to them: See, my sons, it is not the lizard that kills, it is sin that kills!
> D. On that occasion they said: Woe to the man whom a lizard meets, but woe to the lizard which R. Hanina b. Dosa meets! (*Babylonian Talmud, Berakoth* 33a; Epstein ad locum)

In AD, first of all, as Baruch Bokser has emphasized, "the issue is not concentration in prayer but a community in danger," and "the account exemplifies one type of 'miracle story,' familiar from the Hebrew Bible, the New Testament, and other literature. Such stories have three elements: (a) a problem that is brought to the attention of a person who can help; (b) the person's 'superhuman' or miraculous response; and (c) the miraculous removal of the problem" (69–70). And the type usually ends with some laudatory response from those saved. Next, and on the other hand, there are two problems with the presence of BC. One is that, as Bokser again notes, it "interpolates a routine moralizing point . . . [and] it breaks the sequence" between miracle in A and admiration in D. Another, and more serious difficulty is that "it destroys the plot line of a simple miracle story, for if the problem is caused by people's sins, anyone can rescue the community and Hanina—known for his wondrous actions—is not needed" (70). I presume, therefore, that BC is an intrusive moralistic rabbinization with a possible reference to Genesis 3. But that interpretation brings up a final consideration. The *arvad* or *havarbar* was a doubly impure creature since it fell, in any case, under the prescription of Leviticus 11:29 and was also, according to legend, the hybrid offspring of snake and lizard. And Hanina's lizard was now dead, which made it triply impure. Why would the rabbis have had him carry this triply impure object into the house of study? My proposal is that B was already in the tradition. In other words, what the serenely unrabbinical Hanina did was carry around on his shoulders the proof of his victory and the evidence of his magic. He may even have himself proclaimed those twin woes whose aphoristic nature rendered them most memorable. The rabbis, then, confronted with ABD, did their best by inserting C, which probably only made the matter worse. In summary, therefore, ABD was powerful magic, and it would take much more than the intrusion of C to rabbinize it adequately.

The second and much more successful step in appropriating the Lizard's Bite tradition occurs as injunctions to prayerful concentration, such as those in *Mishnah, Berakoth* 5:1, are exemplified by an adaptation of the Hanina story.

> A. One who was standing and reciting the Prayer in a camp or in a wide highway—
>
> B. lo, he may move aside to allow an ass, an ass-driver or a wagon-driver to pass in front of him, but he may not interrupt [his recitation of the Prayer].
>
> C. They related about R. Haninah b. Dosa that once while he was reciting the Prayer, a poisonous lizard [*arvad*] bit him, but he did not interrupt [his recitation].
>
> D. His students went and found it [the lizard] dead at the entrance to its hole.
>
> E. They said, "Woe to the man who is bitten by a lizard. Woe to the lizard that bites Ben Dosa." (*Tosefta, Berakoth* 3:20; Neusner ad locum)

Notice a few details in this second stage. The lizard is still an *arvad*, thus keeping a closer linguistic link with the original miracle story. The prayer that Hanina was reciting was the Tefillah, that is "'prayer' *par excellence*, the 'Shemoneh Esreh,' or the 'Eighteen Benedictions'" (Danby 796). Hanina has students like any other good rabbi. The lizard dead at its hole rather than immediately is somewhat strange, but at least impurity is lessened by not having it die while touching his heel. And in this one case he is simply called "ben Dosa" and not the usual "Rabbi Hanina ben Dosa" (Vermes 1972–73a:340).

The third stage of the tradition's development effects a much closer conjunction between *Mishnah, Berakoth* 5:1 and the Hanina story, but it is also much more critical of Hanina himself. I cite a simplified version of Bokser's translation, but note that the word lizard is now *havarbar* rather than *arvad*.

A. Even if a snake is coiled around his heel, he should not interrupt [= *Mishnah, Berakoth* 5:1] ...

B–D [Scorpions? Snakes not coiled but approaching?]

E. It is taught, (If) one stood and prayed in the road or broad way, lo he passes before the ass and before the wagon, so long as he does not interrupt his tefillah [recall *Tosefta, Berakoth* 3:20]

F. They said concerning R. Hanina ben Dosa that (once) he stood and prayed,

G. and a *lizard* came and bit him, and he did not interrupt his tefillah.

H. And they went and found that lizard dead lying upon the mouth of its hole.

I. They said, "Woe to the person whom a lizard has bitten, Woe to the lizard that has bitten R. Hanina ben Dosa."

J. What is the nature of the lizard?

K. When it injures a human, if the human reaches water first, the lizard dies. And if the lizard reaches water first, the human dies.

L. His students said to him, "Master, did you not feel (anything)?"

M. He said to them "Let (evil) befall me — as my heart was concentrated on the tefillah — if I felt (anything)."

N. Said R. Ishaq b. Eleazar, The Holy One Praised be He created a spring under the soles of his feet to fulfill that which has been written, "He fulfills the wishes of those who fear Him; He hears their cries and saves them." (Psalm 145:19)

(*Palestinian Talmud, Berakoth* 9a; Bokser 55–56)

The essential step is now the conjunction of A and F–I. In H, however, there are now no disciples, but in I Hanina is given his full name and title. The Aramaic addition in JK deflates the whole miracle. He must have, like anyone else, simply got to water in time. Not special magic but general medicine was at work. The second addition in LM could be more neutral, simply underlining the theme of prayerful concentration. But at the same time it removed any idea of magical certitude or miraculous confidence. Finally, N, accepting the popular medicine of JK, underlines that God was in charge of the operation and saved Hanina by making water miraculously available right under his heel.

There are obvious similarities in the processing of the Distant Child and the Lizard's Bite traditions. Both cases start with no mention of prayer, and both cases end with it emphasized. And in both cases there are contradictory tendencies on how to handle Hanina, whether to debunk and deny his magic or to absorb and appropriate it. It is neither safe nor easy to rabbinize a magician.

Those two cases will have to suffice for now because, although there are about a dozen other miracles told of Hanina, including an Aramaic sevenfold set redolent of small village life and small village magic in *Babylonian Talmud, Taanith* 24b–25a, those other cases do not furnish multiple attestations that allow clear glimpses of the rabbinization trajectory. The first miracle of that catena may serve as conclusion.

> A. R. Hanina ben Dosa was journeying on the road when it began to rain. He exclaimed: Master of the Universe, the whole world is at ease, but Hanina is in distress; the rain then ceased. When he reached home he exclaimed: Master of the Universe, the whole world is in distress and Hanina is at ease; whereupon rain fell.
>
> B. (With reference to this incident) R. Joseph remarked: Of what avail was the prayer of the High Priest (on the Day of Atonement) against that of R. Hanina ben Dosa? (*Babylonian Talmud, Taanith* 24b *Yoma* 53b; Epstein ad locos)

No doubt A could be construed as prayer, but it also places Hanina on a par with all the rest of the universe in the sight of God. In any case, B makes the prayer explicit, and, with Hanina safely within the rabbinical fold, it is quite willing to exalt him over the long-gone high priest. The question in B is, however, the eternal question posed by charism to institution and by individual magic to communal ritual.

The Magician as Type

Throughout this second section of the book, and whether talking of protesters, prophets, bandits, messiahs, or revolutionaries, there are clearly enough examples of each to establish them as types of lower-class protagonists in first-century Palestine. But Honi, his two grandsons, and Hanina, four magicians in two centuries — and even granting the Elijah-Elisha tradition as background — seem rather scant evidence for a perduring type.

Geza Vermes has made a strong case for a "holy man" or *hasid* tradition within "charismatic Judaism," a specifically northern or Galilean tradition stemming from Elijah and Elisha, and including not only Honi and Hanina, but Jesus of Nazareth as well (1981:58–82). I consider this a profoundly correct framework for discussion, but, in order to use it, I need also to prune it back a little. First of all, the title *hasid* is not appropriate, since ultra-strict observance of the law does not seem at all part of the constitutive identity of these wonder workers. Terms such as *hasid* or *rabbi* and emphases on prayer or legal observance are all part of the rabbinization process necessary to have these popular and famous magicians included in the rabbinical corpus. But we *are* dealing with a type of wonder worker who operates with certain and secure divine authority not mediated through or dependent on the normal forms, rituals, and institutions through which that divine power usually operates. Next is the question of its predominantly northern or Galilean base. This is certain, of course, for Elijah and Elisha, and, despite their present neutralized position within a southern literary complex, one still senses a basic tension with the Mosaic tradition and possibly with the Temple establishment. And links with the Elijah-Elisha tradition appear among those later wonder workers: Honi brings rain using a circle, as Elisha did in two *separate* miracles on Mount Carmel, the rain in 1 Kings 18:41–45 and the circular trench around the altar in 18:30–38; Hanina prays with his head between his knees in *Babylonian Talmud, Berakoth* 34b, just as Elijah did in 1 Kings 18:42; and he controls the rain in *Babylonian Talmud, Taanith* 24b = *Yoma* 53b, just as Elijah and the Honi family had done. I prefer, however, not to restrict this tradition's later development to a strictly northern provenance since the evidence concerning Honi and Hanina is very doubtful. Indeed, once the healings, multiplications, and even miraculous trivializations of the Elijah and Elisha stories were made part of the Great Tradition, it would be much more difficult to erase magic completely from the Little Tradition, in the north or in the south, or anywhere else in the Jewish world. I presume, therefore, that Jewish magic and miracle working were widespread on the popular and oral levels among the lower classes and that the few detailed cases we know indicate only those most famous figures whose appropriation and absorption was deemed necessary for rabbinical ascendancy. The others are lost to history forever because they did not impinge as curiosities, problems, or values on the upper-class writers, as did, for example, the protesters and prophets, the bandits, messiahs, and revolutionaries who fill out this second section of the book.

In all of this the point is not really Galilee against Jerusalem but the far more fundamental dichotomy of magician as personal and individual power against priest or rabbi as communal and ritual power. Before the Second Temple's destruction, it was magician against Temple, thereafter magician against rabbi. And that opposition could extend all the way from the most implicit to the most explicit. It might well happen that some magicians would not even feel that tension while others might programmatically announce it. But just as we shall later see bandits implicitly challenging the *legitimacy* of political power, so magicians implicitly challenge the *legitimacy* of spiritual power. If a magician's power can bring rain, for what do you need the power of temple priesthood or rabbinical academy?

To Perform the Millennial Dream

Richard Horsley distinguished three different types of prophecy, exegetical, oracular, and millennial, in Josephus (1985, 1986c). The first two are, respectively, elitist and popular, but it is with that third variety that I am concerned at the moment. First of all, however, I warn against presuming that elitist apocalypticism or aristocratic prophecy are the only versions of those genres around. There is also peasant apocalyptic, there is also popular prophecy.

"I am tempted," Jonathan Z. Smith admits, "to describe apocalypticism as *wisdom lacking a royal patron*," and he hopes that "definition . . . will serve at least to question both the 'lachrymose theory' of apocalypticism as growing out of a situation of general persecution and the popular recent theory that it reflects lower-class interests" (1975:149). There is a very serious problem with that formulation. He is absolutely correct, and indeed redundantly correct, to insist that all our Near Eastern texts stem from elitist sources. Ancient literate or scribal millennialism is necessarily elitist. But were there no other forms of apocalypticism in the ancient Near East, no popular or illiterate millennialism? We must at least envision twin modes of the millennial dream, one literate and one illiterate, one of words and one of deeds, one for the upper and one for the lower classes, one for scribes and one for peasants. If we envision twin modes, we will look for them; if we look for them, we might just find them. In any case, it is well to remember, for example, that the natives of the South Pacific who destroyed their crops, built their storage sheds and landing strips, and waited for the cargo to come are not more or less religious or irrational than the scribes of the Near East who wove verbal tapestries of a fictionalized past and a transformed future, imagining perfect roles in a perfect world.

Popular prophecy, and especially its millennial aspect, represents a fascinating transition from those peaceful peasant protests in the preceding chapter to the violent peasant banditry in the next one. Theoretically, at least, there is no reason why millennial prophecy might not instigate an armed revolution or keep its permanent possibility always alive. The Josephan cases, however, seem to be nonviolent on the human level, but, since they seek to seduce or invoke, initiate or create a transcendental violence against the imperial overlords, they are also profoundly ambiguous in any case and usually result in an immediately violent reaction from the colonial authorities.

The background for millennial prophecy is all that was seen earlier about anthropological millennialism and Jewish apocalypticism. But I am concerned here not with the scribal millennialism of the *retainer* class, which resulted in texts, but the popular millennialism of the *peasant* class, which resulted in actions. Apocalypticism belonged, of course, equally to both, but each in its own way. And, need it be said, not all retainers nor all peasants were apocalyptic dreamers or millennial visionaries.

Richard Horsley, distinguishing clearly between millennial prophets and messianic kings as part of his projected "typology of the social forms taken by the various popular movements in the early Roman period," defines the former by three characteristics. First, they "are not solitary figures such as Amos or Jesus ben Hananiah . . . nor are they prophets with several disciples, as apparently John the Baptist or Jesus of Nazareth were . . . they are leaders of sizable *movements* (of hundreds or thousands of people)." Next, "they do not simply announce the will or judgment of God, but lead *actions* of deliverance as agents of God." Finally, "these actions of deliverance are understood as new, eschatological actions that *typologically correspond to* or are informed by the great formative acts of *deliverance led by Moses and Joshua*" (1985:454 & note 42). And all of that should be read against the general background of comparative cultural anthropology. Bryan Wilson, for example, in concluding his study of the interaction between magic and the millennium in religious protest among colonized peoples, notes that "incipient millennialism itself is often heavily infiltrated with magical ideas. . . . Marching natives in Melanesia with imitation rifles need not be planning, perhaps not even envisaging revolution" (493). The logic is not: first we drill with sticks, then we get real rifles, then we attack the imperialists. But: imperialists have power and march around in close-order drill; therefore, if we march around in close-order drill we too will receive power. Comparative anthropology should never obscure discrete historicity, but neither should particular traditions and situations obscure human constancies and continuities. The Jews went back into their own ancient stories and thence ritually reenacted those great inaugural acts of Exodus from bondage in Egypt and arrival in the Promised Land. So also, worlds away and centuries later, the Melanesian natives, seeking to emulate or manipulate the colonial Europeans whose cargo goods they coveted as signs and proofs of superior worth and dignity, proceeded, in the words of Peter Worsley, to "the cultivation of large gardens and the building of stores, sheds, jetties and landing-grounds for the reception of goods which [would] never come" and the preparation of "flagpoles, wirelesses, poles and ladders with which to get into touch with God and the ancestors; flash-lights to see Him with; and books, paper and the Bible as both symbols and means of acquiring the Secret of the Cargo" (1968:247, 251). But whether the popular imagination seeks to retrieve its own traditions against those of the imperialists or seeks to co-opt the very traditions of the imperialists themselves, they write their responses not with pens on paper but with their bodies on the earth. They do something, they enact something, they perform something.

There are, apart from John the Baptist, nine cases to be considered between about 30 and 73 C.E., and, once again, I have summarized the data in appendix 2. Of those, one is Samaritan, and the rest are Jewish, some named and some unnamed, some singled out as individuals and others left in generalized statements. Josephus, by the way, has only derogatory names for these individuals: deceivers, magicians, imposters, or false prophets.

The first case is that of the Samaritan Prophet, an incident that led to the dismissal of Pilate as prefectural governor in 36 C.E.

> A man who made light of mendacity and in all his designs catered to the mob, rallied them [the Samaritans], bidding them go in a body with him to Mount Gerizim, which in their belief is the most sacred of moun-tains. He assured them that on their arrival he would show them the sacred vessels which were buried there, where Moses had deposited them. His hearers, viewing this tale as plausible, appeared in arms. They posted themselves in a certain village named Tirathana, and, as they planned to climb the mountain in a great multitude, they welcomed to their ranks the new arrivals who kept coming. But before they could ascend, Pilate blocked their projected route up the mountain with a detachment of cavalry and heavy-armed infantry, who in the encounter with the firstcomers in the village slew some in a pitched battle and put the others to flight. Many prisoners were taken, of whom Pilate put to death the principal leaders and those who were most influential among the fugitives. (Josephus, *Jewish Antiquities* 18.85–87; no parallel in *Jewish War*)

Afterward, according to 18.88–89, the Samaritan authorities appealed against Pilate to Vitellius, the Syrian legate, "for, they said, it was not as rebels against the Romans but as refugees from the persecution of Pilate that they had met at Tirathana." Vitellius found in their favor and sent Pilate to explain his conduct before Tiberius in Rome, where the emperor's timely death saved his life if not his career. But it is, for the participants, the magical and the millennial not the martial and the militaristic that rules such activities.

There is, however, something wrong or at least missing from that story. If the crowd was really "in arms," it is hard to see what Pilate did wrong, from a Roman point of view, and it is equally hard to see how the Samaritan authorities were able to persuade Vitellius to dismiss him. However, if they were not armed and had only millennial rather than military intentions, the crowd at Tirathana could plausibly be described as "refugees" and the action of Pilate as excessive cruelty. I am inclined, therefore, to doubt quite strongly the veracity of Josephus' "in arms," and for three reasons. One, as just seen, is the Samaritan and Roman reaction. Another is the general expectation that millennial prophets and their followers will be unarmed since they expect divine power to solve a sociocultural problem already far beyond human redress. It is not so much that they are pacific, as that force, power, and violence will be of transcendental rather than human derivation. Their part is to enact or reenact the ritual act that invokes the eschatological scenario. Finally, there is the much more pejorative view of the Samaritans in *Jewish Antiquities* as compared to *Jewish War*, the tendentious theme found only in the former book that, as Shaye Cohen puts it, "the Samaritans are scoundrels" (1979:241). We shall see this in greater detail later on concerning the dismissal of another governor, Cumanus, in 52 C.E.

All in all, then, I am not convinced that the Samaritan Prophet and his multitudes were armed. They were gathering to ascend Mount Gerizim when they were attacked by the Romans, not gathering atop Mount Gerizim to descend and attack the Romans themselves. What might have happened had they discovered the hidden vessels and thereby validated their prophet as Moses reincarnate is, of course, quite moot.

The next incident occurred between 44 and 46 C.E. under Fadus, the first procuratorial governor after all of Palestine came under direct, immediate, and unified Roman control. It involved a prophet known by name both to Josephus and to the New Testament but with better chronological data in the former source. As with the Samaritan Prophet, Josephus' description is typically pejorative for such prophetic leaders.

> A certain imposter named Theudas persuaded the majority of the masses to take up their possessions and to follow him to the Jordan River. He stated that he was a prophet and that at his command the river would be parted and would provide them an easy passage. With this talk he deceived many. Fadus, however, did not permit them to reap the fruit of their folly, but sent against them a squadron of cavalry. They fell upon them unexpectedly, slew many of them and took many prisoners. Theudas himself was captured, whereupon they cut off his head and brought it to Jerusalem. (Josephus, *Jewish Antiquities* 20.97–98; no parallel in *Jewish War*)

For before these days Theudas arose, giving himself out to be somebody, and a number of men, about four hundred, joined him; but he was slain and all who followed him were dispersed and came to nothing. (Acts 5:36)

The original partition of the Red Sea under Moses or of the Jordan River under Joshua meant liberation from Egypt and salvation from the desert into the Promised Land of freedom. One might presume, therefore, that this movement is going back into that desert to prepare thence a new incursion into Palestine, be it, in rational and natural terms, as military invasion, or, in magical and supernatural terms, as divine intervention. But, in the text, they took their possessions with them and were expecting transcendental assistance, apparently, in crossing the Jordan into the desert. If Palestine has now become Egypt, liberation is *not from but into* the desert. Even, however, as an unarmed abandonment of Palestine with, possibly, no intention of returning for "reconquest," there were serious political overtones to any such large-scale peasant departures. Bryan Wilson, for example, speaking of "the response of colonial authorities to new movements that are basically thaumaturgical in orientation," has noted that "such movements may, particularly if they give rise to activities which disturb established routines, be interpreted as political manifestations. Religious behaviour, particularly when it is ecstatic, spasmodic, and extensive, and when it leads to the disruption of normal (particularly work) activities, is readily misunderstood" (366). Indeed, since abstention from normal work may well be part of millennial strategy, the political authorities do not so much misunderstand it as understand it all too well. In such a situation, even the fact that they were unarmed would not have saved them from brutal and bloody reaction.

For Felix's governorship, from 52 to 60 C.E., Josephus has three notations about millennial prophets, and for each he has parallel versions that as usual, must be read in critical comparison with each other.

The first one is extremely important and requires very careful attention. I noted earlier that Josephus had created a first confusion by conflating brigands or bandits with Sicarii, that is, rural bandits with urban terrorists. Now comes a second and equally deliberate conflation, this time between brigands or bandits and prophets or, as he puts it, imposters and deceivers. It is as important to recognize and disentangle this second conflation as it was the first one because each has caused a heritage of scholarly misconceptions as its result. Notice, for example, the general sequence of protagonists in these parallel texts from *Jewish War* 2.253–265 and *Jewish Antiquities* 20.160–172:

(1) Brigands/Bandits:	2.253	= 20.160–161
(2) Sicarii/Terrorists:	2.254–257	= 20.162–166
(3) Imposters/Prophets:	2.258–263	= 20.167–172a
(4) Brigands/Bandits:	2.264–265	= 20.172b

What Josephus did was let the imposters/prophets combine with the brigands/bandits, first, in 20.160b–161 but not in its parallel 2.253b, and, second, in 2.264–265 but not in its twin 20.172b. Here are the texts with italics added so you can see the process at work.

(1) Of the brigands whom he [Felix] crucified, and of the common people who were convicted of complicity with them and punished by him the number was incalculable.

(2) The country [Judea] was again infested with bands of brigands *and imposters who deceived the mob.* Not a day passed, however, but that Felix captured and put to death many of these *imposters and* brigands. (Josephus, *Jewish War* 2.253b = *Jewish Antiquities* 20.160b–161)

(1) The *imposters and* brigands, banding together, incited numbers to revolt, exhorting them to assert their independence, and threatening to kill any who submitted to Roman domination and forcibly to suppress those who voluntarily accepted servitude. Distributing themselves in companies throughout the countryside, they looted the houses of the wealthy, murdered their owners, and set the villages on fire.

(2) And now the brigands once more incited the populace to war with Rome, telling them not to obey them. They also fired and pillaged the villages of those who refused to comply. (Josephus, *Jewish War* 2.264b–265a = *Jewish Antiquities* 20.172b)

Social banditry and millennial prophecy may, indeed, go hand in hand, since as Eric Hobsbawm said, "social banditry and millenarianism—the most primitive forms of reform and revolution—go together historically" (1985:29). What we have in those Josephan texts is not, however, historical combination but literary juxtaposition and tendentious confusion. I intend, therefore, to keep millennial prophecy, in this chapter, and social banditry, in the next chapter, carefully separate *until and unless* there is proper evidence for their combination.

The second mention of millennial prophets under Felix is this general statement about unnamed prophets, again in parallel versions.

(1) Besides these [the Sicarii] there arose another body of villains, with purer hands but more impious intentions, who no less than the assassins ruined the peace of the city. Deceivers and imposters, under

the pretence of divine inspiration fostering revolutionary changes, they persuaded the multitude to act like madmen, and led them out into the desert under the belief that God would there give them tokens of deliverance. Against them Felix, regarding this as but the preliminary to insurrection, sent a body of cavalry and heavy-armed infantry, and put a large number to the sword.

(2) Imposters and deceivers called upon the mob to follow them into the desert. For they said that they would show them unmistakable marvels and signs that would be wrought in harmony with God's design. Many were, in fact, persuaded and paid the penalty of their folly; for they were brought before Felix and he punished them. (Josephus, *Jewish War* 2.258–260 = *Jewish Antiquities* 20.167b–168)

First, notice, of course, the bitingly pejorative language, but even within it appears the admission that the millennial prophets had "purer hands" than the Sicarii from whom, in that text, they are clearly distinguished. In other words, the prophets were not really *violent* rebels. Next, the desert location is again indicative of the Mosaic and Exodus typology and with the same ambiguity, seen before for Theudas, of departure as abandonment of Palestine or departure as preparation for "reconquest." Finally, especially against the background of that Mosaic archetype, two phrases are of special significance (Barnett 682–683; Horsley 1985:455). One is the expression "tokens/signs of deliverance" in *Jewish War* 2.259, which is the same expression used for the plagues that Moses invoked upon Egypt before the Exodus in *Jewish Antiquities* 2.327. Another is the phrase "God's design/providence" in *Jewish Antiquities* 20.168, which is the same phrase used for the miracle with his staff that Moses performed against his Egyptian competitors before the Exodus in *Jewish Antiquities* 2.286. So, despite himself, Josephus puts these prophets in Mosaic continuity.

The third and final example under Felix concerns the Egyptian Prophet, a title that may be merely a nickname of geographical origin or else, as Horsley suggests, "more symbolic, in the typological sense of a leader like Moses or Joshua" (1985:458). Here, as with Theudas earlier, there is also a reference in the New Testament

(1) A still worse blow was dealt at the Jews by the Egyptian false prophet. A charlatan, who had gained for himself the reputation of a prophet, this man appeared in the country, collected a following of about thirty thousand dupes, and led them by a circuitous route from the desert to the mount called the mount of Olives. From there he proposed to force an entrance into Jerusalem and, after overpowering the Roman garrison, to set himself up as tyrant of the people, employing those who poured in with him as his bodyguard. His attack was antici-

pated by Felix, who went to meet him with the Roman heavy infantry, the whole population joining him in the defence. The outcome of the ensuing engagement was that the Egyptian escaped with a few of his followers; most of his force were killed or taken prisoners; the remainder dispersed and stealthily escaped to their several homes.

(2) At this time there came to Jerusalem from Egypt a man who declared that he was a prophet and advised the masses of the common people to go out with him to the mountain called the Mount of Olives, which lies opposite the city at a distance of five furlongs. For he asserted that he wished to demonstrate from there that at his command Jerusalem's walls would fall down, through which he promised to provide them an entrance into the city. When Felix heard of this he ordered his soldiers to take up their arms. Setting out from Jerusalem with a large force of cavalry and infantry, he fell upon the Egyptian and his followers, slaying four hundred of them and taking two hundred prisoners. The Egyptian himself escaped from the battle and disappeared. (Josephus, *Jewish War* 2.261–263 = *Jewish Antiquities* 20.169–171)

(3) "Are you not the Egyptian, then, who recently stirred up a revolt and led the four thousand men of the Assassins [Sicarii] out into the wilderness?" (Acts 21:38)

In Acts, Claudius Lysias, tribune of the Jerusalem forces under Felix, mistook Paul for the escaped Egyptian Prophet. Note, of course, and then ignore Luke's conflation of him with the Sicarii.

From the *combined* Josephan texts, and despite the usual pejorative wording, we get the clearest picture available of a first-century millennial prophet. First, and this may cast some light back on those other desert prophets, he led a multitude from the "countryside" out into the "desert" and thence back to Jerusalem. He seems to have been reenacting the Joshuan destruction of Jericho, so that the "circuitous route" probably meant marching around the walls of the city, after which they were supposed to fall to the ground. Next, the Lukan number is surely closer to the truth than the Josephan one according to which the Egyptian Prophet approached Jerusalem with an "army" about the size that Cestius Gallus, the Syrian legate, led disastrously against the later revolt in the fall of 66 C.E. But we are, in any case, dealing with a very large multitude. Finally, the prophet intended to become a "tyrant" with a "bodyguard" according to *Jewish War* 2.262 but not *Jewish Antiquities* 20.170. That should *not* be used to turn a millennial prophet into a messianic claimant but should be bracketed as part of the Josephan prejudice against "Jewish tyrants" as proclaimed openly in the prologue of *Jewish War* 1.10–11, since, according to Shaye Cohen, one of the "motives" of that work was to argue that "the revolutionary leaders . . . were evil tyrants" (1979:240–241).

Under Festus between 60 and 62 C.E., Josephus has one unnamed prophet, but the details read almost like a vague summary of preceding examples, and, with no parallel version in *Jewish War*, one might be suspicious about its validity.

> Festus also sent a force of cavalry and infantry against the dupes of a certain imposter who had promised them salvation and rest from troubles, if they chose to follow him into the wilderness. The force which Festus dispatched destroyed both the deceiver himself and those who followed him. (Josephus, *Jewish Antiquities* 20.188; no parallel in *Jewish War*)

Again the pejorative language, of course, and again they were going *into* the desert without it being specified whether as final abandonment or preparation for return.

Another unnamed prophet appeared when the Temple was already afire in July or August of 70 C.E.

> [The Romans] proceeded to the one remaining portico of the outer court, on which the poor women and children of the populace and a mixed multitude had taken refuge, numbering six thousand . . . the soldiers, carried away by rage, set fire to the portico from below; with the result that some were killed plunging out of the flames, others perished amidst them, and out of all that multitude not a soul escaped. They owed their destruction to a false prophet, who had on that day proclaimed to the people in the city that God commanded them to go up to the temple court, to receive there the tokens of their deliverance. (Josephus, *Jewish War* 6.283–285)

Although the location is now the Temple rather than the desert, there is again that phrase "tokens/signs of deliverance," as earlier with the prophets at the time of Felix.

Immediately after that account, Josephus generalizes against those millennial prophets and then explains why they existed.

> Numerous prophets, indeed, were at this period suborned by the tyrants to delude the people, by bidding them await help from God, in order that desertions might be checked. . . . Thus it was that the wretched people were deluded at that time by charlatans and pretended messengers of the deity. (Josephus, *Jewish War* 6.286a, 288a)

He continues by contrasting them with the literate, exegetical prophets, "the sacred scribes . . . the learned," who read the portents correctly as indicating not the salvation but the destruction of Jerusalem.

Finally, there is one problematic example at the end of the war in 73 C.E. After the fall of Masada and the Josephan apotheosis of its Sicarii from history into legend if not mythology, he mentions that some Sicarii had earlier escaped from Palestine to Alexandria. There, in *Jewish War* 7.409–419, what happens seems quite consistent with their ideology. But then Josephus turns to Cyrenaica, the next province to the west along the North African coast.

> The madness of the Sicarii further attacked, like a disease, the cities around Cyrene. Jonathan, an arrant scoundrel, by trade a weaver, having taken refuge in that town, won the ear of not a few of the indigent class, and led them forth into the desert, promising them a display of signs and apparitions. . . . Catullus, having dispatched a body of horse and foot, easily overpowered the unarmed crowd, the greater number of whom perished in the encounter, a few being taken prisoners and brought up to Catullus. (Josephus, *Jewish War* 7.437–440)

Jonathan certainly looks more like an unarmed millennial prophet than an armed terrorist leader. Once again, I suspect Josephan conflation. Then, in 7.441–450, the governor Catullus caught Jonathan and "prompted" him to accuse specific wealthy Jews of complicity, extending even as far as Alexandria, Rome, and Josephus himself. He eventually brought "Jonathan and his associates in chains" to Rome, but Vespasian, "on the intercession of Titus," refused to believe the accusations. Jonathan, finally, "was first tortured and then burnt alive." All in all, and despite uncertainty, Jonathan was probably a millennial prophet used by Catullus for his own ends.

✧ 9 ✧

Bandit and Messiah

> David departed from there and escaped to the cave of Adullam;
> and when his brothers and all his father's house heard it, they
> went down there to him. And every one who was in distress,
> and every one who was in debt and every one who was
> discontented, gathered to him; and he became captain over
> them. And there were with him about four hundred men.
>
> *1 Samuel 22:1–2*

> Social banditry ... is one of the most universal social
> phenomena known to history, and one of the most amazingly
> uniform ... wherever societies are based on agriculture
> (including pastoral economies), and consist largely of peasants
> and landless labourers ruled, oppressed and exploited by
> someone else—lords, towns, governments, lawyers, or even
> banks. It is found in one or other of its three main forms ... the
> noble robber ... the primitive resistance fighter or guerilla
> unit ... and possibly the terror-bringing avenger.
>
> *Eric J. Hobsbawm (1985:20)*

Imagine this simplified typology of violence. Protesters and magicians act primarily without any human violence. Millennial prophets avoid human violence because they depend on a far greater and more effective divine violence. Messianic claimants invoke human violence but with divine violence undergirding it. Bandits, finally, operate primarily within human violence alone. But it must always be remembered that any such violence represents response rather than initiative; it is the second rather than the first stage in the spiral of violence. As we move along those first-century trajectories of peasant unrest, we oscillate backward and forward between the second stage, *protest and resistance,* and the fourth stage, open *revolt,* until at last that fourth stage prevails completely (Horsley 1987).

The Unpainted Face of Agrarian Empire

The theoretical basis for what follows is the provocative work of Eric Hobsbawm, a British social historian, who coined the term "social banditry" about thirty years ago. A single chapter in *Social Bandits and Primitive Rebels*, his 1959 work on archaic forms of social protest in the nineteenth and twentieth centuries, was enlarged into a 1969 book, *Bandits*, which remained alive and well enough for a second edition in 1985. That inaugural chapter, "The Social Bandit," by the way, was balanced by another, "The City Mob," in which Hobsbawm noted that "the implicit revolutionism of the 'mob' was primitive; in its way it was the metropolitan equivalent of the stage of political consciousness represented by social banditry in the country-side" (1965:118).

What distinguishes social bandits from, on the one hand, plain robbers and, on the other, robber barons, according to Hobsbawm, "is that they are peasant outlaws whom the lord and state regard as criminals, but who remain within peasant society, and are considered by their people as heroes, as champions, avengers, fighters for justice, perhaps even leaders of liberation, and in any case as men to be admired, helped and supported" (1985:17). Furthermore, as cited in this chapter's epigraph, social banditry "is found in one or other of its three main forms . . . the noble robber or *Robin Hood*, the primitive resistance fighter or guerilla unit of what I shall call the *haiduks*, and possibly the terror-bringing *avenger*" (1985:20).

On a superficial level, one might wonder if Robin Hoods ever really existed. Did they actually rob the rich *in order* to feed the poor? Or did they, at best, simply rob the rich because the poor had nothing worth taking, then give to the poor because they were their own kin or because that is how they acquired the protection of silence and the status of respect? It is worth noting, however, that the less Robin Hoods were historical, the more they were mythical, that is to say, the more they were needed by the peasantry as personifications of a restored justice or a just revenge.

On a more profound level, there is the 1972 criticism leveled by Anton Blok, whose dissertation of that year at the University of Amsterdam was on the Sicilian Mafia: "Hobsbawm's comparative treatment of banditry over-emphasizes the element of social protest and obscures the significance of the links which bandits maintain with established power-holders" (502). There are three main points in this disagreement. The first has to do with class. Blok claims that "the element of class conflict as embodied in certain forms of banditry has received undue emphasis. Rather than actual champions of the poor and the weak, bandits quite often terrorized those from whose ranks they managed to rise, and thus helped to suppress them" (496). The second point has to do with protection. Bandits are peasants grasping for a hold on that most unpeasant phenomenon, power. What if those who already possess power decide not to fight but to recruit, not to suppress but to co-opt, not to destroy but to employ such new claimants? "Protection of bandits," says Blok, "may range from a close though narrow circle of kins-men and affiliated friends to powerful politicians, including those who hold formal office as well as grass-roots politicians. . . . It may be argued that unless bandits find political protection, their reign will be short. . . . *The more successful a man is as a bandit, the more extensive the protection granted him"* (498). Those two points taken together lead into a third one concerning rebellion. "Bandits are not instrumental in turning peasant anarchy and rebellion . . . into sustained and concerted action on a wider scale . . . because their first loyalty is *not* to the peasants" (499). Bandits are not class-conscious peasants who rebel as part, pattern, or paradigm for wider rural rebellion. They are individual peasants who refuse to submit to their lot of poverty at best and indigence at worst. They are peasants who grasp for power, and that moves them into a no-man's-land between those who never had it and those who already possess it.

Hobsbawm insisted in 1972, responding directly to Blok, that he had always underlined the *social ambivalence* involved in the economics and politics of banditry. "The crucial fact about the bandit's social situation is its ambiguity," he said, quoting from the 1969 edition of his book. "He is an outsider and a rebel, a poor man who refuses to accept the normal rules of poverty. . . . This draws him close to the poor: he is one of them. It sets him in opposition to the hierarchy of power, wealth and influence: he is not one of them. . . . At the same time the bandit is, inevitably, drawn into the web of wealth and power, because, unlike other peasants, he acquires wealth and exerts power. He is 'one of us' who is constantly in the process of becoming associated with 'them'" (1985:87–88; 1972:504). Again, a year later, in an anthology on peasant movements, rural protest, and social change, the same emphasis appears. "The social ambiguity of banditry, on which we have insisted in this paper, makes them an uncertain element in social movements which must sooner or later challenge both traditional society and the existing structure of wealth and power, towards which suc-cessful bandits, however popular in origin, belong to [or] are drawn" (1973b:156–157).

Whenever, therefore, I use terms such as *bandit, brigand,* or *outlaw* in this book, either myself or quoting from Josephus, it is Hobsbawm's social banditry that I have in mind. But the meaning of that adjective *social* is less their alleged munificence to the peasantry, or even the approval by the peasantry and disapproval by the aristocracy that he emphasized in his definition of the term in 1969 (1985:17), than it is the ambiguity of their location between unpower and power, between the peasant class and the governing class, that, highlighted by Blok, one can discern in Hobsbawm from 1969 (1985:87–88), through 1972 (504), and into 1973 (1973b:156–157).

In other words, social ambiguity must be elevated into the very definition of social banditry. That is its class aspect, its social aspect, and its fascinating importance.

That social ambiguity of banditry as poised between unpower and power has been pushed to an even deeper level by Brent Shaw in discussing its legal ambiguity between might and right specifically in the Roman Empire. The tone is beautifully set by his article's twin epigraphs. The first is from Augustine's *City of God* 4.4: "Remove justice and what are states but gangs of bandits on a large scale? And what are bandit gangs but kingdoms in miniature?" To political ambiguity is then added religious ambiguity, as the next quotation is from Luke 23:33–43, where Jesus is crucified between two not, as we sometimes say, thieves but bandits. In a world where might was right, how were Sulla returning in the eighties B.C.E. with his spoils from the east and Caesar returning in the fifties B.C.E. from his slaughters in the west not bandits writ large?

Shaw begins with the problem of terminology. The Romans, of course, recognized the form of armed violence known as war, and they divided it, on the one hand, into *bellum iustum,* not a "just war" as Christian ethics understands that term but a "real war," that is, war between sovereign states, and *bellum servile,* that is, "not a real war" but one, say, against a slave uprising or an inadequately civilized foe. They were inclined to call every other type of armed violence "banditry" because of a "severely stunted development of the framework of law dealing with illegitimate use of violent force" (21). Yet even when the term is narrowed to mean "the specific residual form of violence that *we* define as banditry" we are dealing with "a common phenomenon in the societies that constituted the empire in any period one would care to investigate" (8). From private correspondence and public literature, from formulaic phrases on tombstones and exculpatory clauses in contracts, Shaw concludes that banditry "endemic to the countryside, is to be found not only in Italy and Judaea of the first century; it was ubiquitous, though in varying degrees of intensity, in the empire in all periods of its existence" (10).

The conclusion so far is that "whatever their absolute numbers (probably small) bandits were a common phenomenon in the Roman empire" (24), but that raises a major problem. If their number was small and even if their presence was ubiquitous, why is the Roman reaction to them so violent? It is clear, for example, from late but cumulative codes of Roman law that the legalities and penalties for bandits set them apart from common criminals. On legalities: "It is the duty of private individuals to detect, to pursue and to betray bandits to local authorities. In the pursuit of this obligation the private individual was authorized to use force, to injure and even to kill such men. And they were also exempted, in doing this, from normal laws on *iniuria* and homicide" (19). On penalties: "In no case, adds the law, are any of the courtesies normally extended to other criminal defendants, such as respite for sacred or public holidays, to be allowed to such men. At the governor's court the expectation was of summary and savage judgement.... The law sanctioned the most brutal of the death penalties (the *summa supplicia*—throwing to the beasts, burning alive, and crucifixion) as savageries that were necessary 'to set a public example'.... The punishment of bandits was clearly viewed as a form of state retribution and public terrorism" (20–21). The problem presses: why such imperial violence precisely against bandits, especially if there was no real threat that they might overthrow the empire?

The answer becomes very clear in some of Shaw's own examples. Consider three careers across four hundred years of time and from one end of the empire to the other (36). First, Viriathus, in Spain during the 140s and 130s B.C.E., progressed from shepherd to hunter to bandit to general. Next, Tacfarinas, in North Africa during the twenties C.E., proceeded from shepherd to soldier to bandit to general. Finally, Maximinus, from Thrace in the 230s C.E., proceeded from shepherd to bandit to soldier to emperor. That last case, admittedly late, admittedly fleeting, and with its ambiguity beautifully symbolized in his own name, shows the answer with glaring inevitability. What was a bandit but an emperor on the make, what was an emperor but a bandit on the throne? Of course, might was justified as right, force was ratified as justice, but the line between the personalized violence of the bandit gangs and the institutionalized violence of the state armies was far harder to justify in theory than to maintain in practice. The social and juridical ambiguity of the bandit was reaching out to entrap the state itself within its ambivalence. It was doing so because it always had done so and always would do so until the state's monopoly on violence was theoretically as well as practically absolute. One final story from Shaw (43), true maybe as historical fact but certainly as ideological theater.

> A certain robber named Claudius, who was overrunning Judaea and
> Syria and was being very vigorously pursued [by Severus] in conse-
> quence, came to him one day with some horsemen, like some military
> tribune, and saluted and kissed him; and he was neither discovered at
> the time nor caught later. (*Dio's Roman History* 75; Cary 9.199)

There it all is, frozen forever in one perfect tableau. Septimius Severus, trying, in 195 C.E., to establish the legitimacy or at least the security of the imperial throne he had just grasped by force, is kissed as equal by Claudius the bandit. How tell the bandit from the emperor, the gang from the army?

Ramsay MacMullen, discussing bandits as enemies of the Roman order, spoke of how "a widespread sympathy felt, or half-felt, for the lives and deeds of outlaws testifies to a loosening loyalty within civilized society, where to be poor, to be rejected, to scrape a living irregularly in the company of others clinging like oneself to the edge of the respectable world; to envy and then to hate the man of property, and to admire the style of his plunderers; to consort with them, then shield them, and at last join them, were the successive steps leading beyond the boundaries of the law" (1966:193). But Shaw's analysis is, I think, much more acute. The core problem is not what MacMullen terms "loosening loyalty" but what Shaw terms "the inability of the archaic state adequately to define its self-defined mandate of authority" (32). And how could it ever define the difference between, say, the soldier who was an ex-bandit and the bandit who was an ex-soldier, unless and until it could show that emperor and army had, over bandit and gang, a monopoly of violence that was not only practically and quantitatively great but theoretically and qualitatively right.

One could, therefore, find bandits co-opted into any level of Roman official violence, from soldier to emperor, but still find tremendous legal venom expanded on banditry as entrepreneurial violence. "Even in the technical-legal view of the state itself," says Shaw, "*such men were never seen simply as common criminals*. There existed quite separate definitions of them that placed bandits in a penumbral category between persons within the scope of the law (criminal and civil, largely overlapping) and enemies of the state. They were, quite literally, 'out-law.' Hence it was not only the downtrodden peasants who refused to place such men in the same category as common criminals. The state too desisted from this identification. Roman law in general reflects this view. It denies to bandits all legal rights of citizens, even those normally retained by criminal defendants. . . . That is to say, the bandit was a non-person" (22–23). In other words, Hobsbawm's vision of banditry's socioeconomic ambiguity has been deepened by Shaw into one of politicojuridical ambivalence. In final conclusion from his article: "Banditry has been shown to have been generated in very precise historical circumstances necessitating a specific political structure, the state, and the imperfect development of this same structure. Banditry exists only in these conditions and has no necessary connection with the phenomenon of class which both precedes the appearance of banditry and continues to exist long after banditry itself has disappeared as a characteristic form of social violence. It is that peculiar space left by the incomplete domination of archaic states that allows for the existence of an interstitial group of men who must be defined in relation to, and in opposition to, the state. It is the availability of this space that allows these men to be defined as outlaws or bandits in contradistinction to common criminals" (49–50). And that structural space is, of course, not just practical but theoretical, not just a temporary gap in the balance of violence but a permanent gap in the justification of violence. Rural banditry holds up to agrarian empire its own unpainted face, it own unvarnished soul.

A Brigand Chief with a Large Horde

That preceding section flows directly into the present one and is presumed throughout it. I insist, once again, that what is important in the social anthropology of banditry or brigandage is not the purity of its motivations against the rich nor the magnanimity of its benefactions to the poor but rather its corrosive ambiguity, on social, economic, political, and juridical levels.

There are eleven cases to be considered, some very specific with individually named bandit chieftains and others little more than generalizing statements. I have, as with Protesters and Prophets, summarized the data on Bandits for easy reference in appendix 2.

The Borders and Caves of Galilee

The Palestinian civil war of the sixties and fifties B.C.E. found itself eventually subsumed within the Roman civil war of the early forties. "Reappearing as if on a rotating stage," in the deft analogy of George Nickelsburg, "the principals of the Jewish civil war returned time and again to interact disastrously with the renowned figures of the last years of the Roman republic" (1981:196). Of the warring Hasmonean princes, the defeated Judas Aristobulus II was removed by murder in 49 B.C.E.; of the warring Roman generals, the defeated Pompey was removed by murder in 48 B.C.E. That left Caesar victorious in Rome and John Hyrcanus II victorious in Palestine. Not for long, of course. For Caesar, the assassins were already waiting and for the last Hasmoneans, the first Herodians. And what was extraordinary about Antipater and his son Herod was not that they always backed the Romans, but that, when Roman fought Roman, they always backed the loser and came out a winner: first Pompey, then Caesar, then Cassius, then Anthony, until, finally, they got it right with Octavian Augustus.

The first major instance of social banditry under Herod the Great is that of the Galilean border bandits. Against that background of almost twenty years of civil war and social disturbance, Antipater, prime minister under Hyrcanus II, appointed his son Herod as ruler of Galilee in 48 B.C.E. The stage was thus set for a somewhat paradigmatic encounter in Galilee

between Herod the not yet Great and the bandit chief Ezekias (or Hezek-
iah), who had been raiding, in Mary Smallwood's interpretation, "across the
Syrian frontier into the formerly Jewish territory of the Decapolis" (44).

> Discovering that Ezekias, a brigand chief at the head of a large horde,
> was ravaging the district on the Syrian frontier, he caught him and put
> him and many of the brigands to death. (Josephus, *Jewish War* 1.204 =
> *Jewish Antiquities* 14.159)

Josephus, however, records two rather different reactions to that event
from the Jerusalem authorities.

The earlier account, in *Jewish War* 1.208–215, had Herod accused
before Hyrcanus by "a number of malicious persons at court" for having
killed people without trial "in violation of Jewish law." Herod came to
Jerusalem strongly escorted but was acquitted by Hyrcanus upon orders
from Sextus Caesar, the Syrian legate, who thereafter made him governor
of Coele Syria and Samaria. He had, after that promotion, to be dissuaded
by his father from attempting to depose Hyrcanus militarily—a straightforward account, that, of old Hasmoneans against new Herodians, with a weak
Hyrcanus starting and a strong Sextus finishing the problem. The parallel
version in *Jewish Antiquities* 14.163–184, however, contains an item not
found in that earlier account.

> [Hyrcanus'] anger was further kindled by the mothers of the men who
> had been murdered by Herod, for every day in the temple they kept beg-
> ging the people to have Herod brought to judgment in the Synhedrion
> for what he had done. (Josephus, *Jewish Antiquities* 14.168; no parallel in
> *Jewish War*)

What is the value of that assertion? Referring specifically to 14.168,
Shaye Cohen notes that it is a "dramatic" passage and concludes that "we
cannot know whether [it was] invented for the occasion by Josephus or
whether he found [it] in his source" (1979:51). In other words, those mothers might be simply Josephus' own invention intended to heighten the
human theater of the trial. If that were correct, of course, no further use
could be made of the unit. The evidence indicates, however, that 14.168
along with 14.171–176 and 15.3–4 belongs to a new and second source concerning Herod's ascendancy that Josephus had not known or used in the
earlier *Jewish War*. Thus in the *Jewish Antiquities* version, that earlier
account, where everything operates only on the highest levels of Roman
power, is conflated with another one according to which Herod is accused
by "the mothers of the men who had been murdered" in 14.168, is brought
before the Sanhedrin, and is acquitted by them because of fear, despite the

prophecy of Samaias, in 14.171–176. In this second source the Sanhedrin, never mentioned at all in *Jewish War* 1.204–215, is repeatedly emphasized as the venue of the trial, in *Jewish Antiquities* 14.167–168, 170–172, 175, 177–180.

The appeal of the mothers to "the king and the people" for a Sanhedrin trial fits with the image of Ezekias as a popularly supported social bandit leading peasants dislocated by Pompey's Palestinian reconstruction and operating primarily in an area he had transferred from Jewish to Syrian control. I think that is a more convincing explanation of those bandits than Mary Smallwood's suggestion that "the nucleus of the band was no doubt the remnants of Aristobulus' party, always strong in Galilee" (44). A similar proposal was made recently by Seán Freyne, who wrote of the "serious social repercussions especially among the Galilean Hasmonean nobility, and it is to their ranks that we must assign Ezekias, whose acts of banditry were therefore not performed in favor of the Galilean peasantry but were reprisals for the loss of his own possessions and presumably those of other nobles as well" (1988:57). While all Hasmoneans had reason to fear the Herodian ascendancy, it is difficult to imagine supporters of the defeated Hasmonean Aristobulus appealing against Herod to the victorious Hasmonean Hyrcanus in Jerusalem. Indeed, as Richard Horsley notes, "Josephus who provides our only sources for these and related events, writes nothing that would suggest that Ezekias and company were Hasmonean nobles" (1988:186).

The second major instance of social banditry under Herod the Great is that of the Galilean cave bandits. This took place about a decade after the border bandits in 37 B.C.E. In the meantime, in 40 B.C.E., the Parthians had invaded Palestine and deposed Hyrcanus II, declaring Antigonus, son of Aristobulus II, king in his place. Point counterpoint, the Romans then declared Herod king and sent him home to take over his kingdom, if he could. He could, but it took him about three years. Josephus assures us, in *Jewish War* 1.291, that "with few exceptions, all Galilee went over to him" or, in the parallel *Jewish Antiquities* 14.395, that "all Galilee, except for a few of its inhabitants, came over to his side." In what follows, however, we realize that those few exceptions are actually rather formidable foes, with Sepphoris, for example, again supporting Antigonus as earlier it had his father Aristobulus II.

Herod had two objectives in Galilee, but the parallel accounts in *Jewish War* 1.303–313 and *Jewish Antiquities* 14.413–430 both tend to get them a little confused. For his primary objective, "he set out to reduce the remaining strongholds of Galilee and to expel the garrisons of Antigonus" in *Jewish War* 1.303, and so also in *Jewish Antiquities* 14.413. The parallel texts continue.

He pushed on to Sepphoris through a very heavy snowstorm and took possession of the city without a contest, the garrison having fled before his assault. . . . [He] then started on a campaign against the cave-dwelling brigands, who were infesting a wide area and inflicting on the inhabitants evils no less than those of war. Having sent in advance three battalions of infantry and a squadron of cavalry to the village of Arbela [northwest of lakeside Tiberias], he joined them forty days later with the rest of his army. Nothing daunted by his approach, the enemy, who combined the experience of seasoned warriors with the daring of brigands, went armed to meet him. . . . Herod pursued them, with slaughter, to the Jordan and destroyed large numbers of them; the rest fled across the river and dispersed. Thus was Galilee purged of its terrors, save for the remnant still lurking in the caves. (Josephus, *Jewish War* 1.304-307 = *Jewish Antiquities* 14.414-417)

One would presume, on a fast reading of that text, that the bandits came down from their caves, broke Herod's left wing, but were eventually defeated, leaving only a remnant still in the caves. But what has happened, I suggest, is that Josephus has intertwined Herod's two Galilean objectives, a primary move against the troops loyal to Antigonus with his entire army and a secondary move against the cave bandits with a much smaller force. Herod, in other words, sent a smaller force against the bandits near Arbela, and, while it was getting nowhere, he himself defeated Antigonus' forces. It was Josephus' own account that mixed up for us "the experience of seasoned warriors with the daring of brigands," as he puts it in *Jewish War* 1.305 without parallel in *Jewish Antiquities* 14.416. Then, having defeated Antigonus' forces and placed his main army in winter quarters, Herod turned fully to his second objective, and he himself took charge of the attack against the bandits. Notice, by the way, that in the twin accounts of this action in *Jewish War* 1.309-313 and *Jewish Antiquities* 14.421-430 there is no mention of their being but a remnant of those defeated in an earlier battle. There is no significant difference between the parallel versions, although the latter is dramatically expanded and admits that "many" surrendered, while the former says that "not one" did. Josephus balances admiration for Herod's novel commando tactics in defeating the bandits with praise for their own noble deaths. There is even an old man who kills his seven sons and his wife and then hurls himself after their dead bodies over the precipice. Is it cynical of me to recall the Taxo tradition or the Masada legend? Is it even more cynical to recall Josephus' own experience with surrender options in Galilean caves?

One final point, linking back to the earlier one concerning Ezekias' band as Hasmonean nobles or peasant bandits: Seán Freyne has located

Hasmonean nobility rather than peasant banditry in the Arbela caves and claimed that "their banditry can be described as social in that it represents the last efforts of a dying social class to regain its former position of wealth and status within Palestinian life" (1988:58). Throughout his account, however, Josephus makes quite clear and explicit the repeated Galilean attempts by the followers of the Hasmonean Aristobulus II and his sons Alexander and Antigonus to defeat their Hasmonean foe Hyrcanus II and his Herodian supporters. They tried under Alexander in 57, under Aristobulus and Antigonus in 56, under Alexander in 55, under Antigonus in 42, and under Antigonus, backed by the Parthians, in 40 B.C.E. That rebellious movement stemmed clearly from the Hasmonean nobility, and in terms of class, it belonged to them. That does not mean that they had no popular or peasant support but simply that they were in charge of their own rebellion and dictated its strategy. On the other hand, however, the Syrian border bandits in 47 and the Arbela cave bandits in 38 B.C.E. are best interpreted as stemming from the peasantry not the nobility. It is precisely because of their lower-class leadership that Josephus calls them bandits or brigands. Finally, there were those two vaguely specified revolts of 38 B.C.E. mentioned in *Jewish War* 1.315–316 = *Jewish Antiquities* 14.432–433 and *Jewish War* 1.326, 329, 330 = *Jewish Antiquities* 14.450, 452, 453. Although a case might be made that those were peasant operations, it is safer, in the absence of any Josephan mention of bandits, to log them as the last resistance from the long-lost cause of Aristobulus II and his sons. From now on, Herod was efficiently, oppressively, and brutally in charge.

Judea Was Infested with Bandits

Josephus says nothing about bandits between the thirties before and the thirties after the turn of the era. They may well have existed, of course, but I am concentrating here on explicit cases.

In 44 C.E., upon the death of Herod Agrippa I, all of Palestine was reunited under direct Roman administration. From then on, bandits are mentioned under every single prefect save Tiberius Alexander in 46 to 48 C.E. And, as we shall see, at least one was operating then and indeed for a very long time before.

The first governor was Cuspius Fadus between 44 and 46 C.E. In *Jewish War* 2.220 Josephus says only that "Cuspius Fadus . . . by abstaining from all interference with the customs of the country kept the nation at peace." But in his later history he enlarges on that.

> Tholomaeus the arch-brigand [brigand chief], who had inflicted very
> severe mischief upon Idumaea and upon the Arabs, was brought before

him in chains and put to death. From then on the whole of Judaea was purged of robber-bands, thanks to the prudent concern displayed by Fadus. (Josephus, *Jewish Antiquities* 20.5; no parallel in *Jewish War* 2.220)

Tholomaeus, or Ptolemy, was operating, in the mid-forties C.E., primarily on the Idumean and Nabatean borders, just as Ezekias was on the Syrian borders in the early forties B.C.E., and I presume a certain longevity or notoriety for his name to have survived.

Ventidius Cumanus was governor from 48 to 52 C.E., and two cases of relatively peaceful public protest were seen in the last chapter during his short administration. This is now matched by two violent incidents, the second of which was extremely serious. In the first one, concerning an imperial official, there are some significant divergences in Josephus' parallel accounts.

This calamity [the riot about a soldier's disrespect for the Temple] was followed by other disorders originating with brigands. On the public road leading up to Bethoron, some brigands attacked one Stephen, a slave of Caesar, and robbed him of his baggage. Cumanus, therefore, sent troops round the neighboring villages, with orders to bring up the inhabitants to him in chains, reprimanding them for not having pursued and arrested the robbers [brigands]. (Josephus, *Jewish War* 2.228–229)

Their first mourning had not yet ceased when another calamity befell them. For some of the seditious revolutionaries robbed Stephen. . . . Cumanus . . . [gave] orders to plunder the neighboring villages and to bring before him their most eminent men in chains so that he might exact vengeance for their effrontery. After the sacking of the villages . . . (*Jewish Antiquities* 20.113–115)

In citing that second version, I have given only the parts that contain those significant differences. First, the three explicit mentions of "brigands" in the former text are reduced and changed to a single mention of "seditious revolutionaries" in the latter one. Next, it is twice noted that the villages were to be plundered in the second but never in the first version, a feature, by the way, that makes destroying a Torah scroll fit better with that first situation. Finally, it is the "eminent men" and not just the "inhabitants" who are enchained in the later account, and the implied punishment seems more severe there as well. I read all those changes as part of Josephus' deliberate emphasizing, in the *Antiquities* even more than in the *War*, the responsibility of Jewish brigands as revolutionaries and of Roman governors as maladministrators. In any case, punishing nearby villagers is an obvious strategy against the local base of social banditry, and it was well known to the Romans. "The law assumes," notes Brent Shaw, speaking of the later cumulative digests of Roman law, "that bandits cannot operate without a broader network of supporters and that the governor [of a province] cannot hope to put an end to their actions without striking at their base. In the words of the law, 'without them the bandit cannot long remain hidden'" (14–16). It is such local peasant support, as Eric Hobsbawm has seen, that lies behind the myth of bandit invisibility and the truth of betrayal as the main means of capturing them (1985:50–51).

The next incident, probably in 51 C.E., escalated to open warfare and ended with Cumanus' banishment in 52 C.E. The parallel texts are in *Jewish War* 2.232–246 and *Jewish Antiquities* 20.118–136, but in this case there is also an account in Tacitus. There are three immediate problems with ramifications for understanding what actually happened.

The first problem is that Tacitus' much shorter account, in *Annals* 12.54, contradicts Josephus' longer ones on two major points: "the province . . . was so divided that the natives of Galilee were subject to Ventidius, Samaria to Felix," and "the province would have been ablaze with war but for the intervention of Quadratus, the governor of Syria" (Moore & Jackson 3.394–395). I consider the former comment flatly incorrect and explain the conflation of the later Felix with the earlier Cumanus as derived from the *Annals* context. That was an attack on Pallas, freedman financial secretary of the emperor Claudius, rich, powerful, hated, and doomed. His freedman brother Felix is accused of misgovernment as part of that attack because he had in his own governorship of Palestine, "practised," according to Tacitus in his *Histories* 5.9, "every kind of cruelty and lust, wielding the power of king with all the instincts of a slave" (Moore & Jackson 2.190–193). Having no specific details of Felix's Palestinian misdeeds, Tacitus simply slips him in with Cumanus, about whose fate he obviously has some detailed knowledge. My solution, in summary, is to remove everything that has to do with Felix, governor between 52 and 60 C.E., from that text, and read it exclusively about Cumanus, governor between 48 and 52 C.E. It cannot be totally dismissed since it knows about Galilee against Samaria, about bandits, about Quadratus' intervention, and about Cumanus' dismissal. But that means that I have to take seriously Tacitus' assertion that "the province would have been ablaze with war but for the intervention of Quadratus, the governor of Syria."

The second problem is the major differences between Josephus' two texts as these concern the Samaritans, a problem touched on earlier when dealing with the Samaritan Prophet and the dismissal of an earlier governor, Pontius Pilate, in 36 C.E. Shaye Cohen has shown most persuasively that, whereas *Jewish War* "evinces no hostility towards the Samaritans," *Jewish Antiquities* "is decidedly anti-Samaritan." Thus, in a detailed comparison of 2.232–246 and 20.118–136, he gives about a dozen specific examples of this "shift in attitude, from neutrality to hostility" (1979:149). It is almost a classic instance of Josephan tendentiousness. His purpose in those changes is to convince us that "the Samaritans are scoundrels who have always caused trouble for the real Jews" (241). It is thus a facet of his growing religious nationalism and increasing Pharisaic emphasis as he moves from *Jewish War* to *Jewish Antiquities*.

The third problem is another major set of differences between Josephus' two texts as these concern the Jews. In the *Jewish War* the event seems to be a punitive raid against Samaria, but in the *Jewish Antiquities* it appears much more as a revolt against Rome. Granted, of course, such a raid was illegal and to that extent indirectly and secondarily anti-Roman, but had it begun or did it become directly and primarily a revolt against Rome rather than a raid against Samaria? Shaye Cohen, mapping with compelling detail the trajectories of Josephan bias, has shown that the *Jewish War* had "contended that isolated individuals from both sides were responsible for the outbreak of the war, although it assigned far greater guilt to the Jewish bandits than to the Roman procurators" but that the *Jewish Antiquities* "redistribute[d] the guilt more equitably between the Jews and Romans and more broadly within each group." In other words, in the former writing, "not all Jews revolted, only small bands of mad fanatics," but in the latter one, "the Jews as a whole participated in the revolt but were compelled by necessity" (1979:237, 240, 241). Along that same line of change, then, the *Jewish War* account of the Cumanus incident seeks to contain it within the parameters of a reprisal raid against Samaria, despite many details that do not really fit such an event. If Cumanus suppressed the raid, why the great increase in banditry? If Quadratus came only for a requested judicial decision, why the slow procession from Tyre to Caesarea to Lydda to Jerusalem, and why do so many very high authorities end up on trial in Rome? The *Jewish Antiquities* version, on the other hand, is quite willing to admit that it was a revolt against Rome, and, indeed, such an interpretation alone makes sense of the entire proceedings. As always, Josephus gives more than enough evidence to read him against himself.

The opening act is in *Jewish War* 2.232–233 and *Jewish Antiquities* 20.118–119. It concerns only "a Galilean" in 2.232 but is expanded by anti-Samaritanism to "the Galileans" in 20.118. A pilgrim is murdered by Samaritans when passing through their territory to celebrate a festival at Jerusalem. Both texts agree that the Jewish leaders of Galilee went immediately to Cumanus seeking justice. Only in 2.233, however, does this happen because "a considerable crowd assembled in haste in Galilee with the intention of making war on the Samaritans." In other words, the war was only against Samaria not Rome. Then, but only in 20.119, Cumanus neglected to intervene because "[he had] been bribed by the Samaritans."

The middle act of the drama is in *Jewish War* 2.234–23 and *Jewish Antiquities* 20.120–124. The news of what had happened on the borders of Galilee and Samaria was spread abroad by Galilean pilgrims when they reached Jerusalem for the festival.

> The masses were profoundly stirred, and, abandoning the festival, they dashed off to Samaria, without generals and without listening to any of the magistrates who sought to hold them back. The brigands and rioters among the party had as their leaders Eleazar, son of Deinaeus, and Alexander, who, falling upon the borderers of the toparch of Acrabatene, massacred the inhabitants without distinction of age and burnt their villages. (Josephus, *Jewish War* 2.234–235)

> *The Galileans . . . urged the Jewish masses to resort to arms and to assert their liberty; for, they said, slavery was in itself bitter, but when it involved insolent treatment, it was quite intolerable.* Those in authority tried to mollify them. . . . The masses, however, paid no heed to them, but taking up arms and inviting the assistance of Eleazar son of Deinaeus—he was a brigand who for many years had his home in the mountains—they fired and sacked certain villages of the Samaritans. (Josephus, *Jewish Antiquities* 20.120–121; my italics)

Notice, of course, that italicized Galilean speech about liberty, linking literarily if not historically back to the "passion for liberty" of Judas the Galilean in *Jewish Antiquities* 18.23. I accept it as a valid admission that revolt against Rome was already at work but do not necessarily accept Josephus' linkage of the revolt to the fourth philosophy. The leadership in what followed came not from teachers but from bandits, and that underlines the role of Eleazar the bandit chieftain. Alexander is mentioned only in the former text; the latter one is quite deliberately muted in terms of Jewish atrocity. This is the clearest case of the collusion of banditry and peasantry seen so far, as also of the brigand chief as popular righter of wrongs when official authority failed to do so. The first Roman-Jewish War almost broke out under Cumanus in 52 C.E., and it almost broke out from the bottom up, from peasantry led by a very famous bandit chieftain.

As this middle act continued, Cumanus moved against the insurgents with his own auxiliary troops and "made prisoners of many of Eleazar's companions and killed a yet larger number," according to *Jewish War* 2.236, or "slew many, but took more alive," according to *Jewish Antiquities* 20.122. Both accounts then agree that the Jerusalem authorities managed to persuade the rest of the insurgents to lay down their arms and return home. One would presume from Josephus that Cumanus had won. Yet the conclusion in 2.238 is that "many . . . emboldened by impunity, had recourse to robbery [brigandage], and raids and insurrections, fostered by the more reckless, broke out all over the country," and in the parallel version of 20.124 that "from that time the whole of Judaea was infested with bands of brigands." Did Cumanus actually win that contest? He did not succeed in capturing Eleazar, who continued to operate until caught under Felix in 52 to 60 C.E. And why that great increase in banditry mentioned in both texts? Did Cumanus completely defeat a raid against Samaria or simply splinter a revolt against Rome into guerrilla bands across the country?

The final act is in *Jewish War* 2.239–246 and *Jewish Antiquities* 20.125–136. It concerns the intervention by Quadratus from Syria. The basic question is whether he came south to suppress a rebellion, as Tacitus said, or to adjudicate a dispute, as Josephus claimed. Notice, for example, the slow and measured progress to Tyre, to Caesarea, to Lydda, and finally to Jerusalem, more the movements of a general pacifying a country than a judge adjudicating a complaint. Notice also the differences between the twin versions as Quadratus arrives in Jerusalem.

> He left Lydda and went up to Jerusalem; and, finding the people peaceably celebrating the feast of unleavened bread, he returned to Antioch. (Josephus, *Jewish War* 2.244b)

> He himself, fearing a fresh revolution on the part of the Jewish people, visited the city of Jerusalem, which he found at peace and observing one of the traditional religious festivals. Having satisfied himself, therefore, that there would be no revolt on their part, he left them celebrating the festival and returned to Antioch. (Josephus, *Jewish Antiquities* 20.133)

There is no mention of a revolt in the earlier text but a double mention of it in the later one.

Finally, Quadratus sent the highest authorities of the Jews, Jonathan, former high priest in 36 to 37 C.E., Ananias, current high priest in 47–59 C.E., and his son and deputy high priest Ananus, to Rome for trial before Claudius. They were to be accompanied by the highest Samaritan authorities and also the highest Roman authorities involved, Cumanus himself and a tribune named Celer.

The conclusion in the twin versions of *Jewish War* 2.245–246 and *Jewish Antiquities* 20.134–136 is set in Rome. Claudius, persuaded definitely by Agrippa II, possibly by Claudius' wife Agrippina, and maybe even by Pallas, who is mentioned in neither text but whose brother Felix was appointed in Cumanus' place, found in favor of the Jewish side, executed some of the

Samaritan petitioners, banished Cumanus into exile, and ordered Celer to be given over to Jewish authority, dragged around Jerusalem, and beheaded. That extraordinary judgment warns us that we lack certain details on the Roman side of this dispute. We are not told what Celer, a tribune and not to be confused with the lewd soldier in the Temple, did to have deserved such a fate.

I conclude, therefore, that a widespread revolt of peasantry spearheaded by banditry took place in 52 C.E., that Josephus suppressed it much more in *Jewish War* than in *Jewish Antiquities*, and that Quadratus came south, as Tacitus said, to quell an insurrection and not just to adjudicate a complaint. In plain language, the First Roman-Jewish War almost started in 52 C.E., and it almost started among peasants and bandits rather than among aristocrats and retainers. But since, in Roman eyes, those latter were responsible for keeping order, saving them *might* well have meant gaining the support of Pallas, for which the price was Felix his brother as next procurator. That *might* also explain why *Jewish Antiquities* 20.162 records tensions between Jonathan and Felix, even though, as it says demurely, he himself "had requested [Claudius] Caesar to dispatch Felix as a procurator of Judaea." Those, of course, are guesses, but guesses warranted by discrepancies in the records.

Be that as it may, and whatever the reasons, Felix went out as governor of Palestine between 52 and 60 C.E. Josephus mentions banditry twice during his rule, and, in each case, one but not the other of his parallel texts combines and confuses *bandits* with *prophets*. But, as seen earlier, it is necessary to ignore any mention of prophets or, as Josephus prefers to call them, "imposters" and "deceivers," in the following two sets of parallel texts, where I have italicized them for emphasis.

> Felix took prisoner Eleazar, the brigand chief, who for twenty years had ravaged the country, with many of his associates, and sent them for trial to Rome. Of the brigands whom he crucified, and of the common people who were convicted of complicity with them and punished by him, the number was incalculable. (Josephus, *Jewish War* 2.253)

> In Judaea matters were constantly going from bad to worse. For the country was again infested with bands of brigands *and imposters who deceived the mob.* Not a day passed, however, but that Felix captured and put to death many of these *imposters and* brigands. He also, by a ruse, took alive Eleazar the son of Dinaeus, who had organized the company of brigands; for by offering a pledge that he would suffer no harm, Felix induced him to appear before him. Felix then imprisoned him and dispatched him to Rome. (Josephus, *Jewish Antiquities* 20.160–161; my italics)

Two standard themes of social banditry are mentioned, one in each text: the complicity between peasantry and banditry, and the bandit leader's capture by deceit. It also looks as if Felix is concluding problems left over from Cumanus. That Eleazar was sent to Rome rather than summarily executed at home, for instance, underlines the importance of the preceding insurrection under Cumanus and its continuation through banditry under Felix. Also, recall my earlier mention of those accused priests sent to Rome by Felix and defended there by Josephus, according to *Life* 13. They *might* have been part of continued aristocratic insurrectionary tendencies from the time of Cumanus. One final point: we already knew, from *Jewish Antiquities* 20.121, that Eleazar "was a brigand who for many years had his home in the mountains." We now learn, but from *Jewish War* 2.253, that "for twenty years [he] had ravaged the country." That means that renewed banditry did not just begin with the brigand chief Tholomaeus, under Fadus in 44 to 46 C.E., but has to be extended, with Eleazar, back into the thirties, maybe even to the time of Pilate in 26 to 36 C.E. Although, therefore, I wish to emphasize those precise times when we are certain of Palestinian banditry, I never presume that it existed only at those times.

The second pair of twin texts evince that same combination of brigands/ bandits and imposters/prophets in one but not the other source. Remember that their immediately preceding contexts had been speaking about that latter category.

> No sooner were these disorders reduced than the inflammation, as in a sick man's body, broke out again in another quarter. The *imposters and brigands,* banding together, incited numbers to revolt, exhorting them to assert their independence [liberty], and threatening to kill any who submitted to Roman domination and forcibly to suppress those who voluntarily accepted servitude. Distributing themselves in companies throughout the country, they looted the houses of the wealthy, murdered their owners, and set the villages on fire. The effects of their frenzy were thus felt throughout all Judaea, and every day saw this war being fanned into fiercer flame. (Josephus, *Jewish War* 2.264–265; my italics)

> And now the brigands once more incited the populace to war with Rome, telling them not to obey them. They also fired and pillaged the villages of those who refused to comply. (Josephus, *Jewish Antiquities* 20.172b)

Both texts show clearly that banditry is well on its way toward revolution. Note that the slogan of liberty or independence appears here in *Jewish*

War 2.264 under Felix as it had in *Jewish Antiquities* 20.120 under Cumanus. I suggested earlier that the war had almost started under Cumanus in 52 C.E. One could even say that it did and was simply contained or controlled until 66 C.E. Note also that "the war," as Josephus calls this banditry in both texts, was as much against Jewish collaboration as against Roman domination and as much against peasant as against aristocratic subordination to colonialism.

Under Festus, governor in 60 to 62 C.E., there is only a general statement about bandits. The parallel texts in *Jewish War* 2.254–257 and *Jewish Antiquities* 20.163–166 were cited already on chapter 6 under 'Hidden Daggers and Hidden Faces.' It was seen there that Josephus had mixed up, not in the earlier but in the later of his twin versions, the urban Sicarii and the rural bandits. That continues the overall confusion of rebel groups so that urban terrorists ("sicarii"), rural bandits ("brigands"), and millennial prophets ("imposters") are now all combined in one undifferentiated rebellious mass.

There is no mention of rural banditry under Albinus, the next procurator, between 62 and 64 C.E. Josephus is primarily concerned, in that period, with factional strife in Jerusalem itself. Claudius had granted the right to appoint high priests to the Herodian princes in 45 C.E. Ananias son of Nebedaeus was high priest from 48 to 59 C.E. But then, between 59 and 64 C.E., Herod Agrippa II appointed and deposed five high priests: Ismael son of Phabi in 59–61; Joseph Kami son of Simon in 61–62; Ananus son of Ananus in 62; Jesus son of Damnaeus in 62–63; and Jesus son of Gamaliel in 63–64 C.E. To have one high priest for over a decade and then five high priests in about as many years must have greatly destabilized priestly control in Jerusalem.

In his earlier *Jewish War* 2.274–276 he leaves this Jerusalem factionalism deliberately unclear, with pejorative description replacing exact delineation. "Each ruffian," whoever that may be, is "like a brigand chief or tyrant." But in *Jewish Antiquities*, where, as Shaye Cohen shows, he is ready to widen the responsibility for the war and even to condemn "the highest echelons of Jewish society, the high priests and the aristocracy" (1979:156), we get a much clearer picture of who these ruffians are. Factional strife breaks out at the end of Felix's term and continues under Albinus in 20.180: between high priests and ordinary priests in 20.181 and 20.206–207 (doublet?); between deposed and current high priests in 20.213; between high priests and aristocrats in 20.214.

The last procurator was Florus, in 64 to 66 C.E. We saw earlier, with Eric Hobsbawm and Anton Blok, that peasant bandits often bribe members of the upper classes for protection or even use them as fences. What

Josephus says in the texts below is not, therefore, absolutely unbelievable. It may, however, be relatively unbelievable.

> [Florus] stripped whole cities, ruined entire populations, and *almost went the length of* proclaiming throughout the country that all were at liberty to practice brigandage, on condition that he received his share of the spoils. Certainly his avarice brought desolation upon all the cities, and caused many to desert their ancestral haunts and seek refuge in foreign provinces. (Josephus, *Jewish War* 2.278b–279; my italics)

> [Florus] even joined in partnership with brigands. In fact, the majority of people practised this occupation with no inhibitions, since they had no doubt that their lives would be insured by him in return for his quota of the spoils. . . . The ill-fated Jews, unable to endure the devastation by brigands that went on were one and all forced to abandon their own country and flee, for they thought that it would be better to settle among gentiles, no matter where. What more need be said? It was Florus who constrained us to take up war with the Romans, for we preferred to perish together rather than by degrees. (Josephus, *Jewish Antiquities* 20.255b–257)

In any case, with that crescendo of criticism against Florus, the *Jewish Antiquities* and hence the parallelism with the continuing *Jewish War* comes to an end. In view of the ideological anti-imperialism of rural banditry under Felix, it is unlikely that it had, as a whole, started to cooperate with Florus. And, of course, it was aristocracy rather than peasantry that had the luxury of emigration.

A Bandit General of a Bandit Army

Josephus was in Galilee for about six months between the fall of 66 and the summer of 67 C.E., at the very start of the war with Rome. For the period before the arrival of Vespasian and Titus with their legions in the spring of 67 C.E., we have, as noted earlier, a double account in *Jewish War* 2.568–646 and in *Life* 28–406, and that demands, of course, not paraphrastic synthesis but critical analysis.

By September of 66 C.E. the Syrian governor Cestius Gallus had marched southward from Antioch with about thirty thousand troops spearheaded by the XII Fulminata legion at full strength. By November of 66 C.E., however, having somewhat inexplicably raised the siege of Jerusalem, he let his army be trapped in the pass of Beth-horon a few miles northwest of the city and suffered a stunning defeat. As the Jerusalem authorities moved to administer their newly won independence and prepare for the inevitable and full-scale Roman reprisals, they sent Josephus to take charge of Galilee. The parallel accounts of his mission and arrival in Galilee lay clearly bare the divergent tendentiousness of each writing. Here is the earlier version.

> Generals were selected. . . . Josephus, son of Matthias, was given the two Galilees, with the addition of Gamala, the strongest city in that region . . . he made it his first care to win the affection of the inhabitants . . . appointed . . . magistrates of the whole of Galilee . . . he fortified the most suitable places. . . . He, moreover, levied in Galilee an army of upwards of a hundred thousand men, all of whom he equipped with old arms collected for that purpose. (Josephus, *Jewish War* 2.568–576)

The full text, of which the above is but barest outline, gives a picture of Josephus in total control of both Upper and Lower Galilee, with almost unlimited time for both juridical and military matters, for fortifying towns and training recruits, and, above all, for organizing "his army on Roman lines." And all of that was done in a few months and in the middle of winter. That entire description, however, is based, as Shaye Cohen has shown so well, not on the actual situation in Galilee but on the ideal picture of a Roman general (1979:91–97). Josephus is describing himself as a worthy opponent for Vespasian just as the Galileans are worthy opponents for the Romans.

Josephus' Galilean levies of one hundred thousand men furnished him, according to *Jewish War* 2.583, with "an army, ready for action, of sixty thousand infantry and three hundred and fifty cavalry." That army, as I just noted, was organized and trained by Josephus "on Roman lines." Later, in *Jewish War* 3.69, just before digressing into a rhapsody on the Roman army in 3.70–109, Josephus enumerates the forces that Vespasian and Titus had assembled at Ptolemaïs to invade Galilee in the spring of 67 C.E. That army, centered on the V Macedonica, X Fretensis, and XV Apollinaris legions, "amounted to sixty thousand" soldiers. In other words, the generals on both sides are of equal caliber; the forces on both sides are of equal size; the training on both sides is in Roman military discipline. Furthermore, according to *Jewish War* 3.42–43, "the two Galilees have always resisted any hostile invasion, for the inhabitants are from infancy inured to war . . . never did the men lack courage nor the country men," and even the smallest of its villages "contains above fifteen thousand inhabitants." All is appropriately and evenly set for the Great Galilean War against Rome. But here, unfortunately, is its first encounter.

> The troops under the command of Josephus, who were camping beside a town called Garis, not far from Sepphoris, discovering that the war was upon them, and they might at any moment be attacked by the Romans,

dispersed and fled, not only before any engagement, but before they had even seen their foes. (Josephus, *Jewish War* 2.129)

Even, then, just reading *Jewish War* against itself, we must place in complete abeyance that inaugural and imaginary vision of a sixty-thousand-strong Army of the Galilees and of Josephus as the very model of a modern Roman general.

When the parallel passage on Josephus' Galilean mandate in *Life* is added to the discussion, the situation there in the early winter of 66 C.E. becomes much clearer.

> After the defeat of Cestius [Gallus] . . . the leading men in Jerusalem . . . being informed . . . that the whole of Galilee had not yet revolted from Rome, and that a portion of it was still tranquil . . . dispatched me with two other priests, Joazar and Judas, men of excellent character, to induce the disaffected to lay down their arms and to impress upon them, the desirability of reserving these for picked men of the nation. . . .
>
> At Gischala I let my colleagues return to Jerusalem and proceeded to take measures for the provision of arms and the strengthening of the fortifications of the towns. I also summoned the most stalwart of the brigands and, seeing that it would be impossible to disarm them, persuaded the people to pay them as mercenaries; remarking that it was better to give them a small sum voluntarily that to submit to raids upon their property. I then bound them by oath not to enter the district unless they were sent for or their pay was in arrear, and dismissed them with injunctions to refrain from attacking either the Romans or their neighbours; for my chief concern was the preservation of peace in Galilee. (Josephus, *Life* 28–29, 77–78)

On the one hand, that version, in which Josephus is one of a triad of priests sent to preserve the peace in Galilee, is almost as oppositely tendentious as the earlier one, in which he is the lone general sent to prepare Galilee for war. On the other, we catch a glimpse of the minimal power base that Josephus managed to establish for himself and the ranks from which his minimal armed forces were chosen.

Josephus never really controlled Upper Galilee, where Gischala was loyal to John son of Levi. And none of the major cities of Lower Galilee was on his side (Cohen 1979:214–221). Sepphoris was for Rome and against Josephus; Tiberias was split for and against Rome along socioeconomic lines, and, for even the anti-Roman party, Josephus was of secondary consideration. Gabara, near the border with Upper Galilee, was against Rome, but, being for John of Gischala, was also against Josephus. The only large settlement consistently loyal to him was Tarichaeae/Magdala at the southwestern corner of the Sea of Galilee. How, then, did he ever get going and last even the few months he did before the legions arrived?

Shaye Cohen offers this explanation. "Josephus arrived in Galilee with the backing of the revolutionary government of Jerusalem, but without troops or money. He found a peasantry which would support him against the cities, but which was victimized by hordes of bandits. He could have organized the peasantry to destroy the bandits, but this — as he says — would have filled the country with civil war (no doubt many of the peasants had relatives who were bandits) and might have failed. After all, the bandits were experienced, full-time fighters who did not have to return to their farms for a livelihood. Facing this problem, Josephus proposed a brilliant solution: he would persuade the peasantry to provide him with funds to hire the bandits as mercenaries, making it a condition of their employment that they should not harass the peasants" (1979:211–212). I have two major difficulties with that interpretation. They have nothing to do with a belief that bandits are Robin Hoods who never attack the poor and would not therefore have been any threat to the peasantry, and they have nothing to do with a belief that all Jewish bandits were ideologically anti-Roman revolutionaries. We know, for instance, from *Life* 104–111, about "Jesus, the brigand chief, on the borderland of Ptolemaïs . . . with his force, which numbered eight hundred" who was bribed by pro-Roman Sepphoris to destroy Josephus. Josephus entrapped him but allowed him, "if he would show repentance and prove his loyalty to me . . . to reassemble his former force." Josephus, I presume, simply out-bribed Sepphoris by himself hiring Jesus and his band as mercenaries for his own army.

The main problem is that, even if the bandits might have pillaged the peasantry, they certainly endangered the propertied classes and their interests to a far greater extent. One loots, presumably, where the looting is better. And, correspondingly, it is far easier to imagine the propertied classes paying Josephus to hire the bandits as mercenaries than to imagine the peasants doing so. Put simply and succinctly, Josephus taxed, as it were, the propertied classes to support his mercenary army of ex-bandits. Notice a certain deliberate vagueness in the above description. The bandits are paid to become mercenaries and then dismissed — but mercenaries to whom if not to Josephus himself? And, although I disagree with Cohen on who was paying the salaries of those bandits become mercenaries, I agree with him that it was a brilliant move on Josephus' part. It controlled banditry, at least against Jews, gave him a permanent if minimum fighting force, and must have placed many of those propertied classes on his side.

It is interesting, too, in the light of that interpretation to go back and read again some details from the *Jewish War*'s account of Josephus' Galilean army. Immediately after describing how he had trained them in Roman military discipline, he continues as follows:

> That he should test their military discipline, even before they went into action, by noting whether they abstained from their habitual malpractices, theft, robbery and rapine, and ceased to defraud their countrymen and to regard as personal profit an injury sustained by their most intimate friends....
>
> He had now mustered an army, ready for action, of sixty thousand infantry and three hundred and fifty cavalry, besides some four thousand five hundred mercenaries, in whom he placed most confidence; he had also a bodyguard of six hundred picked men about his person. These troops, the mercenaries excepted, were maintained without difficulty by the towns. (Josephus, *Jewish War* 2.581, 583, 584)

I leave aside, once again, that huge main conscript army, be it ideal hope or fictional ideal, formed and supported "without difficulty" by the towns. The only real army is those bandits become mercenaries become revolutionaries. It is they, numbering about four thousand five hundred, whose "habitual malpractices" need the moral rearmament speech, who receive "most confidence" from Josephus, and whose salaries are left unexplained. I wonder, by the way, if that picked bodyguard of six hundred soldiers might have been composed of the reassembled forces of the repentant Jesus now loyal to Josephus himself. Be that as it may, reading *Jewish War* both against itself and against *Life*, Josephus' Galilean army consisted of around five thousand ex-bandits who could, of course, melt back into the peasantry at a moment's notice.

Apart, however, from those bandits conscripted as mercenaries, what about the Galilean peasantry at large? If Josephus' narrower and more immediate power base was derived from a brilliant brokerage of banditry and gentry, his wider and more diffused one was derived from an equally brilliant manipulation of rural and urban interests. This is most evident in Josephan usage for the term "the Galileans."

In itself, of course, "the Galileans" can be a simple geographical designation for all those who live within that territorial area, but Seán Freyne has shown that the phrase has a special meaning in contexts concerned with Josephan leadership there during the winter and spring of 66–67 C.E. We are dealing, he concluded, with "a rather distinctive refinement of this basic meaning . . . the Galileans are the country people as distinct from the inhabitants of the major towns, and they are Josephus' loyal supporters, militantly nationalist, but not essentially revolutionary or subversive . . . aggressive, even militant yes, but revolutionary no" (1979–80:412). I leave aside for now that distinction between militancy and revolution but accept Freyne's reading of "the Galileans," within the context of November 66 to May 67 C.E., as the peasantry of Galilee. Shaye Cohen had a similar conclusion, and I quote him without his detailed references. "Josephus' main strength," he said, "was the peasantry, the Galileans" and he "is fairly clear and consistent on the identity of these Galileans. They come from the countryside and the villages, not the cities. They are distinguished from the men of Sepphoris, Tiberias, and Gabara, that is, from the citizens of the three largest settlements of Galilee who are never called *Galilaioi*" (1979:206–207).

Freyne and Cohen agree on one other major feature of those peasant "Galileans," namely, their hatred of the urban centers. "The cause and extent of Galilean animosity towards the larger towns, especially Sepphoris and Tiberias, and to a lesser extent Gabara and Gischala, cannot just be explained," according to Freyne, "by the pro-Roman stance of these towns alone, since with the exception of Sepphoris their pro-Roman attitudes are never explicit or clear-cut. Other, inner Galilean factors must have been at work to explain this situation" (1979–80:412). Josephus usually explains that animosity by stating that those cities were against him or against the war. But we also catch glimpses elsewhere of a more ancient animosity.

> The Galileans, seizing this opportunity, too good to be missed, of venting their hatred on one [Sepphoris] of the cities which they detested, rushed forward, with the intention of exterminating the population, aliens and all. . . .
> Tiberias, likewise, had a narrow escape from being sacked by the Galileans . . . for they had the same detestation for the Tiberians as for the inhabitants of Sepphoris. . . .
> The Galileans, resenting the miseries which he [they?] had inflicted on them before the war, were embittered against the Tiberians.
> (Josephus, *Life* 375, 384, 392)

What Freyne had termed "inner Galilean factors" is explained by Cohen's commentary. "Sepphoris was, and Tiberias had been, the administrative capital of Galilee; this would exacerbate the tension. . . . [The Galileans'] hatred of the cities undoubtedly included hatred of Rome, the defender of the established order, but it was one thing to attack and plunder Sepphoris or Tiberias, quite another to face the imperial legions. The Galileans were eager for the former, but were afraid of the latter. It is no surprise that their enthusiasm for war waned when the Romans arrived" (1979:207).

It is necessary, finally, to take a look at Freyne's earlier distinction; the Galilean peasantry was militant and nationalistic but not subversive or revolutionary. Compare, for example, the different fates of the war in Judea and in Galilee. In Judea, the irrevocable revolt started in the Temple and was led initially by a high priestly aristocrat. And in Judea the war involved a full-scale social revolution within an even broader political revolution. Things were very different in Galilee. The war had not started there, and when Gallus, marching southward in the fall of 66 C.E., sent forces into Galilee, only one battle against "rebels and brigands" is recorded, "more than two thousand" of them were killed, and there were "no further signs of revolt in Galilee," according to *Jewish War* 2.511–513. Even when other high priestly aristocrats decided to spread the war, through Josephus, into Galilee, the political revolution never really took hold there. Once Josephus arrived in Galilee, the peasantry supported him, at least in theory, and at least until the legions appeared, but, as Shaye Cohen put it, "the Galilean population was in no mood to fight Rome. It was pre-occupied with other matters and . . . [nobody] was able to incite it to a war it did not want" (1979:231). But if political revolution made little headway in Galilee, social revolution might well have done so, were it not for Josephus.

Peasant hatred for administrative centers such as Sepphoris and Tiberias or for Gabara, which was probably a toparchy capital, according to Mary Smallwood (184 note 12), points toward social revolution or, if that term presumes too much class consciousness, at least toward social insurrection. The Galilean peasants might not have been able to imagine a new social order, but they could well imagine a world with certain administrative centers razed to the ground. They were ready in the winter of 66 to 67 C.E. for a social revolution of poor against rich, of peasantry against gentry, of countryside against urban center. Josephus, having successfully brokered between bandit groups and propertied classes, brokered with equal success between peasant countryside and urban centers. Despite all his posturing and self-adulation, there is truth in the claim that he did not become a tyrant and did not start a civil war in Galilee. Had he offered to lead his banditry and peasantry against the major administrative centers and propertied interests, he might have had in Galilee what would later happen in Judea, namely, a social revolution within a political rebellion. I am inclined, therefore, to disagree with Cohen's judgment that Josephus "failed" in Galilee (1979:230). True, of course, he never organized much of a *political* rebellion in the province, and that was his primary mandate. But he did succeed in avoiding a *social* revolution. Unless, of course, one judges it a good thing for the exploited peasantry to slaughter the oppressive gentry while waiting for the Romans to come and slaughter them, it must be conceded that Josephus did very well indeed. As everywhere in these chapters, the delicate and intertwined strands of social revolution and political rebellion must be kept separate even if not separable.

One postscript: Josephus, in *Jewish War* 2.587, calls John of Gischala "a bandit" leading, in 2.593, "his band of brigands." He is never called a bandit or brigand in *Life,* but then, as Shaye Cohen has observed, "one of [*Jewish War's*] major motives . . . is to blacken John" (1979:90). John son of Levi was certainly not a bandit chief from the peasant class. He may, of course, have ended up leading bandit forces in Upper Galilee but so did Josephus in Lower Galilee. Indeed, part of Josephus' antagonism to John is that they are, in many ways, a little too like for comfort. John was actually, in Lenski's stratification terms, from the *merchant* class and important enough to be known to the Jerusalem authorities. It is, for instance, his business acumen that is recounted, with aristocratic disdain and pejorative interpretation, in the parallel texts of *Jewish War* 2.590–592 and *Life* 71–75. John of Gischala, then, represents the one clear case we have of a *merchant* class individual who, as David Rhoads summarized his life, "changed from a pro-Roman position to that of a moderate, like Josephus, and only later became a revolutionary" (124).

The Zealots, as They Called Themselves

Scholars have often talked as if there was a unified Jewish resistance movement against Rome from 6 to 66 C.E., with its theory stemming from the fourth philosophy of Judas the Galilean and its practice centered on an organized group known as the Zealots. This mistaken construct is quite understandable, since Josephus went to some trouble to create it. But as we have already seen, it is necessary to keep urban Sicarii quite distinct from rural bandits, and, as we shall now see, it is also necessary, following the work of Morton Smith (1971), David Rhoads, and Richard Horsley (1979b, 1986b), to link the Zealots not with the former but with the latter phenomenon.

We are quite accustomed in English to the distinction between a conservative and the Conservatives or a democrat and the Democrats. The lowercase word denotes a specific personal attitude, the upper case an organized political party. In reading Josephus' Greek we must also watch the distinction between "a zealot" and "the Zealots." There were always individual zealots around, for instance, in *Jewish Antiquities* 20:47 or *Jewish War* 2.444, 564, 651, but they are not of present concern. In what follows, I am primarily interested in the Zealots as a special organized political group during the war against Rome and with the sustained usage of that term that began when Ananus incited the people against

[t]he Zealots . . . for so these miscreants called themselves, as though
they were zealous in the cause of virtue and not for vice in its basest and
most extravagant format. (Josephus, *Jewish War* 4.160-161)

That is the first and clearest usage of the term *Zealots* for an organized
faction. Note that, as usual, when rebel class goes down, Josephan rhetoric
goes up, when social standing decreases, literary invective increases. But,
moving backward from that moment, Josephus has been talking about
them already in 4.147-159, where they were electing a peasant high priest,
and even earlier in 4.139-146, where they were executing Herodian nobles.
Reading from 4.139 to 4.161, it is not hard to see why Ananus (and
Josephus) is so outraged against them in his speech at 4.162-193. But it is,
still moving backward, only in 4.135-138 that we see clearly who and
whence are these not-yet-named Zealots.

In the end, satiated with their pillage of the country, the brigand chiefs
of all these scattered bands joined forces and, now merged into one pack
of villainy, stole into poor Jerusalem. . . . Fresh brigands from the country
entering the city and joining the yet more formidable gang within,
abstained henceforth from no enormities. (Josephus, *Jewish War* 4.135,
138)

The background and cause of that process may be seen quite clearly in
the following text, where the Roman "scorched earth" and "search and
destroy" policies, as Richard Horsley accurately terms them (1986b:168-
169) are quite clearly evident. Cities and even towns might surrender, but
how did a village surrender? Aristocrats might surrender, but how did peasants surrender?

While the winter lasted, [Vespasian] employed himself in securing with
garrisons the villages and smaller towns which had been reduced, post-
ing decurions in the villages and centurions in the towns; he also rebuilt
many places that had been devastated. Then, at the first approach of
spring, he marched the main body of his army from Caesarea to
Antipatris. After two days spent in restoring order in that town, on the
third he advanced, laying waste and burning all the surrounding
places . . . devastating with fire this and the neighbouring district and the
outskirts of Idumaea . . . he put upwards of ten thousand of the inhabitants to death, made prisoners of over a thousand, expelled the
remainder and stationed in the district a large division of his own troops,
who overran and devastated the whole of the hill country. . . . The mass
of the population, anticipating their arrival, had fled from Jericho to the
hill country over against Jerusalem, but a considerable number remained
behind and were put to death. (Josephus, *Jewish War* 4.442-448)

With Galilee already conquered by Titus, Vespasian moved into Judea in the winter between 67 and 68 C.E. and then, in the spring of 68, continued deeper into Judea and Idumea. The options for the peasantry were death, slavery, flight, or banditry. The Roman advance, in other words, swept larger and larger numbers of peasants off their lands, into brigand bands, and so, relentlessly as the noose tightened, into Jerusalem itself. Thus was created what Richard Horsley rightly called "the peasants-turned-brigands-turned Zealots," (1986b:174), that coalition of bandit groups that appeared for the first time in the winter of 67 to 68 C.E. in Jerusalem. "The roots of the party were," in the summary statement of Morton Smith, "mainly in the Judean peasantry, and the facts that the first things they did were attack the city aristocrats, seize control of the Temple, and elect as High Priest a villager of their own sort—all these fit perfectly with peasant piety" (1971:17).

With the Zealot coalition in Jerusalem, then, rural banditry came explosively to the forefront of the revolt. A social revolution now developed within a political rebellion. And even though the latter did not win, it is not so clear that the former lost.

A King Without a Dynasty?

The nonviolent and millennial movements led by peasant prophets were based on popular recall of the Moses and Joshua stories. The violent and military movements led by peasant messiahs were based on popular recall of the Saul and David stories. For about two hundred years, from Moses to Samuel, the leadership of the Israelite tribes had not been an institutional or dynastic procedure but a much more personal and charismatic one. I understand charisma, by the way, with Peter Worsley, as "a social relationship, not an attribute of individual personality or a mystical quality," that is, on an interactionist model by which "the leader must . . . strike responsive chords in his audience . . . [as] a catalytic personality . . . [who must] convert latent solidarities into active ritual and political action" (1968:xii, xviii).

Then, around 1000 B.C.E., the Philistines, operating with iron weaponry from urban bases on the southern coastal plain, began to make inroads on Israelite territory so serious as to warrant consideration of institutionalized leadership over unified tribal armies—in other words, a king. But, against that background of tribal egalitarianism, might it not be possible to have a sort of charismatic king, a monarch without a dynasty, one with popular election, acclamation, and acceptance as the basis of authority? Might it not be possible to have and not to have a king at the same time, to have all the benefits and none of the liabilities of monarchical leadership? The controversies of that proposal and the ambiguities of that attempt riddle the tortured account of Saul's election as Israel's first experiment in kingship. On the one hand, there is the positive account in 1 Samuel 9:1–10:16, in which the whole idea comes from God, the choice of Saul comes from God, and everything is processed with enthusiasm by the prophet Samuel, who, in 10:1, "took a vial of [olive] oil and poured it on his [Saul's] head, and kissed him and said, 'Has not the Lord anointed you to be prince over his people Israel?'" Notice, however, that the only title used in that positive account is *prince*, or war leader, and not king. On the other hand, there is the negative account that now frames that positive one in 1 Samuel 8:1–22; 10:17–27; 12:1–25. Here the idea for a *king* comes from the people and is seen by both God and Samuel as a rejection of the kingship of God. It is accepted by them both with extreme reluctance and enacted with these safeguards.

> Samuel brought all the tribes of Israel near, and the tribe of Benjamin was taken by lot. He brought the tribe of Benjamin near by its families, and the family of the Matrites was taken by lot; finally he brought the family of the Matrites near man by man, and Saul the son of Kish was taken by lot. . . . Then Samuel told the people the rights and duties of the kingship; and he wrote them in a book and laid it up before the Lord. (1 Samuel 10:20–21a, 25)

Lottery is surely the proper mode of selection in a theocracy since it leaves total control in God's power and also obviates absolutely any human hierarchical conceptions. And, whether true or not as historical record of the selection, it is clear enough as ideological model of radical egalitarianism and theocratic control. The description in that sacred book also sounds like the establishment of a constitutional rather than an absolute monarchy. Buried deep, then, in the origins of Jewish kingship was something flatly antimonarchical and maybe even antirational, the idea of a charismatic or nondynastic king, the implicit possibility, therefore, that the monarchy might be continued not by genes but by lots, leaving it all up to God. And, if theory and story sound at times a little farfetched, one may well see what actually happened by reading 1 Samuel 11, where Saul's successful defeat of the Ammonites probably led to his popular acclamation as king for the war against the Philistines. If lottery is the way of theocracy, acclamation is the way of democracy, and dynasty does not figure prominently in either system.

All those points were reiterated in the transition from Saul to David, with one very important new element added. The time came when, in ideal charismatic theory, Saul should have been retired in favor of David. But Saul refused to accept this nondynastic transition, and David was driven into banditry.

> David departed from there and escaped to the cave of Adullam; and when his brothers and all his father's house heard it, they went down there to him. And every one who was in distress, and every one who was in debt and every one who was discontented, gathered to him; and he became captain over them. And there were with him about four hundred men. (1 Samuel 22:1–2)

So David, the ideal king, was nondynastic, was popularly acclaimed, and had used a base in banditry from which to achieve the kingship. Bandit and king were closely aligned in the Davidic model. Thus, although much biblical writing was expended in obscuring it, "the popular Israelite tradition of kingship" had, as Richard Horsley argues, "three principal characteristics: Kingship was constituted by *popular* election or *anointing*; it was *conditional* on the king's maintenance of a certain social policy and the anointing of a new king was generally a *revolutionary* action" (1984:477).

Messianic claimants surfaced only twice in the period with whose trajectories I am at present concerned, once after the death of Herod the Great in 4 B.C.E. and again during the war with Rome in 66–70 C.E. There are five cases in all, but one of them, that of Menahem the Sicarii leader, concerns a member not of the *peasant* but the *retainer* class. (The data are summarized for fast review in appendix 2.)

Anyone Might Make Himself King

After Herod's death revolt broke out all over Palestine, and its seriousness may be assessed by the fact that the Syrian legate Varus eventually needed three legions and numerous auxiliary troops to suppress it. I leave aside here aristocratic rebellion within the Herodian family (from the parallel texts of *Jewish War* 2.78 and *Jewish Antiquities* 17.298) and also ethnic revolts by Herod's Idumean veterans against his Jewish troops (from the parallel texts of *Jewish War* 2.55b and *Jewish Antiquities* 17:269–270). None of that is particularly surprising, nor would it have needed such massive Roman reprisals. My emphasis is exclusively on messianic claimants, who were, as Richard Horsley said, "all men of humble origins" (1984:484), and whose ubiquity from Galilee to Perea to Judea indicated widespread popular revolt and resulted in two thousand crucifixions. It is precisely the messianism of the revolt that needs to be understood against the background of Herodian dynastic intrigues.

The three messianic claimants are Judas in Galilee, Simon in Perea, and Athronges in Judea, and Josephus seems quite aware that he is working with a triadic set. First of all, each one in *Jewish War* is about twice as long as the preceding one, so is each one in *Jewish Antiquities*, but they are all twice as long as the former set to begin with. There is, as it were, a deliberate climactic progress across the three units. Next, those three parallel accounts in *Jewish War* 2.56–65 and *Jewish Antiquities* 17.271–284 are preceded in the former case but succeeded in the latter one by a general statement.

> (1) The country, also, in various districts, was a prey to disorder, and the opportunity induced numbers of persons to aspire to sovereignty.
>
> (2) And so Judaea was filled with brigandage. Anyone might make himself king as the head of a band of rebels whom he fell in with, and then would press on to the destruction of the community, causing trouble to few Romans and then only to a small degree but bringing the greatest slaughter upon their own people. (*Jewish War* 2.55a = *Jewish Antiquities* 17:285)

Notice two details, one small and one very large. The first statement introduces the triad and generalizes to the entire "countryside" of Palestine. The second one concludes the triad, but, since Athronges of Judea immediately preceded it, the generalization is limited to that area. The more important point, however, is that neither there nor anywhere else does Josephus talk about messianic claimants. He makes no attempt to explain the Jewish traditions of popular kingship that might make a brigand chief or a rural outlaw think not just of rural rebellion but of regal rule. The reason is, of course, quite clear and was seen already. For Josephus, Jewish apocalyptic and messianic promises were fulfilled in Vespasian. It is hardly likely, then, that Josephus would explain too clearly or underline too sharply the existence of alternative messianic fulfillments before Vespasian, especially from the Jewish lower classes. But, just as popular prophets were earlier hidden behind words like *imposters, magicians,* or *deceivers,* so now popular kings are hidden behind words like *diadem, king,* or *sovereignty.* It is interesting, though, that the former receive far more pejorative descriptions than the latter.

The first of the three named messianic claimants is Judas, son of the bandit chieftain Ezekias whom Herod the Great had executed, and not to be confused with another Galilean Judas, founder of the fourth philosophy, with its slogan of no Lord but God.

> (1) At Sepphoris in Galilee . . . [he] raised a considerable body of followers, broke open the royal arsenals, and having armed his companions, attacked the other aspirants to power.

> (2) Judas got together a large number of desperate men at Sepphoris in Galilee and there made an assault on the royal palace, and having seized all the arms that were stored there, he armed every single one of his men and made off with all the property that had been seized there. He became an object of terror to all men by plundering those he came across in his desire for great possessions and his ambition for royal rank, a prize that he expected to obtain not through the practice of virtue but through excessive ill-treatment of others. (Josephus, *Jewish War* 2.56 = *Jewish Antiquities* 17:271–272)

The differences in those versions are rather interesting. First, as Richard Horsley emphasized, that double "at Sepphoris" is literally "in Sepphoris" the first time and "around Sepphoris" the second time (1988:192). If one had only the former phrase, Judas might be considered an urban rebel striking out from a base in Sepphoris. But the latter's Greek makes it much clearer that he gathered his forces "around" Sepphoris, then attacked its royal arsenal, and thereafter returned to the countryside whence he had come. Although, therefore, his social class is not recorded, as is that of Simon and Athronges, he was probably a peasant bandit chieftain whose initial success raised him to the level of messianic claimant. Next, the former text does not mention royalty but makes Judas sound like one bandit chieftain fighting others. The second makes his role more clearly social as well as political. He took not only arms but possessions from Sepphoris, then capital of Galilee, and he continued, leaving aside Josephus' pejorative description, to attack the rich. One must also presume some complicity from the city itself in this entire process since, according to *Jewish War* 2.68 and *Jewish Antiquities* 17.289, the Romans later burned the city and enslaved its people.

The second messianic claimant, with parallel texts in *Jewish War* 2.57–59 and *Jewish Antiquities* 17.273–277a, was Simon, a slave of Herod's, operating in Perea east of the Jordan. His royal aspirations were also known to Tacitus, who says, in *Histories* 5.9, that he "assumed the name of king without waiting for Caesar's decision [about Herod's will and heirs]" (Moore & Jackson 2.190–191).

> (1) Simon . . . proud of his tall and handsome figure, assumed the diadem. Perambulating the country with the brigands whom he had collected he burnt down the royal palace at Jericho and many other stately mansions, such incendiarism providing him with an easy opportunity for plunder. Not a house of any respectability would have escaped the flames, had not . . . the . . . troops gone out to encounter this rascal.
>
> (2) Simon . . . a handsome man, who took pre-eminence by size and bodily strength . . . was expected to go farther. Elated by the unsettled

conditions of affairs, he was bold enough to place the diadem on his head, and having got together a body of men, he was himself also proclaimed king by them in their madness, and he rated himself worthy of this beyond anyone else. After burning the royal palace in Jericho, he plundered and carried off the things that had been seized there. He also set fire to many other royal residences in many parts of the country and utterly destroyed them after permitting his fellow-rebels to take as booty whatever had been left in them. (Josephus, *Jewish War* 2.57–58 = *Jewish Antiquities* 17:273–274)

Popular messianic fervor is obliquely designated by Josephus' pejorative term "madness," as also by his later description in 17.276 of their fighting "a long and heavy battle . . . with more recklessness than science." But what is much more significant is that the description of Saul, Israel's first king, lies behind that of Simon.

Saul [was] a handsome man. There was not a man among the people of Israel more handsome than he; from the shoulders upward he was taller than any of the people. . . . When he stood among the people, he was taller than any of the people from his shoulders upward. (1 Samuel 9:2; 10:23)

Simon, like Saul, was very tall and very handsome, requirements that personalize the necessary military prowess of the charismatic leader and that indicate the difference between popular and dynastic kingship.

Before he moves from Simon to Athronges, however, Josephus adds one interesting apologetic comment.

Such was the great madness that settled upon the nation because they had no king of their own to restrain the populace by his pre-eminence [virtue], and because the foreigners who came among them to suppress the rebellion were themselves a cause of provocation through their arrogance and their greed. (Josephus, *Jewish Antiquities* 17.277b; no *Jewish War* parallel)

That comment, which, as one would expect, has no earlier parallel version, is a very oblique and indirect admission of popular messianic hopes. It was not just a case of upstart royal pretenders, Josephus now adds, but of a people with no king of their own, no monarch preeminent in virtue.

The last of the three messianic claimants and the one who receives the longest account, with parallel texts in *Jewish War* 2.60–65 and *Jewish Antiquities*17.278–284, is Athronges in Judea.

(1) Now, too, a mere shepherd had the temerity to aspire to the throne. He was called Athrongaeus, and his sole recommendations, to

raise such hopes, were vigour of body, a soul contemptuous of death, and four brothers resembling himself. To each of them he entrusted an armed band . . . while he himself, like a king, handled matters of graver moment. It was now that he donned the diadem, but his raiding expeditions continued long afterwards.

(2) There was a certain Athronges, a man distinguished neither for the position of his ancestors nor by the excellence of his character, nor for any abundance of means but merely a shepherd completely unknown to everybody although he was remarkable for his great stature and feats of strength. This man had the temerity to aspire to the kingship, thinking that if he obtained it he would enjoy freedom to act more outrageously; as for meeting death, he did not attach much importance to the loss of his life under such circumstances. He also had four brothers and they too were tall men and confident of being very successful through their feats of strength, and he believed them to be a strong point in his bid for the kingdom. . . . Athronges himself put on the diadem. . . . This man kept his power for a long while, for he had the title of king and nothing to prevent him doing what he wished. (Josephus, *Jewish War* 2.60–62 = *Jewish Antiquities* 17:278)

Apart from the details of their exploits and, of course, the tendentious Josephan language, there is again the significant linkage to Saul and now to David as well. In 1 Samuel 16:11 David is called to be king while he is "keeping the sheep," and, in 17:20, he began the day on which he killed Goliath by leaving "the sheep with a keeper." Josephus is rendered almost speechless by the lowliness of Athronges' status, but it is the model of David the shepherd-king that ideologically undergirds the prolonged and successful military rebellion of Athronges and his brothers.

A Purple Mantle in the Temple

Two leaders in the war of 66 to 73 C.E. were messianic claimants, Menahem (grand ?)son of Judas the Galilean, and, like him, a teacher from the *retainer* class, who was killed by aristocratic Jewish rebels at the very beginning of the war, and Simon son of Gioras, who was ritually executed as the official Jewish leader during the Roman triumph toward its end.

We have already seen above that the teacher Menahem, having armed his Sicarii followers from the captured arsenal of Masada, returned to Jerusalem to break the standoff between the rebel aristocrat Eleazar, son of Ananias, and the loyal aristocratic leadership, which included his father Ananias. It was, however, a short-lived alliance. As soon as Menahem and his followers had murdered the defeated Ananias, Eleazar turned on them, killed Menahem, and drove the surviving Sicarii into retirement atop Masada.

> Menahem . . . took his intimate friends off with him to Masada, where
> he broke into king Herod's armoury and provided arms both for his
> fellow-townsmen and for other brigands; then, with these men for his
> bodyguard, he returned like a veritable king to Jerusalem, became the
> leader of the revolution, and directed the siege of the palace. . . . So they
> laid their plans to attack him in the Temple, whither he had gone up in
> state to pay his devotions, arrayed in royal robes and attended by his
> suite of armed fanatics. (Josephus, *Jewish War* 2.434, 444)

Menahem had returned to Jerusalem not only with his Sicarii followers, Josephus' "fellow-townsmen," but now at the head of a peasant mili-
tia, Josephus' "brigands," as well. For now, however, the important points
are those phrases "a veritable king" and "arrayed in royal robes." It might be
objected that Josephus is simply talking of leadership aspirations rather
than messianic claims. But his standard pejorative expression for such aspirations is tyranny not monarchy. That expression is also used of Menahem:
"an insufferable tyrant" in 2.442 and "his tyranny" in 2.448. Josephus' use of
"king" and "royal" must, therefore, be taken seriously, and Menahem's
leadership, however abortive, should be seen as a messianic program. Its
transcendental status was vindicated, no doubt, by the successful capture
of Masada and was corroborated by its initially successful intervention in
Jerusalem.

I agree, however, with Richard Horsley that "far more serious and
important than the Menahem episode was the messianic movement
focused on Simon bar Giora, who eventually became the principal
political-military commander in the besieged holy city and whom the
Romans recognized as the enemy general or chief of state" (1984:488).
Simon was a native of Gerasa in the Transjordan Decapolis, and his nickname "son of the proselyte" probably indicates humble origins. We first
hear of him as Cestius Gallus, the Syrian legate, was preparing to attack
Jerusalem in October of 66 C.E. After a "frontal attack" from the city had
killed many Romans but was eventually "checked," Simon attacked, according to *Jewish War* 2.521, "from the back of their lines . . . cut up a large part
of their rear-guard, and carried off many of their baggage mules . . . into the
city." Later, in the euphoria after Gallus' final defeat, the aristocratic leadership of the war, in appointing its local commanders, sent one John son of
Ananias to take charge of "Gophna and Acrabetta," areas north of Jerusalem toward the borders with Samaria. But despite 2.568, we find in
2.652–654 and 4.503–507 that it is Simon who is in actual control of Acrabatene. He has "a large band of revolutionaries . . . [and] not content with ran-
sacking the houses of the wealthy, he further maltreated their persons." On
the one hand, political revolution against Rome is being combined with

social revolution against the wealthy. On the other, noting Simon's "physical strength and audacity," we can presume that charismatic has prevailed over official leadership. In any case, with the Jerusalem aristocracy still in charge of the revolution, Simon was forced to take temporary refuge with the equally suppressed Sicarii on Masada.

A year later, when the Zealots and their Idumean allies had destroyed the aristocratic leadership of the revolt in Jerusalem, Simon left Masada and began to organize his own movement, and the David parallels begin to multiply.

> He withdrew to the hills, where, by proclaiming liberty for slaves and rewards for the free, he gathered around him the villains from every quarter.... And now when he was becoming a terror to the towns, many men of standing were seduced by his strength and career of unbroken success into joining him; and his was no longer an army of mere serfs or brigands, but one including numerous citizen recruits, subservient to his command as to a king. (Josephus, *Jewish War* 4.508, 510)

The first link is: bandit to general to king, just like David before him. The next one is just as important. When Simon marched into Idumea, in 4.529, he "first of all by a surprise attack captured the little town of Hebron." That restored to Jewish sovereignty, as Josephus underlines, the ancient town of Abraham. But, much more significantly, it means that Simon started for Jerusalem from Hebron just as David had done, since, as Otto Michel has noted, Hebron is the "city of David" (403).

> After that [the death of Saul and Jonathan] David inquired of the Lord, "Shall I go up into any of the cities of Judah?" And the Lord said to him, "Go up." David said, "To which shall I go up?" And he said, "To Hebron." So David went up there, and his two wives also.... And the men of Judah came, and there they anointed David king over the house of Judah....
>
> All the elders of Israel came to the king at Hebron; and King David made a covenant with them at Hebron before the Lord and they anointed David king over Israel.... At Hebron he reigned over Judah seven years and six months; and at Jerusalem he reigned over all Israel and Judah thirty-three years. (2 Samuel 2:1–4; 5:3–5)

A third parallel derives from that mention of David's wives, which, as becomes clear in 2 Samuel 3:2–5, is intended to emphasize dynastic continuities. It is significant, therefore, that the presence of Simon's wife is repeatedly mentioned: presumably as he fled from Acrabatene to Masada, where "with his band" in 2.653 is specified in the parallel 4.505 as "with his following of women" and certainly in 4.538, where the Zealots "captured

his wife and a large number of her attendants." The reaction of Simon in
4.539–544, even allowing for Josephan exaggeration, bespeaks more than
marital distress.

Even more important, however, because specific to Simon, is the constant reiteration of the stern discipline he imposed upon his entrance into
Jerusalem. This might just reflect good military leadership, but it might also
reflect, as well, the ideology of a holy war. In other words, as David Rhoads
suggested, "it would have been this strict 'discipline in war' which distinguished Simon from the other revolutionary leaders and characterized any
messianic self-understanding he might have had" (146). More than any of
the others, Simon may have imagined not just a political or even a social
but an ideologically holy revolution.

His final act may be especially important for understanding Simon's
messianism. Josephus says, in *Jewish War* 7.26–28, that Simon occupied the
upper city during the siege but that, after the fall of Jerusalem, he took his
closest associates, provisions for several days, and "some stone-cutters . . .
down into one of the secret passages." Hoping to escape, they mined their
way until they ran out of food.

> Thereupon, Simon, imagining that he could cheat the Romans by creat-
> ing a scare, dressed himself in white tunics and buckling over them a
> purple mantle arose out of the ground at the very spot whereon the tem-
> ple formerly stood. The spectators were at first aghast . . . but . . . Simon
> bade them summon the general. (Josephus, *Jewish War* 7.29–31)

Discrepancies abound in that story. To excavate from the western or
upper city, he mined toward the Temple Mount in the east. To escape he
tried to scare the Romans, but, having succeeded, he asks for their general.
And he brings his royal apparel along with him. A somewhat different reading seems equally plausible. Simon deliberately mined eastward in order to
surrender formally on the Temple Mount, and he did so robed in purple as
king of the Jews. It is surely significant, that, in the end, Josephus was willing to glorify the deliberate and calculated suicide of the Sicarii atop
Masada but not the deliberate and calculated martyrdom of Simon as king
of the Jews. Maybe, to Josephus, the former act was safely exotic, unique,
and unlikely to become a model for regular emulation but the latter was all
too possibly open for future imitation. In any case, as Otto Michel suggests,
not everyone may want to follow Josephus' preferences on that question
(408).

Those messianic trajectories between 4 B.C.E. and 70 C.E. must suffice
for now, but two short notes may be added. The Second Roman-Jewish War
of 115 to 117 C.E. in Egypt, Cyrenaica, Cyprus, newly Roman Mesopota-

mia, and possibly even Palestine, was led in North Africa, where it started and whence it spread elsewhere, by one Lucuas, possibly the same as Andreas, who "received the messianic title of 'king'" (Smallwood 397). Finally, between 132 and 135 C.E., in the Third Roman-Jewish War, restricted like the first one to Palestine, its leader Simon bar Cosiba received the nickname "Bar Cochba . . . a messianic title . . . conferred on him by Akiba, one of the leading rabbis, who accepted him as the messiah despite the assurance of a more sceptical rabbi that 'grass will grow on your cheeks, Akiba, before the son of David comes'" (Smallwood 439).

✦ 10 ✦

Rebel and Revolutionary

Scattered across the countryside one may observe certain wild
animals, male and female, dark, livid and burnt by the sun,
attached to the earth which they dig and turn over with
invincible stubbornness. However, they have something like an
articulated voice and when they stand up they reveal a human
face. Indeed, they are human beings. . . . Thanks to them the
other human beings need not sow, labour and harvest in order
to live. That is why they ought not to lack the bread which they
have sown.

Jean la Bruyère, French moralist
of the late seventeenth century (Hobsbawm 1973:6)

We want everybody to work, as we work. There should no
longer be either rich or poor. All should have bread for
themselves and for their children. We should all be equal. I have
five small children and only one little room, where we have to
eat and sleep and do everything, while so many lords (*signori*)
have ten or twelve rooms, entire palaces. . . . It will be enough to
put all in common and to share with justice what is produced.

Unnamed peasant woman from Piana dei Greci,
province of Palermo, speaking to a north Italian journalist
during an 1893 peasant uprising (Hobsbawm 1965:183)

It is clear from the preceding chapters, or from a glance at the summary
appendix 2, that, leaving aside the most inadequately documented trajectories of the magicians, those of the protesters, prophets, bandits, and messiahs all came to a first climax in the mid-sixties C.E. Immediately before
and then during the First Roman-Jewish War, we found in Jerusalem, first,
Sicarii from the *retainer* class, then, protesters, prophets, both oracular and
millennial, bandits, and messiahs, from both *retainer* and *peasant* classes.
The final step, then, is to look at that war, not so much for itself as for the
light it casts back over the types and trajectories of social unrest that
preceded and precipitated it. And I do so with certain comparative historical and sociological models as discipline.

Native Revolts Against Rome

Stephen Dyson has written a fascinating comparative description of five native revolts against the Roman Empire more or less within the hundred years on which this book's second part has been concentrating. The first case, in 52 to 51 B.C.E., was the rebellion of Vercingetorix of the Arverni, who, having united the other Gallic tribes, conducted initially successful guerrilla warfare against Caesar but was eventually trapped at Alesia in Burgundy and executed during the Caesarean triumph of 46 B.C.E. The second example, between 6 and 9 C.E., took place in Dalmatia and Pannonia, between the Adriatic and the Danube. It was led primarily by Bato of the Daesitiates, and it took "four years, an army of fifteen legions plus auxiliaries, and the skills of Rome's best general [Tiberius] . . . to once more bring the territory under Roman control" (250). And Bato was not executed but sent into retirement at Ravenna. The third instance took place in 9 C.E. even as the preceding revolt was finally ending. P. Quinctilius Varus, whom you may last recall crucifying two thousand Jewish insurgents in 4 B.C.E., was lured by Arminius of the Germanic Cherusci out of his summer quarters and into disaster amid the wooded constriction of the Teutoburger Wald. Varus lost his nerve and his three legions and took his own life, and it was six years before Germanicus, nephew of the new emperor Tiberius, returned for revenge. He had to settle, however, for avoiding disasters and claiming victories, so that, in the end, Arminius survived until 19 C.E., when he "was accused of seeking a kingship, an aim that ran counter to the feelings of his countrymen and met his end by assassination" (255). In other words, although or because Arminius' was the only one of the five revolts that was successful, it was also the only one whose leader was assassinated by his own people. The fourth revolt was that of Boudicca, queen of the East Anglian Iceni, who was, in 61 C.E., "one of the few surviving members of the tribal royalty in occupied Britain" (262). After an initial success in which she destroyed one legion, the governor Gaius Suetonius Paulinus returned from an expedition and defeated her forces, she took her own life, and "the revolt continued [but] was finally worn down by a combination of military action, a lack of supplies and the more lenient policy of a new commander" (263). The final rebellion, against the background of Roman civil war in 69 to 70 C.E., was that of Julius Civilis, a chieftain of the Germanic Batavi on the Lower Rhine. Although he did not get as much support from the Gallic tribes as he had expected, Civilis' initial successes were impressive. Once Vespasian had secured control of Rome, however, he sent Petilius Cerialis to oppose Civilis, and, combining both military and diplomatic approaches, he probably forced him to negotiate a surrender with pardon.

In comparing the five revolts, Dyson emphasized those "repeated characteristics which allow us to say that we are dealing with a common social phenomenon, arising from generally the same causes and following a basically similar course" so that we can "create an explainable model of social action." He suggested eight such "repeated characteristics" or "salient features" of native revolts against Rome. First, they occurred after initial Roman control was established but before the older native social structure was completely changed. Second, they happened when Roman control was undergoing fiscal or administrative intensification. Third, they are all dominated by native leaders who established greater tribal unity than was usual beforehand. Fourth, their major and minor leaders "almost always come from the more Romanized native class." Fifth, that unification process may have been assisted, in some cases, by older kingdom systems or more recent meeting patterns. Sixth, the revolts all caught the Romans by surprise because they presumed a pacification process already complete. Seventh, there is some evidence of "mass psycho-religious disturbances," for example, the ritual sacrifice of captured Roman centurions and tribunes in Arminius' revolt or the atrocities against Roman or Romanized upper-class women in Boudicca's. Eighth, although the duration of the revolts varied, those of Vercingetorix and Boudicca continued despite the early defeat of the original charismatic leadership and were, therefore, not totally dependent on it (267–268).

Finally, despite many resemblances, Dyson finds one major divergence between those native rebellions against Rome and nineteenth- or twentieth-century native revolts against European or American imperialism. "The great difference is in the sphere of religious involvement. This reflects a profound difference in the nature of the acculturative process. For the modern native, his response must be both to an overwhelming political, military, economic and social entity, and to a religion that is organized, sophisticated, and missionary. . . . Except in a few cases where they met unpalatable rituals, the Romans were not interested in attacking native religion and in fact syncretism was encouraged" (273). He is surely correct that there is a far more overtly obvious religious component in contemporary native reactions against white colonialism and Christian imperialism, for example, those seen earlier in Bryan Wilson's sociological study of religious movements of protest among tribal and Third-World peoples. And yet, by Dyson's own analysis, religious associations and motivations are "lacking" with Bato, "tenuous at best" with Vercingetorix, "some elements" with Boudicca, "used" by Arminius, and given a "clear association" with Civilis (271). That means that they are there in the last three of those five cases. It might be better, in conclusion, to underline its presence even in that ancient situation where politicocultural colonialism was not accompanied by any explicit religious imperialism.

A Revolution Within a Revolution

It is immediately evident that the Jewish revolt of 66 to 73 C.E. does not fit exactly into that model of other native revolts against Rome. The religious context, obviously, is much more emphatic, but it is in the leadership that the major difference arises. In Dyson's five rebellions the leaders were from the Romanized upper classes of their tribal societies. And, even though discord was by no means unknown within that leadership, it always managed enough unanimity to render its threat extremely dangerous. Think, in contrast, of that marvelously vituperative and magnificently venomous passage in *Jewish War* 7.262–270 where Josephus mentions the five distinct groups within besieged Jerusalem at war both with themselves inside and the Romans outside the walls. He records them in ascending order of wickedness as the Sicarii, John of Gischala, Simon son of Gioras, the Idumeans, and the Zealots. Why, precisely in the Jewish revolt, did the leadership, on the one hand, pass so completely out of control of the Romanized upper classes and, on the other, become so savagely fissiparous within itself? The addition of some other models, wider in scope and broader in time, may be of assistance in answering that question.

In 1938 Crane Brinton published a comparative study of the English, American, French, and Russian revolutions, which started, respectively, in 1640, 1776, 1789, and 1917. Despite its universal title, *The Anatomy of Revolution* warns, at the start, that "a complete sociology of revolutions would have to take account of other kinds of revolution, and notably of three: the revolution initiated by authoritarians, oligarchies, or conservatives — that is, the 'Rightist' revolution; the territorial-nationalist revolution; and the abortive revolution" (21), and, at the conclusion, that "our four revolutions are but one kind of revolution, and we must not attempt to make them bear the strain of generalizations meant to apply to all revolutions" (262). Even within those limitations, however, one notices repeatedly that the American revolution does not fit with the other three as well as they do with one another. Furthermore, the constant usage of "extremists" and "moderates" introduces a terminology whose vagueness of definition renders comparative clarity impossible. Recently, and despite those rather serious shortcomings, two biblical scholars have applied Brinton's typological sequence to the Jewish revolt against Rome. Cecil Roth in 1959 (514) and Tessa Rajak in 1983 (126–143) both argued that the Jewish war followed the five-step outline suggested by Brinton. The first stage is *Economic Reform*, involving reform rather than revolution, and is primarily economic and financial. Next comes an escalation to *Political Revolution*, especially after reform is not forthcoming and some initial military actions are strikingly successful. Then there is the stage of *Social Revolution*, demanding a far more profound change in society than any mere improvements or relocations at the top. Although a political revolution can have its own murderous internal strife, it is especially social revolution that leads to the *Reign of Terror* as the next stage in the process. Finally, and especially in reaction to that preceding anarchy, there is the *Dictatorship*, in which absolute rule is entrusted to one individual in order to save the revolution or, maybe better, to save the political from the social revolution.

It is impressively clear that Brinton's fivefold sequence seems to work quite well for the Jewish war, whether or not it works as well for his four modern revolutions. Indeed, that typology seems to work best for a double revolution, for any one that includes a social revolution wrapped up inside a political one. Thus, for example, when he searches for a "touch of the reign of terror and virtue . . . a touch of social revolution, in our [American] revered revolution," the best he can come up with is the tarring and feathering of "a most incorrigible Tory" (176). It was, no doubt, considerably unpleasant but hardly Robespierre. It is that feature of double revolution that I wish to insist on for the analysis of the Jewish revolt, and I suspect in passing that Brinton's book could be totally redone along the explicit axes of "political" and "social" elements of revolution rather than that of "moderate" and "extremist" proponents of revolution.

In a 1950 work by a political scientist and a philosopher, revolutions were divided into three types: palace, political, and social revolutions. Harold Lasswell and Abraham Kaplan define a *palace revolution* as "a change in governors contrary to the political formula but retaining it" (270), for example, the transition from Caligula to Claudius. They define and compare the other types by noting that "a *political revolution* is a radical change in the regime (authority structure); a *social revolution*, in the rule (control structure). . . . In a political revolution the authority structures alone are changed, the underlying pattern of control remaining unaltered. An example is the replacement of a monarchy by a republic with the same ruling class and the same basis of elite recruitment—for instance, the American Revolution [note R]. In social revolution it is the patterns of control which are changed, as for instance in the Russian revolution [note r]" (272–273;). Also, political revolutions happen continually without entailing social ones, but social ones almost always entail political ones.

Take, then, Lasswell and Kaplan's distinction of political and social revolution and cross it with Lenski's stratification of agrarian societies. A political revolution would take place within his five upper classes, but a social revolution would take place from his four lower against his five upper classes. A successful social revolution in an agrarian society would mean that, for example, the slaves or the peasants assumed and kept control of the government. Thomas Carney has argued that "there were in fact no revolutions in antiquity. . . . The degree of politicization of a peasant in antiquity was, likewise, of a different order to that of his modern counterpart. Indeed, as there were no ideologies developed in antiquity, its peasants and serfs existed in rural stupor" (268–269). Despite that judgment and even against it, I intend, as a conclusion to this chapter's charting of the trajectories of *retainer*, and especially *peasant*, unrest across the century preceding the sixties C.E., to look one final time at the interplay of political and social revolution and to ask what exactly the political and social revolutionaries accomplished amid all that rage and fury, terror, horror, and destruction.

At the opening of the war, reform rather than revolution seemed to be the object. This was, as it were, the *economic reform* stage, during which the people insisted to Herod Agrippa II, in *Jewish War* 2.403, that "they were not taking up arms against the Romans, but against [the governor] Florus, because of all the wrong that he had done them." The king persuaded them to collect the overdue tribute, but they absolutely refused to cooperate with Florus even pending his dismissal. That soon moved into the second stage of *political revolution* with two resounding military successes, first, in 2.449–456, the treacherous annihilation of the Roman cohort stationed in Jerusalem and, next, in 2.540–555, the complete defeat of the legionary forces from Syria under the legate Cestius Gallus.

But even before those victories, there was already an attempt to turn political into *social revolution*. You will recall that the revolt began officially when, in 2.409, Eleazar, deputy high priest and son of the former but still very powerful high priest Ananias, persuaded the lower clergy to abandon the sacrifices offered daily for Rome. This led, in 2.422–424, to a week-long military standoff, with the forces of Eleazar controlling the Temple and the lower city to its south while Ananias and his forces controlled the upper city to the west. So far, however, the stalemate of forces for and against the revolt was controlled on either side by members of the high-priestly aristocracy.

It was then, as you will also recall from 2.408 and what I take as its parallels in 2.425 and 2.433–434, that Menahem, having gained some popular rural following and messianic leadership status from his successful capture of Masada, returned to the city with a mixture of Sicarii and peasant supporters and intervened to break the stalemate in favor of Eleazar.

> Along with some feebler folk, numbers of the *sicarii* ... burst in and set fire to the palaces of Ananias the high-priest and to the palaces of Agrippa and Bernice; they next carried their combustibles to the public archives, eager to destroy the money-lenders' bonds and to prevent the recovery of debts, in order to win over a host of grateful debtors and to cause a rising of the poor against the rich, sure of impunity. The keepers of the Record Office having fled, they set light to the building. ... [A few days later] the high-priest Ananias was caught near the canal in the palace grounds, where he was hiding, and, with his brother Ezechias, was killed by the brigands. (Josephus, *Jewish War* 2.425–427,441)

The facts are quite clear even within Josephus' tendentious description. Menahem attempted to extend the political revolution into a social one but was swiftly assassinated by Eleazar, as we saw earlier in 2.442–448. The *governing* class leadership of the political revolution had successfully prevented *retainer* class leadership from turning it into a social revolution. The Sicarii retired to military impotence and mythological apotheosis atop Masada.

At this point the *governing* class is securely in control of the revolution in Jerusalem; indeed, if anything, it may be more widely in control of it than before. Possibly the specter of social revolution has achieved at least that effect. Such control has to be presumed because, despite overtures by some of the sacerdotal aristocracy to open the gates to Cestius Gallus in 2.533, it is the upper class elite that appoints the generals and directs the war after his inexplicable retreat was turned into a disastrous defeat. In terms of Brinton's fivefold sequence, then, Menahem and his followers failed to turn the second-stage political revolution into the third-stage social revolution. It was not the Sicarii but the Zealots who effected that transition.

The Zealots, as we saw in an earlier discussion concerning the texts of *Jewish War* 4.130–138, 441–451, 486–490, were a coalition of bandit groups swept into Jerusalem between the winter of 67 and the spring of 68 as Vespasian's scorched-earth strategy tightened the noose inexorably around the capital. They were, as Richard Horsley put it, "peasants-turned-brigands-turned-Zealots" (1986b:174). Once inside the city they formed a close liaison with lower-class priests, among whom the most important was Eleazar son of Simon, who may have been among those involved with Eleazar son of Ananias and the initial cessation of the Roman sacrifices and was certainly involved, according to 2.564–565, in the defeat of Cestius Gallus. And with the Zealots arrived not only social revolution but the fourth-stage reign of terror as well.

One incident is forcibly paradigmatic of their social ideology of theocratic egalitarianism, the equality of all under God alone as master. It is told as a doublet by Josephus, first in short form at 4.147–151 and then in greatly expanded form at 4.152–207. Each unit involves the Zealots' selection of a new high priest, the arousal of the people against them by Ananus, former high priest from 62 C.E., and the confinement of the Zealot forces to the inner Temple. Josephus, as usual, gives both a clear description of what happened and an equally pejorative interpretation of its motivation and meaning.

> In the end to such abject prostration and terror were the people reduced and to such heights of madness rose these brigands, that they actually took upon themselves the election to the high-priesthood. Abrogating the claims of those families from which in turn the high priests had *always* been drawn, they appointed to that office ignoble and low born individuals, in order to gain accomplices in their impious crimes. . . .
>
> To these horrors was added a spice of mockery more galling than their actions. For, to test the abject submission of the populace and make trial of their own strength, they essayed to appoint the high priests by lot, although, as we have stated, the succession was hereditary. As pretext for this scheme they adduced ancient custom, asserting that in old days the high priesthood had been determined by lot; but in reality their action was the abrogation of established practice and a trick to make themselves supreme by getting these appointments into their own hands. They accordingly summoned one of the high-priestly clans, called Eniachin, and cast lots for a high priest. By chance the lot fell to one who proved a signal illustration of their depravity; he was an individual named Phanni, son of Samuel, of the village of Aphthia, a man who not only was not descended from high priests, but was such a clown that he scarcely knew what the high priesthood meant. At any rate they dragged their reluctant victim out of the country and, dressing him up for his assumed part, as on the stage, put the sacred vestments upon him and instructed him how to act in keeping with the occasion. To them this monstrous impiety was a subject for jesting and sport, but the other priests, beholding from a distance this mockery of their law, could not restrain their tears and bemoaned the degradation of the sacred honours. (Josephus, *Jewish War* 4.147–148, 153–157; my italics)

First, some background: high priests had been chosen from the family of Zadok from at least the time of Solomon until the early decades of the second century B.C.E. The Hasmoneans, however, eventually assumed the high priesthood themselves, although they were not of Zadokite lineage. And from Herod to the outbreak of the revolt against Rome, the high priests were selected from four families, likewise not of legitimate Zadokite origins (Jeremias 1969:181–198). So much, in other words, for that "always" in Josephus' text. Next, notice what the Zealots did. They first chose one priestly clan, that of Eniachin, not otherwise known but which must be presumed of Zadokite bloodline. Further, their claim to be following "ancient custom" in selecting the specific high priest by lot is quite correct. That, at least, was how the weekly duties of the individual priestly clans were determined in 1 Chronicles 14:3–5, and, as we have seen already, it was how Saul, the first Jewish king, was selected in 1 Samuel 10:21. Such a process bespoke an ideology of egalitarianism under the theocratic rule of God, although, of course, in this case it was already limited within Zadokite legitimacy. That tradition's vitality around the turn of the era is evident, as Richard Horsley has observed, both among the Qumran Essenes, for whom, in their *Community Rule* at 1QS 5:3, "shall the lot come forth . . . [on] all matters concerning the Law or property or justice" and for the early Christians, for whom, in Acts 1:21–26, it was the obvious way to choose a replacement for Judas among the twelve apostles (1986b:183). Behind, then, and despite all of Josephus' tendentious rhetoric, what the Zealots did is quite clear and consistent. They restored the ancient Zadokite line according to theocratic selection by lot, and one presumes, of course, that such was to be the future mode of selection as well. Furthermore, this was probably more than just a new or legitimate high priest. It was also, at least as far as the Zealots were concerned, a new and legitimate government of the city and the country. And within that context the association of a rebel priest such as Eleazar son of Simon with the Zealots becomes very significant. He must have been their liaison with the earlier revolution among the Jerusalem lower classes and also with those priestly circles who objected to the illegitimate priestly aristocracies that had ruled for almost two hundred fifty years. No wonder Ananus reacted so strongly and Josephus wrote so scathingly.

Another major action of the Zealots again underlines their ideological vision and also shows their social revolution becoming a *reign of terror* as they conducted three major purges against the nobility (Horsley 1986b:171–172):

The first wave is recorded in *Jewish War* 4.139–146 as soon as they arrived in the city and even before they selected the new high priest. They imprisoned "Antipas, one of the [Herodian] royal family" who had "charge of the public treasury" and also Levias and Syphas, "both also of royal blood — besides other persons of high reputation throughout the country." These were executed in prison by John son of Dorcas and ten others, who accused them of conspiring to surrender Jerusalem to the Romans.

The second wave is recorded in 4.315–344. The Zealots and their social revolution, initially contained within the inner Temple by a counterattack from Ananus and the aristocratic leadership of the political revolution, were freed by Idumean peasant forces brought into the city for that purpose. The first victims of this new Zealot and Idumean combination were Ananus himself and also Jesus, former high priests of 62 and 63 to 64 C.E. respectively, and heretofore the chief opponents of the Zealots.

> They actually went so far in their impiety as to cast out the corpses without burial, although the Jews are so careful about funeral rites that even malefactors who have been sentenced to crucifixion are taken down and buried before sunset. (Josephus, *Jewish War* 4.317)

Their fate, "cast out naked, to be devoured by dogs and beasts of prey," is mourned by Josephus and compensated for somewhat by a long encomium, especially of Ananus. But then this second wave of terror escalated dramatically. It was focused on the "young nobles" who were imprisoned so that they "would come over to their [the Zealots'] party." Josephus says that all refused, were tortured, and then executed, so that "twelve thousand of the youthful nobility thus perished." The final stage of this second purge involved the show trial of one Zacharias son of Baris, "one of the most eminent of the citizens . . . [and] he was also rich." The Zealots appointed seventy "of the leading citizens" as judges, accused Zacharias of conspiracy with the Romans, and, when he was acquitted, killed him immediately.

The third wave is recorded in 4.353–365 after the Idumeans, presumably judging that the Zealots' *social revolution* and its concomitant *reign of terror* were becoming counterproductive, had left the city. Before they did so, however, they liberated from prison about two thousand captives, who fled the city and joined the growing army of Simon son of Gioras in the countryside. The Zealots first executed Niger the Perean, one of the heroes of the earlier stages of the revolution, and also refused to allow his body any burial. And then, as Josephus generalizes in 4.365, "none escaped save those whose humble birth put them utterly beneath notice, unless by accident." It may or may not have been true that the aristocratic leadership would have betrayed the *political revolution* to the Romans. They would surely have been ready to negotiate a surrender, and judging from other native revolts against Rome, Rome might well have been ready to listen. But they were certainly conspiring to betray the *social revolution*. Thus, from the Zealots' viewpoint, anyone of the upper classes was, by definition, against *their* revolution.

A final major indication of Zealot ideology is their own internal leadership system. Although we do hear, now and then, of specific important members of the Zealot faction, Josephus usually speaks of them in the plural as "the Zealots" and does not consistently single out any one individual as their main leader. This is in marked contrast, for example, to John of

Gischala, who, having brought the defeated remnants of the Galilean revolt southward into Jerusalem just ahead of the Zealots, is always mentioned as the leader of those forces. He had an on-again off-again coalition with the Zealots, but this text is significant.

> John, aspiring to despotic power, began to disdain the position of mere equality in honours with his peers, and, gradually gathering round him a group of the more depraved, broke away from the coalition. Invariably disregarding the decisions of the rest, and issuing imperious orders of his own, he was evidently laying claim to absolute sovereignty. (Josephus, *Jewish War* 4.389–390)

Despite the standard pejorative overtones, Josephus' description of John's break with the Zealot coalition indirectly defines their mode of egalitarian leadership.

Eventually, of course, the Zealots' *reign of terror* gave way to the fifth and final stage of revolution, that of the *dictatorship*, in which Simon son of Gioras was invited by Matthias, the current high priest, to enter Jerusalem, in 4.575, "as one who was to rid the city of the Zealots, acclaimed by the people as their saviour and protector." What had the Zealots achieved between, say, the winter of 67 to 68 and the spring of 69 when, in the lull necessitated by the death of Nero in June of 68 C.E., they controlled Jerusalem? Cecil Roth has suggested that, on the level of symbolism, the change from the coins of revolutionary Year 1 with the inscription Jerusalem the Holy to those of Year 2 with the new slogan, Freedom of Zion, evidences Zealot control of the Jerusalem mint and "reflects the circumstances of the secondary, more extreme revolution which took place in the winter of 67/8, when the priestly moderates who had hitherto been at the head of affairs were ejected in a second, Jacobin, revolutionary movement and the Zealots . . . took control" (1962:41–42). But was that all they achieved?

What they did, brutally but thoroughly, was so to destroy the sacerdotal and lay aristocratic control of the revolution that negotiation with Rome was rendered forever impossible. With their arrival a *political* rebellion became a *social* revolution. With the arrival against them of Simon son of Gioras, a social revolution became a holy and messianic war. Negotiation was only possible at that first stage when a political rebellion might have been bargained into surrender. In Galilee, for example, in *Jewish War* 3.447–452, Vespasian had spared Tiberias once the rebels under Jesus son of Saphat or Sapphias had fled south along the lake to Tarichaeae and "the elders and the more respected of the citizens" had begged him not "to impute to the whole city the madness of a few." Jesus was involved in social as well as political revolution, because Josephus says in *Life* 66 that he was "the ringleader . . . of the party of the sailors and destitute class." What happened to Tiberias might have been a model for the fate of Jerusalem, its Temple, and its people had the Zealots not destroyed any chance of negotiation with Rome. Once that happened, peasants under peasant leaders had opened up an unpredictable future for their people and their religion. There would be no surrender, and, on the other side of a destroyed Temple, there would have to be a new Judaism.

Trajectories of Peasant Turmoil

This book is concerned with Jesus of Nazareth, a peasant who died around 30 C.E., yet I have spent a very large amount of space on what happened long after his death between 66 and 73 C.E. My intention was to chart specific points along trajectories of unrest and turmoil and to show how those lines came to a first and climactic consummation in that revolution. I emphatically do not presume any coordinated and continuous century-long insurrection against Rome led, say, on the ideological level by the fourth philosophy or the Sicarii and on the practical level by the Zealots. That is an unfortunate scholarly construct based on Josephan disinformation. But neither do I think that all was peaceful until the decades immediately preceding the revolt so that, for example, nothing that happened then can tell us anything about the much earlier period when Jesus was alive. That conclusion is confirmed by some considerations derived from Ted Robert Gurr's sociological and cross-cultural analysis of political revolt, a superb (if linguistically male) study for which the following quotation may serve as epigraph: "A survey of the histories of European states and empires, spanning twenty-four centuries [500 B.C.E.–1925 C.E.], shows that they averaged only four peaceful years for each year of violent disturbances" (3).

Gurr distinguishes three basic types or levels of political violence. The first is *turmoil*, defined as "relatively spontaneous, unorganized . . . with substantial popular participation, including violent political strikes, riots, political clashes, and localized rebellions." Next, is *conspiracy*, described as "highly organized . . . with limited participation, including organized political assassinations, small-scale terrorism. small-scale guerrilla wars, coups d'état, and mutinies." Finally, there is *internal war*, designated as "highly organized . . . with wide-spread popular participation, designed to overthrow the regime or dissolve the state and accompanied by extensive violence, including large-scale terrorism and guerrilla wars, civil wars, and revolutions" (11). Using those terms, one could summarize this present chapter by saying that Palestine moved from a century of *turmoil*, first to a period of *conspiracy* in the mid-fifties with the Sicarii, and then into *internal war* by 65 C.E., with all classes involved in open rebellion. Focus just on popular *turmoil*, and look, once more, at the types and trajectories, dates and sequences of protesters, prophets, bandits, and messiahs in appendix 2. No doubt there were other instances besides those enumerated by Josephus, but, for my present purpose, I prefer to speak only of what is explicitly documented by him. First, those cases are spread across the entire period, with the bandits as early as 47 B.C.E., the protesters and messiahs from 4 B.C.E., but the prophets only from the thirties C.E. Second, in terms of violence and nonviolence, the eleven cases of bandits are balanced by the ten cases of prophecy, and the five instances of messiahs are about equalled by the seven instances of protesters. In none of this do I intend to invoke some sort of inevitability, as if one had to move from one level of unrest inexorably to the next. But, on the other hand, if Varus had come down from Syria in 4 B.C.E. with as inadequate a force or as inept a strategy as did Cestius in 65 C.E., the First Roman-Jewish War might have started about seventy years earlier. Be that as it may, Gurr's pattern of turmoil, conspiracy, and war helps us understand that the events of 66 C.E. cast their shadow back over the entire preceding century.

There is also another way of crossing Palestinian peasant unrest with Gurr's cross-cultural model of political violence. He starts from the concept of "relative deprivation" or *perceived deprivation*, "the tension that develops between the 'ought' and the 'is' of collective value satisfaction, and that disposes men to violence" (23). The *ought* indicates value expectations, those goods and conditions a group considers its rightful due. The *is* represents value capabilities, those goods and conditions a group considers it can get and keep. The motivational link between relative deprivation and potential violence lies in frustration-aggression theory, which holds, on empirical evidence, that "there is a biologically inherent tendency, in men and animals, to attack the frustrating agent" (33). That tension or discrepancy between expectations and capabilities can arise in one of three manners or patterns. The first two are: "*decremental deprivation*, in which a group's value expectations remain relatively constant but value capabilities are perceived to decline; [and] *aspirational deprivation*, in which capabilities remain relatively static while expectations increase or intensify" (46). The third one, actually a special case of that second one, is *progressive deprivation*, in which the simultaneous and parallel past rise of expectations and capabilities develops presumptions of continuance that are abruptly disappointed when capabilities either level off or go into decline and expectations continue upward. Hence, the revolution of rising expectations. We can ask, therefore, which type of deprivation led to the Jewish revolution of 66 C.E.?

It is possible, of course, that different classes had different types of perceived deprivation. One could easily imagine a situation in which, in Lenski's stratification, the upper classes experienced progressive deprivation while the lower classes experienced decremental deprivation. But, for here and now, I restrict the question to the peasantry. Which of those three types of relative deprivation led to the massive *peasant* involvement in the double social and political revolution that began in 66 C.E.?

It is here that our types and trajectories from appendix 2 become important once again. Does the Jewish revolution indicate large-scale *progressive* deprivation among the peasantry? That would have meant a rising parallelism of expectations and capabilities in the preceding decades terminating in an abrupt discrepancy between still rising expectations and falling off capabilities in the sixties C.E. The trajectories of those four different types of peasant turmoil tell strongly against such an interpretation. They indicate recurrent trouble in almost every decade of the preceding century. Could it, then, have been a case of *aspirational* deprivation? Maybe millennial prophets raised the expectation of peasants otherwise satisfied with their lot of bare subsistence? But, on the one hand, prophets are only one part of our fourfold typology of popular turmoil, and, on the other, Gurr's cross-cultural model repeatedly emphasizes that "the impoverished worker and peasant . . . must be subjectively aware of his impoverishment before he becomes susceptible to revolutionary ideologies" (104), that "to the extent that men are already discontented . . . they are strongly susceptible to ideological conversion" (121), that "men's susceptibility to these beliefs is a function of the intensity of their discontent" (198), and that "discontented men are much more susceptible to conversion to new beliefs than contented men" (357–358).

That leaves only *decremental* deprivation as an explanation for peasant turmoil leading up to and into the war of 66 C.E., and that explanation agrees with what one would expect from Gurr's model, since "decremental deprivation is probably most common in 'traditional' societies and in traditional segments of transitional societies" (48). The peasantry, in other words, were being pushed below the subsistence level that they considered their normal lot in life. Recall, however, that we are talking about relative or perceived deprivation. The Palestinian peasantry, like all peasants before and after them, lived as close to bare subsistence as those who controlled them could calculate. They had done so under imperial overlords for almost half a millennium, under the Persians, the Ptolemies, the Seleucids, and now the Romans. They had always been double taxed, for foreign empire and indigenous temple; they had always suffered droughts and famines; but they did not, for instance, ever rise against the Persians or the

Ptolemies. They rose against the Seleucids, but that was under extreme religiopolitical provocation, and they were securely led and controlled by the Hasmoneans, a priestly and most likely an aristocratic family from within their own *governing* class. What happened against the Romans was all quite different and requires a very specific explanation, especially since, as Peter Brunt put it, "the revolt of 66 was almost as much directed against native landlords and usurers as against the heathen rulers" (149). It will not do for us to say, therefore, even with some degree of social and political morality, that they revolted because the Romans were imperialists, taxed them harshly, or kept them at subsistence level. For there to have been a *perceived* deprivation, the peasants must have been pushed below the subsistence level, not into poverty, which was "normal," but into indigence and destitution. In Lenski's stratification, large numbers of the *peasant* class were being pushed down among the *unclean, degraded,* and *expendable* classes. And that raises the final question for this chapter, one, however, that may represent very unfinished business. What happened under precisely Roman imperialism that pushed the Jewish peasantry of Palestine below "normal" subsistence level and thus into relative, perceived, and decremental deprivation, resulting eventually in massive peasant rebellion?

The best, and maybe indeed the only, answer to that question has been proposed by Martin Goodman. He began by noting that "it is rash to assume that Roman and Temple taxation of the period was much more oppressive than Palestinian taxation at other times, or contemporary taxes elsewhere in the empire, and this cannot have been the sole factor producing economic crisis." Hence, he suggested instead "that both small independent farmers and the craftsmen and urban plebs of Jerusalem fell heavily into debt as much because the rich landowners needed to invest surplus income profitably as because the poor needed loans to survive" (1982:418–419; see also 1987:56–58). It is important to underline that first point. Recall, for example, Gerhard Lenski's earlier judgment that agrarian empires took about two-thirds of peasant production in rents, tolls, and taxes (267). Compare that with Douglas Oakman's careful analyses for such dues in first-century Palestine, where he concludes to a low figure of about "one-half" and a high figure of about "two-thirds" (1986:72). The question is not, of course, whether such taxation was brutally exploitive or not. It was and it always had been, but was it any worse under the Romans than, say, under the Ptolemies? What was special about the Roman situation that brought on rebellion? Although Goodman's thesis requires much further investigation, it is supported by these considerations.

To begin with, "in Herodian Palestine we know," according to Magen Broshi, "of at least twenty of [Herod's] operations, whose size set world records at the time. . . . It is clear that the country experienced unprecedented prosperity under him, and that considerable surpluses were securable" (31). But, then, as Martin Goodman commented, even if "the effect should have been beneficial . . . in practice it was only the few who benefited, [namely] the rich . . . but . . . because those aristocrats did not know what to do with their wealth, the poor in the end not only did not gain but in many cases actually suffered . . . The Judean economy lacked sufficient enterprises from which a suitable return on invested capital could be assured. . . . There is little evidence of rich aristocrats putting money into new manufacturing industry or long-distance trade. Instead, wealth was invested in either land or loans" (1982:419–421). The former investment squeezed the peasantry from ownership to tenancy to day-laboring or even slavery. But it is the latter investment that was the real villain.

There were, however, two major problems with Jews lending money to Jews. First of all, there was the biblical prohibition of Exodus 22:25 and Deuteronomy 23:20 against taking any interest from a fellow Jew. You could, of course, ignore it, but, if you wished to observe the law, there was a way to observe the law and obtain significant investment increase as well. Indeed, as Victor Tcherikover has stated, "interest-free loans, especially of corn, are older than Biblical law, and it is likely that such loans were commonly made by many agricultural peoples in the ancient Orient. . . . It is worth noting that sometimes loans 'without interest' weighed more heavily on the debtor than did the usual ones, since such loans were usually granted for a very short period and heavy penalties were payable to the lender in cases where repayment did not take place within the stipulated period" (Tcherikover et al. 1.35–36). You could, in other words, do much better by heavy fines for nonrepayment within a set time than you could ever have done with interest alone. Recall, for example, the deposit-loan from Saraeus to Tryphon in chapter 1. Martin Goodman, speaking of such Palestinian deposit-loans without interest, concludes, "If the debtor repaid his loan within the set limit, the lender lost nothing and gained a grateful friend. If repayment was made after the fixed period, as perhaps it was expected to be, the fine charged in the Judean desert documents provided 20% interest" (Goodman 1982:423). The first difficulty, the biblical injunction against interest for fellow Jews, could, in other words, be very easily and even profitably overcome.

The second difficulty is equally important and its solution even more significant. All debts between Jews were to be canceled in the Seventh Year, according to the biblical law of Deuteronomy 15:1–8, and creditors were warned, in 15:9–11, not to refuse loans just on account of its nearness. But obviously, as the Seventh Year approached, creditors would be increasingly reluctant to lend money, and debtors would be increasingly blocked from obtaining it. The solution was the *prosbul*, a document allowing the court to obtain repayment of outstanding loans even during the Seventh Year. Biblical law, it was argued, forbade *individuals* from demanding Seventh Year repayment but said nothing against the *courts* doing so. What is most interesting in all of this is that the creation of the *prosbul* solution was attributed to the great rabbi Hillel, who lived from around the middle of the first century before the common era to the first decade after it. And, again from Martin Goodman, "whether or not Hillel was in fact connected with the prosbul's introduction, a document from the Judean Desert . . . shows the institution to have been in use, and presumably backed by the courts, early in the reign of Nero" (1982:422).

Since, however, the problem of tightened credit from the Seventh Year's imminent advent was there long before Hillel, why was it solved "by" him or at least only in his time? If the poor wanted to borrow and could not do so, that was their problem. But if the rich wanted to lend and could not do so, then it became their problem as well. It was, in other words, the rich who wanted the *prosbul* enacted, and they wanted it enacted precisely at the time when they had much excess wealth to invest in loans. No doubt the poor may have always wanted some way of obtaining loans as the Seventh Year approached, but the law was changed only when the rich needed it even more, namely, at the time if not the instigation of Hillel around the turn of the era.

Goodman's theory, then, is that "Judaean society rotted from within because of the social imbalance caused by excessive wealth attracted during the Pax Romana into the holy city of Jerusalem" (1982:426). He deliberately focuses the economic malaise in Jerusalem and Judea and not in "more distant areas of Palestine such as Galilee [which] lacked such a wide division between economic classes" (1982:417–418). Recall, however, a few items from my earlier discussion of Josephus in Galilee. First, the bandit army led by Josephus and the rural peasantry who supported him were quite ready to attack local capitals such as Sepphoris or Tiberias where taxes were assessed and debts recorded. And, even within Tiberias, the major division for or against the war fell basically along class lines. Second, Josephus' major accomplishment was in preventing the political rebellion from turning into a social revolution. Third, the other major leader in Galilee was John of Gischala, who, as a member of the *merchant* class, was well able, if and as long as he wanted, both to speak with the rich and march with the poor. There was no *reign of terror* in Galilee between 66 and 67 C.E. as there was in Judea and Jerusalem between 68 and 70 C.E. The reason was less the differing socioeconomic tensions than it was the leadership of John and Josephus, neither of whom was interested in either a social war, as were the Zealots, or a holy war, as was Simon son of Gioras. But, of course, in the terrible ambiguities of history, it was through the peasant Zealots that the Jewish aristocracy was destroyed, surrender and negotiation were rendered impossible, the Temple was demolished, and, on the other side of horror, a new Judaism was conceived, a beauty born terribly.

PART III

Brokerless Kingdom

He returned, then, into his beloved Galilee, and found again his
heavenly Father in the midst of the green hills and the clear
fountains — and among the crowds of women and children, who
with joyous soul and the song of angels in their hearts, awaited
the salvation of Israel. . . . The extremely delicate feeling toward
women, which we remark in him, was not separated from the
exclusive devotion which he had for his mission. . . . It is,
however, probable that these loved him more than the work; he
was, no doubt, more beloved than loving. Thus as often
happens in very elevated natures, tenderness of the heart was
transformed in him into an infinite sweetness, a vague poetry,
and a universal charm.

> *Ernest Renan,* The Life of Jesus, *from 1863 (1972:118, 120)*

It is a good thing that the true historical Jesus should overthrow
the modern Jesus, should rise up against the modern spirit and
send upon earth, not peace, but a sword. He was not teacher,
not a casuist; He was an imperious ruler. It was because He was
so in His inmost being that He could think of Himself as the Son
of man. That was only the temporally conditioned expression of
the fact that He was an authoritative ruler. The names in which
men expressed their recognition of Him as such, Messiah, Son
of Man, Son of God, have become for us historical parables. We
can find no designation which expresses what he is for us. He
comes to us as One unknown, without a name, as of old, by the
lake-side, he came to those men who knew Him not. He speaks
to us the same word: "Follow thou me!" and sets us to the tasks
which He has to fulfil for our time. He commands. And to those
who obey, whether they be wise or simple, He will reveal
Himself in the toils, the conflicts, the sufferings which they
shall pass through in his fellowship, and, as an ineffable mystery,
they shall learn in their own experience Who He is.

> *Albert Schweitzer,* The Quest of the Historical Jesus,
> *from 1906 (1968:403)*

Jesus is, for the Jewish nation, *a great teacher of morality and an artist in parable.* . . . It is no ethical code for the nations and the social order of to-day, when men are still trying to find the way to that future of the Messiah and the Prophets, and to the "kingdom of the Almighty" spoken of by the Talmud, an ideal which is of "this world" and which, gradually and in the course of generations, is to take shape in this world. But in his ethical code there is a sublimity, distinctiveness and originality in form unparalleled in any other Hebrew ethical code; neither is there any parallel to the remarkable art of his parables. The shrewdness and sharpness of his proverbs and forceful epigrams serve, in exceptional degree, to make ethical ideals a popular expression. If ever the day should come and this ethical code be stripped of its wrappings of miracles and mysticism, the Book of the Ethics of Jesus will be one of the choicest treasures of the literature of Israel for all time.

Joseph Klausner, Jesus of Nazareth,
from 1922 (1925:411, 412, 414)

✧ 11 ✧

John and Jesus

There is silence all around. The Baptist appears, and cries:
"Repent, for the Kingdom of Heaven is at hand." Soon after
that comes Jesus, and in the knowledge that He is the coming
Son of Man lays hold of the wheel of the world to set it moving
on that last revolution which is to bring all ordinary history to a
close. It refuses to turn, and He throws Himself upon it. Then it
does turn; and crushes Him. Instead of bringing in the
eschatological conditions, He has destroyed them. The wheel
rolls onward, and the mangled body of the one immeasurably
great Man, who was strong enough to think of Himself as the
spiritual ruler of mankind and to bend history to His purpose, is
hanging upon it still. That is His victory and His reign.
Albert Schweitzer, The Quest of the Historical Jesus
(1968:370–371)

At the start of the twentieth century, in a splendidly written and superbly
argued analysis, Albert Schweitzer indicted the preceding century and a half's
quest of the historical Jesus for having created an ethical and moral teacher
to replace the original eschatological and apocalyptic prophet. In that contemporary context other dichotomies were present behind the overt one of
ethical versus eschatological, divisions such as liberal versus conservative, natural versus supernatural, reason versus faith, history versus myth. But, if one
leaves aside those specific and, of course, much more important strands of
Enlightenment debate, the split between Jesus as a sapiential teacher of wisdom versus Jesus as an apocalyptic prophet of eschatology can be traced back
as far as one can ever get in the inaugural Jesus tradition. I emphasize, of
course, that both sides of that first-century dichotomy spoke from supernatural faith and both sides presumed a mythic background to their
interpretation. I also emphasize that one can discover combinations and
conflations of an apocalyptic and a sapiential vision of Jesus. But, where
they are opposed to each other, they bespeak the obvious twin modes of
handling an unacceptable present. One can, in a sapiential mode, go backward into a past and lost Eden, or one can, in an apocalyptic mode, go

227

forward into a future and imminent Heaven. Three cases, all from the
fifties of the first common-era century, serve to establish the problem.

By the Middle of the First Century

The first case can be securely dated in the early fifties and probably in
the winter of 53 to 54 C.E. with Paul writing from Ephesus to quell severe
internal tensions in the church of Corinth. "It is probably not wrong,"
according to Helmut Koester's summary of that crisis, "to call the opponents in Corinth (the 'strong people' in the church) gnostics or proto-
gnostics, if by this we mean to describe their self-consciousness. But we
should not look for a theoretical justification of their views in terms of a
doctrine comparable to the gnostic systems of II [second century] C.E. The
Corinthians were convinced of their possession of divine wisdom and
related its mediation to the specific apostles through whom they had been
initiated into Christianity by baptism. . . . It is also possible that they made
recourse to wisdom sayings of Jesus, since words of Jesus are quoted here
more frequently than in other Pauline letters. . . . The missionaries, indeed
even Jesus himself, thus became mystagogues, and baptism a mystery rite"
(1982:2.121–122). I will consider five examples of such "wisdom sayings of
Jesus" at a later stage, but for now it suffices to note that, by the early fifties
C.E., the Corinthian interpretation of Jesus in sapiential terms is opposed
by Paul's interpretation in apocalyptic terms. "The appointed time," he says
in 1 Corinthians 7:29, "has grown very short," and, in 7:31b, "the form of
this world is passing away."

In that first case, then, Paul wrote to the Corinthians opposing his
future and apocalyptic Jesus to their present and sapiential one. In the second case a sapiential Jesus is opposed to an apocalyptic Jesus. Stevan
Davies has shown that the *Gospel of Thomas* "contains a variety of logia
which are in the form of questions and answers, questions by the disciples
as a group and answers by Jesus. The questions predominantly are about
the time of the end or about the nature of Jesus. In both cases the disciples'
questions seem to indicate their failure to understand" (83). Questions
about the time of the end appear in the complexes 285 *Beginning and End*
[1/1] and 8 *When and Where* [1/5], but the "response given by Jesus is that
what they look for is already present, their error is in awaiting it rather than
seeking to discover it" (83). Questions about the nature of Jesus appear in
21 *The World's Light* [1/4], 37 *New Garments* [1/3], 296 *From My Words* [1/1],
42 *Scriptures and Jesus* [1/3], and 53 *Knowing the Times* [1/3], but "the
answers, Jesus seems to say, are present immediately to the questioner"

(83). One example, from 8 *When and Where* [1/5], will suffice to confirm
Davies's point, since it contains three versions of the same traditional unit.

> (1) Jesus said, "If those who lead you say to you, 'See, the kingdom is
> in the sky,' then the birds of the sky will precede you. If they say to you,
> 'It is in the sea,' then the fish will precede you. Rather, the kingdom is
> inside of you, and it is outside of you."
>
> (2) His disciples said to him, "When will the repose of the dead
> come about, and when will the new world come?"
>
> He said to them, "What you look forward to has already come, but
> you do not recognize it."
>
> (3) His disciples said to him, "When will the kingdom come?"
>
> <Jesus said,> "It will not come by waiting for it. It will not be a
> matter of saying 'Here it is' or 'There it is.' Rather, the kingdom of the
> father is spread out upon the earth, and men do not see it." (*Gospel of
> Thomas* 3:1, 51, 113)

Once again, as with Paul at Corinth, we are dealing with divergent
views of Jesus held within the Christian fold. The *Gospel of Thomas* has
Jesus' own disciples personifying the wrong or apocalyptic viewpoint, and
in 3:1 he even goes so far as to mock derisively "those who lead you" into an
apocalyptic and heavenly future.

After apocalyptic versus sapiential in 1 Corinthians, and sapiential
versus apocalyptic in the *Gospel of Thomas*, the third case involves the
combination of an apocalyptic layer with an earlier sapiential layer in the
Sayings Gospel Q. John Kloppenborg's analysis of that document proposes
a composition with two major strata, indicated as 1Q and 2Q in my inventory of the Jesus tradition (appendix 1). That stratification indicates two
successive stages in the life of the community: the first one in 1Q, despite
expecting opposition to its mission, was extremely serene and hopeful; the
second one in 2Q, much more threatening and vengeful, reflected an
awareness of that mission's failure. We see, in Kloppenborg's summary, a
"community which both preached an ethic which departed markedly from
macro-societal values [hence the primary or sapiential layer], and experienced the failure of its preaching among its contemporaries [hence the secondary or apocalyptic layer]" (1987:325). Kloppenborg does not argue,
however, that those twin strata were *historically* successive interpretations
of Jesus. He considers them only as compositionally successive in the
development of the *Sayings Gospel Q*. "To say that the wisdom components
were formative for Q and that the prophetic judgment oracles and
apophthegms describing Jesus' conflict with 'this generation' are secondary

is *not* to imply anything about the ultimate tradition-historical provenance of any of the sayings. It is indeed possible, indeed probable, that some of the materials from the secondary compositional phase are dominical or at least very old, and that some of the formative elements are, from the standpoint of authenticity or tradition-history, relatively young" (1987:244–245).

Brought together, those three insightful studies, by Koester on 1 Corinthians 1–4, Davies on the *Gospel of Thomas,* and Kloppenborg on the *Sayings Gospel Q* (that is, in my view, from three documents of the fifties C.E.), indicate that sapiential and apocalyptic understandings of Jesus were both well developed and simultaneously present at an extremely early stage. Those twin interpretations, in other words, seem equiprimordial visions of Jesus. That must be kept constantly in mind throughout this chapter. Two other points are, however, equally important and will also reappear later in this chapter.

A first point is that neither the apocalypticism that Paul proposes nor the apocalypticism that the *Gospel of Thomas* opposes knows anything about Jesus as the Son of Man, the avenging judge based on Daniel 7:13. But, on the other hand, the apocalypticism added in the second stratum of the *Sayings Gospel Q* emphatically sees Jesus as the coming Son of Man. That will require further discussion. Another point, from Kloppenborg's stratification of the *Sayings Gospel Q,* is that all the sayings concerning John the Baptist belong to the same second layer as the apocalyptic sayings. In other words, John and apocalyptic arrive together. That will also require further discussion.

John and the Coming One

Around the year 30 C.E., Herod Antipas had, according to Josephus, rejected his first wife in order to marry Herodias, wife of his half-brother Herod, and thereafter had been defeated in battle by his rejected father-in-law, Aretas, king of the Nabateans.

> But to some of the Jews the destruction of Herod's army seemed to be divine vengeance, and certainly a just vengeance, for his treatment of John, surnamed the Baptist. For Herod had put him to death, though he was a good man and had exhorted the Jews to lead righteous lives, to practice justice towards their fellows and piety towards God, and so doing to join in baptism. In his view this was a necessary preliminary if baptism was to be acceptable to God. They must not employ it to gain pardon for whatever sins they committed, but as a consecration of the body implying that the soul was already thoroughly cleansed by right behaviour. When others too joined the crowds about him, because they

were aroused to the highest degree by his sermons, Herod became
alarmed. Eloquence that had so great an effect on mankind might lead
to some form of sedition, for it looked as if they would be guided by
John in everything that they did. Herod decided therefore that it would
be much better to strike first and be rid of him before his work led to an
uprising, than to await for an upheaval, get involved in a difficult situation and see his mistake. Though John, because of Herod's suspicions
was brought in chains to Machaerus . . . and there put to death, yet the
verdict of the Jews was that the destruction visited upon Herod's army
was a vindication of John, since God saw fit to inflict such a blow on
Herod. (Josephus, *Jewish Antiquities* 18.116–19)

That is a most remarkable passage, with Josephus according John
emphatic protection against two forms of misunderstanding.

First of all, there is the ritual aspect. Josephus insists that, in John's
view, baptism was not a magic rite effecting the forgiveness of sins but the
physical symbol of a spiritual reality already established before, without,
and apart from it. Like, in other words, those "ablutions of cold water, by
day and night, for purity's sake" that Josephus himself, according to his *Life*
11, had practiced with Bannus in the desert. If that were true, of course,
one wonders why John's rite ever turned him into "the Baptist." The
interpretation of Morton Smith is surely more correct: "By John's time the
only place in the country where Jews could legally offer sacrifices was
Jerusalem, and its services were expensive. To introduce into this situation
a new, inexpensive, generally available, divinely authorized rite, effective
for the remission of all sins, was John's great invention. His warning of the
coming judgment was nothing new; prophets had been predicting that for
the past eight centuries. The new thing was the assurance that there was
something the average man could easily do to prepare himself for the cata-
strophic coming of the kingdom" (1973b:208).

Next, there is the elimination of any political misunderstanding about
John. Josephus never mentions any apocalyptic preaching but only standard Hellenistic piety. Neither does he mention any desert location or any
contact with the Jordan. Yet John must have been captured within Antipas'
territories, that is, either in Galilee or Perea, and, since he was taken to
Machaerus, a fortress on the very southern borders of that latter area, an
initial location on the Perean or desert side of the Jordan seems most plausible. In other words, Josephus has no mention of what is most politically
explosive about John's rite: people cross over into the desert and are baptized in the Jordan as they return to the Promised Land. And that is dangerously close to certain millennial prophets, well known to Josephus and seen
in detail in chapter 8 above, who, in the period between 44 and 62 C.E.,

invoked the desert and the Jordan to imagine a new and transcendental conquest of the Promised Land (appendix 2). Whatever John's intentions may have been, Antipas was not paranoid to consider a conjunction of prophet and crowds, desert and Jordan, dangerously volatile.

"We may suggest," notes Louis Feldman, "that there is no necessary contradiction between Josephus and the Gospels as to the reason why John was put to death: the Christians chose to emphasize the moral charges that he brought against the ruler, whereas Josephus stresses the political fears that he aroused in Herod" (675). I prefer to think, however, that within 197 *Herod Beheads John* [2/2] the detailed narrative of Mark 6:14–29 is his own creation, allowing him to emphasize certain parallels between the fates of John and Jesus, and especially how both were put to death at the insistence of others by a reluctant civil authority. In that complex, of course, neither Mark nor *Apocryphon of James* 6:1–4 is interested in the politics of John's beheading. But that brings us from the John of Josephus to the John of the Jesus tradition.

Of the eighteen complexes concerning John in the inventory of the Jesus tradition, only six have plural attestation (appendix 3), agreeing, in other words, with the overall two-thirds to one-third balance throughout that entire corpus. I base my analysis only on those six complexes, one of which has just been mentioned.

John Baptizes Jesus

The first and most important complex is, necessarily, 58 *John Baptizes Jesus* [1/3]. It belongs to the primary stratum, has three independent witnesses, and involves nine separate texts. But it also evinces a very large amount of what I term, without any cynicism, theological damage control. The tradition is clearly uneasy with the idea of John baptizing Jesus because that seems to make John superior and Jesus sinful.

The earliest text is in the *Gospel of the Hebrews*, where "the accounts of Jesus' pre-existence, coming, baptism, and temptation, are," in Ron Cameron's summation, "abbreviated mythological narratives. They presuppose a myth of the descent of divine Wisdom, embodying herself definitively in a representative of the human race for the revelation and redemption of humankind. Such a myth was widespread in the Greco-Roman world and underlies many of the earliest christological formulations of believers in Jesus" (1982:84).

> And it came to pass when the Lord was come up out of the water, the whole fount of the Holy Spirit descended upon him and rested on him and said to him: My son, in all the prophets was I waiting for thee that

thou shouldest come and I might rest in thee. For thou art my rest; thou art my first-begotten Son that reignest for ever. (*Gospel of the Hebrews* 2; *NTA* 1.163–164; Cameron 1982:85)

I presume that, to make sense of "coming up out of the water," some account of John's baptism must have preceded that section, but the power of its mythological presentation would have negated any problems about superiority or inferiority.

Similarly, at the start of the second set of texts, Mark 1:9–11 was quite content to tell of the baptism in 1:9 and then conclude with the epiphany in 1:10–11. But those twin elements furnished problem and solution for texts dependent on Mark: one could negate or deny the baptism; one could emphasize or underline the epiphany. Watch the apologetic process across these texts.

Now when all the people were baptized, and when Jesus also had been baptized and was praying . . . (Luke 3:21a)

Then Jesus came from Galilee to the Jordan to John, to be baptized by him. John would have prevented him, saying, "I need to be baptized by you, and do you come to me?" But Jesus answered him, "Let it be so for now; for thus it is fitting to fulfil all righteousness." Then he consented. (Matthew 3:13–15)

John fell down before him and said: "I beseech thee, Lord, baptize thou me." But he prevented him and said: "Suffer it; for thus it is fitting that everything should be fulfilled." (*Gospel of the Ebionites* 4; *NTA* 1.157–158; Cameron 1982:105)

Behold, the mother of the Lord and his brethren said to him: John the Baptist baptizes unto the remission of sins, let us go and be baptized by him. But he said to them: Wherein have I sinned that I should go and be baptized by him? Unless what I have said is ignorance (a sin of ignorance). (*Gospel of the Nazoreans* 2; *NTA* 1.146–147; Cameron 1982:99)

And John bore witness, "I saw the Spirit descend as a dove from heaven and remained on him. I myself did not know him; but he who sent me to baptize with water said to me, 'He on whom you see the Spirit descend and remain, this is he who baptizes with the Holy Spirit.' And I have seen and have borne witness that this is the Son of God." (John 1:32–34)

Notice, to begin with, that the *Sayings Gospel Q*, which is much more interested in John's preaching than John's baptizing, has apparently no mention at all of Jesus' baptism (Kloppenborg 1988:16). Luke barely mentions Jesus' baptism in a syntactical rush toward prayer and the epiphany.

Matthew and the *Gospel of the Ebionites* face the problem and declare its divine necessity. The *Gospel of the Nazoreans* denies it ever happened. But John, probably dependent on the synoptics for his Baptist traditions, never mentions a word about Jesus' baptism in all of 1:19–34 and emphasizes instead John's witness concerning Jesus. With John, then, the baptism of Jesus is gone forever, and only the revelation about Jesus remains.

Finally, there are the two units in the letters of Ignatius of Antioch, both of a semicredal character, giving, as William Schoedel put it, "lists of the events of salvation in the ministry of Jesus" (8).

> Our Lord . . . is truly of the family of David according to the flesh, Son of God according to the will and power of God, truly born of a virgin, baptized by John that all righteousness might be fulfilled by him . . . (Ignatius, *To the Smyrnaeans* 1:1)

> For our God, Jesus the Christ, was carried in the womb by Mary according to God's plan — of the seed of David and of the Holy Spirit — who was born and baptized that by his suffering he might purify the water. (Ignatius, *To the Ephesians* 18:2)

Those texts give two divergent explanations for Jesus' acceptance of John's baptism. The one in the first text has to be dependent on Matthew since it uses "righteousness," a redactional emphasis concerning John in both Matthew 3:14–15 and 21:32. But since, as Helmut Koester has argued, there are no other equally clear indications that Ignatius had read Matthew, it is best to consider this an indirect dependency in which the creed used by Ignatius was already influenced by Matthew's apologetic gloss (1957:59). The explanation in the second text is, in William Schoedel's words, "closer to Ignatius' own theological world" (222). It links Jesus' baptism and passion together mythologically in that Jesus purifies the depths of the water by his baptism and the depths of the earth by his burial.

One conclusion emerges from the texts in that first unit. Jesus' baptism by John is one of the surest things we know about them both. But to see what that baptism meant, we have to look at another unit.

John's Message

This second unit is 115 *John's Message* [1/2]. As you look across the five texts of this traditional unit, you can see how, with growing emphasis, John's message about the advent of God has been deftly and smoothly changed into a witness about the advent of Jesus. The earliest text is from the *Sayings Gospel Q* but without the Lukan frames in 3:15–16a and 18.

> I baptize you with water; but he who is mightier than I is coming, the
> thong of whose sandals I am not worthy to untie; he will baptize you
> with the Holy Spirit and with fire. His winnowing fork is in his hand, to
> clear his threshing floor, and to gather the wheat into his granary, but
> the chaff he will burn with unquenchable fire. (*Sayings Gospel Q*: Luke
> 3:16b–17 = Matthew 3:11–12)

That description of the Coming One points to God as apocalyptic
avenger, and it is only later, after reading 143 *Reply to John* [1/1], that one
thinks of Jesus as the Coming One. Thus the dependent version in Acts
13:23–25, in a sermon placed by Luke on the lips of Paul, can take it for
granted that John was talking about Jesus. Next, the independent version in
Mark 1:7–8 has no parallel to that image of the apocalyptic threshing floor,
and, with that absent and Jesus arriving in the immediately subsequent
1:9–11, one is implicitly guided to read John's message as pointing to Jesus
as the Coming One. Finally, in John 1:24–31, all is emphatically clear.

> I baptize with water; but among you stands one whom you do not know,
> even he who comes after me, the thong of whose sandal I am not worthy
> to untie.... The next day he saw Jesus coming towards him, and said,
> "Behold the Lamb of God, who takes away the sins of the world!" This is
> he of whom I said, "After me comes a man who ranks before me, for he
> was before me." I myself did not know him; but for this I came baptizing
> with water, that he might be revealed to Israel. (John 1:26b–27, 29–31)

That is the process superbly consummated. Far from needing a baptism for remission of his own sins, Jesus takes away the sins of the world.
And the message of John about the Coming One is now explicitly interpreted by John himself as applying to Jesus. But what appears from a careful reading of those texts, somewhat against themselves, is that John's
message was an announcement of imminent apocalyptic intervention by
God and not at all about Jesus. Baptism and message went together as the
only way to obtain forgiveness of one's sins before the fire storm came. I
presume that the religiopolitical overtones of that situation are quite clear.
For baptism you only need water, not necessarily Jordan water, but any
such baptism anywhere would have cast negative aspersions, be they
explicit or implicit, on the Temple cult. But a Transjordanian desert location and a baptism in the Jordan, precisely the Jordan, had overtones,
explicit or implicit, of political subversion. No matter what John's intentions may have been, Antipas had more than enough materials on which to
act. Desert and Jordan, prophet and crowds, were always a volatile mix calling for immediate preventive strikes.

Into the Desert

The third unit, 51 *Into the Desert* [1/3], is much more difficult to analyze both externally and internally. The version in the *Sayings Gospel Q*
includes the twin questions and answer in Luke 7:24–26 = Matthew 11:7–9
and the application of Malachi 3:1 to John in Luke 7:27 = Matthew 11:10.
But, on the one hand, that in *Gospel of Thomas* 78 has the twin questions,
a different answer, but no prophetic application, and, on the other, that in
Mark 1:2–3 has the prophetic application without any twin questions or
answer. Furthermore, the *Thomas* version does not mention John's name. I
consider that two originally independent units have become merged in the
Sayings Gospel Q complex and that those two are still visible in that original
separation at *Gospel of Thomas* 78 and Mark 1:2–3, respectively:

(a) Questions and Answer About John:
   (1) Gos. Thom. 78
   (2) 2Q: Luke 7:24–26 = Matt. 11:7–9
(b) Application of Mal. 3:1 to John:
   (1) 2Q: Luke 7:27 = Matt. 11:10
   (2) Mark 1:2–3

I am now concerned only with that former unit of tradition. I judge
that the better version is in *Sayings Gospel Q* at Luke 7:24–26 = Matthew
11:7–9, where it concluded positively with, "Yes, I tell you, and more than a
prophet." In the parallel version, *Gospel of Thomas* 78, the name of John
has been dropped so that the answer can be generalized, and it now concludes negatively with "and they are unable to discern the truth"; that is,
the rich have wealth but not truth. But, even granted all that, what does
Luke 7:24–26 = Matthew 11:7–9 say about John, why is it said that way, and
could Jesus ever have said any such thing?

In terms of form, the saying is set up as an implicit dialogue, it is
addressed to those presumably sympathetic to John. In terms of content,
the saying sets up a contrast between desert and palace and between their
appropriate and expected inhabitants. But, while a prophet is clearly
named as the one you expect to find in the desert, the palace dweller is not
defined as king or courtier, ruler or minister. He is simply described,
metaphorically, as one who bends to the prevailing wind and, literally, is
dressed in soft, gorgeous, and luxurious garments. But, even if that is a correct reading, why is the saying set up that way? Why compare and contrast
the desert-dwelling prophet with, precisely, the palace-dwelling "man"?
The only answer I can imagine is that the saying intends a comparison
between John and Antipas and that it arose, directly and immediately, from

the crisis engendered among his followers by John's incarceration and execution. It reads like an attempt to maintain faith in John's apocalyptic vision despite John's own execution. He is—he still is—not just another prophet but the last of the prophets, the Prophet of the Coming One. I accept the aphorism, so understood and so engendered, as stemming from Jesus. It confirms what we already know, namely, that Jesus, in submitting himself to John's baptism, must also have accepted John's apocalyptic expectation, must have accepted John as the Prophet of the Coming One. But that conclusion must be taken in conjunction with the next unit.

Greater Than John

The fourth unit, 85 *Greater than John* [1/2], is a very important one because, while a conjunction or even comparison of John and Jesus is not at all unexpected in the *Sayings Gospel Q*, it is very unexpected in the *Gospel of Thomas*.

> Jesus said, "Among those born of women, from Adam until John the Baptist, there is no one so superior to John the Baptist that his eyes should not be lowered (before him). Yet I have said, whichever one of you comes to be a child will be acquainted with the Kingdom and will become superior to John. (*Gospel of Thomas* 46)

> I tell you, among those born of women none is greater than John; yet the least in the kingdom of God is greater than he. (*Sayings Gospel Q:* Luke 7:28 = Matthew 11:11)

If that saying were only in the *Sayings Gospel Q*, it might easily be dismissed as its own creation, born of a need to balance the sapiential traditions about Jesus in 1Q with the apocalyptic traditions about John in 2Q. But it is also in the *Gospel of Thomas*, which has no particular interest in John, less, according to *Gospel of Thomas* 52, in the prophets of Israel, and even less, as we have seen, in apocalyptic hopes and expectations. It is, therefore, as old as anything we can ever get. And its formulation, despite a definite polemical edge, displays little concern with community boundaries but rather with a startlingly paradoxical juxtaposition of greatest and least. Not John in the desert but the child in the Kingdom is the beginning of the future.

I consider that both those statements about John, the first half of 51 *Into the Desert* [1/3] and all of 85 *Greater than John* [1/2], derive from the historical Jesus, and that leaves only one conclusion, namely, that between those twin assertions Jesus changed his view of John's mission and message. John's vision of awaiting the apocalyptic God, the Coming One, as a repentant sinner, which Jesus had originally accepted and even defended in the crisis of John's death, was no longer deemed adequate. It was now a question of being in the Kingdom. "Jesus started his public life," as Paul Hollenbach put it, "with a serious commitment to John, his message and his movement, and . . . Jesus developed very soon his own distinctive message and movement which was very different from John's" (1982:203).

The Apocalyptic Son of Man

There is, it would seem, an immediate and crippling objection to those preceding conclusions. Have we not known, at least from Albert Schweitzer's brilliant analysis at the start of this century, that Jesus repeatedly foretold the coming of the Son of Man, a figure clearly apocalyptic and presumably meaning himself? Jesus was, in other words, just as apocalyptic as John the Baptist. The question thus presses: did Jesus speak of himself or any other protagonist as the coming Son of Man? Was the one who preached of old by the lakeside an apocalyptic visionary?

I begin with a word about terminology. In a recent article, Marcus Borg has defined "eschatological . . . to include as an indispensable element the notion that the world itself will come to an end, including the traditional expectation of last judgment, resurrection, and dawn of the new age. *The eschatological Jesus is one who thought this was imminent.* Thus, with the term 'eschatological,' I do not mean 'end' in more metaphorical senses, either in the sense of a dramatic change in Israel's history, or in the sense of a radical change in the individual's sensitivity which one might describe by speaking of the (old) world coming to an end for that individual" (1986:81 note 1). In my own preferred terminology, however, and to be more precise, that describes the apocalyptic Jesus. I need the term *eschatology* as the wider and generic term for world-negation extending from apocalyptic eschatology, as just described, through mystical or utopian modes, and on to ascetical, libertarian, or anarchistic possibilities. In other words, all apocalyptic is eschatological, but not all eschatology is apocalyptic. The advantage of using the wider, generic term and the narrower, more specific term is that it helps to understand their ready slippage from one to another. In discussing, therefore, those texts about the coming Son of Man, I am speaking about the apocalyptic Jesus and asking whether Jesus saw this figure against the darkening scenario of an imminent end to the world. And by end of the world I mean that the apocalypticist expected a divine intervention so transcendentally obvious that one's adversaries or enemies, oppressors or persecutors would be forced to acknowledge it and to accept conversion or concede defeat.

One Like a Son of Man

The four visions of Daniel 7, 8, 9, and 10–12 were intended to reassure faithful Jews, persecuted between 167 and 164 B.C.E. by the Syrian monarch Antiochus IV Epiphanes, that, just as Babylonians, Medes, Persians, and Greeks had come and gone, so also would the Syrian onslaught swiftly pass. And this, in Daniel's dream-vision by night, is its apocalyptic judgment:

> As I looked, thrones were placed and one that was ancient of days took his seat; his raiment was white as snow, and the hair of his head like pure wool; his throne was fiery flames, its wheels were burning fire. . . . [T]he court sat in judgment, and the books were opened. I looked then because of the sound of the great words which the horn [Antiochus IV Epiphanes] was speaking. And as I looked, the beast [Greek imperialism] was slain, and its body destroyed and given over to be burned with fire. . . . I saw in the night visions, and behold, with the clouds of heaven there came one like a son of man, and he came to the Ancient of Days and was presented before him. And to him was given dominion and glory and kingdom, that all peoples, nations, and languages should serve him; his dominion is an everlasting dominion, which shall not pass away, and his kingdom one that shall not be destroyed. (Daniel 7:9–14)

In that vision, "one like a son of man" is emphatically not a title. It simply contrasts the earlier three empires who were described as "like a lion . . . like a bear . . . like a leopard," that is, like wild beasts from the chaotic depths of the sea, with this superhuman figure who is "like a human being" and comes from the heights of the heavens. In other words, just as English-language male chauvinism uses *man* or *mankind* to describe humanity, so did its Hebrew equivalent use *man* and *son of man*, especially in poetic parallelism, to describe the human race. Examples may be found in Numbers 23:19; Isaiah 51:12; 56:2; Jeremiah 50:40; 51:43; Psalms 80:17; 144:3. The following text, for instance, is cited in Hebrews 2:6:

> What is man that thou art mindful of him,
> and the son of man that thou dost care for him?
> (Psalm 8:4)

After the vision in Daniel 7:2–14 comes its interpretation in 7:17–27, and there, in 7:18, "the saints of the Most High shall receive the kingdom," and, in 7:27, "the kingdom . . . shall be given to the people of the saints of the most high." Thus, as John Collins comments, "the three formulations of Dan 7:14, 18, and 27, in which the one like a son of man, the holy ones of the Most High, and the people of the holy ones are said in turn to receive the kingdom, represent three levels of a multidimensional reality" (1984a:84). The archangel Michael as leader of the heavenly armies, those angelic armies themselves, and the persecuted but faithful Jews are all hierarchically layered within that reality. But I emphasize once again that "one like a son of man" is not a title for Michael as the angelic personification of that apocalyptic victory. It is a simple description: he is, in contrast with the beastlike ones from below, humanlike and from above.

The atitular nature of the phrase "son of man" in Daniel 7:13 is underlined in two Jewish texts from the first common-era century, both of which use and develop that vision.

The first text is the *Book of the Similitudes*, which, as we saw in chapter 6, appears at *1 Enoch* 37–71 as the second part of a composite five-part anthology. This work, from early in the first century, has three parables in 38–44, 45–57, 58–69 and a double conclusion, one in 70 and another in 71. Here is the first appearance of the Son of Man figure.

> At that place, I saw the One to whom belongs the time before time. And his head was white like wool, and there was with him another individual, whose face was like that of a human being.... And I asked ... one ... among the angels ... "Who is this?" ... And he answered me and said to me, "This is the Son of Man, to whom belongs righteousness, and with whom righteousness dwells.... This Son of Man whom you have seen is the One who would remove the kings and the mighty ones from their comfortable seats and the strong ones from their thrones. (*1 Enoch* 46:1–4; *OTP* 1.34)

It is very significant that, as John Collins emphasizes, "the manner in which he is introduced does not presuppose that 'son of man' is a well-known title" (1980:112). Or, indeed, a title at all. Notice, in fact, that the capitalization in that translation makes a title out of what is little more than a reference or an allusion. The text begins with a clear if implicit allusion to Daniel 7:13 and thereafter "the one whose face was like that of a human being" is identified as "this Son of Man" and then specified in various ways. But there is no presupposition that the term *Son of Man* has any meaning or content apart from an allusion to the text of Daniel 7:13. Thus, after this introduction in *1 Enoch* 46:1–4, all subsequent Son of Man texts look back to it and presume its presence. Usually, in fact, the reference is specified as "that Son of Man." In other words, there can only be a specific "Son of Man" in direct dependence on Daniel 7:13. Furthermore, the one entitled Son of Man has other titles such as the Chosen One or the Righteous One (for example, in 53:6) and is possibly, in the later conclusion at 71:14, identified with heavenly Enoch himself. Put crudely: Daniel 7:13 precedes the titular Son of Man, the titular Son of Man does not precede Daniel 7:13. And, once again, titular may be far too strong a word for that situation.

The case of another Jewish apocalyptic writing, this time from the end of the first common-era century, is equally instructive. The author, fictionally imagined as Ezra in Babylonian captivity during the sixth century B.C.E., has seven visions of the future. Here is the sixth, or Man from the Sea, vision:

> After seven days I dreamed a dream in the night; and behold, a wind
> arose from the sea and stirred up all its waves. And I looked, and behold,
> this wind made something like the figure of a man come up out of the
> heart of the sea. And I looked, and behold, that man flew with the
> clouds of heaven; and wherever he turned his face to look, everything
> under his gaze trembled, and whenever his voice issued from his mouth,
> all who heard his voice melted as wax melts when it feels the fire. (4 *Ezra*
> 13:1–4; *OTP* 1.551)

In this vision, and in the preceding fifth, or Eagle, vision, 4 *Ezra* depends on Daniel 7, but, as he explicitly admits in 12:10–12, his own interpretations are quite different from those of "your brother Daniel." The reasons are that he, unlike Daniel, must incorporate the Roman Empire into the sequence of imperialisms and, more importantly, as John Collins notes, that he has introduced "motifs associated with the Davidic messiah, who played no part in Daniel" (1984a:166). But what is important for here and now is how one can go from Daniel 7:13 just as well into "that Man" in 4 *Ezra* 13:3 as into "that Son of Man" in 1 *Enoch* 46:2. Each, *apart from that Danielic association and background,* is a title of absolute vagueness if not vacuity. And each retains a connection with that background by specifying "that" when referring to one like a man or a son of man based on Daniel 7:13. Otherwise it would be like us speaking about "the human one" without any further specification.

To Say, Indirectly, I Myself

If "son of man" is clearly atitular in those preceding Jewish texts based on Daniel 7:13, it is just as clearly titular in the Christian ones where Jesus speaks of the coming, future, or apocalyptic Son of Man. It comes across, indeed, as Jesus' most specific circumlocution for himself. How exactly did that strange transition take place?

One answer is that "son of man" was in fact a circumlocution for "I" in Aramaic usage at the time of Jesus. It was an oblique and surrogate way of indicating the speaker's own self. When, therefore, Jesus said "son of man," everyone would have understood that he was referring to himself. The proposal comes from Geza Vermes (1967; 1973b:163–168, 188–191; 1978a; 1978b), but it has been emphatically denied by Joseph Fitzmyer (1968; 1979a; 1979b). Both scholars agree that there was no such thing as a titular Son of Man designation at the time of Jesus. They also agree that the term was used in a generic or indefinite sense, especially in parallelism with *man*, as a rather chauvinistic way of saying humanity or human beings. The meaning there could range from a generic everyone to an indefinite anyone. We saw an example of that generic usage earlier in the parallelism of *man* and *son of man* in Psalm 8:4, both meaning mankind, that is, humanity in general. But Vermes proposed that apart from such generic (everyone) or indefinite (anyone) usage there was also at the time of Jesus a surrogate or circumlocutional usage, that is, an oblique way of referring to the "I" of the speaker. Thus the phrase *son of man* would have had some of the ambiguity of our *one*: it usually means everyone, but, especially in arch and elitist British usage, means exclusively the "I" of the speaker. Fitzmyer countered that none of Vermes's examples were from texts of the first century and, even more significantly, that "many of the examples cited by Vermes from the Palestinian Talmud and *Genesis Rabbah* and said to mean 'I' or 'me' can just as easily be translated 'a man' or 'man' in an indefinite or generic sense" (1979b:153). Indeed, I would say that all of his examples could and should be so read (Vermes 1967:320–328; 1973b:163–168). I am not even persuaded by the one example Fitzmyer accepts from twin Aramaic translations of Genesis 4:14. In *Targum Neofiti 1* Cain says, "It is impossible for me to hide," but in *Cairo Targum B* he says, "It is impossible for a son of man to hide" (Fitzmyer 1979b:152). That second version might just as well be generic as circumlocutional. One can only tell circumlocutional for sure when generic is impossible, since every generic use implicitly includes a circumlocutional. Everyone and anyone includes my "I," but my "I" does not include anyone or everyone.

Let me pause to emphasize what is at stake here, using *one* to illustrate the point concerning *son of man*. If I say, in American English, "One always protects a child," I mean that everyone should do so and thereby, of course, include myself within that generality. If I say, in British English, "One always flies the Concorde," I mean that I, or at most all those with the good taste to be like me, always do so. In the former case my "I" is included but in no way emphasized; in the latter it is personally or corporately exclusive and emphatically underlined. The only way, in fact, that a circumlocutional usage is sure, is if a generic or indefinite one is not possible. If, therefore, Jesus spoke about "the son of man" in a generic or indefinite sense, he would be, of course, including himself, but if he spoke of "the son of man" in a circumlocutional or surrogate sense he would be exclusively proclaiming himself. In our present New Testament Gospels "Son of Man" has become both titular for Jesus and therefore circumlocutional for himself on the lips of Jesus. But that is the end, not the beginning, of the process. There is as yet no conclusive evidence for "son of man" in Hebrew or Aramaic as a surrogate expression for "I" in any emphatic or exclusive sense. So, with Fitzmyer, "one may well ask whether this usage would ever have been queried or sought for, if it were not for the NT parallels" (1979b:154).

In summary, therefore, if Jesus spoke about a son of man, his audience would not have taken the expression in either a titular or a circumlocutionary sense but, following normal and expected usage, in either a generic (everyone) or an indefinite (anyone) sense. He is talking, they would presume, about human beings, making claims or statements about humanity. An unchauvinistic English translation would be "the human one." The only alternative would be if the context clearly alluded to Daniel 7:13 so that the audience would see that he was identifying the "one like a son of man" (one like a human being) in that mysterious and prophetic scenario. I turn now, to see if that second alternative is persuasive, to specific texts in which Jesus speaks about the apocalyptic Son of Man.

Coming on the Clouds

The inventory for the apocalyptic Son of Man texts contains eighteen traditional complexes, of which six have plural attestation (appendix 4). As usual, I focus my analysis on those latter complexes. But here we run into a very special problem. On the one hand, six out of eighteen complexes appears fairly consistent with the percentage for more than single attestation in the overall tradition. On the other hand, and I emphasize this fact as strongly as possible, there is not a single one of those six complexes in which Son of Man appears in more than a single source. In fact, if you widen the inventory to include not only the apocalyptic Son of Man sayings but all the others as well, you find that out of forty complexes only a single one has Son of Man attested in more than a single source (appendix 4). In other words, while the overall numeric summary for *apocalyptic* Son of Man sayings is 18:6 + 12 and for *all* Son of Man sayings is 40:14 + 26, the true numerical summary for the *phrase* Son of Man itself is, respectively, 18:0 + 18 and 40:1 + 39. That rather striking phenomenon will be of crucial importance for my analysis.

Jesus' Apocalyptic Return

The first complex for study is 2 *Jesus' Apocalyptic Return* [1/6] because of its extremely high attestation status. Notice, however, that the titular Son of Man stems only from one single source, Mark.

In its first source, Paul's converts at Thessalonica are apparently discon-
certed that some of their number have died before the triumphant return
of Jesus at the parousia. Paul insists, presumably from a prophetic word of
the heavenly Lord, that the dead rather than the living will be first to meet
the apocalyptic Christ and so they are, if anything, at somewhat of an
advantage.

> But we would not have you ignorant, brethren, concerning those who
> are asleep, that you may not grieve as others do who have no hope. For
> since we believe that Jesus died and rose again, even so, through Jesus,
> God will bring with him those who have fallen asleep. For this we
> declare to you by the word of the Lord, that we who are alive, who are
> left until the coming of the Lord, shall not precede those who have
> fallen asleep. For the Lord himself will descend from heaven with a cry
> of command, with the archangel's call, and with the sound of the trum-
> pet of God. And the dead in Christ will rise first; then we who are alive,
> who are left, shall be caught up together with them in the clouds to
> meet the Lord in the air; and so we shall always be with the Lord. There-
> fore comfort one another with these words. (1 Thessalonians 4:13–18)

Notice, first and above all, that Paul's title for the returning Jesus is "the
Lord," a title repeated four times within that section. Neither here, nor anywhere else, does he ever mention the "Son of Man." Second, Christ's command, the archangel's call, and God's trumpet are presumably three
different ways of indicating the summons to apocalyptic consummation.
Finally, there is that small phrase "in [the] clouds." And that brings up a possible biblical background in Daniel 7:13.

The only significant contact between 1 Thessalonians 4:13–18 and
Daniel 7 is their common mention of clouds: "with the clouds" for the "one
like a son of man" in the latter and "in [the] clouds" for "the Lord" in the
former. I am almost inclined to dismiss that link as a simple coincidence of
transcendental scenario, but two factors give me pause. One is the redundancy between Paul's "in [the] clouds" and the immediately succeeding "in
[the] air." Granted that the meeting place is between heaven and earth, that
is, in the air, why does Paul need to mention clouds? Another is the importance of "clouds" in other texts, soon to be seen, where a deliberate linkage
with Daniel 7:13 is definitely present. That leads to an inevitable conclusion. If Daniel 7:13 lies behind 1 Thessalonians 4:13–18, then it was perfectly possible for Paul, in 50 C.E., to think of the returning Jesus as the
fulfillment of that prophecy without at all referring to him as "one like a son
of man," let alone entitling him the Son of Man. If this was the only
instance of such a situation, you might respond that Paul has simply

replaced *Son of Man* with *Lord.* But we shall see it again below with *Didache* 16:6–8. What may, therefore, have been initially important was not an individual description or a title but the whole text itself as a way of imagining how Jesus rather than God was to be the agent of apocalyptic judgment. Put it this way: *Son of Man* became important because of Daniel 7:13; Daniel 7:13 did not become important because of *Son of Man.*

All this becomes much simpler in turning to the second source in 2 *Jesus' Apocalyptic Return* [1/6]. Here the background is clearly Daniel 7:13–14, and *the Son of Man* is equally clearly a title for Jesus.

> But in those days, after that tribulation, the sun will be darkened, and the moon will not give its light, and the stars will be falling from heaven, and the powers in the heavens will be shaken. And then they will see the Son of man coming in clouds with great power and glory. And then he will send out the angels, and gather his elect from the four winds, from the ends of the earth to the ends of heaven. (Mark 13:24–27 = Matthew 24:29, 30c–31 = Luke 21:25–28)

Notice also that Mark 13:26 has exactly the same phrase, "in [the] clouds," as did 1 Thessalonians 4:17. In those two texts, then, with relatively clear chronological situations and even with a common background in Daniel 7:13, it is "the Lord" that returns as apocalyptic judge in the much earlier one and "the Son of Man" in the much later one. That requires further discussion. As does also one small point: why is the verb "see" used for the apocalyptic judge here, although not in Paul?

The next two sources in this complex must be considered together as they have a common source behind them. Matthew 24 has combined three separate apocalyptic sources: (1) Matthew 24:1–25, 29, 30b–36 is from Mark 13; (2) Matthew 24:26–28, 37–51 is from 2Q; (3) Matthew 24:10–12, 30a is from a source known also to *Didache* 16:3–8 (Kloppenborg 1979).

> [And] then will appear the sign of the Son of man in heaven, and then all the tribes of the earth will mourn. (Matthew 24:30a)

> And then shall appear the signs of the truth. First the sign spread out in heaven, then the sign of the sound of the trumpet, and thirdly the resurrection of the dead: but not of all the dead, but as it was said, "The Lord shall come and all his saints with him." Then shall the world see the Lord coming on the clouds of heaven. (*Didache* 16:6–8)

That common source is much more visible in *Didache* 16:6–8 because Matthew 24:30a is swallowed up within 24:29–31, which is otherwise entirely from Mark 13:24–27. But what is of present interest is that *Didache* 16:6–8 speaks, as did 1 Thessalonians 4:13–18, of the Lord as apocalyptic

judge but Matthew 24:30a speaks of the Son of Man. Which better represents the title in their common source? It is not clear why *Didache* 16:6–8
would omit the title had it been there, but, on the other hand, Matthew
24:30a, preparing for Matthew 24:30b, which mentions the Son of Man
from Mark 13:26, could easily or even necessarily have added it. I judge
that, once again, the earlier text spoke of the Lord as the apocalyptic judge,
even against a backdrop of Daniel 7:13, whereas the later text changed "the
Lord" to "the Son of Man."

The final two sources in 2 *Jesus' Apocalyptic Return* [1/6] are highly
instructive on this entire process.

> One of the soldiers pierced his side with a spear . . . that the scripture
> might be fulfilled. . . . "They shall look on him whom they have pierced."
> (John 19:34, 36, 37)

> Behold, he is coming with the clouds, and every eye will see him, every
> one who pierced him; and all tribes of the earth will wail on account of
> him. Even so. Amen.
> . . . and in the midst of the lampstands one like a son of man,
> clothed with a long robe and with a golden girdle round his breast . . .
> Then I looked, and lo, a white cloud, and seated on the cloud one
> like a son of man, with a golden crown on his head, and a sharp sickle in
> his hand. (Revelation 1:7, 13; 14:14)

Those first two sources in John 19 and Revelation 1:7 serve to explain
why "see" is so important in Mark 13:26 and *Didache* 16:8. Behind the
former pair, and also Matthew 24:30a, lies another biblical text:

> And I will pour out on the house of David and the inhabitants of Jerusa-
> lem a spirit of compassion and supplication, so that, when they look on
> him whom they have pierced, they shall mourn for him, as one mourns
> for an only child, and weep bitterly over him, as one weeps over a first-
> born. (Zechariah 12:10)

That prophetic promise was declared fulfilled at the crucifixion,
according to John, and, in combination with Daniel 7:13, at the parousia,
according to Revelation 1:7. Those texts have the same verb for "look on"
and "see," the same verb that appears also in Mark 13:26 and *Didache* 16:8.
In other words, the combination of Zechariah 12:10 and Daniel 7:13, totally
absent in John 19:37 but fully and explicitly present in Revelation 1:7, is
implicitly and residually present wherever "see" appears in the parousia
scenario. The arch from passion to parousia was first established by
Zechariah 12:10 and only then was parousia developed in terms of Daniel
7:13.

The final two texts in Revelation 1:13 and 14:14 show explicitly a usage of Daniel 7:13 in which Jesus is still "one like a son of man," that is, not a titular Son of Man but simply identified and equated with the heavenly figure of that apocalyptic vision.

Two major conclusions are indicated from all of that. One is that this whole stream of tradition, far from starting on the lips of Jesus, began only after his crucifixion with meditation on Zechariah 12:10, then moved on to combine Daniel 7:13 with that prophecy, and finally left only the barest vestige of those beginnings in the perdurance of the *see* verb for the apocalyptic judge. Another is that, despite a common background in Daniel 7:13, some early traditions felt no need to speak in a titular way of Jesus as Son of Man even if others did. So, on the one hand, Paul and *Didache* 16 presume Daniel 7:13 but think of Jesus as the returning Lord. Revelation 1:13 and 14:14 presume Daniel 7:13 but think of Jesus as the "one like a son of man" there mentioned. On the other, the *Gospel of the Hebrews*, the *Sayings Gospel Q*, and Mark all see Jesus as the titular Son of Man. Such an early bifurcation is hard to explain if it was Jesus who first spoke of himself as titular Son of Man based on Daniel 7:13.

Before the Angels

The second complex for study is 28 *Before the Angels* [1/4], and, here again, we have a similar problem with the presence or absence of the title Son of Man across those texts. It is present only from Mark.

Over thirty years ago Ernst Käsemann isolated what he termed "sentences of holy law" in the New Testament writings. The set form of those apocalyptic sanctions usually involved the threat and/or promise that if one did something on earth, it would be counterdone to one by God on the last day. The power of the sanction came, rhetorically, from the use of the same verb for here and hereafter, and came, religiously, from a still lively expectation of the imminent judgment. The apocalyptic protagonist was God, mentioned either explicitly as such or implicitly by the passive voice or an anathema. Here are all three cases, respectively, in one of Paul's letters.

> If any one destroys God's temple, God will destroy him ...
> If any one does not recognize this, he is not recognized ...
> If any one has no love for the Lord, let him be accursed ...
> (1 Corinthians 3:17a; 14:38; 16:22a)

Those three cases are all negative threats rather than positive promises. And that negativity continues in Galatians 1:9 and Revelation 22:18–19. But both negative and positive styles are found in those apocalyptic sanctions modeled on the 60 *Measure for Measure* [1/3] format, such as 118 *Judgment for Judgment* [1/2], 370 *Mercy for Mercy* [3/2], 382 *Gift for Gift* [3/2], 441 *Condemnation for Condemnation* [3/1], 481 *Action for Action* [3/1], and 482 *Kindness for Kindness* [3/1]. It would seem that the more original sanctions were negative, but, in any case, it would be very easy to double any single version into a balanced positive and negative version. Thus, for example, in 27 *Forgiveness for Forgiveness* [1/4], Mark's single positive was doubled by Matthew into a balanced positive and negative. In summary, then, apocalyptic sanctions were threats and/or promises whereby the believer's earthly action would be punished or rewarded by God's similar action in heaven. And the initial power of the sentence derived less from the believer's eventual death than the eschaton's imminent advent. It is within that much wider matrix that the Son of Man sayings in 28 *Before the Angels* [1/4] must be reviewed. Take a look, to begin, at these twin versions.

(1) And I tell you, every one who acknowledges me before men, the Son of man also will acknowledge before the angels of God; but he who denies me before men will be denied before the angels of God.

(2) So every one who acknowledges me before men, I also will acknowledge before my Father who is in heaven; but whoever denies me before men, I also will deny before my Father who is in heaven. (*Sayings Gospel Q*, 2Q: Luke 12:8–9 = Matthew 10:32–33)

Those are, clearly enough, apocalyptic sanctions in balanced positive and negative format; nothing surprising there. But there are also two major differences between Luke and Matthew. In Luke the protagonists are the Son of Man and the passive voice, whereas in Matthew they are "I," in other words, Jesus himself, both times. And, while "before men" on earth demands some corresponding "before . . . " in heaven, Luke has the "angels of God" and Matthew has "my Father." What, then, was in the *Sayings Gospel Q* itself? My best answer is the following:

Every one who acknowledges me before men will be acknowledged before the angels of my Father; but he who denies me before men will be denied before the angels of my Father. (Reconstructed *Sayings Gospel Q* 12:8–9)

Thus an original balance of passive and passive became, in Matthew, a balance of "I" and "I" but, in Luke, a balance of "Son of Man" and a still residual passive. It is Luke, in other words, who first introduced the Son of Man into this unit, and he probably did it with an eye to his other or Markan source which already contained it in his version of the aphorism.

(1) For whoever is ashamed of me and of my words in this adulterous and sinful generation, of him will the Son of man also be ashamed, when he comes in the glory of his Father with the holy angels.

(2) For the Son of man is to come with his angels in the glory of his Father, and then he will repay every man for what he has done.

(3) For whoever is ashamed of me and of my words, of him will the Son of man be ashamed when he comes in his glory and the glory of the Father and of the holy angels.

(Mark 8:38 = Matthew 16:27 = Luke 9:26)

But, since Mark is independent of the *Sayings Gospel Q*, could he have retained a more original version of the saying, one that contained the Son of Man as protagonist? That is unlikely, for two reasons. First, because of the formal matrix, it is God or the passive voice that one expects to find as the original protagonist, just as in the reconstructed *Sayings Gospel Q* version. Second, consider the two other versions from later strata of the tradition.

He who conquers shall be clad thus in white garments, and I will not blot his name out of the book of life; I will confess [= acknowledge] his name before my Father and before his angels. (Revelation 3:5)

If we endure, we shall also reign with him; if we deny him, he also will deny us. (2 Timothy 2:12)

The last parts of those two verses contain, respectively, a positive and a negative edition of the aphorism, and in both cases the protagonist is Jesus as "I" or as "he."

In summary and conclusion, therefore, 28 *Before the Angels* [1/4] has passed through three successive stages. The first stage used only the passive voice and is recoverable as a doubled aphorism from the reconstructed *Sayings Gospel Q* text. The second stage moved from passives to Jesus himself as "I" or "he." This is visible in Matthew's rewriting of that *Sayings Gospel Q* version at 10:32–33 and also, as a single negative, in 2 Timothy 2:12b and, as a single positive, in Revelation 3:5c. The third stage is Mark's introduction of the Son of Man into a single negative version at 8:38, and thence it influenced the first or positive half of the *Sayings Gospel Q* version in Luke 12:8–9. In all of this, we are quite removed from the historical Jesus; the form of 28 *Before the Angels* [1/4] is an apocalyptic sanction from the early church; the Son of Man content first entered that form from Mark himself. And Mark, of course, presumed that the reader who had followed him to 8:38 would know quite clearly that the Son of Man was Jesus himself.

Knowing the Danger

The third complex, 12 *Knowing the Danger* [1/4], continues the phenomenon just seen in those first two complexes. Jesus is only Son of Man in one source, and this time it is the *Sayings Gospel Q*.

While *a thief in the night* is a rather obvious metaphor for unexpected danger, it is not exactly the most obvious metaphor for Jesus' apocalyptic return. The origins of that strange usage may be illuminated by these two texts.

> (1) Therefore I say, if the owner of a house knows that the thief is coming, he will begin his vigil before he comes and will not let him dig through into his house of his domain to carry away his goods. You (pl.), then, be on your guard against the world. Arm yourselves with great strength lest the robbers [brigands] find a way to come to you, for the difficulty which you expect will (surely) materialize.
>
> (2) Jesus said, "Fortunate is the man who knows where the brigands will enter, so that [he] may get up, muster his domain, and arm himself before they invade." (*Gospel of Thomas* 21:3, 103)

There seems to be a move from brigands invading a country, with the emphasis on knowing *where* they will strike, as in 103, to a thief breaking into a house, with the emphasis on knowing *when* he will come, as in 21:3 (Crossan 1983a:61–64). Apparently, then, there was an aphorism such as *Gospel of Thomas* 103 that, through an intermediate stage such as *Gospel of Thomas* 21:3, became applied to Jesus, as in the *Sayings Gospel Q*. But compare, now, that latter version with the others in the complex.

> For you yourselves know well that the day of the Lord will come like a thief in the night. (1 Thessalonians 5:2)

> But the day of the Lord will come like a thief, and then the heavens will pass away with a loud noise, and the elements will be dissolved with fire, and the earth and the works that are upon it will be burned up. (2 Peter 3:10)

> But know this, that if the householder had known at what hour the thief was coming, he would not have left his house to be broken into. You also must be ready; for the Son of man is coming at an unexpected hour. (*Sayings Gospel Q*, 2Q: Luke 12:39–40 = Matthew 24:43–44)

> Remember then what you received and heard; keep that, and repent. If you will not awake, I will come like a thief, and you will not know at what hour I will come upon you. (Revelation 3:3)

Lo, I am coming like a thief! Blessed is he who is awake, keeping his garments that he may not go naked and be seen exposed! (Revelation 16:15)

In those three sources and five texts the thief is "the Lord" in 1 Thessalonians 5:2 and in 2 Peter 3:10, a text presumably dependent on Paul. And in Revelation 3:3 and 16:5 the thief is the "I" of Jesus. Only in the *Sayings Gospel Q* is the thief identified as the Son of Man. I conclude that the Son of Man as *Thief* is not at the start of that stream of tradition but was inserted into it only at and by the apocalyptic layer of the *Sayings Gospel Q*.

Revealed to James

The fourth complex is 30 *Revealed to James* [1/3], with again the Son of Man in only one source. These are the three sources.

Then he appeared to James, then to all the apostles. (1 Corinthians 15:7)

The disciples said to Jesus, "We know that you will depart from us. Who is to be our leader?" Jesus said to them, "Wherever you are, you are to go to James the righteous, for whose sake heaven and earth came into being." (*Gospel of Thomas* 12)

And when the Lord had given the linen cloth to the servant of the priest, he went to James and appeared to him. For James had sworn that he would not eat bread from that hour in which he had drunk the cup of the Lord until he should see him risen from among them that sleep. And shortly thereafter the Lord said: Bring a table and bread! . . . He took the bread, blessed it and brake it and gave it to James the Just and said to him: My brother, eat thy bread, for the Son of Man is risen from among them that sleep. (*Gospel of the Hebrews* 7)

I take those three units, despite their quite disparate content, as pointing to the same theme, namely, the preeminence of James for certain early strands of the tradition. What is, however, of present importance is that, once again, Son of Man appears in only one source within a complex. It is hard to know, incidentally, whether Son of Man in that last text is apocalyptic, earthly, or suffering and rising. It probably warns us, in any case, as does the Johannine usage, not to press those distinctions too hard.

Request for Sign

The fifth complex is 122 *Request for Sign* [1/2], and its twin units have the same phenomenon seen in all those preceding complexes: one source mentions the Son of Man, and the other does not. Following the recent analysis of John Kloppenborg (1987:128–134), the earliest recoverable texts are these:

> This generation is an evil generation; it seeks a sign, but no sign shall be given to it except the sign of Jonah. (*Sayings Gospel Q*, 2Q: Luke 11:29b = Matthew 12:39b/16:4)

> Why does this generation seek a sign? Truly, I say to you, no sign shall be given to this generation. (Mark 8:12b)

I once argued that Mark 8:12b was the more original of those twin versions (1973:6), but I am now more persuaded by Kloppenborg that, since "Mark denies public legitimations of Jesus' identity to outsiders . . . he may have abbreviated an originally longer tradition concerning the Sign of Jonah, leaving only the flat refusal of a sign" (1987:129). But, granted that, maybe the earliest text also included the next verse and Mark simply omitted that as well?

> (1) For as Jonah was three days and three nights in the belly of the whale, so will the Son of man be three days and three nights in the heart of the earth.
> (2) For as Jonah became a sign to the men of Nineveh, so will the Son of man be to this generation. (*Sayings Gospel Q*, 2Q:Matthew 12:40 = Luke 11:30)

First, that former version is Matthew's own composition since, as Kloppenborg notes, "Q never explicitly refers to the resurrection" (1987:132). It is Luke who retains the original Q explanation that, for Jonah then as for Jesus now, the only sign is the preaching of judgment itself. Next, the key argument that the *Sayings Gospel Q* itself added that explanatory gloss rather than finding all of 2Q: Luke 11:29b–30 = Matthew 12:39b–40 as a traditionally given unit, depends on two fundamental pieces of research. Over twenty years ago, Richard Edwards drew attention to a stylized form of speech in the *Sayings Gospel Q* that he termed an "eschatological correlative" (1969; 1971). It was the distinctive way that text developed content for the Son of Man expectation. Examples, all unique to that document, are 174 *As with Lightning* [1/1], 175 *As with Noah* [1/1], and 176 *As with Lot* [1/1]. Some event, from either common nature or biblical history, is cited as a model for what the avenging Son of Man will do in the imminent future. So also here, within 122 *Request for Sign* [1/2], that section in 2Q: Luke 11:30 = Matthew 12:40 might be called *As with Jonah*. Edwards claimed that the Q community had created this genre of saying, but it is better to consider it, not their creation, but simply their very distinctive usage. Daryl Schmidt, for example, showed that the Septuagint translation of the Hebrew Scriptures, the Greek Old Testament, has a very specific form he called the "prophetic correlative." Some event, from either common nature

or biblical history, is cited as a model for what the avenging God will do in
the imminent future. Two examples will suffice.

> As the shepherd rescues from the mouth of the lion two legs, or a piece
> of an ear, so shall the people of Israel who dwell in Samaria be rescued,
> with the corner of a couch and part of a bed. (Amos 3:12)

> As my hand has reached to the kingdoms of the idols whose graven
> images were greater than those of Jerusalem and Samaria, shall I not do
> to Jerusalem and her idols as I have done to Samaria and her images?
> (Isaiah 10:10–11)

Combining Edwards and Schmidt but using my own terminology, I
conclude that the *Sayings Gospel Q* adapted that prophetic correlative into
an *apocalyptic correlative* in order to imagine and develop content for the
advent of Jesus as the avenging Son of Man. "As" this or that happened in
general nature or biblical past, "so" would a corresponding this or that happen when the Son of Man returned. Once again, although the Sign of
Jonah is older than either the *Sayings Gospel Q* or Mark, its Son of Man
interpretation came in only from that former Gospel's own apocalyptic
layer.

The Unknown Time

The sixth complex, 188 *The Unknown Time* [2/4], has, instead of the
metaphor of a thief breaking into another's house in 12 *Knowing the Danger* [1/4], the metaphor of a master returning late at night to his own house.
Here are the texts:

> Take heed, watch; for you do not know when the time will come. It is
> like a man going on a journey, when he leaves home and puts his ser-
> vants in charge, each with his work, and commands the doorkeeper to be
> on the watch. Watch therefore—for you do not know when the master
> [lord] of the house will come, in the evening, or at midnight, or at cock-
> crow, or in the morning—lest he come suddenly and find you asleep.
> And what I say to you I say to all: Watch. (Mark 13:33–37)

> Watch therefore, for you do not know on what day your Lord is coming.
> (Matthew 24:42)

> Watch therefore, for you know neither the day nor the hour. (Matthew.
> 25:13)

> Let your loins be girded and your lamps burning, and be like men who
> are waiting for their master [lord] to come home from the marriage feast,
> so that they may open to him at once when he comes and knocks.

Blessed are those servants whom the master [lord] finds awake when he comes; truly, I say to you, he will gird himself and have them sit at table, and he will come and serve them. If he comes in the second watch, or in the third, and finds them so, blessed are those servants! (Luke 12:35–38)

But take heed to yourselves lest your hearts be weighed down with dissipation and drunkenness and cares of this life, and that day come upon you suddenly like a snare; for it will come upon all who dwell upon the face of the whole earth. But watch at all times, praying that you may have strength to escape all these things that will take place, and to stand before the Son of man. (Luke 21:34–36)

Watch over your life: let your lamps be not quenched and your loins be not ungirded, but be ready, for ye know not the hour in which our Lord cometh. (*Didache* 16:1)

First of all, there probably is a single parable behind both Mark 13:33–37 and Luke 12:35–38, although the rhetorical second-person has now drastically intruded inside the parabolic third-person format in both cases. The original image, but changed more in Mark than in Luke, is of servants who must stay awake and be ready to open the door as soon as their master comes home late at night from a feast. The image is, of course, extremely appropriate since the Greek word for "master" is the same as that for "Lord." Notice especially that *Didache* 16:1, which I take as an independent and residual version of that parable, mentions "our Lord" as the protagonist. But what is of present interest is that none of those units save Luke 21:34–36 ever mentions the Son of Man, and that unit is best seen as a Lukan redactional composition developing his own special climactic conclusion instead of Mark 13:33–37, for which he had a parallel earlier in Luke 12:35–38. Notice, by the way, that Luke introduces there a third metaphor for Jesus' apocalyptic return, that of a snare. Once again, in conclusion, the Son of Man enters a traditional complex late, indeed very late, in its development.

I pause for a second to underline what I have done and to emphasize the methodology of my argument. Only six apocalyptic Son of Man texts have more than single attestation. Only with those six is it possible to establish a comparative trajectory and to see thereby the tradition's development. And the conclusion is very surprising. One could easily imagine an apocalyptic judgment in which Jesus was imagined as chief witness for the prosecution or even as the prosecuting attorney. But throughout this tradition Jesus is seen as the apocalyptic judge, and that may well have needed a very early use of Daniel 7:13 so that, just as its one who was ancient of days gave power and dominion to the one who was like a son of man, so now

God cedes apocalyptic judgment to Jesus. *But what is extraordinary is that I could not find a single case within those six complexes in which two independent sources both contained the Son of Man designation for Jesus.*

Finally, there are, of course, twelve other complexes concerning the apocalyptic Son of Man that have but a single attestation. I presume, methodologically, that they must be judged within those preceding conclusions as stemming, independently, from the creativity of either the *Sayings Gospel Q* or Mark or, dependently on them, from either Matthew or Luke. If, however, one wished to base everything on a singly attested text, 405 *Cities of Israel* [3/1] or 490 *The Heavens Opened* [4/1], for example, as an authentic saying of Jesus, one has the advantage that it cannot be disproved, the disadvantage, unfortunately, that it cannot be proved.

Earthly and Heavenly Son of Man

I have argued that the apocalyptic judge's title, the Son of Man, did not stem from Jesus himself or even from the common voice of all those early Christian communities. It is not present, despite allusions to Daniel 7:13, in the apocalyptic expectations of Paul, in the source used by *Didache* 16, or in the apocalyptic visionaries opposed in the *Gospel of Thomas*. But it did arise very early in the tradition, as is clear from its independent presence in the *Sayings Gospel Q*, the *Gospel of the Hebrews*, and Mark. The conclusion is that Jesus' return could be described in the scenario of Daniel 7:13 without anyone using a titular Son of Man. Why, then, did a titular Son of Man ever arise at all, even among those circles in which it did? How did Son of Man become so early, so easily, and even so emphatically a special title for Jesus in certain communities and traditions?

My proposal is that those early traditions also held texts in which Jesus spoke of "son of man" in the generic or indefinite sense and that it was the presence of such texts that facilitated the transition from Jesus as apocalyptic judge from Daniel 7:13 to Jesus as the Son of Man from Daniel 7:13.

Foxes Have Holes

The complex 101 *Foxes Have Holes* [1/2] is very important because, as mentioned before, it is the only case among all of the forty Son of Man complexes in which that phrase is present in two independent sources.

Jesus said, "[The foxes have their holes] and the birds have their nests, but the son of man has no place to lay his head and rest." (*Gospel of Thomas* 86)

As they were going along the road, a man said to him, "I will follow you wherever you go." And Jesus said to him, "Foxes have holes, and birds of

the air have nests; but the Son of man has nowhere to lay his head."
(*Sayings Gospel Q*, 1Q: Luke 9:57–58 = Matthew 8:19–20)

In that second version, Son of Man, as the translator's capitalization indicates, is both titular and circumlocutionary: it means Jesus himself. But it also indicates that the designation is now being used for the earthly and past Jesus, not just for the future and apocalyptic judge. The dialectical format of the unit probably stems from its position in the *Sayings Gospel Q*, where it was embedded in, most likely, three such dialogues (Kloppenborg 1988:64). Note, for example, the structural rhythm of man/Jesus, Jesus/man/Jesus, man/Jesus and the thematic rhythm of "I will follow you . . . Follow me . . . I will follow you" across the three units in Luke 9:57–62.

The first version, however, retains the earlier format of a Jesus saying without any dialogue framework. It also retains, more significantly, a saying in which "son of man" is neither titular nor circumlocutionary. It does not mean Jesus but the generic or indefinite "human being." We can be relatively sure on this point because, while the *Gospel of Thomas* is, as we saw earlier, emphatically anti-apocalyptic, that apocalypticism did not contain the theme of Jesus as the Son of Man, else that Gospel would surely have avoided or glossed this present saying. In other words, *Gospel of Thomas* 86 uses "son of man" for "human being" without any fear of apocalyptic misunderstanding, just as *Gospel of Thomas* 106 uses the plural "sons of man" for "human beings" (Koester 1989a:43). The saying in *Gospel of Thomas* 86 asserts, and it is an assertion capable of diverse interpretations, that the human being, unlike the animal or the bird, has no fixed abode on earth. I leave aside, by the way, that terminal "and rest," which is, in the light of other sayings on rest and repose such as *Gospel of Thomas* 2, 50, 51, 60, a major theological theme within the redaction of that Gospel (Vielhauer). Apart from that final gloss, the saying goes back to Jesus, although, as just mentioned, its meaning will demand much further context for final interpretation. But its existence means that the *Sayings Gospel Q* had at least one traditional unit in which Jesus spoke of "the son of man" and that, in conjunction with the other traditional theme of Jesus as apocalyptic judge from Daniel 7:13, facilitated the creation of Jesus speaking of himself as the apocalyptic Son of Man.

Lord and Sabbath

A similar situation occurs in Mark's Gospel with 220 *Lord and Sabbath* [2/1], but notice that this text has only a single attestation. I am ignoring such complexes in this book and indicate this one only as a form of methodological cheating. Any probative value it has, therefore, must be absolutely dependent on the strength of the preceding and succeeding cases.

> And he said to them, "The sabbath was made for man, not man for the sabbath; so the Son of man is lord even of the sabbath." (Mark 2:27–28 = [!] Matthew 12:8 = [!] Luke 6:5)

On the one hand, as the capitalization rightly emphasizes, Son of Man is, for Mark 2:28 as earlier for 2:10, Jesus' title for himself. But, on the other, and within its present conjunction with 2:27, it somewhat denigrates the sovereignty of Jesus since, logically from 2:27 into 2:28, every human being is lord of the sabbath, not just Jesus. I take it that Matthew 12:8 and Luke 6:5, those first most careful readers of Mark, saw that problem and solved it alike by the complete excision of any parallel to Mark 2:27. I have argued this in more detail elsewhere (1983a:78–85) and repeat only my conclusion here. It is most unlikely that Mark found a traditional unit such as 2:27 and appended 2:28 to it. It is much more likely that he found 2:27–28 together and, wanting the latter verse, tolerated also the former. But that conjunction of 2:27–28 is only explicable at a stage when "son of man" is not yet titular and circumlocutionary for Jesus, when, in other words, it is still used in its ordinary generic or indefinite sense. In paraphrase: the Sabbath was made for human beings, not human beings for the Sabbath; so the human being is lord even of the Sabbath. My methodological discipline in this book forbids the use of single attestations for reconstructing the historical Jesus so I use this unit here only as an example of a traditional unit known to Mark wherein Jesus used "the son of man" and that, in conjunction with the equally traditional theme of Jesus as apocalyptic judge from Daniel 7:13, facilitated the creation of Jesus' speaking of himself as the apocalyptic Son of Man.

All Sins Forgiven

That proposed transition from generic "son of man" to titular "Son of Man" worked quite well in *Gospel of Thomas* 86, worked rather less well in Mark 2:27–28, and was a disastrous operation in a third example where, however, one can actually see it happening even more clearly than in those two cases. The complex in question is 23 *All Sins Forgiven* [1/4], and I give its main texts in the order of their transmissional development

> Truly, I say to you, all sins will be forgiven the sons of men, and whatever blasphemies they utter; but whoever blasphemes against the Holy Spirit never has forgiveness, but is guilty of an eternal sin. (Mark 3:28–29)

Do not test or examine any prophet who is speaking in a spirit, for every sin shall be forgiven, but this sin shall not be forgiven. (*Didache* 11:7)

And every one who speaks a word against the Son of man will be forgiven; but he who blasphemes against the Holy Spirit will not be forgiven. (*Sayings Gospel Q*, 2Q: Luke 12:10 = Matthew 12:32)

Therefore I tell you, every sin and blasphemy will be forgiven men, but the blasphemy against the Spirit will not be forgiven. And whoever says a word against the Son of man will be forgiven; but whoever speaks against the Holy Spirit will not be forgiven, either in this age or in the age to come. (*Sayings Gospel Q* as in Luke 12:10 and Mark 3:28–29 = Matthew 12:31–32)

Jesus said: "Whoever blasphemes against the father will be forgiven, and whoever blasphemes against the son will be forgiven, but whoever blasphemes against the holy spirit will not be forgiven either on earth or in heaven." (*Gospel of Thomas* 44)

I presume as basic to that complex a saying from Jesus such as that in Mark 3:28 which declared that all sins would be forgiven to "the sons of men," that is, to human beings. This was limited very early on by the exclusion of sins against the Holy Spirit, that is, refusals to believe those acting or speaking in the name of God. Mark 3:28–30 applied this to accusations of satanic collusion against Jesus, and *Didache* 11:7 used it for criticism against prophets. But while that latter text simply eliminated the original Semitism of "sons of men" for human beings, others kept it and generated thereby a magnificent stream of theological confusion. Thus generic "sons of men" became titular "Son of Man" in the *Sayings Gospel Q* at Luke 12:10. And Matthew combined both sources by translating the "sons of man" from Mark 3:28 into "men" in Matthew 12:31 but then accepting the *Sayings Gospel Q*'s confusion with "Son of Man" in Matthew 12:32. The result, even if somehow explicable, was surely a most unfortunate distinction of forgivable sins against Jesus as Son of Man but unforgivable sins against the Holy Spirit. And *Gospel of Thomas* 44 compounded and consummated the entire muddle by enlarging it into a Trinitarian formula of forgivable sons against Father and Son but not against the Holy Spirit.

I conclude, therefore, that Jesus' own use of the generic "son(s) of man" greatly facilitated the transition to the titular Son of Man as almost a favorite self-designation in both the *Sayings Gospel Q* and Mark. And in the process it generated three complexes: 101 *Foxes Have Holes* [1/2] with acceptable, 220 *Lord and Sabbath* [2/1] with unacceptable, and 23 *All Sins Forgiven* [1/4] with disastrous theological results. Others, quite possibly, fell completely by the wayside in that process.

Jesus, Himself, did not author or appoint any
Son of Man of the the genuine —
JOHN AND JESUS   259

Finally, once the arch of the term's usage spanned both Jesus as earthly
Son of Man in the past and Jesus as heavenly Son of Man in the future, two
further developments became possible. A first one was the extension of the
phrase on the lips of Jesus to other earthly situations (appendix 4). That happened quite naturally in both the *Sayings Gospel Q* and Mark. The insertion
of Son of Man is always secondary in those cases. A second and much more
significant development came from Mark himself as a major facet of his own
theology, a theology in which acceptance of the humble and hidden, suffering and rejected Jesus was an absolute prerequisite to being accepted by him
in the imminent apocalyptic consummation. It was Mark, therefore, and Mark
alone, who created the suffering and rising Son of Man and placed all those
units in 240 *Passion-Resurrection Prophecy* [2/1] on the lips of Jesus, whence
they were accepted and expanded by both Matthew and Luke (appendix 4).
Another development is the Johannine usage, where the term itself may possibly
derive from the synoptic tradition but where, in any case, it is often given
a quite distinctive emphasis (appendix 4).

Children and Disciples Complain

I have argued that John the Baptist was an apocalyptic prophet preparing his followers for the imminent advent of God as the Coming One but
that Jesus, after having originally accepted that vision, eventually changed
his response some time after the execution of John. He then emphatically
contrasted a follower of John and a member of the Kingdom. He never
spoke of himself or anyone else as the apocalyptic Son of Man, and a tentative hypothesis for the break between John and Jesus is that the latter no
longer accepted the former's apocalyptic message. That hypothesis will
demand, of course, further testing. My final point here is that a difference
between John and Jesus was discerned and expressed in the tradition itself.

The only complex with plural attribution remaining in the Baptist
inventory is 106 *Fasting and Wedding* [1/2], but a look at its twin sources
makes clear a problem.

> They said to Jesus, "Come, let us pray today and let us fast." Jesus said,
> "What is the sin that I have committed, or wherein have I been
> defeated? But when the bridegroom leaves the bridal chamber, then let
> them fast and pray." (*Gospel of Thomas* 104)

> Now John's disciples and the Pharisees were fasting; and people came
> and said to him, "Why do John's disciples and the disciples of the
> Pharisees fast, but your disciples do not fast?" And Jesus said to them,
> "Can the wedding guests fast while the bridegroom is with them? As

long as they have the bridegroom with them, they cannot fast. The days will come, when the bridegroom is taken away from them, and then they will fast in that day." (Mark 2:18–20)

The problem is that a contrast between John and Jesus, refracted through their respective disciples, is present only in the second text. Ordinarily, then, I would methodologically omit it from consideration in this book. But the difficulty is that precisely this contrast of John and Jesus over asceticism comes up again in 144 *Wisdom Justified* [1/1], another text with only single attestation but this time from the *Sayings Gospel Q*.

> To what then shall I compare the men of this generation, and what are they like? They are like children sitting in the market place and calling to one another, "We piped to you, and you did not dance; we wailed, and you did not weep." For John the Baptist has come eating no bread and drinking no wine; and you say, "He has a demon." The Son of man has come eating and drinking; and you say, "Behold, a glutton and a drunkard, a friend of tax collectors and sinners!" Yet wisdom is justified by all her children. (*Sayings Gospel Q*, 2Q: Luke 7:31–35 = Matthew 11:16–19)

We have, in other words, only single attestation for the contrast on fasting between John and Jesus in 144 *Wisdom Justified* [1/1] and 106 *Fasting and Wedding* [1/2], but I cannot ignore them, because they evince double attestation not of the same text but of the same theme.

From 106 *Fasting and Wedding* [21/2] I take only their common assertion by Jesus that now is a time of joy and celebration rather than of mourning and fasting. It is like the time of a wedding. I leave aside the inference in Mark 2:20 that Jesus is himself the Bridegroom soon to be taken away. In 144 *Wisdom Justified* [1/1] I presume, with John Kloppenborg, that "the identification of John and Jesus with the children who do the calling, and 'this generation' with those who refuse to respond, seems the most natural interpretation, especially since v. 35 characterizes John and Jesus as children . . . of Sophia" (1987:111). There is no emphasis here on the superiority of Jesus over John. The evenhanded chiastic construction of piped/wailed //fasted/feasted leaves them on the same level but, of course, the presence of the titular Son of Man with all its apocalyptic overtones underlines the position of Jesus. In any case, and for my present concerns, both the *Sayings Gospel Q* and Mark know a tradition comparing John and Jesus in terms of the former's asceticism and the latter's prodigality. I translate that, as part of my working hypothesis, to mean that John lived an apocalyptic asceticism and that Jesus did the opposite. But, of course, to say that Jesus was not an apocalyptic ascetic does not at all tell us what he was.

Open Commensality

The accusation made against John in 144 *Wisdom Justified* [1/1] is the rather standard one by which unofficial power claimants are officially dismissed before being officially destroyed. The same allegation of witchcraft is later made against Jesus in 121 *Beelzebul Controversy* [1/2]. What is surprising, however, is the allegation made against Jesus in that same 144 *Wisdom Justified* [1/1]. I no more take it at face value than I do the charge against John. But what exactly is its basis? We can see the acts of John that beget the charge of witchcraft. What acts of Jesus begot the charges of gluttony, drunkenness, and keeping very bad company?

An answer may be seen in the parable of 95 *The Feast* [1/2]. I have studied this story in greater detail elsewhere (1985:39–52) and can but summarize those conclusions here. In *Gospel of Thomas* 64 the interpretation is guided by the contextual situation of the three parables in *Gospel of Thomas* 63–65, by the addition of the second invited guest to enlarge the overall number from three to four and thereby the business concerns from two to three, and especially by the concluding aphorism from Jesus: "Businessmen and merchants [will] not enter the places of my father." It is the celibate and world-negating ascetics and not those engaged in the entanglements of ordinary life who attain the feast. In Luke 14:15–24, presuming some deliberate symbolism, it is the "lawyers and Pharisees," among whom Jesus dines in 14:2, who refuse the feast, and it is, first, the outcasts of Israel near at hand and, second, the Gentiles farther afield who are included. Luke, in 14:21 as earlier in 14:12–14, has a fourfold categorization of those outcasts: "the poor and maimed and blind and lame." Finally, Matthew 22:1–14, in deliberate parallelism with his version of 46 *The Tenants* [1/3] in his preceding 21:33–46, develops a full-blown symbolism in which, first, Jerusalem's destruction in 70 C.E. is seen as punishment for Jewish rejection of Matthean Christianity and, second, Matthean Christianity itself is internally divided pending final discrimination by God at the Last Judgment.

All three extant versions have interpreted and applied the parable to their own situations by both contextual connections and intratextual developments. I think, however, that a common structural plot is discernible behind them all. It tells of a person who gives a presumably unannounced feast, sends a servant to invite friends, finds by late in the day that each has a valid but extremely polite excuse, and replaces them with anyone off the streets. I emphasize one point, especially in the light of Luke's parallel fourfold sets in 14:12–14. There, one is not to invite "your friends or

your brothers or your kinsmen or rich neighbors" but to invite "the poor,
the maimed, the lame, the blind." In the first as in the twentieth century, a
person might create a feast for society's outcasts. That could easily be
understood even or especially in the honor and shame ideology of Mediterranean society as a benefaction and one of deliberately high visibility. No
doubt if one did it persistently and exclusively there might be some very
negative social repercussions. But, in itself, to invite the outcasts for a special meal is a less socially radical act than to invite anyone found on the
streets. It is that "anyone" that negates the very social function of table,
namely, to establish a social ranking by what one eats, how one eats, and
with whom one eats. It is the random and open commensality of the parable's meal that is its most startling element. One could, in such a situation,
have classes, sexes, ranks, and grades all mixed up together. The social challenge of such egalitarian commensality is the radical threat of the parable's
vision. It is only a story, of course, but it is one that focuses its egalitarian
challenge on society's mesocosmic mirror, the table as the place where bodies meet to eat. And the almost predictable counteraccusation to such
open commensality is immediate: Jesus is a glutton, a drunkard, and a
friend of tax collectors and sinners. He makes, in other words, no appropriate distinctions and discriminations. He has no honor. He has no shame.
That is also, and quite correctly, the accusation made against Jesus in 113
Eating with Sinners [1/2].

   I cluster seven other complexes around that ideal of open or egalitarian
commensality. As advocated in parable and acted out in practice, it
involved very specific challenges from mesocosmic table to macrocosmic
society. There is, first and above all, 19 *What Goes In* [1/4], a complex that
negates any value to food taboos or table rituals. The same point is made in
102 *Inside and Outside* [1/2]. Together they insist that the inside and what
comes from inside out are more important than the outside and what
comes from outside in. There is no need to presume that Jesus was speaking against the fully developed table rituals of the Pharisaic sect. An open
table and an open menu offend alike against any cultural situation in which
distinctions among foods and guests mirror social distinctions, discriminations, and hierarchies. It would, of course, also offend the Pharisees, but it
was not directed exclusively against them. Next, that it did so offend is clear
from two other complexes, also from the historical Jesus. In 84 *On Hindering Others* [1/2], the version in *Gospel of Thomas* 102 is, as I argued in more
detail elsewhere (1983a:29–36), probably the most original rendition, with
its conjunction of woe, dog-in-the-manger proverb, and metaphor of eating.
And, when 124 *Honors and Salutations* [1/2] is read in conjunction with
that former case, the parallelism between food regulations and social hier-

archies becomes quite clear. Distinctions and discriminations among foods or guests stand or fall with distinctions and discriminations among seats and salutations. We are actually dealing with three cultural levels metonymically and metaphorically interlinked: the microlevel of food, the mesolevel of table, and the macrolevel of society itself. To subvert either of the former is a calculated attack on the latter. Finally, complexes such as 76 *Speck and Log* [1/2], 80 *The Blind Guide* [1/2], and 126 *Salting the Salt* [1/2] were probably said by Jesus not to or against his own followers but about and against those religiopolitical functionaries such as local village scribes, teachers, and whatever Pharisees were around in early first century Galilee.

One postscript: it was obviously possible for the first Christian generations to debate whether Jesus was for or against the ritual laws of Judaism. His position must have been, as it were, unclear. I propose, from those preceding complexes, that he did not care enough about such ritual laws either to attack or to acknowledge them. He ignored them, but that, of course, was to subvert them at a most fundamental level. Later, however, some followers could say that, since he did not attack them, he must have accepted them. Others, contrariwise, could say that, since he did not follow them, he must have been against them. Open commensality profoundly negates distinctions and hierarchies between female and male, poor and rich, Gentile and Jew. It does so, indeed, at a level that would offend the ritual laws of *any* civilized society. That was precisely its challenge.

Another, and even more important postscript: is all of this simply projecting a contemporary democratic idealism anachronistically back onto the performance of the historical Jesus? I emphasize most strongly, for now and the rest of this book, that such egalitarianism stems not only from peasant Judaism but, even more deeply, from peasant society as such. "The popular religion and culture of peasants in a complex society are not only a syncretized, domesticated, and localized variant of larger systems of thought and doctrine. They contain almost inevitably the seeds of an alternative symbolic universe — a universe which in turn makes the social world in which peasants live less than completely inevitable. Much of this radical symbolism can only be explained as a cultural reaction to the situation of the peasantry *as a class.* In fact, this symbolic opposition represents the closest thing to class consciousness in pre-industrial agrarian societies. It is as if those who find themselves at the bottom of the social heap develop cultural forms which promise them dignity, respect, and economic comfort which they lack in the world as it is. A real pattern of exploitation dialectically produces its own symbolic mirror image within folk culture" (1977:224). That quotation is from a fascinating analysis by James Scott, moving from Europe to Southeast Asia, noting the Little Tradition's common reaction to such disparate Great Traditions as Christianity, Buddhism, and Islam, and arguing very persuasively that peasant culture and religion is actually an anticulture, qualifying alike both the religious and political elites that oppress it. It is, in fact, a reflexive and reactive inversion of the pattern of exploitation common to the peasantry *as such*. "The radical vision to which I refer," he continues, "is strikingly uniform despite the enormous variations in peasant cultures and the different great traditions of which they partake. . . . At the risk of overgeneralizing, it is possible to describe some common features of this reflexive symbolism. It nearly always implies a society of brotherhood in which there will be no rich and poor, in which no distinctions of rank and status (save those between believers and non-believers) will exist. Where religious institutions are experienced as justifying inequities, the abolition of rank and status may well include the elimination of religious hierarchy in favor of communities of equal believers. Property is typically, though not always, to be held in common and shared. All unjust claims to taxes, rents, and tribute are to be nullified. The envisioned utopia may also include a self-yielding and abundant nature as well as a radically transformed human nature in which greed, envy, and hatred will disappear. While the earthly utopia is thus an anticipation of the future, it often harks back to a mythic Eden from which mankind has fallen away" (1977:225–226).

✧ *12* ✧

Kingdom and Wisdom

A vast substitution of classes would take place. The kingdom of
God was made — 1st, for children, and those who resemble
them; 2nd, for the outcasts of the world, victims of that social
arrogance which repulses the good but humble man; 3d, for
heretics and schismatics, publicans, Samaritans, and Pagans of
Tyre and Sidon. An energetic parable explained this appeal to
the people and justified it [95 *The Feast* (1/2)]. . . . The doctrine
that the poor . . . alone shall be saved, that the reign of the poor
is approaching—was, therefore, the doctrine of Jesus. . . . This,
however, was not a new fact. The most exalted democratic
movement of which humanity has preserved the remembrance
(the only one, also, which has succeeded, for it alone has
maintained itself in the domain of pure thought), had long
disturbed the Jewish race. . . . The prophets, the true, and, in
one sense, the boldest tribunes, had thundered incessantly
against the great, and established a close relation, on the one
hand, between the words "rich, impious, violent, wicked," and,
on the other, between the words "poor, gentle, humble, pious."
                    Ernest Renan, The Life of Jesus *(1972:194–196)*

The comparison between Son of Man and Kingdom sayings is rather startling, when done, that is, in terms of stratigraphy and attestation. If you
look at complexes with the specific expression in at least one text, the overall inventory for Son of Man is 40:14 + 26 (appendix 4) and for Kingdom is
77:33 + 44 (appendix 5). Obviously, then, and even in crudest statistics,
Kingdom is a more frequent expression and is found in more sayings with
plural attestation. There are, however, other more specific and more significant differences. The inventory for the Son of Man *expression* in plural
attribution was but 40:1 + 39 (appendix 4), but that for the Kingdom *expression* is 77:12 + 65 (appendix 5). There are, in other words, twelve sayings in
which the Kingdom expression itself appears in plural attribution. And of
those, one has multiple, two have triple, and the remaining nine have double attribution (appendix 5). It is on those twelve complexes that I build my
understanding of the Kingdom announced by Jesus. Finally, while Son of

Man was found outside the canonical Gospels only twice, in 2 *Jesus'*
Apocalyptic Return [1/6] and 490 *The Heavens Opened* [4/1], and outside
the New Testament only once, in 386 *Faith Against Sight* [3/2], the Kingdom expression is found, outside the Gospels, thirty times within the New
Testament, and outside the New Testament, eight times in the Apostolic
Fathers (appendix 5). I conclude, therefore, that Kingdom is situated far
more deeply and broadly within the Christian tradition than is Son of Man.

A note on terminology. I am not particularly happy with the word *king-*
dom. It is not only androcentric—that, at least, admits its historical bias—it
is also primarily local or, at least, is readily so interpreted. But what we are
actually talking about is power and rule, a state much more than a place, or,
if you will, a place only because of a state. And, lest one ambiguity replace
another, state means way of life of mode of being, not nation or empire.
The basic question is this: how does human power exercise its rule, and
how, in contrast, does divine power exercise its rule? The kingdom of God
is people under divine rule, and that, as ideal, transcends and judges all
human rule. The focus of discussion is not on kings but on rulers, not on
kingdom but on power, not on place but on state.

A Kingdom of Nobodies

First for consideration, at least in methodological discipline, is 20 *King-*
dom and Children [1/4] because of the striking fourfold independent
attestation (Crossan 1983b). I consider with and after it two other Kingdom
sayings, 43 *Blessed the Poor* [1/3] and 199 *Kingdom and Riches* [1/2].

Kingdom and Children

The first source has a double conjunction, first, of setting and saying,
then, of physical and metaphorical children. It is, in other words, a situation of actual infants that engenders the Kingdom aphorism from Jesus.

Jesus saw infants being suckled. He said to his disciples, "These infants
being suckled are like those who enter the kingdom." (*Gospel of Thomas*
22:1–2)

In this version, however, there follows an integrated gloss, to be seen in
greater detail under 13 *Two as One* [1/4] below, which interprets the meaning of that enigmatic correlation of Kingdom and children by an even more
enigmatic series of sentences.

They [his disciples] said to him, "Shall we then, as children, enter the
kingdom?" Jesus said to them, "When you make the two one, and when

you make the inside like the outside and the outside like the inside, and
the above like the below, and when you make the male and the female
one and the same, so that the male not be male nor the female female;
and you fashion eyes in place of an eye, and a hand in place of a hand,
and a foot in place of a foot, and a likeness in place of a likeness, then
will you enter [the kingdom]." (*Gospel of Thomas* 22:3-4)

You will recall from earlier that the *Gospel of Thomas* derided the idea
of looking into the future for apocalyptic salvation. Instead, it advocated
looking back to the past, not only to an Edenic moment before Adam and
Eve sinned but to an even more primordial moment before they were split
into two beings. Its gaze was not on a male but on an androgynous Adam,
image of its Creator in being neither female nor male. And it was in baptism, precisely in the primitive form of nude baptism, that the initiant,
reversing the saga of Genesis 1-3, took off "the garments of shame" (Smith
1965-66) mandated for a fallen humanity and assumed "the image of the
androgyne" (Meeks). This theology, which is the basic unifying vision of
the *Gospel of Thomas*, can be seen not only in *Gospel of Thomas* 22:1-4 but
also in 21:1-2 and 37:1-2 and in all those sayings, such as 4:2, 11:2, 16, 23, 49,
75, 106, about being or becoming one, a single one, or a solitary (Klijn).
Baptismal regeneration involved the destruction of duality, of that
between the inner soul and the outer body, between the heavenly,
androgynous image of God and its earthly, bifurcated counterpart, but
most especially, for the *Gospel of Thomas*, between female and male, so
that sexual differentiation was negated by celibate asceticism. That fitted,
of course, with the Gospel's overall asceticism, a world-negating isolation
that mocked, in sayings such as *Gospel of Thomas* 6:1+14:1 and 27, ordinary Jewish asceticism in favor of its own far more radical, total, and cosmic
abandonment. It becomes quite clear, against all that background, why an
infant is chosen as metaphor for those entering the Kingdom. The child is
considered asexual or presexual or nonsexual in any operational manner
and is therefore an appropriate image for the ideal Christian in the *Gospel
of Thomas*, a Christian who is, in other words, an ascetic celibate. A kingdom of children is a kingdom of the celibate.

The second source in 20 *Kingdom and Children* [1/4] is Mark 10:13-16
and thence into the other two synoptics, but with Matthew 19:13-15 omitting Mark 10:15, and Luke 18:15-17 omitting Mark 10:16. There is, once
again, an interaction of setting and saying, of literal and metaphorical
children.

[13] And they were bringing children to him, that he might touch them;
and the disciples rebuked them. [14] But when Jesus saw it he was indig-

nant, and said to them, "Let the children come to me, do not hinder
them; for to such belongs the kingdom of God. [15] Truly, I say to you,
whoever does not receive the kingdom of God like a child shall not enter
it." [16] And he took them in his arms and blessed them, laying his hands
upon them. (Mark 10:13–16)

Notice that we have plural "children" in 10:13, 14, 16 but singular
"child" in 10:15, that each unit, 10:13 + 14 + 16 or 10:15, can stand quite well
on its own, and that the presence of both 10:14 and 10:15 creates a slight
redundancy. I presume, therefore, what I argued in greater detail elsewhere, namely, that Mark 10:13–16 was created by Mark in deliberate parallelism with 9:36–39 but using a traditional and given unit in 10:15
(1983b:84–87). What Mark understands by a kingdom of children is to be
seen within that parallelism and especially in its double rebuke to the
pretensions of the disciples who wish to assume first places in and thereby
regulate access to the Kingdom. The "child" of Mark 9:36 and of 10:15 are
deliberately connected images, as indicated by the theme of "embracing" in
both cases. For Mark 9:33–36 and 10:13–16, to be a child is to be "last of all
and servant of all." A kingdom of children is a kingdom of the humble.
The third source is Matthew 18:3, which is an independent version of
the aphorism (Lindars 1980–81). Its preceding presence at 18:3 explains
why Matthew 19:13–15 accepted only Mark 10:13 + 14 + 16 and omitted any
parallel to Mark 10:15.

> At that time the disciples came to Jesus, saying, "Who is the greatest in
> the kingdom of heaven?" And calling to him a child, he put him in the
> midst of them, and said, "Truly, I say to you, unless you turn and
> become like children, you will never enter the kingdom of heaven. Who-
> ever humbles himself like this child, he is the greatest in the kingdom of
> heaven." (Matthew 18:1–4)

Once again, however, the immediate context makes the interpretation
quite clear. A kingdom of children is a kingdom of the humble.
The fourth and final source is just as interesting as all the others and
evinces just as much contextual and compositional interpretation. Its dialogue is framed, ironically, by the twin mentions of teacher, and it proceeds,
as noted below, in three dialogues [A, B, C] but with that of poor Nicodemus [1] getting shorter and shorter, that of Jesus [2] getting longer and
longer.

> [A1] Now there was a man of the Pharisees, named Nicodemus, a ruler
> of the Jews. This man came to Jesus by night and said to him, "Rabbi,

we know that you are a teacher come from God; for no one can do these signs that you do, unless God is with him." [A2] Jesus answered him, "Truly, truly, I say to you, unless one is born anew, he cannot see the kingdom of God." [B1] Nicodemus said to him, "How can a man be born when he is old? Can he enter a second time into his mother's womb and be born?" [B2] Jesus answered, "Truly, truly, I say to you, unless one is born of water and the Spirit, he cannot enter the kingdom of God. That which is born of the flesh is flesh, and that which is born of the Spirit is spirit. Do not marvel that I said to you, 'You must be born anew.' The wind blows where it wills, and you hear the sound of it, but you do not know whence it comes or whither it goes; so it is with every one who is born of the Spirit." [C1] Nicodemus said to him, "How can this be?" [C2] Jesus answered him, "Are you a teacher of Israel, and yet you do not understand this?" (John 3:1–10)

The dialogue is now fully developed, but any actual children are left far behind. Children, as newly born, are like the newly baptized, born of water and the Spirit. A kingdom of children is a kingdom of the baptized.

We have, therefore, three different and contextually created interpretations of Jesus' correlation of kingdom and children. I accept that correlation as historical but all three interpretations as divergent explanations of its quite startling juxtaposition. But what would ordinary Galilean peasants have thought about children? Would "like a child" have immediately meant being humble, being innocent, being new, being credulous? Go back, if you will, to those papyrus fragments quoted in chapter 1 of this book and think for a moment of infants, often female but male as well, abandoned at birth by their parents and saved from the rubbish dumps to be reared as slaves. Pagan writers were, according to Menahem Stern, rather surprised that Jewish parents did not practice such potential infanticide (1976–84:1.33, 2.41), but still, to be a child was to be a nobody, with the possibility of becoming a somebody absolutely dependent on parental discretion and parental standing in the community. That, I think, is the heart of the matter with all other allusions or further interpretations clustering around that central and shocking metaphor. A kingdom of the humble, of the celibate, or of the baptized comes later. This comes first: a kingdom of children is a kingdom of nobodies. And if "it is an insult for an adult to be compared to children" as Wendy Cotter rightly emphasizes concerning 144 *Wisdom Justified* [1/1] and the ancient honor and shame societies of the Mediterranean world (1989:70), what happens when a Kingdom is announced for those alone who are like children? Indeed, a Kingdom of Nobodies seems so untenable an interpretation that it requires immediate corroboration from two other Kingdom sayings that confirm its deliberate challenge.

Blessed the Poor

It is hard to imagine a saying more initially radical than 43 *Blessed the Poor* [1/3] and thereafter more safely relegated to the confines of normalcy if not banality.

> Blessed are the poor [*hēke*], for yours is the kingdom of heaven. (*Gospel of Thomas* 54)

> Blessed are you poor [*ptōchoi*] for yours is the kingdom of God. (*Sayings Gospel Q*, 1Q: Luke 6:20)

> Blessed are the poor [*ptōchoi*] in spirit, for theirs is the kingdom of heaven. (*Sayings Gospel Q*, 1Q: Matthew 5:3)

> Has not God chosen those who are poor [*ptōchous*] in the world to be rich in faith and heirs of the kingdom which he has promised to those who love him? (James 2:5)

The basic problem is not just Matthew's gloss "in spirit," although that certainly diverts attention and interpretation from material to spiritual, from economic to religious poverty. Even when that is left aside as a Matthean addition, there is still a serious problem with the word *poor* itself. First, then, a word about words, and especially about that word *ptōchos* which we translate "poor."

The classic text is in the *Plutus* of Aristophanes, the last play of that great comic dramatist, produced probably in the Athens of 388 B.C.E. Its theme is that, since the evil are rich and the virtuous are poor, the god Wealth, or Plutus, must himself be blind and in need of miraculous healing at the shrine of Asclepius. The point in question occurs with Chremylus arguing for the advantages of Wealth, or Plutus, against Poverty, or Penia, who is personified as a goddess.

CHREMYLUS:
Why, what have *you* got to bestow but a lot
    of burns from the bathing-room station
And a hollow-cheeked rabble of destitute hags,
    and brats on the verge of starvation? . . .
For a robe but a rag, for a bed but a bag
    of rushes which harbour a nation
Of bugs whose envenomed and tireless attacks
    would the soundest of sleepers awaken.
And then for a carpet a sodden old mat,
    which is falling to bits, must be taken.
And a jolly hard stone for a pillow, you'll own;
    and, for griddle-cakes barley and wheaten,

Must leaves dry and lean of the radish or e'en
    sour stalks of the mallow be eaten.
And the head of a barrel, stove in, for a chair;
    and, instead of a trough, for your kneading
A stave of a vat you must borrow, and that
    all broken. So great and exceeding
Are the blessings which Poverty brings in her train
    on the children of men to bestow!

POVERTY:

The life you define with such skill is not mine:
    'tis the life of a beggar [*ptōchōn*], I trow.

CHREMYLUS:

Well, Poverty [*penian*], Beggary [*ptōcheias*], truly the twain
    to be sisters we always declare.

POVERTY:

Aye you! who to good Thrasybulus [deliverer from tyrants] forsooth
    Dionysius the Tyrant declare!
But the life I allot to my people is not,
    nor shall be, so full of distresses.
'Tis the beggar [*ptōchou*] alone who has nought of his own,
    nor even an obol possesses.
My poor [*penētos*] man, 'tis true, has to scrape and to screw
    and his work he must never be slack in;
There'll be no superfluity found in his cot;
    but then there will nothing be lacking.
        (Aristophanes, *Plutus* 535–554; Rogers 3.412–415)

Beggary, or Ptocheia, and those who follow her, are described by Chremylus; but Poverty, or Penia, and those who follow her are described by Poverty herself and emphatically distinguished from the former. Three commentaries, with their cumulative length underlining their cumulative importance, draw out the implications of that contrast between Poverty and Beggary.

A first commentary on that text is taken from Arthur Hands's book on charitable social aid in ancient Greece and Rome. "The Greek and Latin terms commonly translated as 'the poor' seldom imply absolute poverty or destitution. They were applied, in particular, to the vast majority of the people in any city-state who, having no claim to the income of a large estate, lacked that degree of leisure and independence regarded as essential to the life of a gentleman. In many instances such men would own small plots on which they would have to work themselves, though perhaps with the help of hired labourers or slaves. . . . Such language was, of course, appropriate to members of the upper class, from whom almost all of our classical literature comes. Their tone was usually disparaging, but if it was the small farmer whom the speaker had in mind, it might be otherwise, the farmer's status being idealized or even envied. . . . But the terms suggestive of complete destitution — or even of the lot of the class of labourers which possessed no land — are seldom idealized. Such was the Greek term *ptōchos*, a word suggesting 'one who crouches,' and so a 'beggar'" (62–63). A similar linguistic refinement is offered by Sir Moses Finley in his study of the ancient economy. "The Greek words *ploutos* and *penia*, customarily rendered 'wealth' and 'poverty,' respectively, had in fact a different nuance, what [Thorstein] Veblen called [in his *The Theory of the Leisure Class*] 'the distinction between exploit and drudgery' [1934:15]. A *plousios* was a man who was rich enough to live properly on his income (as we would phrase it), a *penēs* was not. The latter need not be propertyless or even, in the full sense, poor: he could own a farm or slaves, and he could have a few hundred drachmas accumulated in a strong-box, but he was compelled to devote himself to gaining a livelihood. *Penia*, in short, meant the harsh compulsion to toil, whereas the pauper, the man who was altogether without resources, was normally called a *ptōchos*, a beggar, not a *penēs*" (41). The final commentary is that of Gildas Hamel's doctoral dissertation on poverty and charity in the early centuries of Roman Palestine. "If the *penēs* was the opponent of the *plousios* . . . he was also on the same side of the fence. Both *plousioi* and *penētes* determined each other's identities, whereas a *ptōchos* was on the margins, and recognized by everyone as such. Poor and rich belonged to the same world and placed themselves on a common, even sliding scale, but beggars could not. The *ptōchos* was someone who had lost many or all of his family and social ties. He often was a wanderer, therefore a foreigner for others, unable to tax for any length of time the resources of a group to which he could contribute very little or nothing at all . . . a *ptōchos* was a shocking reality for the Greco-Roman world. We can see that it was a real difficulty from the fact that many authors of Greek Christian literature sought to explain away the *ptōchos* of the Gospels, and to harmonize the Beatitudes and their own view of society. One solution was to spiritualize the meaning of *ptōchos* in infinitely varied ways. The other was to retranslate it as *penēs*, attaching to it values already present in Hellenistic society, albeit not developed" (8, 39).

The point of all that, from ancient comedy to modern commentary, is quite clear. Aristophanes might create a goddess known as Poverty, the divine personification of the deserving and hard-working poor, and so quite appropriately opposed to the leisured laziness of the idle rich, but he created no goddess known as Beggary, gave no apotheosis to Destitution. That is, however, exactly what Jesus did. He spoke, in shocking paradox, not about a Kingdom of the Poor but about a Kingdom of the Destitute. That is quite clear in the Greek of the *Sayings Gospel Q* behind both Luke 6:20 and Matthew 5:3, where it is not the poor or *penētes* but the destitute or *ptōchoi* who are declared to be blessed. It is also clear in the Coptic of the *Gospel of Thomas* 54, which uses the adjective *hēke*. There is no corresponding Greek fragment for this unit, but both Coptic and Greek versions are available for *Gospel of Thomas* 3 and 29. In both those cases "poverty," but in the negative sense of spiritual poverty, appears as *ptōchia* in Greek and as the abstract formation *mñt-hēke* in Coptic (Emmel 276, 289). We can, therefore, be fairly sure that the Coptic translator found *ptōchoi* in his Greek text for *Gospel of Thomas* 54 just as Luke and Matthew did with the *Sayings Gospel Q*. We can also be very sure that *Thomas*, unlike Matthew, did not think he was talking about spiritual poverty. For *Thomas*, physical poverty was spiritual riches; physical riches were spiritual poverty. Similarly, the invectives against the rich in James 1:9–11 and 5:1–6 emphasize that the destitution of 2:5 is to be taken quite literally and materially.

The beatitude of Jesus declared blessed, then, not the poor but the destitute, not poverty but beggary. Recall, for a moment, Gerhard Lenski's typology of stratification in agrarian societies from the first section of this book. In its terms, Jesus spoke of a Kingdom not of the Peasant or Artisan classes but of the Unclean, Degraded, and Expendable classes.

That reading is supported by considering three other beatitudes, all of which derive from Jesus himself. 59 *Blessed the Sad* [1/3], that is, those who weep or mourn, and 96 *Blessed the Hungry* [1/2] are almost synonymous for 43 *Blessed the Poor* [1/3] and do not add anything particularly new to its already radical content. The fourth beatitude, 48 *Blessed the Persecuted* [1/3], requires some commentary. If that beatitude is read "as a graphic description of the persecution of Christian preachers who speak on behalf of their exalted Lord" it would have to be judged as developmental rather than original, especially "if its formulation reflects the attempt to solidify group boundaries by defining the 'in-group' negatively in terms of rejection by an 'out-group' or positively in terms of attachment to a particular confession or *logos* or by appeal to a transcendental explanation for membership (election, predetermination). Such strong 'boundary language' is hardly thinkable for the Jesus of history, whose appeal seems to have been precisely on the basis of a rejection and destruction of such language" (Kloppenborg 1986:36, 49). Yet a glance at the three independent sources for the beatitude underlines a problem and serves possibly to question the appropriateness of using *persecution* in its title. First, 1 Peter does not mention persecution but only suffering in 3:14a and reproach in 4:14. Second, the *Sayings Gospel Q* may also have lacked persecution: Luke 6:22 has "hate you . . . exclude you . . . revile [reject] you . . . cast out your name as evil"; Matthew 5:11 has "revile you and persecute you and utter all kinds of evil against you." But Matthew 5:10 had just created another persecution beatitude of its own even before giving the *Q* version, so it is at least possible that it was Matthew 5:11 who added the word and that *Q* is better reflected in Luke 6:22b. Third, the word *persecution* is securely present in *Gospel of Thomas* 68 as "hated . . . persecuted . . . persecuted" and in 69:1 as "persecuted." What we seem to have, in summary, is a series of verbs meaning contemptuous abuse and social rejection slowly ceding place to the more lethal single verb of *persecution*. I judge that Jesus said, speaking no doubt from his own experience, something like, "Blessed are the abused and the rejected," and the early communities said, speaking from their own increasingly dangerous situations, "Blessed are the persecuted." As John Kloppenborg put it, having paralleled that beatitude's acceptance of social abuse with similar Cynic experiences, "those who proclaim, 'blessed are the poor' will find themselves hated and reviled" (1986:51).

Kingdom and Riches

The second of the two major Kingdom aphorisms in whose light I read Jesus' correlation of kingdom and children as a kingdom of nobodies is 199 *Kingdom and Riches* [2/2]. There are two independent texts (Koester 1957:244–246), but notice that this is the only Kingdom saying from the second stratum with plural attestation.

> And Jesus looked around and said to his disciples, "How hard it will be for those who have riches to enter the kingdom of God!" And the disciples were amazed at his words. But Jesus said to them again, "Children, how hard it is to enter the kingdom of God! It is easier for a camel to go through the eye of a needle than for a rich man to enter the kingdom of God." And they were exceedingly astonished, and said to him, "Then who can be saved?" Jesus looked at them and said, "With men it is impossible, but not with God; for all things are possible with God." (Mark 10:23–27)

> And the rich cleave with difficulty to the servants of God, fearing that they will be asked for something by them. Such then will enter with difficulties the kingdom of God. For just as it is difficult to walk with naked feet among thistles, so it is also difficult for such men to enter the kingdom of God. (*Shepherd of Hermas, Similitude* 9.20.2b–3)

Mark's triple assertion of that fact coupled with his double statement of the disciples' amazement is muted back by the dependent Matthew 19:23–26 and Luke 18:24–27 to a double statement of the former theme and a single one of the latter. Markan emphasis can be, at times, a little heavy-handed.

The more important fact, however, is that despite the aphorism's radical stance against the rich, it is not nearly as radical as was 43 *Blessed the Poor* [1/2]. Taken alone and by itself, 199 *Kingdom and Riches* [2/2] might have been read as against the rich and for the poor, but not necessarily for the destitute. It is only in conjunction with 20 *Kingdom and Children* [1/4] and also 43 *Blessed the Poor* [1/2], that is, the destitute, the beggars, and the vagrants, that its full implications are evident. And, of course, such a reading will demand constant checking as this study proceeds.

There is double attestation only for the difficulty of the rich entering the Kingdom, not for the camel metaphor itself. I wonder, however, if Hermas also knows the full aphorism, but, because he is already working with a metaphor of the rich being unable to walk on the thorns and thistles of an allegorical third mountain, he is unable to use the full saying lest metaphors become mixed. That cannot be more than a guess. There is, however, a certain saving grace of humor in the camel aphorism. It evinces, be it from Jesus or Mark, a certain lack of venom and vengeance against the rich. The idea of the rich in the Kingdom is not only quite impossible, it is rather hilarious, like getting a camel through the eye of a needle. For my methodology, however, such dark humor must be established from plural attestation elsewhere before it can be accepted as from Jesus here.

Five other complexes cluster within that same criticism of riches. The complex 94 *The Rich Farmer* [1/2], especially as read without Luke 12:21 as commentary, does not presume that the farmer has done anything wrong. He is simply rich and has the planning problems of such a status. But riches do not save you from death's unexpected arrival. The complex 99 *Treasure in Heaven* [1/2] makes the same point but is also heavily developed in its transmission. Speaking of the *Sayings Gospel Q* version, John Kloppenborg says that "the admonition itself finds partial parallels in contemporary Jewish exhortation to collect heavenly treasures by doing good deeds (especially almsgiving), although the disdain for earthy acquisitions is somewhat peculiar" (1987:221). That comment may indicate the saying's trajectory. I imagine an original saying of Jesus put negatively against earthly possessions: Do not lay up treasures because [internally] the moth can attack the purse that hides them and [externally] thieves can break in and steal them. That was changed into a positive version in *Gospel of Thomas* 76:2, developed into a parallel negative and positive or earthly and heavenly dyad as

Matthew 6:19–20 accepted the *Sayings Gospel Q* version, and finally changed into a positive admonition to almsgiving as Luke 12:33 rewrote the *Sayings Gospel Q* version. The complex 86 *Serving Two Masters* [1/2] makes the same point but without the pungent specificity of moth and thief. The complex 103 *Give Without Return* [1/2] is a much more radical statement of the same theme. Give not only without interest but without taking your capital back. But one would soon be destitute. Exactly. Finally, those twin paradoxes in 31 *First and Last* [1/3] and 40 *Have and Receive* [1/3] look to the same situation in which the rich and powerful are classed as poor and powerless. And vice versa.

A Kingdom of Undesirables

There are, in that basic list of twelve complexes with the expression Kingdom in plural attestation, five parables, and, together, they constitute a very strange constellation of metaphors. Once again, of course, I begin with the maximum attestation and work from there.

The Mustard Seed

The parable of 35 *The Mustard Seed* [1/3] is the only case in the entire parabolic corpus attributed to Jesus that has triple independent attestation. These are the three sources, with the *Sayings Gospel Q* version represented primarily by Luke.

> The disciples said to Jesus, "Tell us what the kingdom of heaven is like." He said to them, "It is like a mustard seed. It is the smallest of all seeds. But when it falls on tilled soil, it produces a great plant and becomes a shelter for birds of the sky." (*Gospel of Thomas* 20)

> He said therefore, "What is the kingdom of God like? And to what shall I compare it? It is like a grain of mustard seed which a man took and sowed in his garden; and it grew and became a tree, and the birds of the air made nests in its branches." (*Sayings Gospel Q*, 1or2Q?: Luke 13:18–19 = Matthew 13:31–32)

> And he said, "With what can we compare the kingdom of God, or what parable shall we use for it? It is like a grain of mustard seed, which, when sown upon the ground, is the smallest of all the seeds on earth; yet when it is sown it grows up and becomes the greatest of all shrubs, and puts forth large branches, so that the birds of the air can make nests in its shade." (Mark 4:30–32 = Matthew 13:31–32)

The tradition, in handing on the parable, has steadily changed it along three converging vectors. First, it has emphasized the original contrast between small mustard seed and large mustard plant so that change from smallness to greatness becomes the emphasis, as in Mark's somewhat turgid rendition. Second, it has changed the terminal mustard plant or shrub into a tree, as in the *Sayings Gospel Q* version. Finally, it has, by mentioning the nesting birds, established connections with biblical texts extolling the providence of God, such as Psalm 104:12, or the mighty cedar of Lebanon as a symbol of earthly or heavenly kingdom, as in Daniel 4:10–12 and Ezekiel 31:3, 6. Probably the closest parallel, when tree and nesting birds are combined, is this text.

> Thus says the Lord God: "I myself will take a sprig from the lofty top of the cedar, and will set it out; I will break off from the topmost of its young twigs a tender one, and I myself will plant it upon a high and lofty mountain; on the mountain height of Israel will I plant it, that it may bring forth boughs and bear fruit, and become a noble cedar; and under it will dwell all kinds of beasts; in the shade of its branches birds of every sort will nest. And all the trees of the field shall know that I the Lord bring low the high tree, and make high the low tree, dry up the green tree, and make the dry tree flourish. I the Lord have spoken, and I will do it. (Ezekiel 17:22–24)

That allegory of the cedar imagines tiny Israel as the great apocalyptic tree, and it underlines precisely the problem of Jesus' parable. "This, then, is the crux of the problem," to quote myself from about twenty years ago. "If one intended an image of the apocalyptic advent, the mighty cedar of Lebanon was ready at hand in the tradition. If one needed an image of growth to this advent, the figure of a cedar shoot planted on a high mountain was also in the tradition. The mustard seed can grow only into a bush or shrub and, at its very best, is hardly competition for the Lebanese cedar. When one starts a parable with a mustard seed one cannot end it with a tree, much less the great apocalyptic tree, unless, of course, one plans to lampoon rather rudely the whole apocalyptic tradition" (1973:48). I am therefore in complete agreement with Brandon Scott, who has just published the best recent study of the parables, and who thinks that this story "calls into question and burlesques the expectation of the kingdom under the symbol of the cedar or apocalyptic tree" (386).

Granted, then, that any *positive* allusions to an apocalyptic tree were neither included in the original parable nor too convincingly appended to its later transmission, what exactly is the correlation of kingdom and mustard plant?

Pliny the Elder, who lived between 23 and 79 C.E., wrote about the mustard plant in his encyclopedic *Natural History*.

Mustard . . . with its pungent taste and fiery effect is extremely beneficial for the health. It grows entirely wild, though it is improved by being transplanted: but on the other hand when it has once been sown it is scarcely possible to get the place free of it, as the seed when it falls germinates at once. (Pliny, *Natural History* 19.170–171; Rackham et al. 5.528–529)

There is, in other words, a distinction between the wild mustard and its domesticated counterpart, but even when one deliberately cultivates the latter for its medicinal or culinary properties, there is an ever-present danger that it will destroy the garden. And, apart from those domesticated types, such as *brassica nigra* or *sinapis alba*, there is, as Douglas Oakman emphasizes, the wild mustard, charlock, or *sinapis arvensis*, whose "plants have from time immemorial been found as weeds in grain fields" (1986:124). The mustard plant, therefore, is, as domesticated in the garden, dangerous and, as wild in the grain fields, deadly. The point is not just that it starts small and ends big but that its bigness is not exactly a horticultural or agricultural desideratum.

In the three independent versions of Jesus' parable, only that in the *Sayings Gospel Q* refers to a domesticated mustard plant deliberately sown, for Matthew in a field, for Luke in a garden. The *Gospel of Thomas* and Mark seem to presume one that sows itself, takes over, and grows big enough to attract birds for shade. Within my own methodology, I prefer not to assume that Luke's garden is original, although if it was, as Brandon Scott comments, it would be against the teaching of the *Mishnah*, which, around the year 200 C.E. and precisely because of that tendency for mustard to intrude and mix with other plants, decrees that it should not be planted in a garden but only in a larger field where it can be carefully segregated by itself (374, 380). I prefer, methodologically, to bracket both Luke and the *Mishnah* and to conclude that the core image of the parable is of the mustard plant, whether of the deliberately sown but still relatively dangerous domestic variety or of the intrusive and so absolutely dangerous wild variety. "It is hard," as Douglas Oakman rightly concludes, "to escape the conclusion that Jesus deliberately likens the rule of God to a weed." And he is also surely correct that a peasant audience hearing Jesus speak of birds attracted by the mustard plant would think immediately, as in 34 *The Sower* [1/3] parable, "that birds are natural enemies of the sown" (1986:127).

The point, in other words, is not just that the mustard plant starts as a proverbially small seed and grows into a shrub of three or four feet, or even higher, it is that it tends to take over where it is not wanted, that it tends to get out of control, and that it tends to attract birds within cultivated areas where they are not particularly desired. And that, said Jesus, was what the Kingdom was like: not like the mighty cedar of Lebanon and not quite like a common weed, like a pungent shrub with dangerous takeover properties. Something you would want in only small and carefully controlled doses—if you could control it.

The Planted Weeds

The parable of 90 *The Planted Weeds* [1/2] in Matthew 13:24–30 has been given a detailed allegorical interpretation in 13:36–43a, and, once you read that explanation, it is almost impossible to see the parable except through the lens of its Matthean explanation. Both parable and interpretation could easily and convincingly be assessed as pure Matthean creations —except for the following:

> Jesus said, "The kingdom of the father is like a man who had [good] seed. His enemy came by night and sowed weeds among the good seed. The man did not allow them to pull up the weeds; he said to them, 'I am afraid that you will go intending to pull up the weeds and pull up the wheat along with them.' For on the day of the harvest the weeds will be plainly visible, and they will be pulled up and burned." (*Gospel of Thomas* 57)

There is, of course, no interpretation of that parable in the *Gospel of Thomas*, but its content is substantially the same as in Matthew. Indeed, it seems necessary to presume some mention at least of the servants' intention, as in Matthew, to make full sense of *Thomas's* version. We must, therefore, if we can, bracket the Matthean interpretation entirely and attempt to see the parable afresh before and apart from it.

The specific weed is called *zizania* in both Matthew and the *Gospel of Thomas* and is to be identified, according to Douglas Oakman, "with *lolium temulentum* or darnel, a noxious weed common in the Levant. The grains of this annual grass contain a strong toxin. Therefore, it is not self-evidently wise to harvest darnel with wheat, because mixing the toxic grains of darnel with wheat ruins the quality of the grain and poses a health hazard to anyone eating flour so adulterated. The weed does not grow above 1000 feet in altitude. It is typically a weed infesting the best wheat fields. In wetter than normal years darnel thrives and successfully competes with the good crop. Drier years favor the wheat" (1986:116). Once again, Pliny the Elder is instructive.

> There is a white grass like Italian millet that springs up all over the fields, and is also fatal to cattle. As for darnel, caltrops, thistle and burdock, I should not count these any more than brambles among diseases of

cereals, but rather among pestilences of the soil itself. (Pliny, *Natural History* 18.153; Rackham et al. 5.284–285)

When I first worked on this parable I thought that it intended to praise the wisdom of the landowner's decision caught, as he was, between twin evils (1973:64, 85). But I find Oakman's recent arguments entirely persuasive, as is also his contention that Jesus' hearers are being asked to laugh a little at this relatively well-to-do landowner. Since darnel is a natural problem, only its great extent in a specific field would need to be explained, within the narrative of the parable and not just the paranoia of the owner, as due to an enemy's action. So he is stuck. "Weeding after the appearance of grain might pose the danger of uprooting wheat along with the darnel," according to Oakman, "but it possibly can claim to be the lesser of two evils" (1986:118). And that, says Jesus, is what the Kingdom is like. From the viewpoint of the well-to-do with their fields of best wheat and plural servants, it is a noxious weed. But they are stuck with it. Mustard and darnel, then, stand together, surely with some ironic humor, as twin images of the Kingdom, seen, however, from the angle of the landless poor.

The Leaven

The third image is just as bad or even worse. The parable of 104 *The Leaven* [1/2] involves leaven, a woman, and the act of hiding, all of which have negative connotations in their original social matrix.

Jesus said, "The kingdom of the father is like [a certain] woman. She took a little leaven, [concealed] it in some dough, and made it into large loaves." (*Gospel of Thomas* 96:1)

And again he said, "To what shall I compare the kingdom of God? It is like leaven which a woman took and hid in three measures of flour, till it was all leavened." (*Sayings Gospel Q*, 1or2Q?: Luke 13:20–21 = Matthew 13:33)

The essential point is "that leaven in the ancient world was a symbol of moral corruption," according to Brandon Scott, since it was "made by taking a piece of bread and storing it in a damp, dark place until mold forms. The bread rots and decays . . . modern yeast . . . is domesticated." Furthermore, "in Israel there is an equation that leaven is the unholy everyday, and unleaven the holy, the sacred, the feast" (324). Once again, we are confronted with an image of the Kingdom that is immediately shocking and provocative. And it is compounded by the fact that, again from Scott, "woman as a symbolic structure was associated in Judaism, as in other Mediterranean cultures, with the unclean, the religiously impure. The male was the symbol for purity." Furthermore, "the figurative use of hiding to describe the mixing of leaven and flour is otherwise unattested in Greek or Hebrew" (326). With mustard and darnel, then, stands another and triply shocking image for the Kingdom: a woman hiding leaven in her dough. It's there, it's natural, it's normal, it's necessary, but society has a problem with it.

The Pearl

The fourth image is 98 *The Pearl* [1/2]. In *Gospel of Thomas* 76:1 the merchant "sold the merchandise" to buy the pearl, while in Matthew 13:45–46 he "sold all that he had."

> Jesus said, "The kingdom of the father is like a merchant who had a consignment of merchandise and who discovered a pearl. The merchant was shrewd. He sold the merchandise and bought the pearl alone for himself." (*Gospel of Thomas* 76:1)

> Again, the kingdom of heaven is like a merchant in search of fine pearls, who, on finding one pearl of great value, went and sold all that he had and bought it. (Matthew 13:45–46)

Of those twin versions the former is slightly preferable, since Matthew's "sold all that he had" may have infiltrated from the preceding "sells all that he has" of 108 *The Treasure* [1/2] parable in Matthew 13:44. But even that former operation is quite unusual. What is the merchant going to do with the pearl? As a merchant he buys and sells with, hopefully, some profit each time. He now is left with a pearl, which is, unlike the treasure of the next parable, totally useless to a merchant unless and until it is sold. He now has, as it were, something priceless and also useless. And, that is a rather challenging image of the Kingdom.

The Treasure

The parable of 108. *The Treasure* [1/2] is now extant in two quite different versions, although each is, in different ways, another anomalous image for the Kingdom.

> Jesus said, "The kingdom is like a man who had a [hidden] treasure in his field without knowing it. And [after] he died, he left it to his [son]. The son [did] not know (about the treasure). He inherited the field and sold [it], And the one who bought it went plowing and [found] the treasure. He began to lend money at interest to whomever he wished. (*Gospel of Thomas* 109)

The kingdom of heaven is like treasure hidden in a field, which a man
found and covered up; then in his joy he goes and sells all that he has
and buys that field. (Matthew 13:44)

I proposed in an earlier work that Matthew's version was the more original and that *Thomas*'s was adapted to fit with another ancient Jewish story
about finding hidden treasure (1979:106). Charles Hedrick countered by
arguing for the priority of *Thomas*'s version. And Brandon Scott, most
recently, has suggested that they are both variations on the same original
structure (395).

I would still maintain, theoretically, that Matthew is the more original
version, but, methodologically, they are so different that I cannot use them
as plural attestation for the parable. It is, however, safe to note, with Scott,
that "both treasure parables ascribed to Jesus involve the finder of the treasure in scandal, in impiety; and that may be the most important point"
(393). In Matthew's version the finder obtains treasure by stealth and in
Thomas's version he uses it for money lending. Unlike the case of the pearl,
the story of the treasure is, once again, a rather shocking image for a Kingdom, the obtaining of which involves actions neither socially acceptable
nor morally approved within their environment.

A Kingdom of Here and Now

I already accepted 85 *Greater Than John* [1/2] as originally from Jesus
and also as indicating the break between John's and Jesus' messages. The
aphoristic complex 8 *When and Where* [1/5] specifies in more detail exactly
what the difference was between Jesus' vision of the Kingdom and John's
apocalyptic vision of the Coming One.

When and Where

Although there are five independent versions of this aphorism, only
two sources mention the Kingdom, and it is on those I concentrate. Both
Mark 13:21–23 = Matthew 24:23–25 and 2Q: Luke 17:23 = Matthew 24:26
declare, respectively, that Christ or the Son of Man's future parousia will
not come with forewarning signs, because, respectively, only false Christs
and false prophets give such indications or that advent will be so sudden
and total that, as with a lightning flash, no warnings are possible. In those
sources, the aphorism is not about the Kingdom but about the parousia.
Here, however, are the two most significant versions.

His disciples said to him, "When will the kingdom come?" <Jesus
said,> "It will not come by waiting for it. It will not be a matter of say-

ing 'Here it is' or 'There it is.' Rather the kingdom of the father is spread out upon the earth, and men do not see it." (*Gospel of Thomas* 113)

Being asked by the Pharisees when the kingdom of God was coming, he answered them, "The kingdom of God is not coming with signs to be observed; nor will they say, 'Lo, here it is!' or 'There!' for behold, the kingdom of God is in the midst of you." (Luke 17:20–21)

Notice, first of all, that both those versions are formatted as corrective answers. Signs of future presence are not wrong because they might be incorrect or too late but because the Kingdom is already present. I consider that the polemical edge of that aphorism stems originally from Jesus against John, but, of course, it suits *Gospel of Thomas* 113 just as much. The polemical edge is intensified in two derivative versions, with the former still retaining Kingdom but the latter using two synonyms for its apocalyptic expectation, namely, the "repose of the dead" and "the new world."

> (1) Jesus said, "If those who lead you say to you, 'See, the kingdom is in the sky,' then the birds of the sky will precede you. If they say to you, 'It is in the sea,' then the fish will precede you. Rather, the kingdom is inside of you, and it is outside of you."
> (2) His disciples said to him, "When will the repose of the dead come about, and when will the new world come?" He said to them, "What you look forward to has already come, but you do not recognize it." (*Gospel of Thomas* 3:1, 51)

Closely akin to *Gospel of Thomas* 3:1 is the badly fragmented version in *Dialogue of the Savior* 16. Notice, by the way, that this is not included in the basic *Dialogue Source* of that text, where most of such parallels occur (Pagels & Koester; Emmel et al. 2, 8).

> And I say [to you what] you seek [and] inquire after, [behold it is] within you. (*Dialogue of the Savior* 16; Emmel et al. 57, with possible restoration)

<u>What is needed, then, is not insight into the Kingdom as future but a recognition of the Kingdom as present</u>. For Jesus, a Kingdom of beggars and weeds is a Kingdom of here and now.

A Kingdom of God

The most striking feature of Jesus' Kingdom expression is the wide diversity in its eact and precise attestation. For example, the phrases "Kingdom," "kingdom of God," and "kingdom of Heaven" appear in the three units of 85 *Greater Than John* [1/2] and the phrases *Kingdom of God, His Kingdom* (Christ's), and *Kingdom of my Father* appear within the same unit of 2 *Clement* 12:1–16 from 13 *Two as One* [1/3]. Are there any indications which may have been the more original expression?

In terms of attestation, at least, certain conclusions may be drawn (appendix 5). "Kingdom" alone is never found in two sources. "Kingdom of Heaven" is never found in two sources. "Kingdom of the Father" is only found in two sources if "Father . . . thy Kingdom come" is counted as one such expression in 120 *The Lord's Prayer* [1/3]. But, on the other hand, "kingdom of God" appears certainly in two and possibly in two more cases of double attestation. It is certain in 20 *Kingdom and Children* [1/4] and also 199 *Kingdom and Riches* [2/2]. It is possible in 35 *The Mustard Seed* [1/3] if, as is most likely, Luke 13:18–19 rather than Matthew 13:31–32 repre-sents the original *Sayings Gospel Q* text. It is also possible in 8 *When and Where* [1/5] if, as is most likely, the correct restoration for the fragmented line 15 of Papyrus Oxyrynchus 654 is "king[dom of God]," the same phrase that appears in lines 7–8 of Papyrus Oxyrynchus 1. Both those expressions from the Greek fragments of the *Gospel of Thomas* met with, according to Harold Attridge, "deliberate deletion" in their respective Coptic transla-tions at *Gospel of Thomas* 3 and 27 (100–101, 114, 118). If, therefore, one precise form of the "Kingdom" phrase goes back to Jesus, it is most likely "kingdom of God." But what background would his hearers have brought to that expression? What might they have expected him to be talking about when he used that phrase? There are, in general, two such possible con-texts, the apocalyptic or the sapiential kingdom of God.

The Apocalyptic Kingdom of God

Although the precise phrase "kingdom of God" does not appear as an established expression in Jewish apocalyptic literature before and at the time of Jesus, there is more than enough emphasis on God as king and on a coming kingdom of justice and holiness to make such a phrase quite understandable against an apocalyptic context. Recall, for example, those three writings mentioned at the start of this book's chapter 6, which could be dated most likely between 50 B.C.E. and 50 C.E., in other words, more or less contemporary with Jesus' lifetime.

The *Psalms of Solomon*, assembled sometime after 48 B.C.E. when the murdered body of Pompey lay unburied on an Egyptian beach, "preserve one of the most detailed messianic expectations in the immediate pre-Christian centuries" and, in fact, "there is more substance to the ideas con-cerning the Messiah in the Psalms of Solomon than in any other extant

Jewish writing . . . the Messiah is here identified as a son of David who will come to establish an everlasting kingdom of God" (*OTP* 2.643).

> The kingdom of our God is forever over the
> nations in judgment.
> Lord, you chose David to be king over Israel,
> and swore to him about his descendants forever
> that his kingdom should not fail before you. . . .
> See, Lord, and raise up for them their king,
> the son of David, to rule over your servant Israel
> in the time known to you, O God . . .
> and their king shall be the Lord Messiah.
> (*Psalms of Solomon* 17:3–4, 21, 32; *OTP* 2.665–667)

This everlasting Kingdom is apocalyptic, however, not in the sense of a destroyed earth and an evacuation heavenward for the elect, but rather of something like a heaven on earth over which the Messiah will rule with transcendent and spiritual power for Jew and Gentile alike.

The *Testament of Moses* was, as you will recall, updated from Hasmonean to Herodian times by the addition of chapters 7 and 8. Here, however, the apocalyptic Kingdom is much more otherworldly and does not involve any messianic intermediary.

> Then his kingdom will appear throughout the whole creation. . . .
>
> For the Heavenly One will arise from his kingly throne. . . .
>
> And God will raise you [Israel] to the heights.
> Yea, he will fix you firmly in the heaven of the stars,
> in the place of their habitations.
>
> And you will behold from on high.
> Yea, you will see your enemies on the earth.
> (*Testament of Moses* 10:1, 3, 9; *OTP* 1.931–932)

It seems, in that scenario, that the earth has been abandoned to the wicked and the just have been taken up into immortality.

The third of those three apocalyptic documents closest to the time of Jesus is the *Book of the Similitudes* in *1 Enoch* 37–71. Here, on the one hand, the term *kingdom* (of God) is never used, and God is termed *king* in only one passage.

> In those days, the governors and the kings who possess the land shall
> plead that he may give them a little breathing spell from the angels of
> his punishment to whom they have been delivered; so that they shall fall
> and worship before the Lord of the Spirits, and confess their sins before

him. They shall bless and glorify the Lord of the Spirits and say, "Blessed
is the Lord of the Spirits—the Lord of kings, the Lord of rulers, and the
Master of the rich—the Lord of glory and the Lord of wisdom. . . . Now
we have come to know that we should glorify and bless the Lord of
kings—him who rules over all kings. (1 Enoch 63:1-4; OTP 1.44)

But, on the other hand, *king* and *kingdom* are terms almost too weak
for the ultimate rule and dominion of the Lord of Spirits over the repentant
empires of this world.

There is also, of course, the heavenly figure appointed by God as
apocalyptic judge. He has many names and titles: the Messiah in 48:10 and
52:4, the Righteous One in 38:2, the Righteous and Elect One in 53:6, but
then most often and about equally, either the Elect One or that Son of
Man from Daniel 7:13-14. Thus, for example:

He [the Lord of Spirits] placed the Elect One on the throne of glory; and
he shall judge all the works of the holy ones in heaven above, weighing
in the balance their deeds. . . .
      They shall be terrified and dejected; and pain shall seize them when
they see that Son of Man sitting on the throne of his glory. (These)
kings, governors, and all the landlords shall (try to) bless, glorify, extol
him who rules over everything from the beginning, him who has been
concealed. (1 Enoch 61:8; 62:6-7; OTP 1.43)

Once again, and especially against the background of Daniel 7:13-14, it
is scarcely important that "kingdom of God" is not used. The point is the
final, ultimate, and absolute dominion of the Lord of Spirits and that Son
of Man over a chastened and repentant world.

Recall, however, the problem seen at the start of this book's chapter 6
just after those three texts were first discussed. Josephus had applied the
messianic and apocalyptic tradition of Judaism to Vespasian himself
because he had been declared emperor on Jewish soil. His writings tell us
very little, therefore, about messianic claims or apocalyptic hopes among
Jewish individuals or groups. This is true both for *retainer* elites, such as the
Fourth Philosophy or the Sicarii, and even more so for *peasant* activists,
such as millennial prophets and messianic kings (appendix 2). We cannot
tell, in other words, whether either or both of those lower-class groups
would have used or accepted such a phrase as the "kingdom of God" to
describe their activities. But, in the light of Josephus' calculated reticence,
it must at least be kept open whether both scribes and peasants would have,
within their own Great and Little Traditions, understood kingdom of God
in a basically similar fashion.

One major conclusion from all of that is that the phrase "kingdom of God" could easily have been understood in an apocalyptic sense at the time of Jesus. And, as far as we can tell, that would have been true in both the Great and the Little Traditions, among both *retainer* and *peasant* classes, among both literate elites and illiterate activists. The specific content could be quite open or even vague, for example, with or without an armed revolt, with or without a messiah, with or without a cosmic destruction. But what would have been constant was a coming act of transcendent divine power that, having destroyed all evil and pagan empires, would establish a rule of justice and a dominion of holiness in which humanity would dwell forever.

The Sapiential Kingdom of God

If one emphasizes, however, that "kingdom of God" could have been easily heard as an apocalyptic expression at the time of Jesus, one must just as equally emphasize that it could have been heard instead as a sapiential one. The kingdom of God, in contemporary Jewish thought, could be just as much a present ethical as a future apocalyptic realm, and it could, in that former reading, be just as critical of royal abuse and imperial misrule as was the latter.

"Discourse about *basileia* ('rule') during the Greco-Roman period was not limited to circles of Jewish apocalypticists, nor, for that matter, to those with specifically Jewish interests," according to the forceful argument of Burton Mack. "*Basileia* was a common topic of far-reaching significance throughout Hellenistic culture . . . in the post-Alexander age . . . the critical issues now centered on power and privilege, and on the rights and duties of those who had it. . . . *Basileia* is what kings and rulers had: sovereignty, majesty, dominion, power, domain . . . [and] the abstract models constructed in order to imagine the practical issues inherent in the political structures of society could be used as well to think through basic questions about social ethos in general . . . 'king' no longer needed to refer to the actual king of a city or kingdom. 'King' became an abstract representation of *anthropos* ('human being') at the 'highest' level imaginable, whether of endowment, achievement, ethical excellence, or mythical ideal" (1987:11–12). A word, once again, about words. I have, in this book, retained the term *kingdom* to translate *basileia* because most of the texts I am quoting do so. But what is actually at stake is not kingdom as place, be it here or there, but rule as state, be it active or passive. The problem, in plain language, is power: who rules, and how one should.

The three texts contemporary with Jesus that pointed to the apocalyptic kingdom of God may be complemented with another equally contemporary triad pointing to the sapiential kingdom of God. In fact, to quote Burton Mack once more, "the three instances of the term *basileia tou theou* [kingdom of God] outside of early Christian texts appear in Hellenistic-Jewish literatures" (1987:14; 1988:73 note 16). Although that statement will have to be qualified below, it may stand, for the moment, as challenge to any too-exclusive correlation of kingdom and apocalypse.

The first source is the Jewish philosopher Philo of Alexandria, who lived from about 10 B.C.E. to 45 C.E. A summary sweep across his voluminous writings can begin with the insistence that God is king of the universe.

> Whose is the ring, the pledge of faith, the seal of the universe, the archetypal idea by which all things without form or quality before were stamped and shaped? Whose is the cord, that is, the world-order, the chain of destiny, the correspondence and sequence of all things, with their ever-unbroken chain? Whose is the staff, that is firmly planted, the unshaken, the unbending; the admonition, the chastening, the discipline; the sceptre, the kingship, whose are they? Are they not God's alone? (Philo, *On the Change of Names* 135–136; Colson et al. 5.210–213)

> For the soul of the lover of God does in truth leap from earth to heaven and wing its way on high, eager to take its place in the ranks and share the ordered march of sun and moon and the all-holy, all-harmonious host of the other stars, marshalled and led by the God Whose kingship none can dispute or usurp, the kingship by which everything is justly governed. (Philo, *The Special Laws* 1.207; Colson et al. 7.216–217)

The next development is Philo's equal insistence that the wise participate in divine kinship and are alone truly worthy of being called king. Thus, for example, Adam or Abraham exemplify this royalty of wisdom.

> The first man was wise with a wisdom learned from and taught by Wisdom's own lips, for he was made by divine hands; he was, moreover, a king, and it befits a ruler to bestow titles on his several subordinates [so Adam named the animals]. (Philo, *On the Creation* 148; Colson et al. 1.116–117)

> The Sage who possesses [virtues] is a king, a king appointed not by men but by nature, the infallible, the incorruptible, the only free elector [like Abraham]. . . . And thus they laid down the doctrine for the students of philosophy, that the Sage alone is ruler and king, and virtue a rule and a kingship whose authority is final. (Philo, *On Dreams* 2.243–244; Colson et al. 5.552–553)

Other kingdoms are established among men with wars and campaigns and numberless ills which the ambitious for power inflict on each other in mutual slaughter, with forces of foot and horse and ships which they raise for the strife. But the kingdom of the Sage [like that of Abraham] comes by the gift of God, and the virtuous man who receives it brings no harm to anyone, but the acquisition and enjoyment of good things to all his subjects, to whom he is the herald of peace and order. (Philo, *On Abraham* 261; Colson et al. 6.126–129)

There is, of course, a quiet but explicit critique of human kingship latent in all of that. On the one hand, not only wisdom but goodness confers on its every bearer a kingship of freedom superior to any kingship of force, a natural and inherent royalty superior to any political and acquired dominion.

When [Chaereas, a man of culture] was living in Alexandria, he once incurred the anger of Ptolemy, who threatened him in no mild terms. Chaereas considering that his own natural freedom was not a whit inferior to the other's kingship replied [in a verse adapted from Homer's *Iliad* 1.180–181]: "Be King of Egypt; I care not for you— / A fig for all your anger." For noble souls, whose brightness the greed of fortune cannot dim, have a kingly something, which urges them to contend on an equal footing with persons of the most massive dignity and pits freedom of speech against arrogance. (Philo, *Every Good Man Is Free* 125–126; Colson et al. 9.82–83)

On the other hand, the only valid political kingdom is modeled on the kingdom of God. It is here alone that the full phrase "kingdom of God" occurs, as a human monarch meditates on the laws he makes for his people.

Other kings carry rods in their hands as sceptres but my sceptre is the book of the Sequel to the Law, my pride and my glory, which nothing can rival, an ensign of sovereignty which none can impeach, formed in the image of its archetype the kingship of God. (Philo, *The Special Laws* 4.135–136; Colson et al. 8.110–111)

For Philo, therefore, the wise and the virtuous already partake in the kingdom or kingship of God, and only political dominions with laws modeled on God's are worthy even of the title of kingdom.

The second source is also a Jewish work, the Wisdom of Solomon, written, most likely, during the reign of the emperor Caligula, between 37 and 41 C.E. (Nickelsburg 1981:184; Collins 1983:182). There are two key texts. The first one is directed against the kings of the earth.

For your dominion was given you from the Lord,
and your sovereignty from the Most High,
who will search out your works and inquire into your plans.
Because as servants of his kingdom you did not rule rightly. . . .
The beginning of wisdom is the most sincere desire for instruction
and concern for instruction is love of her,
and love of her is the keeping of her laws,
and giving heed to her laws is assurance of immortality,
and immortality brings one near to God;
so the desire for wisdom leads to a kingdom.

                           (Wisdom of Solomon 6:3–4, 17–20)

The true and lasting rule is not that which the kings of the earth now exercise but that which they would receive if they submitted themselves to wisdom's own rule. They are kings without the real kingdom. But Jacob, on the other hand, possessed the true kingdom, although he was not a king.

When a righteous man fled from his brother's wrath,
she [Wisdom] guided him on straight paths;
she showed him the kingdom of God.

                           (Wisdom of Solomon 10:10)

The kingdom of God is the kingdom of Wisdom eternally present, available, on the one hand, to anyone who heeds her call and, on the other, punitively transcendent to all the evil rulers of the world.

The third example is from the *Sentences of Sextus,* a work that is not Hellenistic-Jewish but whose moral teaching is intensely ascetic, with a highly prominent concern about sexuality. It was those features, no doubt, that made it congenial to those who collected and buried the Nag Hammadi library, whose tractates contained a version of the *Sentences of Sextus* 157–180 and 307–397 (Wisse).

"The external evidence," according to Henry Chadwick, "provides two radically divergent answers to the question concerning the authorship of the collection, the first answer that it is a Christian collection, the second that it is purely of pagan inspiration without trace of Christianity in it. The internal evidence shows that both views are exaggerations of the truth, which is simply that a Christian compiler has edited, carefully revised and modified a previous pagan collection . . . mainly of Pythagorean origin. On the one hand, in content there is a Christianisation of pagan maxims; on the other hand, in form there is also a 'paganisation' of Christian maxims." (1959:138). The sayings or *Sentences of Sextus* is, therefore, a collection of 451 aphorisms that, with minimal and mostly implicit Christianization, became a "best seller . . . which over a period of many centuries found an extensive reading public in four languages among Christians from Britain to Mesopotamia" (1959:ix). "The single theme of the maxims, running through them in all forms and variations, is the way to achieve moral and spiritual perfection" and, upon the one who has achieved this summit, "a divine freedom has been conferred ... so that he, being wholly surrendered to the dominion of God, exercises in turn dominion over the world and his fellow-men. . . . He and he alone possesses the true freedom which is transcendence over against all his environment" (1959:97–98).

> Whatever you honor most will rule you.
> Honor what is best that you may be governed by what is best.
> If you are governed by what is best, you yourself will govern whatever
>   you choose.
> The knowledge and imitation of God is the best way to honor Him. . . .
> A wise man presents God to humanity.
> Of all his works God is most proud of a sage.
> Next to God, nothing is as free as a wise man.
> Whatever God possesses belongs also to the sage.
> A wise man shares in the kingdom of God.
>   (*Sentences of Sextus* 41–44, 307–311; Edwards & Wild 20–21, 50–51)

Although it might be possible that "kingdom," which appears only here in the collection, was inserted by a Christian editor, Chadwick does not list that line among "the category of maxims which could have had no other origin than a Christian author" (1959:139). And notice, by the way, how "wise man" or "sage" and "god" appears in every single line of that fivefold series.

All that can safely be said about the date of the pagan collection was that it was available for Christian reading by the second century at the latest. But what is most striking about that aphorism in line 311 is that the life of ethical perfection and moral wisdom unites one with God and gives one a share in the kingdom of God. Thus, even for a pagan sage, let alone a Jewish or a Christian one, an ethical or sapiential kingdom of God was as clear a possibility as an apocalyptic one.

A Typology for the Kingdom

It is now both possible and necessary to imagine a basic fourfold typology of the kingdom of God in Jewish usage contemporary with Jesus. It is obtained by crossing the thematic distinction of apocalyptic and sapiential with the class distinction of retainers and peasants. And for this purpose apocalyptic and sapiential modes are defined as separate types of understanding. They could and were often combined, but they are taken here as disjunctive rather than conjunctive options.

The apocalyptic is a future Kingdom dependent on the overpowering action of God moving to restore justice and peace to an earth ravished by injustice and oppression. Believers can, at the very most, prepare or persuade, implore or assist its arrival, but its accomplishment is consigned to divine power alone. And despite a serene vagueness about specifics and details, its consummation would be objectively visible and tangible to all, believers and unbelievers alike, but with appropriately different fates.

The sapiential Kingdom looks to the present rather than the future and imagines how one could live here and now within an already or always available divine dominion. One enters that Kingdom by wisdom or goodness, by virtue, justice, or freedom. It is a style of life for now rather than a hope of life for the future. This is therefore an ethical Kingdom, but it must be absolutely insisted that it could be just as eschatological as was the apocalyptic Kingdom. Its ethics could, for instance, challenge contemporary morality to its depths. It would be a gross mistake to presume that, in my terminology, a sapiential kingdom of God was any less world-negating than an apocalyptic one.

Earlier, however, a distinction was made between what I term *proclaimed* apocalypses written by rebellious retainers and *performed* apocalypses enacted by millennial prophets and possibly even by messianic claimants. The scribal elites wrote because that was what they could do, and the peasant leaders marched because that was what they could do. I do not presume that either mode is in any way better than the other. The Great Tradition writes and proclaims; the Little Tradition marches and performs. But, of course, the former is a slightly safer activity. In any case, and be that as it may, those twin modes of the millennial vision should be matched with twin modes of the sapiential dream.

We know quite well how the Great Tradition imagined the kingdom of God as an ideal mode of human existence here and now. It is clear, for instance, in Philo. But we are still lacking one section of the fourfold typology. What did the sapiential kingdom of God entail for peasants? How could they imagine such an eventuality from within the Little Tradition? My proposal is that when we cross apocalyptic and sapiential with scribes and peasants, it becomes necessary to locate Jesus in the quadrant formed by sapiential and peasant. What was described by his parables and aphorisms as a here and now Kingdom of the nobodies and the destitute, of mustard, darnel, and leaven, is precisely a Kingdom performed rather than just proclaimed. That, at least, is the hypothesis taken from this chapter to be tested in the next one. But, before that, there are still two of those twelve plurally attested kingdom of God complexes that have not yet been considered.

From Kingdom to Liturgy

Two complexes, 120 *The Lord's Prayer* [1/3] and 13 *Two as One* [1/4], are the only ones of the twelve plurally attested kingdom of God complexes that I do not attribute to the historical Jesus. And that needs careful explanation and justification. Both of them concern ritual activity, and this may indicate that such was a generative matrix for early and plurally attested materials that do not, despite that status, go back to Jesus himself.

The Lord's Prayer

There are probably three rather than two independent versions of 120 *The Lord's Prayer* [1/2]. One version is in Luke 11:2–4, with an address to the "Father" followed by five petitions. This is presumably the version from the *Sayings Gospel Q* but with a situational opening from Luke himself in 11:1 (Kloppenborg 1987:205–206; 1988:84).

> He was praying in a certain place, and when he ceased, one of his disciples said to him, "Lord, teach us to pray, as John taught his disciples."
> And he said to them, "When you pray, say: 'Father, hallowed be thy name. Thy kingdom come. Give us each day our daily bread; and forgive us our sins, for we ourselves forgive every one who is indebted to us; and lead us not into temptation." (1Q: Luke 11:1–4 = [!] Matthew 6:9–13)

A second version is in Matthew 6:9–13 but with an address to "Our Father who art in heaven [plural]" followed by seven petitions. The extra two requests are "Thy will be done, On earth as it is in heaven" and "But deliver us from evil." It seems very unlikely that Matthew redacted the version he found in the *Sayings Gospel Q* but much more likely that he replaced its text with the prayer's format as used in his own community. This possibility is strengthened by the third version, in *Didache* 8:2b, which has, like Matthew, seven rather than five petitions. But it opens with an address to "Our Father who art in heaven [singular]," and, since it lacks Matthew's redactional plural there, it is most likely an independent rendition of the same version known to Matthew himself (Koester 1957:203–209).

Does the prayer in either version come from the historical Jesus? On the one hand, as Joseph Fitzmyer has written, it "is a thoroughly Jewish prayer, for almost every word of it could be uttered by a devout Jew . . . even though many of the Jewish prayers that are often used for such comparisons . . . date from centuries well after the New Testament." On the other, "Gal. 4:6 and Rom. 8:15, which preserve an early tradition about Spirit-inspired prayer, not only include the Aramaic counterpart of the address, 'abbā,' but reflect a recollection about how Jesus himself addressed God—in a way exclusive to himself and otherwise unknown in pre-Christian Palestinian tradition" (1981–85:900, 898). Furthermore, and from my point of view, the petitions fit very well as a prayer for that sapiential or radically ethical Kingdom seen in the other dually attested complexes. This is especially so if "daily" bread be taken precisely as such, that is, enough and no more material bread for one's daily needs, and mutual forgiveness of debts be taken precisely as erasure of monetary debts. "Bread and debt were, quite simply," in the words of John Kloppenborg, "the two most immediate problems facing the Galilean peasant, day labourer and non-elite urbanite. Alleviation of these two anxieties were the most obvious benefits of God's reign" (1990:192). The debt petition is especially significant, since 27 *Forgiveness for Forgiveness* [1/4], 60 *Measure for Measure* [1/3], and 118 *Judgment for Judgment* [1/2] all bespeak a close interaction between the way humans treat each other and the way God treats them. This is an even more radical suggestion than 33 *The Golden Rule* [1/3]. Those three aphorisms suggest that we do unto others as God does onto us and that God does unto us as we do unto others. The point, however, is not sequentiality or causality, "we do in order that God does," but rather simultaneity and mutuality, "we do and God does." God forgives us our debts, that is, the offerings or punishments due for our sins, and we forgive our neighbors their debts, that is, the returns or penalties due for their loans.

Still, despite the fact that the Lord's Prayer must be a very early summary of themes and emphases from Jesus' own lifetime, I do not think that such a coordinated prayer was ever taught by him to his followers. And neither do I think that it was a diverse set of miniature prayers later collected into one sequence. If there had been a special prayer, specifically and emphatically taught to his followers by Jesus himself, I would expect an even wider attestation for it and also a more uniform version of its contents. Also, and this may be even more important, the establishment of such a prayer seems to represent the point where a group starts to distinguish and even separate itself from the wider religious community, and I do not believe that point was ever reached during the life of Jesus. I repeat, however, that there is nothing apocalyptic about the Lord's Prayer, and it serves, unless rendered too exclusively spiritual, as a beautiful summary of the themes and emphases in Jesus' vision of the kingdom of God.

I contrast that composite prayer with an aphorism on the same subject from Jesus himself. The most plurally attested saying in my inventory is 4 *Ask, Seek, Knock* [1/6]. But, apart maybe from the triadic structure, it is almost a proverbial platitude. I cannot quite believe, in the light of such transmissional multiplicity, that a simple proverb has been placed on the lips of the historical Jesus by the tradition itself. I take it, especially in its original triadic formulation, as a serene statement of the absolute and unmediated access to God that Jesus' movement proclaims. Thereafter, of course, its triple insistence was broken up, with the "seek" unit going one way, the "ask" going another, and the less pliable "knock" disappearing (Crossan 1988b; Koester 1980b:238–244).

The parable of 34 *The Sower* [1/3] is an equally obvious or platitudinous image. Any peasant would recognize its balance of three, that is, multiple, losses and gains in the normal process of sowing. Yet its serene message of gains despite losses and even of multiple forms of gain puts in narrative format the same message of assured success. The roots of that assurance become clear in 82 *Against Anxieties* [1/2], where God's care for nature's birds and flowers should obviate human worries about food and clothing. The parallels to Stoic-Cynic admonitions are, as F. Gerald Downing indicates, quite striking (1988:70–71). The serenity and security passed by Jesus to his followers derives not from knowing hidden mysteries of past or present but from watching nature's rhythms of here and now.

Two as One

The 13 *Two as One* [1/4] complex was already touched upon under 20 *Kingdom and Children* [1/4] above. Apart from the version in *Gospel of Thomas* 22.3–4, there are three other independent versions.

> (1a) For as many of you as were baptized into Christ have put on Christ. There is neither Jew nor Greek, there is neither slave nor free, there is neither male nor female; for you are all one in Christ Jesus. (Galatians 3:27–28)

> (1b) For by one Spirit we were all baptized into one body—Jews or Greeks, slaves or free—and all were made to drink of one Spirit. (1 Corinthians 12:13)

> (1c) You have put off the old nature with its practices and have put on the new nature, which is being renewed in knowledge after the image of its creator. Here there cannot be Greek and Jew, circumcised and uncircumcised, barbarian, Scythian, slave, free man, but Christ is all, and in all. (Colossians 3:9b–11)

> (2) When Salome asked when what she had inquired about would be known, the Lord said, "When you have trampled on the garment of shame and when the two become one and the male with the female (is) neither male nor female." (*Gospel of the Egyptians* 5b; NTA 2.168; Cameron 1982:52)

(3) For when the Lord himself was asked by someone when his kingdom would come, he said: "When the two shall be one, and the outside
as the inside, and the male with the female neither male nor female."
Now "the two are one" when we speak with one another in truth, and
there is but one soul in two bodies without dissimulation. And by "the
outside as the inside" he means this, that the inside is the soul, and the
outside is the body. Therefore, just as your body is visible, so let your
soul be apparent in your good works. And by "the male with the female
neither male nor female" he means this, that when a brother sees a sister he should have no thought of her as female, nor she of him as male.
When you do this, he says, the kingdom of my Father will come.
(2 Clement 12:2-6)

First of all, the baptismal situation of this Edenic recapitulation is
emphatically evident in the Pauline tradition, but, as seen already for the
Gospel of Thomas, it is absolutely implicit in the other texts as well. Next,
there is a triadic formulation with three sets of socioreligious distinctions in
Galatians 3:27-28, but only the first two sets reappear in the authentically
Pauline 1 Corinthians 12:13 and the fictionally Pauline Colossians 3:19b-11.
A quite different but still triadic formulation appears in both Gospel of the
Egyptians 5b and 2 Clement 12:2-6. Finally, in what follows, I accept the
expert analysis of those texts in Dennis Ronald MacDonald's 1978 doctoral
dissertation at Harvard University.

The most original version of this saying was probably a triadic version,
as divergently exemplified in Gospel of the Egyptians 5b or 2 Clement
12:2-6 and as greatly expanded in Gospel of Thomas 22:3-4. But originally
that triad indicated not three discriminations but three ways of saying the
same thing. And, whatever the exact formulation and no matter how many
dualities were enumerated, they all served to focus the baptismal regeneration and cosmic recapitulation on celibate and ascetic negation of sexuality. Paul, however, deliberately rephrased the content in Galatians 3:27-28
so that there were now three different discriminatory sets, with male-
female as simply the last of the triad. There are linguistic traces of his
editorial activity in that the first two sets, Jew-Greek and slave-free, form a
structurally balanced ("there is no x or y") and chiastically closed (superior/
inferior//inferior/superior) pair. But the more original male/female
appears outside that closed chiasm in superior/inferior sequence and with
"there is no x and y." Furthermore, and even more significantly, when Paul
repeats the unit from Galatians 3:27-28 in 1 Corinthians 12:13, you get
another structural balance ("whether x or y") within the same chiastically
closed construction (superior/inferior//inferior/superior). Finally, those

are the only two distinctions adopted and rephrased from 1 Corinthians 12:13 into the deutero-Pauline letter of Colossians 3:10–11.

Paul, in other words, is much more concerned with the Jew-Greek and free-slave distinctions than with the male-female one. That latter dichotomy came to Galatians 3:27–28 from received tradition and was dropped thereafter in the Pauline transmission. Two tremendous ambiguities clash with each other here, especially as read in terms of modern gender equality.

First there is the Pauline ambiguity. He could insist in 1 Corinthians 11:2–16, based on an atrocious reading of Genesis 1–2, that the Corinthian women not appear in church with unveiled heads, yet insert within that awful argument its own refutation. Compare the texts:

> For man was not made from woman, but woman from man. Neither was man created for woman, but woman for man. . . .
> Nevertheless, in the Lord woman is not independent of man nor man of woman; for as woman was made from man, so man is now born of woman. And all things are from God. (1 Corinthians 11:8–9, 11–12)

It is no wonder that all of 1 Corinthians 11:3–16 has been called an interpolation (Walker). That is probably a surgery too radical for acceptance, and, besides, the ambiguity is still there, even if now within an interpolation and therefore less explicable. Notice, first, how the chiastic sequence of man/woman//woman/man is repeated in that order twice in 11:8–9 but appears twice in the reversed sequence of woman/man//man/woman in 11:11–12. Recall, second, the fine impartiality and reciprocity of female/male and male/female sequences in 1 Corinthians 7. I conclude that Paul's general sense of female-male equality within Christianity had been badly unnerved by the unveiled and presumably ecstatic prayer of women at Corinth and had led him into a remarkably ambiguous position. It was, however, at least ambiguous; the later deutero-Pauline tradition would remove any ambiguity and establish strict inequality of women and men within Christianity.

The ascetic and celibate ambiguity is, I think, much more serious. The theme of the original androgyne sounds, at first note, a remarkably reciprocal equality. But all too often, in practice and sometimes even in theory, the androgyne was imagined as an original archetypal male. In such a context, women had to "become men" in order to obtain equality. And, indeed, such a discriminatory formulation was probably behind the unveiled heads at Corinth: the women were acting like men. The classic example of this ambiguity, which makes the Pauline one appear almost innocent, appears in this interchange:

Simon Peter said to them, "Let Mary leave us, for women are not worthy of Life." Jesus said, "I myself shall lead her in order to make her male, so that she too may become a living spirit resembling you males. For every woman who will make herself male will enter the Kingdom of Heaven." (*Gospel of Thomas* 114)

The eventual trajectories of both those ambiguities would resolve alike into male supremacy reasserted and restored. On the one hand, it is surely unfortunate that Paul did not reverse the sequence of his triad in Galatians 3:27–28 and pay as much attention to gender difference as to religious difference. On the other, ascetic celibacy, especially as it moved along a Gnostic trajectory, offered, at best, an equality which was often chauvinistic and, at worst, an equality which denigrated the human body in general and the female body in particular.

The original baptismal denial of sexual differentiation and its consequent life of celibate asceticism, evident in *Gospel of Thomas* 22:3–4 and *Gospel of the Egyptians* 5b, was expanded in Galatians 3:27–28 and, with those expansions remaining, was itself removed in 1 Corinthians 12:13 and Colossians 3:10–11. That was one tactic; another was to moralize it away as in 2 *Clement* 12:2–6. Either way, it was gone. But did it come from Jesus himself? "The precise origin of the saying itself still lies," according to Dennis MacDonald, "in the penumbral past, even though it was attributed to Jesus in the *Gospel of the Egyptians, 2 Clement,* and the *Gospel of Thomas.* The anthropology and Genesis speculation implied by the saying were foreign to Jesus, but were quite at home in Alexandrian Judaism — for example, Philo — and in Corinthian Christianity by the time Paul wrote 1 Corinthians (53/54 C.E.). Perhaps these ideas were introduced in Corinth by Apollos, who like Philo was a Hellenistic Jewish biblical scholar from Alexandria" (127–128).

I agree that this complex does not stem from the historical Jesus, but I also think that it is an interpretation of something that does. Jesus' Kingdom of nobodies and undesirables in the here and now of this world was surely a radically egalitarian one, and, as such, it rendered sexual and social, political and religious distinctions completely irrelevant and anachronistic. Different Christian groups could and did focus that radical egalitarianism on this or that distinction, for example, the Corinthians on sex and gender, or Paul on religion and freedom. Usually and eventually such a single focus betrayed egalitarianism even in that one limited area. But radical lack of social differentiation remained as a permanent challenge to all other specifications, interpretations, and actualizations of the Kingdom proclaimed by Jesus.

Against the Patriarchal Family

How does such radical social egalitarianism relate to the family? Is there some relationship between that general vision of the kingdom of God and those several complexes in which Jesus speaks almost virulently against the family?

The twin narratives in 24 *Blessed the Womb* [1/4?] and 105 *Jesus' True Family* [1/2] are both transmitted as dialogues rather than simple aphorisms.

> A woman from the crowd said to him, "Blessed are the womb which bore you and the breasts which suckled you." He said to [her], "Blessed are those who have heard the word of the father [Luke has: "of God"] and have truly kept it." (*Gospel of Thomas* 79:1–2)

> The disciples said to him, "Your brothers and your mother are standing outside." He said to them, "Those here who do the will of my father [Mark has: "of God"] are my brothers and my mother. It is they who will enter the kingdom of my father." (*Gospel of Thomas* 99)

Those texts speak of the "word" or "will" of God, phrases synonymous with the "kingdom" of God, an equation made explicit in that final sentence added only by the *Gospel of Thomas*. In the second complex, 105 *Jesus' True Family* [1/2], Mark, in keeping with his very severe criticism of the family of Jesus, has made the encounter much more inimical by the intercalation of 3:19b–21, 31–35 with 3:22–30. He has also added in "sister" in 3:35 to connect with the following equally inimical encounter in 6:3. But, apart from that addition, both *Gospel of Thomas* 99 and Mark 3:31–35 agree on "brothers and mother" twice in the former case and on "mother and brothers" three times, with "brother . . . and mother" once, in the latter case. They agree on excluding the father. That exclusion might be interpreted in many different ways: Joseph was busy that day, was already dead, or was omitted to protect either the virgin birth or God as Jesus' true Father. I underline, therefore, less the father's exclusion than the mother's inclusion. Jesus declares his followers to be a replacement family. Notice, for example, that the dependent version in 2 *Clement* 9:11 speaks only of "my brethren," a much less striking usage than "my mother and brothers." And, however we explain the literal absence of Jesus' father, his new metaphorical family lacks one as well.

In 74 *Peace or Sword* [1/2] that alternation of physical and spiritual family cuts across the generations of the patriarchal family itself.

Do you think that I have come to give peace on earth? No, I tell you, but
rather division; for henceforth in one house there will be five divided,
three against two and two against three; they will be divided, father
against son and son against father, mother against daughter and daughter against her mother, mother-in-law against her daughter-in-law and
daughter-in-law against her mother-in-law. (*Sayings Gospel Q*, 2Q: Luke
12:51–53 = Matthew 10:34–36)

The family imagined there has five members, father, mother, son,
daughter, and son's wife, all living together in the one household. "Note," as
Bruce Malina advises, "that there is no mention of son-in-law, since it was
the new wife who moved into her husband's house, not the husband into
the wife's family" (1981:101). I emphasize immediately that this is not simply saying that families will be split over Jesus, with some believing and
some disbelieving. The division imagined cuts between the generations,
the two parents against the three children, and vice versa. But it does not
tell us which group is on Jesus' side. We cannot presume that parents are
against Jesus and children are for him, or vice versa. Indeed, the point is not
belief or disbelief at all. It is, just as in Micah 7:6, the normalcy of familial
hierarchy that is under attack. The strife is not between believers and non-
believers but quite simply, and as it says, between the generations and in
both directions. Jesus will tear the hierarchical or patriarchal family in two
along the axis of domination and subordination. Second, and even more
significant, is that the division imagined cuts across sex and gender. That
point is underlined by the version in *Gospel of Thomas* 16, which, despite
having "five in a house: three will be against two, and two against three"
gives only one example, and that the dominant male one: "the father
against the son, and the son against the father." That obscures the saying's
point: the split is *between* the generations but *across* the genders. There can
be women just as much as men on the side of Jesus, or on the other side for
that matter. I return to that point below in considering Jesus' missionaries,
but even now it is already apparent: what happens to women if the patriarchal family is split asunder?

A similar point is made with 89 *Hating One's Family* [1/2], although the
protagonist of the saying is given in masculine gender. The opposition is
with one's "father and mother . . . brothers and sisters" in *Gospel of Thomas*
55:1–2, "father and mother" in *Gospel of Thomas* 101, "father or mother . . .
son or daughter" in Q/Matthew 10:37, and "father and mother and wife
and children and brothers and sisters" in Q/Luke 14:26. In other words,
whatever number of generations are mentioned, both genders are always in
question. I incline, therefore, to read 89 *Hating One's Family* [1/2] in the
light of 74 *Peace or Sword* [1/2] as referring, despite its male format, to both

genders. Jesus, on the other hand, refuses to get involved in 97 *The Disputed Inheritance* [1/2], in which sons disagree over the father's inheritance. He is not that kind of divider.

Finally, there is 15 *Against Divorce* [1/4], an especially well attested saying of Jesus. The formulation of the divorce law in Deuteronomy 24:1-4 is strictly androcentric: "when a man takes . . . marries . . . writes . . . puts . . . sends . . . " It concerns how a husband divorces a wife and says nothing whatsoever about how a wife divorces a husband. It does not have to do so, because the law does not allow it. Unlike, say, Greek, Roman, or Egyptian law at the time of Jesus, Jewish law did not allow the wife to initiate divorce proceedings. Adultery, furthermore, was also androcentric. It was always a crime against male honor and male rights. Seen against such a cultural situation, the texts in 15 *Against Divorce* [1/4] are strikingly anomalous. That is not because both 1 Corinthians 7:10-11 and Mark 10:10-12, but not its parallel Matthew 19:9, have adapted Jesus' saying to a wider Greco-Roman ambiance—they therefore forbid divorce either by husband of wife or by wife of husband—it is because the saying of Jesus situates itself directly in the androcentric tradition of Jewish Palestine but says,

> (1) Every one who divorces his wife and marries another commits adultery, and he who marries a woman divorced from her husband commits adultery. (*Sayings Gospel Q*, 1[or 2?]Q: Luke 16:18 = Matthew 5:31-32)

> (2) Whoever divorces his wife and marries another, commits adultery against her. (Mark 10:11)

> (3) If he put his wife away and marry another he also commits adultery himself. (*Shepherd of Hermas, Mandate* 4.1:6b)

John Kloppenborg has seen most clearly the implications of the term "adultery" against the Mediterranean background of an androcentric or even phallocentric honor and shame ideology. "By saying that the *male* who disembeds his wife and remarries commits adultery *against her* . . . Jesus implies that honour is not (only?) *androcentric*—I use the term descriptively rather than pejoratively—but (also or equally) *gynecentric*. Honour is still understood as a pseudo-commodity but it belongs as much to a woman as it does to a man. Hence a man can 'steal' his own wife's honor by divorcing her and remarrying. . . . In the Palestine of Jesus' day, which did not permit women to initiate a divorce, the dignity of women was not . . . easily guarded. It is for this reason that Jesus uses the dramatic term 'adultery' in so surprising a way. He thus brought sharply into focus the wife's honour. It is as much to be protected and respected as the husband's honour and the woman is as vulnerable to damage as the male." (1990:195). The opposition here is not just to divorce. To forbid divorce one has only to say that divorce is never legal. That is exactly what happens in the much less radical 252 *Moses and Divorce* [2/1]. The attack is actually against "androcentric honour whose debilitating effects went far beyond the situation of divorce. It was also the basis for the dehumanization of women, children and non-dominant males" (1990:196). When 74 *Peace or Sword* [1/2] is read in conjunction with 15 *Against Divorce* [1/4], Jesus sets parents against children and wife against husband, sets, in other words, the Kingdom against the Mediterranean. But not just against the Mediterranean alone.

✧ *13* ✧

Magic and Meal

The complete visionary and mystic exerts an influence only
upon other visionaries like himself, and his influence soon
passes. The man of practical wisdom, alert in worldly matters
only, merely influences the brain while leaving the heart
untouched; and never in this world was anything great achieved
unless the heart, deeply stirred, has played its part. Only where
mystic faith is yoked with practical prudence does there follow a
strong, enduring result. And of such a nature was the influence
exerted by Jesus of Nazareth upon his followers, and through
them, upon succeeding generations.
                    Joseph Klausner, Jesus of Nazareth *(1925:411)*

At this point four major strands are coming together, and I underline that
conjunction before proceeding. The first and most profound strand derives
from Bryan Wilson's sevenfold anthropological and cross-cultural typology
of protest movements among colonial peoples. "Men may seek salvation from
evil conceived in many forms—from anxiety; illness; inferiority feelings; grief;
fear of death; concern for the social order. What they seek may be healing;
the elimination of evil agents; a sense of access to power; the enhancement
of status; increase of prosperity; the promise of life hereafter, or reincarna-
tion, or resurrection from the grave, or attention from posterity; the transformation of the social order (including the restoration of a real or imagined
past social order). . . . Of the various theodicies that organize appropriate
promises and command the appropriate activities to cope with these specific
apprehensions of evil, two responses are widely found among the less-
developed peoples—the thaumaturgical and the revolutionist" (492). Furthermore, "the thaumaturgical response . . . is a recurrent, and as yet inextinguish-
able, characteristic of religion. It outcrops in all the great religious traditions,
and—more vigorously and with far fuller expectation of effectiveness—in the
movements which espouse a different deviant response to the world. It stands
in tension, often, with the revolutionist response" (131). We saw much about
revolutionists in the second part of this book, the emphasis in the present
chapter is on the *thaumaturgists,* the miracle workers, the magicians.

The second strand comes from the tension seen in this book's first part between what might be termed the yuppies and the hippies of the first century C.E. The early decades of the Roman Empire generated not only opportunities for vast wealth even for a freed slave like the fictional but representative Trimalchio, but also deliberate and programmatic poverty for another freed slave like the saintly Epictetus. Cynicism represented a countercultural phenomenon and especially in its popular and performancial aspects would have been known and recognized wherever Greco-Roman culture had penetrated. The subtitle of Gerald Downing's 1988 book *Christ and the Cynics* is, for example, *Jesus and Other Radical Preachers in First-Century Tradition.*

The third strand comes from the situation of first-century Palestinian peasantry outlined in this book's second part. If you map Dick Horsley's list of peasant protesters, prophets, bandits, and messiahs between 40 B.C.E. and 70 C.E. (see appendix 2) onto Ted Robert Gurr's sociological and cross-cultural analysis of political revolt into three successive stages of *turmoil, conspiracy,* and *internal war,* it is clear that before, during, and after Jesus, the Palestinian peasantry was in a state of political *turmoil,* Gurr's technical term for unrest that is "relatively spontaneous, unorganized . . . with substantial popular participation, including violent political strikes, riots, political clashes, and localized rebellions" (11).

The fourth and final strand is Jesus' invocation of the kingdom of God not as an apocalyptic event in the imminent future but as a mode of life in the immediate present. So far, however, that challenge seems more a poetic vision than a social program. The next step is to bring those strands together and to see the Kingdom not as an individual dream but as a corporate plan. My wager is that *magic and meal* or *miracle and table* constitutes such a conjunction and that it is the heart of Jesus' program. That intersection of magic and meal, miracle and table is pointed directly and deliberately at the intersection of patronage and clientage, honor and shame, the very heart of ancient Mediterranean society. If that is incorrect, this book will have to be redone.

Magic as Religious Banditry

Recall from earlier how Eric Hobsbawm's concept of the Robin Hood element in social banditry was severely criticized by Anton Blok. Blok was, I argued, superficially correct but profoundly wrong. Bandits may seldom rob the rich *and* give to the poor and even more seldom rob the rich *to* give to the poor, but the validity and perdurance of the Robin Hood mystique is based firmly on the fact that they do rob the monopoly of violence from the rich and distribute it to the poor, and, more significantly, they rob aristocratic and structural violence of the veneer of morality under which it operates. They force the question: what is the moral difference between a gang and an army, a peasant bandit on the make and an imperial entrepreneur on the throne.

I propose now that magic is to religion as banditry is to politics. As banditry challenges the ultimate legitimacy of political power, so magic challenges that of spiritual power. Magic and religion can be mutually distinguished, in the ancient world or in the modern one, by political and prescriptive definitions but not by substantive, descriptive, or neutral descriptions. Religion is official and approved magic; magic is unofficial and unapproved religion. More simply: "we" practice religion, "they" practice magic. The question is not whether magicians are for or against official religion. Their very existence, totally apart from such intentions, is a challenge to its validity and exclusivity. Thus, for example and as we have seen, great Jewish magicians such as Honi the Circle-Maker or Hanina ben Dosa had to be carefully sanitized in terms of prayer and study before they were acceptable to the growing hegemony of the rabbinical tradition.

Because of magic's position as subversive, unofficial, unapproved, and often lower-class religion, I have deliberately used the word *magic* rather than some euphemism in the preceding and present parts of this book. Elijah and Elisha, Honi and Hanina, were magicians, and so was Jesus of Nazareth. It is endlessly fascinating to watch Christian theologians describe Jesus as miracle worker rather than magician and then attempt to define the substantive difference between those two. There is, it would seem from the tendentiousness of such arguments, an ideological need to protect religion and its miracles from magic and its effects.

Hans Dieter Betz, in introducing the invaluable translated collection of Greek and Demotic papyri "containing a variety of magical spells and formulae, hymns and rituals . . . from the second century B.C. to the fifth century A.D" that he edited, asks, in conclusion, why "magic . . . from time immemorial . . . has survived throughout history, through the coming and going of entire religions, the scientific and technological revolutions, and the triumphs of modern medicine." His answer uses terms such as "fraud" and "delusion" once apiece, "deception" or "deceive" eight times, and the expression "props .. fads .. and gobbledygook" once. Yet those pejorative descriptions intertwine with sentences like this: "Magic is the art that makes people who practice it feel better rather than worse, that provides the illusion of security to the insecure, the feeling of help to the helpless, and the comfort of hope to the hopeless." And notice the ambivalence in these final sentences: "Of course, it is all deception. But who can endure naked reality, especially when there is a way to avoid it? This is why magic has worked and continues to work, no matter what the evidence may be. Those whose lives depend on deception and delusion and those who provide them have formed a truly indissoluble symbiosis. Magic makes an unmanageable life manageable for those who believe in it, and a profession profitable for those who practice the art" (1986:xli, xlvii–xlviii). Would one be as willing to say exactly the same about, say, Jesus' miracles in particular and religion's promises in general? And, if not, why not?

The next case is Howard Clark Kee's comparison of medicine, miracle, and magic in New Testament times. "*Medicine* is a method of diagnosis of human ailments and a prescription for them based on a combination of theory about and observation of the body, its functions and malfunctions. *Miracle* embodies the claim that healing can be accomplished through appeal to, and subsequent action by the gods, either directly or through a chosen intermediary agent. *Magic* is a technique, through word or act, by which a desired end is achieved, whether that end lies in the solution to the seeker's problem or in damage to the enemy who has caused the problem" (1986:3). In other words, "if the technique is effective of itself in overcoming a hostile force, then the action is magical. If it is viewed as the intervention of the god or goddess, then it is miraculous. If it is a facilitating of the natural function of the body, then it is medical" (1986:4). Those definitions are fair and unprejudicial, although I am not certain I can thereby distinguish miracle from magic unless one presumes that all gods are absent from the latter and all techniques from the former activity. But, in any case, what actually happens as his book progresses is that magic is repeatedly described as coercive or exploitive, although that element was not at all part of the initial definition. In his section on the Greco-Egyptian magical papyri, for instance, he interprets them as "coercive" or "peremptory" even while admitting that "some of the papyri are more nearly petitionary in nature, rather than demanding or coercive," and he concludes with one that is "wholly free of . . . coercive elements." His final summary on those texts says that "clearly the line is breaking down between religion and magic, but it is the latter which is the dominant feature in this material, since the purpose of the formulae is to coerce the desired results by means of repeating the appropriate words or acts. What is sought is not to learn the will of the deity, but to shape the deity's will to do the bidding of the one making the demands or to defeat the aims of the evil powers" (1986:107–112). The distinction between beseeching or imploring and coercing or exploiting is surely a valid one, but where is the evidence that religious miracle is always the former and magical ritual always the latter?

The third and final example is the thesis of A. A. Barb that "the fundamental difference between magic and religion is still the same as it always was. On the one hand, we have the religious man, offering his adorations in humble submission to the deity; always careful to add to any supplication the reservation 'if it be according to Thy will.' On the other hand, we have the magician, attempting to force the supernatural powers to accomplish what he desires and avert what he fears," and so, despite the last century's fashionable evolutionary hypothesis, "religion does not evolve from primitive magic; on the contrary magic derives from religion, which, as it becomes tainted by human frailty, deteriorates into so-called white magic (the Greeks called it *theurgia*—working things divine), gradually losing its whiteness and turning from more or less dirty grey into black magic, called in Greek *goētia*, from the evil-sounding recitation of spells" (101). The classical distinction between petitioning and forcing, beseeching and coercing supernatural powers is, once again, a valid one, but is it an adequate one to distinguish magic from religion? In any case, that at least debatable distinction is totally overshadowed by the fact that, throughout her lecture, she consistently uses the metaphor of authorities who must protect their people from rotten or poisonous food masquerading as good or healthy produce. The rhetoric of invective is fascinating to watch: "rotten food . . . refuse-heap . . . unfit for human consumption . . . deadly poison . . . refuse-heap . . . slightly putrid . . . refuse . . . decomposing garbage . . . decayed and decomposing" (101, 102, 107, 117, 124). Or, in greater detail: "food-poisoning is caused more frequently by imported food than by home-grown stuff; just so we find again and again that the closest connexion exists between magic and alien imported cults" (102). And again: "the task of a Roman emperor as health officer in things supernatural became increasingly difficult when the syncretistic, rotting refuse-heap of the dead and dying religions of the whole ancient world grew to mountainous height while wholesome supernatural food became scarce" (104). I submit that argumentation has yielded to vituperation because the theoretical basis for substantive distinction between magic and religion is inadequate. But, if I may borrow Barb's own analogy, if it is good for religiopolitical authorities to protect their people from rotten bread, it is also good to watch carefully who is claiming that function while seeking or establishing an exclusive monopoly on the local bakery.

There have always been other voices, however, that wonder how, then or now, one can tell "our" miracle worker from "their" magician or "our" miracle from "their" magic. John Hull, comparing Hellenistic magic and the synoptic tradition, admitted that "the category of miracle, although an indispensable form in the mythological expressions of faith found in the ancient world, was for the ancients difficult to separate from the category of magic. For us today it is impossible to separate magic from miracle without seriously modifying the strictly miraculous part of the miracle" (60). Morton Smith, comparing terms such as *son of god* or *divine man* or *magician* in the early Roman Empire, concludes that "the difference between these figures is one of social status and success . . . once the requirements of social status and decorum are met, the same man will customarily be called a [divine man], or son of a god, by his admirers, a magician by his enemies. Within this area all three refer to a single social type, and that type is characterized by the actions . . . which make up by far the greater part of the Gospels' reports about Jesus" (1973b:228–229). Eugene Gallagher, working specifically on the problem of classification raised by Celsus' attack and Origen's defense of Jesus, concludes that, in the Hellenistic religious world, "the fervent proclamation of miracle working ability is frequently countered by the ascription of the results to magic. Where the supporters of a given figure would perceive his actions as miraculous, his detractors would see them as magical. . . . It will not be the performance of certain actions, but the evaluation of them, that will provide keys to the range of criteria. The deed which demonstrates divinity for one audience may well demonstrate the malign influence of demons to another. In dealing with the criteria, judgments rather than actions should be paramount" (32–33). The spectrum, in other words, from religion to magic, or from a son of god, a divine man, a miracle worker, to a magician, is not one of description but prescription, not one of differentiation but of acclamation. And the discriminant is the political one of official, approved, and accepted, as against unofficial, unapproved, or unaccepted activities. A similar conclusion, based again on a study of pagan-Christian conflicts in the second century, is argued in even greater detail by Harold Remus. "Viewed from the perspective of language, the conflicts can be seen as competitions in naming: affirming miracle of the extraordinary phenomena of one's own group and denying the name to those of rival groups. That is a sociological judgment, and our study has shown that social and cultural factors play a basic role in such conflicts and should figure into attempts to understand them" (182–183).

The clearest and finest discussion of magic in terms both of anthropological theory and Greco-Roman history is the comprehensive 1980 study by David Aune. He starts from "the emerging *communis opinio* among modern anthropologists that the older dichotomy between magic and religion is not only misleading, but that, regarded as strict categories, [they are] totally unworkable" (1511). He concludes, from a survey of socioanthropo-

logical theories on deviance and labeling that "magic is defined as that form
of religious deviance whereby individual or social goals are sought by
means alternate to those normally sanctioned by the dominant religious
institution." But, then, to that first criterion he adds a second: "goals sought
within the context of religious deviance are magical when attained through
the management of supernatural powers in such a way that results are
virtually guaranteed" (1515). I think it better once and for all to bury that
discriminant of guarantee. On the one hand, magicians do not give money-
back guarantees, and when they make absolute claims it is simply the
necessity of publicity and propaganda, the exigency of entrepreneurial
competition and unauthorized individuality. On the other hand, religious
rites, such as the Roman Catholic Mass, guarantee eucharistic transubstan-
tiation and could easily be accused of magic by inimical onlookers. That
first criterion is quite sufficient without the second one, and, in fact, when
Aune sums up on the next page, he ignores it. "(1) Magic and religion are so
closely intertwined that it is virtually impossible to regard them as discrete
socio-cultural categories. (2) The structural-functional analysis of magico-
religious phenomena forbids a negative attitude toward magic. (3) Magic is
a phenomenon which exists only within the matrix of particular religious
traditions; magic is not religion only in the sense that the species is not the
genus. A particular magical system coheres within a religious structure in
the sense that it shares the fundamental religious reality construction of
the contextual religion. (4) Magic appears to be as universal a feature of religion as deviant behavior is of human societies" (1516). He ignores it again,
in closing the article, by noting that he has used the term *magic* "without
any pejorative connotations, referring only to the pragmatic and religious
deviant features of magic as a necessary and universally present sub-
structure in religious systems" (1557). Religion as unguaranteed request
and magic as guaranteed coercion is a distinction long overdue for final burial. Magic, simply, is what any socioreligious ascendancy calls its deviant
shadow. We return, in other words, to Marcel Mauss's definition of almost
ninety years ago: "A magical rite is *any rite which does not play a part in
organized cults* — it is private, secret, mysterious and approaches the limit of
a prohibited rite . . . We do not define magic in terms of the structure of its
rites, but by the circumstances in which these rites occur, which in turn
determine the place they occupy in the totality of social customs" (24).

In conclusion, first, there are aspects of magic that are evil, inhuman,
pathological, and pernicious. There are also such elements in religion, and
they should, in both cases, be located and named. There are also, no doubt,
frauds, cheats, and charlatans in both areas, and they also should, in both
cases, be located and named. Such facts do not invalidate either phenome-

non any more than quacks do doctors. Second, efficacy and utility can and should, no doubt, be debated for both magic and religion, and distinctions must be drawn between direct results, such as cure, healing, or restoration, and indirect results, such as hope, meaning, or consolation, but they must be drawn alike for both. Third, hocus-pocus or mumbo jumbo may be found not only in ritual acts but also in philosophical theories, ideological claims, and theological systems. There may be, in other words, one gobbledygook, to use Betz' term, for the oral masses and another for the scribal elites, but it is still gobbledygook in each case. Finally, Jesus as a popular first-century Jewish magician in the tradition, say, of Elijah and Elisha, may well be different from the professional magicians who owned those magical papyri, but that should be established by comparing their actions, not presuming their motives. In summary, religion and magic, the religious miracle and the magical effect, are in no way substantively distinct. Distinctions can and should be made, but they are within magic/religion and not between magic and religion. Above all, the prescriptive distinction that states that *we* practice religion but *they* practice magic should be seen for what it is, a political validation of the approved and the official against the unapproved and the unofficial.

A Gospel of Miracles?

There is something very strange about the miracles of Jesus, not about their facticity but about their attestation. The problem can be underlined by a comparison. In proposing "the sources of the gospels," Helmut Koester suggested three separate items: collections of sayings, collections of miracle stories, and a passion narrative (1982:2.48). That first claim is based both on a text, the *Gospel of Thomas,* and a reconstruction, the *Sayings Source Q.* The second claim is much harder to substantiate. We have no textual Gospel of miracles similar to that textual Gospel of sayings. Furthermore, while we have as high as sixfold independent attestation in the primary stratum of the sayings, we never get higher than twofold for that of the miracles. And the closest we get to a triple attestation is in the second stratum (appendix 6). One might almost conclude that miracles come into the tradition later rather than earlier, as creative confirmation rather than as original data. I think, however, that such a conclusion would be completely wrong. The better explanation is just the opposite. Miracles were, at a very early stage, being washed out of the tradition and, when retained, were being very carefully interpreted (Hull). A full proof of that assertion would demand wider studies on the four intracanonical Gospels than presently possible, but it is at least substantiated by the miracles under consideration.

I hold, in summary, that Jesus, as magician and miracle worker, was a very problematic and controversial phenomenon not only for his enemies but even for his friends.

There are, as usually analyzed, seven miracles in John 1–11 (Mack 1988:221). These are 349 *Water into Wine* [2/1], 119 *Distant Boy Cured* [1/2], 127 *Sickness and Sin* [1/2], 3 *Bread and Fish* [1/2], 128 *Walking on Water* [1/2], 129 *Blind Man Healed* [1/2], and 130 *Dead Man Raised* [1/2]. It has also been proposed that those miracles came to John from a sequential source primarily because of the deliberate connections between the first two cases. The openings of that first pair are linked: "on the third day there was a marriage at Cana in Galilee" in 2:1 looks to "after the two days he departed to Galilee . . . so he came again to Cana in Galilee, where he had made the water wine" in 4:43, 46. And so are the endings; "this, the first of his signs, Jesus did at Cana in Galilee" in 2:11 looks to "this was now the second sign that Jesus did when he had come from Judea to Galilee" in 4:54. Thus, "the miracles source has been most clearly detected in John 2:1–12a (the wedding at Cana) followed directly by John 4:46b–54a (the healing of the son of the official from Capernaum)" according to James Robinson (Robinson & Koester 242). I admit, however, that when authors start counting I am inclined to see redaction rather than tradition, final author rather than original source. For example, after the 190 *Fishing for Humans* [2/3] miracle, John 21:14 concludes that "this was now the third time that Jesus was revealed to the disciples after he was raised from the dead." But that backward linkage with John 20:19–23 and 26–29 indicates not an original triad of three appearances but a later editorial addition of John 21 to the already closed unity of John 20.

I suspect, therefore, that something similar has occurred with that set of seven miracles. Those careful numerical cross-references, which are only given for the first two miracles in the catena, serve less to prove that there was an original sevenfold linked source than that 349 *Water into Wine* [2/1] and 119 *Distant Boy Cured* [1/2] were added on at the start of an original fivefold linked source. I am persuaded of that fivefold sequence's existence by the fact that the Markan and Johannine traditions have those miracles in the same order:

127. *Sickness and Sin* [1/2]	Mark 2:1–12	John 5:1–18
3. *Bread and Fish* [1/6]	Mark 6:33–44	John 6:1–15
128. *Walking on Water* [1/2]	Mark 6:45–52	John 6:16–21
129. *Blind Man Healed* [1/2]	Mark 8:22–26	John 9:1–7
130. *Dead Man Raised* [1/2]	*Secret Mark* 1v20–2r11a	John 11:1–57

That common sequence could, of course, be sheer coincidence, but, at least hypothetically, I hold on to it as the only evidence we have for early collections of miracles similar to those more certain and equally early collections of sayings. Whether such collections were ever brought together into a Gospel of miracles is too speculative for present discussion.

I am deliberately not using one other argument for such a fivefold catena of miracles. Paul Achtemeier has argued, in two very fine articles, that there are twin fivefold sets of miracles absorbed and restructured within the present text of Mark 4:35–8:26. Here is their original sequence, which Mark has followed with but one major transposition in each set. He combined the two female cures into one unit as 229 *Two Women Cured* [2/1], and he relocated 129 *Blind Man Healed* [1/2] to an earlier position:

128. *Walking on Water* [1/2] as Mark 4:35–41	128. *Walking on Water* [1/2] as Mark 6:45–52
228. *The Gerasene Demoniac* [2/1] Mark 5:1–20	129. *Blind Man Healed* [1/2] Mark 8:22–26
229. *Two Women Cured* [2/1] as Mark 5:21–24a,35–43	237. *Distant Girl Cured* [2/1] Mark 7:24–30
229. *Two Women Cured* [2/1] as Mark 5:24b–34	238. *Deaf Mute Cured* [2/1] Mark 7:31–37
3. *Bread and Fish* [1/6] as Mark 6:33–44	3. *Bread and Fish* [1/6] as Mark 8:1–10

In each set a sea miracle is followed by three cures involving one exorcism and two healings and is concluded by a feeding miracle. That is a very powerful proposal, especially when the framing dyads are seen against a background of Moses and the inside triads against one of Elijah and Elisha. There is, however, one very major problem. It is even more likely that what we have in Mark 4:35–8:26 is a deliberate and creative doubling, within 3 *Bread and Fish* [1/6], of the miracle from Mark 6:33–44 into that in 8:1–10 and also, within 128 *Walking on Water* [1/2], of the miracle in Mark 6:45–52 into that in 4:35–41. On the level of words and phrases, doublets are, of course, characteristically Markan (Neirynck 1970; 1982:83–142), and on the level of composition and theology, those twin crossings and twin feedings lead up to the climactic failure of apostolic understanding in 8:14–21 and, in fact, double its culpability and inexcusability. Jesus brings one bread that is more than enough for Jews and Gentiles together (Kelber 45–65). I prefer, therefore, to take those parallel accounts not as evidence of twinned data but of deliberate Markan duplication.

There is, in summary, only one very plausible collection of miracles evident in our sources, and that is the common source that lies behind Mark and John and is most clearly evident in that fivefold sequential set. No doubt there may have been other such sets as well. But we still need much more evidence to postulate a Gospel of miracles similar to the already established Gospels of sayings. Maybe, of course, it was there very early and erased very fast?

Possessed by Demonic Imperialism

The British anthropologist Mary Douglas proposed, in a marvelously fecund intuition, that the physical body is a microcosm of the social body so that there is a dialectic between the personal and the social, the individual and the corporate, with regard to taboos and boundaries, with regard to the acceptable, the permissible, and the tolerable. "The human body is common to us all. Only our social condition varies. The symbols based on the human body are used to express different social experiences" (vii). Sheldon Isenberg and Dennis Owen, commenting on that intuition, note that "the individual's body is presented to him, taught to him by society, usually in the manifestation of parents, and then by peers, perhaps also by schools. Our attitudes about our bodies arise from society's image of itself. So if we can learn how a person understands the workings of that complex system called the body, its organization, its spatial arrangement, and its priorities of needs, then we can guess much about the total pattern of self-understanding of the society, such as its perception of its own workings, its organization, its power structure, and its cosmology" (3). And, of course, vice versa.

Think, now, of demonic possession. George Nickelsburg, speaking of the *Book of the Similitudes/Parables of Enoch* in 1 *Enoch* 37–71, a work that he dates "around the turn of the era," says that "on the one side are God, the heavenly entourage, the agents of his judgment . . . and God's people. . . . On the other are the chief demon Azazel, his angels, and the kings and the mighty . . . [who] would have their counterparts among the Roman generals, governors, triumvirs, and monarchs whose activities in Judea are well documented in the sources. The author might also have had in mind the late Hasmoneans and the Herods" (1981:215, 223). For this representative of the Great Tradition, then, Roman imperialism meant that God's people were possessed by demons on the social level. Notice, by the way, the somewhat schizophrenic implications of demonic control: it indicates a power admittedly greater than oneself, admittedly "inside" oneself, but that one declares to be evil and therefore beyond any collusion or cooperation. Yet one must surely, at some level, envy it or at least desire its power in order to destroy it. How did that look on the level of the Little Tradition; how did that social possession appear, if Mary Douglas' basic intuition is correct, on the individual level of the physical body?

I begin with twin examples, one ancient and one modern. The ancient example is 228 *The Gerasene Demoniac* [2/1], but I use it with this caution. It is from the second stratum, has only single attestation, and is being used only for general background, not specific foreground. No claim is being made about the historical Jesus.

> They came to the other side of the sea, to the country of the Gerasenes. And when he had come out of the boat, there met him out of the tombs a man with an unclean spirit, who lived among the tombs; and no one could bind him any more, even with a chain; for he had often been bound with fetters and chains, but the chains he wrenched apart, and the fetters he broke in pieces; and no one had the strength to subdue him. Night and day among the tombs and on the mountains he was always crying out, and bruising himself with stones. And when he saw Jesus from afar, he ran and worshiped him; and crying out with a loud voice, he said, "What have you to do with me, Jesus, Son of the Most High God? I adjure you by God, do not torment me." For he had said to him, "Come out of the man, you unclean spirit!" And Jesus asked him, "What is your name?" He replied, "My name is Legion; for we are many." And he begged him eagerly not to send them out of the country. Now a great herd of swine was feeding there on the hillside; and they begged him, "Send us to the swine, let us enter them." So he gave them leave. And the unclean spirits came out, and entered the swine; and the herd, numbering about two thousand, rushed down the steep bank into the sea, and were drowned in the sea. The herdsmen fled, and told it in the city and in the country. And people came to see what it was that had happened. And they came to Jesus, and saw the demoniac sitting there, clothed and in his right mind, the man who had had the legion; and they were afraid. And those who had seen it told what had happened to the demoniac and to the swine. And they began to beg Jesus to depart from their neighborhood. (Mark 5:1-17)

An individual is, of course, being cured, but the symbolism is also hard to miss or ignore. The demon is both one and many; is named Legion, that fact and sign of Roman power; is consigned to swine; and is cast into the sea. A brief performancial summary, in other words, of every Jewish revolutionary's dream! And it may be left open whether the exorcist is asked to depart because a cured demoniac is not worth a herd of swine or because the people see quite clearly the political implications of the action.

The political dialectic between possessed individual and possessed society, between demonic microcosm and demonic macrocosm, in 228 *The Gerasene Demoniac* [2/1] is confirmed by my second and contemporary example. Among the Lunda-Luvale tribes of the Barotse in what was then Northern Rhodesia there existed, according to Barrie Reynolds, traditional ailments called *mahamba* that resulted "from possession by ancestral spirits." But there also developed a special modern version called *bindele* "caused by possession by other spirits [that] may be considered to reflect a tension between the society of the victim and that of the group represented by the spirit. Sufferers from *bindele,* which is the Luvale word for 'European', are believed to be possessed by the spirit of an European" (133). He goes on to tell how, in 1944, an exorcist called Rice Kamanga, later called Chana I, founded a church dedicated to curing *bindele,* "a lengthy process that may take from one to five months" (135). *Legion,* I think, is to colonial Roman Palestine as *bindele* was to colonial European Rhodesia.

Ioan Lewis has drawn attention to the close connection between possession and oppression, whether that subjugation be the sexual and familial one of women by men or the racial and imperial one of some people by other people. In that first case, "women's possession cults are . . . thinly disguised protest movements directed against the dominant sex. . . . In its primary social function, peripheral possession thus emerges as an oblique aggressive strategy" (31, 32). In that second case, "those societies in which central possession cults persist are usually those composed of small, fluid, social units exposed to particularly exacting physical conditions, or conquered communities lying under the yoke of alien oppression" (35). Lewis calls such possession groups "oblique redressive strategies" or "protest cults" or even "ritual rebellions" (88, 127). Three powerful ambiguities appear regularly across Lewis's cross-cultural corpus of cases. There is, first of all, the phenomenon of shamans as healed healers, female or male persons who, having gained control of their own possessing spirits or deities, gather around them a group of others whose possessors they can likewise control. Next, there are those particular instances in which the possessing being desires or demands precisely the signs and tokens of the oppressing forces themselves. The possessed woman demands male attire; the slave demands the whip of the master. Finally, there is "the paradox of the shaman's position [in] that he is credited with being capable of causing what he has learnt through suffering to cure" (201). This is, of course, the obvious backlash of the overprovoked oppressor. "It seems that the irritation aroused by the game of possession amongst the ranks of the manipulated establishment fastens most securely on those who in assuming a positive, active, and above all, militant role are indeed in danger of exceeding the bounds of tolerance. These leaders of mutinous women or depressed men who, in diagnosing and treating possession afflictions amongst their colleagues, perpetuate the whole system are the most dangerous agents of dissent and potential subversion. Hence it is they who are held in check by accusations of witchcraft which seem designed to discredit them and to diminish their status" (122).

That general overview seems confirmed by specific contemporary case studies. Gananath Obeyesekere, recounting the case of Alice Nona from western Ceylon, says, "'Repression,' 'projection,' 'depression,' 'lowering of self worth' are abstract terms which help to explain certain psychological processes; the demonological idiom by contrast reifies and anthropomorphises these processes and relates them to the larger religious world view of the people. The inaccessible experiences of the patient are brought into the open and made existentially more real for both the patient and the larger culture. In the modern West mental illness is often looked upon as idiosyncratic pathology; here it is transformed into a publicly intelligible cultural idiom. The public idiom facilitates communication between patient, ritual specialist, the family and the larger community" (104). In a similar vein, Colleen Ward and Michael Beaubrun, working with four cases in a Trinidadian Pentecostal context, "suggest that the predisposing cultural mores, beliefs, traditions, and superstitions, coupled with highly emotional stress situations, constitute the precipitating factors of demonic possession" (207). Those are powerful cross-cultural explanations of possession cults in situations of depression or oppression, but they also presume an environment where possession is not viewed in a predominantly negative way, where, in other words, possession cults and groups can form and flourish. But what if one's religion itself militates against such options?

In 1921, for example, Traugott Konstantin Oesterreich, then head of Tübingen's Department of Philosophy, published a vast and fascinating collection of possession cases "among primitive races, in antiquity, the middle ages, and modern times." He began with that Gerasene narrative and used it almost as an archetypal instance (3). Erika Bourguignon, however, in a superb cross-cultural study of possession, noted that, though "Oesterreich . . . remarks on the striking similarity between the New Testament accounts and cases of possession reported in later times, and . . . suggests that this similarity enhances the credibility of the gospels . . . that . . . similarity is undoubtedly in part due to the fact that subsequent cases of possession were indeed modeled on these earlier ones." Thus "the phenomenon of split consciousness or of compulsive action against which the victim appears to be helpless appears primarily in Christian and Jewish cases of possession. In fact, in a review of the ethnographic literature on hundreds of societies, we have not encountered this phenomenon. Rather, we are more likely to find a total transformation, the apparent substitution of one personality for another" (3, 6). That means, of course, that those New Testament cases represent, from both individual and social viewpoint, a far more virulent situation and a far more disturbing problem.

Recently, Paul Hollenbach, basing his discussion on how "the phenomena of possession and exorcism are now examined and understood via the social sciences as common world-wide phenomena throughout most of history" (1981:567), has returned again to that almost archetypal Gadarene example. He makes three major points in summing up its cross-cultural and trans-temporal background. First, in sociopsychological explanations, "situations of social tension such as the following are often indicated as the causal context of possession: class antagonisms rooted in economic exploitation, conflicts between traditions where revered traditions are eroded, colonial domination and revolution" (573). He illustrates this from *The Wretched of the Earth*, Franz Fanon's famous 1963 analysis of mental illness during the Algerian revolutionary war against France. Especially significant is Fanon's comment that "the native is an oppressed person whose permanent dream is to become the persecutor" (Hollenbach 573). With such divided minds, split personalities, and schizoid dreams, it is no wonder "that the colonial situation of domination and rebellion nourishes mental illness in extraordinary numbers of the population" (575). Next, there is the fact that "mental illness can be seen as a socially acceptable form of oblique protest against, or escape from, oppressions." This "salvation by possession" is, of course, both "a 'fix' for people who saw no other way to cope with the horrendous social and political conditions in which they found their lot cast" and also "a way that does not at all threaten the social position of . . . powerful oppressors, the state, the police, the employer, the tax collector" (576). Finally, and most pointedly for the Beelzebul accusation, because it is obvious that the possessed are deviants, it becomes just as obvious that deviants must be possessed. There is thus a "symbiotic relationship" between "possession as protest" from the weak to the strong and accused possession as control from the strong to the weak (577). Hence the illogical logic of the possessed exorcist.

In discussing Jesus' exorcisms, therefore, two factors must be kept always in mind. One is the almost schizoid position of a colonial people. If they submit gladly to colonialism, they conspire in their own destruction. If they hate and despise it, they admit that something more powerful than themselves, and therefore to some extent desirable, is hateful and despicable. And what does that do to them? Another is that colonial exorcisms are at once less and more than revolution; they are, in fact, individuated symbolic revolution.

Beelzebul Controversy

In terms of my methodology only one exorcism, 121 *Beelzebul Controversy* [1/2], can be considered, but it is, admittedly, a very powerful case. In Mark, that unit leads into 81 *Strong One's House* [1/2], but in the *Sayings Gospel Q* it leads first into 150 *By Whose Power* [1/1] and then into 81 *Strong One's House* [1/2]. It is debated whether 81 *Strong One's House* [1/2] was actually in the *Sayings Gospel Q* or was simply and independently inserted from Mark by both Matthew and Luke into their versions of the *Sayings Gospel Q*. I presume that second option (1983a:189), although others, as noted by John Kloppenborg (1988:92), and especially Philip Sellew (100), have argued for the first. The present analysis would not be affected in either case.

There is only one major difference between the Markan and *Sayings Gospel Q* versions of the controversy itself. In Mark 3:22–26 the accusation is not connected to any specific exorcism, but Q/Luke 11:14–15, 17–18 begins, "He was casting out a demon that was dumb; when the demon had gone out, the dumb man spoke." Matthew wanted to obtain two miracles from this single instance, so Q/Matthew 9:32–34 begins, "A dumb demoniac was brought to him. And when the demon had been cast out, the dumb man spoke." But then Q/Matthew 12:22–26 begins, to be different, "A blind and dumb demoniac was brought to him, and he healed him, so that the dumb man spoke and saw." Matthew also refers to this incident in between at 10:25b. Most likely, however, the traditional unit had some such specific introduction that Mark omitted because of the parallelism he was creating within 3:21–35 between inimical family members and inimical Jerusalem authorities

> Now he was casting out a demon that was dumb; when the demon had gone out, the dumb man spoke, and the people marveled. But some of them said, "He casts out demons by Beelzebul, the prince of demons". . . . But he, knowing their thoughts, said to them, "Every kingdom divided against itself is laid waste, and a divided household falls. And if Satan also is divided against himself, how will his kingdom stand?" (*Sayings Gospel Q*, 2Q: Luke 11:14–15, 17–18a = Matthew 9:32–34; 12:22–26)

The first important element is that, in both sources, the accusation is preserved in strikingly similar language and the accusatory term begins as

Beelzebul and ends as Satan. The former word preserves, as Joseph Fitz-myer notes, "the name of an old Canaanite god, meaning 'Baal, the Prince,' or 'Baal of the Exalted Abode'" (1981–85:920). But that unique epithet is the voice, surely, of the Little Tradition, an attack that bespeaks a village environment. Beelzebul needed to be rephrased as Satan when the transmissional process began to move from that original location.

A second important element is the conjunction that Jesus creates between kingdom, house, and Satan. Although those first two expressions could be taken as innocent and random examples of division begetting destruction, they could also be taken as underlining the politicosocial dimensions of exorcism. Satan now rules, as Douglas Oakman has suggested, through kingdoms and houses, maybe, for example, the house of Herod or the kingdom of Rome (1988:115). The association is delicate, indirect, and implicit but probably neither accidental nor innocuous.

A final consideration: one wonders how Jesus' opponents left themselves open for such a devastating rejoinder. How could one even imagine casting out demons by demonic possession? One answer was seen already in Ioan Lewis' work as establishments struck back somewhat desperately at shamanistic curers of possession by accusing them of witchcraft, that is, of causing what they cured. Another answer may lie in George Peter Murdock's survey of illness in a statistically valid sample of the world's cultures. He distinguishes between *disease,* "suggesting primarily the communicable virus-borne or bacteria-borne phenomena," and *illness,* "embracing any impairment of health serious enough to arouse concern, whether it be due to communicable disease, psychosomatic disturbance, organic failure, aggressive assault, or alleged accident or supernatural interference" (6). He concedes "that supernatural causes of illness far outweigh natural causes in the belief systems of the world's peoples" (26) but never really wonders about that fact, it being enough apparently to say that "magic is illusory technique whereas science is the most admirable component of man's ideational environment" (53). Be that as it may, he notes that, among the supernatural causes of illness, "*spirit-aggression* ... the direct hostile, arbitrary, or punitive action of some malevolent or affronted supernatural being" (20) is a "quasi-universal ... rated as important (i.e., predominant or significant) ... most markedly so in ... the Circum-Mediterranean" (73–74). Yet there is another, separate, and different explanation, *witchcraft,* which "is practically universal in the Circum-Mediterranean region but surprisingly rare elsewhere in the world" (21) so that "there are fairly substantial grounds for regarding the Circum-Mediterranean as a culture area in which one of the most characteristic and deep-seated traits is the belief in the causation of illness by witchcraft" (58). It is those twin explanations, one a quasi-universal and the other a regional emphasis, that clash in the Beelzebul incident. The sick man is possessed, and is therefore a victim of spirit-aggression. Jesus cures him, so how can one denigrate Jesus? He is a witch, himself possessed by or possessive of an evil spirit (Malina & Neyrey). Unfortunately, however, you cannot have it both ways for the same event at the same time.

Event and Process in Miracle

"The miracle tradition of the gospels contains," in David Aune's fully documented summary, "accounts of six exorcisms, seventeen healings, and eight so-called nature miracles. Next in importance are the generalized descriptions of Jesus' program of wonder working, allusions to miracles performed by his disciples, references to specific miracles which are alluded to but not narrated, and various feats of Jesus wherein he appears to exercise supernatural powers. Finally we have what appear to be the remnants of accusations levelled at the historical Jesus to the effect that he practised magic" (1523–1524; see also Theissen 1983; Kee 1983).

My own inventory for Jesus' miracles contains thirty-two items, of which nine have plural attestation (appendix 6). Within that fuller corpus I focus exclusively on those nine, one of which, 121 *Beelzebul Controversy* [1/2], has already been seen. Three others are usually classed as nature miracles rather than healing miracles. These are 3 *Bread and Fish* [1/6], 128 *Walking on Water* [1/2], and 190 *Fishing for Humans* [2/3]. David Aune has said that most of the nature miracles are "creations out of whole cloth by the early church" (1538). I agree, but that description still needs explanation. I postpone explanation until the last chapter of this book, where the question of nature miracle and apostolic authority can be considered in much greater detail. That leaves five miracles for immediate consideration.

I am concerned with two processes at work within that corpus, one moving from event to process and the other in the opposite direction from process to event. By *event* I mean the actual and historical cure of an afflicted individual at a moment in time. By *process* I mean some wider socioreligious phenomenon that is symbolized in and by such an individual happening. But just as event can give rise to process so process can give rise to event.

There is nothing very surprising in all of this. The basic symbolic interaction postulated by Mary Douglas's body-society parallelism means that social symbolism is always latent in bodily miracle and that bodily miracle always has social signification. It is very easy and indeed inevitable to move in both directions, from body to society or event to process and from society to body or process to event. And it is very possible not to be certain at times in which way one is moving. There is no such thing as a simple miracle. There is no such thing as private magic.

Event to Process

I consider, under the rubric of event to process, three miracles from the ninefold plurally attested corpus: 110 A *Leper Cured* [1/2], 127 *Sickness and Sin* [1/2], and 129 *Blind Man Healed* [1/2].

A *Leper Cured*

The story of 110 A *Leper Cured* [1/2] may possibly have only a single attestation and so should be methodologically excluded from this present study. I proposed earlier that Mark "may well be . . . dependent" on the *Egerton Gospel* (1985:75), and Frans Neirynck rejoined, to the contrary, that the *Egerton Gospel* "is post-Synoptic and that the writer probably had some acquaintance with the three Synoptic gospels and almost certainly with Luke" (1985:159; see also 1989:161–167). Either way, there would be only single attestation. Whether Mark knew the *Egerton Gospel* or not is probably beyond proof or disproof and therefore without interest, so I am willing to withdraw the proposal. But I am still quite completely convinced that the *Egerton Gospel* did not know the intracanonical Gospels. In other words, Mark (and John) knew *not* the *Egerton Gospel* itself but simply the traditions it contained. Provisionally, then, the leper's cure appears in two independent sources, the *Egerton Gospel* and Mark.

> And behold a leper drew near [to him] and said: "Master Jesus, wandering with lepers and eating with [them was I(?)] in the inn; I also [became] a le[per]. If [thou] therefore [wilt], I am made clean." Immediately the Lord [said to him]: "I will, be thou made clean." [And thereupon] the leprosy departed from him [And the Lord said to him]: "Go [thy way and show th]yself to the [priests] . . . and offer [concerning the cle]ansing as [Moses] com[manded and] si[n n]o more. . . . (*Egerton Gospel* 1r35–47 [P. Eger. 2 + P. Köln 255]; Bell & Skeat 1935a:10–11; 1935b:30 + Gronewald 140; *NTA* 1.96–97; Cameron 1982:74; Neirynck 1989:163–164; Daniels 25)

> And a leper came to him beseeching him, and kneeling said to him, "If you will, you can make me clean." Moved with pity, he stretched out his hand and touched him, and said to him, "I will; be clean." And immediately the leprosy left him, and he was made clean. And he sternly charged him, and sent him away at once, and said to him, "See that you say nothing to any one; but go, show yourself to the priest, and offer for your cleansing what Moses commanded, for a proof to the people

[literally: to them]." But he went out and began to talk freely about it, and to spread the news, so that Jesus could no longer openly enter a town, but was out in the country; and people came to him from every quarter. (Mark 1:40–45 = Matthew 8:1–4 = Luke 5:12–16)

Both texts agree on two major points. There is, first of all, the request and reply formulation with its unusual "if you will" and "I will." What exactly does that add to a straightforward request and immediate responsive cure? It seems to underline a striking ambiguity between "declared clean" and "made (healed) clean." This sets Jesus' power and authority on a par with or even above that of the Temple itself. It is not just a simple request for and granting of a cure. Jesus can, if he wants, both cure and declare cured. There is also, however, and to the contrary, that terminal injunction to submit to the legal purity regulations of the Temple itself. Leviticus 13–14 begins, "When a man has on the skin of his body a swelling or an eruption or a spot, and it turns into a leprous disease on the skin of his body, then he shall be brought to Aaron the priest or to one of his sons the priests, and the priest shall . . . " Thereafter, the instructions mention only "the priest," but, as is clear from that opening phrase, one could send the cured person to "the priest" as in Mark 1:44a (but notice the plural "them" in 1:44b) or "the priests" as in the *Egerton Gospel*. Jesus, accordingly, is carefully obedient to the purity regulations on leprosy, as in Deuteronomy 24:8–9. Those two points must derive from the common source available to the *Egerton Gospel* as well as to Mark, but they seem in flat contradiction with one another. Jesus both is and is not a conscientious and obedient observer of levitical purity regulations. How is that to be explained?

I propose a four-step process. The *original story* of the leper's cure involved only that first point, and it showed Jesus precisely as an authoritative healing and purifying alternative to the Temple. Thereafter, that story, so reminiscent of the encounters with leprosy recorded of both Moses in Numbers 12:1–15 and Elisha in 2 Kings 5:14, is pulled in two opposite directions.

The *common source* version had already reversed and rectified the image of Jesus as an alternative to or negation of Mosaic purity regulations by that terminally appended injunction to legal fidelity. The twin texts now available to us move that *common source* in opposing directions. The *Egerton Gospel* continues and intensifies the vision of Jesus as law-observant teacher. The leper's opening autobiographical admission shows him as one either ignorant of or disobedient to legal purity regulations. And Jesus' final admonition, "sin no more," a phrase found also in John 5:14 and 8:11, indicates that Jesus does not agree with such "sinning." Mark, on the other hand, continues and intensifies the thrust of the *original story* over and against that of the *common source*. He has the leper deeply reverential to Jesus, has Jesus actually touch the leper, and qualifies the fulfillment of the purity regulations with the confrontation challenge "as a witness to (against) them," namely, the priests. Do it, in other words, to show them who I am and what I can do. For Mark, then, Jesus is precisely *not* a law-observant Jew.

Three footnotes to that analysis. That Jesus actually "touched" the leper could be redactionally Markan, his own addition to the original story in the common source. It could also have been part of the original story in the common source and may well have been what necessitated such specific terminal injunctions to legal obedience lest Jesus be "misunderstood" as neglectful of legal purity. The *Egerton Gospel* would then have omitted it while Mark retained it. David Aune has noted, "While Jesus' exorcistic and healing technique does not follow a rigid or invariable pattern, at least two generalizations can be made about it: (1) Jesus never touched demon-possessed individuals; on the other hand, the technique of touching was the characteristic way in which he healed the sick and infirm. (2) Jesus' own use of the authoritative word of command was perhaps the most characteristic technique which he used to effect both exorcisms and healings" (1529). Yet, "In Hellenistic traditions, touch as a healing rite is used by the gods in legends and stories, but only rarely by human miracle workers" (1533). If touch, then, was a characteristic magical technique used by Jesus, what would happen when he was confronted by a leper? He would touch him, of course, and thus show little respect or concern for purity regulations. I keep open, then, at least the possibility that the "touch" of the leper was traditional and not just editorial. Next, that "touch" may have necessitated the textual alternative of "angered" for "moved with pity" in Mark 1:41a and may even have effected the scribal addition of 1:43, "And he sternly charged him, and sent him away at once," or better, "And being angry at him, he tossed him out right way." There is no direct textual evidence that 1:43 is not Markan, but, on the one hand, it is not found in the parallels at Matthew 8:3 or Luke 5:13, and, on the other, if it was written by Mark, nobody has a very good explanation of its purpose.

Sickness and Sin

It is possible to regard the cures in Mark 2:1–12 and John 5:1–7, 14 as quite separate events (Brown 1966–70:1.209). I prefer, despite the obvious differences in place and detail, to consider that a single traditional event lies behind 127 *Sickness and Sin* [1/2]. The overriding similarities are, for me: the malady; the mention of the sufferer's getting or not getting somebody to carry him; the injunction to rise, carry his pallet, walk; and, finally and most especially, the conjunction of sickness and sin. This last item is programmatic in Mark 2:5-9 and irrelevantly residual in John 5:14, but, since it contradicts John's own theology in 9:1-3, I presume it comes from tradition rather than redaction.

There is, first and above all, a terrible irony in that conjunction of sickness and sin, especially in first-century Palestine. Excessive taxation could leave poor people physically malnourished or hysterically disabled. But since the religiopolitical ascendancy could not blame excessive taxation, it blamed sick people themselves by claiming that their sins had led to their illnesses. And the cure for sinful sickness was, ultimately, in the Temple. And that meant more fees, in a perfect circle of victimization. When, therefore, John the Baptist with a magical rite or Jesus with a magical touch cured people of their sicknesses, they implicitly declared their sins forgiven or nonexistent. They challenged not the medical monopoly of the doctors but the religious monopoly of the priests. All of this was religiopolitically subversive.

In the Markan version, the man does have somebody to carry him, and they carry him, with heroic effort, to Jesus.

> And when Jesus saw their faith, he said to the paralytic, "My son, your sins are forgiven." Now some of the scribes were sitting there, questioning in their hearts, "Why does this man speak thus? It is blasphemy! Who can forgive sins but God alone?" And immediately Jesus, perceiving in his spirit that they thus questioned within themselves, said to them, "Why do you question thus in your hearts? Which is easier, to say to the paralytic, 'Your sins are forgiven,' or to say, 'Rise, take up your pallet and walk'?" (Mark 2:5-9 = Matthew 9:2b-5 = Luke 5:20-23)

That, of course, makes the whole challenge quite explicit. The authorities are trapped in their own theology. If sickness is a divine punishment for sin, then the one who cures sickness has forgiven sin and manifested divine power.

The Johannine redaction is rather different, and now, with equal extremity, the sufferer cannot find any carriers. Then there is the unexplained sentence in 5:14, "Afterward, Jesus found him in the temple, and said to him, 'See, you are well! Sin no more, that nothing worse befall you.'" John is not interested in the subject of sin and its forgiveness. He moves instead, in 5:9b-18, to raise, first, the fact that Jesus had the man carry his pallet on the Sabbath and, then, that Jesus was "making himself equal to God." The Sabbath is a totally new theme, found neither in Mark 2:1-12 nor John 5:1-9a, 14. But the "equal to God" is implicitly present in the accusation of blasphemy from Mark 2:7.

I think, in other words, that the transmission had moved, already in the common source behind both Mark and John, from event to process, from curing sickness, to forgiving sins, to wondering about questions of divine power. But in the beginning was the lame paralytic.

Blind Man Healed

As with that preceding miracle, so here also there might be two quite separate events behind 129 *Blind Man Healed* [1/2] in Mark 8:22–26 and John 9:1–7 (Brown 1966–70:379). Once again, but even more tentatively, I take them as independent versions of the same source primarily because of the conjunction of blindness and spittle.

The Markan story was not accepted by either Matthew or Luke. They also refused to accept 238 *Deaf Mute Cured* [2/1]. Since both miracles mention Jesus' use of his spittle, in Mark 7:33 and 8:23, that seems the most likely reason for their avoidance. Morton Smith mentions spittle as an instance of how "the miracle stories in the Gospels show a great many of the minor traits of magical procedures" (1973b:223) and David Aune places it among "techniques . . . well-known to both Jewish and Graeco-Roman magical practitioners" (1537).

> And they came to Bethsaida. And some people brought to him a blind man, and begged him to touch him. And he took the blind man by the hand, and led him out of the village; and when he had spit on his eyes and laid his hands upon him, he asked him, "Do you see anything?" And he looked up and said, "I see men; but they look like trees, walking." Then again he laid his hands upon his eyes; and he looked intently and was restored, and saw everything clearly. And he sent him away to his home, saying, "Do not even enter the village." (Mark 8:22–26)

The magic features of that process are also emphasized by the private nature of the cure, "out of the village." The concluding injunction not to reenter the village may well be Markan redaction, another of those injunctions to silence that indicate the danger of misunderstanding Jesus' miracles. But the opening separation is part of the traditional story, and it underlines the dangerously deviant nature of magical healing.

John had great difficulty in using that miracle. It is almost too physical, despite the symbolic spiritual development that he gives it in the drama of John 9:8–41. In this case he is unable first to give the traditional story and then to append the commentary that renders it a sign. He keeps interrupting himself, as it were, to make certain we do not lose the spirit in the spittle.

> As he passed by, he saw a man blind from his birth. *And his disciples asked him, "Rabbi, who sinned, this man or his parents, that he was born*

blind?" Jesus answered, "It was not that this man sinned, or his parents,
but that the works of God might be made manifest in him. We must work
the works of him who sent me, while it is day; night comes, when no one
can work. As long as I am in the world, I am the light of the world." As he
said this, he spat on the ground and made clay of the spittle and
anointed the man's eyes with the clay, *saying to him, "Go, wash in the*
pool of Siloam" (which means Sent). So he went and washed and came
back seeing. (John 9:1–7)

My italics show how the symbolic meaning of the miracle is given in
summary even before the cure is completed. Even before the spittle, Jesus
is the Sent One. And after the spittle, it is Siloam/Sent that consummates
the cure. Once again, and brilliantly, a physical event for one man becomes
a spiritual process for the world. But still, in the beginning was the spittle.

Process to Event

I consider, under the rubric of process to event, two miracles from the
ninefold plurally attested corpus: 119 *Distant Boy Cured* [1/2] and 130 *Dead
Man Raised* [1/2]. These two cases could be understood under the preceding rubric as moving from event to process; my own view, however, is that
they are actually moving from process to event.

Distant Boy Cured

The story of 119 *Distant Boy Cured* [1/2] appears in John 4:46b–53 and
in the *Sayings Gospel Q* at Luke 7:1–2[3–5]6–10 and Matthew 8:5–10, 13. In
that latter case Luke 7:3–5 is probably his own creation and Matthew
8:11–12 his own relocation (Kloppenborg 1988:50). Recall, by the way, the
somewhat similar miracle at a distance by Hanina ben Dosa in chapter 8 of
this book.

And at Capernaum there was an official whose son was ill. When he
heard that Jesus had come from Judea to Galilee, he went and begged
him to come down and heal his son, for he was at the point of death.
Jesus therefore said to him, "Unless you see signs and wonders you will
not believe." The official said to him, "Sir, come down before my child
dies." Jesus said to him, "Go; your son will live." The man believed the
word that Jesus spoke to him and went his way. As he was going down,
his servants met him and told him that his son was living. So he asked
them the hour when he began to mend, and they said to him, "Yesterday
at the seventh hour the fever left him." The father knew that was the
hour when Jesus had said to him, "Your son will live"; and he himself
believed, and all his household. (John 4:46b–53)

As he entered Capernaum, a centurion came forward to him, beseeching him and saying, "Lord, my servant is lying paralyzed at home, in terrible distress." And he said to him, "I will come and heal him." But the
centurion answered him, "Lord, I am not worthy to have you come
under my roof; but only say the word, and my servant will be healed. For
I am a man under authority, with soldiers under me; and I say to one,
'Go,' and he goes, and to another, 'Come,' and he comes, and to my
slave, 'Do this,' and he does it." When Jesus heard him, he marveled, and
said to those who followed him, "Truly, I say to you, not even in Israel
have I found such faith. . . . " And to the centurion Jesus said, "Go; be it
done for you as you have believed." And the servant was healed at that
very moment. (*Sayings Gospel Q*: Matthew 8:5–10, 13 = Luke 7:1–2,
6b–10)

There is clearly a common source behind those twin accounts since
the Greek term *pais*, or "boy," can be read to mean "child," as in John or to
mean "servant," as in the *Sayings Gospel Q*.

Those twin accounts, however, have actually pulled the story in two
contradictory directions, from one event to two divergent processes. In
John the father is not designated a Gentile and so is presumably a Jewish
official of Herod Antipas. He speaks directly to Jesus without any intermediaries. But, like the Jerusalem Jews of 2:23–25 and the Galilean Jews of
4:44–45, he is criticized in 4:48 for believing only on account of "signs and
wonders." In John's usage he is a symbol of wrong belief, of belief in miracles as wonders rather than in miracles as signs. Exactly the opposite symbolism is given by the *Sayings Gospel Q*. There, after his extraordinary
"Lord I am not worthy" speech, Jesus commends him for greater faith than
anyone in Israel. It underlines that Gospel's turn toward the Gentiles, at
least to criticize Israel's refusal to believe (Kloppenborg 1987:117–121).

First of all, then, this miracle is told, divergently, to incarnate inadequate faith and to incarnate extraordinary faith. But there is also a second
process at work, this time in terms of Jews and Gentiles. John, who is
criticizing Jewish misunderstanding of miracles, does not say the official is
a Gentile and lets us implicitly consider him a representative Galilean Jew.
In the *Sayings Gospel Q* he is explicitly a Gentile and serves to exemplify
Gentile acceptance over Jewish refusal of Jesus. But Luke moves that process even further.

The petitioner gets, in John and *Q*/Matthew, to speak directly to Jesus,
and Jesus replies to him. But in Luke 7:3–6a there is a double buffer
between them so that petitioner and Jesus never get to speak to each other
directly.

> When he heard of Jesus, he sent to him elders of the Jews, asking him to
> come and heal his slave. And when they came to Jesus, they besought
> him earnestly, saying, "He is worthy to have you do this for him, for he
> loves our nation, and he built us our synagogue." And Jesus went with
> them. When he was not far from the house, the centurion sent friends
> to him, saying to him, "Lord . . . I am not worthy . . . " (Luke 7:3–6a)

In this instance Matthew 8:5–10, 13 must be the version in the *Sayings
Gospel Q* and Luke 7:3–6a his own creative redaction (Fitzmyer
1981–85:648–649). By its insertion, on the one hand, Jesus and a Gentile
believer never come directly into contact with each other, and, on the
other, the Gentile God-fearers of the Acts of the Apostles and especially
the centurion of Acts 10:1–11:18 receive a proleptic presence. Luke, in other
words, adds on a symbolic specification in preparation for his own vision of
the Gentile mission.

One final question: 119 *Distant Boy Cured* [1/2] and 237 *Distant Girl
Cured* [2/1] are the only two miracles that Jesus performed for Gentiles and
performed at a distance. And, although this is not unique to those cases,
they are performed for a child rather than the child's parent. It is hard not
to consider those twin miracles, requested by a father for his son and a
mother for her daughter, as programmatic defenses of the later Gentile
mission, as Jesus' proleptic initiation of that process. It is quite likely, it
seems to me, that those cases are not at all a movement from event to process but actually from process to event. Early Christian communities symbolically retrojected their own activities back into the life of Jesus.

Dead Man Raised

The *Secret Gospel of Mark* is known only from quotations in a letter
from Clement of Alexandria, who lived between about 150 and 215 C.E., to
one Theodore, otherwise unknown. That letter is known only from a fragment copied, in the mid-eighteenth century, onto the three end-pages of a
seventeenth-century collection of Ignatius of Antioch's letters at the Greek
Orthodox monastery of Mar Saba, halfway between Bethlehem and the
Dead Sea. And that copy is known only from photographs taken by its dis-
coverer, Morton Smith of Columbia University, in 1958 (1973b:445–453).

The two units that Clement cites are 130 *Dead Man Raised* [1/2] and
255 *Raised Man's Family* [2/1]. The core problem is whether those units are
expansions of *Secret Mark* over canonical Mark, as Clement explained, or
whether they are contractions by canonical Mark of *Secret Mark,* as certain
contemporary scholars maintain (Koester 1983; Schenke 1984). Which, in
other words, was the first edition of Mark: *Secret Mark* or canonical Mark?

Here is the former of those two units, the one with which we are presently concerned.

> And they come into Bethany. And a certain woman whose brother had
> died was there. And, coming, she prostrated herself before Jesus and says
> to him, "Son of David, have mercy on me." But the disciples rebuked
> her. And Jesus, being angered, went off with her into the garden where
> the tomb was, and straightway a great cry was heard from the tomb. And
> going near Jesus rolled away the stone from the door of the tomb. And
> straightway, going in where the youth was, he stretched forth his hand
> and raised him, seizing his hand. But the youth, looking upon him, loved
> him and began to beseech him that he might be with him. And going
> out of the tomb they came into the house of the youth, for he was rich.
> And after six days Jesus told him what to do and in the evening the
> youth comes to him, wearing a linen cloth over his naked body. And he
> remained with him that night, for Jesus taught him the mystery of the
> kingdom of God. And thence, arising, he returned to the other side of
> the Jordan. (*Secret Gospel of Mark* 1v20–2r11a; Smith 1973b:445–453;
> Cameron 1982:70–71)

I have argued elsewhere and in some detail my own position on that unit (1985:89–121; 1988a:283–284), and I ask your indulgence to allow here only summary assertions and specifications of that interpretation. First, canonical Mark is a censored version of *Secret Mark*, so that 130 *Dead Man Raised* [1/2] was present in the first edition of Mark, the one that Clement calls *Secret Mark*. Second, it was probably used in the nude baptismal practice of his community and thereby received an erotic interpretation among some believers. The second-century Carpocratians known to Clement were not, in other words, the only or even the first early Christians with homosexual understandings of such baptisms. Proto-Carpocratians existed, as it were, within the immediate time and place of Mark's first composition. Third, and for that reason, the story was excised completely from the second edition, the one that we call canonical Mark. Fourth, I think that process happened very swiftly and that both editions may well have been done by Mark himself. Fifth, that censorship not only excised the story, it dismembered it, so that the miraculous raising devolved into Mark 16:1–8 within 275 *The Empty Tomb* [2/1] and the nocturnal initiation devolved into Mark 14:51–52 within 130 *Dead Man Raised* [1/2]. Such dismemberment indicates the censorship's strategy of making the story look like a pastiche rather than an excision from canonical Mark. Sixth, all three "versions" continued in existence, so that, at least in Alexandria around the year 200 C.E., there was a *Secret Mark*, a canonical Mark, and an erotic Mark. Seventh, and finally, *Secret Mark* must have been important in the baptismal liturgy, or the simplest solution would have been to destroy it completely.

That baptismal importance was based on two elements. Jesus, unlike John, was not a baptizer but a healer. The tradition, therefore, had no baptism-by-Jesus stories that could be used in their baptismal liturgies. But a story about a miraculous or physical raising from death could be used or created as a symbol for baptismal or spiritual raising from death. In church practice, then, the convert would hear that story and experience its reenactment during baptismal preparation in the night and nude baptism in the dawn. "The mystery of the kingdom of God" was the meaning of baptismal rebirth as a movement backward discarding the garments of shame from Genesis 3 and arising as a new creation through the waters of chaos from Genesis 1. "After six days" is not from the historical life of Jesus but the baptismal practice at Alexandria for, as Thomas Talley noted, "a peculiar aspect of the Coptic tradition is that it identifies the baptismal day, the sixth day of the sixth week, with a tradition which asserted that that was the day on which Jesus baptized his disciples" (44).

One final point. In order to put the sacred homosexuality of baptismal eroticism in perspective, a parallel from Lucian of Samosata may be helpful. You will recall from the case of Peregrinus Proteus that invective ranging from satirical to savage was Lucian's way of handling those he disliked. Here that vilification is turned on Alexander, priest of Asclepius at Abonoteichus, modern Inebolu on the mid-southern Black Sea coast. There, between 150 and 170 C.E., Alexander established an Asclepian cult focused on that god's incarnation in a human-headed snake named Glycon and emphasizing oracles rather than healings.

> Although he cautioned all to abstain from intercourse with boys on the ground that it was impious, for his own part this pattern of propriety made a clever arrangement. He commanded the cities in Pontus and Paphlagonia to send choir-boys for three years' service, to sing hymns to the god in his household; they were required to examine, select, and send the noblest, youngest, and most handsome. These he kept under ward and treated like bought slaves, sleeping with them and affronting them in every way. He made it a rule, too, not to greet anyone over eighteen years with his lips, or to embrace and kiss him; he kissed only the young, extending his hand to the others to be kissed by them. They were called "those within the kiss." (Lucian, *Alexander, the False Prophet* 41; Harmon et al. 4.227–228)

The accusation, you will note, is more against the hypocrisy of the injunction than the homosexuality of the intercourse. But even if that con-

summation is deemed rhetorical libel, the entire phenomenon has overtones of sacred homosexuality, in which the divine power could emanate
physically from Alexander to his protégés and thence to their native places
on their return home. The magical and the mystical, the physical and the
erotic merged in that initiation intimacy between master and disciple. That
is the background against which an erotic reading of the baptismal rite
must be understood. And it may have been prevalent as early as Corinth in
the early fifties C.E.; one must wonder where the line between the mystical
and the physical should be located in these words of Paul:

> For it has been reported to me by Chloe's people that there is quarreling
> among you, my brethren. What I mean is that each one of you says, "I
> belong to Paul," or "I belong to Apollos," or "I belong to Cephas," or "I
> belong to Christ." Is Christ divided? Was Paul crucified for you? Or were
> you baptized in the name of Paul? I am thankful that I baptized none of
> you except Crispus and Gaius; lest any one should say that you were
> baptized in my name. (I did baptize also the household of Stephanas.
> Beyond that, I do not know whether I baptized any one else.) For Christ
> did not send me to baptize but to preach the gospel, and not with elo-
> quent wisdom, lest the cross of Christ be emptied of its power. (1 Corin-
> thians 1:11-17)

Jesus himself was not a baptizer and, in any case, nude baptism was not
at all inherently erotic. Such baptism is, for example, at the heart of the
Gospel of Thomas, a text stressing celibate asceticism as the Christian ideal.
But it could easily—very, very easily—be interpreted along the lines of
sacred sexuality and even homosexual intimacy as initiation ritual. It was
such an interpretation that necessitated the drastic textual dismemberment of 130 *Dead Man Raised* [1/2] as Mark's Gospel went from its first or
secret to its probably quite immediate second or canonical edition.

Process led to event in *Secret Mark*. The spiritual and baptismal process
led to the creation of a physical and miraculous event. I would argue that a
similar trajectory holds for the use of this story in John 11. But now the
event is the gift of eternal life through Jesus.

> Martha said to Jesus, "Lord, if you had been here, my brother would not
> have died. And even now I know that whatever you ask from God, God
> will give you." Jesus said to her, "Your brother will rise again." Martha
> said to him, "I know that he will rise again in the resurrection at the last
> day." Jesus said to her, "I am the resurrection and the life; he who
> believes in me, though he die, yet shall he live, and whoever lives and
> believes in me shall never die. Do you believe this?" She said to him,

"Yes, Lord; I believe that you are the Christ, the Son of God, he who is coming into the world." (John 11:21–27)

It seems most probable that John is an intensely redacted version of the same story found in *Secret Mark*, although no direct relationship need be postulated. I presume that 130 *Dead Man Raised* [1/2] was simply the last in the collection of miracles used alike and independently by Mark and John. The former added the nocturnal initiation; the latter added the dialogue on eternal life. Both simply specified what was already latent in the story: Jesus raises the dead to life. Abiding spiritual process is incarnated in single physical event.

From Miracle to Table

Jesus was both an exorcist and a healer: I take 121 *Beelzebul Controversy* [1/2], 110 A *Leper Cured* [1/2], 127 *Sickness and Sin* [1/2], and 129 *Blind Man Healed* [1/2] as not only typically but actually historical. His vision of the Kingdom was but an ecstatic dream without immediate social repercussions were it not for those exorcisms and healings. Those latter were what the Kingdom looked like at the level of political reality. But none of those plurally attested miracles make any connection between Kingdom and cure. That connection must be investigated next within a framework that makes its programmatic social function very clear.

There are two plurally attested complexes to be considered from the first stratum, 1 *Mission and Message* [1/7] and 50 *Harvest Is Great* [1/3]. Lest that former's sevenfold annotation be misleading, the core of the argument, the conjunction of magic and meal, miracle and table, compassion and commensality is found in three independent sources:

When you go into any land and walk about in the districts, if they receive you, eat what they will set before you, and heal the sick among them. (*Gospel of Thomas* 14:2)

After this the Lord appointed seventy [or: seventy-two?] others, and sent them on ahead of him, two by two, into every town and place where he himself was about to come. And he said to them, "The harvest is plentiful, but the laborers are few; pray therefore the Lord of the harvest to send out laborers into his harvest. . . . Carry no purse, no bag, no sandals; and salute no one on the road. Whatever house you enter, first say, 'Peace be to this house!' And if a son of peace is there, your peace shall rest upon him; but if not, it shall return to you. And remain in the same house, eating and drinking what they provide, for the laborer deserves his wages; do not go from house to house. Whenever you enter a town

and they receive you, eat what is set before you; heal the sick in it and
say to them, 'The kingdom of God has come near to you.' But whenever
you enter a town and they do not receive you, go into its streets and say,
'Even the dust of your town that clings to our feet, we wipe off against
you; nevertheless know this, that the kingdom of God has come near.'"
(*Sayings Gospel Q,* 1Q: Luke 10:(1), 4–11 = Matthew 10:7, 10b, 12–14)

And he called to him the twelve, and began to send them out two by
two, and gave them authority over the unclean spirits. He charged them
to take nothing for their journey except a staff; no bread, no bag, no
money in their belts; but to wear sandals and not put on two tunics. And
he said to them, "Where you enter a house, stay there until you leave
the place. And if any place will not receive you and they refuse to hear
you, when you leave, shake off the dust that is on your feet for a testimony against them." So they went out and preached that men should
repent. And they cast out many demons, and anointed with oil many
that were sick and healed them. (Mark 6:7–13 = Matthew 10:1, 8–10a, 11
= Luke 9:1–6)

That first and fleeting mention in *Gospel of Thomas* 14:2 is quite significant, since that document shows no interest elsewhere in healing. The
version in the *Sayings Gospel Q* is most clearly seen in Luke 10:(1), 4–11.
The third version, in Mark 6:7–13, was copied thence into Luke 9:1–6, so
that Luke now has two versions of the "mission discourse." Matthew, on the
other hand, combined together both his Q and his Markan sources, alternating them in small units, so that Matthew 10:1, 7–14 now has a single
conflated version of the "mission discourse" (Kloppenborg 1988:72). Those
three texts are the core of the argument and the place, I propose, where
one can see the heart of the Jesus movement most clearly.

Mission

I use the term *mission* quite deliberately. We are dealing with more
than a life-style, even one with a message implied by it or attached to it. Yet,
on the other hand, we should be very careful not to read into it the full
panoply of the Pauline mission, let alone all the implications of later Christian evangelization.

Who exactly is being sent on this mission? It seems most likely that
Gospel of Thomas 14:1–3, rather than 6:2–4, was once the direct answer to
Gospel of Thomas 6:1:

(1) His disciples questioned him and said to him, (a) "Do you want
us to fast? (b) How shall we pray? (c) Shall we give alms? (d) What diet
shall we observe?"

(2) Jesus said to them, (a)"If you fast, you will give rise to sin for yourselves; (b) and if you pray, you will be condemned; (c) and if you give alms, you will do harm to your spirits. (d) When you go into any land and walk about in the districts, if they receive you, eat what they will set before you, and heal the sick among them. For what goes into your mouth will not defile you, but that which issues from your mouth — it is that which will defile you. (*Gospel of Thomas* 6:1 + 14:1–3)

If that fourfold correlation is correct, the admonition of 14:2 is addressed to "his disciples." But that does not take us very far. In its present context, of course, 14:2 does not concern mission but diet.

The *Sayings Gospel Q* is even less helpful in its present state. Q/Luke 10:1 is a Lukan composition (Kloppenborg 1988:72; Fitzmyer 1981–85:842), and Matthew 10:1 is derived from Mark 6:7. We have no idea, in other words, to whom those mission instructions were addressed in the *Sayings Gospel Q.*

In Mark 6:7, and thence directly into Matthew 10:1 = Luke 9:1 and indirectly into Luke 22:35, the missionaries are the Twelve. But that association has but a single attestation, and so, in the methodology of this book, I do not use it. Also, "there is no conclusive evidence," as Jirair Tashjian noted, "that for Q the Twelve were significant" (188), so we cannot even argue that it was once present but now dropped from the opening of that document's mission discourse.

In summary, therefore, the missionaries can only be identified in very general terms as followers or disciples of Jesus. They should not be identified as Luke's Seventy (two) or Mark's Twelve. I do not even presume one particular, special, or unique sending out of missionaries. The "mission" may well have been a more or less standard phenomenon for those who wished to participate more actively in the Jesus movement. Nor, in the confines of Lower Galilee, do we have to imagine very long journeys. "One is never," as Andrew Overman reminds us, "more than a day's walk from anywhere in lower Galilee, if that" (165). I wonder, but this is a pure guess, if what we are initially or primarily dealing with is *healed healers?* Is this what Jesus did with those whom he himself healed and who wanted to join his movement? He sent them out to do likewise? And, would a cross-cultural anthropology of thaumaturgical movements help to answer that question?

There is one small residual problem, small but maybe very, very significant. In Mark 6:7 "the twelve" are sent out "two by two," a specification not copied into either Matthew 10:1 or Luke 9:1. It also appears, however, in Luke 10:1 as "two by two," but with a slightly different Greek expression. In view of the highly redactional nature of Luke 10:1, it seems most unlikely

that the *Sayings Gospel Q* contained this element. It is safer to presume
that Luke 10:1 is simply a rephrased version of Mark 6:7. And Mark could
then be explained in terms of the two-by-two travel practice "famous in the
later rabbinical tradition" (Fitzmyer 1981–85:846) and based, presumably,
on the requirement of two witnesses according to Deuteronomy 19:15 and
Numbers 35:30. But "later" is a most important qualification, since, as
"there is no evidence for the existence of itinerant rabbis before the
destruction of the Temple" (Liefeld 119), there could not have been any
two-by-two custom of rabbinical itinerancy by the time Mark wrote, almost
immediately after 70 C.E. In any case, and whatever its origin and explanation, if Mark 6:7 is the only independent attestation for the "two by two"
phrase, by my methodology, it would have to be ignored.

What gives me pause, however, is Paul's statement in the same context
as 1 Corinthians 9:14, which is another independent attestation of this missionary theme,

> Do we not have the right to be accompanied by a wife (*adelphēn
> gynaika*), as the other apostles and the brothers of the Lord and Cephas?
> (1 Corinthians 9:5)

The English version makes the problem a simple one of support for both
the missionary and his wife, with the literal "sister wife" collapsed into the
translational "wife." But is Paul talking about real, married wives, and, if so,
how exactly are we to imagine what happened to their children in such situations? My proposal is that a "sister wife" means exactly what it says: a female
missionary who travels with a male missionary as if, for the world at large,
she were his wife. The obvious function of such a tactic would be to furnish
the best social protection for a traveling female missionary in a world of male
power and violence. Was that the original purpose and focus of the "two by
two" practice, namely, to allow for and incorporate safely the possibility of
female missionaries? I am utterly aware of how tentative that suggestion must
remain. But I am convinced that it must be made for two reasons. First, Paul's
expression "sister wife" must be given some more adequate interpretation
than "(Christian) wife." Second, if, as suggested earlier, Jesus advocated *open*
commensality, that would involve both women and men. If, then, the missionaries included women, how could that possibly have worked in the context of Galilean peasant society? I do not think they could have gone out to
houses alone, and a "sister wife" relationship might have been not only the
best but the only way to effect it. If society got wind of it, the term for such
women would be *whores*, the standard description for any women outside normal social convention or out of normal social control. Jesus, of course, would
then be consorting with "whores."

The complex in 50 *Harvest Is Great* [1/3] does not assist very much in any precise identification of the missionaries.

(1) Jesus said: "The harvest is great but the laborers are few. Beseech the Lord, therefore, to send out laborers to the harvest." (*Gospel of Thomas* 73)

(2) And he said to them, "The harvest is plentiful, but the laborers are few; pray therefore the Lord of the harvest to send out laborers into his harvest." (*Sayings Gospel Q*, 1Q: Luke 10:2 = Matthew 9:37–38)

(3) Do you not say, "There are yet four months, then comes the harvest"? I tell you, lift up your eyes, and see how the fields are already white for harvest. (John 4:35)

Although that third version may not be the same unit of tradition, the agreement between the former two sources is quite striking. I see no reason why it could not refer to the same mission situation as does 1 *Mission and Message* [1/7], and I have no presumption that such a missionary situation happened only once in the life of Jesus. It seems much more likely that what lies behind both those complexes is a standard procedure in the early Jesus movement.

In any case, I understand the success both of Jesus and his missionaries against the background of what Arthur Kleinman and Lilias Sung call "the cross-cultural investigation of indigenous healing" in medical anthropology (7). They distinguish, as did Murdock above, between "*disease* [as] any primary malfunctioning in biological and psychological processes . . . and . . . *illness* [as] the secondary psychosocial and cultural responses to disease, e.g. how the patient, his family, and social network react to his disease. Ideally, clinical care should treat both disease and illness. Up until several decades ago, when their ability to control sickness began to increase dramatically, physicians were interested in treating both disease and illness. At present, however, modern professional health care tends to treat disease but not illness; whereas, in general, indigenous systems of healing tend to treat illness, but not disease" (8). In other words, for disease you are better off with the doctor and the dispensary, but for illness you are better off with the shaman and the shrine. Their argument is based on a contemporary study of about twenty-five shamans in urban and rural Taiwan and on about five hundred patients treated by them, including both initial and follow-up studies. "Based upon the material we have presented, we draw the perhaps startling conclusion that in most cases indigenous practitioners must heal" because they "primarily treat three types of disorders: (1) acute, self-limited (naturally remitting) diseases; (2) non–life threatening, chronic diseases in which management of the illness is a larger component of clinical management than biomedical treatment of the disease; and (3) secondary somatic manifestation (somatization) of minor psychological disorders and interpersonal problems. The treatment of disease plays a small role in the care of these disorders. . . . The equally startling corollary of this argument is that in most cases modern professional clinical care *must* fail to heal" because "the physician is trained to systematically ignore illness. This represents a profound distortion of clinical work which is built into the training of physicians. It pays off on the application of biomedical technology to the control of disease, a less common but crucial clinical function, while it founders on the psychosocial and cultural treatment of illness, which is a much more common clinical function" (24). There is, of course, the obvious danger that, in a disease like cancer, the shaman may so replace or postpone the doctor that the patient dies. But, on the other hand, when the doctor abandons the patient to terminal cancer, it is again the shaman who takes over the process.

It may even be advisable, as suggested in a recent survey of medical anthropology by Allan Young, to enlarge that double distinction between *disease* and *illness* to a triple one among *disease*, for "organic pathologies and abnormalities," *illness*, for "how disease and sickness are brought into the individual consciousness," and *sickness*, for "the process through which worrisome behavioral and biological signs, particularly ones originating in disease, are given socially recognizable meanings" (270). Illness personalizes disease, and sickness socializes them both. Young does not suggest a term for that total and triadic process, but it might well be *unhealth*. The presumption is that *unhealth*, as Peter Worsley wrote in another recent survey, takes place "not within a biomechanistic framework which separates nature from the supernatural, the social world from the world of Nature, and the physical individual from his or her social matrix, but which precisely postulates an interdependence of all four: Nature, supernature, society, and person" (1982:317). That is the still observable situation in most of the modern world, and where it is not, as in high-technology Western medicine, it may well represent a very serious liability and limitation for *health* care. In any case, it is against that contemporary background in medical anthropology and its understanding of the personal, familial, local, and psychosocial nature of unhealth that I understand the success of the earliest Jesus movement's healing activity. Then, as now, of course, the healed greatly expanded both the actuality and capacity of their healers' power. But enthusiasm and exaggeration, publicity and propaganda, do not, either then or now, destroy the basis of success on which it rests.

Dress

The general background for the dress and equipment codes is the countercultural Cynic life-style seen in chapter 4. Parallel texts have also been assembled for those "other radical preachers in first-century tradition" by F. Gerald Downing (1988:47–48) and for the wider "ethos and ethics of an itinerant intelligence" by Leif Vaage (1987:314–326). I presume both those immensely helpful studies in all that follows.

Gospel of Thomas 14:2 has nothing about any dress or equipment code. Q/Luke 10:4 has four prohibitions: purse, bag, sandals, greeting. Mark 6:8–9 has four prohibitions: bread, bag, money, two tunics; and two permissions: staff, sandals. Matthew conflating and Luke duplicating those twin sources end up alike with five prohibitions and no permissions. Matthew 10:9–10 forbids money, bag, two tunics, sandals, staff. He skips Mark's no-bread because it is, presumably, included in no-bag. Luke 9:3 forbids staff, bag, bread, money, two tunics. He skips Mark's positive sandals to avoid a contradiction with Q's negative sandals. Both of them, in other words, are but different attempts to handle the contradictions between the all-negatives of the *Sayings Gospel Q* and the some-positives of Mark. I take it for granted, by the way, that the move here is from negative and radical to positive and normal. I find it most unlikely that anyone would bother to permit a staff and sandals unless, previously, somebody else had forbidden them. Finally *Didache* 11:6 allows bread but forbids money for the road: "And when an Apostle goes forth let him accept nothing but bread till he reach his night's lodging; but if he ask for money, he is a false prophet"

In summary, then, there are seven items mentioned in the above texts: money/purse, sandals, bag, bread, staff, two tunics, greeting. There is a tendency to mitigate some of those negatives into positives, for example, on the sandals as you move from the *Sayings Gospel Q* to Mark or on bread as you move from Mark to the *Didache*. But, more importantly, the last three of those seven items appear only in a single source: the staff and two tunics are from Mark, the greeting from Q/Luke. I focus therefore on the first four items, which appear in more than two independent sources: money/purse, sandals, bag, bread. And immediately one notices a very striking anomaly precisely against the general background of Greco-Roman Cynicism.

One finds, for money/purse and sandals, that, as Leif Vaage's parallels prove, "the abnegation of money belongs to the primary characterization of the way of life of the Cynic in terms of poverty" and "to go barefoot was a constitutive feature of their way of life" (1987:318, 321). Yet the situation with bag and bread is exactly the opposite. I presume, by the way, that no bag implicitly means no bread, that is, no food for the journey. And that is the heart of the problem, because, again from Leif Vaage, the purse or *pēra* was "typical of the Cynic . . . was supposed to indicate their self-sufficiency. Signaled thereby was their abnegation of the conventional forms of social security" (1987:319–320). They carried their world at their waist and needed no more. It was, like the staff, a highly important symbol of their counter-cultural life-style. Yet the *Sayings Gospel Q* and Mark indicate that such a bag was forbidden in the common dress and equipment code known to them both. I propose that its prohibition goes back to Jesus and that it must be explained in terms of the functional symbolism of the social movement he was establishing.

Place

Notice, in those three key texts cited above, how the exact place to which the messengers go changes from one text to the other or even within the same text itself.

Gospel of Thomas 14:2 is somewhat anomalous. It mentions "any land" but then specifies, with a Greek loanword *chōra,* the rural "districts," that is, the countryside rather than the city. Mark specifically mentions a "house" in 6:10 and then a "place" in 6:11 as he establishes an antithesis of reception or nonreception, but, in context, one presumes that he is speaking on the same geographical level. But Q/Luke has a double and parallel antithesis of reception or nonreception, first for a "house" in 10:5–7 and then for a "town," actually a city or *polis,* in 10:8–11. I once considered those to be sep-arate strands of tradition (Crossan 1986:53–54) but would now consider them as reflecting a historical growth from house-mission to city-mission. Notice three small details. First, even when they "enter a town/city" in Q/Luke 10:8, they are to "eat what is set before you," an activity surely presuming a house situation. Second, as Matthew conflates the *Sayings Gospel Q* and Mark, he recognizes that disjunction and says, in 10:11–12a, "whatever town/city or village you enter, find out who is worthy in it, and stay with him until you depart. As you enter the house, salute it." And again later, in 10:14, "shake off the dust from your feet as you leave that house or town/city." Three, Luke, following Mark but also preparing for the Q source in his next chapter, speaks of entering a "house" in 9:4 but leaving a "town" or city in 9:5. In other words, while Mark speaks only of a house-mission, a house-mission has been developed into a city-mission, and both stages reside now side by side in Luke 10:5–7 and 10:8–11. Need it be said that wiping the dust off one's bare feet is somewhat more effective before the door of a refusing house than at the gate of a refusing city?

There is an antithetical balance of positive and negative, of reception and rejection, in all three sources. It is but implicit in the "if" of *Gospel of*

Thomas 14:2, it is explicit for the house in Mark, and it is explicit for both house and city in the *Sayings Gospel Q*:

(1) Reception:	Mark 6:10	Q/Luke 10:5, 6a, 7	Q/Luke 10:8–9
(2) Rejection:	Mark 6:11	Q/Luke 10:6b	Q/Luke 10:10–11

I understand those differences as a systematic expansion of the original place from house to town (literally: city) to land: "whatever house/city/land you enter, eat what you get." And the expansion is in that precise direction, because one receives a meal from a house not from a town, let alone a land or presumably rural district. That process may have already begun with Mark's house/place, although that latter term is not absolutely sure textually. I conclude, therefore, that the one feature common to the *Sayings Gospel Q* and Mark, namely, house, is most original. Jesus sent those messengers on a mission to houses, not to towns, or cities, or lands.

That precise location is of significance when you compare it, for instance, with the standard strategies of what Walter Liefeld termed "the wandering preacher as a social figure in the Roman Empire." He mentions three "basic methods . . . preaching in the open air . . . lecturing indoors . . . conversing with individuals" and cites this text as illustration (183–184):

> Some among that company [of philosophers] do not appear in public at all and prefer not to make the venture, possibly because they despair of being able to improve the masses; others exercise their voices in what we call lecture-halls, having secured as hearers men who are in league with them and tractable. And as for the Cynics, as they are called . . . these Cynics, posting themselves at street-corners, in alleyways, and at temple-gates, pass round the hat and play on the credulity of lads and sailors and crowds of that sort, stringing together rough jokes and much tittle-tattle and that low badinage that smacks of the market place. (Dio Chrysostom, *Discourses* 32:8–9; Cohoon & Crosby 3.178–181)

But it is the town or city that is presumed behind such options. Popular philosophers and preachers had, especially and perforce, to head for the city and its marketplace or the festival and its crowd. As you can see from that text and as Liefeld notes, "the Cynics avoided rural areas, preferring the greater audiences (and probably support) found in larger cities" (213).

Jesus, however, is establishing a rural rather than an urban mission. Call it, if you will, Jewish and rural Cynicism rather than Greco-Roman and urban Cynicism. And its destination also explains why there is no bag. It is deliberately made not self-sufficient but, rather, dependent in a very particular fashion on commensality with those it would heal.

Commensality

We are still dealing with those initial three texts. And what is important now is the insistence, in all three sources, that we are not just dealing with almsgiving but with a shared table, with commensality. The missionaries do not carry a bag because they do not beg for alms or food or clothing or anything else. They share a miracle and a Kingdom, and they receive in return a table and a house. Here, I think, is the heart of the original Jesus movement, a shared egalitarianism of spiritual and material resources. I emphasize this as strongly as possible, and I insist that its materiality and spirituality, its facticity and symbolism cannot be separated. The mission we are talking about is not, like Paul's, a dramatic thrust along major trade routes to urban centers hundreds of miles apart. Yet it concerns the longest journey in the Greco-Roman world, maybe in any world, the step across the threshold of a peasant stranger's home.

Shared home and common meal must be understood against the cross-cultural anthropology of food and commensality. In the words of Gillian Feeley-Harnik, "it is owing precisely to the complex interrelationship of cultural categories that food is commonly one of the principal ways in which differences among social groups are marked" (10). And Lee Edward Klosinski, having "reviewed the significant anthropological and sociological literature which . . . discussed food and eating" concluded that "sharing food is a transaction which involves a series of mutual obligations and which initiates an interconnected complex of mutuality and reciprocity. Also, the ability of food to symbolize these relationships, as well as to define group boundaries, surfaced as one of its unique properties. . . . Food exchanges are basic to human interaction. Implicit in them is a series of obligations to give, receive and repay. These transactions involve individuals in matrices of social reciprocity, mutuality and obligation. Also, food exchanges are able to act as symbols of human interaction. Eating is a behavior which symbolizes feelings and relationships, mediates social status and power, and expresses the boundaries of group identity" (56–57, 58). I cannot emphasize this too strongly: commensality is not almsgiving; almsgiving is not commensality. Generous almsgiving may even be conscience's last great refuge against the terror of open commensality.

But just as radical equipment codes ceded eventually to more liberal ones, and just as houses ceded eventually to cities, so also did commensality give way to support. This is a crucial point because while commensality implies support, support does not imply commensality.

Jesus' injunction to commensality was already glossed in the *Sayings Gospel Q* with the presumably proverbial saying, "the laborer deserves his food" in Matthew 10:10b, or "the laborer deserves his wages" in Luke 10:7b. I am inclined, rather tentatively, to presume that "food" was the word in the *Sayings Gospel Q* for reasons to be seen below.

Another, and very interesting move, is that of Paul in 1 Corinthians 9:1–18. There was, as Ronald Hock has shown, a debate among Greco-Roman popular philosophers on whether charging, begging, or working was the proper way for a teacher to live. Paul himself, like certain Cynics, and despite or against the common contempt for work in the Greco-Roman world, refused to live off the communities he was actually converting. "In fact," concludes Hock, "it might be said that what was only a Cynic ideal was realized in Paul's working and preaching" (1974:165). That is the point of 1 Cor 9:1–18. Paul refuses to accept, in 9:4, "the right to our food and drink" enjoyed by the other apostles despite the fact that, as he says in 9:14, "the Lord commanded that those who proclaim the gospel should get their living by the gospel." I presume that he refers to that interpretative proverb, "the laborer deserves his food," cited as Jesus' position. But Jesus enjoined commensality, not alms, wages, charges, or fees, and Paul, in refusing those latter interpretative options, was arguing with the Jesus *tradition* and not with Jesus himself. The logic of Jesus' original mission moved not toward charity but toward commensality. And that was a vision of egalitarian community that Paul would have understood quite well.

A different and much more complex move occurs in *Didache* 11–13, and it represents that community's eventual preference for residency over itinerancy, and for local bishops and deacons over wandering apostles, prophets, and teachers. Stephen Patterson's doctoral dissertation has traced that community's progress through a stratigraphic analysis of those three chapters (249–259). The first and oldest stratum is in *Didache* 11:4–12 concerning itinerant apostles and prophets. It presumes hospitality and commensality but for two days at the very most. Apostles, as we saw before, are to receive hospitality for an absolute maximum of two days in 11:3 and to take nothing but bread for their onward journey in 11:6. Next, that older stratum is now embedded in 11:1–12:2a, which includes the problem of wandering teachers in 11:1–2 and notes, in absorbing 11:4–12, that, "concerning the Apostles and Prophets act thus according to the ordinance of the Gospel." A third stage is reached as 11:1–12:2a is expanded into 12:2b–13:7, where the problem is refugees (from Roman Palestine?), ordinary workers as well as prophets and teachers, who wish to *settle* in the community.

But every true prophet who wishes to settle among you is worthy of his food. Likewise a true teacher is himself worthy, like the workman, of his food. Therefore thou shalt take the firstfruit of . . . winepress . . . threshing-floor . . . oxen and sheep . . . bread . . . wine or oil . . . money . . . clothes . . . all your possessions . . . and give according to the commandment. (*Didache* 13:1–7)

Whatever the social realities behind those rapturous injunctions, it is resident and not itinerant prophets and teachers who are to benefit from them. Maybe that change from the suspicious reception of *Didache* 11 to the rapturous reception of *Didache* 13 is explained by the community's greater stability, stemming now, as Patterson suggests, from a resident and local authority structure (258):

Appoint therefore for yourselves bishops and deacons worthy of the Lord, meek men, and not lovers of money, and truthful and approved, for they also minister to you the ministry of the prophets and teachers. Therefore do not despise them, for they are your honourable men together with the prophets and teachers. (*Didache* 15:1–2)

Residency has succeeded itinerancy, bishops and deacons have succeeded prophets and teachers, and it is some time now since, in Patterson's deft formulation, "with the knock of the wandering radical, the old world has already passed away, and the Kingdom has arrived" (11).

Finally, there is the case in 1 Timothy 5:18b, which cites the proverb as Scripture but applies it to the elders of the community:

Let the elders who rule well be considered worthy of double honor, especially those who labor in preaching and teaching; for the scripture says, "You shall not muzzle an ox when it is treading out the grain," and, "The laborer deserves his wages." (1 Timothy 5:17–18)

But, once again, no matter how perfectly valid and even necessary such decrees may have been, commensality is a much more specific phenomenon than support.

We have, then, it would seem, three stages in this movement from commensality to salary:

Commensality: (1) *Gos. Thom.* 14:2; (2) *Q*/Luke 10:7; (3) Mark 6:10.

Food (proverb): (1) 1 Cor. 9:4; (2) *Q?*/Matt. 10:10b; (3) *Did.* 13:1; (4) *Dial. Sav.* 53b.

Wages (proverb): (1) *Q?*/Luke 10:7b; (2) 1 Tim. 5:18b.

The Coptic *Dialogue of the Savior* 53b has the Greek loanword *trophē* for "food" (Emmel et al. 78), and it is those three mentions of food in that second series rather than the single one in the third that persuades me to read the *Sayings Gospel Q* as "food" not "wages." Nevertheless, even though the food version of the proverb was far closer to commensality than was the wages version, it facilitated the eventual move from commensality to salary, a move made final, however, only in Luke and 1 Timothy.

For Jesus, however, commensality was not just a strategy for supporting the mission. That could have been done by alms, wages, charges, or fees of some sort. It could have been done, for instance, by simple begging in good Cynic fashion. Commensality was, rather, a strategy for building or rebuilding peasant community on radically different principles from those of honor and shame, patronage and clientage. It was based on an egalitarian sharing of spiritual and material power at the most grass-roots level. For that reason, dress and equipment appearance was just as important as house and table response.

Healing

All three of the core texts agree on the mission's healing function and even use the same verb. The Coptic *Gospel of Thomas* 14:2 uses the Greek loanword *therapeuō* for "heal the sick," and that is the same verb used in *Q*/Luke 10:9, "heal the sick." The account in Mark 6:7b mentions "authority over the unclean spirits," and 6:13 records that "they cast out many demons, and anointed with oil many that were sick and healed them." Even though Mark has heavily redacted those verses and changed the healing account from second-person injunction to third-person description, the verb "heal" still appears even in his revision. As with the healing medium of spittle in Mark 8:22–26, the healing medium of oil in Mark 6:13 is omitted by both Matthew 10:1 and Luke 9:1,6.

Healing is not at all in the forefront of the other texts within 1 *Mission and Message* [1/7] complex. Paul speaks not of healing but of preaching the gospel in 1 Corinthians 9:12, 14, 16, 18; *Didache* 13 is primarily interested in resident prophecy; and 1 Timothy 5:18 is concerned mostly with elders who preach and teach. Such changes are probably inevitable since, as Bryan Wilson has argued from his sevenfold typology of religious resistance to imperial aggression, "thaumaturgical movements, focusing so intensely on the state of individual grace and wholesomeness, find organization, direction, and permanence difficult to achieve" (91). It is much more difficult for them to establish "stable sect organization of the type found in conversionist, revolutionist, and introversionist movements" (100). But that combination of magic and meal, miracle and table, with its egalitarian commonality of spiritual powers and material possessions laid at least a foundation on which the future could build.

Kingdom

All three of the basic texts agreed on the dyad of magic and meal, healing and eating, compassion and commensality, spiritual and material egalitarianism. The triad of meal, miracle, Kingdom is not at all that secure. The Kingdom is not mentioned in *Gospel of Thomas* 14:2. It is explicitly present in the *Sayings Gospel Q*, where the same Greek verb *ēggiken* is translated somewhat differently as "the kingdom of God has come near" in Luke 10:9 and "the kingdom of heaven is at hand" in Matthew 10:7. Mark 6:12 has only that "they went out and preached that men should repent." I think, however, that Mark 6:12 must be read in the light of Jesus' inaugural message according to the summary of Mark 1:14–15, "Now after John was arrested, Jesus came into Galilee, preaching the gospel of God, and saying, 'The time is fulfilled, and the kingdom of God is at hand (*ēggiken*); repent, and believe in the gospel.'" That formulation is, as Matthew 4:17's reformulation and Luke's omission indicate, a distinctively Markan statement. Its emphatically Markan theology presumes, as Werner Kelber has shown so well, that the Kingdom is here and now present but in a mode of hiddenness and humility that demands repentance before acceptance is even possible (7–11). So, for Mark, with 1:14–15 read in conjunction with 6:12, the message is the gospel of the Kingdom's hidden presence, and the response is repentance and faith. I propose, therefore, that preaching the Kingdom's presence was in Mark's source for 6:6b–13 but that, having used it as a programmatic summary in 1:14–15, he used a more laconic mini-summary in 6:12. There are two other small details that support such a proposal. The exact same phrase "the kingdom of God is at hand/near (*ēggiken*)" appears in both Mark 1:15a and Q/Luke 10:9(11b) = Matthew 10:7. Furthermore, as Luke 9:2, 6 copies Mark 6:12, he rephrases it as "to preach the kingdom of God" and "preaching the gospel."

One final point. That Greek verb *eggiken* is in the perfect, a tense that in Greek may "be expected to refer to an event which happened in the past but continues to be of relevance for the present" (Kelber 11). Insofar as that perfect verb, common to the *Sayings Gospel Q* and Mark, reflects the message of Jesus, it states that the Kingdom is at hand or near in the sense not of promise but of presence and that its power is made visible in the commonality of shared miracle and shared meal.

Itinerancy

Ever since the ground-breaking studies of Gerd Theissen in the early seventies, the itinerant radicalism of Jesus and of the original Jesus movement has been a major topic of discussion and controversy. What exactly does it mean, and how does it stand with what has just been seen in those preceding units?

Itinerant radicalism means that one's itinerancy or even vagrancy is a programmatic part of one's radical message. Granted, of course, that dress and message could cohere in their radicality, how exactly did itinerancy become radical? If nobody else traveled from place to place, then travel itself would be radical. But, as we have seen earlier from Walter Liefeld's doctoral dissertation, "the wandering preacher" was "a social figure in the Roman Empire." Is itinerancy, therefore, a simple functional necessity of mission, or does it actually have a radical sociosymbolic meaning? If you respond that itinerancy or vagrancy sends a message of no fixed abode, of being atopic wanderers within an alien world, I reply that such a message is far better sent by staying in one place where everybody knows who you are and living, for example, in a barrel.

My proposal is that the itinerancy of Jesus' movement is radical because it is a symbolic representation of unbrokered egalitarianism. Neither Jesus nor his followers are supposed to settle down in one place and establish there a brokered presence. And, as healers, we would expect them to stay in one place, to establish around them a group of followers, and to have people come to them. Instead, they go out to people and have, as it were, to start anew each morning.

Let me cheat a little and exemplify from something that I use only as a general example, similar to my earlier cheating use of 228 *The Gerasene Demoniac* [2/1]. Only Mark 1:16–38 has the sequence of an inaugural day in Capernaum. Methodologically, therefore, I cannot use it, and, historically, I doubt very much it actually was a day in the life of the historical Jesus. I cite it only to exemplify my point about itinerant radicalism as unbrokered egalitarianism. Jesus calls Peter and others in 1:16–20 and then impresses those in the synagogue with his authority in 1:21–28. Next he enters the house of Peter and heals his mother-in-law in 1:29–31. Finally, the whole city and all its sick are gathered together at Peter's door once the Sabbath has ended. Any Mediterranean person would recognize what should happen or is already happening. Peter's house is becoming a brokerage place for Jesus' healing, and Peter will broker between Jesus and those seeking help. What happens?

> And in the morning, a great while before day, he rose and went out to a lonely place, and there he prayed. And Simon and those who were with him pursued him, and they found him and said to him, "Every one is searching for you." And he said to them, "Let us go on to the next

towns, that I may preach there also; for that is why I came out."
(Mark 1:35–38)

Luke 4:43 spoils that last sentence by rephrasing it as "for I was sent for this purpose." But Peter, if Mark had granted him a reply, would have said that it makes much more sense to stay right here at Capernaum, let the word go forth along the peasant grapevine, and await the crowds that would come to his door. It would also make much more sense in the psychosociology of healing and the anthropology of magic. It was, after all, what John the Baptist had done. But all Jesus says is that he "came out" from Peter's house. That entire day is a Markan creation opposing Jesus to Peter and showing their, from Mark's point of view, incompatible visions of mission. I take from it only its opposition of itinerancy and brokerage and its usefulness for seeing what is radical about *itinerant* radicalism. In the light of the preceding sections on the mission, such itinerancy is radical in its conjunction with healing, magic, and miracle working. The egalitarian sharing of spiritual and material gifts, of miracle and table, must be atopic else it will inevitably become another hierarchical operation.

I conclude with two legitimate complexes that I read as statements of unbrokered egalitarianism coming from the historical Jesus and not just from Mark's dislike of Peter. First, there is the well-attested complex 22 *Prophet's Own Country* [1/4]. What exactly is the tension between Jesus, hometown Nazareth, and his family, especially his brothers? The obvious answer is that they did not believe in him and that Jesus responded by repudiating them and the patriarchal family in general. The equally obvious objection is that, very soon after Jesus' death, his family, especially James, had considerable authority in the early church. How did James, for example, move so swiftly from disbelief to leadership? My suggestion is that the tension is not about belief but about brokerage. If Jesus was a well-known magician, healer, or miracle worker, first, his immediate family, and, next, his village, would expect to benefit from and partake in the handling of that fame and those gifts. Any Mediterranean peasant would expect an expanding ripple of patronage-clientage to go out from Jesus, through his family and his village, to the outside world. But what Jesus did, in turning his back on Nazareth and on his family, was repudiate such brokerage, and that, rather than belief or disbelief, was the heart of the problem. The complex 22 *Prophet's Own Country* [1/4] is simply Jesus' own experience of what we already heard aphoristically in 74 *Peace or Sword* [1/2].

This antibrokerage activity is confirmed, finally, by the very well attested complex 10 *Receiving the Sender* [1/5]. It was difficult, in discussing the mission of Jesus' followers in the last chapter, not to read back into it all the developmental complexities of the later urban mission to the Gentiles. The same happens with this complex. It could be seen, first of all, as presuming a very advanced theology of Jesus' heavenly preexistence prior to his being "sent" to earth. But, "sent" need not have any such connotation. Recall, for example, the self-referential statement of Epictetus cited earlier: "See, God has sent you a man to show you that it [voluntary poverty] is possible." Second, the complex could be seen as establishing a clear missionaries-Jesus and Jesus-God hierarchy. Far from establishing a hierarchy of mission, however, the texts actually negate any such patronal mediators or brokered mediations. But that is only clear when the full dyadic structure is preserved: missionaries are to Jesus as Jesus is to God. It is always the Sender who is received. That emphasis on God rather than the missionary is undermined when only one half of the saying is preserved. And of the ten texts from five sources making up this complex, only half preserve that double structure. The sequence of, by whatever name, missionary/Jesus//Jesus/God appears in Luke 10:16 = Matthew 10:40 from the *Sayings Gospel Q*, in Mark 9:36-37 and thence into Luke 9:47-48a but not Matthew 18:2, 5, and in John 13:20. But missionary/Jesus alone is in *Didache* 11:4-5 and Ignatius' *Letter to the Ephesians* 6:1 and Jesus/God alone is in John 5:23b and 12:44b. There is one other feature that underlines that same delicate change across the transmission. Both Mark 9:37, with "whoever receives me, receives not me but him who sent me," and John 12:44b, with "believes not in me but in him who sent me," have an emphatic negation in the Jesus/God half of the double saying. Yet neither Matthew 18:5 nor Luke 9:48 accept that negation in copying Mark's text. And, of course, neither John 5:23b nor 13:20 have any negation parallel to that in John 12:44b. It was, presumably, a little too strong. I propose, in summary, that the double saying, possibly even with a double emphatic negation ("not you but me, not me but God"), stems from the historical Jesus and was intended to keep the emphasis on God and not on either the missionary or on Jesus himself. Thereafter, of course, it could easily be read in quite different ways, especially when the dyadic structure was broken. On the other hand, 61 *Disciple and Servant* [1/3] probably comes from a later stage of the tradition when disciples needed to be told not that they were equal to Jesus before God but that they were not above Jesus and should handle their status as he had done before them.

The Message of an Open Secret

Although I deliberately used the term *mission* (and *missionaries*) in the previous section, I take that term in a very wide sense to include both the way Jesus lived and acted and the way his followers did as well. I presume, in other words, that dress and itinerancy, miracle and table, healing and commensality, characterized Jesus just as much as his missionaries and that they characterized them not just once but all the time. "Mission" is thus much more than a single one-time sending of some set group. In this final section, then, I look at sets of complexes that speak alike to the situation of Jesus and of his followers, that speak, in other words, of the movement as such. I emphasize, once more, that the historical Jesus had both an ideal vision and a social program.

The first set of complexes focuses on the openness of that message. The enigmatic injunction 9 *Who Has Ears* [1/5] should be interpreted in the simplest possibly way. It means, on the lips of the historical Jesus, "You have ears, use them; what I say is as clear and obvious as I can make it; all you have to do is listen. It is not cryptic, hidden, mysterious; it is obvious, maybe that is its problem, it is too obvious. Listen!" A similar point is made in 53 *Knowing the Times* [1/3?] but shifting there from ear to eye. What Jesus shows them is as open to anyone as the sky's indications of impending weather; Jesus' message is just as obvious. That image's appeal to common nature rather than special Scripture goes back to Jesus, although the present emphases on the messenger rather than the message in *Gospel of Thomas* 91:2 and on the inimical situation in Matthew 16:2–3 are their own developments.

Four other complexes reflect this same theme but moving the emphasis, possibly, from Jesus to follower, maybe even to missionaries as healed healers. The complex 21 *The World's Light* [1/4] shifts now within its sources from the missionaries to Jesus as the light of the world. I read its original and almost ecstatic overstatement as coming from Jesus and as concerning them rather than himself. The complex 36 *Lamp and Bushel* [1/3] makes the same case but with a more limited and less rhapsodic metaphor. The complexes 78 *The Mountain City* [1/2] and 79 *Open Proclamation* [1/2] speak the same vision. The missionaries have a message that is neither private nor clandestine, neither hidden nor occult, neither secret nor mysterious.

Five other complexes are less likely to come from the historical Jesus, although they actually extend that general theme against the background of early sapiential development. The complex 66 *Wise and Understanding* [1/2] is already defining such absolute access to God over against others who do not have it. The complexes 45 *Father and Son* [1/3] and 52 *Yoke and Burden* [1/3] shift the emphasis to Jesus himself. The complex 67 *Hidden Since Eternity* [1/2] emphasizes the present revelation of something hidden since creation. The complex 14 *Eye, Ear, Mind* [1/4] is especially interesting since its multiple attestation requires careful explanation, but, as William Stroker has shown, it "was originally a Jewish tradition . . . attributed to Jesus in several different circles and at different times" (1970: 278–279). Indeed, Helmut Koester has argued persuasively that all five of those complexes stem from "a lost sapiential writing which the Corinthians knew and used in the context of their wisdom theology," that it was written "under the authority of an Old Testament figure," and that, finally, "material from this sapiential book—once it had been used by gnosticizing Christians in the time of Paul—was incorporated into the tradition of sayings of Jesus" (1980b:249–250). Jesus' serene assertion of open and unmediated access to God has been developed and interpreted as a secret and eternally hidden wisdom now revealed to the simple and the humble. The same, I presume, has happened in 92 Knowing the Mystery [1/2].

Similar to that preceding quintet is the case of 32 Hidden Made Manifest [1/3], which underlines very well the ambiguities of those preceding cases. It could be read apocalyptically, as in Mark 4:22, to indicate that what is hidden now will be made manifest at an imminent future consummation. It could also be read sapientially, as in Gospel of Thomas 5:2 and 6:4, to indicate that what has been hidden since creation is revealed at the present time. It could also be taken commonsensically, as with Jesus and maybe even in Q/Luke 12:2, to indicate that his message is of something that should be open and obvious to all. I take it in that last understanding as coming from the historical Jesus.

A second set of complexes emphasizes the clash between the message of the inaugural Jesus movement and its alternatives. This clash is found, of course, throughout all the layers of the Jesus tradition, but it is presented here in very general or metaphorical images. The twin complexes about 87 Drinking Old Wine [1/2] and 88 Patches and Wineskins [1/2], for example, speak of the clash between old and new but are far less specific than the ones that criticize the patriarchal family or the powerfully rich. They were thus susceptible to very precise applications as their transmission progressed. But originally they used obvious, everyday, and even commonsensical images to underline the radical alternatives proposed by Jesus.

The same theme of clash and choice, challenge and response appears in the three parables of 71 The Fishnet [1/2], 75 The Harvest Time [1/2], and 107 The Lost Sheep [1/2]. The first image is, in Gospel of Thomas 8:1, a fairly obvious example of making the right choice. In Matthew 13:47–50 it is a full-blown allegory of Matthean Christianity and its eschatological consummation. The second image is now equally but divergently interpreted by its contextual frames in Gospel of Thomas 21:4 and Mark 4:26–29. Nothing could illustrate more clearly the problem of deciding original materials even within the first stratum. Jesus could use a more or less proverbial or parabolic image that is radical only in its application, namely, that his vision, his message, or his challenge is as obvious, ordinary, or necessary as this or that action. It is as clear as a fisherman choosing the better fish or a harvester choosing the right moment to begin reaping. But the transmission could just as easily interpret common sense as sapiential mystery hidden from the dawn of creation or eschatological secret to be revealed at the imminent eschaton. Jesus, like the Cynics, would claim that their life was simply the wisdom of common sense open to all with eyes to see and ears to hear. So also with 107 *The Lost Sheep* [1/2], but here the commonsensical aspect is not at all so evident. Would a shepherd actually leave ninety-nine sheep presumably unattended to go looking for a single lost one? That may well be the problem seen in *Gospel of Thomas* 107, which makes it "the largest" sheep to which the shepherd says, "I care for you more than the ninety-nine." From the historical Jesus the original parable simply inverts the obviousness of radicality into the radicality of obviousness. What if the one sheep is as important as the ninety-nine? What if one refuses to make a hierarchical decision? What if, for example, the kingdom of God is a kingdom of equality?

Finally, within this second set, there are the complexes concerning 46 *The Tenants* [1/3] and 47 *The Rejected Stone* [1/3]. I presume two developmental stages for those complexes before the earliest textual evidence. First, *The Tenants* originally told the story of a son, with absolutely no self-reference to Jesus whatsoever. Next, there was the obvious step of allegorizing the son of the parable as Jesus himself. And that development could then go in one of two directions. Either make the whole story positive as in the *Shepherd of Hermas, Similitude* 5.2:4–7, so that tenants (= servant) and son jointly inherit the vineyard. Or, if the son's death was kept as an allegory of the passion of Jesus, some reference to resurrection had to be added. That could not be done within the narrative realism of the parable itself, so *The Rejected Stone* was added in conclusion, thereby solving the allegorical application but also creating two different images, one of Jesus as Son and another of Jesus as Stone. That earlier second-stage conjunction is evidenced in our present texts by two divergent processes. In Mark 12:1–12 the twin units are already further integrated through the rhetorical question in 12:9a and the punishment answer in 12:9b. In *Gospel of Thomas* 65–66, however, an editor either accidentally or deliberately divided that prior conjunction into two quite separate units. I am concerned here only with 46 *The Tenants* [1/3], which comes from Jesus, and not with 47 *The Rejected Stone* [1/3], which, as *Barnabas* 6:4 indicates, comes from the early church. What could such a parable have meant from Jesus himself?

It is not impossible, first of all, that Jesus could have told the parable about his own fate, as a metaphorical vision of his own possible death. After the execution of John, and in the context of what he himself was doing, such a prophecy required no transcendental information. Indeed, if the idea never crossed Jesus' mind, he was being very naive indeed. I find that explanation less plausible, however, because I cannot see how its narrative logic coincides with the situation of Jesus himself. How, in terms of Jesus' own life, would the tenants *acquire the vineyard* by his murder? The story, on the other hand, is absolutely understandable as spoken to peasants who know all about absentee landlords and what they themselves have thought, wished, and maybe even planned. I am inclined, then, but somewhat tentatively, to read it as one of those places where the political situation breaks most obviously on the surface of the text. Presuming that the original parable ended with the son's death, how would a Galilean peasant audience have responded? Maybe like this. Some: they did right. Others: but they will not get away with it. Some: he got what he deserved. Others: but what will the father do now? Some: that is the way to handle landlords. Others: but what about the soldiers?

The third set of complexes proposes even more clearly than any of those preceding cases the opposition, hostility, rejection, and danger involved in accepting either the vision or the mission of Jesus. Even in the instructions for that inaugural mission in the last chapter, there was always a dual possibility: if they receive you, stay and eat in their house; if they refuse you, shake off their dust from your feet. I do not think, by the way, that such barefooted dust shaking need be read as solemn eschatological curse. "Indeed," as Leif Vaage said, "it is rather an amusing, if not hilarious, gesture when literally imagined. Perhaps, the humour was not unintended" (1987:342). Read to mean "if they refuse you, forget it," the response is like Jesus' own reaction in 55 *Caesar and God* [1/3]. When the questioners sought to trap him between refusing or advocating submission to Caesar's taxation, he simply pointed to Caesar's head on the coin they held in their hands and answered with a phrase that can be as absolutely superficial or as absolutely profound as one wishes to make it. In all of this, however, there is, as yet, no evidence of external indictments against any clearly opposing group and no evidence of internal worries about group boundaries or sectarian delineations. Such an "over against them" attitude may be already present, say, in 54 *Dogs and Swine* [1/3], and that would make it later than Jesus himself. But there is also no delusion that the entire world is but waiting for the light to dawn or is happy to hear of its advent. The image of 72 *Fire on Earth* [1/2] is hardly a neutral one. Fire-starters are not always welcome, and authorities usually like to extinguish fires. The complex 81

Strong One's House [1/2] is another such warning, but notice how it presumes difficulty rather than impossibility and danger rather than failure. The complex 38 *Serpents and Doves* [1/3] could be original against such a background, but the same can hardly be said for 62 *Spirit Under Trial* [1/3]. In that latter case the promised Spirit who will speak in their defense indicates development from casual opposition to juridical prosecution.

Finally, in this third set, there are the twin warnings of 63 *Saving One's Life* [1/3] and 44 *Carrying One's Cross* [1/3]. The warning of crisis and danger is quite explicit in that former complex, but watch, once again, the move from tradition to development.

> (1) Whoever seeks to gain his life will lose it, but whoever loses his life will preserve it. (*Sayings Gospel Q*, 1Q: Luke 17:33 = Matthew 10:39)

> (2) For whoever would save his life will lose it; and whoever loses his life *for my sake and the gospel's* will save it. (Mark 8:35 = Matthew 16:25 = Luke 9:24; my italics)

> (3) He who loves his life loses it, and he who hates his life *in this world* will keep it *for eternal life*. (John 12:25; my italics)

The italicized Markan and Johannine glosses are almost predictable development, but the original saying, as in the *Sayings Gospel Q* version, goes back to Jesus. To be rich is to be poor; to be poor is to be rich. To lose one's life is to save it; to save one's life is to lose it.

The complex 44 *Carrying One's Cross* [1/3] could be dismissed almost immediately as a retrojection of Jesus' death back onto his own prophetic lips. That would be especially persuasive if it were found only in Mark 8:34, but it is found in both *Gospel of Thomas* 55:2b and the *Sayings Gospel Q* at Luke 14:27 = Matthew 10:38, neither of which show any great interest in the historical crucifixion of Jesus. On the other hand, there is the following text:

> If you want to be crucified, just wait. The cross will come. If it seems reasonable to comply, and the circumstances are right, then it's to be carried through, and your integrity maintained. (Epictetus, *Discourses* 2.2.20; Oldfather 1.228–231)

There is, therefore, no need to take Jesus' saying as either retrojected or projected prophecy. Jesus, "was discussing," as Leif Vaage put it about Epictetus, "the (possible) consequences of following a certain philosophy . . . The cost of adopting a particular way of life is . . . graphically imagined . . . The fate portrayed . . . certainly seems a conceivable outcome of the kind of social challenge and outrageous behavior" (1989:173) seen so often throughout this chapter.

✧ *14* ✧

Death and Burial

Rest now in thy glory, noble initiator. Thy work is completed;
thy divinity is established. Fear no more to see the edifice of thy
efforts crumble through a flaw. Henceforth, beyond the reach of
frailty, thou shalt be present, from the height of thy divine
peace, in the infinite consequences of thy acts. At the price of a
few hours of suffering, which have not even touched thy great
soul, thou hast purchased the most complete immortality. For
thousands of years the world will extol thee. Banner of our
contradictions, thou wilt be the sign around which will be
fought the fiercest battles. A thousand times more living, a
thousand times more loved since thy death than during the days
of thy pilgrimage here below, thou wilt become to such a degree
the corner-stone of humanity, that to tear thy name from this
world would be to shake it to its foundations. Between thee and
God, men will no longer distinguish. Complete conqueror of
death, take possession of thy kingdom, whither, by the royal
road thou has traced, ages of adorers will follow thee.
      Ernest Renan, The Life of Jesus *(1972:368–369)*

Jonathan Smith, in a superb article on "the second century autobiography
of Thessalos, the magician," has suggested that a profound change was
already taking place in the ancient world "as early as the second century
(B.C.)." The focal points of that shift were the Temple and the Magician.
"Rather than a sacred place, the new center and chief means of access to
divinity will be a divine man, a magician, who will function, by and large, as
an entrepreneur without fixed office and will be, by and large, related to
'protean deities' of relatively unfixed form whose major characteristic is
their sudden and dramatic autophanies. . . . It is revealing that the Hebrew
Scriptures, in the two great traditions that cherish them, do not end, in
their present Late Antique redactions, with the same passage. The Jewish
collection ends with the promise of 2 Chronicles 36:23 of a rebuilt Temple
and restored cultus. The Christian collection ends with the promise to
Malachi 4:5 of the return of the *magus* Elijah—a promise fulfilled in the
figure of John the Baptist who reinterprets the archaic water-ritual of puri-

fication into a magic ritual that saves. The Temple and the Magician were one of the characteristic antinomies of Late Antique religious life; the tension between them contributed much to its extraordinary creativity and vitality" (1977:233, 238–239). But, of course, once institutionalized Temple was replaced by institutionalized Magician, that latter would have another name — rabbi, priest, or monk — and the role of magician would be once again open for alternative investment or subversive opposition.

Not only John the Baptist but, even more, Jesus, fit within that wider and profounder antinomy. John offered an alternative to the Temple but from another fixed location, from desert and Jordan rather than from Zion and Jerusalem. Jesus was, as we have seen, atopic, moving from place to place, he coming to the people rather than they to him. This is an even more radical challenge to the localized univocity of Jerusalem's Temple, and its itinerancy mirrored and symbolized the egalitarian challenge of its protagonist. No matter, therefore, what Jesus thought, said, or did about the Temple, he was its functional opponent, alternative, and substitute; his relationship with it does not depend, at its deepest level, on this or that saying, this or that action. But what I now ask is much more specific even though it presumes all of the preceding. First, is there evidence that Jesus actually said or did anything inimical to Jerusalem's Temple? Second, is there evidence that such words or deeds led to his crucifixion and death?

I Will Destroy This House

The complex 49 *Temple and Jesus* [1/3] is extremely complicated and controversial. The problems start with the first version:

> I shall [destroy this] house, and no one will be able to build it[. . .].
> (*Gospel of Thomas* 71)

There is, obviously, no mention of the Temple in that saying, but, as Stephen Patterson has recently argued, "its structural similarity to [the other texts in *Temple and Jesus*] permits the assumption that it is indeed a version of the so-called 'temple word'. . . . Whether the lack of any reference to the temple in [*Gospel of Thomas*] 71 is a secondary feature, or a primitive touch is difficult to decide. I would suspect, however, that Thomas' ending: 'and no one will be able to rebuild it' is secondary over against references to rebuilding the Temple in the various other versions. The fact that the Temple never was rebuilt would eventually prove awkward for such predictions. One way to ease off the problem would be to allegorize it, as does John, in terms of the resurrection (2:21); another way would be to ease off the prediction itself (so Thomas)" (109–110).

I agree with the first two points of that analysis but not with its third one. Despite its ambiguities, "house" is best seen as referring originally to the Temple at Jerusalem, even if the *Gospel of Thomas* may now understand it in some other way. Next, the structural balance of destroying/rebuilding is common to all three sources in the complex and must be taken very seriously. But I reverse the sequence presumed by Patterson's analysis. I take *Gospel of Thomas* 71 as the most original version we have, and it simply states emphatically: I will destroy this house so utterly that rebuilding will be impossible. The rebuilding does not, initially, reflect any spiritual substitution but is merely an emphatic way of stating utterly, completely, totally, and forever. It is not this version that has eased off the rebuilding, taken negatively, but the other versions that have developed the rebuilding, taken positively. It is most significant, therefore, that the *Gospel of Thomas*, which has no interest in the passion of Jesus, still retains this saying. But that cuts both ways. It may mean that it is very good historical Jesus tradition but also that the connection with the passion was not at all on the same level.

The problems continue with the Markan tradition, which involves not only the texts in 49 *Temple and Jesus* [1/3] but all of Mark 13 as well. I begin with that chapter itself, following its analysis by Werner Kelber (109–128). Mark insists that, while Jesus foretold the physical destruction of Jerusalem's Temple in 13:1–2, he never said he himself would do it, that is, that it would be coincident with his parousiac return. He said, according to Mark 13:24, that there would be a clear but not prolonged interval between the Temple's destruction and his own return. Mark's community was living in that interval, having rejected those false but Christian prophets who, in 13:5–8 and 21–23, had proclaimed Jesus' return at and as the destruction of the Temple in the First Roman-Jewish War of 66–70 C.E. Mark, in other words, clearly and deliberately separates all that led up to the destruction of the Temple in 13:5–23 from all that will lead up to the parousia of Jesus in 13:24–37. And all is placed on the prophetic lips of Jesus himself. That, says Mark, was what he actually said.

This polemical emphasis reappears in Mark 14:55–59 and 15:29–32a as well. Jesus is accused before the "chief priests and the whole council" of having said:

> (1) I will destroy this temple that is made with hands, and in three days I will build another, not made with hands.
> (2) I am able to destroy the temple of God, and to build it in three days. (Mark 14:58 = Matthew 26:61)

Mark insists four times in 14:55, 56, 59 that their accusation was false: "false witness against him . . . their witness did not agree . . . false witness against him . . . not even so did their testimony [witness] agree." For Mark, the destroying/rebuilding dyad means the destruction/parousia and the "three days" means "soon afterwards." Matthew changes that to a general claim of divine power, and Luke omits it completely. But as far as Mark is concerned it is absolutely and emphatically false to say that Jesus foretold any conjunction of the Temple's fall and his own return. Finally, it is only mocking unbelievers beneath the cross who say,

> Aha! You who would destroy the temple and build it in three days, save yourself, and come down from the cross! (Mark 15:29b–30 = Matthew 27:40–41)

One should not, Mark insists, believe either false witnesses or mocking enemies. But all of that intensive damage control in Mark 13–15 simply underlines the fact that certain Christian circles, first, believed Jesus had said or done something concerning his destruction of the Temple and, second, interpreted that as the conjunction of siege and parousia in 70 C.E. Where did such an idea come from?

The answer lies in Mark 11:15–19, which is often and quite incorrectly called the purification of the Temple. It is not at all a purification but rather a symbolic destruction. First of all, and in general, there was absolutely nothing wrong with any of the buying, selling, or money-changing operations conducted in the outer courts of the Temple. Nobody was stealing or defrauding or contaminating the sacred precincts. Those activities were the absolutely necessary concomitants of the fiscal basis and sacrificial purpose of the Temple. Second, Mark himself knows that Jesus was not just purifying but symbolically destroying the Temple because he carefully framed his action with the fruitless fig tree's cursing in 11:12–14 and withering in 11:20. As the useless fig tree was destroyed, so, symbolically, was the useless Temple.

> (A) And they came to Jerusalem. And he entered the temple and began to drive out those who sold and those who bought in the temple, and he overturned the tables of the money-changers and the seats of those who sold pigeons; and he would not allow any one to carry anything through the temple.
> (B) And he taught, and said to them, "Is it not written, 'My house shall be called a house of prayer for all the nations'? [= Isaiah 56:7]. But you have made it a den of robbers [= Jeremiah 7:11]." (Mark 11:15–16)

Notice, first of all, the dyad of deed and word, action and comment. That action is not, of course, a physical destruction of the Temple, but it is a deliberate symbolical attack. It "destroys" the Temple by "stopping" its fiscal, sacrificial, and liturgical operations. The comment is drawn from two Old Testament passages, and the former one twice mentions the Temple as the "house" of God. The interpretative words in Mark 11:17 may well bespeak his own interests, but the use of "house" gives one, in the light of *Gospel of Thomas* 71, at least pause. If one compares, however, the destructive *word* in *Gospel of Thomas* 71 and the destructive *deed* in Mark 11:15–16, which way did the tradition develop? Was it from word to deed or from deed to word? Did the deed generate the word as its summary or the word generate the deed as its symbol?

Even more problems arise from the account in John, but its content may also help to answer those preceding questions.

> (A) In the temple he found those who were selling oxen and sheep and pigeons, and the money-changers at their business. And making a whip of cords, he drove them all, with the sheep and oxen, out of the temple; and he poured out the coins of the money-changers and over-turned their tables. And he told those who sold the pigeons, "Take these things away;
>
> (B) you shall not make my Father's house a house of trade."
>
> *His disciples remembered* that it was written, "Zeal for thy house will consume me [= Psalm 69:9]"
>
> (C) The Jews then said to him, "What sign have you to show us for doing this?" Jesus answered them, "Destroy this temple, and in three days I will raise it up." The Jews then said, "It has taken forty-six years to build this temple, and will you raise it up in three days?" But he spoke of the temple of his body.
>
> When therefore he was raised from the dead, *his disciples remembered* that he had said this; and they believed the scripture and the word which Jesus had spoken. (John 2:14–22, my italics)

That is surely a fascinating unit. Its importance is signaled by the double "his disciples remembered" after each of its two component parts. That gloss indicates, I presume, some trouble with those twin units, some initial lack of understanding or misunderstanding that had to be explained by later comprehension.

First of all, however, is the fact that "house" appears in all three independent sources, in *Gospel of Thomas* 71 as the total focus of interest and without any action by Jesus, then in both Mark 11:17 (twice from Isaiah 56:7) and John 2:16 (twice from Jesus himself and once from Psalm 69:9). In both those latter cases it is appended as immediate explanation of the *action* of Jesus. I conclude, provisionally, that the *action* was originally— that is, at least prior to those three sources—accompanied by some saying about "house."

Second, that double "his disciples remembered" in John 2:17, 22 draws attention to the fact that his account has both an *action* accompanied by a "house" *saying* to be explained by later remembrance in 2:14–17 and, separately, another *saying* to be explained also by later remembrance in 2:18–22. And that second saying is "Destroy this temple, and in three days I will raise it up." You will notice the resemblance to Mark 14:58, "I will destroy this temple that is made with hands, and in three days I will build another, not made with hands." For Mark, of course, it is a false accusation coupling the Temple's actual destruction and Jesus' parousiac return. For John, it is not a prophecy, whether true or false, but a challenge. It is not something that Jesus will do to their Temple but something that they will do to his body.

Behind all of that development, I propose the following trajectory. The earliest recoverable stratum involved an *action* symbolically destroying the Temple, as in Mark 11:15–16 and John 2:14–16a, and a *saying* announcing what was happening, "I will destroy this house utterly beyond repair," as in *Gospel of Thomas* 71. Thereafter, the tradition tended to separate *action* and *saying* along separate lines of interpretation. That original *saying* was replaced by positive but divergent biblical references attached to and explaining the *action*. And the original but now separated *saying* itself was recast to apply either to parousia, as rejected by Mark, or to resurrection, as accepted by John, in whom both streams are present.

I conclude, therefore, that an action and equal saying involving the Temple's symbolic destruction goes back to the historical Jesus himself but that any biblical references or applications to the Temple's actual destruction, the resurrection, or the parousia are later explanations of an action considered enigmatic to begin with and rendered even more so by the Temple's actual destruction in 70 C.E.

I am quite convinced of that analysis but much less secure about whether that action/saying led directly to Jesus' arrest and execution. There is clearly no connection at all in *Gospel of Thomas* 71. There is an equally clear connection in the immediately consequent Mark 11:18, "And the chief priests and the scribes heard it and sought a way to destroy him; for they feared him, because all the multitude was astonished at his teaching." But then there is the problem of John. In Mark, as everyone knows, Jesus goes up to Jerusalem only once, at the end. In John, on the other hand, he seems to be up there almost every chapter. I think, however, that the units of the *Signs Gospel* at the base of our present John often concentrated on Jerusalem as the place of opposition and consummation, so that many units happened, as it were, "in Jerusalem." It was only when the entire unity was read as a sequential narrative composition that Galilean, or Samaritan, or Judean locations had to be correlated, so that onc is now left with an overall impression that Jesus was constantly going to and from Jerusalem. None of that, however, proves that Mark's single ascent is any less artificial and compositional.

I have, in other words, no plural attestation *linking* the Temple's symbolic destruction and Jesus' execution. I will make, however, one tentative and possibly unmethodological proposal. I am not sure that poor Galilean peasants went up and down regularly to the Temple feasts. I think it quite possible that Jesus went to Jerusalem only once and that the spiritual and economic egalitarianism he preached in Galilee exploded in indignation at the Temple as the seat and symbol of all that was nonegalitarian, patronal, and even oppressive on both the religious and the political level. His symbolic destruction simply actualized what he had already said in his teachings, effected in his healings, and realized in his mission of open commensality.

But the confined and tinder-box atmosphere of the Temple at Passover, especially under Pilate, was not the same as that in the rural reaches of Galilee, even under Antipas, and the soldiers would have moved in immediately at any disturbance. None of that can be grounded in this book's methodology, so it must be taken very carefully. Without it, however, we are reduced to even greater guesswork in answering why then, why there, why thus? In summary, therefore, I think the symbolic destruction was but the logical extension of the miracle and table conjunction, of open healing and open eating; I think that it actually happened and, *if* it happened at Passover, *could* easily have led to arrest and execution.

Do This in Memory of Me

We have already seen two cases, 120 *The Lord's Prayer* [1/2] and 13 *Two as One* [1/4], that, although they are plurally attested in the first stratum and although they summarize principles or practices, themes or emphases, of the historical Jesus, stem not from him but from the liturgical creativity of the early communities. A third case occurs now with 16 *Supper and Eucharist* [1/4]. But even to hear this case demands that you hold in abeyance two thousand years of eucharistic theology and a similar amount of Last Supper iconography. Prior to those developments, I propose five major preliminary stages. John 6:51–58 is actually a sixth stage, but that would lead the argument further afield than is necessary to show that 16 *Supper and Eucharist* [1/4] does not derive from the historical Jesus.

The first stage is the general anthropology of eating and the more specific historical customs of Greco-Roman commensality. "The chief insight gleaned from the anthropology of food," according to Lee Edward Klosinski, summing up his 1988 doctoral dissertation, "is that food has the

capacity both to serve as the object of human transactions and to symbolize human interaction, relationships and relatedness. Giving and receiving
food creates obligations. It involves the creation of matrices of reciprocity
and mutuality. It defines relationships and the contours of group boundaries.... In Greco-Roman antiquity ... commensality gave concrete expression to the boundaries of the group, facilitated social identification,
and provided a means to mediate social status and social power" (205–206).
Furthermore, according to Dennis Smith's 1980 doctoral dissertation,
"meals in the setting of a private home, a philosophical gathering, a
sacrifice, a club, or a Christian assembly did not differ in their forms so
much as they differed in the interpretations given to those forms according
to the contexts in which the meals took place" (2). Within that common
form, "the meal proper consisted of two courses, the *deipnon* and the *sym-
posion* ... [the former course] might consist of bread and various vegetables, with fish or meat if the meal was especially extravagant. There were
many grades and varieties of breads since it was the staple of the diet ...
[and for the latter course] it is clear that, at the least, a ritual libation and
removal of the tables commonly marked the transition from the eating to
the drinking part of the meal" (11–13). Such a background means that a two-
part sequence of eating and drinking, of breaking bread and then pouring
a libation before drinking wine, or more simply, of bread and wine, summarizes and symbolizes the entire process of a Greco-Roman formal meal.

The second stage is the *open* commensality, that is to say, in the light
of the preceding paragraph, the radical social egalitarianism practiced by
Jesus and his followers and expected of others to whom they brought their
free and itinerant healing. Obviously, in such a situation, Jesus and those
closest to him would have had a last supper, that is, a meal that later and in
retrospect was recognized as having been their last one together. That is all
that happened before the death of Jesus. I do not presume any distinctive
meal known beforehand, designated specifically, or ritually programmed as
final and forever. My reason for that position is a consideration of *Didache*
9–10 within the trajectory of 16 *Supper and Eucharist* [1/4].

The third stage, then, is the *Didache* or *Teaching of the Twelve Apostles*,
which is "the oldest Christian church order, written," according to Helmut
Koester," in Syria at the end of I [first century] C.E." (1982:2.158). There are
now two quite separate eucharistic celebrations given in *Didache* 9–10,
with the earlier one now put in second place (Riggs 93). That there are two
originally separate liturgies is evident from the common fourfold format of
each as well as from certain common themes and even phrases. I draw
attention to that commonality by italicizing them in my quotations. That
Didache 10 is more primitive than *Didache* 9 is clear from the titles used for

Jesus. In *Didache* 10 he is Jesus the Child (or Servant) of God, a title that goes back, according to Joachim Jeremias, to "the earliest Palestinian community" but that lived on "in the Gentile Church . . . only as a fixed liturgical formula anchored in the eucharistic prayer, the doxology and the confession" (1967: 703). In *Didache* 9 he is still Child (Servant) of God in 9:2–3, but in 9:4 he is Jesus Christ. In what follows I give both rituals but divided up into their fourfold structure and with *Didache* 10 always preceding *Didache* 9. I emphasize, however, that in neither case is there any hint of a Passover meal, of a Last Supper, or of either connection to or celebration of the death of Jesus.

The opening common element is an *introductory command*. Notice, by the way, that the translator gives exactly the same Greek verb as "hold Eucharist" in *Didache* 9:1 and "give thanks" in *Didache* 10:1.

> (1) But after you are satisfied with food, thus give thanks.
>
> (2) And concerning the Eucharist, hold Eucharist thus. (*Didache* 10:1; 9:1)

The earlier ritual is simply a thanksgiving prayer *after* a common meal. In the latter practice it is integrated within the meal's twin parts.

The second common element is a *double thanksgiving*. Notice the duality of "we give thanks . . . to thee be glory for ever." I have italicized those phrases and other ones common to the earlier and later versions of the liturgy.

> (1) *"We give thanks to thee,* O Holy *Father,* for thy Holy Name which thou didst make to tabernacle in our hearts, and for the *knowledge* and faith and immortality *which thou didst make known to us through Jesus thy Child. To thee be glory for ever.* Thou, Lord Almighty, didst create all things for thy Name's sake, and didst give food and drink to men for their enjoyment, that they might give thanks to thee, but us hast thou blessed with spiritual food and drink and eternal light through thy Child. Above all *we give thanks to thee* for that thou art mighty. *To thee be glory for ever."*
>
> (2) First concerning the Cup. *"We give thanks to thee,* our *Father,* for the Holy Vine of David thy child, *which thou didst make known to us through Jesus thy child; to thee be glory for ever."* And concerning the broken Bread: "We give thee thanks, our Father, for the life and *knowledge which thou didst make known to us through Jesus thy child. To thee be glory for ever."* (*Didache* 10:2–4; 9:2–3; my italics)

On the one hand, the later version has simply quarried the earlier one for its contents. On the other, and very significantly, the earlier prayer's double thanksgiving was for, first, spiritual gifts such as knowledge, faith, and immortality and, then, material gifts such as food and drink. This has now been specified, so that the first thanksgiving is for the cup, the second for the bread. There was absolutely no mention of bread and wine or bread and cup in that earlier prayer. But why, in the later prayer, is it in the sequence of cup and bread? The structure of the Greco-Roman meal makes one expect bread and wine(cup), yet that reversed order reappears twice in 1 Corinthians 10:15, 21 and also, but with textual problems expertly summarized by Bruce Metzger (173–177), in Luke 22:17–19a. But, as Aaron Milavec has noted, "the Didache provides structures of prayer which parallel, in both ritual and rhetoric, the oldest Jewish prayers. It is significant, for instance, that both the *Didache* and the Mishnah require a separate blessing for the wine and the bread, with the blessing over the cup preceding the blessing over the bread in both cases." It is most likely that, in the light of such *Mishnah* sections as *Berakoth* 6:1, 7:3, and especially 8:8, "local practice in the first century was diversified," so that a sequence of bread/cup or cup/bread blessing was equally possible in a Jewish and thence into a Jewish Christian context (112–113).

In any case, and for my present purpose, *Didache* 9 shows the infiltration of a postmeal Eucharist within the meal and associated separately with its twin parts, in whatever order. I emphasize again, however, that at this point there is absolutely no connection with Passover meal, Last Supper, or even the death of Jesus in general.

The third common element is an *apocalyptic prayer* that is, as you will notice, much more explicit in the earlier *Didache* 10 than the later *Didache* 9.

> (1) Remember, Lord, *thy Church* to deliver it from all evil and to make it perfect in thy love, and *gather it together* in its holiness *from* the four winds *to thy kingdom* which thou hast prepared for it. *For thine is the power and the glory for ever.* Let grace come and let this world pass away. Hosannah to the God of David.
>
> (2) As this broken bread was scattered upon the mountains, but was brought together and became one, so let *thy Church* be *gathered together from* the ends of the earth *into thy kingdom, for thine is the glory and the power* through Jesus Christ *for ever.* (*Didache* 10:5–6a; 9:4; my italics)

It is clear, in that case, how "through Jesus Christ" is inserted by the later version within a doxology from the former one. Jesus the Child (Servant) of God is now Jesus the Christ. Even more significant is the fact that, even when the bread is developed symbolically in *Didache* 9, that symbolism still has nothing to do with the death of Jesus. As many grains, scattered by sowing over the mountainside plots, come together as one bread, so let God's church be gathered together into heaven.

The fourth common element is the *worthiness warning*. In the older text it is linked closely with implicit apocalyptic sanctions, but in the later one it is baptism that is mentioned.

(1) If any man be holy, let him come! if any man be not, let him repent: Maran atha, Amen.
(2) But let none eat or drink of your Eucharist except those who have been baptised in the Lord's name. For concerning this also did the Lord say, "Give not that which is holy to the dogs." (*Didache* 10:6b; 9:5)

The earlier text looks inside to the community and, despite its heightened apocalyptic awareness, always holds out repentance to the unholy. The later one looks outside, draws group boundaries based on baptism, and relegates outsiders to canine status. That confirms, therefore, the proposal made above that 54 *Dogs and Swine* [1/3] is not from the historical Jesus himself.

I have spent time and space on *Didache* 9–10 to emphasize two points. First, the older prayer in *Didache* 10 indicates a eucharistic meal with no ritualization of bread and wine/cup, let alone anything else. The newer prayer in *Didache* 9 does have a ritualization of cup and bread, but, even late in the first century C.E., at least some (southern?) Syrian Christians could celebrate a Eucharist of bread and wine with absolutely no hint of Passover meal, Last Supper, or passion symbolism built into its origins or development. I cannot believe that they knew all about those elements and studiously avoided them. I can only presume that they were not there for everyone from the beginning, that is, from solemn, formal, and final institution by Jesus himself. Already, of course, *Didache* 9–10 represents a ritualization of the open commensality of Jesus and his first followers. There is nothing necessarily wrong with such a development, but, especially as one follows that *worthiness warning* from *Didache* 10:6b into 9:5, it is hard not to acknowledge a loss: the holy ones are now at table, and the dogs are not to be fed.

The fourth stage in the eucharistic development is represented by Paul's use of pre-Pauline tradition in 1 Corinthians 10–11. My argument is not, despite its terminology of stages, that the *Didache* communities and the pre-Pauline communities must be on a single and sequential chronological trajectory or even that this is earlier and that is later. It is simply that their dual existence renders most unlikely a Last Supper with its passion symbolism institutionalized and commanded to repetition by Jesus himself on the eve of his death. Paul himself has a strong sense of egalitarian commensality, and he upbraids the Corinthians for not following it. "It would appear," according to Dennis Smith, "that there were three aspects to the schisms at the meal at Corinth: eating separately, eating different amounts of food, and taking positions of rank and status" (194). But, on the other hand, Paul knows from received tradition a eucharistic meal that has the bread and wine symbolize the body and blood of the Lord.

> For I received from the Lord what I also delivered to you, that the Lord Jesus on the night when he was betrayed [literally: handed over, presumably by God] took bread, and when he had given thanks, he broke it, and said, "This is my body which is for you. Do this in remembrance of me." In the same way also the cup, after supper, saying, "This cup is the new covenant in my blood. Do this, as often as you drink it, in remembrance of me." For as often as you eat this bread and drink the cup, you proclaim the Lord's death until he comes. (1 Corinthians 11:23–26)

Notice how, in correct Greco-Roman practice for a formal meal, the wine appears "after supper." But, as Burton Mack emphasizes, "the combination here of the terms body and blood as symbols for a death is an important clue. They only make sense within the tradition of martyrological thought. The otherwise normal combination when referring to a self would be body and soul; flesh and blood are the terms that go together when referring to the physical body. But body and blood occur in martyrological texts" (1988:118). When bread and wine become body and blood, one necessarily "proclaims the Lord's *death*." We have now moved from, first, open commensality during the lifetime of Jesus through, second, general eucharistic meal without and then with a bread and wine(cup) emphasis and on, third, to specific passion remembrance, celebration, and participation. And this later specification is given as Jesus' direct and explicit institution on, appropriately, the eve of his death.

The fifth and final stage is in Mark 14:22–25, which is copied into Matthew 26:26–29 and into Luke 22:15–19a but with some textual conflation from 1 Corinthians 11:23–26 in Luke 22:19b–20 (Mack 1988:300–301).

> And as they were eating, he took bread, and blessed, and broke it, and gave it to them, and said, "Take; this is my body." And he took a cup, and when he had given thanks he gave it to them, and they all drank of it. And he said to them, "This is my blood of the covenant, which is poured out for many. Truly, I say to you, I shall not drink again of the fruit of the vine until that day when I drink it new in the kingdom of God." (Mark 14:22–25)

The ritual is, as in Paul, explicitly connected with Jesus' passion both in its timing as a last supper and in its bread and wine, body and blood symbolism, and especially in the far greater emphasis given to cup/blood than to bread/body. It is now, however, a Passover meal as well. And, even though the ritual now seems completely separated from the Greco-Roman formal meal tradition, with, for example, no mention of the wine-cup "after supper" as in Paul, the phrase "poured out" appropriates the libation moment of the Greco-Roman sequence even more precisely than does Paul. What is most striking, however, is that Mark has no double command for repetition and remembrance but instead that terminal and emphatic "truly, I say to you," with its apocalyptic reference. What we are actually dealing with is, for Mark, almost an anti- or de-institutionalization of the eucharistic meal, as Burton Mack (1988:298–306) and his doctoral student Lee Edward Klosinski (193–213) have shown so clearly. On the wider structural level Mark 14:22–25 brings to a climax the disciples' failure to understand Jesus' meal symbolism. "Mark has," according to Klosinski, "organized three of the boat trips of Jesus and his disciples (4:35–41; 6:45–52; and 8:13–21), three healings (7:31–37; 8:22–26; and 10:46–52), and the two feeding miracles and the last supper (6:3–44; 8:1–10; 14:17–26) into progressive, triadic structures. A feature of this structure is that the final member serves as a climax of the previous two" (207–208). On the narrower sequential level, Mark 14:22–25 is brutally linked, externally, to the preceding prophecy of Judas' betrayal by a triple repetition: "they were at table eating . . . one who is eating with me . . . one of the twelve, one who is dipping bread into the dish with me." And, internally, Mark insists at 14:23 that "they all drank of it," as if to associate all the disciples with the betrayer himself. Following those clues, and reading Mark 14:21–25 in the context of Mark's compositional, polemical, and climactic theology, I conclude that Mark is opposing an institutionalized eucharistic ritual that does not allow for Jews and Gentiles at the same table (Kelber 45–65) and that emphasizes the presence of Jesus *now* rather than the coming of Jesus *soon* within that liturgy. We have come, as it were, full circle. "Mark is caught," as Klosinski summarizes his doctoral dissertation, "between two understandings of Christian commensality. One understanding envisions commensality as a continuation of the type of table-fellowship remembered from the time of Jesus. Another understands commensality in terms of the eucharistic elements of the Christ cult. Mark employs the language of the Christ cult, but subverts its earlier meaning" (203).

A final point. "In the straitened Mediterranean, the kingdom of Heaven had to have something to do with food and drink." But, Peter Brown continues, "it may be that one of the deepest changes of mentality associated with the rise of Christianity in the Mediterranean world is the rise to prominence of one single meal (the Eucharist), which, though heavy with associations of interpersonal bonding in a single *human* society, was carefully shorn, from an early time, of any overtones of organic, non-human abundance. Previously, a widespread frame of mind had tended to take for granted the solidarity of any settled community around the rare commodities of food and relaxation, and had intended, through moments of high and leisurely eating, to shame the dull world of Nature out of its accustomed stinginess" (22–23). It is necessary to calculate very carefully what was lost and what gained in moving from Jesus' real meal with open commensality to its continuance in a ritual meal with Christian commensality. It is also necessary to ponder, as we have never done, the differences in ritualization between crowds having bread and fish and disciples having bread and wine. I shall return to that former case below but underline even now that the smell of the crowd and, even more, the smell of the fish keep our feet firmly on the ground of Mediterranean want and human need. Brown's final warning is salutary. "A Christian church, patronized largely by the well-fed and increasingly led by austere men such as [Origen, in the third century], whose restricted diet was the result of choice and not of necessity, found itself, in the next centuries, increasingly tempted to treat sexuality (a drive which frequently assumes leisure and regular eating habits), rather than greed and greed's dark shadow in a world of limited resources and famine, as the most abiding and disquieting symptom of the frailty of the human condition. Maybe the time has come to look again at the seemingly absurd dreams of abundance of ancient Mediterranean men, to find, through their concerns, one way, at least, to more humane and more commonsensical objects of anxiety" (24). In memory of me, to be sure, but not real food, not open commensality, not for the crowds, and not with baskets filled left over.

The Passion as Narrative

Here at last, says common sense, there should be few problems. Whatever about the divergent versions of Jesus' sayings and miracles rendered the previous chapters so difficult, we have, in the passion narrative, a coherent story whose four accounts can be easily integrated into a single consecutive saga. The prepassion Gospel narratives were constructed from units of tradition whose divergent forms and contents, locations and interpretations underlined the artificiality of the narrative frames that now encompass them. No such situation exists for the passion accounts. Here the narrative units are found in this fourfold saga and nowhere else. That saga has, in painting and sculpture, in play and film, in explicit citation and implicit allusion, and in acceptance as well as rejection, become profoundly sedimented into the Western imagination. Narrative realism has become equated with historical accuracy. How else, asks common sense, could there be so much agreement in sequence and content save for eyewitness consistency marred, at most, here by special emphasis or there by individual memory lapse? There are, however, problems that indicate a deeper and more basic difficulty lying beneath the harmonious parallelism of the fourfold passion account in Matthew, Mark, Luke, and John.

Prophecy or History?

Three short detours before proceeding. A first one visits in more detail those Qumran Essenes mentioned before but only in passing. As that dissident community, led, in Lenski's typology, by members of the *priestly* class, meditated upon its past history and future destiny, it moved to correlate tradition and situation. The point of such activity was not primarily external apologetics or polemics, although, of course, it could be used to those ends. It was much more internal ideology and self-understanding, the attempt to justify the present and project the future based on the only grounding possible, their own rereading of the past, that is, of the biblical tradition. Two main methods were used in such correlative exegeses, as indicated in Geza Vermes's more recent presentation of the Qumran documents. He cites "a first group of exegetical writings [that] comment on single scriptural books" and gives seventeen examples of such cases. There is also "another collection in which the exposition is based on bringing diverse texts together with a view to explaining one by another," but here only six examples can be given (1985:66). I call those twin processes, respectively, *sequential* and *testimonial* commentary.

The first method, for which we have much more evidence so far, was to take a biblical text verse by verse and apply it to the group's story. Such *sequential exegeses* are called in Hebrew *pesherim*, or interpretations. An example is the sequential interpretation of the biblical prophet Nahum 2:11–3:1, from which I cite only that on 2:11b–12, deliberately chosen for its somewhat unusual explicit references. Notice how the biblical unit, given here in italics, is followed in each case by "interpreted, this concerns . . . "

> *Whither the lion goes, there is the lion's cub, [with none to disturb it]* (Nahum 2:11b). [Interpreted, this concerns Deme]trius king of Greece who sought, on the counsel of those who seek smooth things, to enter Jerusalem. [But God did not permit the city to be delivered] into the hands of the kings of Greece, from the time of Antiochus until the coming of the rulers of the Kittim. But then she shall be trampled under their feet. . . .
>
> *The lion tears enough for its cubs and it chokes prey for its lionesses* (Nahum 2:12a). [Interpreted, this] concerns the furious young lion who strikes by means of his great men, and by means of the men of his council.

[*And chokes prey for its lionesses; and it fills*] *its caves* [*with prey*] *and its dens with victims* (Nahum 2:12ab). Interpreted, this concerns the furious young lion [who executes revenge] on those who seek smooth things and hangs men alive, [a thing never done] formerly in Israel. (4QpNah 1; Vermes 1968:231– 232)

The event is the Battle of Shechem in 88 B.C.E., when the Hasmonean monarch Alexander Jannaeus (103–76 B.C.E.), having defeated the Syrian ruler Demetrius III Eucerus (95–78 B.C.E.), took a terrible revenge on the Pharisees, "those who seek smooth things," who had invited the latter south as their supporter. That terrible revenge was massive live crucifixion, restoring that last line's lacuna not as Vermes did above but as Fitzmyer did later: "[as it was thus done] from of old in Israel" (1978:500). Notice, by the way, that in sequential exegeses it is relatively easy to distinguish between biblical text and historical application.

The second method, with far fewer examples, is to select individual biblical verses on some specific theme or event from different books and/or different places in the same book and present them as a catena or anthology. Such strings of collected proof-texts are often called in Latin *testimonia* or *florilegia*. One example, found in the fourth of the Qumran document caves, is called *4Q Testimonia* by Allegro (1956), or *A Messianic Anthology* by Vermes (1968:247–249). It contains a fivefold string involving Deuteronomy 5:28–29; 18:18–19; Numbers 24:15–17; Deuteronomy 33:8–11; and an expanded version of Joshua 6:26. Joseph Fitzmyer, comparing *4Q Testimonia* with the *Robert Papyrus*, a fourth-century C.E. anthology from the Egyptian Fayyûm, noted that both "are strung together without introductory formulas and intervening comments on the text. And he concluded that, "while the collections of *testimonia* that are found in patristic writers might be regarded as the result of early Christian catechetical and missionary activity, *4Q Testimonia* shows that the stringing together of OT texts from various books was a pre-Christian literary procedure, which may well have been imitated in the early stage of the formation of the NT. It resembles so strongly the composite citations of the NT writers that it is difficult not to admit that *testimonia* influenced certain parts of the NT" (1957:531, 534).

But then, just as the *sequential biblical texts* generated interlacing commentaries, so could those *testimonial biblical texts* likewise generate interlacing commentaries. An example is, possibly, what Allegro calls *4Q Florilegium* (1958) and Vermes calls *A Midrash on the Last Days* (1968:245–247; 1985:80). It involves a threefold catena of 2 Samuel 7:10–14, Psalm 1:1, and Psalm 2:1, but it is also interlaced with both commentary and other explicitly cited biblical texts. Here is one particularly intense unit.

> Explanation of *How blessed is the man who does not walk in the counsel of the wicked* (Psalm 1:1). Interpreted, this saying [concerns] those who turn aside from the way [of the people]; as it is written in the book of Isaiah the prophet concerning the last days, *It came to pass that [the Lord turned me aside, as with a mighty hand, from walking in the way of] this people* (Isaiah 8:11). They are those of whom it is written in the book of Ezekiel the Prophet, *The Levites [strayed far from me, following] their idols* (Ezekiel 44:10). They are the sons of Zadok who [seek their own] counsel and follow [their own inclination] apart from the Council of the Community. (*4Q Florilegium*; Vermes 1968:246–247)

Our own added italics and parenthetical citations help us to see, in the above text, where Bible ends and commentary begins and, of course, the original specific attributions help even more so. But as text merges with text and as event merges with citation, it could easily get extremely difficult to know where anything starts and something else finishes. Prophecy and history could begin to interweave, mutually influencing and even creating each other. Obviously, of course, all such activity demands a most sophisticated scribal and exegetical capability. But the referent of that capacity could be, for some, the Teacher of Righteousness and his Qumran Essenes and, for others, Jesus of Nazareth and his Galilean followers.

A second detour is through 139 *Jesus Tempted Thrice* [1/1], a complex whose single attestation keeps it methodologically bracketed and that is therefore used only for illustrative purposes. The basis of that triple temptation is an opposition between magic and exegesis, between miraculous activity and exegetical citation. Miracles are dismissed, obliquely, as self-serving acts such as turning stones into bread when one is hungry, as divine temptations such as descending from the pinnacle of the Temple, or as demonic collusion such as gaining the world by obeying Satan. Jesus overcomes Satan, and even his quotation of Psalm 91:11–12, by three separate quotations from Deuteronomy 8:3, 6:16, and 6:13. But that opposition between magic and exegesis also represents a distinction in class. Even though, in Lenski's typology, the *peasant* class is not the only one that could appreciate magic, it would take the *retainer* class to appreciate the scribal exactitude of such exegetical quotations. Peasants would know, in their Little Tradition, the general themes and dominant emphases of the Great Tradition. But their illiteracy would preclude the duel of citation practiced here by Satan and Jesus. All such precise search and verbatim application presume not only developed literacy but also exegetical dexterity. A retainer-class believer is now interpreting the peasant-class Jesus.

A third detour concerns 26 *Jesus Virginally Conceived* [1/4] and 7 *Of David's Lineage* [1/5], two heavily attested complexes neither of which gives us any biographical information about the historical Jesus.

If you compare the long narrative accounts of Jesus' birth in Matthew 1–2 and Luke 1–2 , the only common features, apart from the names of Jesus, Mary, and Joseph, are the virginal conception and the birth at Bethlehem. Matthew links those twin events with explicit prophetic citation. John links only the second one and with summary rather than citation:

> All this took place to fulfil what the Lord had spoken by the prophet: "Behold, a virgin shall conceive and bear a son, and his name shall be called Emmanuel" (which means, God with us). (Matthew 1:22–23, based on Isaiah 7:14)

> They told him, "In Bethlehem of Judea; for so it is written by the prophet: 'And you, O Bethlehem, in the land of Judah, are by no means least among the rulers of Judah; for from you shall come a ruler who will govern my people Israel.'" (Matthew 2:5–6, based on Micah 5:2)

> Others said, "This is the Christ." But some said, "Is the Christ to come from Galilee? Has not the scripture said that the Christ is descended from David, and comes from Bethlehem, the village where David was?" (John 7:41–42)

But Luke has no such explicit or even general allusions. His use of Isaiah 7:14 in 1:27, 31 is, as Barnabas Lindars put it, "a much more polished and allusive composition" (1961:214). But when you turn to the Bethlehem birth, you can see quite clearly what Luke is doing. If the prophetic background has been almost completely hidden, the historical foreground has been greatly enhanced.

> In those days a decree went out from Caesar Augustus that all the world should be enrolled. This was the first enrollment, when Quirinius was governor of Syria. And all went to be enrolled, each to his own city. And Joseph also went up from Galilee, from the city of Nazareth, to Judea, to the city of David, which is called Bethlehem, because he was of the house and lineage of David, to be enrolled with Mary, his betrothed, who was with child. And while they were there, the time came for her to be delivered. And she gave birth to her first-born son and wrapped him in swaddling cloths, and laid him in a manger, because there was no place for them in the inn. (Luke 2:1–7)

That seems a brilliant explatation of why Jesus of Nazareth was born at Bethlehem, unless, of course, one knows anything of Roman history and Roman, or indeed any, bureaucracy (Schürer-Vermes 1.399–427). First, there never was a worldwide census under Augustus. Second, the Palestinian census was undertaken by the Syrian legate, P. Sulpicius Quirinius, in 6 to 7 C.E., about a decade after the birth of Jesus. You will recall, from chapter 6 above, that its occasion was the annexation of Archelaus' territories under a direct Roman prefecture. Third, and above all, even if Augustus had ordained a complete census of the Roman world, and even if Quirinius had overseen its administration in Archelaus' territories, the Roman custom was to count you in the place of your domicile or work and not in that of your ancestry or birth. That is little more than common sense. Census was for taxation; to record people in their ancestral rather than their occupational locations would have constituted a bureaucratic nightmare. That agrees with the younger Tryphon's documentary papyri seen from Roman Egypt in chapter 1 above. His brother Thoönis was registered at one year of age among the extended family of the elder Tryphon in 11 to 12 C.E. But, later, in 44 C.E., it is certified legally that he is out of work and has left the area.

Luke, however, is interested in portraying Jesus in close interaction with major events of "Roman history," interested, that is, in the historicization of prophecy, of rephrasing prophetic allusion as "historical" narrative. If the details are all wrong, or if one gets into convoluted arguments on their historical verisimilitude or administrative plausibility, so much the better. One is still arguing over Augustus and Jesus, and, then or now, Luke has succeeded in his project. We shall see exactly the same process below when the *Cross Gospel* attempts to write, from prophetic allusions, a first "historical narrative" about the passion of Jesus. Hide the prophecy, tell the narrative, and invent the history.

Under Pontius Pilate

I take it absolutely for granted that Jesus was crucified under Pontius Pilate. Security about the *fact* of the crucifixion derives not only from the unlikelihood that Christians would have invented it but also from the existence of two early and independent non-Christian witnesses to it, a Jewish one from 93–94 C.E. and a Roman one from the 110s or 120s C.E.

The Jewish witness is the description of Jesus in Flavius Josephus' *Jewish Antiquities* 18:63, which seems to be presumed before and by the passing mention in 20:200. This *Testimonium Flavianum* has generated an immense bibliography, annotated recently and superbly by Louis Feldman

(679–703), and an intense controversy, reviewed recently and superbly by John Meier. The problem is that Josephus' account is too good to be true, too confessional to be impartial, too Christian to be Jewish. It is either a total or a partial interpolation by the Christian editors who preserved Josephus' works. Here are the two Josephan texts; notice how the second one seems to presume at least some earlier and more detailed one.

> (1) About this time there lived Jesus, a wise man, *if indeed one ought to call him a man.* For he was one who wrought surprising feats and was a teacher of such people as accept the truth gladly. He won over many Jews and many of the Greeks. *He was the Messiah.* When Pilate, upon hearing him accused by men of the highest standing amongst us, had condemned him to be crucified, those who had in the first place come to love him did not give up their affection for him. *On the third day he appeared to them restored to life, for the prophets of God had prophesied these and countless other marvellous things about him.* And the tribe of the Christians, so called after him, has still to this day not disappeared.
>
> (2) And so he [Ananus, the high priest] convened the judges of the Sanhedrin [in 62 C.E. during the interregnum between the prefects Festus and Albinus] and brought before them a man named James, the brother of Jesus who was called the Christ, and certain others. (Josephus, *Jewish Antiquities* 18:63; 20:200)

The words in bold italic represent interpolations deliberately but delicately Christianizing, in the words of John Meier, the "fairly neutral—or even purposely ambiguous—tone" of Josephus' original description.

In 1971 Shlomo Pines of Jerusalem's Hebrew University drew attention to an Arabic version of that first Josephan text preserved in the *Kitāb al'Unwān* or *Book of the Title*, a history of the world written around the middle of the tenth century by Agapius, Melkite bishop of Phrygian Hierapolis in Asia Minor.

> Similarly Josephus [Yūsīfūs], the Hebrew. For he says in the treatises that he has written on the governance [?] of the Jews: "At this time there was a wise man called Jesus. *His conduct was good, and [he] was known to be virtuous [or: his learning/knowledge was outstanding].* And many people from among the Jews and the other nations became his disciples. Pilate condemned him to be crucified and to die. But those who had become his disciples did not abandon his discipleship. **They reported that he had appeared to them three days after his crucifixion, and that he was alive; accordingly he was perhaps the Messiah, concerning whom the prophets have recounted wonders.**" (Shlomo Pines 10–11, 16; my emphases)

It is possible to argue that, despite Christian preservation and translation from Greek to Syrian to Arabic all under Christian auspices, we have
here the original and uninterpolated text of Josephus. But notice what I have
placed in bold type. The italic bold words could indicate a simple summary
of Josephus' sentence about Jesus' deeds and words, miracles and teachings.
But the words in roman bold pick up two of the same three Christianizations
seen in our official Josephan version. "We are thus left," in Pines's conclusion,
"with two possibilities: either the version of Agapius is the product of Christian censorship applied to the original text in a less thoroughgoing form than
in the case of the vulgate recension, or it did not undergo censorship at all. . . .
The first hypothesis seems to me to be the more probable one, but for no
very conclusive reason. At the moment this is anybody's guess" (70). But we
can probably go beyond that. A good interpolation, as distinct from an
editorial comment, is a delicate process. "They reported" about the resurrection and "perhaps" about the Messiah, in the Arabic text, are better, because
more oblique, Christianizations of a Jewish text that one wants to retain as
a Jewish witness than are the more overtly confessional inserts in the Greek
text. And by the same token, the omission of "men of the highest standing
amongst us" is probably not just scribal error but ideological deletion. I agree,
therefore, with James Charlesworth's admission, albeit amidst somewhat over-
heated enthusiasm, that "some Christian alterations are found in the Arabic recension, even if they are more subtle in the Arabic version than in the
Greek" (1988:96). It is probably better, actually, to relegate the Arabic text of
Agapius to a footnote, as John Meier does with the comment, "I am doubtful that this 10th-century Arabic manuscript preserves the original form of
the *Testimonium,* especially since it contains sentences that . . . are probably later expansions or variants of the text" (89 note 36). We are left, in other
words, with that Greek text of Josephus but minus the boldface Christian
inserts. And all that debate should not diminish the importance of Josephus'
commentary. That is how Jesus and early Christianity looked to a very prudent, diplomatic, and cosmopolitan Roman Jew in the early last decade of
the first century: miracles and teachings, Jews and Greeks, our "men of
highest standing" and Pilate, crucifixion and continuation.

The Roman witness is Cornelius Tacitus, who, having detailed the Flavian decline in his *Histories,* described the Julio-Claudian one in his *Annals.*
The former study was written in the second century's first decade, the latter in its second and maybe even into its third decade. He has just told how
a rumor blamed Nero for the disastrous fire that swept Rome in 64 C.E.

Therefore to scotch the rumour, Nero substituted as culprits, and
punished with the utmost refinements of cruelty, a class of men, loathed

for their vices, whom the crowd styled Christians. Christus, the founder
of the name, had undergone the death penalty in the reign of Tiberius,
by sentence of the procurator Pontius Pilatus, and the pernicious superstition was checked for the moment, only to break out once more, not
merely in Judaea, the home of the disease, but in the capital itself,
where all things horrible or shameful in the world collect and find a
vogue. (Tacitus, *Annals* 15.44; Moore & Jackson 4.282–283)

My point, then, is not that there is the slightest doubt about the *fact* of
Jesus' crucifixion under Pontius Pilate. The point is the provenance of
those specific details, quoted dialogues, narrative connections, and almost
journalistic hour-by-hour accounts of the passion of Jesus. Is the passion
narrative from history or from prophecy? from the prophetization of history or the historicization of prophecy? from applying prophecy to an
underlay of detailed history or from applying an overlay of history to
detailed prophecy? I remind you of the difference between prophecy and
history by comparing these twin texts on the passion of Jesus:

(1) For I delivered to you as of first importance what I also received,
that Christ died for our sins in accordance with the scriptures. (1 Corinthians 15:3)
(2) Our Lord is ... truly nailed [to a tree: *not in the Greek text*] in the
flesh for our sakes under Pontius Pilate and Herod the Tetrarch.
(Ignatius of Antioch, *To the Smyrnaeans* 1:2)

In both cases Jesus died for us, but in the former according to the
Scriptures, in the latter according to the decree of Pilate and Antipas.

What follows now depends on my earlier and much more complete
study on the origins of the passion and resurrection narratives (1988a). I
proposed that, first of all, Jesus' closest followers knew nothing more about
the passion than the fact of the crucifixion, that they had fled and later had
no available witnesses for its details, and that they were concerned, in any
case, with far more serious matters, such as whether that death negated all
that Jesus had said and done, all that they had accepted and believed. Second, what followed *in one very literate and highly sophisticated stream of tradition* was an intense search of the Scriptures, similar to that at Qumran. It
discovered verses and images each of which could be applied to the passion
as a whole but not, of course, to its individual details, for no such details
existed in their memories. Third, those individual scriptural connections
and specific prophetic fulfillments could be organized into a coherent and
sequential story. But, for this, some overarching form, shape, pattern, or
genre had to be conceived or adopted. Finally, once such a narrative had
been achieved, its historicity could be improved by more accurate

verisimilitude and refined by more precise detail. The process developed, in other words, over these primary steps. First, the *historical passion,* composed of minimal knowledge, was known only in the general terms recorded by, say, Josephus or Tacitus. Next, the *prophetic passion,* composed of multiple and discrete biblical allusions and seen most clearly in a work like the *Epistle of Barnabas,* developed biblical applications over, under, around, and through that open framework. Finally, those multiple and discrete exercises were combined into the *narrative passion* as a single sequential story. I proposed, furthermore, that the narrative passion is but a single stream of tradition flowing from the *Cross Gospel,* now embedded within the *Gospel of Peter,* into Mark, thence together into Matthew and Luke, and thence, all together, into John. Other reconstructions are certainly possible, but that seems to me the most economical one to explain all the data (see appendix 7).

The Sacrificed Goats

To test my hypothesis, I ask you to imagine yourself on the first Holy Saturday, *a day which is going to last about, say, five or ten years.* And you are located among certain followers of Jesus who are not at all peasants, are not at all interested in miracles, are not at all interested in collecting, preserving, or creating Jesus sayings, but are very, very interested in studying the Scriptures to understand your past, reclaim your present, and envisage your future. What do you find, what do you produce? I focus on 131 *Mocking of Jesus* [1/2] as something of a paradigmatic case for such intense exegetical study.

The *Epistle of Barnabas* is, according to Helmut Koester, an "example among the early Christian writings for an allegorical interpretation of the Old Testament in the genre of scriptural gnosis. . . . Its interpretive method is closely related to Hebrews, and *Barnabas* also strives for a scriptural understanding of the soteriological significance of Jesus' death, all the while holding to the apocalyptic expectation. . . . New Testament writings are never used in *Barnabas,* neither explicitly nor tacitly, which would argue for an early date, perhaps even before the end of I [first century] C.E. . . . The material presented by Barnabas represents the initial stages of the process that is continued in the *Gospel of Peter,* later in Matthew, and is completed in Justin Martyr" (1982:2.276–77). What is most interesting, however, is that *Barnabas* 7 presents a biblical basis not just *for the passion of Jesus but for the passion and parousia as a linked and related dyad.* It is not just a case of biblical texts interpreted as prophecies of Jesus' passion but of coordinating such texts as prophecies of the passion-parousia trajectory, that is, of arching those passion texts toward the future apocalyptic consummation.

I ask you, if you have a copy of *Barnabas* 7, to read that entire chapter over and over again, to forget for a moment the detailed narrative "knowledge" you have of the passion from the four intracanonical evangelists, and to try and imagine early Christians who knew no more about it than what you read in that chapter. And yet they could still write a whole chapter, and many others like it, about that event. I cannot quote it all, but a focus on one section may suffice.

> Note what was commanded: "Take two goats, goodly and alike, and offer them, and let the priest take the one as a burnt offering for sins."
>
> (a) But what are they to do with the other? "The other," he says, "is accursed." Notice how the type of Jesus is manifested: "And do ye all spit on it, and goad [pierce] it, and bind the scarlet wool about its head, and so let it be cast into the desert." And when it is so done, he who takes the goat into the wilderness drives it forth, and takes away the wool, and puts it upon a shrub which is called Rachél, of which we are accustomed to eat the shoots when we find them in the country: thus of Rachél alone is the fruit sweet.
>
> (b) What does this mean? Listen: "**the first goat is for the altar, but the other is accursed**," and note that the one that is accursed is crowned because then *"they will see him on that day" with the long scarlet robe "down to the feet" on his body,* and they will say, "Is not this he whom we once crucified and rejected and *pierced* and spat upon? Of a truth it was he who then said that he was the **Son** of God."
>
> (c) But how is he like the goat? For this reason: "**the goats shall be alike, beautiful, and a pair**," in order that when *they see him* come at that time they may be astonished at the likeness of the goat. See then the type of Jesus destined to suffer.
>
> (d) But why is it that they put the wool in the middle of the thorns? It is a type of Jesus placed in the Church, because whoever wishes to take away the scarlet wool must suffer much because the thorns are terrible and he can gain it only through pain. Thus he says, "those who will see me, and attain to my kingdom must lay hold of me through pain and suffering." (*Barnabas* 7:6–12; my emphases : I discuss first the italic bold and then the roman bold in what follows)

There are two quite separate and I think successive layers visible across that text's four questions, and I have noted each by separate typographical markings.

There is, first of all, a layer from the prophet Zechariah, and it may well have developed from a combination of two sublayers, one from 12:10–14 and the other from 3:1–5. I have indicated them both with italic bold. The use of the former unit, Zechariah 12:10–14, is known explicitly from Matthew

24:10–12, 30a, a source independent of Mark 13:25–26 (Kloppenborg 1979), and also from John 19:34–37.

> (1) And I will pour out on the house of David and the inhabitants of Jerusalem a spirit of compassion and supplication, so that, **when they look on him whom they have pierced**, they shall **mourn** for him, as one mourns for an only child, and weep bitterly over him, as one weeps over a first-born [son?]. . . . The land shall mourn, each family [tribe] by itself; the family [tribe] of . . . the family [tribe] of . . . the family [tribe] of . . . the family [tribe] of . . . and all the families *[tribes]* that are left, each by itself, and their wives by themselves. (Zechariah 12:10–14)

> (2) then will appear the sign of the Son of man in heaven, and then *all the tribes of the earth will mourn*. (Matthew 24:30a)

> (3) But one of the soldiers pierced his side with a spear, and at once there came out blood and water. He who saw it has borne witness—his testimony is true, and he knows that he tells the truth—that you also may believe. For these things took place that the scripture might be fulfilled, "Not a bone of him shall be broken." And again another scripture says, *"They shall look on him whom they have pierced."* (John 19:34–37)

Notice how, in that single prophetic application, a dyad of "piercing *and* looking/mourning," that is, of passion *and* parousia linked irrevocably together, has been achieved. And that combination is emphasized and developed when the first sublayer, Zechariah 12:10–14, is connected with the second one, Zechariah 3:1–5, a text that originally applied to Joshua (Jesus!), the first high priest after the Babylonian Exile's conclusion in 538 B.C.E. He was thus an obvious type of the destruction/deliverance dyad. The usage of Zechariah 12:10 combined with 3:1–5 is also known independently from Revelation 1:7 as followed by the vision of Christ in 1:13.

> (1) Now Joshua was standing before the angel, clothed with filthy garments. And the angel said to those who were standing before him, "Remove the filthy garments from him." And to him he said, "Behold, I have taken your iniquity away from you, and I will clothe you with rich apparel [in Greek: *a long robe*]." And I said, "Let them put a clean turban on his head." So they put a clean turban on his head and clothed him with garments; and the angel of the Lord was standing by. (Zechariah 3:3–5)

> (2) Behold, he is coming with the clouds, and *every eye will see him, every one who pierced him, and all the tribes of the earth will wail [mourn]* on account of him. Even so. Amen.

> ... and in the midst of the lampstands one like a son of man,
> clothed with *a long robe* and with a golden girdle round his breast.
> Revelation 1:7, 13)

The advantage of that combination's intensive intertextuality is that passion (piercing) and parousia (looking/mourning) from Zechariah 12:10–14 is expanded by passion (disrobing) and parousia (rerobing, crowning) in Zechariah 3:1–5. Notice, by the way, that the conjunction is passion and parousia not passion and resurrection. And those applications from passion prophecy, furnishing the combined motifs of piercing, robing, and crowning, all came to *Barnabas* already worked out by the tradition.

The combination of a second layer with that former or Zechariah one was also worked out by the tradition prior to *Barnabas'* use of it. The twin states of Joshua/Jesus as first clothed in filthy garments and then regally robed and crowned were correlated with the twin goats from the Day of Atonement. I have indicated that second layer with roman bold in *Barnabas* 7 above. This combination is also known in the independent version of Justin Martyr from around the middle of the second century. In fact, you can see it there much more clearly.

> And the **two goats** which were ordered to be offered during the fast, of
> which one was sent away as the scape [goat], and the other sacrificed,
> were similarly declarative of the two appearances of Christ: the first, in
> which the elders of your people, and the priests, having laid hands on
> Him and put Him to death, sent him away as the scape [goat]; and His
> second appearance, because in the same place in Jerusalem *you shall*
> *recognize Him whom you have dishonoured,* and who was an offering
> for all sinners willing to repent, and keeping the fast which Isaiah speaks
> of, loosening the terms of the violent contracts, and keeping the other
> precepts, likewise enumerated by him, and which I have quoted, which
> those believing in Jesus do. And further, you are aware that the offering
> of the **two goats,** which was enjoined to be sacrificed at the fast, was not
> permitted to take place similarly anywhere else, but only in Jerusalem.
> (Justin Martyr, *Dialogue with Trypho* 40; ANF 1.215)

What is fascinating here, returning to *Barnabas* 7, is that its verse-by-verse commentary, similar to the *pesher*-style of the Qumran Essenes, is not based on the very general ritual given in Leviticus 16 but on a much more specific one that we would almost suspect *Barnabas* had himself invented to suit his typology were it not known from several passing allusions in the *Mishnah,* the rabbinical Oral Torah codified at the end of the second century C.E. From those allusions we know that the two goats had to be alike and equal, that scarlet wool was placed on the scapegoat's head, that it was abused as it was hurried toward the desert, and that before it was killed there the scarlet wool was attached between a rock and its horns (Crossan 1988a:118–119). He is, then, combining Zechariah not with Leviticus 16 but with its specific and detailed ritualization, which he probably knows from a textual source.

That combination required some textual pyrotechnics and exegetical gymnastics from the robing and crowning of Joshua to the "robing" and "crowning" of the scapegoat. The "red wool on its head" furnished, with an admirable ingenuity working in two different directions simultaneously, "a scarlet robe" from the "red wool" and a "crown" from "on its head." And the scapegoat has merged with Joshua and Joshua with Jesus in his parousia.

One final and very significant point. *Barnabas* 7:8 must be some kind of linguistic confusion between rocky height and thorny shrub (Prigent 105), but, however it may have happened, he ends with a ritual involving the red wool placed on a thorny shrub. And that is, he concludes,

> a type of Jesus placed in the Church, because whoever wishes to take away the scarlet wool must suffer much because the thorns are terrible and he can gain it only through pain. Thus he says, "those who will see me, and attain to my kingdom must lay hold of me through pain and suffering." (*Barnabas* 7:11b)

That final aphorism, 483 *Only Through Suffering* [3/1], is attributed to Jesus by nobody else. It may possibly be a free rendition of the theme or idea contained in a saying such as 44 *Carrying One's Cross* [1/3]. Be that as it may, I consider that to have known the story of Jesus' crowning with thorns and to have changed that crown *of* thorns to a crown *among* thorns would be a singularly obtuse or even perverse operation. In what follows, to the contrary, I propose to show how Jesus as a crown among thorns became Jesus crowned with thorns and how Jesus as Rejected Scapegoat became Jesus as Mocked King.

However brilliant one deems the intertextual dexterity of *Barnabas* 7 and however supportive or probative one deems it is for the passion-parousia destiny of Jesus, it can hardly be called a good story or even a narrative sequence, let alone an historical memoir. Compare, for example and by contrast, the following historical anecdote. Philo recounts how the Alexandrian mob mocked the Jewish Agrippa I when, having been made king by Gaius Caligula, he sailed home via Alexandria in August of 38 C.E.

> There was a certain lunatic Carabas, whose madness was not of the fierce and savage kind, which is dangerous both to the madmen themselves and those who approach them, but of the easy-going, gentler style. He spent day and night in the streets naked, shunning neither

heat nor cold, made game of by the children and the lads who were
idling about. The rioters drove the poor fellow into the gymnasium and
set him up on high to be seen by all and put on his head a sheet of
byblos spread out wide for a diadem, clothed the rest of his body with a
rug for a royal robe, while someone who had noticed a piece of the
native papyrus thrown away in the road gave it to him for his sceptre.
And when in some theatrical farce he had received the insignia of kingship and had been tricked out as a king, young men carrying rods on
their shoulders as spearmen stood on either side of him in imitation of a
bodyguard. Then others approached him, some pretending to salute
him, others to sue for justice, others to consult him on state affairs.
Then from the multitude standing round him there rang out a tremendous shout hailing him as Marin, which is said to be the name for "lord"
in Syria. For they knew that Agrippa was both a Syrian by birth and had
a great piece of Syria over which he was king. (Philo of Alexandria,
Flaccus 32–34, 36–39; Colson 320–25)

Carabas' mockery as pseudo-king does not involve physical abuse or
torture but rather a theatrical mime involving throne, crown, robe, scepter,
bodyguard, salutation and consultation, and especially his proclamation as
lord.

Supposing, now, that one took a prophetic exegesis such as that of *Barnabas* 7 and a historical story such as that of poor Carabas and fused them
together. One would get, I propose, again summarizing my earlier study
(1988a:114–159), a text such as the following one from the *Gospel of Peter*
3:6–9, a text whose detailed chiastic structure indicates where and how the
composer wished its emphases understood:

(A) So they took the Lord and pushed him in great haste
and said, "*Let us* hale *the Son of God* now that we have gotten power
  over him."
(B) And they put upon him a purple robe
(C) and set him on the judgment seat and said, "Judge righteously, O
  King of Israel!"
(B') And one of them brought a crown of thorns and put it on the Lord's
  head.
(A') And others who stood by spat on his face, and others buffeted him
  on the cheeks,
others nudged him with a reed, and some scourged him,
saying, "With such honour **let us** honour **the Son of God**."

                                                   (*Gospel of Peter* 3:6–9)

There is nothing whatsoever on the surface of that description that pre-
cludes it being a simple journalistic description of the historical scourging

of Jesus. It is interrupted by no direct and explicit prophetic allusions: "and so was fulfilled what was spoken by the prophet" . . . I underline, however, that while prisoners were quite usually scourged before being crucified, the scourging is not exactly made central or emphasized in the above process. But, on the other hand, every line of that description is redolent with prophetic allusions and with ones whose presence can be vindicated from direct and explicit quotations elsewhere in early Christian literature. Besides a possible one from Psalm 118:13 in A, a more secure one from Isaiah 58:2 in C, and a definite one from Isaiah 50:6–7 (spitting, buffeting/striking, nudging/piercing) in A', all those seen above from Zechariah 3:1–5 and 12:10 (robing, crowning, piercing) are also present. And even the scapegoat background is still evident in that phrase "nudged him *with a reed*," a qualification not present in *Barnabas* 7.

I present that as a paradigmatic case for the transition from prophetic to narrative passion. Passion meditation began with isolated prophecies, for example, Isaiah 50:6–7, each applied to the passion of Jesus *as a whole*. Notice, for example, the words "whom we once crucified" in *Barnabas* 7:9. It was not, I emphasize, that each prophecy was applied to specific details of the passion, for no such specific details *yet* existed. Those individual prophetic passages were also organized around typological applications that allowed for extended meditative exegesis. Read, for example, the correlation between the sacrifice of the red heifer and the death of Jesus in *Barnabas* 8, with its assertion, in 8:2, that "the calf is Jesus." But those exegeses still emphasized only the passion. Next, then, dyadic structures organized and developed the isolated prophecies toward a balanced emphasis on passion and parousia, for example, in Zechariah 12:10–14, 3:1–5, or the Day of Atonement's detailed ritual for the two goats. That was, of course, a tremendously important achievement involving a complete trajectory from past, through present, into future. I insist, once again, that those processes were initially not just apologetic and polemical but constitutive and foundational. Finally, historicized narratives were created out of those prophetic complexes, stories so good that their prophetic origins were almost totally obliterated. I consider it quite possible that a unit such as *Gospel of Peter* 3:6–9 may have arisen even before the larger complex of which it is now a part. The reason is the prior existence of the Carabas case, or at least the model behind it, and also the polished chiastic and titular construction of that particular unit. In any case, once the abusing of Jesus was so told in *Gospel of Peter* 3:6–9, it was copied thence into the entire intracanonical tradition. It seems to me quite possible that, even before a fuller passion narrative was completed, that inaugural move from prophecy to "history," from Jesus as the twin goats from the Day of Atonement to

Jesus as the Mocked King, had already been made as an independent endeavor. But that was still a long way from a complete and detailed story of the passion, a step-by-step and even hour-by-hour drama of events.

Models for a Passion Narrative

As you read through those multiplied prophetic applications and typological correlations of the *Epistle of Barnabas,* you realize how difficult it was, then and now, to communicate such scholarly exegeses to people not interested in minute, learned, and sophisticated textual exercises. But what model could be used to organize them not just into a large exegetical synthesis but into a larger *narrative* framework, into a story understandable by anyone who heard it? There was, however, one model that was not only available for such a development but almost predictable in its usage.

By the middle of the first century, other Christians, basing themselves not so much on prophetical and liturgical as on proverbial and sapiential models, were involved in the collection, development, and creation of Jesus sayings. Two examples of such Gospels are still extant from that period, and each bears traces of at least two layers in its formation. The *Gospel of Thomas,* in three fragmentary Greek texts from Oxyrhynchus and a complete Coptic text from Nag Hammadi, "*may* suggest," according to Stephen Patterson, that a collection made before the death of James in 62 C.E. was afterward expanded to its present scope (171). The *Sayings Gospel Q,* now embedded in Matthew and Luke, may also have undergone expansion as an original sapiential layer was amplified by the intercalation of an apocalyptic one, representing the before and the after of its failed Jewish mission (Kloppenborg 1987). We might have there for Palestine, respectively the southern or Jerusalem, and northern or Galilee traditions of the sayings' collections, which later migrated to become, again respectively but now in Syria, the eastern or Edessa, and western or Antioch streams of that great tradition. But regardless, it is at least certain that, by the middle of the first century, some early Christians were collecting the sayings of Jesus as words of divine wisdom and thence moving toward considering Jesus as Wisdom incarnate. That is but one model for a sapiential understanding of Jesus, however, and it would not assist much in creating a narrative framework for the passion.

There is also another model, still well within the sapiential tradition, that might be distinguished from that *anthological* or collection model by terming it a *narratological* or story model. And their mutuality, that is, the common sapiential roots of both the *anthological* and the *narratological* models can be seen in *Ahiqar,* "one of the best known and most widely disseminated tales in the ancient Mediterranean world," dating from the seventh to sixth centuries B.C.E. "The work is in two parts. The first is the story of Ahiqar, wise scribe and counselor to the kings of Assyria. The sage, advanced in years and having no son to succeed him, decides to adopt his nephew Nadin and teach him all his wisdom. The young man is educated and presented to Esarhaddon [681–669 B.C.E.], and in time takes his uncle's place at court. Nadin, instead of dealing kindly with his uncle, plots to discredit him and manages to convince Esarhaddon that the old man is scheming to overthrow the throne. In a rage, the king orders Ahiqar killed. However, the officer sent to carry out the death sentence turns out to be an old friend of Ahiqar, whom the latter once rescued from death. The two of them concoct a plan by which a slave is substituted for Ahiqar and killed in his place. Evidently the plan succeeds, but the end of the story is lost. Presumably, it related the restoration of Ahiqar to favor and the punishment of Nadin. The second part contains the wisdom of Ahiqar, a collection of slightly over a hundred aphorisms, riddles, fables, instructions, and other brief sayings of various kinds, arranged in a more or less haphazard manner. . . . They cover a wide range of topics such as family discipline, respect for the king, prudent speech, and righteous behavior, and many of the individual sayings are similar to proverbs known from the Bible and wisdom of the ancient Near East" (*OTP* 2.479–480).

However one explains the origins of *Ahiqar*'s twin parts, their very early juxtaposition furnished a duplex model for later sapiential traditions within the biblical tradition. But that duplex model was usually split into one or the other of its component but possibly composite parts. On the one hand, as James Robinson has shown, the *anthological* model flowed through Jewish collections like Proverbs and Ecclesiastes into Christian compilations like the *Sayings Gospel Q* and the *Gospel of Thomas* (Robinson & Koester 71–113). On the other, as George Nickelsburg has shown, the *narratological* model flowed through Jewish stories like Joseph in Genesis 37–50 and the martyrs in 2 Maccabees 7 into Christian accounts of the passion like the *Gospel of Peter* and Mark 14–15 (1972; 1980). It is with that latter proposal that we are now concerned.

In my earlier study of the passion traditions, I suggested that Nickelsburg's *narratological* model actually involved two successive submodels and that they should be kept distinct to understand their development both in Jewish and early Christian tradition (1988a:297–334). I call those submodels *innocence rescued* and *martyrdom vindicated*, and I divide Nickelsburg's examples among them as follows.

The theme and indeed genre of *innocence rescued* is precisely that archetypal story just seen in *Ahiqar*. It has five standard motifs. There is a *Situation* wherein an innocent one, often at court, receives a false *Accusa-*

tion and thence an unjust *Condemnation* to death. But before the death sentence is actually or fully executed, there occurs a *Deliverance*, after which the innocent one gains a *Restoration* to former or even greater status while the unjust accusers are appropriately punished. That is the generic structure of the Joseph saga from Genesis 37–50 and Psalm 105:16–22, of Tobit from Tobit 1:18–22, of Daniel himself in the lions' den from Daniel 3 and of his three companions in the fiery furnace from Daniel 6, of Esther from the book of that name, of Susanna from the supplementary stories added to the Greek translation of Daniel, and of Egyptian Jewry from 3 *Maccabees*. That is a very long stream of tradition, extending from the middle of the first millennium B.C.E. to the middle of the first century C.E. But in all those cases we are always dealing with *innocence rescued*, with virtue saved by divine intervention from most imminent danger of death. It is a tradition, one imagines, most persuasive to those under social pressure and discrimination but not under sustained and lethal persecution.

The theme of *martyrdom vindicated* is something of a deliberate corrective to that rather optimistic vision of *innocence rescued*. It promises salvation not from death but after death, not preservation here below in this world but hereafter in heaven. And it is there, not here, that one's unjust enemies and evil persecutors will be punished. That is the fate of the mother and her seven sons from 2 Maccabees 7 and of the archetypal Just One from Wisdom 1–5. Despite their innocence, God does not intervene to save them from death and punish their accusers and condemners. Salvation and punishment are in the hereafter and can be seen from here not by sight but only by faith.

Innocence Rescued

I propose, still following my earlier study (1988a:297–334), that the first model applied to organize all those discrete prophetic applications to a full passion narrative was that of *innocence rescued*. But that process not only "historicized" the prophetic passion, it allowed the "historicization" of *passion and resurrection* so that resurrection, which was of course taken absolutely for granted in earlier dyadic *passion and parousia* prophecies, could now become part of the story and receive full focus in its own right. This is the model used to present what I call the *Cross Gospel*, the original passion narrative now found in the following three closely linked units within the multilayered *Gospel of Peter*:

(1) Crucifixion and Deposition   in *Gos. Pet.* 1:1–2 and 2:5b–6:22
(2) Tomb and Guards   in *Gos. Pet.* 7:25 and 8:28–9:34
(3) Resurrection and Confession   in *Gos. Pet.* 9:35–10:42 and 11:45–49

Those three acts have a tight narrative continuity: Jesus is crucified by the people themselves; but the miracles at Jesus' death lead the people to wonder about his identity; this forces their leaders to guard the tomb; there are thus Jewish leaders and Roman soldiers there to witness the resurrection; and that allows for confession from the Roman leadership but dissimulation against their own people by the Jewish leadership.

First, the fivefold structure of the *innocence rescued* genre is the organizing principle of that story:

(1) Situation	presumably in materials lost prior to present fragmented opening at *Gos. Pet.* 1:1
(2) Accusation	also lost but residually indicated by "King of Israel" and "Son of God" titles at *Gos. Pet.* 3:6, 7b, 9
(3) Condemnation	abuse, crucifixion, guarded tomb at *Gos. Pet.* 1:1–2; 2:5b–6:22; 7:25; 8:28–9:34
(4) Deliverance	resurrection in presence of his enemies at *Gos. Pet.* 9:35–10:42
(5) Restoration	centurion and Pilate confess Jesus as Son of God at *Gos. Pet.* 11:45–49

What is crucial to that generic argument is that the Deliverance and Restoration must take place before and against the accused one's enemies. Think, for example, of Daniel in the lions' den from Daniel 6. Using the model of *rescued innocence*, Jesus' enemies must be at the tomb to see him rise and must, in fact, confess before Pilate that he has risen. The full restoration occurs, obviously, as official Roman power declares Jesus to be the Son of God. That is, by the way, a breathtaking act of faith for the middle of the first century, maybe breathtaking even to the middle of the fourth century. I take up below the fact that Jesus' Deliverance is "from" death in a very special way.

Next, all the prophetic allusions are now buried under the narrative surface. If you did not know the prophetic passion you would not even recognize them, for example:

(1) The authorities at the trial	in *Gos. Pet.* 1:1	from Ps. 2:1
(2) The abuse and torture	in *Gos. Pet.* 3:9	from Isa. 50:6–7 and Zech. 12:10
(3) The death among thieves	in *Gos. Pet.* 4:10a	from Isa. 53:12
(4) The silence	in *Gos. Pet.* 4:10b	from Isa. 50:7; 53:7

(5) The garments and lots	in *Gos. Pet.* 4:12	from Ps. 22:18
(6) The darkness at noon	in *Gos. Pet.* 5:15	from Amos 8:9
(7) The gall and vinegar drink	in *Gos. Pet.* 5:16	from Ps. 69:21
(8) The death cry	in *Gos. Pet.* 5:19	from Ps. 22:1

The ordinary reader, then or now, might well find claims to their presence quite gratuitous were it not that their explicit citation is found within the *prophetic passion,* that stream of prophetic fulfillment that started independently before, existed independently during, and continued independently after the period of intracanonical Gospel formation (Crossan 1988a).

Finally, much of that narrativization or historicization is beautifully and serenely naive or else, possibly, quite deliberately apologetical and polemical. I take it for granted that early Christianity knew nothing about the passion beyond the fact itself. And reading Psalm 2:1, for example, would help a little but not much in trying to imagine the story of a trial. The author(s) of the *Cross Gospel* wrote from a viewpoint strongly favorable to Roman political authority and strongly critical of Jewish religious authority, blaming it, in fact, for the Jewish people's ignorance of what had really happened. But they also presumed that Herod Antipas could be in charge of a crucifixion near Jerusalem and that people not soldiers could carry it out. I find both of those presuppositions highly unlikely, but they might well bespeak the outlook of a literate Galilean Christianity centered, say, at Sepphoris in the middle of the first century C.E. That city had been the Roman capital of Lower Galilee from 57–55 B.C.E. until 19 C.E., when Herod Antipas gave that privilege to his newly constructed Tiberias on the lake. But, around 54, under the Roman procurator Felix, it was restored to its former position, and it remained firmly pro-Roman in the First Roman-Jewish War of 66, even issuing Eirenopolis or City of Peace coins in 67–68 (Meyers et al. 1986:6). For such Sepphoran Christians, the emphasis was on Galilee not Jerusalem and on Roman procurators not Herodian monarchs. They composed their story, be it politically naive or polemically astute, accordingly.

The Harrowing of Hell

I drew attention above to one very obvious difference between the standard tales of *innocence rescued* and that generic model's application to the case of Jesus in the *Cross Gospel.* Jesus' story agrees with the model in having his enemies see and admit his restoration here on earth and not in the promised or threatened hereafter. But, even if the word for death is avoided, Jesus is "taken up" in *Gospel of Peter* 5:19b. He is not, as it were, rescued from the cross—that is, before death—as were the protagonists in other narratives of that genre. The actual death, of course, was part of the historical passion that could not be denied. But, Jesus' followers must have asked themselves, if he was to rise from the dead more or less immediately, what was the point of such an almost pseudo-death, such an almost unreal demise? The early, and I think it was very, very early, Christian answer was 29 *Descent into Hell* [1/5?].

According to Jean Daniélou, "the descent into hell was a subject of central importance for Jewish Christianity" (1.233), and according to Henry Chadwick, speaking of the late first century *Odes of Solomon,* "the harrowing of Hades was the decisive moment in the redemptive process" (1970:268). It was in Sheol, Hades, or Hell, that the souls of holy and righteous, persecuted and martyred Jews awaited their final and promised deliverance. And it was there that Jesus descended in burial to deliver *those that slept,* as they were called, in triumphant resurrection and communal ascension. But, important as all that once was, it may not even be mentioned in the New Testament (Dalton 1965), and it is but residually present in the apostolic creed's terse statement, "he descended into Hell." There are four reasons why this very early theme was steadily marginalized. First, it is an intensely Jewish Christian one, and the future did not lie with that stream of tradition. Second, it is also intensely mythological, with three linked motifs: a *deception* in which the demons were allowed to crucify Jesus not knowing who he was; a *descent* that was the actual reason for his death and burial; and a *despoiling* whereby Jesus, as Son of God, broke open the prison of Hell and released both himself and all the righteous ones who had preceded him there. Third, it created many doctrinal problems as Christianity developed: did the righteous have to repent? were they baptized? were they given special treatment? how did their redemption relate to that of ordinary Christians? Finally, and I suspect most important, how was it possible to have Jesus "manifested," on the one hand, to the spirits below so he could lead them straight into heaven, and, on the other, to the disciples here on earth so that, between resurrection and ascension, he could give them their official mandate and apostolic authority? It was probably that last problem that irrevocably doomed the descent into Hell to Christian marginality, as can be seen very clearly in the following somewhat desperate solution:

> These apostles and teachers, who preached in the name of the Son of God, having fallen asleep in the power and faith of the Son of God, preached also to those who had fallen asleep before them, and themselves gave to them the seal of the preaching [baptism]. (*Shepherd of Hermas, Similitude* 9.16:5).

The apostolic mandate, in other words, extended not only to the future but to the past, and it was they, rather than Jesus, who exercised it. But that was later, with doctrine becoming embarrassed by mythology. For the *Cross Gospel*, the story was simpler. In *Gospel of Peter* 10:39–42 Jesus leaves his tomb in triumphant resurrection-ascension and behind him, presumably in a huge cruciform procession, come the holy ones. God says or asks Jesus if he "has preached to them that sleep," and they, rather than Jesus, respond in the affirmative. I return to that scene in the next chapter, but, for now, it suffices to note that it is the harrowing of hell, the despoiling of the demonic regions, that is used to explain why Jesus must die and be buried and still, in the genre of *innocence rescued,* be saved "from death" before the very eyes of his enemies.

Martyrdom Vindicated

It was, then, the signal achievement of the *Cross Gospel* to move from the *prophetic passion* to the *narrative passion,* to create from discrete prophetic allusions and composite prophetic fulfillments a coherent and sequential story. It also moved from a dyadic focus on passion and parousia to one on passion and resurrection-ascension. And it even tried to describe the indescribable: Jesus ascending to heaven at the head of the holy ones released from Hell. And the result: Jesus rises, Rome converts.

The first writer to use and develop the *Cross Gospel* composition was, in my judgment on the extant texts, the evangelist Mark himself. I see no convincing evidence that Mark has any other basis for his passion narrative than that source and his own theological creativity. But in following it, he made three profound changes. The first and most basic one was to change the overarching model from *innocence rescued* to *martyrdom vindicated.* No salvific miracle *seen here below* would save Jesus before, during, or after death. Only at the parousia would the resurrectional victory become visible, according to Mark 13:26 and 14:62. And that was true not only for the crucified Jesus but also for his persecuted followers. Salvation was not from but through death, not in the here below but in the imminent hereafter. It was not salvific miracle but exemplary death that counted. Mark had, therefore, to negate completely both the visible resurrection and the subsequent Roman confession from the *Cross Gospel.* He did it by retrojecting both back into preceding sections of his Gospel. Jesus' resurrection-ascension accompanied by two heavenly beings was rewritten as his transfiguration accompanied by Elijah and Moses in Mark 9:2–8. And the centurion, far from confessing Jesus because of having seen the resurrection, as in *Gospel of Peter* 11:45, now does so when he "saw that he thus breathed his last" in Mark 15:39.

The second major change was the duplication of the trial process from a single, composite, and general one in *Gospel of Peter* 1:1–2, based on Psalm 2:1, to distinct religious and political ones before, respectively, the Jewish Sanhedrin and the Roman governor. That explains how the trial's responsibility moves between Pilate and Antipas in the texts of 65 *Pilate and Antipas* [1/3] and other early Christian traditions (Crossan 1988a:33–113). I do not believe, once again, that Jesus' followers knew anything about such details beyond what they could extrapolate from general expectations and prophetic texts such as Psalm 2:1. And I am very unsure what level of Roman bureaucratic authority was empowered to eradicate a peasant nuisance like Jesus. I doubt that "trial" is even a good description of that process even when taken at its most minimal connotation. It is difficult for the Christian imagination, then or now, to accept the brutal informality with which Jesus was probably condemned and crucified. But, in any case, Mark was very interested in how Christians should behave before both religious and political persecution, as we know from Mark 13:9, and in Jesus' passion he gave them a model for both situations. It is impossible, in my mind, to overestimate the creativity of Mark, but those twin trials must be emphasized for what they are, namely, consummate theological fictions. It is also impossible, to my mind, to overestimate the terrible consequences of relocating such abuse as spitting, striking, and goading from an original situation involving Jesus as the Day of Atonement's scapegoat in *Barnabas* 7:8–9, to Jesus with the people in *Gospel of Peter* 2:5b–3:9, to Jesus under separate Jewish and Roman trial in Mark 14:65 and 15:19. It is magnificent theological fiction, to be sure, but entailing a dreadful price for Judaism.

The third major change made by Mark was a better "historicization" of the *Cross Gospel*'s account. Herod Antipas is removed completely from the story, and Pontius Pilate is now in full charge. And soldiers, not people, conduct the crucifixion. But that raises a problem, since Mark wants to have it both ways. Pilate must be in charge, since nothing else is historically plausible, but he must also be innocent of any wrongdoing in the unjust sentencing of Jesus. Mark's solution is to create the Barabbas incident in 15:6–15. I do not believe for a second that it actually happened, that there ever was or ever could be any such open and preset Passover amnesty, or that Pilate deviated on this occasion from his normal crowd-control tactics. When Philo, for instance, is discussing what decent governors do for crucified criminals on festival occasions he can mention only two possibilities: postponing but not abrogating sentences or allowing familial burial to the crucified.

> Rulers who conduct their government as they should and do not pretend to honour but do really honour their benefactors make a practice

of not punishing any condemned person until those notable celebrations in honour of the birthdays of the illustrious Augustan house are over.... I have known cases when on the eve of a holiday of this kind, people who have been crucified have been taken down and their bodies delivered to their kinsfolk, because it was thought well to give them burial and allow them the ordinary rites. For it was meet that the dead also should have the advantage of some kind treatment upon the birthday of the emperor and also that the sanctity of the festival should be maintained. But Flaccus gave no orders to take down those who had died on the cross. Instead he ordered the crucifixion of the living, to whom the season offered a short-lived though not permanent reprieve in order to postpone the punishment though not to remit it altogether. (*Flaccus* 81–84; Colson 9.346–49)

Speaking against the behavior of the Egyptian governor Flaccus in the anti-Jewish pogroms during Gaius Caligula's birthday on August 31 of 38 C.E., Philo can reach, in contrast, only to postponement but not abrogation of sentence. There is no way, I believe, that Pilate, or any other Roman governor, could allow out of prison on a festival occasion *anyone the crowd demanded.* But the Passover amnesty is a magnificent solution, since, for Mark, it symbolically sums up the events of the preceding decades. The people were asked to choose between a bandit or Jesus. They chose the bandit. They chose the leadership of the violent revolutionary over the pacific Jesus, and thereby, for Mark, came the war of 66 C.E. against Rome. The Barabbas incident is true as process even if it never actually happened as event.

Once Mark had made that crucial move from *innocence rescued* to *martyrdom vindicated* as the dominant model for the passion narrative, the other evangelists followed his example. I see no reason to postulate any independent passion tradition for Matthew, Luke, or John beyond what was available to them in both the *Cross Gospel* and Mark. They also clearly preferred, except for specific details chosen by each from the *Cross Gospel*, to follow the lead of Mark.

A Member of the Council

We know from Josephus that thousands of Jewish victims were crucified outside the walls of Jerusalem in the first common era century, from "two thousand" by Varus in 4 B.C.E., according to *Jewish Antiquities* 2.75, to "five hundred or more" a day by Titus in 70 C.E., according to *Jewish War* 5.450. Yet only one crucified skeleton has so far been found in that area from that or any other period (Haas; Naveh; Tzaferis; Yadin). The twenty-four to twenty-eight-year-old man found in northeastern Jerusalem during June of 1968 had died with his arms tied to the crossbar, with a foot nailed on either side of the upright, with legs unbroken, and he was found with an iron nail still impaled through his right heel. He had been buried in one of the niches within a rock-cut tomb and, after his flesh had decomposed, his bones had been reburied in an ossuary (Zias & Sekeles). Apart even from the tomb itself, ossuaries or small boxes used for the secondary burial of bones "were an expensive luxury, and . . . not every Jewish family could afford them" (Tzaferis 1970:30). He was probably, in other words, an exception. His family had enough money, power, or influence, not to save his life but at least to regain his body for proper burial. It recalls the exceptional situation, in which, as in Philo's text above, a governor might allow proper burial in honor of a festive occasion.

What must have happened normally was that the soldiers who executed the crucifixion guarded the cross until death and made sure it was over by burying the crucified one themselves. Guarding was necessary to make certain that nobody intervened to save the crucified person and to ensure the full public effect of the slow and horrible death. Josephus, for example, tells us that he managed to get three friends of his taken down from crosses after the fall of Jerusalem, and though "two of them died in the physicians' hands; the third survived" (*Life* 421). In most cases, however, ordinary families were probably too afraid or too powerless to get close to a crucified body even after death.

All of that would have presented early Christianity with an almost intolerable problem, one that is very clear across the texts of 70 *Burial of Jesus* [1/2]. If, as I maintain, Jesus' followers had fled upon his arrest and knew nothing whatsoever about his fate beyond the fact of crucifixion itself, the horror was not only that he had been executed but that he might not even have been decently buried. But then there was the law of Deuteronomy 21:22–23:

> And if a man has committed a crime punishable by death and he is put
> to death, and you hang him on a tree, his body shall not remain all night
> upon the tree, but you shall bury him the same day, for a hanged man is
> accursed by God; you shall not defile your land which the Lord your
> God gives you for an inheritance. (Deuteronomy 21:22–23)

The unspoken hope and the unspoken presupposition behind the *Cross Gospel* is that Jesus would have been buried, out of piety, by the *Jews* who had crucified him. It never actually describes that burial, but it presumes that those who executed Jesus are totally in control of death, burial, and tomb.

Now it was midday and a darkness covered all Judaea. And they became anxious and uneasy lest the sun had already set, since he was still alive. <For> it stands written for them: the sun should not set on one that has been put to death. And one of them said, "Give him to drink gall with vinegar." And they mixed it and gave him to drink. And they fulfilled all things and completed the measure of their sins on their head.... And then the Jews drew the nails from the hands of the Lord and laid him on the earth. And the whole earth shook and there came a great fear. Then the sun shone <again>, and it was found to be the ninth hour. (*Cross Gospel* in the *Gospel of Peter* 5:15–17; 6:21–22)

The complex 11 *Climax of Sins* [1/4] is there interpreted as a deliberate poisoning of Jesus to hasten his death and enable a burial before sunset. But then, writer and reader hope, Jesus must at least have been given decent burial even if only by his enemies.

The trajectory of the burial tradition sought, after that rather negative beginning, to move from burial by enemies to burial by friends, from inadequate and hurried burial to full, complete, and even regal embalming. The first problem was how to create a story in which Jesus was buried by his friends. If they had power, they were not his friends; if they were his friends, they had no power. Mark, once again, made the crucial preliminary step. He created and sent to Pilate, in 15:43, one "Joseph of Arimathea, a respected member of the council, who was also himself looking for the kingdom of God." That is a perfect in-between figure, at once within the Jewish leadership elite as "respected" and still connected to Jesus as "looking." Need I say that Mark's naming him renders him more not less suspect as an historical figure in my eyes? Both Luke and Matthew are, however, a little nervous with that creation, especially with how Joseph can have a solid and powerful foot in both camps, can be, as it were, at once "Jewish authority" and "Christian believer." Matthew 27:57 solves the ambiguity by stressing Joseph's Christian rather than his Jewish credentials: "When it was evening, there came a rich man from Arimathea, named Joseph, who also was a disciple of Jesus." Luke 23:50–51 focuses on the other half and explains his Jewish rather than his Christian credentials: "Now there was a man named Joseph from the Jewish town of Arimathea. He was a member of the council, a good and righteous man, who had not consented to their purpose and deed, and he was looking for the kingdom of God." John 19:38 solves the problem in his own way by speaking of "Joseph of Arimathea, who was a disciple of Jesus, but secretly, for fear of the Jews." But then, in 19:39, he adds "Nicodemus also, who had at first come to him by night, came bringing a mixture of myrrh and aloes, about a hundred pounds' weight." Jesus, now, is regally embalmed, and there is no mention of a simple linen shroud and a hurried burial. Finally, as the *Gospel of Peter* sought to integrate the *Cross Gospel* with the intracanonical tradition (appendix 7), that is, to correlate Antipas' control with Pilate's control, it created this marvelous solution:

> Now there stood there Joseph, the friend of Pilate and of the Lord, and knowing that they were about to crucify him he came to Pilate and begged the body of the Lord for burial. And Pilate sent to Herod and begged his body. And Herod said, "Brother Pilate, even if no one had begged him, we should bury him, since the Sabbath is drawing on. For it stands written in the law: the sun should not set on one that has been put to death." (*Gospel of Peter* 2:2–5a)

Joseph is now a friend of Pilate and Jesus; the route is now Joseph to Pilate to Antipas. But all of those industrious redactions set out to solve one simple problem. *Nobody knew what had happened to Jesus' body.* And the best his followers could initially hope for was that he had been buried out of Jewish piety toward Deuteronomy 21:22–23. If you turn from the burier to the tomb, exactly the same phenomenon occurs. In Mark 15:46 it was "a tomb which had been hewn out of the rock." In Matthew 27:60 it is Joseph's "own new tomb." In Luke 23:53 it is "a rock-hewn tomb, where no one had ever been laid." In John 19:41 it is "a garden, and in the garden a new tomb where no one had ever been laid." But no amount of damage control can conceal what its intensity only confirms. With regard to the body of Jesus, by Easter Sunday morning, those who cared did not know where it was, and those who knew did not care. Why should even the soldiers themselves remember the death and disposal of a nobody? Still, Matthew 27:19 records, in a unit taken possibly from the *Cross Gospel*'s lost opening, that Pilate's wife had troubled dreams the previous night. That never happened, of course, but it was true nonetheless. It was a most propitious time for the Roman Empire to start having nightmares.

✧ 15 ✧

Resurrection and Authority

> Men feared that to admit the claims of eschatology would
> abolish the significance of His words for our time; and hence
> there was a feverish eagerness to discover in them any elements
> that might be considered not eschatologically conditioned. . . .
> But in reality that which is eternal in the words of Jesus is due
> to the very fact that they are based on an eschatological
> worldview, and contain the expression of a mind for which the
> contemporary world with its historical and social circumstances
> no longer had any existence. They are appropriate, therefore, to
> any world, for in every world they raise the man who dares to
> meet their challenge, and does not turn and twist them into
> nothingness, above his world and his time, making him inwardly
> free, so that he is fitted to be, in his own world and in his own
> time, a simple channel of the power of Jesus. . . . Why spare the
> spirit of the individual man its appointed task of fighting its way
> through the world-negation of Jesus, of contending with Him at
> every step over the value of material and intellectual goods — a
> conflict in which it may never rest?
> *Albert Schweitzer*, The Quest of the Historical Jesus (1968:402)

Even a reader totally innocent of questions about source or genre notices a
drastic change in moving from the passion and burial stories to the resurrection and apparition ones. More specifically, it is very simple to compose
a single harmonized version of the former narratives up to the finding of
the empty tomb but flatly impossible to compose one for the latter traditions. If all those accounts derived from composite memory and historical
recall, it is quite remarkable that an almost hour-by-hour remembrance
prevailed for the death and burial of Jesus but an almost total discrepancy
prevailed for what was, I would presume, even more important, namely, the
extraordinary return of Jesus from beyond the grave to give the disciples
their missionary mandate and apostolic commission.

I am still working here from my earlier explanation for that phenomenon (1988a:335–403). I propose a single stream of tradition for the passion-
resurrection traditions from the *Cross Gospel* into Mark, from both of them

into both Matthew and Luke, and from all of them into John. But although, in general, all later versions accepted the *Cross Gospel*'s passion sequence, none of them was willing to accept its resurrection account. Mark would not do so because his theology was based on a dyad of passion and parousia. The resurrection was simply the departure of Jesus pending a now imminent return in glory. Between passion and parousia was, for Jesus, the time of absence and nonintervention, and, for the community, the time of waiting in faith and of suffering in imitation. There were to be no apparitions within that period, and to speak of them after the passion was to invite and commit the same mistake made by the false prophets and false Christs of Mark 13:5–6 and 13:21–22. Instead, for Mark, as seen above, Roman power believed not because of Jesus' resurrectional apparition but because of Jesus' exemplary death, and the Transfiguration, a foretaste not of resurrection but of parousia according to 9:9–10, was a rewritten relocation of the *Cross Gospel*'s resurrectional apparition back into the earthly life of Jesus. But Matthew, Luke, and even John, on the other hand, do have postresurrectional apparitions. Why then does none of them accept the *Cross Gospel*'s account of Jesus' combined resurrection, apparition, and ascension? It is not, I think, because they disapprove of apparitions. John 20:19–29 allows them even after the ascension in order to say that you should not need them! It is, rather, that a glorious revelation to the righteous dead in order to lead them into heaven is very hard to reconcile with one to the apostolic authorities in order to send them forth to preach. One will have Jesus either appearing after rather than before the resurrection-ascension, or else the liberated dead will have to wait somewhere while Jesus meets with the apostles. The *Cross Gospel*, in other words, could say with serene simplicity that Jesus rose and Rome converted. But others were concerned with how that process was actualized. Who led it, who was in charge, and who was in charge of those in charge?

Meal and Sea

If I am correct that Mark programmatically retrojected Jesus and the two heavenly beings' apparition from the *Cross Gospel* back into the earthly life as what we call the Transfiguration, there is one obvious question. Were any other postresurrectional manifestations or apparitions given a like retrojection? I propose three such cases: 3 *Bread and Fish* [1/6], 190 *Fishing for Humans* [2/3], and 128 *Walking on Water* [1/2]. Behind that proposal lie two linked hypotheses. My first hypothesis recalls the earlier discussion about Jesus' miracles and suggests that those three complexes represent cases with process creating event rather than event creating process. The second hypothesis recalls the earlier distinction between the healing miracles and nature miracles of Jesus. I suggest that those latter stories, including the above trilogy, had nothing originally to do with demonstrating the power of Jesus over nature but rather with establishing the power of leadership over the church and especially of some leaders over others. Notice, for example, that, while the disciples are mostly a choral background for the healing miracles, they are either direct recipients or active mediators in the nature miracles.

I begin with 1 Corinthians 15:1-11 because it shows how resurrectional apparition could be summarized by Paul as early as the winter of 53 to 54 C.E.

> Now I would remind you, brethren, in what terms I preached to you the gospel, which you received, in which you stand, by which you are saved, if you hold it fast—unless you believed in vain. For I delivered to you as of first importance what I also received, that Christ died for our sins in accordance with the scriptures, that he was buried, that he was raised on the third day in accordance with the scriptures, and that he appeared to Cephas, then to the twelve. Then he appeared to more than five hundred brethren at one time, most of whom are still alive, though some have fallen asleep. Then he appeared to James, then to all the apostles. Last of all, as to one untimely born, he appeared also to me. For I am the least of the apostles, unfit to be called an apostle, because I persecuted the church of God. But by the grace of God I am what I am, and his grace toward me was not in vain. On the contrary, I worked harder than any of them, though it was not I, but the grace of God which is with me. Whether then it was I or they, so we preach and so you believed. (1 Corinthians 15:1-11)

First of all, notice the double "in accordance with the scriptures," which recalls the biblical basis that, as I have argued, furnished the creative matrix for the earliest passion and resurrection traditions. Second, notice with what emphasis Paul insists that he too is an apostle. Even if latest and least, he is still equal to those earlier ones. Revelation from Christ is, for Paul, the determining factor in apostolic authority. It makes no difference when or where it occurs. There is nothing about before or after any ascension, before or after any closed off and determined period for mandated mission. An apostle, apparently, could be called by God and Christ at any time or any place. Finally, notice the other personages to whom Christ has appeared, apart from Paul himself: Cephas or Simon Peter, the Twelve; the five hundred brethren; James, all the apostles.

The most striking element in that listing is, as has often been noted, the almost parallel or competitive balance of Cephas and the Twelve, James and the apostles. It also seems that there are three types of protagonists within that set. One is a *general community*, the five hundred brethren, designated only by a single large enumeration. Another is a *leadership group* designated divergently as it accompanies a *specific leader*, either the Twelve with Cephas or the apostles with James. Those three categories of *general community*, *leadership group*, and *specific leader* will be used hereafter to analyze the nature miracle complexes not just as manifestations of the Risen Lord but much more precisely as demonstrations of mission and mandate, community and leadership, power and authority. My idea is to cross those three categories of *community*, *group*, and *leader* with the three complexes of 3 *Bread and Fish* [1/6], 190 *Fishing for Humans* [2/3], and 128 *Walking on Water* [1/2] in order to suggest a trajectory of revelatory apparition moving the emphasis slowly but steadily from *community* to *group* to *leader*.

Bread and Fish

I argued earlier that, if Jesus himself had ritualized a meal in which bread and wine were identified with his own body and blood, it would be very difficult to explain the complete absence of any such symbolization or institutionalization in the eucharistic texts of *Didache* 9–10. It was, therefore, open commensality during his life rather than Last Supper before his death that was the root of any such later ritualization. This is confirmed by the bread and fish Eucharists in the early tradition. For how could such have ever been created if a bread and wine symbolization had already officially antedated them? But, despite the eventual ascendancy of the bread and wine Eucharist, it is impossible to emphasize too greatly the early importance of the bread and fish alternative. Richard Hiers and Charles Kennedy, for instance, have shown how "paintings on the walls of the earliest Christian catacombs in Rome, dating from slightly before 200 A.D., characteristically depict seven or eleven male figures, presumably apostles, seated at table, about to partake of two fish and five loaves . . . [and] two fish also appear accompanied often by five loaves of bread, in . . . early Christian funerary carvings and inscriptions" (21–23). They judge it to "be fairly certain . . . that either for Jesus himself or for quite early, and probably, Jewish Christians, the meal of bread and fish, of which we learn in the gospels, was understood as a eucharistic anticipation if not epiphanic participation in the blessed life of table-fellowship in the Kingdom of God" (45). Furthermore, "there are no known Last Supper scenes in catacomb or sarcophagus art" (Irwin 25). For me, then, two different traditions, one of bread and fish, another of bread and wine, symbolically ritualized, after his death, the open commensality of Jesus' lifetime. That disjunction possibly represented a Jewish Christian and a Gentile Christian development. It might be considered, however, whether bread and fish for the crowd and abundant fragments left over is a better ritualization of Jesus' own life than bread and wine for the believers with abundance now completely irrelevant.

What is, however, of present interest is to watch how *general community, leadership group,* and *specific leader* intertwine with that Eucharist of 3 *Bread and Fish* [1/6]. And in what follows I make no distinction between bread and fish Eucharists before or after the death of Jesus. There are two independent versions of the former, in Mark 6:33–44 and John 6:1–15, and two independent versions of the latter, in Luke 24:30–31, 42–43 and John 21:9, 12–13. Those bread and fish Eucharists and their institutionalization stories went back before anyone ever thought of writing a biographical narrative of Jesus and hence of having to decide what happened "before" and what "after" his death.

First of all, then, consider Jesus' bread and fish Eucharist with the *general community.* This is the most difficult of the three relationships, and it must remain by far the most speculative. But that is quite understandable if it is also the most suppressed. What we are dealing with here is the possibility of very early traditions about a resurrectional and ritualized meal of bread and fish involving Jesus and the believing *community* as a whole, that is, about the eucharistic presence of the Risen Lord but without any discriminating emphasis on leadership in general or on any one leader in particular. On the one hand, there are the five hundred brethren of 1 Corinthians 15:6, clearly distinguished from leadership groups and specific leaders, but with no mention of bread and fish anywhere. On the other, there are the two travelers of Luke 24:13–35, at best a minimally symbolic community, but possibly with an original connection to a bread and fish Eucharist. That latter narrative requires more detailed scrutiny.

In Luke 24 a bread and fish Eucharist is separated over two scenes. In the first scene Jesus appears to "two of them" between Jerusalem and Emmaus and is recognized during a eucharistic meal in which only bread is mentioned in 24:30. But, after their return to Jerusalem, while they are still speaking to "the eleven . . . and those who were with them" in 24:33, Jesus appears again, and this time "they gave him a piece of broiled fish and he took it and ate before them" in 24:42–43. Notice, however, the chiastic structure of Luke's composition:

(A) *Scriptures:* And he said to them, "O foolish men, and slow of heart to believe all that the prophets have spoken! Was it not necessary that the Christ should suffer these things and

enter into his glory?" And beginning with Moses and all the
prophets, he interpreted to them in all the scriptures the
things concerning himself (24:25–27).

(B) *Bread:* When he was at table with them, he took the bread
and blessed, and broke it, and gave it to them. And their eyes
were opened and they recognized him; and he vanished out
of their sight (24:30–31).

(C) *Simon Peter:* And they rose that same hour and returned to
Jerusalem; and they found the eleven gathered together and
those who were with them, who said, "The Lord has risen
indeed, and has appeared to Simon!" (24:33–34).

(B′) *Fish:* And while they still disbelieved for joy, and wondered,
he said to them, "Have you anything here to eat?" They gave
him a piece of broiled fish, and he took it and ate before
them (24:41–43).

(A′) *Scriptures:* Then he said to them, "These are my words
which I spoke to you, while I was still with you, that everything written about me in the law of Moses and the prophets and the psalms must be fulfilled." Then he opened their
minds to understand the scriptures, and said to them, "Thus
it is written, that the Christ should suffer and on the third
day rise from the dead" (24:44–46).

On the one hand, and despite some syntactical strain, those three
apparitions are so structured that Simon Peter takes central place and the
reader is left deliberately uncertain if his apparition might not even have
chronologically preceded the Emmaus one. On the other, the two remaining apparitions, linked by bread and fish, involve either "two of them" or
"the eleven . . . and those who were with them," that latter phrase recalling
"the eleven and .. all the rest" of 24:9. In other words, those apparitions are
not specified as being for the *leadership group* but are for the *general community* comprising a Jerusalem core from which others go out by twos.
Even the missionary mandate in 24:47–49 is addressed to that *general community*, including, of course, the eleven apostles but not at all restricted to
them.

I think, in other words, that Luke himself broke a bread and fish
Eucharist originally associated with the *general community* into a bread
Eucharist of resurrectional presence and a fish vindication of resurrectional physicality, but still connected with *general community* as Luke envisioned it, that is, a Jerusalem core group from which missionaries went out

in twos. That the bread Eucharist in Luke 24:13–35 is a Lukan formulation can be seen from his description of the Eucharist as "the breaking of bread" in Acts 2:42, 46; 20:7, 11; 27:35. That the fish proof in Luke 24:36–43 is a Lukan formulation can be seen from its absence in other versions of that same scene, both from the dependent John 20:19–21 and the independent Ignatius, *Letter to the Smyrnaeans* 3.2b–3, from 18 *Revealed to Disciples* [1/4]. Later, of course, as those narratives were summarily rewritten in Acts 1:1–26, the mention of eating together would remain in 1:4, but there was now a far greater emphasis on the apostles, first eleven in 1:2, then twelve in 1:26, as a leadership group. Indeed, we now have a clear hierarchy of *general community* in 1:14–15, *leadership group* in 1:2, 26, and *specific leader* in 1:15. But still, behind Luke 24:13–43, and even though the broiled fish is now simply a naively physical proof of resurrectional reality, there must have been originally a bread and fish Eucharist, a meal in which the risen Lord was present to the *general community* as a whole.

Next, and much more clearly, there is Jesus' bread and fish Eucharist with a *general community* but with a *leadership group* as significant intermediaries. I am dealing here, still within the 3 *Bread and Fish* [1/6] complex, with the common source behind the multiplication of loaves and fishes in Mark 6 and John 6. First, however, there is the Markan doublet in 6:33–44 and 8:1–10. Frans Neirynck has already annotated in great detail the "duplicate expressions in the gospel of Mark" (1970; 1982:83–142), but there are also units and even sections that show a similar preference for parallelism, balance, and duality. This is one such duplicate event, and it is a dualism created deliberately by Mark himself. Although Robert Fowler has suggested that 8:1–10 is traditional and 6:33–44 is Mark's own redactional creation, I would argue exactly the opposite process. The miracle in Mark 6:33–44 came to him, as it did to John 6:1–15, from that fivefold *Miracles Source* seen earlier. Thereafter Mark composed 8:1–10 as a doublet whose presence greatly increased the culpable incomprehension of the disciples and emphasized their climactic failure in 8:14–21. For now, therefore, that secondary bread and fish miracle may be left aside as a Markan development. What is of present concern, in any case, is the movement, within both Mark and John, from Jesus to disciples to crowds or, in my terms, from Jesus to *leadership group* to *general community*. There are five main elements in the narrative: the *question* comes from the disciples in Mark 6:35 but from Jesus in John 6:5; the *food* comes from the disciples in Mark 6:38 but from "a lad" in John 6:9; the *preparation* comes from Jesus directly in Mark 6:39 but from Jesus through the disciples in John 6:10; the *distribution* comes from Jesus through the disciples in Mark 6:41 but from Jesus directly in John 6:11; and the *collection* of fragments comes from an unidentified "they" in Mark 6:43 but from Jesus through the disciples in John 6:12. The lack of even a single agreement on any one element makes it impossible to be sure what was in the common source for that element. Yet the coincidence in process is quite striking. There must have been a trajectory of change from action *by Jesus directly* toward action *by Jesus through the disciples* along both branches of the transmission. The tradition of a bread and fish Eucharist for the *general community* directly becomes one for the *general community* through a *leadership group*. There may even be a hint of *specific leaders* in the mention of Philip and Andrew in John 6:7–8.

Finally, there is one case of a bread and fish Eucharist between Jesus and the disciples but with no mention whatsoever of any *general community*. The emphasis here is on the *leadership group* itself. The case is John 21:9, 12–13, from 3 *Bread and Fish* [1/6], which is complicated because of its present redactional connection with John 21:1–8, from 190 *Fishing for Humans* [2/3]. Their original separation appears in the divergent Greek words used for fish: in 21:1–8 it is *ichthys*, but in 21:9, 12–13 it is *opsarion*. In the conjunctive and integrative hinge of 21:10–11 it is *opsarion* in 21:10 and *ichthys* in 21:11. That could all be mere coincidence except that, on the one hand, *ichthys* is the word for fish in the parallel to John 21:1–8 at Luke 5:1–11, and, on the other, *opsarion* is the word for fish in the eucharistic "multiplication" at John 6:9, 11. Furthermore, notice how Peter does in the editorial 21:11 what the disciples as a whole do in 21:8. By that redactional stage *specific leaders* have come to the forefront of the story.

In summary, therefore, the bread and fish Eucharist was originally a postresurrectional confession of Jesus' continued presence at the ritualized meals of the believing community. Open commensality survived as ritualized meal. Once narrative Gospels were composed that tradition was placed both before the resurrection, in the common source for Mark 6 and John 6, and after the resurrection, in Luke 24 and John 21. Even more fascinating, however, are those fleeting but tantalizing glimpses we catch across the bread and fish tradition as it moves from *general community* toward *leadership group* and on to *specific leaders*.

There is one final and very important point. Hierarchical rank rather than egalitarian commonality was emphasized symbolically in the ritual meals of the Qumran Essenes. That priestly led group withdrew from Jerusalem's Temple to a "monastery" on the Dead Sea's northwest coast, judging that the Temple was polluted after the usurpation of the high priesthood by the Hasmonean rulers, Jonathan and Simon, between 152 and 134 B.C.E. Here are two examples found in the first of the caves (1Q) where the group hid their precious library during the First Roman-Jewish War of 66–73 C.E. The first one is taken from the *Rule of the Community*, or *Manual of Discipline,* and the second one from its badly fragmented appendix, *The Rule of the Congregation,* or *Messianic Rule,* both from manuscripts dated to about 100 B.C.E.

> And when the table has been prepared for eating, and the new wine for drinking, the Priest shall be the first to stretch out his hand to bless the first-fruits of the bread and new wine. (1QS 6:4–5; Vermes 1968:81)

> And [when] they shall gather for the common [tab]le, to eat and [to drink] new wine, when the common table shall be set for eating and the new wine [poured] for drinking, let no man extend his hand over the first-fruits of bread and wine before the Priest; for [it is he] who shall bless the first fruits of bread and wine, and shall be the first [to extend] his hand over the bread. Thereafter, the Messiah of Israel shall extend his hand over the bread, [and] all the Congregation of the Community [shall utter a] blessing, [each man in the order] of his dignity. (1QSa 2; Vermes 1968:121)

There the emphasis is on hierarchy, precedence, and the order of dignity. A very different emphasis appears in Jesus' commensality. The four key verbs of *take, bless, broke, gave* from Mark 6:41 reappear at the Last Supper in Mark 14:22; similarly, the four verbs of *take, give thanks, broke, gave* from the Last Supper in Luke 22:19 reappear as *take, blessed, broke, gave* in Luke 24:30; and the expression "took ... given thanks ... distributed ... so also the fish" from John 6:11, within a eucharistic context underlined by 6:53–58, reappears as "took ... gave ... so with the fish" in John 21:13. I think, therefore, that even as early communities ritualized the contents of Jesus' open commensality, they also continued one major feature that has not been mentioned so far. Recall what was said earlier about the anthropology of eating as the absolutely vital matrix for Jesus' own meal symbolism. In summary, from Peter Farb and George Armelagos: "In all societies, both simple and complex, eating is the primary way of initiating and maintaining human relationships ... Once the anthropologist finds out where, when, and with whom the food is eaten, just about everything else can be inferred about the relations among the society's members ... To know what, where, how, when, and with whom people eat is to know the character of their society" (4, 211). Dennis Smith, for example, speaking from the Greco-Roman context, notes that "the posture of reclining required that one be served, thus tending to associate it ... with a class who owned servants" and that "sometimes status among guests would be indicated by the host by serving a lower quality of food or wine to those at his table whom he considered to be of lower rank" (35, 37). Verbs such as *took, blessed, broke, gave* have, therefore, profound symbolic connotations and may well stem from that inaugural open commensality itself. They indicate, first of all, a process of *equal sharing* whereby whatever food is there is distributed alike to all. But they also indicate something even more important. The first two verbs, *took* and *blessed,* and especially the second, are the actions of the master; the last two, *broke* and *gave,* and especially the second, are the actions of the servant. Jesus, as master and host, performs instead the role of servant, and all share the same food as equals. There is, however, one further step to be taken. Most of Jesus' first followers would know about but seldom have experienced being served at table by slaves. The male followers would think more experientially of females as preparers and servers of the family food. Jesus took on himself the role not only of servant but of female. Not only *servile* but *female hosting* is symbolized by those four verbs. Far from reclining and being served, Jesus himself serves the meal, serves, like any housewife, the same meal to all including himself. Later, of course, and quite legitimately, it would happen that just as the female both serves food and becomes food, so Jesus would both have served food here below and would become food hereafter (Bynum). But long before Jesus was host, he was hostess.

Walking on Water

The thesis of this chapter is that the "nature" miracles of Jesus are actually credal statements about ecclesiastical authority, although they all have as their background Jesus' resurrectional victory over death, which is, of course, the supreme "nature" miracle. If those who accepted Jesus during his earthly life had not continued to follow, believe, and experience his continuing presence after the crucifixion, all would have been over. That *is* the resurrection, the continuing presence in a continuing community of the past Jesus in a radically new and transcendental mode of present and future existence. But how to *express* that phenomenon? And, just as significantly for any human process involving a now-dead founder, what was, by Jesus' will, to be the direction of that community, what was to be its authority structure, and who was to be in charge? But how to express *that* phenomenon?

Recall the spectrum of commentary seen already at various places. Tacitus, a derisive opponent, said that "the pernicious superstition" spread from Judea to Rome. Josephus, in a more prudently neutral statement, said that "those who had in the first place come to love him did not give up their affection for him. . . . And the tribe of the Christians, so called after him, has still to this day not disappeared." Paul ransacked metaphor in 1 Corinthians 15 to explain Jesus' resurrectional mode of existence but insisted that "flesh and blood cannot inherit the kingdom of God, nor does the perishable inherit the imperishable." Still, Luke 24:39 and Ignatius, *Letter to the Smyrnaeans* 3.2b–3 could talk of touching and feeling the risen Jesus and of having literal rather than symbolical, actual rather than eucharistic meals in his continued company. But, then again, John 20:24–29, in 386 *Faith Against Sight* [3/2], created the doubting Thomas incident almost as a satire on such literality: "Blessed are those who have not seen and yet believe."

We have just seen one way of putting that faith and that experience into narrative as 3 *Bread and Fish* [1/6]. Another such credal narrative is 128 *Walking on Water* [1/2], but, unlike that preceding case, this is not located after as well as before the crucifixion. Nevertheless, it was already linked to 3 *Bread and Fish* [1/6] in the common *Miracles Source* used by both Mark and John. There are also some residual indications of its original resurrectional function when Mark, for example, is contrasted with those other narratives, 3 *Bread and Fish* [1/6] and 190 *Fishing for Humans* [2/3], that are located both before and after the resurrection in the present Gospel sequences. First, Jesus came "about the fourth watch," that is, toward morning, in Mark 6:48b, just what happened "as day was breaking" in John 21:4. He came in the dawn of their fruitless or dangerous night. Next, "he meant to pass them by" in Mark 6:49 just as in Luke 24:28–29. The disciples must make the initial overture. Then, "they thought it was a ghost, and cried out; for they . . . were terrified" in Mark 6:50a, just as "they were startled and frightened, and supposed that they saw a spirit" in Luke 24:37. Finally, Jesus reassured them with "it is I" in both Mark 6:50b and Luke 24:39.

The original symbolism of the narrative is clearer in John 6:16–21 than in Mark 6:45–52. In the former case the emphasis is on the disciples. Sailing without Jesus they make no headway against the wind, but once they "take him into the boat [it] immediately . . . was at the land to which they were going." It is not even certain, as Julian Hills of Marquette University mentioned to me in conversation, that Jesus walked *on* the sea in this story. The Greek word is *epi*, and that is translated as "on the sea" in John 6:19 but "by the sea" in John 21:1. Thus John 6:16–21, apart from its parallel version in Mark 6:45–52, can be taken to mean that they were forced along the shore by the contrary winds until they finally picked up Jesus "three or four miles" from where they had started. The point is not to diminish the miracle but to keep the focus where it should be, not on the general power of Jesus but on the specific impotence of the disciples without him. In Mark, however, the emphasis has shifted to underline the majestic power of Jesus, hence, of course, to increase their culpable misunderstanding. That is clearly Mark's own redactional theology maintaining, as is its wont, that the disciples were impotent not only without Jesus but even with him. The original point, however, was not just that Jesus could walk on and calm the raging sea but that he could and would do it to help the disciples succeed in their mission. And, of course, such a walk was itself a beautiful symbol of resurrection, of victory over death. It was the risen Jesus who assisted and thereby validated their authority.

Mark's own polemical theology also explains the parallelism between the earlier sea miracle in Mark 4:35-41 and the present one in 6:45-52. I propose that, just as he doubled the meal miracle from Mark 6:33-44 into Mark 8:1-10 so also did he double the sea miracle from 6:45-52 into 4:35-41. That gives him a double sequence of sea and meal, first in 4:35-41 and 6:33-44, then in 6:45-51 and 8:1-10. But the biting point of that duplication becomes clear from the climactic sea/meal conversation in 8:14-21. The disciples have been through it all twice, and they still do not understand that there is but one single bread and it is more than enough for Jews and Gentiles alike and together (Kelber 45-65).

Two final points. First, I move for a moment outside the inventoried corpus used in this book. The sequence of sea and meal, rather than meal and sea, appears in a section of the Christian *Sibylline Oracles,* a work of uncertain date (*OTP* 1.416), that, I think, is independent of the canonical Gospels:

> With a word shall he make the winds to cease, and calm the sea
> While it rages walking on it with feet of peace and in faith.
> And from five loaves and fish of the sea
> He shall feed five thousand men in the desert,
> And then taking all the fragments left over
> He will fill twelve baskets for a hope of the people.
> (*Sibylline Oracles* 8:273-278; NTA 2.734; OTP 1.424)

Not only is the sequence there sea and meal rather than meal and sea, but the sea miracle includes both facets, the wind and the waves, later split by Mark over 6:45-52 (wind) and 4:35-41 (wind, waves). Furthermore, the *Epistula Apostolorum,* a work dating from 160 to 170 C.E., but definitely dependent on the canonical Gospels, has a long and carefully constructed account of Jesus' miracles in *Epistula Apostolorum* 4-5 (NTA 1.193-194; Cameron 1982:134-135). That account, however, seems to be combining *stories* of miracles that are intracanonically dependent with *lists* of miracles that are intracanonically independent. The structure is as follows, amending somewhat the seminal analysis of Julian Hills (1985:61-62; 1990a:46; see also 1990b):

(1) Single detailed miracle with dialogue: student
    + "then" + single detailed miracle without dialogue and
    three undetailed miracles: Cana, dead, lame, hand.

(2) Single detailed miracle with dialogue: hemorrhage
    + "then" + four undetailed miracles: deaf, blind, exorcism,
    leper.

(3) Single detailed miracle with dialogue: Legion
    + "then" + single [?] detailed miracle without dialogue: sea.

(4) Single detailed miracle with dialogue: denarius
    + "then" + single detailed miracle without dialogue: five
    thousand fed.

I placed a question mark after that sea miracle. Is it single or double?
The text reads: "Then he walked on the sea, and the winds blew, and he
rebuked them, and the waves of the sea became calm." The general structure leads one to expect a single miracle in that slot. The author, despite
possible knowledge of the Markan dyad, has, I think, presented them as a
single miracle. If the sea miracles were, before and apart from Mark, an
original single miracle, that might also explain why early Christian miracle
lists treat them, as Julian Hills has shown, like "companion pieces, quite
independent of their NT counterparts though likely derived from them"
(1985:68; 1990a:50). The creative interaction of *intracanonically independent miracle lists* and *intracanonically dependent miracle stories* requires
much fuller investigation (see Frankfurter; and Hills 1990b).

Second, and in conclusion, it seems possible that 128 *Walking on Water*
[1/2] developed from 3 *Bread and Fish* [1/6] as a natural dyad based on the
balance and sequence of sea and meal miracles from the Exodus tradition,
as summarized, for example, in Psalm 78:13, 21–29. If that was so, the order
of meal and sea in the *Miracles Source* used by Mark and John may have
been reversed under the influence of the non-Exodus situation and
sequence in Psalm 107:4–9, 23–32.

Fishing for Humans

The last of the three complexes is 190 *Fishing for Humans* [2/3], and
like 3 *Bread and Fish* [1/6] but unlike 128 *Walking on Water* [1/2] it is found
independently both "before" and "after" the crucifixion and resurrection.
In my thesis, therefore, it was originally another symbolical, resurrectional
validation of apostolic authority. None of the three was an illusion, halluci-
nation, vision, or apparition. Each was a symbolic assertion of Jesus' continued presence to the *general community,* to *leadership groups,* or to
specific and even competing *individual leaders.*

With regard to 190 *Fishing for Humans* [2/3], the quite unmiraculous
story in Mark is copied closely by Matthew but replaced by a completely
different and miraculous version in Luke:

And passing along by the Sea of Galilee, he saw Simon and Andrew the brother of Simon casting a net in the sea; for they were fishermen. And Jesus said to them, "Follow me and I will make you become fishers of men." And immediately they left their nets and followed him. And going on a little farther, he saw James the son of Zebedee and John his brother, who were in their boat mending the nets. And immediately he called them; and they left their father Zebedee in the boat with the hired servants, and followed him. (Mark 1:16–20 = Matthew 4:18–22)

While the people pressed upon him to hear the word of God, he was standing by the lake of Gennesaret. And he saw two boats by the lake; but the fishermen had gone out of them and were washing their nets. Getting into one of the boats, which was Simon's, he asked him to put out a little from the land. And he sat down and taught the people from the boat. And when he had ceased speaking, he said to Simon, "Put out into the deep and let down your nets for a catch." And Simon answered, "Master, we toiled all night and took nothing! But at your word I will let down the nets." And when they had done this, they enclosed a great shoal of fish; and as their nets were breaking, they beckoned to their partners [*metochois*] in the other boat to come and help them. And they came and filled both the boats, so that they began to sink. But when Simon Peter saw it, he fell down at Jesus' knees, saying, "Depart from me, for I am a sinful man, O Lord." For he was astonished, and all that were with him, at the catch of fish which they had taken; *and so also were James and John, sons of Zebedee, who were partners* [*koinōnoi*] *with Simon.* And Jesus said to Simon, "Do not be afraid; henceforth you will be catching men." *And when they had brought their boats to land, they left everything and followed him.* (Luke 5:1–11; my emphases)

The Markan account is a deliberate diptych, in which, first, Simon and Andrew cast their nets and then leave them, and second, James and John sit with their father in the boat and then leave them both. The metaphor that rules the double transition is this: as they once fished for fish, so they will now fish for human beings. It is not, incidentally, the happiest possible choice of metaphor.

The Lukan account is more subtle. It is located a little later in his narrative and combines sections from Mark 1:16–20 and 4:1–2 with a quite independent miracle-story in Luke 5:4–9a. The opening and closing of that original unit are lost behind the combination of Markan source and Lukan redaction in the verses italicized above (see Fitzmyer 1981–85:559–569). It is still clear, however, that the story's focus is on Simon and that, apart from Mark's influence in 5:10, no other disciples are mentioned by name. Indeed, Simon alone is actually called in 5:10b and, despite its Lukan formulation, that verse probably reflects the source's original emphasis. The metaphor is now much better as well. By themselves Peter and his companions catch nothing, but when Jesus appears and commands them, they catch a huge haul. The transition is not from catchers of fish to fishers of humans but from acting unsuccessfully without Jesus' mandate to acting successfully with it. Indeed, it may well have been Mark himself who, in omitting the symbolic miracle, replaced it with a less than fortunate metaphorical saying.

The last version of this episode is even more strikingly separated from those preceding versions in Mark and Luke.

> After this Jesus revealed himself again to the disciples by the Sea of Tiberias; and he revealed himself in this way. Simon Peter, Thomas called the Twin, Nathanael of Cana in Galilee, the sons of Zebedee, and two others of his disciples were together. Simon Peter said to them, "I am going fishing." They said to him, "We will go with you." They went out and got into the boat; but that night they caught nothing. Just as day was breaking, Jesus stood on the beach; yet the disciples did not know that it was Jesus. Jesus said to them, "Children, have you any fish?" They answered him, "No." He said to them, "Cast the net on the right side of the boat, and you will find some." So they cast it, and now they were not able to haul it in, for the quantity of fish. That disciple whom Jesus loved said to Peter, "It is the Lord!" When Simon Peter heard that it was the Lord, he put on his clothes, for he was stripped for work, and sprang into the sea. But the other disciples came in the boat, dragging the net full of fish, for they were not far from the land, but about a hundred yards off. When they got out on land, they saw a charcoal fire there, with fish lying on it, and bread. Jesus said to them, "Bring some of the fish that you have just caught." So Simon Peter went aboard and hauled the net ashore, full of large fish, a hundred and fifty-three of them; and although there were so many, the net was not torn. Jesus said to them, "Come and have breakfast." Now none of the disciples dared ask him, "Who are you?" They knew it was the Lord. Jesus came and took the bread and gave it to them, and so with the fish. (John 21:1–13)

The miraculous catch is but a variant of Luke 5:4–9a, as can be seen from both the general structural similarity as well as the particular use of the name Simon Peter in Luke 5:8 and John 21:7. There are now seven disciples in question, but Simon Peter is mentioned first in 21:2, starts the process in 21:3, and, despite the redactional intrusion of the Beloved Disciple in 21:7, is consistently in the forefront of both catch in 21:7 and meal in 21:11.

Recalling the chronological sequence of the Gospels from Mark to Luke to John, one might easily judge that 190 *Fishing for Humans* [2/3] developed from a nonmiraculous saying of Jesus in Mark, to a miraculous symbolization in Luke, to be finally displaced into a more climactic post-resurrectional setting in John. All the internal evidence, however, points in exactly the opposite direction. The unit's trajectory is from John to Luke to Mark, and the miracle, far from a later insertion, is a later deletion. Notice, for example, that Peter's confession of his sinfulness in Luke 5:8 makes far less sense there than in a postresurrectional situation after he had denied Jesus during his trial. Thus, at a "charcoal fire" in John 21:9, 15–17, Peter will thrice affirm Jesus just as earlier, at another "charcoal fire" in 18:17–18, 25–26, he had thrice denied him. The complex 190 *Fishing for Humans* [2/3] is therefore a companion piece to 128 *Walking on Water* [1/2] and carries exactly the same meaning and message. To row all night without Jesus is to get nowhere; to fish all night without Jesus is to catch nothing. But, of course, it is the leadership group of the disciples who are both rowing and fishing, and it is to them that Jesus' resurrectional assistance is forthcoming. *They*, also, administer the bread and fish and gather the fragments after the meal (but not, by the way, in the independent *Sibylline Oracles* 8: 275–278 just quoted above).

The Named and the Unnamed

The discipline of this book is to work primarily with plurally attested complexes from the primary stratum of the Jesus tradition. Conclusions from that investigation form the bedrock for further explorations of later strata and single attestations. But there is one item that falls somewhat between the cracks of such a method, and that is the presence of named individuals within a complex, source, or unit. I am not speaking here of the well-known tendency to give unnamed protagonists later names as the transmission grows and develops. I refer to what we just saw in reading 1 Corinthians 15:5, 7. There the names of Cephas and James, especially as read within such complexes as 6 *Revealed to Peter* [1/5] or 30 *Revealed to James* [1/3], indicate questions, debates, and even controversies over direction, leadership, and authority within the early communities. And such tensions involved discussions not just of personage but of type and gender of leadership as well.

Personage clashes were already evident by the early fifties in a text such as Galatians 1–2, with Paul asserting his independent and equal ascendancy against the Jerusalem and Antioch authorities. They also appear in *Gospel of Thomas* 13–14. The transition from James as leader in *Gospel of Thomas* 13 to Thomas as leader in *Gospel of Thomas* 14 seems a peaceful and nonpolemical transition, but, in that latter text, Thomas himself is exalted to preeminence in contrast to both Peter and Matthew.

Type clashes may well be behind the dialectic between Peter and the Beloved Disciple throughout John 20–21. Is some debate over, say, institutional as against charismatic, hierarchical as against egalitarian, patronal as against servile leadership behind those scenes in John 20–21?

Gender clashes are evident in who gets to ask Jesus questions in the discourse Gospels. In the *Gospel of Thomas*, for example, "the disciples" offer Jesus questions, comments, or requests in 6, 12, 18, 20, 24, 37, 43, 51, 52, 53, 99, 113. But named disciples also raise questions in three units: Mary in 20, Salome in 61, and Peter in 114. And that final one is extremely significant:

> Simon Peter said to them, "Let Mary leave us, for woman are not worthy of life." Jesus said, "I myself shall lead her in order to make her male, so that she too may become a living spirit resembling you males. For every woman who will make herself male will enter the kingdom of heaven." (*Gospel of Thomas* 114)

In the *Gospel of Thomas* two female disciples are named questioners, and the only male questioner asks that one of them be removed precisely because she is a woman. To question is to lead, to be a questioner is to be a leader, and Simon Peter seeks to deny a leadership role to Mary. Historically he succeeds.

There is one obvious objection to all this. What about the named women and the empty tomb? What about the fact that Jesus appeared first to named women in Matthew 28:8–10 and John 20:14–18? Does that not admit their importance in and for the early communities? What, especially, about Mark 16:1–8, where the first of the canonical Gospels concludes with named female disciples at the empty tomb and no apparitions to named male disciples afterward? I conclude this book with a look at the named and the unnamed in the original ending of Mark. I do not refer to the fact that, as Bruce Metzger has summarized the situation, "four endings of the Gospel according to Mark are current in the manuscripts" (122). My question is not whether there was a further ending originally appended to 16:1–8 but whether 16:1–8 was itself the original ending. And my reason for that question is the problem posed by the *Secret Gospel of Mark*.

Secret Mark is, as we have seen before, a version of Mark's Gospel mentioned in a fragmentary letter of Clement of Alexandria from the end of the second century. It was discovered in 1958 by Morton Smith of Columbia University in the Greek Orthodox Monastery of Mar Saba between Bethlehem and the Dead Sea (1960; 1973a; 1973b; 1982). Although we can only guess at other differences, we are sure that it diverges from our present canonical Mark in at least two important locations (Smith 1973b:446–453; Cameron 1982:70–71). First, after the present or canonical Mark 10:32–34, it narrates a more primitive version of John 11 in which an unnamed young man is raised from the dead by Jesus and then comes to him by night robed as befits a candidate for baptism, which, as you will recall from an earlier discussion, was necessarily nude. Second, after the present or canonical Mark 10:46a, it narrates Jesus' refusal to meet the family of the young man:

> And they came to Jericho; and as they were leaving Jericho with his disciples . . . (Mark 10:46ab)

> And he comes to Jericho. And the sister of the youth whom Jesus loved and his mother and Salome were there, and Jesus did not receive them. (*Secret Gospel of Mark* 2r14–16)

It is especially those last two units that raise a very basic problem. According to Clement's own explanation, public or canonical Mark, intended for catechumens or "those who were being instructed" in Christianity prior to baptism, was written first, and *Secret Mark*, intended as "a more spiritual Gospel for the use of those who were being perfected" by baptism, was the later version. A glance at those two citations cited above makes that explanation somewhat unlikely. It reads much more like canonical Mark's total excision of some event already partially excised by either *Secret Mark* itself or else by Clement's description. Indeed, the more one compares the two versions, the more likely it seems that, as Helmut Koester put it, "Canonical Mark is derived from Secret Mark. The basic difference between the two seems to be that the redactor of canonical Mark eliminated the story of the raising of the youth and the reference to this story in Mk 10:46. . . . Clement of Alexandria believed that Mark first wrote the 'canonical' (or 'public') Gospel, and later produced the 'secret' version of this writing. My observations, however, lead to the conclusion that 'canonical' Mark was a purified version of that 'secret' Gospel, because the traces of the author of Secret Mark are still visible in the canonical Gospel of Mark" (1983:56–57). Several other scholars, such as Hans-Martin Schenke (1984), Marvin Meyer (1990), and myself (1985; 1990), agree that Clement gives the sequence incorrectly and that canonical Mark is a development of *Secret Mark* rather than the reverse. But we also disagree rather fundamentally on how that process worked.

Helmut Koester, for example, noting that, with regard to citations, "there is no certain quotation from Mark before Irenaeus and Clement of Alexandria" at the end of the second century and that, with regard to manuscripts, "Mark appears for the first time in the mid-third-century in P[apyrus] 45 which contains the text of all four canonical gospels" (1983:37), concludes that "there should be no question that the oldest accessible text of the Gospel of Mark is preserved in most instances in which Matthew and Luke agree in their reproduction of their source—even if the extant Markan manuscript tradition presents a different text. These instances ... include cases in which Matthew and Luke agree in the wording of a phrase or sentence that is different from Mark's text; and cases in which Markan words, sentences, or entire pericopes are absent from both Matthew and Luke" (1990:21). That conclusion led Koester to postulate three successive versions of Mark's Gospel. First came *Proto-Mark*, known to Matthew and Luke in longer and shorter editions. Next, came *Secret Mark*, a theologically motivated redaction containing not only the two units now known from Clement's letter but many other details still present in canonical Mark but lacking from *Proto-Mark*, as indicated by their double absence in Matthew and Luke. Finally, there is *canonical Mark*, a version that censored out those twin units mentioned in Clement's letter because, presumably, they had led to the erotic interpretation favored by the Carpocratians.

Koester is surely correct that "textual critics of the New Testament writings have been surprisingly naïve" in presuming that our earliest Markan manuscripts accurately reflect their autographical archetype (1989b:19). But, first of all, and with regard to his basic principle, major and minor agreements of Matthew and Luke against Mark cannot automatically be taken as evidence for their Markan source. In every single case, and case by case, coincidental redaction by both of them must be weighed against later corruption in the Markan tradition. That is not just special pleading for the accuracy of the Markan manuscript tradition. I take it for granted that Koester is quite correct on the inevitability of such scribal corruption. But, the Two Source theory of synoptic literary relations accepts the coincidence that both Matthew and Luke, separately and independently, decided to unite Mark and the *Sayings Source Q* and decided, again separately and independently, to swallow both into their own new textual and theological compositions. They did not, in other words, like Mark as a narrative Gospel. They rewrote it and would probably be very surprised to find it today wedged in between them. The more Markan something is, either in the peculiarities of its Greek syntax or the peculiarities of its distinctive theology, the more likely Matthew and Luke are to change it. And, in such cases, they are as likely to change it the same way as to change it in different ways. That is, in my view, the overwhelming result of the monumental inventory of "minor agreements" analyzed by Frans Neirynck (1974). Once again, and after Koester's admonition, we will have to be much more critical about the possibility of Markan textual change being indicated by the minor agreements of Matthew and Luke against our present text, but coincidental redactional change will have to be assessed as an alternative in every single case. Next, with regard to the possibility of *Proto-Mark*, I find the postulation of different editions, one with Mark 6:45–8:26 known to Matthew and one without it known to Luke, very hard to accept. Are we talking of addition or subtraction from the autograph? If *subtraction* in the version used by Luke, I would accept it as an open possibility but not one of great interest. If *addition* in the version used by Matthew, the problems begin to multiply. How and why did that addition occur? What was the textual, theological, and generic integrity before and after that addition? What caused the addition of 6:45–8:26 to the shorter version? Was it a prior unity? What, in any case, was the reason for its addition? The suggestion of an original version of Mark lacking 6:45–8:26 raises far more profound difficulties than does its alternative, namely, that Luke, probably with a view to the second volume of his Gospel, which we call the Acts of the Apostles, and also in a desire to mitigate the virulence of Mark's attack on the disciples that comes to a first climax in that section, simply omitted it entirely from his own composition. It was not that he disliked emphatic redundancy, think of Peter in Acts 10:1–48 and 11:1–18 or Paul in Acts 9:1–29; 22:1–21 and 26:9–23, but rather that he needed space, disliked some of Mark 6:45–8:26, and what he liked he wanted kept for his second volume. Finally, in this theory, I do not understand the logic of canonical Mark's final redaction, which, to counteract the Carpocratian interpretation, censored out, after Mark 10:34, the young man's raising from the dead by Jesus, surely the least dangerous part of the story, but kept, at Mark 14:51–52, the young man's nakedness in the garden with Jesus, surely its more dangerous part. And it kept him also, in this reading, at 16:5, within the Gospel's climactic ending.

My own counterproposal involves only two versions of Mark. The original one could be accurately called the *Secret Gospel* because it contained the twin episodes of the young man's raising and naked initiation as well as that involving his family. My strong suspicion is that the latter incident was given much more fully in Clement's copy and that the phrase "Jesus did not receive them" represents Clement's own summarized and possibly already censored commentary. Be that as it may, the former incident led, I presume immediately, to erotic interpretations from the side of libertine pre- or proto-Gnosticism. I presume that such forces were already operative by the middle of the first century, as evidenced by some of Paul's opponents at Corinth (MacRae 1978; 1980). I have, in other words, no presumption that the "Carpocratian" interpretation had to wait for Carpocrates in the second century to become a problem for the Markan text. It was not enough simply to excise the offending passage from a new "edition" of Mark. Opponents already had the fuller text and could easily prove, however we are to imagine such a textual war, that they were right in their interpretation since they were right in their text. The solution, as I have argued elsewhere in more detail, was not only to remove the offending text but to scatter its dismembered parts throughout the Markan Gospel (1985:89–121). Thereafter, its presence in any version of Mark could be counterclaimed as pastiche from such residue. Marvin Meyer, by the way, describes that as "a rather idiosyncratic theory" (137). It is, to be sure, but does the idiosyncrasy reside with me or with Mark?

My theory, then, is that canonical Mark dismembered *Secret Mark*'s story of the young man's resurrection and initiation so that only Mark 14:51–52 residually evidenced the initiation and Mark 16:1–8 residually evidenced the resurrection. Thus, for example, the "tomb" in Mark 16:2, 3, 5, 8 comes from the "tomb" in *Secret Mark* 1v26; 2r1, 2, 6; "who will roll away the stone for us from the door of the tomb" in Mark 16:3 comes from "rolled away the stone from the door of the tomb" in *Secret Mark* 2r1–2; and, especially, the "young man" in the tomb in Mark 16:5 comes from the "young man" in the tomb in *Secret Mark* 2r3, 4, 6. But that raises a question I did not realize earlier (1976; 1988a:283–284). When you remove those elements, what is actually left for a conclusion to *Secret Mark*? How did *Secret Mark*, the first version of Mark's Gospel, actually end? If the young man in the tomb was created by canonical Mark, what was there before that creation? Did *Secret Mark* conclude with *any* story about finding the empty tomb?

The obvious answer is that of course it did. There are still the women. But now I notice a curious coincidence that I missed before. There are three women identified in *Secret Mark* 2r14–16 as "the sister of the youth whom Jesus loved and his mother and Salome." There are also three women mentioned in Mark 15:40 as "Mary Magdalene, and Mary the mother of James the younger and of Joses, and Salome," in 15:47 as "Mary Magdalene and Mary the mother of Joses," and in 16:1 as "Mary Magdalene, and Mary the mother of James, and Salome." Is that too much coincidence? There are, obviously, far more names given in canonical Mark, but it and *Secret Mark* agree, respectively, on a triad involving, first, a named or unnamed woman, second, a named or unnamed mother, and, third, Salome. I think that, once again, canonical Mark has simply relocated the textual debris of a censored incident from *Secret Mark*. So do even the three women, inaugurally and therapeutically enveloped among many other women in 15:40–41, come from the creativity of canonical Mark? The three women were not, any more than the young man in the tomb, part of the conclusion to *Secret Mark*. The question presses, then, how did it end?

My proposal is that the original version of Mark's Gospel ended with the centurion's confession in 15:39. What comes afterward, from 15:40

through 16:8, was not in *Secret Mark* but stems from canonical Mark. I realize, of course, that such a claim lacks any external or manuscript evidence unless one retrojects the fact that redoing the ending of Mark became a small industry in the early church. The evidence for it is internal and circumstantial, tentative, hypothetical, and clearly controversial. But it fits very well with a Markan theology in which faith and hope despite persecution and death is much more important than visions, apparitions, and even revelations.

If that reading is correct, Mark framed the passion of Jesus with the confession of the unnamed woman in 14:3–9 and that of the unnamed centurion in 15:39. Jesus had repeatedly told the disciples about his forthcoming death and immediate resurrection. They had not believed him, especially about the former event. But that unnamed woman believed in his imminent death, and she anointed him in symbolic preparation for it since, as *Secret Mark* knew full well, there would be no chance for an anointing after it. Her reward is the stunningly emphatic and uniquely explicit statement of Jesus, "truly, I say to you, wherever the gospel is preached in the whole world, what she has done will be told in memory of her," a quotation from Mark 14:9 beautifully underlined as the title of Elisabeth Schüssler Fiorenza's book. One could surely, by the way, make a better case for Mark-as-a-woman obliquely signing her manuscript by that sentence at 14:9 than one ever did for Mark-as-a-man obliquely signing his by that flapping nightshirt in the garden at 14:51–52.

The centurion, named Petronius in the *Cross Gospel*, at *Gospel of Peter* 8:31, which was, in my opinion, known and used by Mark, is left unnamed by him at the end of the passion narrative in parallelism to the unnamed woman at its inception. In the end, therefore, Mark decided to give little credit to named disciples, not to Peter, James, and John, and likewise not to Mary Magdalene, Mary mother of James and Joses, and Salome, but rather to an unnamed woman and an unnamed man, possibly a Jewish woman and probably a Gentile man. The future of Jesus lay, for Mark, with both genders alike but more with the unnamed than with the named in each.

Epilogue

When Narcissus died, the flowers of the field were desolate and
asked the river for some drops of water to weep for him. "Oh!"
answered the river, "if all my drops of water were tears, I should
not have enough to weep for Narcissus myself. I love him."
"Oh!" replied the flowers of the field, "how could you not have
loved Narcissus? He was beautiful." "Was he beautiful?" said the
river. "And who should know better than you? Each day, leaning
over your bank, he beheld his beauty in your waters." "If I loved
him," replied the river, "it was because, when he leaned over my
waters, I saw the reflection of my waters in his eyes."
> Oscar Wilde, "The Disciple" (Ellmann 356–357)

Charisma as a term expresses less a quality of person than of
relationship; it contains the acceptability of a leader by a
following, the endorsement of his personality, and the social
endowment of power. . . . *Charisma* is a sociological, and not
a psychological concept . . . [it] expresses the balance of claim
and acceptance — it is not a dynamic, causally explanatory,
concept; it relates to an established state of affairs, when the
leader is already accepted, not to the power of one man to
cause events to move in a particular direction.
> Bryan Wilson (499)

The historical Jesus must be understood within his contemporary Judaism.
But that contemporary Judaism was, as modern scholarship insists ever
more forcibly, a richly creative, diverse, and variegated one. By the end of
the second century C.E. rabbinic Judaism, like catholic Christianity, was
deeply involved in retrojecting its ascendancy onto earlier history so that it
would later be as difficult to discern that earlier plurality in one as in the
other. But it is certainly quite incorrect to see Jesus' current Judaism as uni-
formly, normatively, or even predominantly rabbinical. And neither is the
distinction between Palestinian Judaism and Diaspora Judaism a particularly useful or helpful one. It is a geographical distinction but not an ideological one. What, for instance, is the ideological difference between those

417

two first-century Jews, the Diaspora's Philo of Alexandria and Palestine's Josephus of Jerusalem? There was, in the world and time of Jesus, only one sort of Judaism, and that was Hellenistic Judaism, Judaism responding with all its antiquity and tradition to a Greco-Roman culture undergirded by both armed power and imperial ambition.

Jesus and Judaism

There is, however, one distinction within Hellenistic Judaism that still seems valid and useful; that is the difference between *exclusive* and *inclusive* Judaism, between exclusive and inclusive reactions to Hellenism. I insist immediately that those terms are intended quite neutrally. I have no presumption that exclusivity is always wrong or inclusivity always right. Exclusivity, at its extreme, can mean petrification, isolation, and irrelevance. Inclusivity, at its extreme, can mean abdication, betrayal, and disintegration. By exclusive I mean a Judaism seeking to preserve its ancient traditions as conservatively as possible with minimal conjunction, interaction, or synthesis with Hellenism on the ideological level. By inclusive I mean a Judaism seeking to adapt its ancestral customs as liberally as possible with maximal association, combination, or collaboration with Hellenism on the ideological level. That distinction is, of course, really a continuum with manifold gradations, and, I repeat, a religion, a culture, or a people could lose its soul at the extremity of either direction.

One way to test that distinction's validity is to read three great multivolume textual collections in chronological simultaneity. If you compare Victor Tcherikover's *Corpus Papyrorum Judaicarum*, Menahem Stern's *Greek and Latin Authors on Jews and Judaism*, and James Charlesworth's *The Old Testament Pseudepigrapha* for any same general period you can see the documentary and literary evidence for what Jews were saying about Gentiles and Gentiles about Jews at that moment. It is not always nice reading — in either direction. But at times it is positive, and, in any case, it always bespeaks at least a forced interaction on both sides. Indeed, the savagery of pagan anti-Judaism seems often to stem from the successes of Jewish missionary activity. Recall the bitter comment of Seneca the philosopher, son of Seneca the Elder, writing in the sixties of the first common-era century, that "the customs of this accursed race have gained such influence that they are now received throughout all the world. The vanquished have given laws to their victors" (*De Superstitione*; Stern 1.431). Two examples must suffice as summary for a total synoptic reading of those three immensely valuable collections.

First, on God. In the last part of the second century B.C.E., an Alexandrian Jew composed the fictional *Letter of Aristeas to Philocrates,* a work that has been described, by George Nickelsburg, as presenting "in the whole of our literature . . . the most positive estimate of the Greeks and Greek culture and of the possibility for peaceful and productive coexistence between Jews and Greeks" (1981:165), and, by John Collins, as "a manifesto of the self-sufficiency of Diaspora Judaism" (1983:85). Its Jewish author, speaking fictionally through a pagan, says that the Jews "worship the same God—the Lord and Creator of the Universe, as all other men, as we ourselves, O king, though we call him by different names, such as Zeus or Dis" (*Aristeas* 15; APOT 2.96 rather than the translation in OTP 2.13). That quite extraordinary admission from a Jew about paganism is matched in the next century by a pagan, Marcus Terentius Varro, speaking about Judaism. Although a Pompeian, pardoned by Caesar and then proscribed by the Second Triumvirate, he escaped to become, as Menahem Stern put it, "the greatest scholar of republican Rome and the forerunner of the Augustan religious restoration" (1.207). Most of his prodigious work is no longer extant, but Saint Augustine reports that "Varro . . . thought the God of the Jews to be the same as Jupiter, thinking that it makes no difference by what name he is called, so long as the same thing is understood. . . . Since the Romans habitually worship nothing superior to Jupiter . . . and they consider him the king of all the gods, and as he perceived that the Jews worship the highest God, he could not but identify him with Jupiter" (*Res Divinae*; Stern 1.210).

On the other hand, of course, Jews could mock pagans for worshiping "clay idols of dead gods" (*Sibylline Oracles* 3:588; OTP 1.375), and pagans could talk of Jews adoring an ass's head in their temple at Jerusalem (Apion, *Aegyptiaca*; Stern 1.410).

Second, on morality. As with images, so with ethics. Jewish texts could look at the worst of paganism and vaunt their own superiority. They could also look at the best of paganism and proclaim their mutuality. And vice versa. In the middle of the second century B.C.E., the *Third Sibylline Oracle* could claim that Phoenicians, Egyptians, Romans, Greeks, Persians, Galatians, and Asians transgressed "the holy law of the immortal God" on adultery, homosexuality, and infanticide (3:594–600, 764–766; OTP 1:375, 379). But then, on precisely those same three actions, an unknown Jew, writing in Ionic hexameters, probably in Alexandria between about 30 B.C.E. and 40 C.E., could advocate the Jewish position with the pen of a pagan teacher, taking on the fictional identity of a famous poet from Miletus in the middle of the sixth century B.C.E. The *Sentences of Pseudo-Phocylides* speaks against "the adulterous bed," against letting "a woman destroy the unborn babe in her belly," against "throw[ing] it before the dogs and the vultures as a prey," and against "intercourse of male with male" (178, 184, 185, 191; *OTP* 2.580–581). Those *Sentences* are, of course a fiction, or, if one prefers, a forgery, but they are based on a more inclusive vision of Judaism and paganism, a more irenic vision presuming a superior ethic not only from exclusively Jewish revelation but from commonly available natural law. And what, once again, of the other side?

Diodorus the Sicilian, a writer of the first century B.C.E., records what happened when, between 134 and 132 B.C.E., the Hasmonean John Hyrcanus found himself hopelessly besieged in Jerusalem by Antiochus VII Sidetes and sued for peace. The anti-Jewish advisers of the Syrian monarch, reminding him how his predecessor Antiochus IV Epiphanes had attacked the Temple, proposed instead an immediate genocide. Their reason was that "Moses, the founder of Jerusalem and organizer of the nation . . . had ordained for the Jews their misanthropic and lawless customs." And so they advised him "to make an end of the race completely, or, failing that, to abolish their laws and force them to change their ways" (*Bibliotheca Historica*; Stern 1.183). But, then, to the contrary, Numenius of Apamea in Syria, follower of Pythagoras and Plato and main precursor of the Neoplatonists, writing in the second half of the second century C.E., gave Judaism this supreme philosophical accolade. "What is Plato," he asked, "if not Moses speaking in Attic Greek?" (Stern 2.209).

If you try to envisage that early first common-era century without any of the unified simplifications that later rabbinic Judaism, or catholic Christianity, would retroject upon it, three questions must be faced. Faced, I emphasize again, despite the fact that we have been taught to consider them unthinkable. First, left to itself, what would have happened to the dialectic of exclusive and inclusive Judaism? Second, left to itself, would Judaism have been willing to compromise on, say, circumcision, in order to increase missionary possibilities among Greco-Roman pagans? Or, again, if paganism conceded on divinity and morality, could Judaism have conceded on intereating and intermarrying? Third, left to itself, could Judaism have converted the Roman Empire? Moot questions, to be sure, but worth asking if only to counteract the influence of a rabbinic Judaism and a catholic Christianity that have taught us not to ask them. Moot questions because, of course, the process was not left to itself. Within sixty-five years, first in 70–73, next in 113–115, and finally in 132–135 C.E., Judaism in, respectively, Palestine, Egypt and its environs, and Palestine again, rose against Rome. There were two results from those three wars, possibly of equal importance for the future of Judaism and Christianity. First, the Temple of Jerusalem was destroyed and Judea was proscribed to Jews. Second, Egyptian Judaism was destroyed. That facilitated the move from levitical to rabbinical Judaism and also the ascendancy of exclusive over inclusive Judaism. I understand that assessment, whether correct or incorrect, as a neutral judgment of historical fact and not as an implicit moral indictment or indirect religious criticism.

A Peasant Jewish Cynic

Those moot questions are important for two reasons. One is that Jesus has been interpreted, in this book, against the background of inclusive rather than exclusive Judaism. It is not, however, the elite, literary, and sophisticated philosophical synthesis of a Philo of Alexandria. It is, rather, the peasant, oral, and popular philosophical praxis of what might be termed, if adjective and noun are given equal weight, a Jewish Cynicism. What a Cynic was is clear from this book's fourth chapter. It involved practice and not just theory, life-style and not just mind-set in opposition to the cultural heart of Mediterranean civilization, a way of looking and dressing, of eating, living, and relating that announced its contempt for honor and shame, for patronage and clientage. They were hippies in a world of Augustan yuppies. Jesus and his followers, but not John the Baptist and his, fit very well against *that* background. Greco-Roman Cynics, however, concentrated primarily on the marketplace rather than the farm, on the city dweller rather than the peasant. And they showed little sense of collective discipline, on the one hand, or of communal action, on the other. Jesus and his followers do not fit well against *that* background. This book's second part suggested a fivefold popular typology against a backdrop of first-century Palestinian peasant turmoil. It ranged from the human violence of the bandit leader, through the human and divine violence of the messianic claimant, to the exclusively divine violence of the millennial prophet, and the nonviolence of the protester. But it also contained the magician, a type barely discernible behind and despite later rabbinical prophylaxis. Jesus is closest to that fifth type rather than to, say, a millennial or apocalyptic prophet like John the Baptist, who, even if he never led crowds *from* the Jordan, certainly gathered crowds *at* the Jordan. Moreover, baptizing *in the Jordan* was never just a matter of water but of history, never just a matter of purificatory baptism but of freedom from imperial slavery. We are forced, then, by the primary stratum itself, to bring together two disparate elements: healer and Cynic, magic and meal.

The historical Jesus was, then, a *peasant Jewish Cynic*. His peasant village was close enough to a Greco-Roman city like Sepphoris that sight and knowledge of Cynicism are neither inexplicable nor unlikely. But his work

was among the farms and villages of Lower Galilee. His strategy, implicitly
for himself and explicitly for his followers, was the combination of *free healing and common eating*, a religious and economic egalitarianism that
negated alike and at once the hierarchical and patronal normalcies of Jewish religion and Roman power. And, lest he himself be interpreted as simply
the new broker of a new God, he moved on constantly, settling down neither at Nazareth nor Capernaum. He was neither broker nor mediator but,
somewhat paradoxically, the announcer that neither should exist between
humanity and divinity or between humanity and itself. Miracle and parable, healing and eating were calculated to force individuals into unmediated physical and spiritual contact with God and unmediated physical and
spiritual contact with one another. He announced, in other words, the
brokerless kingdom of God.

Jesus and Christianity

This is a book about the historical Jesus and not about the history of
earliest Christianity. But it is impossible to conclude without some more
direct comments on what happened after Jesus.

I think, first, that both those preceding sections are necessary to
explain the rather swift spread of Christianity. It took both the ideological
orientation and practical missionary experience of inclusive Judaism *as well
as* the enabling vision and abiding presence of Jesus to create that effect.
Jesus, as a peasant Jewish Cynic, was already moving, but on a popular
level, within the ambience of inclusive Judaism's synthesis of Jewish and
Gentile tradition. But the wider surges, from countryside to city, from
Palestine to Diaspora, and from, maybe, Aramaic to Greek, also moved
along the well-established routes and strategies of inclusive, missionary
Judaism. By the end of the first century two great religions, rabbinic Judaism and early Christianity, were emerging from a common matrix. Each
claimed to be its only legitimate continuation, and each had texts and traditions to prove that claim. Each, in fact, represented an equally valid,
equally surprising, and equally magnificent leap out of the past and into
the future. It would, in truth, be difficult to say, had Moses awoke from
slumber around 200 C.E., which of the two would have surprised him the
more. I insist once more that in linking exclusive Judaism with rabbinic
Judaism and inclusive Judaism with early Christianity I am not making a
comparison pejorative in either direction. To be human is to balance particularity and universality, and, although the balance may always tip one
way or the other, either extreme is equally inhuman. You can lose your soul
at either end of the spectrum, and one can and should ask, with equal

legitimacy: did Judaism give too little in failing to convert the Roman Empire? did Christianity give too much in succeeding?

That brings up a second point. Is an understanding of the historical Jesus of any permanent relevance to Christianity itself? I propose that at the heart of any Christianity there is always, covertly or overtly, a dialectic between a historically read Jesus and a theologically read Christ. Christianity is always, in other words, a Jesus/Christ/ianity. The New Testament itself contains a spectrum of divergent theological interpretations, each of which focuses on different aspects or clusters of aspects concerning the historical Jesus, or better, different historical Jesuses. It may be, for example, only the sayings, or only the miracles, or only the death, that is of primary concern for a given tradition, but any of those emphases presumes divergent historical Jesuses who said something, did something, and died in a certain way. I think, therefore, that different visions of the historical Jesus present a certain dialectic with different theological interpretations and that the New Testament itself is an obvious expression of that plurality's inevitability. But any analysis of a historical Jesus must be open to the disciplined historical methods of its *contemporary* world and must be able to stand up to its judgments without special pleading. It may also help, of course, to overturn those methods and judgments, because, if scientific history cannot handle somebody that important, it may well be thereby indicating its own vacuity. Need I say, at this point, that the way in which the nineteenth century dreamed of uncommitted, objective, dispassionate historical study should be clearly seen for what it was, a methodological screen to cover various forms of social power and imperialistic control? This book challenges the reader on the level of formal method, material investment, and historical interpretation. It presumes that there will always be divergent historical Jesuses, that there will always be divergent Christs built upon them, but, above all, it argues that the structure of a Christianity will always be: *this is how we see Jesus-then as Christ-now.* I am proposing that the dialectic between Jesuses and Christs (or Sons, or Lords, or Wisdoms, or . . .) is at the heart of both tradition and canon, that it is perfectly valid, has always been with us and probably always will be.

But how, at least, can one ever reconcile speaking of a brokerless Kingdom, of Jesus proclaiming the unmediated presence of God, with such Christian interpretations as, for instance, "For there is one God, and there is one mediator between God and men, the man Christ Jesus," from 1 Timothy 2:5, or, "Therefore he is the mediator of a new covenant, so that those who are called may receive the promised eternal inheritance, since a death has occurred which redeems them from the transgressions under the first covenant," and, "Jesus, the mediator of a new covenant . . . the sprinkled blood that speaks more graciously than the blood of Abel," from Hebrews 9:15 and 12:24? Christianity, however, when it attempted to define as clearly as it could the meaning of Jesus, insisted that he was "wholly God" and "wholly man," that he was, in other words, himself the unmediated presence of the divine to the human. I find, therefore, no contradiction between the historical Jesus and the defined Christ, no betrayal whatsoever in the move from Jesus to Christ. Whether there were ultimate betrayals in the move from Christ to Constantine is another question. It is even possible that, most inappropriately and unfortunately, imagining Jesus as broker or mediator facilitated that latter move (see Malina 1987). It is hard, indeed, not to get very, very nervous in reading this description of the imperial banquet celebrating the Council of Nicaea's conclusion:

> Detachments of the body-guard and troops surrounded the entrance of the palace with drawn swords, and through the midst of them the men of God proceeded without fear into the innermost of the Imperial apartments, in which some were the Emperor's companions at table, while others reclined on couches arranged on either side. One might have thought that a picture of Christ's kingdom was thus shadowed forth, and a dream rather than reality. (Eusebius, *Vita Constantini* 3.15; Brown 1982: 16)

The meal and the Kingdom still come together, but now the participants are the male bishops, and they recline, with the Emperor himself, to be served by others. Maybe, Christianity is an inevitable and absolutely necessary "betrayal" of Jesus, else it might all have died among the hills of Lower Galilee. But did that "betrayal" have to happen so swiftly, succeed so fully, and be enjoyed so thoroughly? Might not a more even dialectic have been maintained between Jesus and Christ in Jesus Christ?

Finally, then, there is the problem of reconstruction. This book is one scholar's reconstruction. And what, after all, does scholarly reconstruction have to do with ecclesiastical faith, what does the university have to do with the church?

This problem became very obvious a few years ago when Robert Funk of the Westar Institute convened the Jesus Seminar to try and establish some scholarly consensus on the historical Jesus. Scholars who accepted his open invitation met twice a year for over five years at various seminaries or universities and worked toward an inventory of what they considered as originally from Jesus, separating such units from what they considered the creation of earlier tradition or later evangelist. After presenting papers and discussing arguments, they voted on each item. They voted with colored beads for one of four options: red meant "Jesus said it"; pink meant "Jesus said something like it"; gray meant "Jesus didn't say it, but it contains his ideas"; black meant "Jesus didn't say it, the content or perspective is from a later or different tradition." Colored beads and ballot boxes were intended, no doubt, to catch the media's attention, since one of the Seminar's purposes was popular education about the problems and difficulties, results and conclusions of contemporary historical Jesus research. But actual objections, from laity and scholars alike, often spoke against the whole idea of voting on Jesus or against the legitimacy, validity, or usefulness of any reconstructed historical Jesus. It was as if a final vote by a scholarly committee was somehow inappropriate in relation to Jesus. It was scorned as presumptuous or dismissed as blasphemous to grade the Jesus tradition on a fourfold scale. Yet scholars know, even if the laity does not, that the very Greek text of the New Testament on which any modern translation must be based is itself a reconstruction and the result, however executed, of a scholarly vote in a committee of experts. And that too is based on a fourfold scale. The United Bible Societies' third edition of *The Greek New Testament* grades disputed readings as A, B, C, or D in the critical apparatus at the bottom of each page. "By means of the letters A, B, C, and D," explains the introduction, "the Committee has sought to indicate the relative degree of certainty, arrived at on the basis of internal considerations as well as the external evidence, for the reading adopted as the text. The letter A signifies that the text is virtually certain, while B indicates that there is some degree of doubt. The letter C means that there is a considerable degree of doubt whether the text or the apparatus contains the superior reading, while D shows that there is a very high degree of doubt concerning the reading selected for the text" (Aland et al. xii–xiii). Thus, for example, the account of the Last Supper in Luke 22:17–20 is graded a C, and Bruce Metzger, in his commentary for the committee, speaks of majority and minority opinions (173–177). Grading by color or grading by letter makes no substantial difference to the process. Beads or ballots, hands raised or heads nodded does not change the ultimate fact of scholarly reconstruction. Furthermore, to make the matter worse, that scholarly reconstruction is made by collating manuscripts, all of which date, with one tiny and textually insignificant exception, from around 200 C.E. or after. Hence this warning from Helmut Koester: "The problems for the reconstruction of the textual history of the canonical Gospels in the first century of transmission are immense. The assumption that the reconstruction of the best archetype for the manuscript tradition is more or less identical with the assumed autograph is precarious. The oldest known archetypes are separated from the autographs by more than a century. Textual critics of classical texts know that the first century of their transmission is the period in which the most serious corruptions occur. Textual critics of the New Testament writings have been surprisingly naïve in this respect" (1989b:19). And again, from François Bovon: "We must learn to consider the gospels of the New Testament canon, in the form in which they existed before 180 C.E., in the same light in which we consider the apocrypha. At this earlier time the gospels were what the apocrypha never ceased to be. Like the apocrypha, the gospels of the New Testament were not yet canonical; they did not circulate together [for example, only Luke and John are present in Papyrus 45], and when they did, they did not always appear in the same sequence [for example, the order Matthew, John, Luke, Mark in Codex Bezae]" (20).

This book, then, is a scholarly reconstruction of the historical Jesus. And if one were to accept its formal methods and even their material investments, one could surely offer divergent interpretative conclusions about the reconstructable historical Jesus. But one cannot dismiss it or the search for the historical Jesus as *mere* reconstruction, as if reconstruction invalidated somehow the entire project. Because there is *only* reconstruction. For a believing Christian both the life of the Word of God and the text of the Word of God are alike a graded process of historical reconstruction, be it red, pink, gray, black or A, B, C, D. If you cannot believe in something produced by reconstruction, you may have nothing left to believe in.

Appendix 1

An Inventory of the Jesus Tradition by Chronological Stratification and Independent Attestation

A. Chronological Stratification

First Stratum [30–60 C.E.]

1. First Letter of Paul to the Thessalonians [1 Thess.]. Written from Corinth in late 50 C.E. (Koester 1982:2.112).

2. Letter of Paul to the Galatians [Gal.]. Written from Ephesus possibly in the winter of 52–53 C.E. (Koester 1982:2.116).

3. First Letter of Paul to the Corinthians [1 Cor.]. Written from Ephesus in the winter of 53–54 C.E. (Koester 1982:2.121).

4. Letter of Paul to the Romans [Rom.]. Written from Corinth in the winter of 55–56 C.E. (Koester 1982:2.138).

5. *Gospel of Thomas* I [*Gos. Thom.* I]. A serial collection of Jesus' sayings with limited individual linkage by means of theme, word, or expression. Although it has several dialogues, it has no miracles, no narrative connections, and no passion-resurrection account. It is known in three fragmentary Greek copies from Oxyrhynchus (P. Oxy. 1, 654, 655; van Haelst ##593–595) and in a Coptic translation (CG II,2) among the Nag Hammadi codices (Lambdin; Cameron 1982: 23–27). There may be at least two separate layers in it. One was composed by the fifties C.E., possibly in Jerusalem, under the aegis of James's authority (see *Gos. Thom.* 12). After his martyrdom in 62 C.E., the collection and maybe also its community, migrated to Syrian Edessa. There a second layer was added, possibly as early as the sixties or seventies, under the aegis of the Thomas authority (see *Gos. Thom.* 13). The collection is independent of the intracanonical Gospels (Davies; Crossan 1985; but esp. Patterson). Those twin layers are identified, but tentatively and experimentally, as follows: the earlier James-

427

layer is now discernible primarily in those units with independent attestation elsewhere and is placed in the first stratum (*Gos. Thom.* I), the Thomas-layer is now discernible primarily in that which is unique to this collection, or at least to the general Thomas tradition, and is placed in the second stratum (*Gos. Thom.* II). That rather crude stratification underlines the need for a better one, but it also emphasizes how much of this collection is very, very early.

6. **Egerton Gospel [*Eger. Gos.*].** The *Egerton Gospel* is known from a single codex now separated over two locations: (a) Papyrus Egerton 2 (P. Lond. Christ 1; van Haelst #586) contains eighty-seven damaged lines on two large fragments, one much smaller one, and a scrap; (b) Papyrus Köln 255 (Inv. 608) adds twelve lines of completion or addition to the bottom of fragment 1. The *Egerton Gospel* must now be taken as presented and numbered not by Bell and Skeat (1935a:8–12; 1935b:29–32; *NTA* 1.96–97; Cameron 1982:74–75) but by Gronewald (138–142 & plate 5). He, however, presuming the *Egerton Gospel*'s intracanonical dependence, changed the order of the fragments to 1, 3, 2. The standard order of 1, 2, 3 is probably more neutral and preferable, hence the best available edition is now that of Daniels (12–16). The codex copy has been dated from the early second to the early third century, but the original composition, which is independent of all the intracanonical Gospels, could be as early as the fifties C.E.

7. **Papyrus Vindobonensis Greek 2325 [P. Vienna G. 2325].** A tiny seven-line text from a third-century papyrus (scroll?) is commonly known as the Fayum Fragment because it was discovered among provincial archives from the Egyptian Fayum acquired by the Archduke Rainer for the library of the Austro-Hungarian Empire in Vienna (van Haelst #589). The *editio princeps* is either Bickell (1887) or Wessely (1946, from 1907). It is, as argued by Bickell, Wessely, and Harnack (1889), independent of the intracanonical Gospels, a fact more evident in the Greek original than in English translations (Hennecke et al. 1.115–116; James 25)

8. **Papyrus Oxyrhynchus 1224 [P. Oxy. 1224].** Two fragments from a Greek papyrus book of the early fourth or maybe even the late third century were discovered by B. P. Grenfell and A. S. Hunt in 1903–4 and published by them in 1914. The pages are numbered, and the thirty pages between fragments 1 and 2 make it possible that they might not even be from the same document (Grenfell & Hunt 1914:1–10 & plate 1; van Haelst #587). Fragment 1 is very small, but fragment 2 is large enough to indicate that it is independent of the intracanonical Gospels.

9. **Gospel of the Hebrews [*Gos. Heb.*].** There are no extant fragments; it is known only from seven patristic citations and is independent of the intracanonical Gospels (Koester 1982:2.223–224). Composed by the fifties

C.E., in Egypt, it depicted the preexistence, advent, sayings, and resurrectional appearance of Jesus as the incarnation of divine Wisdom.

10. **Sayings Gospel Q.** Now embedded within the Gospels of Matthew and Luke. A serial collection of Jesus' sayings but with more compositional organization than the *Gospel of Thomas.* Composed by the fifties, and possibly at Tiberias in Galilee, it contains no passion or resurrection account but presumes the same myth of divine Wisdom as do the *Gospel of Thomas* and the *Gospel of the Hebrews.* There may be three successive layers in its development: a sapiential layer (1Q), an apocalyptic layer (2Q), and an introductory layer (3Q), and it is inventoried within those three rubrics (Kloppenborg 1987; 1988).

11. **Miracles Collection.** Now embedded within the Gospels of Mark and John. Of the seven miracles in John 2–9, the five in John 5, 6 (two), 9, 11 that have Markan parallels appear in the same order in Mark 2, 6 (two), 8 and *Secret Mark.* Collections of Jesus' deeds, like collections of Jesus' words, were already being composed by the fifties C.E.

12. **Apocalyptic Scenario.** Now embedded in *Didache* 16 and Matthew 24. There is a common apocalyptic source behind both *Did.* 16:3–8 and Matt. 24:10–12, 30a that was not known or used by Mark 13 (Kloppenborg 1979).

13. **Cross Gospel.** Now embedded in the *Gospel of Peter* [*Gos. Pet.*]. It contained, at least, a linked narrative of Crucifixion and Deposition in 1:1–2 and 2:5b–6:22, of Tomb and Guards in 7:25 and 8:28–9:34, and of Resurrection and Confession in 9:35–10:42 and 11:45–49. Composed by the fifties C.E., and possibly at Sepphoris in Galilee, it is the single source of the intracanonical passion accounts (Crossan 1985; 1988a). A major alternative proposal is that a single Passion Source was used independently by Mark, John, and the *Gospel of Peter* (Koester 1990:220).

Second Stratum [60–80 C.E.]

14. **Gospel of the Egyptians [Gos. Eg.].** There are no extant fragments, it is known only from six patristic citations, and is independent of the intracanonical Gospels. Its dialogue format is more developed than that in the *Gospel of Thomas* (Koester 1980b:255–256) but both contain the same theology of celibate asceticism as necessary to restore the pre-Adamic split into male and female (MacDonald). It was composed in Egypt, possibly by the sixties C.E. .

15. **Secret Gospel of Mark [Secret Mark].** The first version of the Gospel of Mark contained the accounts of 130 *Dead Man Raised* [1/2] in 1v20–2r11a after Mark 10:32–34 and of 255 *Raised Man's Family* [2/1] in 2r14b–216 after Mark 10:35–46a (Smith 1973a; 1973b). This version was

composed in the early seventies C.E., but those units were immediately interpreted by libertine Gnostics, proleptic Carpocratians as it were, similar to those Paul encountered at Corinth (Crossan 1985).

16. Gospel of Mark [Mark]. The second version of Mark expurgated those passages but left their textual debris strewn across its text. That may well have been done, with the minimal rewriting necessary, by the end of the seventies C.E. (Crossan 1985; but see Koester 1983).

17. Papyrus Oxyrhynchus 840 [P. Oxy. 840]. This fragmented account of a debate between Jesus and a Pharisaic chief priest is formally more developed than the debates in the *Egerton Gospel* or Mark 7, so it may be dated tentatively around the eighties (Cameron 1982:53).

18. *Gospel of Thomas* II [*Gos. Thom.* II]. See comments earlier under *Gospel of Thomas* I [*Gos. Thom.* I].

19. *Dialogue Collection.* Now embedded within the *Dialogue of the Savior* (CG III,5). The dialogues between Jesus, Judas, Matthew, and Mariam, which constitute more than half this document, are created by expanding a collection of Jesus' sayings that is independent of the intracanonical Gospels. This source is still clearly distinguishable in *Dial. Sav.* 124.23–127.18; 131.19–132.15; 137.3–147.22 (Pagels & Koester; Emmel et al.) and shows a more developed dialogue format than in the *Gospel of Thomas* or the *Sayings Gospel Q* (Koester, 1980b:255–256).

20. *Signs Gospel* or *Book of Signs.* Now embedded within the Gospel of John. In John 2–14 the distinctive theology involves a combination of miracle and discourse wherein the earlier *Miracles Collection* is integrated with an independent collection of the sayings of Jesus so that physical miracles become signs pointing, through their attendant discourses, to spiritual realities. It is independent of the three Synoptic Gospels of Mark, Matthew, and Luke. A more difficult question is whether it had anything about John the Baptist and an even more difficult one is whether it had any passion and resurrection account. If it had neither, their later presence might be due to and dependent on the Synoptic accounts.

21. Letter to the Colossians [Col.]. Written most likely not by Paul himself but posthumously by one of his students in his name (Koester 1982:2.261–267).

Third Stratum [80–120 C.E.]

22. Gospel of Matthew [Matt.]. Written around 90 C.E. and possibly at Syrian Antioch, it used, apart from other data, the Gospel of Mark and the *Sayings Gospel Q* for its prepassion narrative, and the Gospel of Mark and the *Cross Gospel* for its passion and resurrection account (Crossan 1988a).

23. Gospel of Luke [Luke]. Written possibly as early as the nineties but before John 1–20, which used its passion and resurrection account. Like the Gospel of Matthew, it used, apart from much other data, the Gospel of Mark and the *Sayings Gospel Q* for its prepassion narrative, and the Gospel of Mark and the *Cross Gospel* for its passion and resurrection account (Crossan 1988a).

24. Revelation/Apocalypse of John [Rev.]. Written in Asia Minor toward the end of the first century C.E. by a church leader named John exiled to the island of Patmos presumably under Domitian (Koester 1982:2.250).

25. *First Letter of Clement* [*1 Clem.*]. Written on behalf of the Church at Rome by Clement, its secretary, to the church at Corinth, soon after the Domitian persecution in 96–97 C.E. It is independent of the intracanonical Gospels (Koester 1957:4–23; 1982:2.287–292).

26. *Epistle of Barnabas* [*Barn.*]. Written toward the end of the first century C.E., it probes the Hebrew Scriptures not only for a deeper understanding of ritual law but especially for biblical bases concerning the suffering and death of Jesus. It is independent of the intracanonical Gospels and indicates the prophetic interpretation from which the narrative tradition of the *Cross Gospel* was created (Koester 1957:124–158; 1982:2.276–279; Crossan 1988a).

27. *Didache* 1:1–3a and 2:2–16:2 [*Did.*]. The earliest church order was written in Syria toward the end of the first century C.E. It explains virtues and vices, rituals and prayers, offices and functions, and is, apart from the later insertion of 1:3b–2:1 (Layton 1968), independent of the intracanonical Gospels. Indeed, to the converse, the apocalyptic source behind *Did.* 16:3–5 may have been known by Mark 13 (Koester 1957:159–241; 1982:2.158–160) or, more likely, by Matthew 24 (Kloppenborg 1979).

28. *Shepherd of Hermas* [*Herm. Vis.; Herm. Man.; Herm Sim.*]. Written at Rome around 100 C.E., and divided into *Visions, Mandates,* and *Similitudes,* it proposes an apocalyptic ordering of moral life. It is independent of the intracanonical Gospels (Koester 1957:242–256; 1982:2.257–261).

29. Letter of James [James]. Written in Syria possibly around 100 C.E., it indicates the continuing importance of James of Jerusalem in terms of ethics and offices. It criticizes misinterpretations of Paul's teachings (Koester 1982:2.156–157).

30. Gospel of John I [John]. The first edition of the Gospel of John was composed, very early in the second century C.E. and under the pressure of Synoptic ascendancy, as a combination of the Johannine *Signs Gospel* and the Synoptic traditions about the passion and resurrection. It is dependent, but very creatively so, on the *Cross Gospel* and the Synoptic Gospels for its

passion and resurrection account (Crossan 1988a). The earliest extant fragment of John is dated to about 125 C.E.

**31–37. *Letters of Ignatius, To the Ephesians* [Ign. *Eph.*]; *To the Magne-
sians* [Ign. *Mag.*]; *To the Trallians* [Ign. *Trall.*]; *To the Romans* [Ign. *Rom.*]; *To
the Philadelphians* [Ign. *Phil.*]; *To the Smyrnaeans* [Ign. *Smyrn.*]; *To Polycarp*
[Ign. *Pol.*].** Written by Ignatius, bishop of Syrian Antioch, from Smyrna and
Troas around 110 C.E., as he was being taken under guard across Asia Minor
to martyrdom at Rome. They are independent of the intracanonical Gospels. (Koester 1957:24–61; 1982:2.279–287).

38. First Letter of Peter [1 Pet.]. Written from Rome and pseudepigraphically attributed to Peter, it was sent to encourage persecuted Christians around 112 C.E. in the situation known from the letters of Pliny the
Younger to Trajan (Koester 1982:2.292–297).

39. *Letter of Polycarp to the Philippians* 13–14 [Pol. Phil.]. Polycarp,
already bishop of Smyrna in Ignatius' time, was martyred around 160 C.E.
Pol. 13–14 is an earlier letter than *Pol.* 1–12 and was sent, soon after
Ignatius' martyrdom, to accompany a copy of the Ignatian letters requested
by the church at Philippi (Harrison 1936; Koester, 1957:112–123;
1982:2.306–308).

40. First Letter of John [1 John]. Interpretations, catholic against
gnostic, of the Gospel of John caused a split within the Johannine community, and this letter was written to underline the catholic reading of that
text (Brown 1979; 1982). The opposite reading may be seen in the Acts of
John 87–105 (Koester 1982:2.192–198; Cameron 1982:87–96).

Fourth Stratum [120–150 C.E.]

41. Gospel of John II [John]. A second edition of the Gospel of John is
indicated most clearly by the appended John 21, which underlines not only
Synoptic but Petrine ascendancy. Many other additions, such as 1:1–18;
6:51b–58; 15–17 and the Beloved Disciple passages, may also have been
added at this late stage.

42. Acts of the Apostles [Acts]. Although probably conceived, along
with the Gospel of Luke, as the second part of a two-volume writing, this
part was probably written some time after its predecessor.

43. *Apocryphon of James* [Ap. Jas.]. There is an intracanonically independent tradition of Jesus' sayings going back to the fifties C.E. behind this
document, but it is no longer possible to separate them as a unified first-
century source. The final composition of this Nag Hammadi writing (CG
1,2) dates from the first half of the second century (Cameron 1982:55–57;
1984; Williams 1985).

44. First Letter to Timothy [1 Tim.]. The three Pastoral Letters of 1 Timothy, 2 Timothy, and Titus were composed by the same author in the general Aegean area during the peaceful years after 120 C.E. and were pseudepigraphically attributed to Paul; 1 Timothy is concerned with ethics and offices as a defense against gnostic inroads (Koester 1982.2:297–305).

45. Second Letter to Timothy [2 Tim.]. Written in the format of a last will and testament, 2 Timothy was originally the last of the three Pastoral Letters but with the same emphasis on ethics and offices found in all three (Koester 1982:2.297–305).

46. Second Letter of Peter [2 Pet.]. Pseudepigraphically attributed to Peter, this letter, which uses 1 Peter and Jude, was written in the second quarter of the second century C.E. (Koester 1982:2.295–297).

47. *Letter of Polycarp to the Philippians* 1–12 [*Pol.*]. This section of the document was originally written a few decades after Pol. *Phil.* 13–14, around 140 C.E., on the occasion of a crisis in the church at Philippi. It is dependent on the intracanonical Gospels of Matthew and Luke (Harrison 1936; Koester 1957:112–123; 1982:2.306–308).

48. *Second Letter of Clement* [2 *Clem.*]. A treatise, attributed to the author of 1 *Clement* by its manuscripts but written around 150 C.E. Dependent on the intracanonical Gospels of Matthew and Luke but in harmonized excerpts, it may well be the earliest anti-gnostic writing known from Egypt (Koester 1957:62–111; 1982:2.233–236).

49. *Gospel of the Nazoreans [Gos. Naz.*]. About twenty-three excerpts from an expansive translation of the Greek Gospel of Matthew into either Aramaic or Syriac are known from patristic citations and marginal notations in a family of thirty-six manuscripts stemming from a "Zion Gospel" edition of about 500 C.E. The translation dates from around the middle of the second century C.E. (Koester 1982:2.201–202; Cameron 1982:97–98).

50. *Gospel of the Ebionites [Gos. Eb.*]. All seven excerpts from this Gospel are cited by Epiphanius at the end of the fourth century C.E. The text, written around the middle of the second century C.E., was dependent on a harmonized version of the Gospels of Matthew, Luke, and possibly Mark as well (Koester 1982:202–203; Cameron 1982:103–104).

51. *Didache* 1:3b–2:1 [*Did.*]. An inserted section, from the middle of the second century, that depends on the Gospels of Matthew, Mark, and Luke and that carefully and rhetorically harmonizes their versions of specific Jesus' sayings (Layton 1968).

52. *Gospel of Peter [Gos. Pet.*]. Extant middle second-century C.E. text is redacted from the *Cross Gospel* and intracanonical units such as Joseph and Burial in 6:23–24, Women and Youth in 12:50–13:57, and Disciples and

Apparition in 14:60. Those new units are redactionally prepared for by, respectively, Request for Burial in 2:3–5a, Arrival of Youth in 11:43–44, and Action of Disciples in 7:26–27 and 14:58–59. It indicates, as do the two editions of the Gospel of John, the Synoptic and Petrine ascendancy within the western Syrian traditions (Crossan 1988a).

B. Independent Attestation

Numbers in square brackets indicate the number of items in that category. The + separation sharply distinguishes items with more than one independent attestation to its left from those with only a single attestation to its right. There are 522 items in all. Of those, 180 have more than one independent attestation: 33 have multiple, 42 have triple, 105 have double attestation. There are 342 with only a single attestation. In summary: only about one-third have more than a single attestation [522:180 + 342].

Complexes have been marked with a plus (+) or minus (-) sign according as I judge them to be from the historical Jesus or from the later Jesus tradition. The plus sign does not, of course, refer to all sources and units in a given complex but means that, despite any later changes and developments, the core of the complex derives from Jesus himself. Such sigla work better for words and sayings than for actions and happenings. They do not work at all for processes dramatically or symbolically incarnated in events. In order to draw particular attention to those latter phenomena, I use the sign ±. It means that the action or happening did not occur as an event at one moment in time or place (hence -) but that it represents a dramatic historicization of something that took place over a much longer period (hence +).

This book's basic database, that is, complexes with plural attestation in the first stratum is given here in list format for easy reference. All other complexes are cited in a more compact fashion.

First Stratum [186:131 + 55]

(a) Multiple Independent Attestation [29]

1+. Mission and Message: (1a) 1 Cor. 9:14; (1b) 1 Cor. 10:27; (2) *Gos. Thom.* 14:2; (3) 1Q: Luke 10:(1), 4–11 = Matt. 10:7, 10b, 12–14; (4) Mark 6:7–13 = Matt. 10:1, 8–10a, 11 = Luke 9:1–6; (5) *Dial. Sav.* 53b [139:9–10]; (6) *Did.* 11–13 [see 11:4–6 & 13:1–2]; (7) 1 Tim. 5:18b.

2-. Jesus' Apocalyptic Return: (1) 1 Thess. 4:13–18; (2) *Did.* 16:6–8; (3) Matt. 24:30a; (4) Mark 13:24–27 = Matt. 24:29, 30b–31 = Luke 21:25–28; (5a) Rev. 1:7; (5b) Rev. 1:13; (5c) Rev. 14:14; (6) John 19:37.

3±. Bread and Fish: (1?) 1 Cor. 15:6; (2) John 6:1–15; (3a) Mark 6:33–44 = Matt. 9:36; 14:13b–21 = Luke 9:11–17; (3b) Mark 8:1–10 = Matt. 15:32–39; (4) Luke 24:13–33, 35; (5) Luke 24:41–43; (6) John 21:9, 12–13

4+. Ask, Seek, Knock: (1a) Gos. Thom. 2 & P. Oxy. 654:2; (1b) Gos. Thom. 92:1; (1c) Gos. Thom. 94; (2) Gos. Heb. 4ab; (3) 1Q: Luke 11:9–10 = Matt. 7:7–8; (4) Mark 11:24 = Matt. 21:22; (5a) Dial. Sav. 9–12; (5b) Dial. Sav. 20d; (5c) Dial. Sav. 79–80 ; (6a) John 14:13–14; (6b) John 15:7; (6c) John 15:16; (6d) John 16:23–24; (6e) John 16:26.

5+. Crucifixion of Jesus: (1) 1 Cor. 15:3b; (2a) Gos. Pet. 4:10–5:16, 18–20; 6:22; (2b) Mark 15:22–38 = Matt. 27:33–51a = Luke 23:32–46; (2c) John 19:17b–25a, 28–36; (3) Barn. 7:3–5; (4a) 1 Clem. 16:3–4 (= Isaiah 53:1–12); (4b) 1 Clem. 16.15–16 (= Psalm 22:6–8); (5a) Ign. Mag. 11; (5b) Ign. Trall. 9:1b; (5c) Ign. Smyrn. 1.2.

6±. Revealed to Peter: (1) 1 Cor. 15:5a; (2a) Luke 24:12; (2b) John 20:2–10; (3) Luke 24:34; (4) Ign. Smyrn. 3.2a; (5) John 21:15–23.

7±. Of David's Lineage: (1a) Rom. 1:3; (1b) 2 Tim. 2:8; (2) Matt. 2:1–12; (3) Luke 2:1–20; (4) John 7:41–42; (5a) Ign. Smyrn. 1:1a; (5b) Ign. Eph. 18:2c; (5c) Ign. Trall. 9:1a.

8+. When and Where: (1a) Gos. Thom. 3:1 & P. Oxy. 654.3:1; (1b) Gos. Thom. 51; (1c) Gos. Thom. 113; (2) 2Q: Luke 17:23 = Matt. 24:26; (3) Mark 13:21–23 = Matt. 24:23–25; (4?) Dial. Sav. 16; (5) 1Q?: Luke 17:20–21.

9+. Who Has Ears: (1a) Gos. Thom. 8:2; (1b) Gos. Thom. 21:5; (1c) Gos. Thom. 24:2; (1d) Gos. Thom. 63:2; (1e) Gos. Thom. 65:2; (1f) Gos. Thom. 96:2; (2a) Mark 4:9 = Matt. 13:9 = Luke 8:8b; (2b) Mark 4:23 =Matt. 13:43b; (3) Matt. 11:15; (4) Luke 14:35b; (5) Rev. 2:7, 11, 17, 29; 3:6, 13, 22; 13:9

10+. Receiving the Sender: (1) 1Q: Luke 10:16 = Matt. 10:40; (2) Mark 9:36–37 = Matt. 18: 2, 5 = Luke 9:47–48a; (3) Did. 11:4–5; (4a) John 5:23b; (4b) John 12:44–50; (4c) John 13:20; (5) Ign. Eph. 6:1.

11-. Climax of Sins: (1) 1 Thess. 2:15; (2) Gos. Pet. 5:17; (3) Matt. 23:32–33; (4a) Barn. 5:11; (4b) Barn. 14:5.

12-. Knowing the Danger: (1a) 1 Thess. 5:2; (1b) 2 Pet. 3:10; (2a) Gos. Thom. 21:3; (2b) Gos. Thom. 103; (3) 2Q: Luke 12:39–40 = Matt. 24:43–44; (4a) Rev. 3:3b; (4b) Rev. 16:15a.

13-. Two as One: (1a) Gal. 3:27–28; (1b) 1 Cor. 12:13; (1c) Col. 3:10–11; (2) Gos. Thom. 22:3–4; (3) Gos. Eg. 5b; (4) 2 Clem. 12:1–6.

14-. Eye, Ear, Mind: (1a) 1 Cor. 2:9a; (1b) 1 Clem. 34:8; (2) Gos. Thom. 17; (3) 2Q: Luke 10:23–24 = Matt. 13:16–17; (4) Dial. Sav. 57a [140:1–4].

15+. Against Divorce: (1) 1 Cor. 7:10–11; (2) 1or2?Q: Luke 16:18 = Matt. 5:31–32; (3) Mark 10:10–12 = Matt. 19:9; (4) Herm. Man. 4.1:6b, 10.

16-. Supper and Eucharist: (1a) 1 Cor. 10:14–22; (1b) 1 Cor. 11:23–25; (2)

Mark 14:22–25 = Matt. 26:26–29 = Luke 22:15–19a [19b–20]; (3) *Did.* 9:1–4; (4) John 6:51b–58.

17±. **Resurrection of Jesus:** (1) 1 Cor. 15:4b; (2) *Gos. Pet.* 9:35–10:40; (3) *Barn.* 15:9; (4a) Ign. *Mag.* 11:1c; (4b) Ign. *Trall.* 9:2a; (4c) Ign. *Smyrn.* 1.2b.

18±. **Revealed to Disciples:** (1) 1 Cor. 15:5b, 7b; (2) Matt. 28:16–20; (3a) Luke 24:36–39; (3b) John 20:19–21; (4) Ign. *Smyrn.* 3.2b–3

19+. **What Goes In:** (1) *Gos. Thom.* 14:3; (2) Mark 7:14–15; (3) Matt. 15:10–11; (4a) Acts 10:14b; (4b) Acts 11:8b.

20+. **Kingdom and Children:** (1) *Gos. Thom.* 22:1–2; (2) Mark 10:13–16 = Matt. 19:13–15 = Luke 18:15–17; (3) Matt. 18:3; (4) John 3:1–5, 9–10.

21+. **The World's Light:** (1) *Gos. Thom.* 24:1–3 & P. Oxy. 655:24d; (2) Matt. 5:14a; (3a?) *Dial. Sav.* 14 (3b?) *Dial. Sav.* 34; (4a) John 8:12; (4b) John 11:9–10; (4c) John 12:35–36.

22+. **Prophet's Own Country:** (1) *Gos. Thom.* 31 & P. Oxy. 1.31; (2) Mark 6:1–6a = Matt. 13:53–58; (3) Luke 4:16–24; (4) John 4:44.

23+. **All Sins Forgiven:** (1) *Gos. Thom.* 44; (2) 2Q: Luke 12:10 = Matt. 12:32a; (3) Mark 3: 28–30 = Matt. 12:31, 32b; (4) *Did.* 11:7.

24+. **Blessed the Womb:** (1) *Gos. Thom.* 79:1–2; (2) 1Q?: Luke 11:27–28; (3?) John 13:17; (4?) James 1:25b.

25-. **Peter's Betrayal Foretold:** (1) P. Vienna G. 2325; (2a) Mark 14:26–31 = Matt. 26:30–35; (2b) John 13:36–38; (3) Luke 22:31–34; (4) *Barn.* 5:12

26±. **Jesus Virginally Conceived:** (1) *Gos. Heb.* 1; (2) Matt. 1:18–25; (3) Luke 1:26–38; (4a) Ign. *Eph.* 7:2; (4b) Ign. *Eph.* 18:2a; (4c) Ign. *Eph.* 19:1; (4d) Ign. *Smyrn.* 1:1b.

27+. **Forgiveness for Forgiveness:** (1) 1Q: Luke 11:4a = Matt. 6:12; (2) Mark 11:25 (26) = Matt. 6:14–15; (3) Luke 6:37c; (4a) *1 Clem.* 13:2b; (4b) Pol. *Phil.* 2:3b.

28-. **Before the Angels:** (1a) 2Q: Luke 12:8–9 = Matt. 10:32–33; (1b) 2 *Clem.* 3:2 [from Matt. 10:32]; (2) Mark 8:38 = Matt. 16:27 = Luke 9:26; (3) Rev. 3:5; (4) 2 Tim. 2:12b.

29±. **Descent into Hell:** (1a) *Gos. Pet.* 10:41–42; (1b) Matt. 27:52–53; (2) *Herm. Sim.* 9.16:5; (3) Ign. *Mag.* 9:2; (4a?) 1 Pet. 3:19–20; (4b?) 1 Pet. 4:6.

(b) Triple Independent Attestation [36]

30±. **Revealed to James:** (1) 1 Cor. 15:7a; (2) *Gos. Thom.* 12; (3) *Gos. Heb.* 7.

31+. **First and Last:** (1) *Gos. Thom.* 4:2 & P. Oxy. 654.4:2; (2) 2Q: Luke 13:30 = Matt. 20:16; (3) Mark 10:31 = Matt. 19:30.

32+. **Hidden Made Manifest:** (1a) *Gos. Thom.* 5:2 & P. Oxy. 654.5:2; (1b) *Gos. Thom.* 6:4 & P. Oxy. 654.6:4; (2) 1Q: Luke 12:2 = Matt. 10:26; (3) Mark 4:22 = Luke 8:17.

33-. The Golden Rule: (1) Gos. Thom. 6:3a & P. Oxy. 654.6:3a; (2) 1Q:
Luke 6:31 = Matt. 7: 12; (3) Did. 1:2b.

34+. The Sower: (1) Gos. Thom. 9; (2) Mark 4:3–8 = Matt. 13:3b–8 =
Luke 8:5–8a; (3) 1 Clem. 24:5.

35+. The Mustard Seed: (1) Gos. Thom. 20:1–2; (2) 1or2?Q: Luke
13:18–19 = Matt. 13:31–32 ; (3) Mark 4:30–32 = Matt. 13:31–32.

36+. Lamp and Bushel: (1) Gos. Thom. 33:2; (2) 2Q: Luke 11:33 =
Matt. 5:15; (3) Mark 4:21 = Luke 8:16.

37-. New Garments: (1) Gos. Thom. 37 & P. Oxy. 655.37; (2a) Dial. Sav.
49–52; (2b) Dial. Sav. 84–85; (3) Gos. Eg. 5a.

38+. Serpents and Doves: (1) Gos. Thom. 39:2 & P. Oxy. 655.39:2; (2a)
Matt. 10:16b; (2b) Gos. Naz. 7; (3) Ign. Pol. 2:2.

39-. Plant Rooted Up: (1) Gos. Thom. 40; (2) Matt. 15:12–13; (3a) Ign.
Trall. 11:1b; (3b) Ign. Phil. 3:1b.

40+. Have and Receive: (1) Gos. Thom. 41; (2) 2Q: Luke 19:(25–)26 =
Matt. 25:29; (3) Mark 4:25 = Matt. 13:12 = Luke 8:18b.

41-. Trees and Hearts: (1) Gos. Thom. 45; (2a) 1Q: Luke 6:43–45 = Matt.
7:16–20; (2b) Matt. 12:33–35; (3) Ign. Eph. 14:2b.

42-. Scriptures and Jesus: (1) Gos. Thom. 52; (2) Eger. Gos. 1 [5–23]; (3a)
John 5:39–47; (3b) John 9:29.

43+. Blessed the Poor: (1) Gos. Thom. 54; (2a) 1Q: Luke 6:20 = Matt.
5:3; (2b) Pol. Phil. 2:3e; (3) James 2:5.

44+. Carrying One's Cross: (1) Gos. Thom. 55:2b; (2) 1Q: Luke 14:27 =
Matt. 10:38; (3) Mark 8:34 = Matt. 16:24 = Luke 9:23

45-. Father and Son: (1) Gos. Thom. 61:4; (2) 2Q: Luke 10:22 = Matt.
11:27; (3a) John 3:35b; (3b) John 13:3a.

46+. The Tenants: (1) Gos. Thom. 65; (2) Mark 12:1–9, 12 = Matt.
21:33–41, 43–46 = Luke 20:9–16, 19; (3) Herm. Sim. 5.2:4–7.

47-. The Rejected Stone: (1) Gos. Thom. 66; (2) Mark 12:10–11 = Matt.
21:42 = Luke 20: 17–18; (3) Barn. 6:4.

48+. Blessed the Persecuted: (1a) Gos. Thom. 68; (1b) Gos. Thom. 69:1;
(2a) 1+2Q: Luke 6:22–23 = Matt. 5:11–12 ; (2b) Matt. 5:10; (2c) Pol. Phil.
2:3f; (3a) 1 Pet. 3:14a; (3b) 1 Pet. 4:14.

49+. Temple and Jesus: (1) Gos. Thom. 71; (2a) Mark 14:55–59 = Matt.
26:59–61; (2b) Mark 15:29–32a = Matt. 27:39–43 = (!) Luke 23:35–37; (2c)
Acts 6:11–14; (3) John 2:18–22.

50+. Harvest Is Great: (1) Gos. Thom. 73; (2) 1Q: Luke 10:2 = Matt.
9:37–38; (3) John 4:35.

51+. Into the Desert: (1) Gos. Thom. 78; (2) 2Q: Luke 7:24–27 = Matt.
11:7–10; (3) Mark 1:2–3 = Matt. 3:3 = Luke 3:4–6 = (?) John 1:19–23.

52-. Yoke and Burden: (1) *Gos. Thom.* 90; (2) Matt. 11:28–30; (3) *Dial. Sav.* 65–68.

53+. Knowing the Times: (1) *Gos. Thom.* 91:1–2; (2a) 2Q: Luke 12:54–56 = Matt. 16:2–3; (2b) *Gos. Naz.* 13; (3?) John 6:30.

54-. Dogs and Swine: (1) *Gos. Thom.* 93; (2) Matt. 7:6; (3) *Did.* 9:5.

55+. Caesar and God: (1) *Gos. Thom.* 100; (2) *Eger. Gos.* 3a [50–57a]; (3) Mark 12:13–17 = Matt. 22:15–22 = Luke 20:20–26.

56-. Lips Without Hearts: (1) *Eger. Gos.* 3c [61b–66]; (2) Mark 7:6–7 = Matt. 15:7–9; (3) *1 Clem.* 15:2.

57+. For and Against: (1) P. Oxy. 1224, 2 r i, lines 2b–5; (2) 2Q: Luke 11:23 = Matt. 12:30; (3) Mark 9:40 = Luke 9:50b.

58+. John Baptizes Jesus: (1) *Gos. Heb.* 2; (2a) Mark 1:9–11 = Matt. 3:13–17 = Luke 3:21–22; (2b) *Gos. Naz.* 2; (2c) *Gos. Eb.* 4; (2d) John 1:32–34; (2e) Ign. *Smyrn.* 1:1c; (3) Ign. *Eph.* 18:2d.

59+. Blessed the Sad: (1) 1Q: Luke 6:21b = Matt. 5:4; (2) *Dial. Sav.* 13–14 ; (3) John 16:20, 22.

60-. Measure for Measure: (1a) 1Q: Luke 6:38bc = Matt. 7:2b; (2) Mark 4:24b; (3a) *1 Clem.* 13:2g; (1a/3b) Pol. *Phil.* 2:3d.

61-. Disciple and Servant: (1) 1Q: Luke 6:40 = Matt. 10:24–25; (2) *Dial. Sav.* 53c; (3a) John 13:16; (3b) John 15:20.

62-. Spirit Under Trial: (1) 1Q: Luke 12:11–12 = Matt. 10:19–20; (2) Mark 13:11 = Matt. 10: 19–20 = Luke 21:14–15; (3) John 14:26.

63+. Saving One's Life: (1) 1Q: Luke 17:33 = Matt. 10:39; (2) Mark 8:35 = Matt. 16:25 = Luke 9:24; (3) John 12:25–26.

64-. The Last Days: (1) *Did.* 16:3–5; (2) Matt. 24:10–12; (3a) Mark 13:3–10, 12–20 = Matt. 24:3–22 = Luke 21:7–13, 16–24; (3b) Matt. 10:17–18; (3c) Luke 17:31–32.

65-. Pilate and Antipas: (1a) *Gos. Pet.* 1:1 & 11:46; (1b) Matt. 27:24–25; (1c) Luke 23:6–16; (2) Ign. *Smyrn.* 1:2; (3) Acts 4:24–28.

(c) Double Independent Attestation [66]

66-. Wise and Understanding: (1) 1 Cor. 1:19; (2a) 1Q: Luke 10:21 = Matt. 11:25–26; (2b) *Gos. Naz.* 9.

67-. Hidden Since Eternity: (1) 1 Cor. 2:7; (2) Matt. 13:35.

68±. Hidden from Demons: (1) 1 Cor. 2:8; (2) Ign. *Eph.* 19:1b.

69-. Faith and Mountain: (1) 1 Cor. 13:2; (2) Mark 11:22–23 = Matt. 21:21.

70+. Burial of Jesus: (1) 1 Cor. 15:4a; (2a) *Gos. Pet.* 5:15b; 6:21; (2b) Mark 15:42–47 = Matt. 27:57–61 = Luke 23:50–56; (2c) John 19:38–42; (2d) *Gos. Pet.* 2:3–5a; 6:23–24.

71+. The Fishnet: (1) *Gos. Thom.* 8:1; (2) Matt. 13:47–48.

72 +. **Fire on Earth:** (1) Gos. Thom. 10; (2) 1Q?: Luke 12:49.

73 -. **Who Is Jesus?** (1) Gos. Thom. 13; (2a) Mark 8:27–30 = Matt. 16:13–20 = Luke 9:18–21; (2b) Gos. Naz. 14; (2c) John 6:67–69.

74 +. **Peace or Sword:** (1) Gos. Thom. 16; (2) 2Q: Luke 12:51–53 = Matt. 10:34–36.

75 +. **The Harvest Time:** (1) Gos. Thom. 21:4; (2) Mark 4:26–29.

76 +. **Speck and Log:** (1) Gos. Thom. 26 & P. Oxy. 1. 26; (2) 1Q: Luke 6:41–42 = Matt. 7:3–5.

77 -. **Two or Three:** (1) Gos. Thom. 30 & P. Oxy. 1. 30; (2) Matt. 18:20.

78 +. **The Mountain City:** (1) Gos. Thom. 32 & P. Oxy. 1. 32; (2) Matt. 5:14b.

79 +. **Open Proclamation:** (1) Gos. Thom. 33:1; (2) 1Q: Matt. 10:27 = Luke 12:3.

80 +. **The Blind Guide:** (1) Gos. Thom. 34; (2) 1Q: Luke 6:39 = Matt. 15:14b.

81 +. **Strong One's House:** (1) Gos. Thom. 35; (2) Mark 3:27 = Matt. 12:29 = Luke 11:21–22.

82 +. **Against Anxieties:** (1) Gos. Thom. 36 & P. Oxy. 655. 36; (2) 1Q: Luke 12:22–31 = Matt. 6:25–33.

83 -. **Seeking Too Late:** (1) Gos. Thom. 38:2; (2) John 7:34a, 36b.

84 +. **On Hindering Others:** (1a) Gos. Thom. 39:1 & P. Oxy. 655. 39:1; (1b) Gos. Thom. 102; (2) 2Q: Luke 11:52 = Matt. 23:13.

85 +. **Greater Than John:** (1) Gos. Thom. 46; (2) 2Q: Luke 7:28 = Matt. 11:11.

86 +. **Serving Two Masters:** (1) Gos. Thom. 47:2; (2a) 1or2?Q: Luke 16:13 = Matt. 6:24; (2b) 2 Clem. 6:1.

87 +. **Drinking Old Wine:** (1) Gos. Thom. 47:3; (2) Luke 5:39.

88 +. **Patches and Wineskins:** (1) Gos. Thom. 47:4; (2) Mark 2:21–22 = Matt. 9:16–17 = Luke 5:36–38.

89 +. **Hating One's Family:** (1a) Gos. Thom. 55:1–2a; (1b) Gos. Thom. 101; (2) 1Q: Luke 14:25–26 = Matt. 10:37.

90 +. **The Planted Weeds:** (1) Gos. Thom. 57; (2) Matt. 13:24–30.

91 -. **Taken or Left:** (1) Gos. Thom. 61:1; (2) 2Q: Luke 17:34–35 = Matt. 24:40–41.

92 -. **Knowing the Mystery:** (1) Gos. Thom. 62:1; (2a) Secret Mark f2r10; (2b) Mark 4:10–12 = Matt. 13:10–11, 13–15 = Luke 8:9–10.

93 -. **On Secrecy:** (1) Gos. Thom. 62:2; (2) Matt. 6:3b.

94 +. **The Rich Farmer:** (1) Gos. Thom. 63:1; (2) 1Q?: Luke 12:16–21.

95 +. **The Feast:** (1) Gos. Thom. 64:1–2; (2) 2Q: Luke 14:15–24 = Matt. 22:1–13.

96+. *Blessed the Hungry:* (1) *Gos. Thom.* 69:2; (2) 1Q: Luke 6:21a = Matt. 5:6.

97+. *The Disputed Inheritance:* (1) *Gos. Thom.* 72:1–3; (2) 1Q?: Luke 12:13–15.

98+. *The Pearl:* (1) *Gos. Thom.* 76:1; (2) Matt. 13:45–46.

99+. *Treasure in Heaven:* (1) *Gos. Thom.* 76:2; (2) 1Q: Luke 12:33 = Matt. 6:19–20 .

100-. *Jerusalem Mourned:* (1) *Gos. Thom.* 79:3; (2) Luke 23:27–31.

101+. *Foxes Have Holes:* (1) *Gos. Thom.* 86; (2) 1Q: Luke 9:58 = Matt. 8:19–20 .

102+. *Inside and Outside:* (1) *Gos. Thom.* 89; (2) 2Q: Luke 11:39–41 = Matt. 23:25–26.

103+. *Give Without Return:* (1) *Gos. Thom.* 95; (2a) 1Q: Luke 6:30, 34, 35b = Matt. 5:42; (2b) *Did.* 1:4b, 5a.

104+. *The Leaven:* (1) *Gos. Thom.* 96:1; (2) 1or2?Q: Luke 13:20–21 = Matt. 13:33.

105+. *Jesus' True Family:* (1) *Gos. Thom.* 99; (2a) Mark 3:19b–21, 31–35 = Matt. 12:46–50 = Luke 8:19–21; (2b) *2 Clem.* 9:11; (2c) *Gos. Eb.* 5.

106+. *Fasting and Wedding:* (1) *Gos. Thom.* 104; (2) Mark 2:18–20 = Matt. 9:14–15 = Luke 5:33–35.

107+. *The Lost Sheep:* (1) *Gos. Thom.* 107; (2) 1or2?Q: Luke 15:3–7 = Matt. 18:12–14.

108+. *The Treasure:* (1) *Gos. Thom.* 109; (2) Matt. 13:44.

109-. *Hour Not Come:* (1) *Eger. Gos.* 2a [26–34]; (2a) John 7:30; (2b) John 8:20; (2c) John 10:31; (2d) John 10:39.

110+. *A Leper Cured:* (1) *Eger. Gos.* 2b [35–47]; (2a) Mark 1:40–45 = Matt. 8:1–4 = Luke 5:12–16; (2b) Luke 17:11–19.

111-. *Invocation Without Obedience:* (1) *Eger. Gos.* 3b [57b–61a]; (2a) 1Q: Luke 6:46 = Matt. 7:21; (2b) *2 Clem.* 4:2.

112-. *Jesus' New Teaching:* (1) P. Oxy. 1224, 2 v i, lines 1–5; (2) Mark 1:27b.

113+. *Eating with Sinners:* (1) P. Oxy. 1224, 2 v ii, lines 1–7; (2a) Mark 2:13–17a = Matt. 9:9–12 = Luke 5:27–31; (2b) *Gos. Eb.* 1c; (2c) Luke 15:1–2.

114+. *Love Your Enemies:* (1) P. Oxy. 1224, 2 r i, lines 1–2a; (2a) 1Q: Luke 6:27–28, 35a = Matt. 5:43–44; (2b) *Pol. Phil.* 12:3a; (2c) *Did.* 1:3b.

115+. *John's Message:* (1a) 2Q: Luke 3:15–18 = Matt. 3:11–12; (1b) Acts 13:24–25; (1c) John 1:24–31; (2) Mark 1:7–8.

116±. *Jesus Tempted:* (1) 3Q: Luke 4:1–2a = Matt. 4:1–2a; (2) Mark 1:12–13.

117-. *Better Than Sinners:* (1a) 1Q: Luke 6:32–35 = Matt. 5:45–47; (1b) *2 Clem.* 13:4a [from Luke 6:32]; (1c) *Did.* 1:3b; (2) Ign. *Pol.* 2:1.

118-. Judgment for Judgment: (1a) 1Q: Luke 6:37a = Matt. 7:1–2a; (2a) *1 Clem.* 13:2e; (2b) Pol. *Phil.* 2:3a.

119±. Distant Boy Cured: (1) 2Q: Luke 7:1–2 [3–6a] 6b–10 = Matt. 8:5–10, 13; (2) John 4:46b–53.

120-. The Lord's Prayer: (1a) 1Q: Luke 11:(1)2–4 = (!) Matt. 6:9–13; (1b) *Gos. Naz.* 5; (1c) Pol. *Phil.* 7:2a; (2) *Did.* 8:2b.

121+. Beelzebul Controversy: (1a) 2Q: Luke 11:14–15, 17–18 = Matt. 12:22–26; (1b) Matt. 9:32–34; (2) Mark 3:22–26.

122-. Request for Sign: (1a) 2Q: Luke 11:29–30 = Matt. 12:38–40; (1b) Matt. 16:4a; (1c) *Gos. Naz.* 11; (2a) Mark 8:11–13 = Matt. 16:1, 4b = Luke 11:16.

123-. The Body's Light: (1) 2Q: Luke 11:34–36 = Matt. 6:22–23; (2) *Dial. Sav.* 8.

124+. Honors and Salutations: (1) 2Q: Luke 11:43 = Matt. 23:6b–7a; (2) Mark 12:38–40 = Matt. 23:5–7 = Luke 20:45–46.

125-. Gnashing of Teeth: (1a) 2Q: Luke 13:28a = Matt. 8:12b; (1b) Matt. 13:42b; (1c) Matt. 13:50b; (1d) Matt. 22:13b; (1e) Matt. 24:51b; (1f) Matt. 25:30b; (2) *Dial. Sav.* 14e.

126+. Salting the Salt: (1) 1Q: Luke 14:34–35a = Matt. 5:13; (2) Mark 9:50a.

127+. Sickness and Sin: (1) John 5:1–9a, 14; (2) Mark 2:1–12 = Matt. 9:1–8 = Luke 5:17–26.

128±. Walking on Water: (1) John 6:16–21; (2a) Mark 6:45–52 = Matt. 14:22–27; (2b) Mark 4:35–41 = Matt. 8:18, 23–27 = Luke 8:22–25.

129+. Blind Man Healed: (1) John 9:1–7; (2) Mark 8:22–26.

130±. Dead Man Raised: (1) John 11:1–57; (2a) *Secret Mark* 1v20–2r11a; (2b) Mark 14:51–52.

131-. Mocking of Jesus: (1a) *Gos. Pet.* 3:6–9; (1b) Mark 15:16–20a = Matt. 27:27–31a; (1c) John 19:1–3; (2a) *Barn.* 5:14; (2b) *Barn.* 7:7–11.

(d) Single Attestation [55]

132-. A Sowing Miracle: (1) *Eger. Gos.* 4 [67–82]; **133-. Vision of Jesus:** (1) P. Oxy. 1224, 2 r ii, lines 1–5. **134-. Spirit as Mother:** (1) *Gos. Heb.* 3; **135-. Joy in Love:** (1) *Gos. Heb.* 5; **136-. Grieving Another:** (1) *Gos. Heb.* 6; **137+. John's Warning:** (1) 2Q: Luke 3:7–9a = Matt. 3:7–10b; **138-. Tree Cut Down:** (1a) 2Q: Luke 3:9b = Matt. 3:10b, (1b) Matt. 7:19; **139-. Jesus Tempted Thrice:** (1a) 3Q: Matt. 4:2b–11 = Luke 4:2b–13, (1b) *Gos. Naz.* 3; **140+. The Other Cheek:** (1a) 1Q: Luke 6:29 = Matt. 5:38–41, (1b) *Did.* 1:4a; **141-. As Your Father:** (1a) 1Q: Luke 6:36 = Matt. 5:48, (1b) Pol. *Phil.* 12:3b; **142-. Rock or Sand:** (1) 1Q: Luke 6:47–49 = Matt. 7:24–27; **143-. Reply to John:** (1) 2Q: Luke 7:18–23 = Matt. 11:2–6; **144-. Wisdom Justified:** (1) 2Q:

Luke 7:31-35 = Matt. 11:16-19; **145+. Leave the Dead:** (1) 1Q: Luke 9:59-60 = Matt. 8:21-22; **146+. Looking Backward:** (1) 1Q?: Luke 9:61-62; **147+. Lambs Among Wolves:** (1a) 1Q: Luke 10:3 = Matt. 10:16a, (1b) 2 *Clem.* 5:2; **148-. Cities of Woe:** (1) 2Q: Luke 10:12-15 = Matt. 11:15, 20-24; **149+. Good Gifts:** (1) 1Q: Luke 11:11-13 = Matt. 7:9-11; **150+. By Whose Power:** (1) 2Q: Luke 11:19-20 = Matt. 12:27-28; **151-. The Returning Demon:** (1) 2Q: Luke 11:24-26 = Matt. 12:43-45; **152-. Judgment by Pagans:** (1) 2Q: Luke 11:31-32 = Matt. 12:41-42; **153-. Tithing and Justice:** (1) 2Q: Luke 11:42 = Matt. 23:23; **154-. Like Graves:** (1) 2Q: Luke 11:44 = Matt. 23:27-28 ; **155-. Helping with Burdens:** (1) 2Q: Luke 11:45-46 = Matt. 23:4; **156-. The Prophets' Tombs:** (1) 2Q: Luke 11:47-48 = Matt. 23:29-31; **157-. Wisdom's Envoys:** (1a) 2Q: Luke 11:49-51 = Matt. 23:34-36, (1b) *Gos. Naz.* 17; **158-. Whom to Fear:** (1a) 1Q: Luke 12:4-5 = Matt. 10:28, (1b) 2 *Clem.* 5:4b; **159+. God and Sparrows:** (1) 1Q: Luke 12:6-7 = Matt. 10:29-31; **160+. Heart and Treasure:** (1) 1Q: Luke 12:34 = Matt. 6:21; **161-. Master and Steward:** (1) 2Q: Luke 12:42-46 = Matt. 24:45-51a; **162-. Before the Judgment:** (1a) 2Q: Luke 12:57-59 = Matt. 5:25-26, (1b) *Did.* 1:5b; **163-. The Narrow Door:** (1) 1Q: Luke 13:23-24 = Matt. 7:13-14; **164-. The Closed Door:** (1) 2Q: Luke 13:25 = Matt. 25:1-12; **165-. Depart from Me:** (1a) 2Q: Luke 13:26-27 = Matt. 7:22-23, (1b?) 2 *Clem.* 4:5, (1c?) *Gos. Naz.* 6; **166-. Patriarchs and Gentiles:** (1) 2Q: Luke 13:28-29 = Matt. 8:11-12; **167-. Jerusalem Indicted:** (1) 2Q: Luke 13:34-35 = Matt. 23:37-39; **168+. Kingdom and Violence:** (1a) 1or2?Q: Luke 16:16 = Matt. 11:12-14, (1b) *Gos. Naz.* 8; **169-. Not One Iota:** (1) 1or2?Q: Luke 16:17 = Matt. 5:1; **170-. Woe for Temptation:** (1) 1or2?Q: Luke 17:1 = Matt. 18:7; **171-. Reproving and Forgiving:** (1) 1or2?Q: Luke 17:3 = Matt. 18:15; **172+. Unlimited Forgiveness:** (1a) 1or2?Q: Luke 17:4 = Matt. 18:21-22, (1b) *Gos. Naz.* 15ab; **173-. Faith's Power:** (1) 1or2?Q: Luke 17:5-6 = Matt. 17:20; **174-. As with Lightning:** (1) 2Q: Luke 17:24 = Matt. 24:27; **175-. As with Noah:** (1) 2Q: Luke 17:26-27 = Matt. 24:37-39a; **176-. As with Lot:** (1) 2Q: Luke 17:28-30 = Matt. 24:39b; **177-. Corpse and Vultures:** (1) 2Q: Luke 17:37 = Matt. 24:28; **178+. The Entrusted Money:** (1a) 2Q: Luke 19:(11)12-24, 27 = Matt. 25:14-28, (1b) *Gos. Naz.* 18; **179-. On Twelve Thrones:** (1) 2Q: Luke 22:28-30 = Matt. 19:28; **180-. Pilate's Question:**(1a) *Gos. Pet.* pre-1:1 from later 3:6, 9 (Son of God) & 3:7; 4:11 (King of Israel), (1b) Mark 15:1-5 = Matt. 27:1-2, 11-14 = Luke 23:1-5, (1c) John 18:28-38; 19:4-16; **181-. The People Repent:** (1a) *Gos. Pet.* 7:25(!); 8:28, (1b) Luke 23:48; **182-. Jesus' Tomb Guarded:** (1a) *Gos. Pet.* 8:29-33, (1b) Matt. 27:62-66, (1c) *Gos. Naz.* 22; **183-. Crowds Visit Tomb:** (1) *Gos. Pet.* 9:34; **184±. Transfiguration of Jesus:** (1a) *Gos. Pet.* 9:35-10:40, (1b) Mark 9:2-10 = Matt. 17:1-9 = Luke 9:28-36, (1c) 2 Pet. 1:17-18; **185-. The Guards**

Report: (1) Gos. Pet. 11:45–49, (1b) Matt. 28:11–15; **186±.** **Apostolic Grief:** (1) Gos. Pet. 7:26–27; 14:58–59

Second Stratum [178:26 + 152]

(a) Multiple Independent Attestation [3]

187-. **Righteous and Sinners:** (1a) Mark 2:17b = Matt. 9:13b = Luke 5:32, (1b) 2 Clem. 2:4, (2) Luke 19:10, (3) Barn. 5:9, (4) 1 Tim. 1:15b; **188-.** **The Unknown Time:** (1a) Mark 13:33–37; (1b) Matt. 24:42; (1c) Matt. 25:13; (2) Luke 12:35–38; (3) Luke 21:34–36; (4) Did. 16:1. **189-.** **Better Not Born:** (1) Mark 14:17–21 = Matt. 26:20–25 = Luke 22:14, 21–23, (2) 1 Clem. 46:8a, (3) Herm. Vis. 4.2:6b, (4a) John 6:70–71, (4b) John 13:18–19, (4c) John 13:21–30.

(b) Triple Independent Attestation [5]

190±. **Fishing for Humans:** (1a) Mark 1:16–20 = Matt. 4:18–22, (1b) Gos. Eb. 1b, (2) Luke 5:4–11, (3) John 21:1–8; **191+.** **Leader as Servant:** (1a) Mark 9:33–35 = Matt. 18:1, 4 = Luke 9:46, 48b, (1b) Mark 10:41–45 = Matt. 20:24–28, (1c) Matt. 23:11, (2) Luke 22:24–27, (3) John 13:1–17; **192+.** **Woman with Ointment:** (1a) Mark 14:3–9 = Matt. 26:6–13, (2a) Luke 7:36–50, (1b/2b) John 12:1–8, (3) Ign. Eph. 17:2; **193-.** **Pharisees as Blind:** (1) P. Oxy. 840. 2b, (2a) Matt. 15:14a, (2b) Matt. 23:16a, 17a, 19a, 24a, 26a, (3) John 9:41b. **194-.** **Flesh and Spirit:** (1) John 3:6–8; (2) Ign. Phil. 7:1; (3) Dial. Sav. 35.

(c) Double Independent Attestation [18]

195-. **Woman and Birth:** (1a) Gos. Eg. 1, (1b) Gos. Eg. 2, (1c) Gos. Eg. 3, (1d) Gos. Eg. 4, (1e) Gos. Eg. 6, (2a) Dial. Sav. 58–59, (2b) Dial. Sav. 90–95; **196±.** **From the Boat:** (1) Mark 4:1–2 = Matt. 13:1–3a = Luke 8:4, (2?) Luke 5:1–3; **197+.** **Herod Beheads John:** (1) Mark 6: 17–29 = Matt. 14:3–12a = (!) Luke 3:19–20, (2) Ap. Jas. 6:1–4; **198-.** **Millstone for Temptation:** (1) Mark 9:42 = Matt. 18:6 = Luke 17:2, (2)1 Clem. 46:8b; **199+.** **Kingdom and Riches:** (1a) Mark 10:23–27 = Matt. 19:23–26 = Luke 18:24–27, (1b) Gos. Naz. 16b, (2) Herm. Sim. 9. 20:1–4; **200-.** **Hundredfold Reward:** (1) Mark 10:28–30 = Matt. 19:27, 29 = Luke 18:28–30, (2) Ap. Jas. 4:1a; **201-.** **The Chief Commandment:** (1) Mark 12:28–34 = Matt. 22:34–40, 46b = Luke 10:25–28, (2) Did. 1:2a; **202-.** **Son of David:** (1) Mark 12:35–37 = Matt. 22:41–46a = Luke 20:41–44, (2) Barn. 12:10–11; **203-.** **Prayer Against Temptation:** (1a) Mark 14:32–42 = Matt. 26:36–46 = Luke 22:39–46, (1b) John 12:27, (1c) Pol. Phil. 7:2b, (2) Ap. Jas. 4:1b; **204-.** **Living Water:** (1) P. Oxy. 840. 2c, (2) John 4:14; **205-.** **Not Taste Death:** (1) Gos. Thom. 1 & P. Oxy. 654. 1; (2) John 8:51–52; **206-.** **Knowing Oneself:** (1) Gos. Thom. 3:2 &

P. Oxy. 654. 3:2; (2) *Dial. Sav.* 30; **207-. Buried and Resurrected:** (1) P. Oxy. 654. 5; (2) Oxyrhynchus shroud [von Haelst #596; *NTA* 1.300]; **208-. Life and Death:** (1a) *Gos. Thom.* 11:1–2a; (1b) *Gos. Thom.* 111:1; (2) *Dial. Sav.* 56–57; **209-. The Bridal Chamber:** (1) *Gos. Thom.* 75; (2) *Dial Sav.* 50b; **210-. Place of Life:** (1) *Dial. Sav.* 27–30, (2) John 14:2–12; **211-. The Day's Evil:** (1) *Dial. Sav.* 53a, (2) Matt. 6:34b; **212-. Blessed for Doing:** (1) John 13:17, (2) James 1:25b.

(d) Single Attestation [152]

213+. John the Baptist: (1a) Mark 1:4–6 = Matt. 3:1, 4–6 = Luke 3:1–3, (1b) *Gos. Eb.* 2–3a; **214-. Kingdom and Repentance:** (1a) Mark 1:14–15 = Matt. 4:12, 17 = Luke 4:14–15 = (?) John 4:1–3, (1b) Matt. 3:2; **215±. In Capernaum's Synagogue:** (1a) Mark 1:21–28 =(!) Matt. 4:13–16 = Luke 4:31–37, (1b) Matt. 7:28–29, (1c) John 2:12; **216±. Simon's Mother-in-Law:** (1a) Mark 1:29–31 = Matt. 8:14–15 = Luke 4:38–39, (1b) *Gos. Eb.* 1a; **217±. Healings and Exorcisms:** (1) Mark 1:32–34 = Matt. 8:16–17 = Luke 4:40–41; **218±. To Other Places:** (1a) Mark 1:35–39 = Matt. 4:23 = Luke 4:42–44, (1b) John 2:12; **219-. Grain and Sabbath:** (1) Mark 2:23–26 = Matt. 12:1–7 = Luke 6:1–4; **220±. Lord and Sabbath:** (1) Mark 2:27–28 = Matt. 12:8 = Luke 6:5; **221-. Hand and Sabbath:** (1a) Mark 3:1–6 = Matt. 12:9–14 = Luke 6:6–11, (1b) *Gos. Naz.* 10; **222±. Crowds Are Cured:** (1) Mark 3:7–10 = Matt. 4:24–25 = Luke 6:17–19; **223-. Demons Are Silenced:** (1) Mark 3:11–12 = Matt. 12:15–16 = Luke 4:41; **224-. Twelve Disciples Chosen:** (1a) Mark 3:13–19a = Matt. 10:2–4 = Luke 6:12–16, (1b) *Gos. Eb.* 1d, (1c) Acts 1:13b; **225-. Interpreting the Sower:** (1) Mark 4:13–20 = Matt. 13:18–23 = Luke 8:11–15; **226-. Hear and Heed:** (1) Mark 4:24a = Luke 8:18a; **227-. Speaking in Parables:** (1) Mark 4:33–34 = Matt. 13:34; **228±. The Gerasene Demoniac:** (1) Mark 5:1–20 = Matt. 8:28–34 = Luke 8:26–39; **229+. Two Women Cured:** (1) Mark 5:21–43 = Matt. 9:18–26 = Luke 8:40–56; **230+. Among the Villages:** (1) Mark 6:6b = Matt. 9:35 = Luke 8:1; **231-. Herod on Jesus:** (1) Mark 6:14–16 = Matt. 14:1–2 = Luke 9:7–9; **232-. The Disciples Return:** (1) Mark 6:30–32 = Matt. 14:12b–13a = Luke 9:10; **233±. Healings at Gennesaret:** (1) Mark 6:53–56 = Matt. 14:34–36; **234-. Unwashed Hands:** (1a) Mark 7:1–5 = Matt. 15:1–2, (1b) Luke 11:37–38; **235-. Commandment and Tradition:** (1a) Mark 7:8–13 = Matt. 15:3–6, (1b) *Gos. Naz.* 12; **236-. What Comes Out:** (1) Mark 7: 17–23 = Matt. 15:15–20; **237±. Distant Girl Cured:** (1) Mark 7:24–30 = Matt. 15:21–23, 25–28; **238+. Deaf Mute Cured:** (1) Mark 7:31–37 [see Matt. 15:29–31]; **239-. Leaven of Pharisees:** (1) Mark 8:14–21 = Matt. 16:5–12 = (!) Luke 12:1; **240-. Passion-Resurrection Prophecy:** (1a) Mark 8:31–33 = Matt. 16:21–23 = Luke 9:22, (1b) Mark 9:9b = Matt. 17:9b, (1c) Mark 9:12b = Matt. 17:12b,

(1d) Mark 9:30–32 = Matt. 17:22–23 = Luke 9:43b–45, (1e) Luke 17:25, (1f) Mark 10:32–34 = Matt. 20:17–19 = Luke 18:31–34, (1g) Matt. 26:1–2, (1h) Mark 14:21 = Matt.26:24 = Luke 22:22, (1i) Mark 14:41 = Matt. 26:45b, (1j) Luke 24:7; **241-. What Profit?** (1a) Mark 8:36 = Matt. 16:26a = Luke 9:25, (1b) 2 *Clem.* 6:2; **242-. Life's Price:** (1) Mark 8:37 = Matt. 16:26b; **243-. Some Standing Here:** (1) Mark 9:1 = Matt. 16:28 = Luke 9:27; **244-. Elijah Has Come:** (1) Mark 9:11–13 = Matt. 17:10–13; **245±. Possessed Boy Cured:** (1) Mark 9:14–29 = Matt. 17:14–21 = Luke 9:37–43a; **246+. Stranger as Exorcist:** (1) Mark 9:38–39 = Luke 9:49–50a; **247-. Cup of Water:** (1) Mark 9:41 = Matt. 10:42; **248-. Hand, Foot, Eye:** (1a) Mark 9:43–48 = Matt. 18:8–9, (1b) Matt. 5:29–30; **249-. Salted with Fire:** (1) Mark 9:49; **250-. Salt and Peace:** (1) Mark 9:50b; **251-. Jesus to Judea:** (1) Mark 10:1 = Matt. 19:1–2 =(!) Luke 9:51; **252-. Moses and Divorce:** (1) Mark 10:2–9 = Matt. 19:3–8; **253-. The Rich Man:** (1a) Mark 10:17–22 = Matt. 19:16–22 = Luke 18:18–23, (1b) *Gos. Naz.* 16a; **254-. Jesus' Baptism:** (1a) Mark 10:35–40 = Matt. 20:20–23, (1b) Luke 12:50; **255+. Raised Man's Family:** (1a) *Secret Mark* 2r14b–16, (1b) Mark 10:46a; **256±. Healing of Bartimaeus:** (1a) Mark 10:46b–52 = Matt. 20:29–34 = Luke 18:35–43, (1b) Matt. 9:27–31; **257-. Entry into Jerusalem:** (1a) Mark 11:1–10 = Matt. 21:1–9 = Luke 19:28–40, (1b) John 12:9–19; **258-. Entry into Temple:** (1) Mark 11:11a = Matt. 21:10–11; **259-. Bethany at Night:** (1) Mark 11:11b = Matt. 21:17 = Luke 21:37–38; **260-. Cursed Fig Tree:** (1) Mark 11:12–14, 20–21 = Matt. 21:18–20; **261-. By What Authority?** (1) Mark 11:27–33 = Matt. 21:23–27 = Luke 20:1–8; **262-. On the Resurrection:** (1) Mark 12:18–27 = Matt. 22:23–33 = Luke 20:27–40; **263-. Widows' Houses:** (1) Mark 12:40 = Matt. 23:14 = Luke 20:47; **264-. Widow's Mite:** (1) Mark 12:41–44 = Luke 21:1–4; **265-. Within This Generation:** (1) Mark 13:28–32 = Matt. 24:32–36 = Luke 21:29–33; **266-. Plot Against Jesus:** (1) Mark 14:1–2 = Matt. 26:3–5 = Luke 22:1–2; **267-. Judas Promised Money:** (1a) Mark 14:10–11 = Matt. 26:14–16 = Luke 22:3–6, (1b) John 13:27a; **268-. The Passover Preparation:** (1a) Mark 14:12–16 = Matt. 26:17–19 = Luke 22:7–14, (1b) *Gos. Eb.* 7; **269±. Jesus Arrested:** (1a) Mark 14:43–50 = Matt. 26:47–56 = Luke 22:47–53, (1b) John 18:1–12, 20; **270-. Priest's Question:** (1a) Mark 14: 53, 60–65 = Matt. 26:57, 62–68 = Luke 22:54a, 63–71, (1b) John 18:13–14, 19–24; **271-. Peter's Three Denials:** (1a) Mark 14:54, 66–72 = Matt. 26:58, 69–75 = Luke 22:54b–62, (1b) *Gos. Naz.* 19, (1c) John 18:15–18, 25–27; **272-. Release of Barabbas:** (1a) Mark 15:6–15 = Matt. 27:15–23, 26 = Luke 23:18–25, (1b) John 18:39–40, (1c) Acts 3:13–14, (1d) *Gos. Naz.* 20; **273-. Simon of Cyrene:** (1a) Mark 15:20b–21 = Matt. 27:31b–32 = Luke 23:26, (1b!) John 19:17a; **274-. Women at Crucifixion:** (1a) Mark 15:40–41 = Matt. 27:55–56 = Luke 23:49, (1b) John 19: 25b–27; **275-. The Empty Tomb:** (1a) Mark 16:1–8 =

Matt. 28:1–10 = Luke 24:1–11, (1b) John 20:1, 11–18, (1c) *Gos. Pet.* 11:44; 12:50–13:57; **276-. *The Great Torment:*** (1) P. Oxy. 840. 1; **277. *Purification by Water?*** (1) P. Oxy. 840. 2a; **278-. *Man and Child:*** (1) *Gos. Thom.* 4:1 & P. Oxy. 654. 4:1; **279-. *In Your Sight:*** (1) *Gos. Thom.* 5:1 & P. Oxy. 654. 5:1; **280-. *On Telling Lies:*** (1) *Gos. Thom.* 6:2 + 3b & P. Oxy. 654. 6:2 + 3b; **281-. *Man and Lion:*** (1) *Gos. Thom.* 7 & P. Oxy. 654. 7; **282-. *Two and One:*** (1) *Gos. Thom.* 11:2b; **283-. *Fasting, Praying, Almsgiving:*** (1) *Gos. Thom.* 6:1 + 14:1; **284-. *Your Father:*** (1) *Gos. Thom.* 15; **285-. *Beginning and End:*** (1) *Gos. Thom.* 18:1–3; **286-. *Before One's Creation:*** (1) *Gos. Thom.* 19:1; **287-. *Stones and Trees:*** (1) *Gos. Thom.* 19:2; **288-. *Children in Field:*** (1) *Gos. Thom.* 21:1–2; **289-. *The Chosen Few:*** (1) *Gos. Thom.* 23; **290 +. *Love Your Brother:*** (1) *Gos. Thom.* 25; **291-. *Fasting and Sabbath:*** (1) *Gos. Thom.* 27 & P. Oxy. 1.27; **292-. *Drunk, Blind, Empty:*** (1) *Gos. Thom.* 28; **293-. *Flesh as Poverty:*** (1) *Gos. Thom.* 29; **294-. *Desire to Hear:*** (1) *Gos. Thom.* 38:1 & P. Oxy. 655. 38:1; **295 +. *Become Passersby:*** (1) *Gos. Thom.* 42; **296-. *From My Words:*** (1) *Gos. Thom.* 43; **297 +. *Horses and Bows:*** (1) *Gos. Thom.* 47:1; **298-. *Unity and Mountain:*** (1a) *Gos. Thom.* 48, (1b) *Gos. Thom.* 106; **299-. *Solitary and Elect:*** (1) *Gos. Thom.* 49; **300-. *If They Ask:*** (1) *Gos. Thom.* 50; **301-. *The True Circumcision:*** (1) *Gos. Thom.* 53; **302-. *Superior to World:*** (1a) *Gos. Thom.* 56, (1b) *Gos. Thom.* 80; **303 +. *Blessed the Sufferer:*** (1) *Gos. Thom.* 58; **304-. *Take Heed Now:*** (1) *Gos. Thom.* 59; **305-. *Samaritan and Lamb:*** (1) *Gos. Thom.* 60; **306-. *Jesus and Salome:*** (1) *Gos. Thom.* 61:2–5; **307-. *Knowing the All:*** (1) *Gos. Thom.* 67; **308-. *From Within Yourselves:*** (1) *Gos. Thom.* 70; **309-. *The Cistern:*** (1) *Gos. Thom.* 74; **310-. *Light and All:*** (1) *Gos. Thom.* 77:1; **311 +. *Stone and Wood:*** (1) *Gos. Thom.* 77:2 & P. Oxy. 1. 77:2; **312-. *Riches and Power:*** (1) *Gos. Thom.* 81; **313-. *Near the Fire:*** (1) *Gos. Thom.* 82; **314-. *The Father's Light:*** (1) *Gos. Thom.* 83; **315-. *The Primordial Images:*** (1) *Gos. Thom.* 84; **316-. *Adam's Death:*** (1) *Gos. Thom.* 85; **317-. *Body and Soul:*** (1) *Gos. Thom.* 87; **318-. *Angels and Prophets:*** (1) *Gos. Thom.* 88; **319-. *Then and Now:*** (1) *Gos. Thom.* 92:2 ; **320 +. *The Empty Jar:*** (1) *Gos. Thom.* 97; **321 +. *The Assassin:*** (1) *Gos. Thom.* 98; **322-. *A Harlot's Son:*** (1) *Gos. Thom.* 105; **323-. *From My Mouth:*** (1) *Gos. Thom.* 108; **324 +. *Finding the World:*** (1) *Gos. Thom.* 110; **325. *Finding Oneself:*** (1) *Gos. Thom.* 111:2; **326-. *Flesh and Soul:*** (1) *Gos. Thom.* 112; **327-. *Peter and Mary:*** (1) *Gos. Thom.* 114; **328-. *Wise and Righteous:*** (1) *Dial. Sav.* 4–7; **329-. *Renouncing Power:*** (1) *Dial. Sav.* 19–20; **330-. *This Impoverished Cosmos:*** (1) *Dial. Sav.* 25–26; **331-. *Stone and Word:*** (1) *Dial. Sav.* 31–34; **332-. *Vision of God:*** (1) *Dial. Sav.* 41–46; **333-. *The True Rule:*** (1) *Dial. Sav.* 47–50; **334-. *Fullness and Deficiency:*** (1) *Dial. Sav.* 54–55; **335-. *Living and Dead:*** (1) *Dial. Sav.* 56–57; **336-. *Place of Absence:*** (1) *Dial. Sav.* 60–64; **337-. *Love and Goodness:*** (1) *Dial. Sav.* 73–74; **338-. *Treasures of Cosmos:*** (1)

Dial. Sav. 69–70; **339-.** *The Perfect Victory:* (1) *Dial. Sav.* 71–72; **340-.** *Love and Goodness:* (1) *Dial. Sav.* 73–74; **341-.** *Faith and Knowledge:* (1) *Dial. Sav.* 75–76; **342-.** *Reaching the Place:* (1) *Dial. Sav.* 77–78; **343-.** *Understanding Everything:* (1) *Dial. Sav.* 81–82; **344-.** *Your Father:* (1) *Dial. Sav.* 86–87; **345-.** *Left Over:* (1) *Dial. Sav.* 88–89; **346-.** *The Dissolved Works:* (1) *Dial. Sav.* 97–98; **347-.** *Spirit and Light:* (1) *Dial. Sav.* 99–102; **348-.** *Understanding the Works:* (1) *Dial. Sav.* 103–104; **349-.** *Water into Wine:* (1) John 2:1–11; **350-.** *Jesus to Nicodemus:* (1) John 3:11–21; **351-.** *The Samaritan Woman:* (1) John 4:1–42; **352-.** *On the Father:* (1) John 5:19–38; **353-.** *Bread of Life:* (1) John 6:22–50; **354-.** *Division over Jesus:* (1) John 6:59–66; **355-.** *Jesus at Tabernacles:* (1) John 7:1–52 & 8:12–59; **356-.** *Blindness and Sight:* (1) John 9:8–41; **357-.** *Life for Others:* (1a) John 10:1–21, (1b) John 15:13, (1c) 1 John 3:16; **358-.** *Feast of Dedication:* (1) John 10:22–42; **359-.** *Pagans Visit Jesus:* (1) John 11:20–36a; **360-.** *Belief in Jesus:* (1) John 11:36b–50; **361-.** *Hour of Glory:* (1) John 12:20–24, 28–34; **362-.** *Prophecies of Disbelief:* (1) John 12:37–43; **363-.** *Jesus' Supper Discourse:* (1) John 13:31–17:26; **364±.** *These Are Written:* (1a) John 20:30–31, (1b) John 21:25

Third Stratum [123:23 + 100]

(a) Multiple Independent Attestation [1]

365-. *Giving and Receiving:* (1) 1 *Clem.* 2:1, (2) *Did.* 1:5, (3) *Herm. Man.* 2:4b, (4) Acts 20:35b.

(b) Triple Independent Attestation [1]

366-. *Blessed the Meek:* (1) Matt. 5:5, (2) *Barn.* 19:4, (3) *Did.* 3:7.

(c) Double Independent Attestation [21]

367±. *Birth of Jesus:* (1a) Matt. 1–2, (1b) *Gos. Naz.* 1, (2a) Luke 1–2, (2b) *Gos. Eb.* 3b; **368-.** *Genealogy of Jesus:* (1) Matt. 1:1–17, (2) Luke 3:23–38; **369-.** *Star of Revelation:* (1) Matt. 2:1–12, (2) Ign. *Eph.* 19:2–3; **370-.** *Mercy for Mercy:* (1) Matt. 5:7, (2a) 1 *Clem.* 13:2a, (2b) Pol. *Phil.* 2:3c; **371+.** *Prayer and Forgiveness:* (1) Matt. 5:23–24, (2) *Did.* 14:2; **372+.** *Against Oaths:* (1a) Matt. 5:33–37, (1b) Matt. 23:22, (2) James 5:12; **373-.** *On Prayer:* (1) Matt. 6:5–6, (2) *Did.* 8:2a; **374-.** *On Fasting:* (1) Matt. 6:16–18, (2) *Did.* 8:1; **375-.** *Binding and Loosing:* (1a) Matt. 16:19, (1b) Matt. 18:18, (2) John 20:23; **376-.** *Power of Prayer:* (1) Matt. 18:19, (2) Ign. *Eph.* 5:2b; **377-.** *Able to Receive:* (1) Matt. 19:12b, (2) Ign. *Smyrn.* 6:1b; **378-.** *Called and Chosen:* (1) Matt. 22:14, (2) *Barn.* 4:14b; **379+.** *Exaltation and Humiliation:* (1) Matt. 23:12, (2a) Luke 14:11, (2b) Luke 18:14; **380-.** *Suicide of Judas:* (1) Matt. 27:3–10, (2)

Acts 1:15–20a; **381±. Teach and Baptize:** (1) Matt. 28:16–20, (2) *Did.* 7:1; **382-. Gift for Gift:** (1) Luke 6:38a, (2) *1 Clem.* 13:2d; **383-. The Servant's Duty:** (1) Luke 17:7–10, (2) *Herm. Sim.* 5.2, 4–7; **384-. Hate Hypocrisy:** (1) *Did.* 4:12, (2) *Ap. Jas.* 6:7; **385-. Faith's Final Profit:** (1) *Did.* 16:2b, (2) *Barn.* 4:9; **386-. Faith Against Sight:** (1) John 20:24–29, (2a) *Ap. Jas.* 8:3, (2b) *Ap. Jas.* 3:3–5; **387-. Place from Which:** (1) *Gos. Pet.* 13:56b, (2a) *Ap. Jas.* 2:2a, (2b) *Ap. Jas..* 9:5b.

(d) Single Attestation [100]

388-. Sermon on Mount: (1) Matt. 5:1–2; **389-. Blessed the Pure:** (1) Matt. 5:8; **390-. Blessed the Peacemakers:** (1) Matt. 5:9; **391-. Your Good Works:** (1) Matt. 5:16; **392-. Not to Abolish:** (1) Matt. 5:17; **393-. The Least Commandment:** (1) Matt. 5:19; **394-. Greater Righteousness:** (1) Matt. 5:20; **395-. Against Anger:** (1a) Matt. 5:21–22, (1b) *Gos. Naz.* 4; **396-. Against Lust:** (1) Matt. 5:27–28; **397-. Piety Before Men:** (1) Matt. 6:1; **398-. On Almsgiving:** (1) Matt. 6:2–3a, 4; **399-. Gentiles and Prayer:** (1) Matt. 6:7–8; **400-. Tomorrow's Anxiety:** (1) Matt. 6:34a; **401-. In Sheep's Clothing:** (1) Matt. 7:15; **402-. Mercy Not Sacrifice:** (1) Matt. 9:13a; **403-. Israel's Lost Sheep:** (1a) Matt. 10:5b–6, (1b) Matt. 15:24; **404-. Give Without Pay:** (1) Matt. 10:8b; **405-. Cities of Israel:** (1) Matt. 10:23; **406-. Master and Household:** (1) Matt. 10:25b; **407-. Reception and Reward:** (1) Matt. 10:41; **408-. Teaching and Preaching:** (1) Matt. 11:1; **409-. My Chosen Servant:** (1) Matt. 12:17–21; **410-. By Your Words:** (1) Matt. 12:36–37; **411-. Planted Weeds Explained:** (1) Matt. 13:36–43a; **412-. The Fishnet Explained:** (1) Matt. 13:49–50; **413-. Peter Sinks:** (1) Matt. 14:28–33; **414-. At His Feet:** (1) Matt. 15:29–31 [see Mark 7:31–37]; **415-. The Humble Child:** (1) Matt. 18:4; **416-. Despising Little Ones:** (1) Matt. 18:10; **417-. Church Excommunication:** (1) Matt. 18:16–17; **418+. The Unmerciful Servant:** (1) Matt. 18:23–34; **419+. The Vineyard Laborers:** (1) Matt. 20:1–15; **420-. On Moses' Seat:** (1) Matt. 23:1–3; **421-. On Titles:** (1) Matt. 23:8–10; **422-. For a Proselyte:** (1) Matt. 23:15; **423-. Against Casuistry:** (1) Matt. 23:16–22; **424-. Gnat and Camel:** (1) Matt. 23:24; **425-. The Last Judgment:** (1) Matt. 25:31–46; **426-. The Kingdom's Scribe:** (1) Matt. 13:51–52; **427+. Kingdom and Eunuch:** (1) Matt. 19:10–12a; **428+. The Two Sons:** (1) Matt. 21:28–32; **429-. The Temple Tax:** (1) Matt. 17:24–27; **430-. The Children's Confession:** (1) Matt. 21:14–16; **431-. Conception of John:** (1) Luke 1:5–25; **432-. Birth of John:** (1) Luke 1:57–80; **433-. Jesus at Twelve:** (1) Luke 2:41–52; **434-. John's Ethic:** (1) Luke 3:10–14; **435-. Gentiles Preferred:** (1) Luke 4:25–27; **436-. On Sabbath Labor:** (1) After Luke 6:1–4 in Codex Beza [D]; **437-. Woe Against Riches:** (1) Luke 6:24; **438-. Woe Against Satiety:** (1) Luke 6:25a; **439-. Woe Against Laughter:** (1) Luke 6:25b; **440-. Woe Against Praise:** (1) Luke 6:26; **441-.**

Condemnation for Condemnation: (1) Luke 6:37b; 442-. *Widow's Son Raised:* (1) Luke 7:11–17; 443-. *Having Rejected John:* (1) Luke 7: 29–30; 444±. *Women with Jesus:* (1) Luke 8:2–3; 445-. *Inhospitable Samaritans:* (1) Luke 9:52–55; 446-. *The Seventy Return:* (1) Luke 10:17–20; 447+. *The Good Samaritan:* (1) Luke 10:29–37; 448-. *Martha and Mary:* (1) Luke 10:38–42; 449+. *Friend at Midnight:* (1) Luke 11:5–8; 450-. *Adversaries Watch Jesus:* (1) Luke 11:53–54; 451-. *Little Flock:* (1) Luke 12:32; 452-. *Much and More:* (1) Luke 12:47–48; 453-. *Repent or Perish:* (1) Luke 13:1–5; 454+. *The Barren Tree:* (1) Luke 13:6–9; 455-. *Cripple and Sabbath:* (1) Luke 13:10–17; 456-. *Going to Jerusalem:* (1) Luke 13:22; 457-. *Jesus and Herod:* (1) Luke 13:31–33; 458-. *Dropsy and Sabbath:* (1) Luke 14:1–6; 459-. *Place at Table:* (1) Luke 14:7–10; 460-. *Inviting the Outcasts:* (1a) Luke 14:12–14, (1b) Luke 14:21b; 461+. *The Tower Builder:* (1) Luke 14:28–30; 462+. *The Warring King:* (1) Luke 14:31–32; 463-. *Renouncing All:* (1) Luke 14:33; 464+. *The Lost Coin:* (1) Luke 15:8–10; 465+. *The Prodigal Son:* (1) Luke 15:11–32; 466+. *The Unjust Steward:* (1) Luke 16:1–7; 467-. *This World's Sons* (1) Luke 16:8; 468-. *Unrighteous Mammon:* (1) Luke 16:9; 469-. *Faithful and Unfaithful:* (1a) Luke 16:10–12, (1b) 2 *Clem.* 8:5b [from Luke 16:10a]; 470-. *Exaltation and Abomination:* (1) Luke 16:14–15; 471+. *Rich Man and Lazarus:* (1) Luke 16:19–31; 472-. *Days Are Coming:* (1) Luke 17:22; 473+. *The Unjust Judge:* (1) Luke 18:1–8; 474+. *Pharisee and Publican:* (1) Luke 18:9–14; 475-. *Salvation for Zaccheus:* (1) Luke 19:1–9; 476-. *The Disciples' Confession:* (1) Luke 19:28–40; 477-. *Jerusalem Destroyed:* (1) Luke 19:41–44; 478-. *Two Swords Enough:* (1) Luke 22:35–38; 479-. *The Promised Spirit:* (1a) Luke 24:44–49, (1b) Acts 1:1–8, (1c) John 20:19–22; 480±. *Ascension of Jesus:* (1a) Luke 24:50–52, (1b) Acts 1:9–11; 481-. *Action for Action:* (1) 1 *Clem.* 13:2c; 482-. *Kindness for Kindness:* (1) 1 *Clem.* 13:2f; 483-. *Only Through Suffering:* (1) *Barn.* 7: 11b; 484-. *Gatherings in Preparation:* (1) *Did.* 16:2a; 485-. *Disciples Find Disciples:* (1) John 1:35–42; 486-. *Jesus and Nathaniel:* (1) John 1:43–51; 487-. *Jesus Baptizing:* (1) John 3:22–36.

Fourth Stratum [35:0 + 35]

(a) Single Attestation [35]

488-. *In the Beginning:* (1) John 1:1–18; 489-. *Matthias Replaces Judas:* (1) Acts 1:20b–26; 490-. *The Heavens Opened:* (1) Acts 7:55–56; 491-. *Kingdom and Fullness:* (1) Ap. Jas. 2:1–4; 492-. *Become Full:* (1) Ap. Jas. 3:6–9; 493-. *Kingdom and Cross:* (1) Ap. Jas. 4:1b–5:5; 494-. *Head of Prophecy:* (1) Ap. Jas. 6:1–4; 495-. *Secretly and Openly:* (1) Ap. Jas. 6:5; 496-. *Go Before Me:* (1) Ap. Jas. 6:6; 497-. *The Palm Shoot:* (1) Ap. Jas. 6:8; 498-. *Ascension*

and Parables: (1) *Ap. Jas.* 6:9–10; **499-.** *Grain of Wheat:* (1) *Ap. Jas.* 6:11;
500-. *Son Needs Father:* (1) *Ap. Jas.* 6:15b; **501-.** *On Persecuting Oneself:* (1)
Ap. Jas. 6:16; **502-.** *It Is Easier:* (1) *Ap. Jas.* 6:17; **503-.** *Grief and Sorrow:* (1)
Ap. Jas. 6:18; **504-.** *Had It Been:* (1) *Ap. Jas.* 6:19; **505-.** *Jesus as Intercessor:*
(1) *Ap. Jas.* 6:22b; **506-.** *Intercessor Not Needed:* (1) *Ap. Jas.* 7:2b; **507-.** *Be
Like Strangers:* (1) *Ap. Jas.* 7:3a; **508-.** *Soul and Flesh:* (1) *Ap. Jas.* 7:7; **509-.**
Few in Heaven: (1) *Ap. Jas.* 7:8; **510-.** *Ear of Grain:* (1) *Ap. Jas.* 8:1–2; **511-.**
House for Shelter: (1) Ap. Jas. 8:4; **512-.** *To the Father:* (1) *Ap. Jas.* 8:5; **513-.**
Who Are Not: (1) *Ap. Jas.* 8:6; **514-.** *Kingdom Becomes Desert:* (1) *Ap. Jas.*
8:7a; **515-.** *Being Like Jesus:* (1) *Ap. Jas.* 8:7b; **516-.** *Kingdom and Life:* (1)
Ap. Jas. 9:1–4; **517-.** *Thrice Blessed Ones:* (1) *Ap. Jas.* 9:9; **518-.** *Small and
Great:* (1) 2 *Clem.* 8:5a; **519-.** *Chosen and Given:* (1) *Gos. Naz.* 23; **520-.**
Wrath for Sacrifice: (1) *Gos. Eb.* 6; **521-.** *Adulterous Woman Forgiven:* (1)
John 7:53–8:11; **522-.** *Later Markan Endings:* (1) Shorter Ending (after
Mark 16:1–8); (2) Longer Ending (= Mark 16:9–20); (3) Freer Logion (after
Mark 16:14).

Appendix 2

Types and Trajectories
of Peasant Unrest
in Early Roman Palestine

A. Protesters [7 cases between 4 B.C.E. and 65 C.E.]

[1] 4 B.C.E.: To Archelaus, about taxes and prisoners, in JW 2:4 = JA 17.204–205; [2a] 16–17 C.E.: To Pilate, about iconic standards in Jerusalem, in JW 2:169–174 = JA 18.55–59; [= 2b?] 16–17 C.E.: To Pilate, about aniconic shields in Jerusalem, in Philo, *Embassy to Gaius* 299–305; [3] 26–36 C.E.: To Pilate, about using Temple funds for Jerusalem aqueduct, in JW 2.175–177 = JA 18.60–62; [4] 39–41 C.E.: To Petronius, about Caligula's statue in the Temple, in JW 2.185–203 = JA 8.261–309 and Philo, *Embassy to Gaius* 203–348; [5] 48–52 C.E.: To Cumanus, about Roman soldier's indecency in the Temple, in JW 2.224–227 = JA 20.108–112; [6] 48–52 C.E.: To Cumanus, about Roman soldier's disrespect for Torah scroll, in JW 2.229–231 = JA 20.115–117; [7] 65 C.E.: To Cestius Gallus, about the governor Florus, in JW 2.280–281.

B. Prophets [10 cases between c.30 C.E. and 73 C.E.]

[1] c.30 C.E.: John the Baptist, in JA 18.116–119; [2] 36 C.E.: The Samaritan Prophet, in JA 18.85–89; [3] 44–46 C.E.: Theudas, in JA 20.97–98 and Acts 5:36; [4] 52–60 C.E.: Unnamed prophets (generalizing statement), in JW 2.258–260 = JA 20.167b–168; [5] 52–60 C.E.: The Egyptian Prophet, in JW 2.261–263 = JA 20.169–171 and Acts 21:38; [6] 60–62 C.E.: Unnamed prophet, in JA 20.188; [7] 62–70 C.E.: Jesus son of Ananias, in JW 6.300–309; [8] 70 C.E.: Unnamed prophet, in JW 6.283–285; [9] 70 C.E.: Unnamed prophets (generalizing statement), in JW 6.286; [10?] 73 C.E.: Jonathan the Weaver, in JW 6.437–450.

C. Bandits [11 cases between 47 B.C.E. and 68–69 C.E.]

[1] 47 B.C.E.: Ezekias the bandit leader, in JW 1.204–207 = JA 14.159–179; [2] 37 B.C.E.: Galilean cave bandits, in JW 1.304–313 = JA 14.414–430; [3] 44–46 C.E.: Tholomaeus the bandit leader, in JA 20.5; [4] 48–52 C.E.: Bandits near Beth-horon, in JW 2.228–229 = JA 20.113–114; [5] 51–52 C.E.: Eleazar, son of Deinaeus, and Alexander lead revolt, in JW 2.232–246 = JA 20.118–136; [6] 52–60 C.E.: Eleazar son of Deinaeus caught after twenty-year career as bandit chief, in JW 2.253 = JA 20.161; [7] 60–62 C.E.: Unnamed bandits (generalizing statement), in JW 2.271 = JA 20.185; [8] 64–66 C.E.: Unnamed bandits (generalizing statement), in JW 2.278b–279 = JA 20.255b–257; [9] 66–67 C.E.: Bandit army under Josephus in Galilee, in JW 2.568–576 = Life 77–78; [10] 66–67 C.E.: Jesus the bandit leader near Ptolemais, in Life 104–111; [11] 68–69 C.E.: Zealots as coalition of bandit groups in Jerusalem, in JW 4.135–138 (note 4.442–448).

D. Messiahs [5 cases between 4 B.C.E. and 68–70 C.E.]

[1] 4 B.C.E.: Judas, son of the bandit leader Ezekias, in Galilee, in JW 2.56 = JA 17:271–272; [2] 4 B.C.E.: Simon, the Herodian slave, in Perea, in JW 2.57–59 = JA 17.273–277a; [3] 4 B.C.E.: Athronges, the shepherd, in Judea, in JW 2.60–65 = JA 17.278–284; [4] 66 C.E.: Menahem, (grand)son of Judas the Galilean (retainer leading peasants), in JW 2.433–434 [= 408, 425], 444; [5] 68–70 C.E.: Simon son of Gioras (bar Giora), in JW 2.521; 2.652–654 = 4.503–507; 4.508–510; 4.529; 7.26–36, 154.

Appendix 3

Inventory for
John the Baptist Sayings [18:6+12]

First Stratum [8:5+3]

[1] 58. *John Baptizes Jesus* [1/3]; [2] 51. *Into the Desert* [1/3]; [3] 115. *John's Message* [1/2]; [4] 85. *Greater Than John* [1/2]; [5] 106. *Fasting and Wedding* [1/2]; [6] 143. *Reply to John* [1/1]; [7] 144. *Wisdom Justified* [1/1]; [8] 168. *Kingdom and Violence* [1/1].

Second Stratum [5:1+4]

[1] 197. *Herod Beheads John* [2/2]; [2] 213. *John the Baptist* [2/1]; [3] 231. *Herod on Jesus* [2/1]; [4] 244. *Elijah Has Come* [2/1]; [5] 261. *By What Authority?* [2/1].

Third Stratum [5:0+5]

[1] 428. *The Two Sons* [3/1]; [2] 431. *Conception of John* [3/1]; [3] 432. *Birth of John* [3/1]; [4] 443. *Having Rejected John* [3/1]; [5] 487. *Jesus Baptizing* [3/1].

Appendix 4

Inventory for
Son of Man Sayings [40:14 + 26]

This inventory must be read very carefully because of one important aspect. Wherever there are two or more sources, in every case but one, Son of Man is present in only one of those sources. And sometimes it is only present in one unit of a source. I indicate in each case which source or unit contains the expression. If no such annotation appears, it means that all texts of a given source contain it. In other words, that 40:14 + 26 summary does not mean fourteen cases of multiple independent attestation for the Son of Man *expression* but merely for complexes in which it occurs at least once. There is only one single case where the Son of Man *expression* occurs in multiple independent attestation; that single exception is 101. *Foxes Have Holes* [1/2], which contains Son of Man in two independent sources. For the *phrase Son of Man itself*, therefore, the numerical summary is actually 40:1 + 39.

A. Apocalyptic Son of Man Sayings [18:6 + 12]

First Stratum [9:5 + 4]

[1] 2. *Jesus' Apocalyptic Return* [1/6] but with Son of Man only in Mark; [2] 28. *Before the Angels* [1/4] but with Son of Man only in Mark; [3] 12. *Knowing the Danger* [1/4] but with Son of Man only in Q; [4] 30. *Revealed to James* [1/3] but with Son of Man only in *Gos. Heb.* 7; [5] 122. *Request for Sign* [1/2] but with Son of Man only in Q; [6] 179. *On Twelve Thrones* [1/1]; [7] 174. *As with Lightning* [1/1]; [8] 175. *As with Noah* [1/1]; [9] 176. *As with Lot* [1/1].

Second Stratum [3:1 + 2]

[1] 188. *The Unknown Time* [2/4] but with Son of Man only in Luke 21:34–36; [2] 243. *Some Standing Here* [2/1]; [3] 270. *Priest's Question* [2/1].

454

Third Stratum [5:0 + 5]

[1] 411. *Planted Weeds Explained* [3/1]; [2] 405. *Cities of Israel* [3/1]; [3] 425. *The Last Judgment* [3/1]; [4] 472. *Days Are Coming* [3/1]; [5] 473. *The Unjust Judge* [3/1].

Fourth Stratum [1:0 + 1]

[1] 490. *The Heavens Opened* [4/1].

B. Earthly Son of Man Sayings [10:8 + 2]

First Stratum [5:4 + 1]

[1] 101. *Foxes Have Holes* [1/2] and with Son of Man in both; [2] 23. *All Sins Forgiven* [1/4] but with Son of Man only in Q; [3] 73. *Who Is Jesus?* [1/2] but with Son of Man only in Matt. 16:13-20; [4] 48. *Blessed the Persecuted* [1/3] but with Son of Man only in Luke 6:22-23; [5] 144. *Wisdom Justified* [1/1] but with Son of Man only in Q.

Second Stratum [4:3 + 1]

[1] 187. *Righteous and Sinners* [2/4] but with Son of Man only in Luke 19:10; [2] 191. *Leader as Servant* [2/3] but with Son of Man only from Mark; [3] 127. *Sickness and Sin* [2/2] but with Son of Man only from Mark; [4] 220. *Lord and Sabbath* [2/1].

Third Stratum [1:1 + 0]

[1] 386. *Faith Against Sight* [3/2] but with Son of Man only in *Ap. Jas.* 3:3-5.

C. Suffering and Rising Son of Man Sayings [2:0 + 2]

Second Stratum [2:0 + 2]

[1] 240. *Passion-Resurrection Prophecy* [2/1] but with Son of Man only from Mark; [2] 269. *Jesus Arrested* [2/1] but with Son of Man only in Luke 22:47.

D. Johannine Son of Man Sayings [10:0 + 10]

Second Stratum [10:0 + 10]

[1] 486. *Jesus and Nathaniel* [2/1]; [2] 350. *Jesus to Nicodemus* [2/1]; [3] 352. *On the Father* [2/1]; [4] 353. *Bread of Life* [2/1]; [5] 354. *Division over*

Eucharist [2/1]; [6] 355. *Jesus at Tabernacles* [2/1]; [7] 356. *Blindness and Sight* [2/1]; [8] 361. *Hour of Glory* [2/1]; [9] 362. *Prophecies of Disbelief* [2/1]; [10] 363. *Jesus' Supper Discourse* [2/1]

Appendix 5

Inventory for
Kingdom Sayings [77:33 + 44]

This inventory must be read just as carefully as the Son of Man list and for the same reason. It is also much more complicated. The general inventory at A gives all complexes in which Kingdom appears in at least one unit of a source. I indicate in each case which source or text contains the expression. If no such annotation appears, it means that all texts of a given source contain it. But, once again, a special inventory (B) is required to list those cases in which the Kingdom expression itself appears in more than one independent source per complex. Thus, while the numerical summary for complexes that include Kingdom somewhere within their texts is 77:33 + 44, the numerical summary for those with Kingdom in at least two independent sources is 77:12 + 65.

A. General Inventory for Kingdom Sayings [77:33 + 44]

First Stratum [43:28 + 15]

[1] 1. *Mission and Message* [1/7] but with Kingdom only in Q or possibly Mark's source as well; compare Mark 6:12 with 1:15, and note Luke 9:2; [2] 3. *Bread and Fish* [1/6] but with Kingdom only in Luke 9:11; [3] 5. *Crucifixion of Jesus* [1/5] but with Kingdom only in Luke; [4] 8. *When and Where* [1/5] but with Kingdom only in two sources: 1a, 1c, 5; [5] 16. *Supper and Eucharist* [1/4] but with Kingdom only from Mark; [6] 13. *Two as One* [1/4] but with Kingdom in two sources: 1, 3; [7] 20. *Kingdom and Children* [1/4] with Kingdom in all four sources; [8] 26. *Jesus Virginally Conceived* [1/4] but with Kingdom only in Luke; [9] 35. *The Mustard Seed* [1/3] with Kingdom in all three sources; [10] 46. *The Tenants* [1/3] but with Kingdom only in Matthew; [11] 43. *Blessed the Poor* [1/3] with Kingdom in all three sources; [12] 48. *Blessed the Persecuted* [1/3] but with Kingdom only from Matt. 5:10; [13] 120. *The Lord's Prayer* [1/2] with Kingdom in both sources:

457

1a, 2; **[14]** 70. *Burial of Jesus* [1/2] but with Kingdom only from Mark; **[15]** 111. *Invocation Without Obedience* [1/2] but with Kingdom only in Matthew; **[16]** 71. *The Fishnet* [1/2] but with Kingdom only in Matthew; **[17]** 73. *Who Is Jesus?* [1/2] but with Kingdom only in Matthew; **[18]** 75. *The Harvest Time* [1/2] but with Kingdom only in Mark; **[19]** 82. *Against Anxieties* [1/2] but with Kingdom only from Q; **[20]** 84. *On Hindering Others* [1/2] but with Kingdom only in Matt. 23:13; **[21]** 85. *Greater Than John* [1/2] with Kingdom in both sources; **[22]** 90. *The Planted Weeds* [1/2] with Kingdom in both sources; **[23]** 92. *Knowing the Mystery* [1/2] but with Kingdom only in Mark; **[24]** 95. *The Feast* [1/2] but with Kingdom only from Q; **[25]** 98. *The Pearl* [1/2] with Kingdom in both sources; **[26]** 104. *The Leaven* [1/2] with Kingdom in both sources; **[27]** 105. *Jesus' True Family* [1/2] but with Kingdom only in *Gos. Thom.* 99; **[28]** 108. *The Treasure* [1/2] with Kingdom in both sources; **[29]** 291. *Fasting and Sabbath* [1/1]; **[30]** 299. *Solitary and Elect* [1/1]; **[31]** 313. *Near the Fire* [1/1]; **[32]** 320. *The Empty Jar* [1/1]; **[33]** 321. *The Assassin* [1/1]; **[34]** 327. *Peter and Mary* [1/1]; **[35]** 145. *Leave the Dead* [1/1] but with Kingdom only in Luke; **[36]** 146. *Looking Backward* [1/1]; **[37]** 150. *By Whose Power* [1/1]; **[38]** 164. *The Closed Door* [1/1] but with Kingdom only in Matthew; **[39]** 166. *Patriarchs and Gentiles* [1/1]; **[40]** 168. *Kingdom and Violence* [1/1]; **[41]** 178. *The Entrusted Money* [1/1] but with Kingdom only in Luke; **[42]** 179. *On Twelve Thrones* [1/1] but with Kingdom only in Luke; **[43]** 180. *Pilate's Question* [1/1] but with Kingdom only in John.

Second Stratum [14:5 + 9]

[1] 191. *Leader as Servant* [2/3] but with Kingdom only in Matt. 18:1, 4; **[2]** 64. *The Last Days* [2/3] but with Kingdom only in Matt. 24:14 and Luke 21:31; **[3]** 199. *Kingdom and Riches* [2/2] with Kingdom in both sources; **[4]** 200. *Hundredfold Reward* [2/2] but with Kingdom only in Luke; **[5]** 201. *The Chief Commandment* [2/2] but with Kingdom only in Mark; **[6]** 214. *Kingdom and Repentance* [2/1] but with Kingdom only in Mark and Matthew; **[7]** 218. *To Other Places* [2/1] but with Kingdom only in Matthew and Luke; **[8]** 225. *Interpreting the Sower* [2/1] but with Kingdom only in Matthew; **[9]** 230. *Among the Villages* [2/1] but with Kingdom only in Matthew and Luke; **[10]** 243. *Some Standing Here* [2/1] with Kingdom in all from Mark; **[11]** 248. *Hand, Foot, Eye* [2/1] but with Kingdom only in Mark; **[12]** 254. *Jesus' Baptism* [2/1] but with Kingdom only in Matthew; **[13]** 257. *Entry into Jerusalem* [2/1] but with Kingdom only in Mark; **[14]** 265. *Within This Generation* [2/1] but with Kingdom only in Luke.

Third Stratum [10:0 + 10]

[1] 393. *The Least Commandment* [3/1]; **[2]** 394. *Greater Righteousness*

[3/1]; **[3]** 411. *Planted Weeds Explained* [3/1]; **[4]** 426. *The Kingdom's Scribe* [3/1]; **[5]** 418. *The Unmerciful Servant* [3/1]; **[6]** 427. *Kingdom and Eunuch* [3/1]; **[7]** 419. *The Vineyard Laborers* [3/1]; **[8]** 428. *The Two Sons* [3/1]; **[9]** 425. *The Last Judgment* [3/1]; **[10]** 451. *Little Flock* [3/1].

Fourth Stratum [10:0+10]

[1] 491. *Kingdom and Fullness* [4/1]; **[2]** 492. *Become Full* [4/1]; **[3]** 493. *Kingdom and Cross* [4/1]; **[4]** 497. *The Palm Shoot* [4/1]; **[5]** 499. *Grain of Wheat* [4/1]; **[6]** 502. *It Is Easier* [4/1]; **[7]** 509. *Few in Heaven* [4/1]; **[8]** 510. *Ear of Grain* [4/1]; **[9]** 514. *Kingdom Becomes Desert* [4/1]; **[10]** 516. *Kingdom and Life* [4/1].

B. Special Inventory for Kingdom Sayings

This inventory lists only the twelve complexes where at least two independent sources contain the Kingdom expression. This is indicated in the numerical coding after the complex's title with $[x/y = z]$ where, as usual, x is stratum and y is attestation for the saying, but then z is attestation for the specific Kingdom expression. The complexes are given according to numerical plurality of that latter attestation. An asterisk designates the source or unit that contains the Kingdom expression, and the square parentheses indicate which Kingdom expression is used: K = Kingdom, KG = kingdom of God, KF = kingdom of the Father, KH = kingdom of Heaven.

First Stratum [11]

[1] 20. *Kingdom and Children* [1/4 = 4]: *(1) *Gos. Thom.* 22:1-2 [K]; *(2) Mark 10:13-16 [KG] = Matt. 19:13-15 [KH] = Luke 18:15-17 [KG]; *(3) Matt. 18:3 [KH]; *(4) John 3:1-10 [KG].

[2] 35. *The Mustard Seed* [1/3 = 3]: *(1) *Gos. Thom.* 20:1-2 [KH]; (2) 1or2?Q: Luke 13:18-19 [KG] = Matt. 13:31-32 [KH]; (3) Mark 4:30-32 [KG] = Matt. 13:31-32 [KH].

[3] 43. *Blessed the Poor* [1/3 = 3]: *(1) *Gos. Thom.* 54 [KH]; *(2a) 1Q: Luke 6:20 [KG] = Matt. 5:3 [KH]; *(2b) Pol. *Phil.* 2:3e [KG]; *(3) James 2:5 [K].

[4] 8. *When and Where* [1/5 = 2]: *(1a) *Gos. Thom.* 3:1 [K] & P. Oxy. 654.3:1 [K(G?)/(H?)]; (1b) *Gos. Thom.* 51 [-]; *(1c) *Gos. Thom.* 113 [KF]; (2) 2Q: Luke 17:23 [-] = Matt. 24:26 [-]; (3) Mark 13:21-23 [-]= Matt. 24:23-25 [-]; (4?) *Dial. Sav.* 16 [-]; *(5) Luke 17:20-21 [KG].

[5] 13. *Two as One* [1/4 = 2]: (1a) Gal. 3:27-28; (1b) 1 Cor. 12:13; (1c) Col. 3:10-11; *(2) *Gos. Thom.* 22:3-4 [K]; (3) *Gos. Eg.* 5b [-]; *(4) 2 *Clem.* 12:1-6 [KG, his K, KmyF].

[6] 120. *The Lord's Prayer* [1/2 = 2]: *(1a) 1Q: Luke 11:(1)2–4 [KF] = (!)
Matt. 6:9–13 [KF]; (1b) *Gos. Naz.* 5 [-]; (1c) Pol. *Phil.* 7:2a [-]; *(2) *Did.* 8:2b
[KF].

[7] 85. *Greater Than John* [1/2 = 2]: *(1) *Gos. Thom.* 46 [K]; *(2) 2Q:
Luke 7:28 [KG] = Matt. 11:11 [KH].

[8] 90. *The Planted Weeds* [1/2 = 2]: *(1) *Gos. Thom.* 57 [KF]; *(2) Matt.
13:24–30 [KH].

[9] 98. *The Pearl* [1/2 = 2]: *(1) *Gos. Thom.* 76:1 [KF]; *(2) Matt.
13:45–46 [KH].

[10] 104. *The Leaven* [1/2 = 2]: *(1) *Gos. Thom.* 96:1 [KF]; *(2) 1or2?Q:
Luke 13:20–21 [KG] = Matt. 13:33 [KG]

[11] 108. *The Treasure* [1/2 = 2]: *(1) *Gos. Thom.* 109 [K]; *(2) Matt.
13:44 [KH].

Second Stratum [1]

[1] 199. *Kingdom and Riches* [1/2 = 2]: *(1a) Mark 10:23–27 [KG] =
Matt. 19:23–26 [KH/KG] = Luke 18:24–27 [KG]; *(1b) *Gos. Naz.* 16b [KH];
*(2) *Herm. Sim.* 9.20:1–4 [KG].

C. Inventory for Other Kingdom Texts

(1) Acts of the Apostles 1:3, 6; 8:12; 14:22; 19:8; 20:25; 28:23, 31; (2) Paul:
1 Thess. 2:12; Gal. 5:21; 1 Cor. 4:20; 6:9–10; 15:24, 50; Rom. 14:17; (3)
Pseudo-Paul: 2 Thess. 1:5; Eph 5:5(!); Col. 1:13(!); 2 Tim 4:1, 18; (4) Other
New Testament texts: Heb. 2:8; 11:23; 12:28; James 2:5; 2 Pet. 1:11(!); Rev.
1:6, 9; 5:10; 11:15(!); 12:10; (5) Apostolic Fathers: *1 Clem.* 42:3; 50:3; *2 Clem.*
9:6; Ign. *Phil.* 3:3 [from 1 Cor. 6:9–10]; Pol. *Phil.* 5:3 [from 1 Cor. 6:9–10];
Barn. 4:13; *Herm. Sim.* 9.15:3; 9.29:2.

Appendix 6

Inventory for Jesus' Miracles [32:9+23]

First Stratum [9:8+1]

[1] 3. *Bread and Fish* [1/6]; [2] 110. *A Leper Cured* [1/2]; [3] 119. *Distant Boy Cured* [1/2]; [4] 121. *Beelzebul Controversy* [1/2]; [5] 127. *Sickness and Sin* [1/2]; [6] 128. *Walking on Water* [1/2]; [7] 129. *Blind Man Healed* [1/2]; [8] 130. *Dead Man Raised* [1/2]; [9] 184. *Transfiguration of Jesus* [1/1].

Second Stratum [19:1+18]

[1] 190. *Fishing for Humans* [2/3]; [2] 215. *In Capernaum's Synagogue* [2/1]; [3] 216. *Simon's Mother-in-Law* [2/1]; [4] 217. *Healings and Exorcisms* [2/1]; [5] 221. *Hand and Sabbath* [2/1]; [6] 222. *Crowds Are Cured* [2/1]; [7] 223. *Demons Are Silenced* [2/1]; [8] 228. *The Gerasene Demoniac* [2/1]; [9] 229. *Two Women Cured* [2/1]; [10] 231. *Herod on Jesus* [2/1]; [11] 233. *Healings at Gennesaret* [2/1]; [12] 237. *Distant Girl Cured* [2/1]; [13] 238. *Deaf Mute Cured* [2/1]; [14] 245. *Possessed Boy Cured* [2/1]; [15] 246. *Stranger as Exorcist* [2/1]; [16] 256. *Healing of Bartimaeus* [2/1]; [17] 260. *Cursed Fig Tree* [2/1]; [18] 269. *Jesus Arrested* [2/1]; [19] 349. *Water into Wine* [2/1].

Third Stratum [4:0+4]

[1] 428. *The Temple Tax* [3/1]; [2] 441. *Widow's Son Raised* [3/1]; [3] 454. *Cripple and Sabbath* [3/1]; [4] 457. *Dropsy and Sabbath* [3/1].

Appendix 7

Strata in the Gospel of Peter

There are three distinguishable strata in the present *Gospel of Peter* (Crossan 1988a). Their contents and titles are given in the following summary table.

Original Stratum	Redactional Stratum	Intracanonical Stratum
(1a) Crucifixion and Deposition (1:1–2 & 2:5b–6:22)	(2a) Request for Burial (2:3–5a) = Preparation for 3a	(3a) Joseph and Burial (6:23–24)
(1b) Tomb and Guards (7:25 & 8:28–9:34)	(2b) Arrival of Youth (11:43–44) = Preparation for 3b	(3b) Women and Youth (12:50–13:57)
(1c) Resurrection and Confession (9:35–10:42 & 11:45–49)	(2c) Action of Disciples (7:26–27 & 14:58–59) = Preparation for 3c	(3c) Disciples and Apparition (14:60 . . .)

Here is the text of the *Gospel of Peter* (NTA 1.183–187; Cameron 1982: 78–82) with those those various subtitles and divergent strata indicated as follows: the original stratum or Cross Gospel in 1abc is in ordinary print; the redactional or connective stratum in 2abc is in roman bold, the intracanonical stratum in 3abc is in italic bold.

(1a) Crucifixion and Deposition [started]

[1:1] But of the Jews none washed their hands, neither Herod nor any one of his judges. And as they would not wash, Pilate arose. [1:2] And then Herod the king commanded that the Lord should be marched off, saying to them, "What I have commanded you to do to him, do ye."

(2a) Request for Burial

[2:3] Now there stood there Joseph, the friend of Pilate and of the Lord, and knowing that they were about to crucify him he came to Pilate and begged the body of the Lord for burial. [2:4] And Pilate sent to Herod and begged his body. [2:5a] And Herod said, "Brother Pilate, even if no one had begged him, we should bury him, since the Sabbath is drawing on. For it stands written in the law: the sun should not set on one that has been put to death."

(1a) Crucifixion and Deposition [completed]

[2:5b] And he delivered him to the people on the day before the unleavened bread, their feast. [3:6] So they took the Lord and pushed him in great haste and said, "Let us hale the Son of God now that we have gotten power over him." [3:7] And they put upon him a purple robe and set him on the judgment seat and said, "Judge righteously, O King of Israel!" [3:8] And one of them brought a crown of thorns and put it on the Lord's head. [3:9] And others who stood by spat on his face, and others buffeted him on the cheeks, others nudged him with a reed, and some scourged him, saying, "With such honour let us honour the Son of God." [4:10] And they brought two malefactors and crucified the Lord in the midst between them. But he held his peace, as if he felt no pain. [4:11] And when they had set up the cross, they wrote upon it: this is the King of Israel. [4:12] And they laid down his garments before him and divided them among themselves and cast the lot upon them. [4:13] But one of the malefactors rebuked them, saying, "We have landed in suffering for the deeds of wickedness which we have committed, but this man, who has become the saviour of men, what wrong has he done you?" [4:14] And they were wroth with him and commanded that his legs should not be broken, so that he might die in torments. [5:15] Now it was midday and a darkness covered all Judaea. And they became anxious and uneasy lest the sun had already set, since he was still alive. <For> it stands written for them: the sun should not set on one that has been put to death. [5:16] And one of them said, "Give him to drink gall with vinegar." And they mixed it and gave him to drink. [5:17] And they fulfilled all things and completed the measure of their sins on their head. [5:18] And many went about with lamps, <and> as they supposed that it was night, they went to bed (or: they stumbled). [5:19] And the Lord called out and cried, "My power, O power, thou hast forsaken me!" And having said this he was taken up. [5:20] And at the same hour the veil of the temple in Jerusalem was rent in two. [6:21] And then the Jews drew the nails from the hands of the Lord and laid him on the earth. And the whole earth shook and there came a great fear.[6:22] Then the sun shone < again >, and it was found to be the ninth hour.

(3a) Joseph and Burial

[6:23] *And the Jews rejoiced and gave his body to Joseph that he might bury it, since he had seen all the good that he (Jesus) had done. [6:24] And he took the Lord, washed him, wrapped him in linen and brought him into his own sepulchre, called Joseph's Garden.*

(1b) Tomb and Guards [started]

[7:25] Then the Jews and the elders and the priests, perceiving what great evil they had done to themselves, began to lament and to say, "Woe on our sins, the judgment and the end of Jerusalem is drawn nigh."

(2c) Action of Disciples [started]

[7:26] But I mourned with my fellows, and being wounded in heart we hid ourselves, for we were sought after by them as evildoers and as persons who wanted to set fire to the temple. [7:27] Because of all these things we were fasting and sat mourning and weeping night and day until the Sabbath.

(1b)Tomb and Guards

[8:28] But the scribes and Pharisees and elders, being assembled together and hearing that all the people were murmuring and beating their breasts, saying, "If at his death these exceeding great signs have come to pass, behold how righteous he was!" [8:29] The elders were afraid and came to Pilate, entreating him and saying, [8:30] "Give us soldiers that we may watch his sepulchre for three days, lest his disciples come and steal him away and the people suppose that he is risen from the dead, and do us harm."[8:31] And Pilate gave them Petronius the centurion with soldiers to watch the sepulchre. [8:32] And with them there came elders and scribes to the sepulchre. And all who were there, together with the centurion and the soldiers, rolled thither a great stone and laid it against the entrance to the sepulchre [8:33] and put on it seven seals, pitched a tent and kept watch. [9:34] Early in the morning, when the Sabbath dawned, there came a crowd from Jerusalem and the country round about to see the sepulchre that had been sealed.

(1c) Resurrection and Confession [started]

[9:35] Now in the night in which the Lord's day dawned, when the soldiers, two by two in every watch, were keeping guard, there rang out a loud voice in heaven, [9:36] and they saw the heavens opened and two men come down from there in a great brightness and draw nigh to the sepulchre. [9:37] That stone which had been laid against the entrance to the sepulchre started of itself to roll and give way to the side, and the sepulchre was opened, and both the young men entered in. [10:38] When now the soldiers saw this, they awakened the centurion and the elders — for they also were there to assist at the watch. [10:39] And whilst they were relating what they had seen, they saw again three men come out from the sepulchre, and two of them sustaining the other and a cross following them, [10:40] and the heads of the two reaching to heaven, but that of him who was led of them by the hand overpassing the heavens. [10:41] And they heard a voice out of the heavens crying, "Thou has preached to them that sleep," [10:42] and from the cross there was heard the answer, "Yea."

(2b) Arrival of Youth

[11:43] Those men therefore took counsel with one another to go and report this to Pilate. [11:44] And whilst they were still deliberating, the heavens were again seen to open, and a man descended and entered the sepulchre.

(1c)Resurrection and Confession [completed]

[11:45] When those who were of the centurion's company saw this, they hastened by night to Pilate, abandoning the sepulchre which they were guarding, and reported everything they had seen, being full of disquietude and saying, "In truth he was the Son of God." [11:46] Pilate answered and said, "I am clean from the blood of the Son of God, upon such a thing have you decided." [11:47] Then all came to him, beseeching him and urgently calling upon him to command the centurion and the soldiers to tell no one what they had seen. "For it is better for us," they said, "to make ourselves guilty of the greatest sin before God than to fall into the hands of the people of the Jews and be stoned."Pilate therefore commanded the centurion and the soldiers to say nothing.

(3b) Women and Youth

[12:50] *Early in the morning of the Lord's day Mary Magdalene, a woman disciple of the Lord—for fear of the Jews, since (they) were inflamed with wrath, she had not done at the sepulchre what women are wont to do for those beloved of them who die—took [12:51] with her her women friends and came to the sepulchre where he was laid. [12:52] And they feared lest the Jews should see them, and said, "Although we could not weep and lament on that day when he was crucified, yet let us now do so at his sepulchre. [12:53] But who will roll away for us the stone also that is set on the entrance of the sepulchre, that we may go in and sit beside him and do what is due?—[12:54] For the stone was great,—and we fear lest any one see us. And if we cannot do so, let us at least put down at the entrance what we bring for a memorial to him and let us weep and lament until we have again gone home." [13:55] So they went and found the sepulchre opened. And they came near, stooped down and saw there a young man sitting in the midst of the sepulchre, comely and clothed with a brightly shining robe, who said to them, [13:56] "Wherefore are ye come? Whom seek ye? Not him that was crucified? He is risen and gone. But if ye believe not, stoop this way and see the place where he lay, for he is not here. For he is risen and is gone thither whence he was sent." [13:57] Then the women fled affrighted.*

(2c) Action of Disciples

[14:58] Now it was the last day of unleavened bread and many went away and repaired to their homes, since the feast was at an end. [14:59] But we, the twelve disciples of the Lord, wept and mourned, and each one, very grieved for what had come to pass, went to his home.

(3c) Disciples and Apparition

[14:60] *But I, Simon Peter, and my brother Andrew took our nets and went to the sea. And there was with us Levi, the son of Alphaeus, whom the Lord . . .*

Bibliography

Abbreviations

AAA = American Anthropological Association; **AnBib** = Analecta Biblica; **ANF** = *The Ante-Nicene Fathers* (Roberts et al.); **ANRW** = *Aufstieg und Niedergang der römischen Welt* (Temporini & Haase); **APOT** = *The Apocrypha and Pseudepigrapha of the Old Testament* (Charles); **ARA** = *Annual Review of Anthropology*; **BA** = *Biblical Archaeologist*; **BAR** = *Biblical Archeology Review*; **BASOR** = *Bulletin of the American Schools of Oriental Research*; **BETL** = Bibliotheca Ephemeridum Theologicarum Lovaniensium; **BZNW** = Beihefte zur ZNW; **CA** = *Current Anthropology*; **CAH** = *The Cambridge Ancient History* (Cook et al.); **CBQ** = *Catholic Biblical Quarterly*; **CRINT** = *Compendia Rerum Iudaicarum ad Novum Testamentum* (Safrai & Stone); **ETL** = *Ephemerides Theologicae Lovanienses*; **HR** = *History of Religions*; **HTR** = *Harvard Theological Review*; **HTS** = Harvard Theological Studies; **IEJ** = *Israel Exploration Journal*; **JA** = Josephus' *Jewish Antiquities* (Thackeray); **JAAR** = *Journal of the American Academy of Religion*; **JBL** = *Journal of Biblical Literature*; **JJS** = *Journal of Jewish Studies*; **JR** = *Journal of Religion*; **JSJ** = *Journal for the Study of Judaism*; **JSNT** = *Journal for the Study of the New Testament*; **JSS** = *Journal of Semitic Studies*; **JSSR** = *Journal for the Scientific Study of Religion*; **JW** = Josephus' *Jewish War* (Thackeray); **LCL** = Loeb Classical Library; **NMS** = Nag Hammadi Studies; **NT** = *Novum Testamentum*; **NTA** = *New Testament Apocrypha* (Hennecke, Schneemelcher, & Wilson); **NTS** = *New Testament Studies*; **OTP** = *The Old Testament Pseudepigrapha* (Charlesworth); **PEQ** = *Palestine Exploration Quarterly*; **P.Oxy** = Oxyrhynchus Papyri; **SBL** = Society of Biblical Literature; **SBLDS** = SBL Dissertation Series; **SBLMS** = SBL Monograph Series; **SBLRBS** = SBL Resources for Biblical Study; **SBLSBS** = SBL Sources for Biblical Studies; **SBLSCS** = SBL Septuagint and Cognate Studies; **SBLSP** = SBL Seminar Papers; **SBLTT** = SBL Texts and Translations; **SBT** = Studies in Biblical Theology; **SC** = *The Second Century*; **SNTSMS** = Society for New Testament Studies Monograph Series; **SSM** = *Social Science and Medicine*; **TS** = *Theological Studies*; **TU** = Texte und Untersuchungen zur Geschichte der altchristlichen Literatur; **ZkT** = *Zeitschrift für katholische Theologie*; **ZNW** = *Zeitschrift für die neutestamentliche Wissenschaft*; **ZTK** = *Zeitschrift für Theologie und Kirche*.

Achtemeier, Paul J. 1970. "Toward the Isolation of Pre-Markan Miracle Catenae." *JBL* 89: 265–291.

———. 1972. "The Origin and Function of the Pre-Markan Miracle Catenae." *JBL* 91: 198–221.

Aland, Kurt, et al. 1975. *The Greek New Testament.* 3d ed. New York: United Bible Societies.

Allegro, John. 1956. "Further Messianic References in Qumran Literature." *JBL* 75: 182–187.

———. 1958. "Fragments of a Qumran Scroll of Eschatological Midrāšîm." *JBL* 77: 350–354.

Attridge, Harold W. 1989. "The Gospel According to Thomas: Appendix: The Greek Fragments." In *Nag Hammadi Codex II,2–7*, 2 vols., edited by Bentley Layton, vol. 1, pp. 96–128. Nag Hammadi Studies 20–21. The Coptic Gnostic Library. Leiden: Brill.

Aune, David E. 1980. "Magic in Early Christianity." ANRW 2.23.1507–1557.

Avi-Yonah, M. 1964. "The Caesarea Inscription of the Twenty-four Priestly Courses." In *The Teacher's Yoke: Studies in Memory of Henry Trantham*, edited by E. Jerry Vardaman and James Leo Garrett, Jr., pp. 46–57. Waco, TX: Baylor Univ. Press.

Bagatti, Bellarmino. 1969. *Excavations in Nazareth*. Vol. 1, *From the Beginning till the XII Century*, translated by E. Hoade. Publications of the Studium Biblicum Franciscanum 17. Jerusalem: Franciscan Printing Press.

Bailey, D. R. Shackleton. 1971. *Cicero*. New York: Scribner's.

Barb, A. A. 1963. "The Survival of the Magic Arts." In *The Conflict Between Paganism and Christianity in the Fourth Century*, edited by Arnaldo Momigliano, pp. 100–125. Oxford-Warburg Studies. Oxford: Clarendon Press.

Barnett, P. W. 1980–81. "The Jewish Sign Prophets—A.D. 40–70: Their Intentions and Origin." *NTS* 27: 679–697.

Basore, J. W., R. M. Gummere, T. H. Corcoran, and F. J. Miller, trans. 1917–72. *Seneca*. 10 vols. LCL. Cambridge, MA: Harvard Univ. Press.

Bell, H. Idris, and T. C. Skeat. 1935a. *Fragments of an Unknown Gospel and Other Early Christian Papyri*. London: Oxford Univ. Press.

———. 1935b. *The New Gospel Fragments*. London: Oxford Univ. Press.

Berman, Dennis. 1979. "Hasidim in Rabbinic Traditions." In *SBLSP 1979*, 2 vols., edited by Paul J. Achtemeier, vol. 2, pp. 15–33. SBLSP 17. Missoula, MT: Scholars Press.

Betz, Hans Dieter, ed. 1986. *The Greek Magical Papyri in Translation, Including the Demotic Spells*. Chicago and London: Univ. of Chicago Press.

Bickell, Gustav. 1885. "Ein Papyrusfragment eines nichtkanonischen Evangeliums." *ZkT* 9: 498–504.

———. 1886. "Zu dem Papyrusevangelium." *ZkT* 10: 208–209.

———. 1887. "Das nichtkanonishe Evangelienfragment." In *Mittheilungen aus der Sammlung der Papyrus Erzherzog Rainer*, edited by Joseph Karabacek, vol. 1, nos. 3–4, pp. 53–61. Vienna: Verlag der k. k. Hof- und Staatsdruckerei. = *Papyrology on Microfiche*, series 2, vol. 40, no. 1. Missoula, MT: Scholars Press (for the American Society of Papyrologists).

Blok, Anton. 1972. "The Peasant and the Brigand: Social Banditry Reconsidered." *Comparative Studies in Society and History* 14: 494–503.

Boissevain, Jeremy. 1969. "Patrons as Brokers." *Sociologische Gids* 16: 379–86.

———. 1974. *Friends of Friends: Networks, Manipulators and Coalitions*. New York: St. Martin's Press.

Boissevain, Jeremy, et al. 1979. "Toward an Anthropology of the Mediterranean." *CA* 20: 81–93.

Bokser, Baruch M. 1985. "Wonder-Working and the Rabbinic Tradition: The Case of Hanina ben Dosa." *JSJ* 16: 42–92.

Borg, Marcus J. 1984. *Conflict, Holiness and Politics in the Teachings of Jesus.* Studies in the Bible and Early Christianity 5. New York and Toronto: Edwin Mellen Press.

———. 1986. "A Temperate Case for a Non-eschatological Jesus." *Forum* 2/3: 81–102.

Bourguignon, Erika. 1976. *Possession.* Chandler and Sharp Series in Cross-cultural Themes. San Francisco: Chandler and Sharp.

Bovon, François. 1988. "The Synoptic Gospels and the Noncanonical Acts of the Apostles." *HTR* 81: 19–36.

Brandon, S. G. F. 1967. *Jesus and the Zealots: A Study of the Political Factor in Primitive Christianity.* New York: Scribner's.

Braudel, Fernand. 1972. *The Mediterranean and the Mediterranean World in the Age of Philip II.* 2 vols. Translated by Siân Reynolds. New York: Harper & Row.

Brinton, Crane. 1938. *The Anatomy of Revolution.*

Broshi, Magen. 1987. "The Role of the Temple in the Herodian Economy." *JJS* 38: 31–37.

Brown, Peter R. L. 1982. Response to "The Problem of Miraculous Feedings in the Graeco-Roman World," by Robert M. Grant. In *Protocol of the Forty-second Colloquy* (14 March 1982), pp. 16–24. Berkeley, CA: Center for Hermeneutical Studies in Hellenistic and Modern Culture, The Graduate Theological Union and the Univ. of California.

Brown, Raymond E. 1966–70. *The Gospel According to John: I–XII and XIII–XXI.* 2 vols. with continuous pagination. Garden City, NY: Doubleday.

———. 1974. "The Relation of 'The Secret Gospel of Mark' to the Fourth Gospel." *CBQ* 36: 466–485.

———. 1979. *The Community of the Beloved Disciple.* New York: Paulist Press.

Brunt, Peter A. 1977. "Josephus on Social Conflicts in Roman Judaea." *Klio* 59: 149–153.

Büchler, A. 1968. *Types of Jewish-Palestinian Piety from 70 B.C.E.–70 C.E.: The Ancient Pious Man.* New York: Ktav. (First published 1922.)

Bynum, Caroline Walker. 1982. *Jesus as Mother: Studies in the Spirituality of the High Middle Ages.* Publications of the Center for Medieval and Renaissance Studies, UCLA, 16. Berkeley and Los Angeles: Univ. of California Press.

———. 1987. *Holy Feast and Holy Fast: The Religious Significance of Food to Medieval Women.* Berkeley and Los Angeles: Univ. of California Press.

Cameron, Ronald D. 1982. *The Other Gospels: Non-canonical Gospel Texts.* Philadelphia: Westminster Press.

———. 1984. *Sayings Traditions in the Apocryphon of James.* HTS 34. Philadelphia: Fortress Press.

———. 1988. "Seeing Is Not Believing: The History of a Beatitude in the Jesus Tradition." *Forum* 4/1: 47–57.

Carney, Thomas F. 1975. *The Shape of the Past: Models and Antiquity.* Lawrence, KS: Coronado Press.

Carrier, Constance. 1963. *The Poems of Propertius.* Bloomington: Indiana Univ. Press.

Cary, Earnest, ed. 1905–06. *Dio's Roman History.* 9 vols. LCL. Cambridge, MA: Harvard Univ. Press.

Chadwick, Henry. 1959. *The Sentences of Sextus: A Contribution to the History of Early Christian Ethics.* Texts and Studies, new series. Cambridge: Cambridge Univ. Press.

———. 1970. "Some Reflections on the Character and Theology of the Odes of Solomon." In *Kyriakon*, Festschrift Johannes Quasten, 2 vols., edited by Patrick Granfield and Josef A. Jungmann vol. 1, pp. 266–270. Münster: Aschendorff.

Charles, R. H., ed. 1913. *The Apocrypha and Pseudepigrapha of the Old Testament.* 2 vols. Oxford: Clarendon Press.

Charlesworth, James H. 1988. *Jesus Within Judaism: New Light from Exciting Archeological Discoveries.* The Anchor Bible Reference Library. New York: Doubleday.

Charlesworth, James H., ed. 1983–85. *The Old Testament Pseudepigrapha.* 2 vols. Garden City, NY: Doubleday.

Chilton, Bruce D. 1984. *A Galilean Rabbi and His Bible: Jesus' Use of the Interpreted Scripture of His Time.* Wilmington, DE: Glazier.

Cohen, Shaye J. D. 1979. *Josephus in Galilee and Rome: His Vita and Development as a Historian.* Columbia Studies in the Classical Tradition 8. Leiden: Brill.

———. 1987. *From the Maccabees to the Mishnah.* Library of Early Christianity. Philadelphia: Westminster Press.

———. 1988. "Roman Domination. The Jewish Revolt and the Destruction of the Second Temple." In *Ancient Israel: A Short History from Abraham to the Roman Destruction of the Temple*, edited by Hershel Shanks, pp. 205–235. Washington, DC: Biblical Archeology Society.

Cohoon, James Wilfred, and H. Lamar Crosby, trans. 1932–51. *Dio Chrysostom.* 5 vols. LCL. Cambridge, MA: Harvard Univ. Press.

Collins, John J. 1980. "The Heavenly Representative: The 'Son of Man' in the Similitudes of Enoch." In *Ideal Figures in Ancient Judaism: Profiles and Paradigms*, edited by John J. Collins and George W. E. Nickelsburg, pp. 111–133. SBLSCS 12. Chico, CA: Scholars Press.

———. 1983. *Between Athens and Jerusalem: Jewish Identity in the Hellenistic Diaspora.* New York: Crossroad.

———. 1984a. *The Apocalyptic Imagination: An Introduction to the Jewish Matrix of Christianity.* New York: Crossroad.

———. 1984b. *Daniel with an Introduction to Apocalyptic Literature.* Forms of the Old Testament Literature 20. Grand Rapids: Eerdmans.

Colson, F. H., et al. 1929–62. *Philo.* 12 vols. LCL. Cambridge: Harvard Univ. Press.

Cook, S. A., F. E. Adcock, and M. P. Charlesworth. 1934. *The Augustan Empire, 44 B.C. to A.D. 70.* Vol. 10 of *CAH*. Cambridge: Cambridge Univ. Press.

Corbett, Philip B. 1970. *Petronius.* Twayne's World Authors Series 97. New York: Twayne Publishers.

Cotter, Wendy J. 1987. "The Children in the Market-place." *NT* 24: 289–304.

———. 1989. "Children Sitting in the Agora: Q(Luke) 7:31–35." *Forum* 5/2: 63–82.

Crossan, John Dominic. 1973. *In Parables: The Challenge of the Historical Jesus.* New York: Harper & Row.

———. 1976. "Empty Tomb and Absent Lord (Mark 16:1–18)." In *The Passion in Mark: Studies on Mark 14–16*, edited by Werner H. Kelber, pp. 135–152. Philadelphia: Fortress Press.

———. 1979. *Finding Is the First Act: Trove Folktales and Jesus' Treasure Parable.* Semeia Supplements 9. Missoula, MT: Scholars Press; Pittsburgh: Fortress Press.

———. 1983a. *In Fragments: The Aphorisms of Jesus.* San Francisco: Harper & Row.

———. 1983b. "Kingdom and Children: A Study in the Aphoristic Tradition." *Semeia* 29: 75–95.

———. 1985. *Four Other Gospels: Shadows on the Contours of Canon.* Minneapolis: Winston Press, Seabury Books.

———. 1986. *Sayings Parallels: A Workbook for the Jesus Tradition.* Foundations and Facets. Philadelphia: Fortress Press.

———. 1988a *The Cross That Spoke: The Origins of the Passion Narrative.* San Francisco: Harper & Row.

———. 1988b. "Aphorism in Discourse and Narrative." *Semeia* 43: 121–140.

———. 1990. "Thoughts on Two Extracanonical Gospels." *Semeia* 49: 155–168.

Dalton, George. 1972. "Peasantries in Anthropology and History." *CA* 13: 385–415.

Dalton, William Joseph. 1965. *Christ's Proclamation to the Spirits: A Study of 1 Peter 3:18–4:6.* AnBib 23. Rome: Pontifical Biblical Institute.

Danby, H. 1967. *The Mishnah.* London: Oxford Univ. Press.

Daniélou, Jean. 1964–77. *A History of Early Christian Doctrine Before the Council of Nicaea.* translated by John Austin Baker and David Smith. 3 vols. Philadelphia: Westminster Press.

Daniels, Jon B. 1989. "The Egerton Gospel: Its Place in Early Christianity." Ph.D. diss., Claremont Graduate School, under James M. Robinson. Ann Arbor, MI: University Microfilms International (forthcoming).

Danker, Frederick W. 1982 *Benefactor: Epigraphic Study of a Graeco-Roman and New Testament Semantic Field.* St. Louis, MO: Clayton Publishing House.

Davies, Stevan L. 1983. *The Gospel of Thomas and Christian Wisdom.* New York: Seabury Press.

Davis, John. 1977. *The People of the Mediterranean: An Essay in Comparative Social Anthropology.* Library of Man. London: Routledge & Kegan Paul.

Davis, W. Hersey. 1933. *Greek Papyri of the First Century.* Chicago: Ares Publishers.

Davisson, William I., and James E. Harper. 1972. *European Economic History.* Vol. 1, *The Ancient World.* New York: Appleton-Century-Crofts.

de Ste. Croix, G. E. M. 1954. "Suffragium: From vote to Patronage." *British Journal of Sociology* 5: 33–48.

———. 1975. "Karl Marx and the History of Classical Antiquity." *Arethusa* 8: 7–41.

Douglas, Mary. 1970. *Natural Symbols: Explorations in Cosmology.* New York: Random House, Pantheon Books.

Downing, F. Gerald. 1984. "Cynics and Christians." *NTS* 30: 584–593.

———. 1987. *Jesus and the Threat of Freedom.* London: SCM Press.

———. 1988. *Christ and the Cynics: Jesus and Other Radical Preachers in First-Century Tradition.* JSOT Manuals 4. Sheffield: Sheffield Academic Press (JSOT Press).

Dudley, Donald Reynolds. 1967. *A History of Cynicism: From Diogenes to the 6th Century A.D.* Hildesheim: Olms. (First published 1937.)

Duff, James D., trans. 1928. *Lucan: The Civil War (Pharsalia).* LCL. Cambridge, MA: Harvard Univ. Press.

Durry, Marcel. 1950. *Éloge funèbre d'une matrone romaine (Éloge dit de Turia)*. Paris: Société d'Édition "*Les Belles Lettres.*"

Dyson, Stephen L. 1971. "Native Revolts in the Roman Empire." *Historia* 20: 239–274.

Eddy, Samuel K. 1961. *The King Is Dead: Studies in the Near Eastern Resistance to Hellenism, 334–31 B.C.* Lincoln: Univ. of Nebraska Press.

Edwards, Douglas R. 1988. "First Century Urban/Rural Relations in Lower Galilee: Exploring the Archeological and Literary Evidence." In *SBLSP 1988*, edited by David J. Lull, pp. 169–182. SBLSP 27. Atlanta: Scholars Press.

Edwards, Richard A. 1969. "The Eschatological Correlative as a *Gattung* in the New Testament." ZNW 60: 9–20.

———. 1971. *The Sign of Jonah in the Theology of the Evangelists and Q.* SBT 2/18. Naperville, IL: Allenson.

Edwards, Richard A., and Robert A. Wild. 1981. *The Sentences of Sextus.* SBLTT 22: Early Christian Literature 5. Chico, CA: Scholars Press.

Eisenstadt, Shlomo N., and René Lemarchand, eds. 1981. *Political Clientelism, Patronage and Development.* Contemporary Political Sociology 3. Beverly Hills, CA: Sage.

Eisenstadt, Shlomo N., and Louis Roniger. 1980. "Patron-Client Relations as a Model of Structuring Social Exchange." *Comparative Studies in Society and History* 22: 42–77.

———. 1984. *Patrons, Clients and Friends: Interpersonal Relations and the Structure of Trust in Society.* Themes in the Social Sciences. Cambridge: Cambridge Univ. Press.

Ellmann, Richard. 1988. *Oscar Wilde.* New York: Knopf.

Emmel, Stephen. 1989. "Indexes of Words and Catalogues of Grammatical Forms." In *Nag Hammadi Codex II,2–7*, 2 vols., edited by Bentley Layton, vol. 1, pp. 261–336. NHS 20–21. The Coptic Gnostic Library. Leiden: Brill.

Emmel, Stephen, Helmut Koester, and Elaine Pagels. 1984. *Nag Hammadi Codex III,5: The Dialogue of the Savior.* NHS 26. The Coptic Gnostic Library. Leiden: Brill.

Epstein, I., ed. 1935–52. *The Babylonian Talmud.* 35 vols. London: Soncino.

Fairclough, Henry Rushton. 1926. *Horace: Satires, Epistles, Ars Poetica.* LCL. Cambridge, MA: Harvard Univ. Press.

Falk, Harvey. 1985. *Jesus the Pharisee: A New Look at the Jewishness of Jesus.* New York: Paulist Press.

Farb, Peter, and George Armelagos. 1980. *Consuming Passions: The Anthropology of Eating.* Boston: Houghton Mifflin.

Feeley-Harnik, Gillian. 1981. *The Lord's Table: Eucharist and Passover in Early Christianity.* Symbol and Culture. Philadelphia: Univ. of Pennsylvania Press.

Feldman, Louis H. 1984. *Josephus and Modern Scholarship (1937–1980).* New York: Walter de Gruyter.

Finegan, Jack. 1969. *The Archaeology of the New Testament: The Life of Jesus and the Beginning of the Early Church.* Princeton, NJ: Princeton Univ. Press.

Finley, Sir Moses I. 1973. *The Ancient Economy.* Berkeley and Los Angeles: Univ. of California Press.

Fiorenza, Elisabeth Schüssler. 1983. *In Memory of Her: A Feminist Theological Reconstruction of Christian Origins.* New York: Crossroad.

Fitzgerald, Robert, trans. 1981. *Virgil: The Aeneid.* New York: Random House.

Fitzmyer, Joseph A. 1957. "'4Q Testimonia' and the New Testament." *TS* 18: 513–537.

———. 1968. Review of *An Aramaic Approach to the Gospels and Acts,* 3rd ed., by Matthew Black. *CBQ* 30: 417–428.

———. 1978. "Crucifixion in Ancient Palestine, Qumran Literature, and the New Testament." *CBQ* 40: 493–513.

———. 1979a. "Another View of the 'Son of Man' Debate." *JSNT* 4: 58–68.

———. 1979b. "The New Testament Title 'Son of Man' Philologically Considered." In his *A Wandering Aramean: Collected Aramaic Essays,* pp. 143–160. SBLMS 25. Missoula, MT: Schoars Press.

———. 1981–85. *The Gospel According to Luke.* 2 vols. with continuous pagination. Anchor Bible 28–28A. Garden City, NY: Doubleday.

Fowler, Robert M. 1981. *Loaves and Fishes: The Function of the Feeding Stories in the Gospel of Mark.* SBLDS 54. Chico, CA: Scholars Press.

Frankfurter, David T. M. 1990. "The Origin of the Miracle-List Tradition and Its Medium of Circulation." In *SBLSP 1990,* edited by David J. Lull, pp. 344–374. SBLSP 29. Atlanta: Scholars Press.

Freyne, Seán. 1979–80. "The Galileans in the Light of Josephus' Vita." *NTS* 26: 397–413.

———. 1980a. *Galilee from Alexander the Great to Hadrian, 323 B.C.E. to 145 C.E.: A Study of Second Temple Judaism.* University of Notre Dame Center for the Study of Judaism and Christianity in Antiquity 5. Wilmington, DE: Glazier; Notre Dame, IN: Univ. of Notre Dame Press.

———. 1980b. "The Charismatic." In *Ideal Figures in Ancient Judaism: Profiles and Paradigms,* edited by John J. Collins and George W. E. Nickelsburg, pp. 223–258. SBLSCS 12. Chico, CA: Scholars Press.

———. 1988. "Bandits in Galilee: A Contribution to the Study of Social Conditions in First-Century Palestine." In *The Social World of Formative Christianity and Judaism,* edited by Jacob Neusner, Peder Borgen, Ernest S. Frerichs, Richard Horsley, pp. 50–68. Philadelphia: Fortress Press.

Gallagher, Eugene V. 1982. *Divine Man or Magician? Celsus and Origen on Jesus.* SBLDS 64. Chico, CA: Scholars Press.

Gellner, Ernest, and John Waterbury, eds. 1977. *Patrons and Clients in Mediterranean Societies.* London: Duckworth.

Gilmore, David D. 1982. "Anthropology of the Mediterranean Area." *ARA* 11: 175–205.

Gilmore, David D., ed. 1987. *Honor and Shame and the Unity of the Mediterranean.* Special Publication of the AMA 22. Washington, DC: AMA.

Goodman, Martin. 1982. "The First Jewish Revolt: Social Conflict and the Problem of Debt." *JJS* 33: 422–434.

———. 1983. *State and Society in Roman Galilee, A.D. 132–212.* Oxford Centre for Post-graduate Hebrew Studies. Totowa, NJ: Rowman and Allanheld.

———. 1987. *The Ruling Class of Judaea: The Origins of the Jewish Revolt Against Rome A.D. 66–70.* Cambridge: Cambridge Univ. Press.

Green, William Scott. 1979. "Palestinian Holy Men: Charismatic Leadership and Rabbinic Tradition." *ANRW* 2.19.619–647.

Grenfell, Bernard Pyne, and Arthur Surridge Hunt. 1898–99. *The Oxyrhynchus Papyri.* Parts 1–2, Nos. 1–207, 208–400. London: Oxford Univ. Press.

———. 1914. "Uncanonical Gospel." In *The Oxyrhynchus Papyri*, part 10, nos. 1224–1350, pp. 1–10 and plate 1. London: Oxford Univ. Press.

Gronewald, Michael. 1987. "Unbekanntes Evangelium oder Evangelienharmonie (Fragment aus dem 'Evangelium Egerton') pp. 136–145 in *Kölner Papyri (P. Köln)*, Band 6. Abhandlungen der Rheinisch-Westfälischen Akademie der Wissenschaften, Sonderreihe Papyrologica Coloniensia 7. Opladen: Westdeutscher Verlag

Gurr, Ted Robert. 1970. *Why Men Rebel.* Princeton, NJ: Princeton Univ. Press.

Haas, Nico. 1970. "Anthropological Observations on the Skeletal Remains from Giv'at ha Mivtar." *IEJ* 20: 38–59, plates 18–24.

Haines, Charles Reginald, trans. 1919–20. *The Correspondence of Marcus Cornelius Fronto with Marcus Aurelius Antoninus, Lucius Verus, Antoninus Pius, and Various Friends.* LCL. Cambridge, MA: Harvard Univ. Press.

Hamel, Gildas H. 1983. *Poverty and Charity in Roman Palestine, First Three Centuries C.E.* Ann Arbor, MI: University Microfilms International.

Hands, Arthur Robinson. 1968. *Charities and Social Aid in Greece and Rome.* Aspects of Greek and Roman Life. London: Thames & Hudson.

Harmon, A. M., K. Kilburn, and M. D. Macleod, trans. 1913–67. *Lucian.* 8 vols. LCL. Cambridge, MA: Harvard Univ. Press.

Harnack, Adolf. 1889. "Anhang: Das Evangelienfragment von Fajjum." In *Agrapha. Aussercanonische Evangelienfragmente.*, by Alfred Resch, pp. 481–497. TU 4. Leipzig: Hinrichs.

Harrington, Daniel J. 1987a. "The Jewishness of Jesus: Facing Some Problems." *CBQ* 49: 1–13.

———. 1987b. "The Jewishness of Jesus." *Bible Review* 3.1 (Spring): 33–41 [This article is an "adapted and expanded" version of 1987a.]

Harrison, P. N. 1936. *Polycarp's Two Epistles to the Philippians.* Cambridge: Cambridge University Press.

Hedrick, Charles W. 1986. "The Treasure Parable in Matthew and Thomas." *Forum* 2/2: 41–56.

Hellholm, David, ed. 1983. *Apocalypticism in the Mediterranean World and the Near East.* Proceedings of the International Colloquium on Apocalypticism, Uppsala, August 12–17, 1979. Tübingen: Mohr, Siebeck.

Hennecke, Edgar, and Wilhelm Schneemelcher, eds., R. McL. Wilson, trans. and ed. 1963–65. *New Testament Apocrypha.* 2 vols. Philadelphia: Westminster Press.

Heseltine, Michael, trans. 1913. *Petronius.* LCL. Cambridge, MA: Harvard Univ. Press.

Hicks, R. D., ed. 1925. *Diogenes Laertius: Lives of Eminent Philosophers.* 2 vols. LCL. Cambridge, MA: Harvard Univ. Press.

Hiers, Richard H., and Charles A. Kennedy. 1976. "The Bread and Fish Eucharist in the Gospels and Early Christian Art." *Perspectives in Religious Studies* 3: 20–47.

Hills, Julian Victor. 1985. *Tradition and Composition in the "Epistula Apostolorum."* Ann Arbor, MI: University Microfilms International.

————. 1990a. *Tradition and Composition in the Epistula Apostolorum.* Harvard Dissertations in Religion 24. Minneapolis: Fortress Press.

————. 1990b. "Tradition, Redaction, and Intertextuality: Miracle Lists in Apocryphal Acts as a Test Case." In *SBLSP 1990,* edited by David J. Lull, pp. 375–390. SBLSP 29. Atlanta: Scholars Press.

Hobsbawm, Eric John. 1965. *Primitive Rebels: Studies in Archaic Forms of Social Movement in the 19th and 20th Centuries.* New York: Norton. [Originally published in 1959 as *Social Bandits and Primitive Rebels*].

————. 1972. "Social Banditry: Reply." *Comparative Studies in Society and History* 14: 503–505.

————. 1973a. "Peasants and Politics." *Journal of Peasant Studies* 1: 3–22.

————. 1973b. "Social Banditry." In *Rural Protest: Peasant Movements and Social Change,* edited by Henry A. Landsberger, pp. 142–157. New York: Barnes & Noble.

————. 1985. *Bandits.* 2d ed. Middlesex: Penguin Books. (First published 1969.)

Hock, Richard F. 1974. *The Working Apostle: An Examination of Paul's Means of Livelihood.* Ann Arbor, MI: University Microfilms International.

————. 1976. "Simon the Shoemaker as an Ideal Cynic." *Greek, Roman, and Byzantine Studies* 17: 41–53.

Höistad, Ragnar. 1948. *Cynic Hero and Cynic King.* Uppsala: Bloms.

Hollenbach, Paul W. 1981. "Jesus, Demoniacs, and Public Authorities: A Socio-Historical Study." *JAAR* 99: 567–588.

————. 1982. "The Conversion of Jesus: From Jesus the Baptizer to Jesus the Healer." *ANRW* 2.25.196–219.

Hooper, William Davis, and Harrison Boyd Ash, eds. 1934. "Marcus Porcius Cato: On Agriculture" and "Marcus Terentius Varro: On Agriculture." In *Cato and Varro: De Re Rustica,* pp. 1–157 and 159–529. LCL. Cambridge, MA: Harvard Univ. Press.

Hopkins, Ian W. J. 1980. "The City Region in Roman Palestine." *PEQ* 12: 19–32.

Horsfall, Nicholas. 1983. "Some Problems in the 'Laudatio Turiae.'" *Bulletin of the Institute of Classical Studies* (London) 30: 85–98 and plates 9–15.

Horsley, Gregory H. R., ed. 1981–87. *New Documents Illustrating Early Christianity: A Review of the Greek Inscriptions and Papyri published in 1976–79,* 4 vols. North Ryde, N.S.W., Australia: The Ancient History Documentary Research Centre of Macquarie University.

Horsley, Richard A. 1979a. "Josephus and the Bandits." *JSJ* 10: 37–63.

————. 1979b. "The Sicarii: Ancient Jewish Terrorists." *JR* 59: 435–458.

————. 1981. "Ancient Jewish Banditry and the Revolt against Rome, A.D. 66–70." *CBQ* 43: 409–432.

————. 1984. "Popular Messianic Movements Around the Time of Jesus." *CBQ* 46: 471–493.

————. 1985. "Like One of the Prophets of Old: Two Types of Popular Prophets at the Time of Jesus." *CBQ* 47: 435–463.

————. 1986a "High Priests and the Politics of Roman Palestine: A Contextual Analysis of the Evidence in Josephus." *JSJ* 17: 23–55.

————. 1986b. "The Zealots, Their Origin, Relationships and Importance in the Jewish Revolt." *NT* 28: 159–192.

————. 1986c. "Popular Prophetic Movements at the Time of Jesus, Their Principal Features and Social Origins." *JSNT* 26: 3–27

————. 1987. *Jesus and the Spiral of Violence: Popular Jewish Resistance in Roman Palestine.* San Francisco: Harper & Row.

————. 1988. "Bandits, Messiahs, and Longshoremen: Popular Unrest in Galilee around the Time of Jesus." In *SBLSP 1988*, edited by David J. Lull, pp. 183–199. SBLSP 27. Atlanta: Scholars Press.

————. 1989. *Sociology and the Jesus Movement.* New York: Crossroad.

Horsley, Richard A., and John S. Hanson. 1985. *Bandits, Prophets, and Messiahs: Popular Movements in the Time of Jesus.* New Voices in Biblical Studies, edited by Adela Yarbro Collins and John J. Collins. Minneapolis: Winston Press, Seabury Books.

Hull, John M. 1974. *Hellenistic Magic and the Synoptic Tradition.* SBT 2/28. Naperville, IL: Allenson.

Humphries, Rolfe. 1957. *The Loves, The Art of Beauty, The Remedies for Love, and The Art of Love.* Bloomington, IN: Indiana Univ. Press.

Hunt, A. S., and C. C. Edgar. 1932–41. *Select Papyri.* 3 vols. LCL. Cambridge, MA: Harvard Univ. Press.

Irwin, K. M. 1982. Response to "The Problem of Miraculous Feedings in the Graeco-Roman World," by Robert M. Grant. In *Protocol of the Forty-second Colloquy* (14 March 1982), pp. 25–27. Berkeley, CA: Center for Hermeneutical Studies in Hellenistic and Modern Culture, The Graduate Theological Union and the Univ. of California.

Isenberg, Sheldon R. 1975. "Power Through Temple and Torah in Greco-Roman Palestine." In *Christianity, Judaism and Other Greco-Roman Cults,* Studies for Morton Smith at Sixty, edited by Jacob Neusner, part 2, Early Christianity, pp. 24–52. Studies in Judaism in Late Antiquity 12:2. Leiden: Brill.

Isenberg, Sheldon R., and Dennis E. Owen. 1977. "Bodies, Natural and Contrived: The Work of Mary Douglas." *Religious Studies Review* 3: 1–17.

James, Montague Rhodes. 1953. *The Apocryphal New Testament.* Oxford: Clarendon Press. [First edition, 1924. Coreected edition, 1953].

Jeremias, Joachim. 1967. *"Pais Theou."* In *Theological Dictionary of the New Testament,* edited by Gerhard Friedrich and Geoffrey W. Bromiley, vol. 5, pp. 677–717. Grand Rapids: Eerdmans.

————. 1969. *Jerusalem in the Time of Jesus: An Investigation into Economic and Social Conditions during the New Testament Period.* Philadelphia: Fortress Press.

Johnson, Luke T. 1989. "The New Testament's Anti-Jewish Slander and the Conventions of Ancient Polemic." *JBL* 108: 419–441.

Käsemann, Ernst. 1969. "Sentences of Holy Law in the New Testament." In his *New Testament Questions of Today,* pp. 66–81. Philadelphia: Fortress Press, 1969.

Kee, Howard Clark. 1963. "'Becoming a Child' in the Gospel of Thomas." *JBL* 82: 307–314.

————. 1983. *Miracle in the Early Christian World: A Study in Sociohistorical Method.* New Haven, CT: Yale Univ. Press.

————. 1986. *Medicine, Miracle and Magic in New Testament Times.* SNTSMS 55. New York: Cambridge Univ. Press.

Kelber, Werner H. 1974. *The Kingdom in Mark: A New Place and a New Time.* Philadelphia: Fortress Press.

Kierdorf, Wilhelm. 1980. *Laudatio Funebris: Interpretationen und Untersuchungen zur Entwick-lung der römischen Leichenrede.* Beiträge zur klassischen Philologie 106. Meisenheim am Glan: Hain.

King, J. E., trans. 1927. *Cicero: Tusculan Disputations*, vol. 18 of 28. LCL. Cambridge, MA: Harvard Univ. Press.

Klausner, Joseph. 1925. *Jesus of Nazareth.* Translated by Herbert Danby. New York: Macmillan. (First published 1922.

Kleinman, Arthur, and Lilias H. Sung. 1979. "Why Do Indigenous Practitioners Successfully Heal?" *SSM* 13B/1: 7–26.

Klijn, A. F. J. 1962. "The 'Single One' in the Gospel of Thomas." *JBL* 81: 271–278.

Kloppenborg, John S. 1979 "Didache 16:6–8 and Special Matthean Tradition." *ZNW* 70: 54–67.

———. 1986. "Blessing and Marginality; The 'Persecution Beatitude' in Q, Thomas and Early Christianity." *Forum* 2/3: 36–56.

———. 1987. *The Formation of Q: Trajectories in Ancient Wisdom Collections.* Studies in Antiquity and Christianity. Philadelphia: Fortress Press.

———. 1988. *Q Parallels: Synopsis, Critical Notes, and Concordance.* Foundations and Facets Reference Series. Sonoma, CA: Polebridge Press.

———. 1990. "Alms, Debt and Divorce: Jesus' Ethics in Their Mediterranean Context." *Toronto Journal of Theology* 6: 182–200.

Klosinski, Lee Edward. 1988. *The Meals in Mark.* Ann Arbor, MI: University Microfilms International.

Koester, Helmut. 1957. *Synoptische Überlieferung bei den Apostolischen Vätern.* TU 65. Berlin: Akademie.

———. 1980a. "Apocryphal and Canonical Gospels." *HTR* 73: 105–130.

———. 1980b. "Gnostic Writings as Witnesses for the Development of the Sayings Tradition." In *The Rediscovery of Gnosticism*, Proceedings of the International Conference on Gnosticism at Yale, New Haven, CT, March 28–31, 1978, vol 1, pp. 238–256 (discussion, pp. 256–261). The School of Valentinus. Studies in the History of Religions: Supplements to *Numen* XLI/1. Leiden: Brill.

———. 1982. *Introduction to the New Testament.* 2 vols. Hermeneia: Foundations and Facets. Philadelphia: Fortress Press.

———. 1983. "History and Development of Mark's Gospel (From Mark to Secret Mark and 'Canonical' Mark)." In *Colloquy on New Testament Studies: A Time for Reappraisal and Fresh Approaches*, edited by Bruce Corley, pp. 35–57 (see also "Seminar Dialogue with Helmut Koester," pp. 59–85). Macon, GA: Mercer Univ. Press.

———. 1989a. "Tractate 2. The Gospel According to Thomas: Introduction." In *Nag Hammadi Codex II,2–7*, 2 vols., edited by Bentley Layton, vol. 1, pp. 38–49. NHS 20–21, The Coptic Gnostic Library. Leiden: Brill.

———. 1989b. "The Text of the Synoptic Gospels in the Second Century." In *Gospel Traditions in the Second Century: Origins, Recensions, Text, and Transmission*, edited by William L. Petersen, pp. 19–37. Christianity and Judaism in Antiquity 3. Notre Dame, IN: Univ. of Notre Dame Press.

———. 1990. *Ancient Christian Gospels: Their History and Development*. London: SCM Press; Philadelphia: Trinity Press International.

Kroeber, A. L. 1948. *Anthropology. Race, Language, Culture, Psychology, Prehistory*. New York: Harcourt, Brace.

Lake, Kirsopp, trans. and ed. 1912–13. *The Apostolic Fathers*. 2 vols. LCL. Cambridge, MA: Harvard Univ. Press.

Lambdin, Thomas O. 1989. "The Gospel According to Thomas." In *Nag Hammadi Codex II,2–7*, 2 vols., edited by Bentley Layton, vol. 1, pp. 52–93. NHS 20–21, The Coptic Gnostic Library. Leiden: Brill.

Lanternari, Vittorio. 1963. *The Religions of the Oppressed: A Study of Modern Messianic Cults*. Translated by Lisa Sergio (from 1960 edition). New York: Knopf, New American Library Mentor Books.

Lasswell, Harold D., and Abraham Kaplan. 1950. *Power and Society: A Framework for Political Inquiry*. New Haven, CT: Yale Univ. Press.

Layton, Bentley. 1968. "The Sources, Date and Transmission of *Didache* 1.3b-2.1." *HTR* 61: 343–383.

Lefkowitz, Mary R., and Maureen B. Fant. 1982. *Women's Life in Greece and Rome: A Source Book in Translation*. Baltimore: Johns Hopkins Press.

Lémonon, Jean-Pierre. 1981. *Pilate et le gouvernement de la Judeé: Textes et Monuments*. Études Bibliques. Paris: Gabalda.

Lenski, Gerhard E. 1966. *Power and Privilege: A Theory of Social Stratification*. New York: McGraw-Hill.

Levick, Barbara. 1985. *The Government of the Roman Empire: A Sourcebook*. London: Croom Helm.

Lewis, Ioan M. 1971. *Ecstatic Religion: An Anthropological Study of Spirit Possession and Shamanism*. Pelican Anthropology Library. Baltimore: Penguin Books.

Lewis, Naphtali. 1983. *Life in Egypt Under Roman Rule*. Oxford: Clarendon Press.

Liefeld, Walter Lewis. 1967. *The Wandering Preacher as a Social Figure in the Roman Empire*. Ann Arbor, MI: University Microfilms International.

Lind, Leni Robert, ed. 1957. *Latin Poetry in Verse Translation: From the Beginnings to the Renaissance*. Boston: Houghton Mifflin, Riverside Editions.

Lindars, Barnabas. 1961. *New Testament Apologetic: The Doctrinal Significance of the Old Testament Quotations*. London: SCM Press.

———. 1980–81. "John and the Synoptic Gospels: A Test Case." *NTS* 27: 287–294.

Lindsay, Jack, Trans. 1960. *The Satyricon and Poems of Gaius Petronius*. London: Elek.

Longstaff, Thomas R. W. 1990. "Nazareth and Sepphoris: Insights into Christian Origins." *Anglican Theological Review* 11: 8–15.

Lutz, Cora E. 1947. *Musonius Rufus "The Roman Socrates."* Yale Classical Studies 10. New Haven, CT: Yale Univ. Press.

MacDonald, Dennis Ronald. 1987. *There Is No Male and Female: The Fate of a Dominical Saying in Paul and Gnosticism*. Harvard Dissertations in Religion 20. Philadelphia: Fortress Press.

Mack, Burton L. 1987. "The Kingdom Sayings in Mark." *Forum* 3/1: 3–47.

———. 1988. *A Myth of Innocence: Mark and Christian Origins*. Philadelphia: Fortress Press.

MacMullen, Ramsay. 1966. *Enemies of the Roman Order: Treason, Unrest, and Alienation in the Empire*. Cambridge, MA: Harvard Univ. Press.

———. 1974. *Roman Social Relations: 50 B.C. to A.D. 384.* New Haven, CT; London: Yale Univ. Press.

MacRae, George W. 1978. "Nag Hammadi and the New Testament." In *Gnosis, Festschrift für Hans Jonas,* edited by B. Aland et al., pp. 144–157. Göttingen: Vandenhoeck and Ruprecht.

———. 1980. "Why the Church Rejected Gnosticism?" In *Jewish and Christian Self-Definition,* vol 1, *The Shaping of Christianity in the Second and Third Centuries,* edited by E. P. Sanders, pp. 126–133. Philadelphia: Fortress Press.

Malherbe, Abraham J. 1977. *The Cynic Epistles: A Study Edition.* SBLSBS 12. Missoula, MT: Scholars Press.

Malina, Bruce J. 1981. *The New Testament World: Insights from Cultural Anthropology.* Atlanta: John Knox Press.

———. 1987. "Patron and Client: The Analogy behind Synoptic Theology." *Forum* 4/1: 2–32.

Malina, Bruce J., and Jerome H. Neyrey. 1988. *Calling Jesus Names: The Social Value of Labels in Matthew.* Social Facets. Sonoma, CA: Polebridge Press.

Mauss, Marcel. 1975. *A General Theory of Magic.* Translated by Robert Brain. The Norton Library. New York: Norton. (First published 1902–3.)

Meeks, Wayne A. 1974. "The Image of the Androgyne: Some Uses of a Symbol in Earliest Christianity." *HR* 13: 165–208.

Meier, John P. 1990. "Jesus in Josephus: A Modest Proposal." *CBQ* 52: 76–103.

Melmoth, William, trans. 1915. *Pliny: Letters.* Revised by W. M. L. Hutchinson. LCL. 2 vols. Cambridge, MA: Harvard Univ. Press.

Metzger, Bruce M. 1971. *A Textual Commentary on the Greek New Testament.* New York: United Bible Societies.

Meyer, Marvin W. 1990. "The Youth in the Secret Gospel of Mark." *Semeia* 49: 129–153.

Meyers, Eric M. 1975–76. "Galilean Regionalism as a Factor in Historical Reconstruction." *BASOR* 220/221: 93–101.

———. 1979. "The Cultural Setting of Galilee: The Case of Regionalism and Early Judaism." *ANRW* 2.19.686–702.

Meyers, Eric M., Ehud Netzer, and Carol L. Meyers. 1986. "Sepphoris, 'Ornament of all Galilee.'" *BA* 49: 4–19.

Meyers, Eric M., and James F. Strange. 1981. *Archaeology, the Rabbis, and Early Christianity: The Social and Historical Setting of Palestinian Judaism and Christianity.* Nashville: Abingdon.

Michel, Otto. 1967–68. "Studien zu Josephus." *NTS* 14: 402–408.

Michie, James. 1963. *The Odes of Horace.* New York: Orion Press.

Milavec, Aaron. 1989. "The Pastoral Genius of the Didache: An Analytical Translation and Commentary." In *Religious Writings and Religious Systems: Systemic Analysis of Holy Books in Christianity, Islam, Buddhism, Greco-Roman Religions, Ancient Israel, and Judaism,* vol. 2, *Christianity,* edited by Jacob Neusner, Ernest S. Frerichs, and A. J. Levine, pp. 89–125. Brown Studies in Religion 2. Atlanta: Scholars Press.

Miller, Walter, trans. 1913. *Cicero: De Officiis.* LCL. Vol. 21 of 28. Cambridge, MA: Harvard Univ. Press.

Moore, Clifford. H., and John Jackson. 1925–37. *Tacitus: Histories and Annals.* 4 vols. LCL. Cambridge, MA: Harvard Univ. Press.

Mumford, Lewis. 1961. *The City in History: Its Origins, Its Transformations, and Its Prospects.* New York: Harcourt, Brace & World.

Murdock, George Peter. 1980. *Theories of Illness: A World Survey.* Pittsburgh: Univ. of Pittsburgh Press.

Naveh, J. 1970. "The Ossuary Inscriptions from Giv'at ha-Mivtar." *IEJ* 20: 33–37, plates 11–17.

Neirynck, Frans. 1970. *Duality in Mark: Contributions to the Study of the Markan Redaction.* BETL 31. Leuven: Leuven Univ. Press.

―――. 1974. *The Minor Agreements of Matthew and Luke Against Mark with a Cumulative List.* BETL 37. Gembloux: Duculot.

―――. 1982. *Evangelica: Gospel Studies—Études d'Évangile. Collected Essays.* Edited by F. Van Segbroeck. BETL 60. Leuven: Leuven Univ. Press.

―――. 1985. "Papyrus Egerton 2 and the Healing of the Leper." *ETL* 61: 153–160.

―――. 1989. "The Apocryphal Gospels and the Gospel of Mark." In *The New Testament in Early Christianity* (La réception des écrits néotestamentaires dans le christianisme primitif), edited by Jean-Marie Sevrin, pp. 123–175. BETL 86. Leuven: Leuven Univ. Press.

Neusner, Jacob. 1977–86. *The Tosefta, Translated from the Hebrew.* New York: Ktav.

Nickelsburg, George W. E. 1972. *Resurrection, Immortality, and Eternal Life in Intertestamental Judaism.* HTS 26. Cambridge, MA: Harvard Univ. Press; London: Oxford Univ. Press.

―――. 1980. "The Genre and Function of the Markan Passion Narrative." *HTR* 73: 153–184.

―――. 1981. *Jewish Literature Between the Bible and the Mishnah.* Philadelphia: Fortress Press.

Oakman, Douglas E. 1985. "Jesus and Agrarian Palestine: The Factor of Debt." In *SBLSP 1985,* edited by Kent Harold Richards, pp. 57–73. SBLSP 24. Atlanta: Scholars Press.

―――. 1986. *Jesus and the Economic Questions of His Day.* Studies in the Bible and Early Christianity 8. Lewiston, NY and Queenston, Ontario: Edwin Mellen Press.

―――. 1988. "Rulers' Houses, Thieves, and Usurpers: The Beelzebul Pericope." *Forum* 4/3: 109–123.

Obeyesekere, Gananath. 1970. "The Idiom of Demonic Possession: A Case Study." *SSM* 4: 97–111.

Oesterreich, Traugott Konstantin. 1966. *Possession Demoniacal and Other Among Primitive Races, in Antiquity, the Middle Ages, and Modern Times,* translated by D. Ibberson. New Hyde Park, NY: University Books, 1930. (First published in German, 1921.)

Oldfather, W. A. 1925–28. *Epictetus: The Discourses as Reported by Arrian, the Manual, and Fragments.* 2 vols. LCL. Cambridge, MA: Harvard Univ. Press.

Oldfather, C. H., C. L. Sherman, C. Bradford Welles, Russell M. Geer, and Francis R. Walton. 1933–67. *Diodorus of Sicily: Library of History.* 12 vols. LCL. Cambridge, MA: Harvard Univ. Press.

Overman, J. Andrew. 1988. "Who Were the First Urban Christians? Urbanization in Galilee in the First Century." in *SBLSP 1988,* edited by David J. Lull pp. 160–168. SBLSP 27. Atlanta: Scholars Press.

Pagels, Elaine, and Helmut Koester. 1978. "Report on the Dialogue of the Savior." In *Nag Hammadi and Gnosis: Papers Read at the First International Congress on Coptology* (Cairo, December 1976), edited by R. McL. Wilson pp. 66–74. NHS 14. Leiden: Brill.

Patterson, Stephen John. 1988. *The Gospel of Thomas Within the Development of Early Christianity.* Ann Arbor, MI: University Microfilms International.

Peristiany, John G., ed. 1965. *Honour and Shame: The Values of Mediterranean Society.* London: Weidenfeld & Nicolson; Chicago: Univ. of Chicago Press, 1966, Midway Reprints, 1974.

Pines, Shlomo. 1971. *An Arabic Version of the Testimonium Flavianum and Its Implications.* Publications of the Israel Academy of Sciences and Humanities. Jerusalem: Israel Academy of Sciences and Humanitites.

Pitt-Rivers, Julian A. 1954. *The People of the Sierra.* New York: Criterion Books.

———. 1977. *The Fate of Shechem or the Politics of Sex: Essays in the Anthropology of the Mediterranean.* Cambridge Studies in Social Anthropology 19. Cambridge: Cambridge Univ. Press.

Potter, Jack M., May N. Diaz, and George M. Foster. eds. 1967. *Peasant Society: A Reader.* Boston: Little, Brown.

Pound, Ezra. 1934. *Homage to Sextus Propertius.* London: Faber & Faber.

Prigent, Pierre. 1961. *L'Épître de Barnabé I–XVI et ses sources: Les Testimonia dans le Christianisme primitif.* Paris: Gabalda.

Rackham, H., W. H. S. Jones, and D. E. Eichholz. 1938–63. *Natural History.* 10 vols. LCL. Cambridge: Harvard Univ. Press.

Rajak, Tessa. 1983. *Josephus: The Historian and His Society.* London: Duckworth.

Redfield, Robert. 1956. *Peasant Society and Culture.* Chicago: Univ. of Chicago Press.

Remus, Harold. 1983. *Pagan-Christian Conflict over Miracle in the Second Century.* Patristic Monograph Series 10. Cambridge, MA: The Philadelphia Patristic Foundation.

Renan, Ernest. 1972. *The Life of Jesus.* New York: Random House, Modern Library. (First published 1863.)

Reynolds, Barrie. 1963. *Magic, Divination and Witchcraft Among the Barotse of Northern Rhodesia.* Robins Series 3. Berkeley and Los Angeles: Univ. of California Press.

Rhoads, David M. 1976. *Israel in Revolution.* Philadelphia: Fortress Press.

Riggs, John W. 1984. "From Gracious Table to Sacramental Elements: The Tradition-History of Didache 9 and 10." *SC* 4: 83–101.

Roberts, Alexander, James Donaldson, and A. Cleveland Coxe. 1926. *The Ante-Nicene Fathers.* 10 vols. American Reprint of the Edinburgh Edition. New York: Scribner's.

Robinson, James M., and Helmut Koester. 1971. *Trajectories Through Early Christianity.* Philadelphia: Fortress Press.

Rogers, Benjamin Bickley, trans. 1924. *Aristophanes.* 3 vols. LCL. Cambridge: Harvard Univ. Press.

Rolfe, John C., trans. 1927. *The Attic Nights of Aulus Gellius.* 3 vols. LCL. Cambridge: Harvard Univ. Press.

Rostovtzeff, Mikhail Ivanovich. 1957. *The Social and Economic History of the Roman Empire.* 2nd ed. Revised by P. M. Fraser. 2 vols. with continuous pagination. Oxford: Oxford Univ. Press. (First published 1926.)

Roth, Cecil 1959 "The Jewish Revolt Against Rome: The War of 66–70 C.E." *Commentary* 27: 513–522.

———. 1962. "The Historical Implication of the Jewish Coinage of the First Revolt." *IEJ* 12:33–46.

Rouse, W. H. D. 1910. *The Moral Discourses of Epictetus.* New York: Dutton.

Safrai, S. 1965. "The Teaching of Pietists in Mishnaic Literature." *JSS* 16: 15–33.

Safrai, Schmuel, and Michael E. Stone, eds. 1974–. *Compendia Rerum Iudaicarum ad Novum Testamentum.* 10 vols. Assen: Van Gorcum; Philadelphia: Fortress Press.

Saller, Richard P. 1982. *Personal Patronage Under the Early Empire.* Cambridge: Cambridge Univ. Press.

Sanders, E. P. 1985. *Jesus and Judaism.* Philadelphia: Fortress Press.

Sayre, Farrand. 1948. *The Greek Cynics.* Baltimore: Furst.

Schenke, Hans-Martin. 1984. "The Mystery of the Gospel of Mark." *SC* 4: 65–82.

Schiffman, Lawrence H. 1983. *Sectarian Law in the Dead Sea Scrolls: Courts, Testimony and the Penal Code.* Chico, CA: Scholars Press.

Schmidt, Daryl. 1977. "The LXX Gattung 'Prophetic Correlative.'" *JBL* 96: 517–522.

Schmidt, Steffen W., Laura Guasti, Carl H. Landé, and James C. Scott, eds. 1977. *Friends, Followers, and Factions: A Reader in Political Clientelism.* Berkeley and Los Angeles: Univ. of California Press.

Schneider, Jane. 1971. "Of Vigilance and Virgins: Honor, Shame and Access to Resources in Mediterranean Societies" *Ethnology* 9: 1–24.

Schoedel, William R. 1985. *Ignatius of Antioch: A Commentary on the Letters of Ignatius of Antioch.* Hermeneia: A Critical and Historical Commentary on the Bible. Philadelphia: Fortress Press.

Schürer, Emil. 1973–87. *The History of the Jewish People in the Age of Jesus Christ (175 B.C.–A.D. 135).* 3 vols. New English Version, revised and edited by Geza Vermes, Fergus Millar, Matthew Black, Martin Goodman, and Pamela Vermes. Edinburgh: Clark.

Schweitzer, Albert. 1968. *The Quest of the Historical Jesus: A Critical Study of Its Progress from Reimarus to Wrede.* Introduction by James M. Robinson. New York: Macmillan. (First published 1906.)

Scott, Bernard Brandon. 1989. *Hear Then the Parable: A Commentary on the Parables of Jesus.* Minneapolis: Fortress Press.

Scott, James C. 1977. "Protest and Profanation: Agrarian Revolt and the Little Tradition." *Theory and Society* 4: 1–38 and 211–246.

———. 1985. *Weapons of the Weak: Everyday Forms of Peasant Resistance.* New Haven, CT: Yale Univ. Press.

———. 1990. *Domination and the Arts of Resistance: Hidden Transcripts.* New Haven, CT: Yale Univ. Press.

Sellew, Philip H. 1988. "Beelzebul in Mark 3: Dialogue, Story, or Sayings Cluster?" *Forum* 4/3: 93–108.

Shaw, Brent D. 1984. "Bandits in the Roman Empire." *Past and Present* 105: 5–52.

Sherwin-White, A. N. 1966. *The Letters of Pliny: A Historical and Social Commentary*. Oxford: Clarendon Press.

Shipley, Frederick William. 1924. *Velleius Paterculus: Compendium of Roman History and Res Gestae Divi Augusti*. LCL. Cambridge, MA: Harvard Univ. Press.

Smallwood, E. Mary. 1976. *The Jews Under Roman Rule: From Pompey to Diocletian*. Studies in Judaism in Late Antiquity 20. Leiden: Brill.

Smith, Dennis Edwin. 1980. "Social Obligation in the Context of Communal Meals: A Study of the Christian Meal in 1 Corinthians in Comparison with Graeco-Roman Communal Meals." Th.D. diss., Harvard University (photocopy).

Smith, Jonathan Z. 1965–66. "The Garments of Shame." *HR* 5: 217–238.

———. 1975. "Wisdom and Apocalyptic." Pp. 131–156 in *Religious Syncretism in Antiquity: Essays in Conversation with Geo Widengren*, edited by Birger A. Pearson. Missoula, MT: Scholars Press.

———. 1977. "The Temple and Magician." In *God's Christ and His People: Studies in Honour of Nils Alstrup Dahl*, edited by J. Jervell and Wayne A. Meeks, pp. 233–247. Oslo: Universitetsforlaget. Found also in *Map Is Not Territory*, by J. Z. Smith, pp. 172–189. Studies in the History of Religions. Leiden: Brill, 1978.

Smith, Morton. 1956. "Palestinian Judaism in the First Century." In *Israel: Its Role in Civilization*, edited by Moshe Davis, pp. 67–81. New York: Harper & Row.

———. 1960. "Monasteries and their Manuscripts." *Archaeology* 13: 172–177.

———. 1971. "Zealots and Sicarii, Their Origins and Relation." *HTR* 64:1–19.

———. 1973a. *The Secret Gospel: The Discovery and Interpretation of the Secret Gospel According to Mark*. New York: Harper & Row.

———. 1973b. *Clement of Alexandria and a Secret Gospel of Mark*. Cambridge, MA: Harvard Univ. Press.

———. 1978. *Jesus the Magician*. New York: Harper & Row.

———. 1982. "Clement of Alexandria and Secret Mark: The Score at the End of the First Decade." *HTR* 75: 449–461.

Stern, Menahem. 1976–84. *Greek and Latin Authors on Jews and Judaism*. 3 vols. Publications of the Israel Academy of Sciences and Humanities, Section of Humanities. Fontes Ad Res Judaicas Spectantes. Jerusalem: The Israel Academy of Sciences and Humanities.

Stroker, William Dettwiller. 1970. *The Formation of Secondary Sayings of Jesus*. Ann Arbor, MI: University Microfilms International.

———. 1989. *Extracanonical Sayings of Jesus*. SBLRBS 18. Atlanta: Scholars Press.

Stuart, Duane Reed. 1923. *Tacitus: The Agricola*. New York: Macmillan.

Syme, Sir Ronald. 1939. *The Roman Revolution*. London: Oxford Univ. Press. (2d impression 1952.)

Talley, Thomas J. 1982. "Liturgical Time in the Ancient Church: The State of Research." *Studia Liturgica* 14: 34–51.

Tashjian, Jirair S. 1987. *The Social Setting of the Mission Charge in Q*. Ann Arbor, MI: University Microfilms International.

Tcherikover, Victor A., Alexander Fuks, and Menahem Stern, eds. 1957–64. *Corpus Papyrorum Judaicarum*. 3 vols. Cambridge, MA: Harvard Univ. Press.

Temporini, Hildegard, and Wolfgang Haase. 1972–. *Aufstieg und Niedergang der römischen Welt: Geschichte und Kultur Roms im Spiegel der neueren Forschung.* 3 parts. Berlin and New York: Walter de Gruyter.

Thackeray, H. St. J., et al. 1926–65. *Josephus.* 9 vols. LCL. Cambridge: Harvard Univ. Press.

Theissen, Gerd. 1974–75. "Legitimation und Lebensunterhalt: Ein Beitrag zur Soziologie urchristlicher Missionare." *NTS* 21: 192–221.

———. 1975. "Itinerant Radicalism: The Tradition of Jesus Sayings from the Perspective of the Sociology of Literature." *Radical Religion* 2: 84–93. (Originally published in 1973. "Wanderradikalismus: Literatursoziologische Aspekte der überlieferung von Worten Jesu im Urchristentum." *ZTK* 70: 245–271.)

———. 1978. *Sociology of Early Christianity.* Translated by J. Bowden. Philadelphia: Fortress Press.

———. 1983. *The Miracle Stories of the Early Christian Tradition.* Translated by Francis McDonagh, edited by John Riches. Philadelphia: Fortress Press. (From 1972 and 1974 editions.)

Thrupp, Sylvia L., ed. 1970. *Millennial Dreams in Action: Studies in Revolutionary Religious Movements.* New York: Schocken.

Tzaferis, Vassilios. 1970. "Jewish Tombs at and near Giv'at ha-Mivtar, Jerusalem." *IEJ* 20: 18–32, plates 9–17.

———. 1985. "Crucifixion—The Archaeological Evidence." *BAR* 11/1 (Jan–Feb) 44–53.

Vaage, Leif Eric. 1987. *Q: The Ethos and Ethics of an Itinerant Intelligence.* Ann Arbor, MI: University Microfilms International.

———. 1989. "Q1 and the Historical Jesus: Some Peculiar Sayings (7:33–34; 9:57–58, 59–60; 14:26–27)." *Forum* 5/2: 159–176.

van Haelst, Joseph. 1976. *Catalogue des Papyrus Littéraires Juifs et Chrétiens.* Série Papyrologie 1. Paris: Publications de la Sorbonne.

Vardaman, E. Jerry. 1964. "Introduction to the Caesarea Inscription of the Twenty-four Priestly Courses." In *The Teacher's Yoke: Studies in Memory of Henry Trantham,* edited by E. Jerry Vardaman and James Leo Garrett, Jr., pp. 42–45. Waco, TX: Baylor Univ. Press.

Vermes, Geza. 1967. "The Use of בר נש/בר נשא in Jewish Aramaic." In *An Aramaic Approach to the Gospels and Acts,* 3rd ed., by Matthew Black, pp. 310–328. Oxford: Clarendon Press. Found also in *Post-Biblical Jewish Studies,* by Geza Vermes, pp. 310–328. Leiden: Brill, 1975.

———. 1968. *The Dead Sea Scrolls in English.* Rev. ed. Baltimore: Penguin Books.

———. 1972–73a. " Hanina ben Dosa: A Controversial Galilean Saint from the First Century of the Christian Era." *JSS* 23: 28–50 and 24: 51–64.

———. 1973b. *Jesus the Jew: A Historian's Reading of the Gospels.* New York: Macmillan.

———. 1978a. "The 'Son of Man' Debate." *JSNT* 1:19–32.

———. 1978b. "The Present State of the 'Son of Man' Debate." *JJS* 29: 123–134 (reprint of 1978a with extended footnotes).

———. 1981. *Jesus the Jew.* Rev. ed. Philadelphia: Fortress Press.

———. 1984. *Jesus and the World of Judaism.* Philadelphia: Fortress Press.

———. 1985. *The Dead Sea Scrolls: Qumran in Perspective.* With Pamela Vermes. Rev. ed. Philadelphia: Fortress Press.

Veyne, Paul. 1961. "Vie de Trimalcion." *Annales* 16: 213–47.

Vielhauer, Philip. 1964. "ANAPAUCIC: Zum gnostischen Hintergrund des Thomasevangeliums." In *Apophoreta*, Festschrift für Ernst Haenchen zu seinem siebzigsten Geburtstag am 10 Dezember 1964, edited by W. Eltester and F. H. Kettler, pp. 281–299. BZNW 30. Berlin: Töpelmann.

Walker, William O., Jr. 1983. "The 'Theology of Woman's Place' and the 'Paulinist' Tradition." *Semeia* 28: 101–112.

Ward, Colleen A., and Michael H. Beaubrun. 1980. "The Psychodynamics of Demon Possession." *JSSR* 19: 201–207.

Wender, Dorothea. 1980. *Roman Poetry from the Republic to the Silver Age*. Carbondale, IL: Southern Illinois Press.

Wengst, Klaus. 1987. *Pax Romana and the Peace of Jesus Christ*. Translated by John Bowden. Philadelphia: Fortress Press.

Wessely, Charles. 1946. "Le fragment relatif au reniement de Saint Pierre appartenant a la collection de l'Archiduc Rainer." In *Les plus anciens monuments du Christianisme écrits sur papyrus: Textes grecs édités traduits et annotés*, vol. 1, pp. 173–177. *Patrologia Orientalis*, vol. 4, part 2, edited by R. Graffin. Paris: Firmin-Didot. (First published 1907.)

White, John L. 1986. *Light from Ancient Letters*. Foundations and Facets, New Testament. Philadelphia: Fortress Press.

Williams, Francis E. 1985. "The Apocryphon of James." Vol. 1, pp. 13–53, and vol. 2, pp. 7–37 in *Nag Hammadi Codex I (The Jung Codex)*. 2 vols. Ed. Harold W. Attridge. NHS 22–23. The Coptic Gnostic Library. Leiden: Brill.

Williams, W. Glynn, trans. 1927–29. *Cicero: Letters to His Friends, etc.* 4 vols. LCL, vols. 25–28 of vols. 1–28. Cambridge, MA: Harvard Univ. Press.

Wilson, Bryan R. 1973. *Magic and the Millennium: A Sociological Study of Religious Movements of Protest Among Tribal and Third-World Peoples*. New York: Harper & Row.

Winstedt, E. O., trans. 1912–18. *Cicero: Letters to Atticus*. 3 vols. LCL. Vols. 22–24 of 1–28. Cambridge, MA: Harvard Univ. Press.

Wisse, Frederik. 1977. "The Sentences of Sextus (XII,1)." In *The Nag Hammadi Library in English*, James M. Robinson, director, edited by Marvin M. Meyer, pp. 454–459. New York: Harper & Row.

Wistrand, Erik. 1976. *The So-called Laudatio Turiae: Introduction, Text, Translation, Commentary*. Studia Graeca et Latina Gothoburgensia 34. Göteborg: Acta Universitatis Gothoburgensis; Lund: Berlingska Boktryckeriet.

Wolf, Eric R. 1966. *Peasants*. Foundations of Modern Anthropology Series. Englewood Cliffs, NJ: Prentice-Hall.

Worsley, Peter. 1968. *The Trumpet Shall Sound: A Study of "Cargo" Cults in Melanesia*. 2d, augmented ed. New York: Schocken Books.

———. 1982. "Non-Western Medical Systems." *ARA* 11: 315–48.

Wright, Wilmer Cave. 1913–23. *Julian*. 3 vols. LCL. Cambridge, MA: Harvard Univ. Press

Yadin, Yigael. 1973. "Epigraphy and Crucifixion." *IEJ* 23: 18–22.

Young, Allan. 1982. "The Anthropologies of Illness and Sickness." *ARA* 11: 257–85.

Zias, Joseph, and Eliezer Sekeles. 1985. "The Crucified Man from Giv'at ha-Mivtar: A Reappraisal." *IEJ* 35: 22–27.

Author Index

487

Text Index

I. Jewish Texts

1. Bible

II. *Pagan Texts*

III. Christian Texts

1. Intracanonical Writings

Complex Index